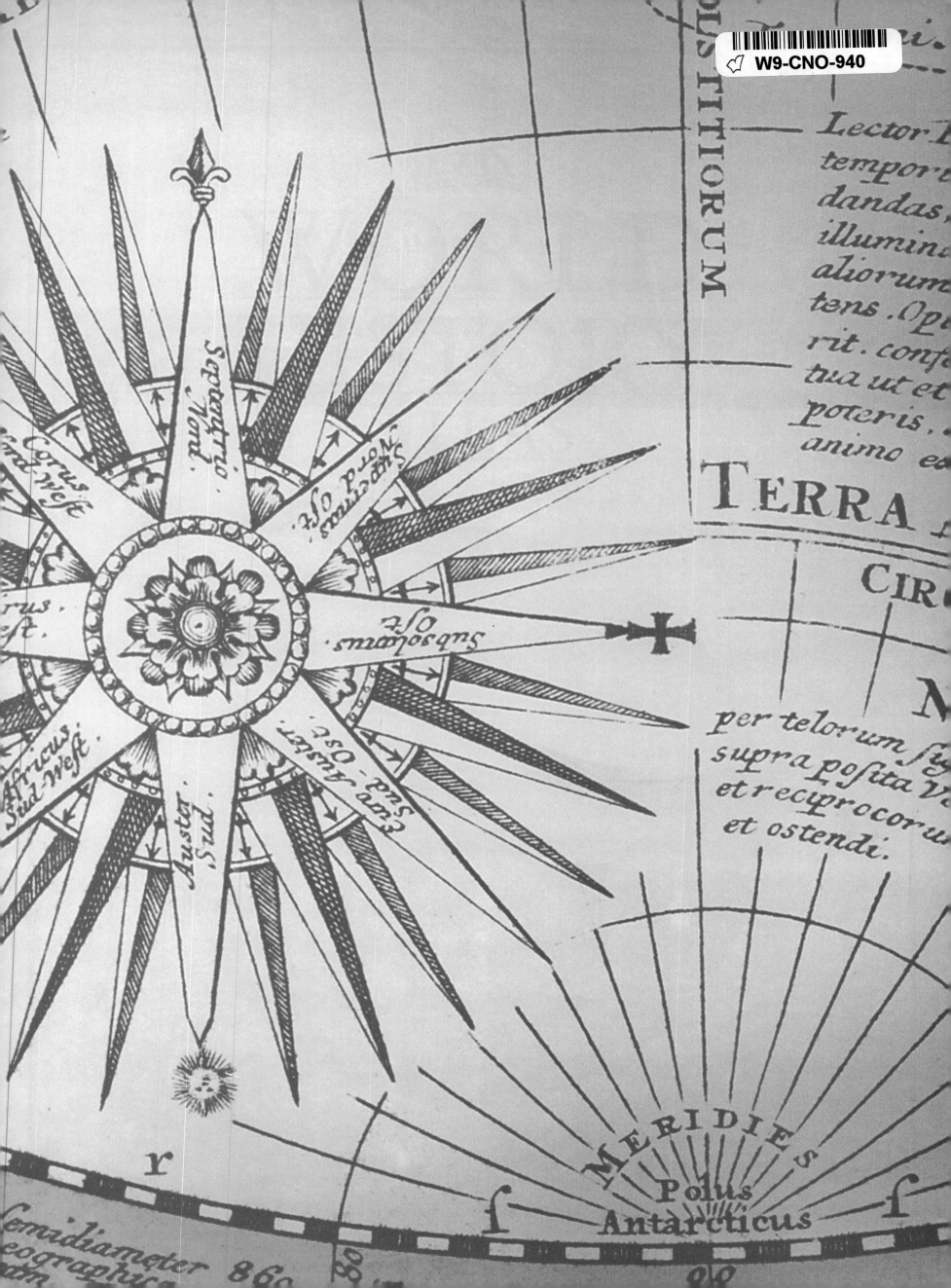

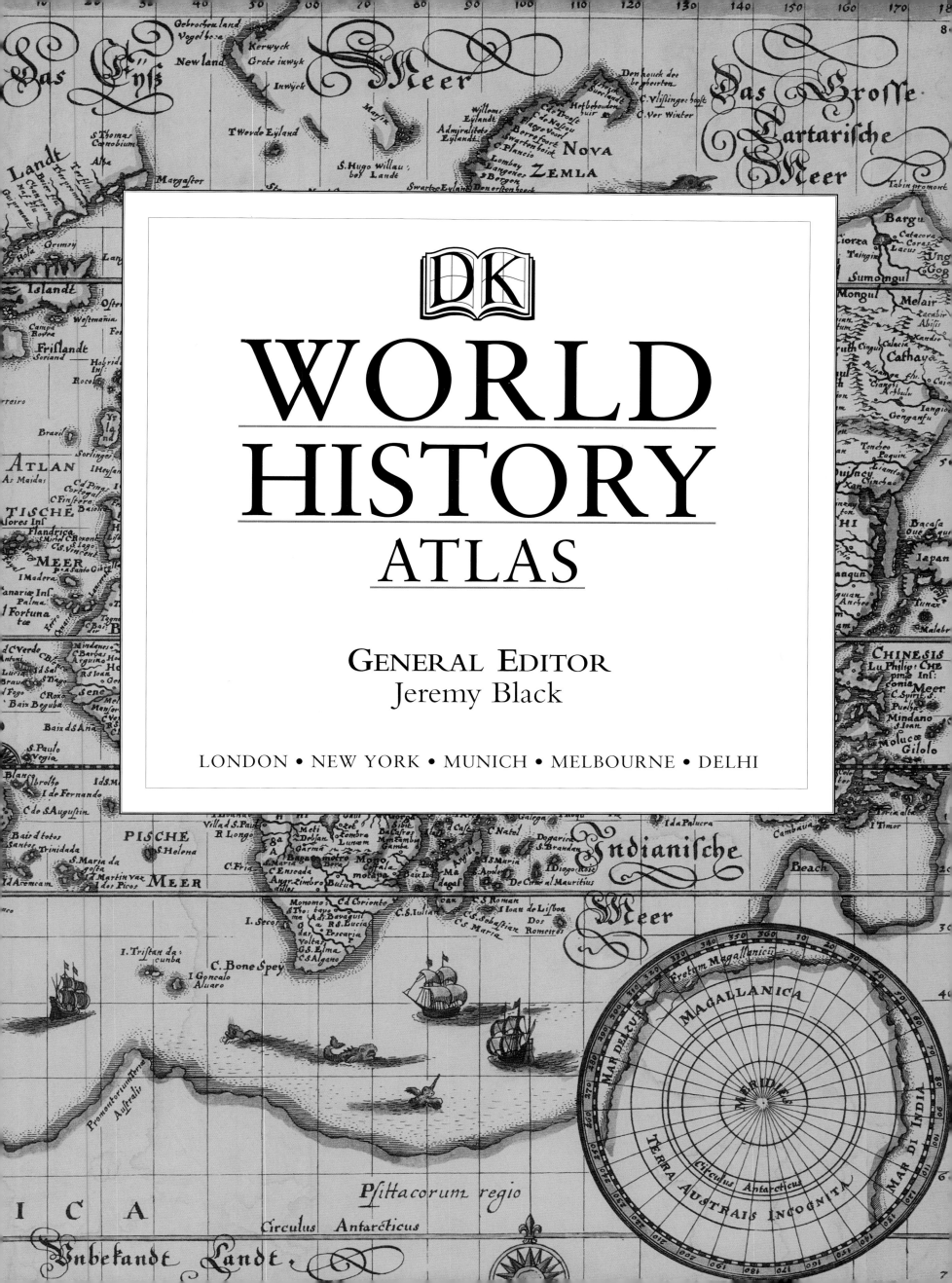

DK

WORLD HISTORY
ATLAS

GENERAL EDITOR
Jeremy Black

LONDON • NEW YORK • MUNICH • MELBOURNE • DELHI

A DORLING KINDERSLEY BOOK
www.dk.com

CONSULTANTS

GENERAL EDITOR Professor Jeremy Black, Department of History, University of Exeter, UK

WORLD HISTORY

Professor Jerry Bentley, Department of History, University of Hawaii, USA
Professor James Chambers, Department of History,
Texas Christian University, USA
Dr John France, Department of History, University of Swansea, UK
Dr Guy Halsall, Department of History, Birkbeck College, London, UK
Dr Chris Scarre, Department of Archaeology, Cambridge University, UK
H. P. Willmott, Royal Military Academy, Sandhurst, UK

NORTH AMERICA

Professor Donald S. Frazier, Department of History,
McMurray University, Texas, USA
Professor Ross Hassig, Department of Anthropology,
Oklahoma State University, USA
Dr Kendrick Oliver, Department of History, University of Southampton, UK
Professor George Raudzens, Department of History,
Macquarie University, Sydney, Australia
Dr Brian Ward, Department of History, University of Florida, USA

SOUTH AMERICA

Dr Edwin F. Early, Department of Economics, University of Plymouth, UK
Dr Anthony McFarlane, Department of History, University of Warwick, UK
Dr Nicholas James, Cambridge, UK
Professor Neil Whitehead, Department of Anthropology,
University of Wisconsin, USA

AFRICA

Professor John Thornton, Department of History, Millersville University, USA

EUROPE

Professor Richard Britnell, Department of History, University of Durham, UK
Dr Michael Broers, School of History, University of Leeds, UK
Professor Brian Davies, Department of History,
University of Texas, San Antonio USA

EUROPE (continued)

Professor Michael Jones, Department of History,
University of Nottingham, UK
Dr Don McRaild, Department of History, University of Sunderland
Dr Susan Rose, Department of History, Roehampton Institute, London, UK
Professor Peter Waldron, Department of History, University of Sunderland, UK
Dr Peter Wilson, Department of History, University of Sunderland, UK
Professor Spencer Tucker, Department of History,
Virginia Military Institute, USA
Professor Edward M. Yates, Department of Geography,
King's College, London, UK

WEST ASIA

Dr Ahron Bregman, Webster University, Regent's College, London, UK
Professor Ian Netton, School of Arabic Studies, University of Leeds, UK
Sajjid Rizvi, Department of Oriental Studies, Cambridge University, UK

SOUTH AND SOUTHEAST ASIA

Professor Joseph E. Schwartzberg, Department of Geography,
University of Minnesota, USA
Dr Sunil Kumar, Department of Medieval History,
University of New Delhi, India

NORTH AND EAST ASIA

Professor Gina Barnes, Department of East Asian Studies,
University of Durham, UK

AUSTRALASIA AND OCEANIA

Dr Steven Roger Fischer, Institute of Polynesian Languages and Literatures,
Auckland, New Zealand

*The publishers would like to acknowledge additional contributions and advice
from the following people: Professor Richard Overy, Professor Geoffrey Parker,
Gordon Marsden, Professor Kenneth Kiple, Paul Keeler.*

FOR THE SECOND EDITION

EDITORIAL DIRECTION Ailsa Heritage

Dr Paul Cornish, Centre for Defence Studies. King's College, London, UK
Dr Jane McIntosh
CIRCA Research and Reference Information, Cambridge, UK
Calum Macleod, Director, Great Britain – China Centre, London, UK

DORLING KINDERSLEY CARTOGRAPHY

EDITOR-IN-CHIEF Andrew Heritage

MANAGING EDITOR Lisa Thomas

SENIOR EDITOR Ferdie McDonald

PROJECT EDITORS Margaret Hynes, Elizabeth Wyse,
Ailsa Heritage, Caroline Chapman,
Debra Clapson, Wim Jenkins

ADDITIONAL EDITORIAL ASSISTANCE
Louise Keane, Adele Rackley

SENIOR MANAGING ART EDITOR Philip Lord

PRINCIPAL DESIGNER Nicola Liddiard

PROJECT ART EDITORS Rhonda Fisher,
Carol Ann Davis, Karen Gregory

CARTOGRAPHIC MANAGER David Roberts

SENIOR CARTOGRAPHIC EDITOR Roger Bullen

CARTOGRAPHIC DESIGN John Plumer

DIGITAL MAPS CREATED BY Rob Stokes

PROJECT CARTOGRAPHERS Pamela Alford, James Anderson,
Dale Buckton, Tony Chambers, Jan Clark, Tom Coulson, Martin
Darlison, Jeremy Hepworth, Chris Jackson,
Julia Lunn, John Plumer, Alka Ranger, Ann Stephenson,
Julie Turner, Peter Winfield

ADDITIONAL CARTOGRAPHY Advanced Illustration Ltd.,
Arcadia Ltd., Lovell Johns Ltd.

HISTORICAL CARTOGRAPHIC CONSULTANT
András Bereznay

PICTURE RESEARCH Deborah Pownall, Louise Thomas, Anna
Bedewell

JACKET DESIGNER Bob Warner

JACKET COPYWRITER Adam Powley

JACKET EDITOR Mariza O'Keeffe

INDEXING Julia Lynch, Janet Smy,
Jo Russ, Sophie Park,
Ruth Duxbury, Zoë Ellinson

DATABASE CONSULTANT Simon Lewis

SYSTEMS MANAGER Philip Rowles

PRODUCTION Stuart Masheter

First published in the United States as Atlas of World History by Dorling Kindersley Publishing Inc., 375 Hudson Street, New York, New York 10014
Copyright © Dorling Kindersley Limited, London 2000. Reprinted with Revisions 2001. Second Edition 2005
A Penguin Company

Library of Congress Catalog Card Number: 99-057342

Printed and bound by Star Standard, Singapore

Picture information: *p.1* Andreas Cellarius, rector of the Latin school at Hoorn in northern Holland, produced this map of the eastern hemisphere in 1708 as part of his exquisite atlas of the heavens, *Atlas Coelestis; seu Harmonia
Macrocosmica.* The map illustrates the seasons of the year and the various climate zones from pole to pole. *pp.2–3* Produced in 1646, by Matthäus Merian, a Swiss engraver. The geography in the map is based on world maps using the
influential Mercator projection, produced by the Dutch Blaeu family, a dynasty of master cartographers. *p.5* This 1598 Dutch engraving shows a cartographer at work, probably Rogerius Bullenius.

The emergence and spread of early humans

The first representative of the *Homo* genus, *Homo habilis* ("handy man"), emerged about 2.5 million years ago and was distinguished by the ability to make and use tools. *Homo ergaster*, which appeared about 1.8 million years ago, had a still larger brain capacity, tall, long-legged physique and ability to walk fully upright, and adapted successfully to a wide range of environments, rapidly spreading as far as East Asia, where it evolved into *Homo erectus*. The earliest fossil remains of fully modern humans, *Homo sapiens sapiens,* found in Africa, date to c.150,000 years ago. Resourceful and inventive, modern humans colonized the most marginal regions, and became the sole surviving human species.

Fossils of *Homo habilis* were discovered in the Olduvai Gorge in the 1960s, and are dated to 2.5 million years ago.

The fossils found at Koobi Fora in Kenya, dating to 1.7 million years ago, are amongst the earliest finds of *Homo ergaster*, and clearly demonstrate a marked increase in brain size.

Modern humans reached Europe from Africa c.45,000 years ago and replaced the Neanderthal population by 28,000 years ago. This skull was found at the site of Predmostí in eastern Europe.

SEE ALSO:

North America: pp.120–121

South America: pp.142–143

Africa: pp.160–161

Europe: pp.174–175

West Asia: pp.220–221

South and Southeast Asia: pp.240–241

North and East Asia: pp.258–259

Australasia and Oceania: pp.278–279

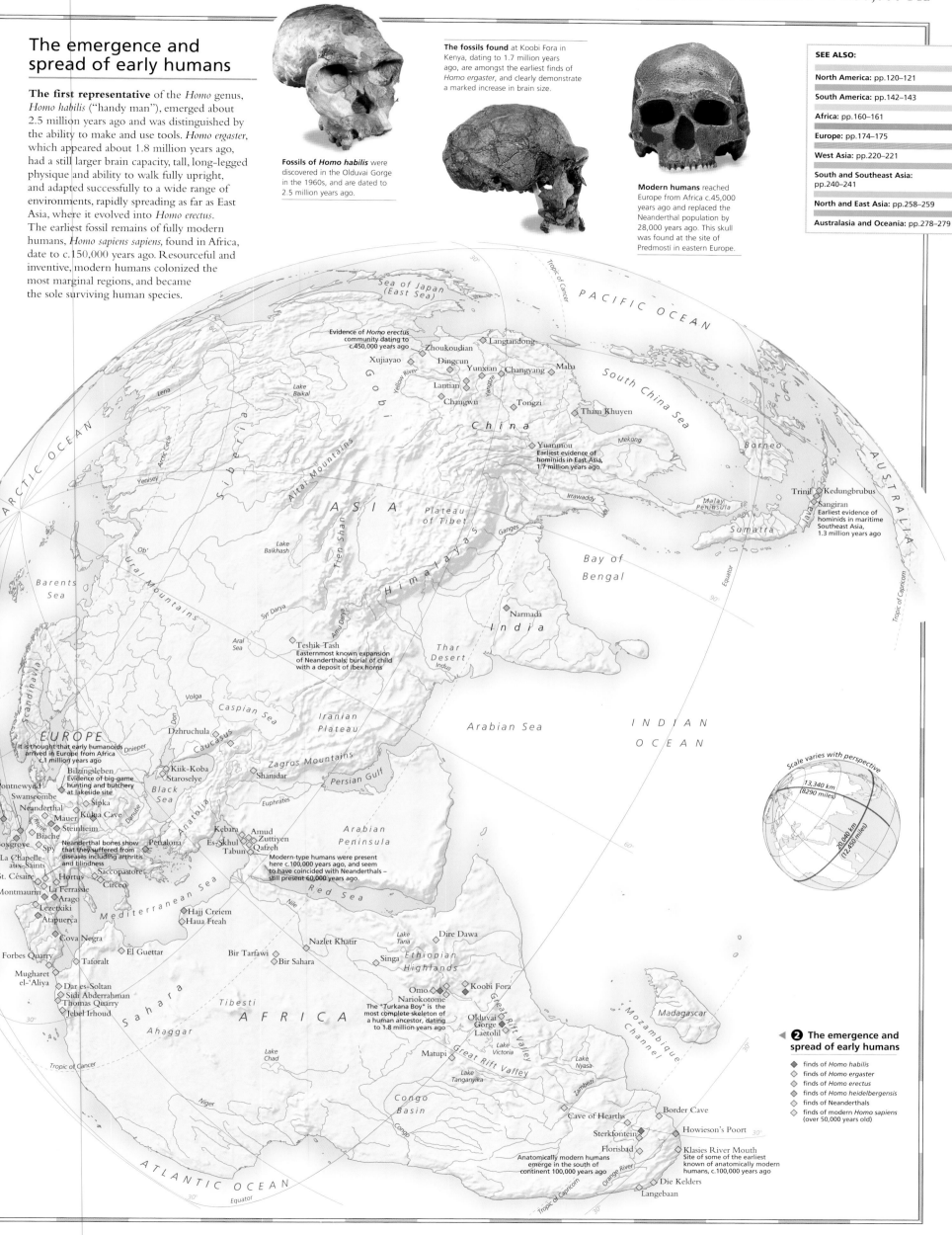

Evidence of *Homo erectus* community dating to c.450,000 years ago

Yuanmou Earliest evidence of hominids in East Asia, 1.7 million years ago

Sangiran Earliest evidence of hominids in maritime Southeast Asia, 1.3 million years ago

Teshik-Tash Easternmost known expansion of Neanderthals; burial of child with a deposit of ibex horns

EUROPE It is thought that early humanoids arrived in Europe from Africa c.1 million years ago

Bilzingsleben Evidence of big-game hunting and butchery at lakeside site

Neanderthal bones show that they suffered from diseases including arthritis and blindness

Modern-type humans were present here c.100,000 years ago, and seem to have coincided with Neanderthals – still present 60,000 years ago

Nariokotome The "Turkana Boy" is the most complete skeleton of a human ancestor, dating to 1.8 million years ago

Anatomically modern humans emerge in the south of continent 100,000 years ago

Klasies River Mouth Site of some of the earliest known of anatomically modern humans, c.100,000 years ago

Scale varies with perspective

13,340 km (8290 miles)

20,040 km (12,450 miles)

2 The emergence and spread of early humans

◆ finds of *Homo habilis*
◆ finds of *Homo ergaster*
◇ finds of *Homo erectus*
◆ finds of *Homo heidelbergensis*
◆ finds of Neanderthals
◇ finds of modern *Homo sapiens* (over 50,000 years old)

THE WORLD FROM PREHISTORY TO 10,000 BCE

FULLY MODERN HUMANS evolved in Africa between 200,000 and 100,000 years ago. With their tool-making skills and abilities to communicate and organize themselves into groups, these early hunter-gatherers were uniquely well-equipped to explore and settle new environments. By 30,000 years ago, they had colonized much of the globe. When the last Ice Age reached its peak 20,000 years ago, they were able to adapt; they refined their tool technology, enabling them to fully exploit the depleted resources, and used sturdy shelters and warm clothing to survive the harsh conditions. As the temperatures rose and the ice sheets retreated, plants and animals became more abundant and new areas were settled. By 9000 BCE larger populations and intense hunting had contributed to the near-extinction of large mammals, such as mastodons and mammoths. By 8000 BCE, in the Near East, groups of hunter-gatherers were living in permanent settlements, harvesting wild cereals and experimenting with the domestication of local animals. The transition to agriculture was under way.

HUNTER-GATHERERS AND THE ENVIRONMENT

Hunter-gatherers, whether semi-settled in one location or constantly on the move in search of food, would have carried a detailed mental map of important local landmarks. Precious water or food sources may have become centers of cultic activity, as in the rock painting below. Though its meaning is far from clear, the wavy vertical lines seem to represent cascades of water. The painting may even be a representation of a specific sacred site.

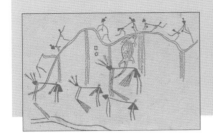

This painting, discovered at Kalhotia in Central India, seems to show a lizard or crocodile, cascades, a stream, and people carrying bundles of stone-tipped arrows.

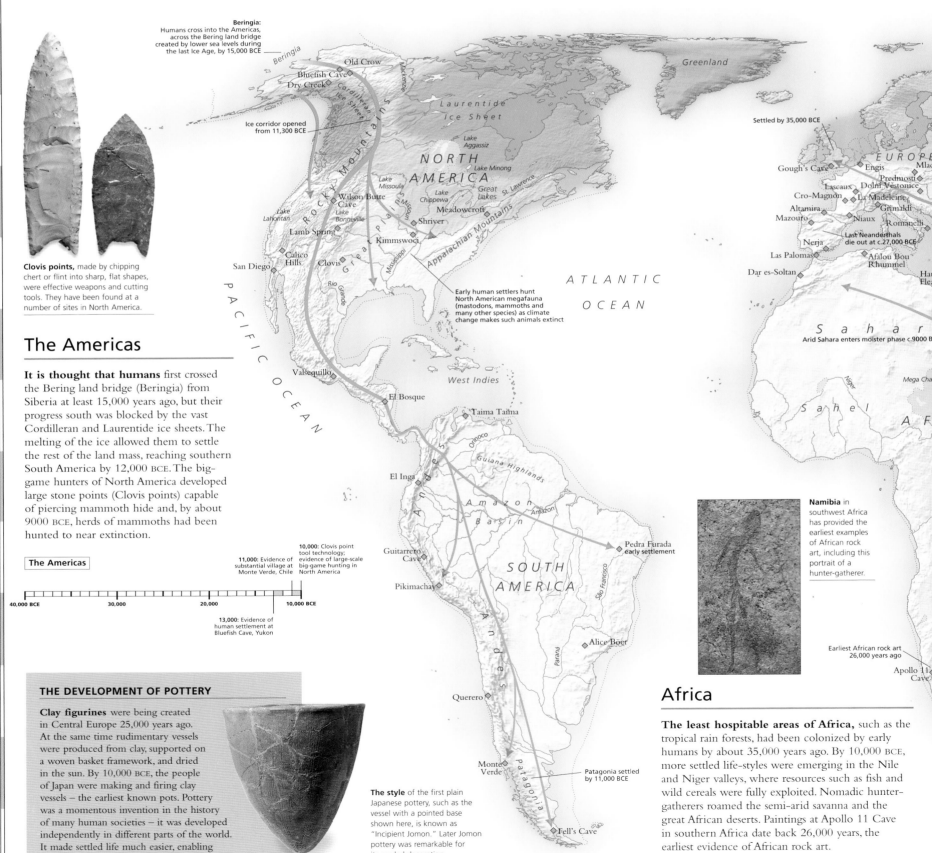

Clovis points, made by chipping chert or flint into sharp, flat shapes, were effective weapons and cutting tools. They have been found at a number of sites in North America.

The Americas

It is thought that humans first crossed the Bering land bridge (Beringia) from Siberia at least 15,000 years ago, but their progress south was blocked by the vast Cordilleran and Laurentide ice sheets. The melting of the ice allowed them to settle the rest of the land mass, reaching southern South America by 12,000 BCE. The big-game hunters of North America developed large stone points (Clovis points) capable of piercing mammoth hide and, by about 9000 BCE, herds of mammoths had been hunted to near extinction.

The Americas

40,000 BCE   30,000   20,000   10,000 BCE

13,000: Evidence of human settlement at Bluefish Cave, Yukon

11,000: Evidence of substantial village at Monte Verde, Chile

10,000: Clovis point tool technology; evidence of large-scale big-game hunting in North America

Beringia: Humans cross into the Americas, across the Bering land bridge created by lower sea levels during the last Ice Age, by 15,000 BCE

Ice corridor opened from 11,300 BCE

Early human settlers hunt North American megafauna (mastodons, mammoths and many other species) as climate change makes such animals extinct

Settled by 35,000 BCE

Last Neanderthals die out at c.27,000 BCE

Arid Sahara enters moister phase c.9000 BCE

Namibia in southwest Africa has provided the earliest examples of African rock art, including this portrait of a hunter-gatherer.

Earliest African rock art 26,000 years ago

THE DEVELOPMENT OF POTTERY

Clay figurines were being created in Central Europe 25,000 years ago. At the same time rudimentary vessels were produced from clay, supported on a woven basket framework, and dried in the sun. By 10,000 BCE, the people of Japan were making and firing clay vessels – the earliest known pots. Pottery was a momentous invention in the history of many human societies – it was developed independently in different parts of the world. It made settled life much easier, enabling people to store and carry food and water.

The style of the first plain Japanese pottery, such as the vessel with a pointed base shown here, is known as "Incipient Jomon." Later Jomon pottery was remarkable for its corded decoration.

Africa

The least hospitable areas of Africa, such as the tropical rain forests, had been colonized by early humans by about 35,000 years ago. By 10,000 BCE, more settled life-styles were emerging in the Nile and Niger valleys, where resources such as fish and wild cereals were fully exploited. Nomadic hunter-gatherers roamed the semi-arid savanna and the great African deserts. Paintings at Apollo 11 Cave in southern Africa date back 26,000 years, the earliest evidence of African rock art.

Portable art objects – sculptures and engravings of animals, like these chamois, on bone and antler, or small stone slabs or plaques – were being produced in Europe by 25,000 years ago.

Europe

Settled by modern humans by about 45,000 BCE, Ice Age conditions over much of Europe tested their ingenuity; wood, bone, hide, and antler were all used to build a range of shelters, and new tools – bows and arrows, spear-throwers, and harpoons – were used to hunt big game. As the climate stabilized, some sites were occupied year round, while others were used by seasonal hunters.

Europe

c.45,000: Fully modern humans settle continent; new tool technology

c.26,000: Extinction of Neanderthals

10,000: Retreat of glaciers; temperate deciduous woodland spreads northward. Rich array of marine and land resources

110,000 BCE — 90,000 — 70,000 — 50,000 — 30,000 — 10,000 BCE

120,000: Neanderthals present from western Europe to Central Asia

c.10,000: Large mammals, such as woolly rhinoceros, giant deer, and mammoth gradually become extinct

West Asia

The world's earliest known burial, at Qafzeh Cave in Israel, dates back 100,000 years and is evidence of human self-awareness and ritual activity. By 13,000 BCE people from Wadi en-Natuf, also in Israel, were intensively harvesting, grinding, and storing the abundant wild grains which grew there. The same people also hunted gazelle herds, using drive lanes leading to traps.

This bone and shell necklace was one of the personal items found at a burial in Mugharet el-Kebara in Israel.

West and South Asia

100,000: World's first known burial at Qafzeh Cave, Israel

40,000: Neanderthals still present alongside modern humans in southwest Asia

13,000: Intensive harvesting of wild cereals by Natufian people, Israel

11,000: Dogs domesticated in Middle East; the world's first domesticated animals

110,000 BCE — 90,000 — 70,000 — 50,000 — 30,000 — 10,000 BCE

45,000: Aurignacian flint tool technology developed in Israel and spreads across southern Europe

17,000: Evidence of wild cereal gathering in the Middle East

12,000: First use of grindstones in Middle East

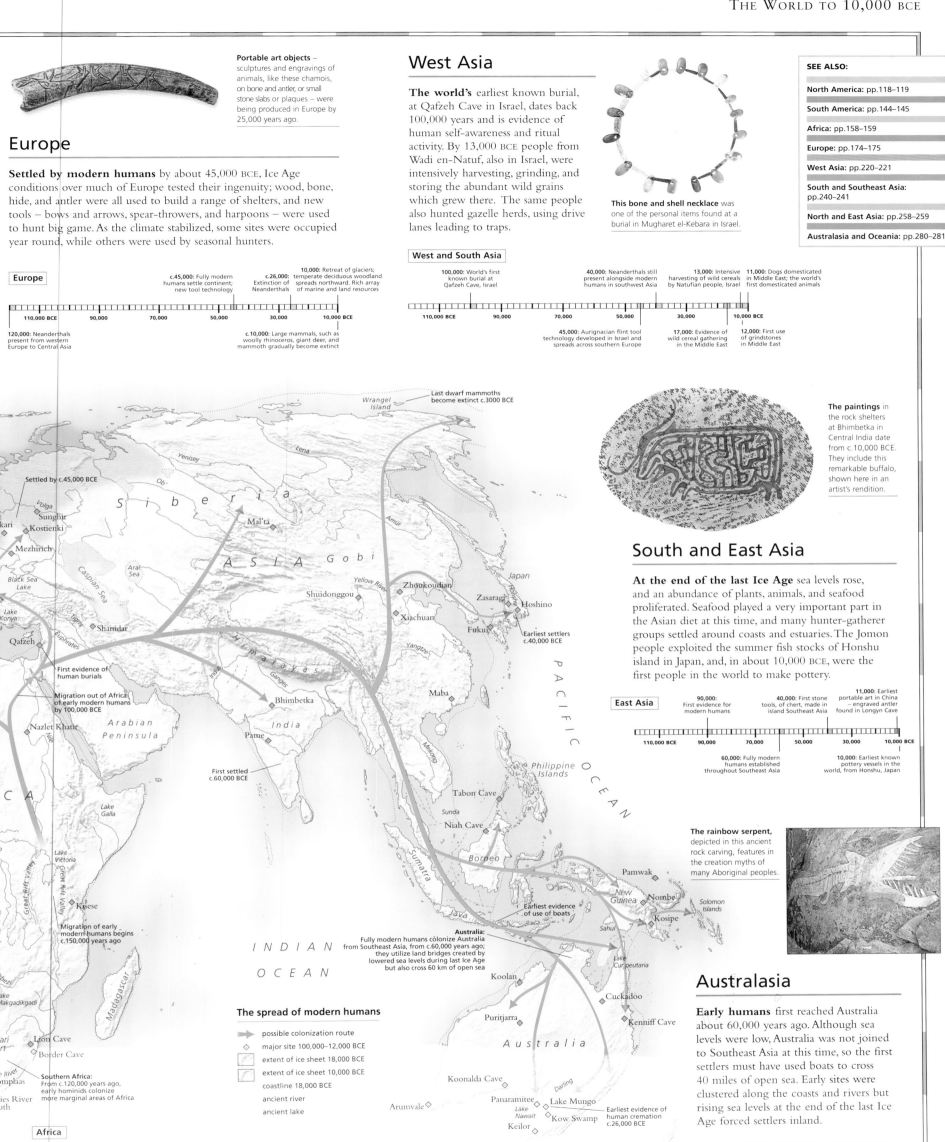

The paintings in the rock shelters at Bhimbetka in Central India date from c.10,000 BCE. They include this remarkable buffalo, shown here in an artist's rendition.

South and East Asia

At the end of the last Ice Age sea levels rose, and an abundance of plants, animals, and seafood proliferated. Seafood played a very important part in the Asian diet at this time, and many hunter-gatherer groups settled around coasts and estuaries. The Jomon people exploited the summer fish stocks of Honshu island in Japan, and, in about 10,000 BCE, were the first people in the world to make pottery.

East Asia

90,000: First evidence for modern humans

40,000: First stone tools, of chert, made in island Southeast Asia

11,000: Earliest portable art in China – engraved antler found in Longyn Cave

110,000 BCE — 90,000 — 70,000 — 50,000 — 30,000 — 10,000 BCE

60,000: Fully modern humans established throughout Southeast Asia

10,000: Earliest known pottery vessels in the world, from Honshu, Japan

The rainbow serpent, depicted in this ancient rock carving, features in the creation myths of many Aboriginal peoples.

Australasia

Early humans first reached Australia about 60,000 years ago. Although sea levels were low, Australia was not joined to Southeast Asia at this time, so the first settlers must have used boats to cross 40 miles of open sea. Early sites were clustered along the coasts and rivers but rising sea levels at the end of the last Ice Age forced settlers inland.

The spread of modern humans

→ possible colonization route
◇ major site 100,000–12,000 BCE
⬚ extent of ice sheet 18,000 BCE
⬚ extent of ice sheet 10,000 BCE
—— coastline 18,000 BCE
—— ancient river
—— ancient lake

Africa

130,000: Earliest evidence of modern humans in eastern and southern Africa

70,000: Evidence of burials at site of Klasies River Mouth, southern Africa

30,000: New tool technology; development of microliths

26,000: Painted rock slabs at Apollo 11 Cave, Namibia

130,000 BCE — 110,000 — 90,000 — 70,000 — 50,000 — 30,000 — 10,000 BCE

42,000: Red ocher being mined from Lion Cave, southern Africa; probably used for body decoration

20,000: Terra-cotta figurines from Algeria. Engraved objects from Border Cave, South Africa

Australasia

45,000: World's first known rock art, from Panaramitee, South Australia

16,000: Extinction of giant marsupials caused by changing climate

110,000 BCE — 90,000 — 70,000 — 50,000 — 30,000 — 10,000 BCE

60,000: Settlement of Australia by groups from Southeast Asia

20,000: Settlement extends to southern coast of Tasmania

Map labels: Wrangel Island; Last dwarf mammoths become extinct c.3000 BCE; Lena; Yenisey; Ob; Siberia; Settled by c.45,000 BCE; Volga; Sunghir; Kostienki; shkari; Mezhirich; Black Sea Lake; Caspian Sea; Aral Sea; Mal'ta; ASIA; Gobi; Amur; Yellow River; Shuidonggou; Zhoukoudian; Japan; Zasaragi; Hoshino; Xiachuan; Fukui; Earliest settlers c.40,000 BCE; Yangtze; Maba; PACIFIC OCEAN; Lake Konya; Shanidar; Tigris; Euphrates; Qafzeh; First evidence of human burials; Himalayas; Indus; Ganges; Bhimbetka; Migration out of Africa of early modern humans by 100,000 BCE; Nazlet Khatir; Arabian Peninsula; India; Patne; First settled c.60,000 BCE; Mekong; Philippine Islands; Tabon Cave; Sunda; Niah Cave; Borneo; Sumatra; Pamwak; Nile; Lake Galla; Java; Sahul; New Guinea; Nombe; Solomon Islands; Kosipe; Earliest evidence of use of boats; ngo; Great Rift Valley; Great Rift Valley; Kisese; Lake Victoria; Migration of early modern humans begins c.150,000 years ago; Madagascar; INDIAN OCEAN; Australia: Fully modern humans colonize Australia from Southeast Asia, from c.60,000 years ago; they utilize land bridges created by lowered sea levels during last Ice Age but also cross 60 km of open sea; Lake Curpeutaria; Koolan; Lake Makgadikgadi; ahari sert; Lion Cave; Border Cave; Puritjarra; Cuckadoo; Kenniff Cave; Australia; nge River oomphas; Southern Africa: From c.120,000 years ago, early hominids colonize more marginal areas of Africa; lasies River Mouth; Koonalda Cave; Koolan; Darling; Panaramitee; Lake Mungo; Lake Nawait; Kow Swamp; Earliest evidence of human cremation c.26,000 BCE; Arumvale; Keilor; Tasmania; New Zealand; Beginner's Luck Cave; Bone Cave

THE WORLD 10,000 – 5000 BCE

IN THE MORE HOSPITABLE CLIMATE and terrain of the post-glacial world, groups of hunter-gatherers began to experiment with the domestication of wild cereals and animals. By 7000 BCE, farming was the main means of subsistence in West Asia, although hunter-gathering remained the most common form of subsistence elsewhere. Over the next 5000 years farming became established independently in other areas. The impact of the agricultural revolution on early societies was immense. Farming could support much larger populations, so settlement sizes increased significantly. Larger communities generated new demands and possibilities, and a class of specialized craftsmen evolved. Trade in raw materials and manufactured goods increased contact between farming communities. Communal ventures, such as irrigation, encouraged cooperation. All these developments paved the way for the much larger cities and states which were soon to follow.

THE FIRST USE OF METAL

The discovery that metals can be isolated from ore-bearing rocks by heating appears to have been made independently in West Asia and southeastern Europe between 7000–5000 BCE. Copper, gold, and lead, all soft metals that melt at relatively low temperatures, were the first metals in use. In early copper-using societies, most copper objects were decorative items that denoted the status of the owner: tools made from the new material could not compete with those of flint and stone.

This horned bull, fashioned from sheet gold is one of a pair from a rich set of grave goods unearthed at a cemetery in Varna, southeast Europe.

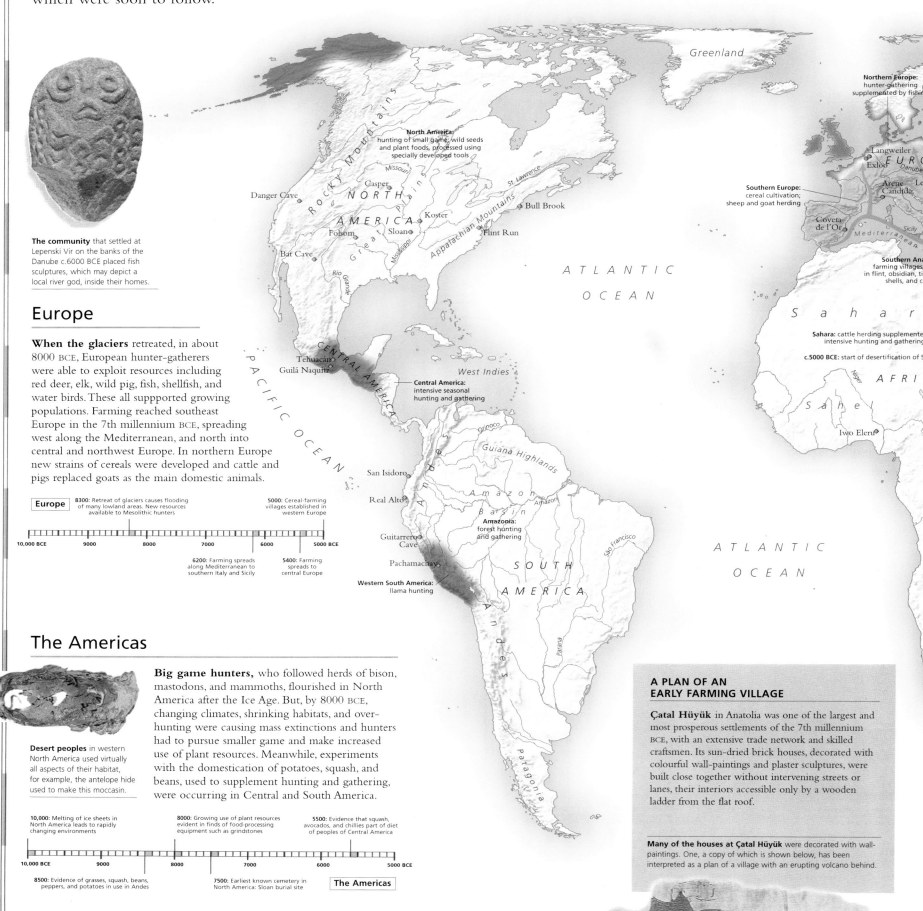

The community that settled at Lepenski Vir on the banks of the Danube c.6000 BCE placed fish sculptures, which may depict a local river god, inside their homes.

Europe

When the glaciers retreated, in about 8000 BCE, European hunter-gatherers were able to exploit resources including red deer, elk, wild pig, fish, shellfish, and water birds. These all supported growing populations. Farming reached southeast Europe in the 7th millennium BCE, spreading west along the Mediterranean, and north into central and northwest Europe. In northern Europe new strains of cereals were developed and cattle and pigs replaced goats as the main domestic animals.

Europe		
8300: Retreat of glaciers causes flooding of many lowland areas. New resources available to Mesolithic hunters		**5000:** Cereal-farming villages established in western Europe

10,000 BCE — 9000 — 8000 — 7000 — 6000 — 5000 BCE

6200: Farming spreads along Mediterranean to southern Italy and Sicily

5400: Farming spreads to central Europe

The Americas

Big game hunters, who followed herds of bison, mastodons, and mammoths, flourished in North America after the Ice Age. But, by 8000 BCE, changing climates, shrinking habitats, and over-hunting were causing mass extinctions and hunters had to pursue smaller game and make increased use of plant resources. Meanwhile, experiments with the domestication of potatoes, squash, and beans, used to supplement hunting and gathering, were occurring in Central and South America.

Desert peoples in western North America used virtually all aspects of their habitat, for example, the antelope hide used to make this moccasin.

			The Americas
10,000: Melting of ice sheets in North America leads to rapidly changing environments	**8000:** Growing use of plant resources evident in finds of food-processing equipment such as grindstones	**5500:** Evidence that squash, avocados, and chillies part of diet of peoples of Central America	

10,000 BCE — 9000 — 8000 — 7000 — 6000 — 5000 BCE

8500: Evidence of grasses, squash, beans, peppers, and potatoes in use in Andes

7500: Earliest known cemetery in North America: Sloan burial site

A PLAN OF AN EARLY FARMING VILLAGE

Çatal Hüyük in Anatolia was one of the largest and most prosperous settlements of the 7th millennium BCE, with an extensive trade network and skilled craftsmen. Its sun-dried brick houses, decorated with colourful wall-paintings and plaster sculptures, were built close together without intervening streets or lanes, their interiors accessible only by a wooden ladder from the flat roof.

Many of the houses at Çatal Hüyük were decorated with wall-paintings. One, a copy of which is shown below, has been interpreted as a plan of a village with an erupting volcano behind.

Map labels

Greenland

Northern Europe: hunter-gathering supplemented by fishing

North America: hunting of small game; wild seeds and plant foods, processed using specially developed tools

Rocky Mountains

Danger Cave

Casper

NORTH AMERICA

Missouri

St. Lawrence

Bull Brook

Koster

Folsom

Sloan

Appalachian Mountains

Flint Run

Bat Cave

Great Plains

Rio Grande

Mississippi

ATLANTIC OCEAN

Langweiler

Exloo

EUROPE

Danube

Arene Candide

Lepenski Vir

Southern Europe: cereal cultivation; sheep and goat herding

Coveta de l'Or

Mediterranean Sea

Sicily

Southern Anatolia: farming villages trade in flint, obsidian, timber, shells, and copper

Sahara

Sahara: cattle herding supplemented by intensive hunting and gathering

c.5000 BCE: start of desertification of Sahara

AFRICA

Niger

Sahel

Iwo Eleru

Tehuacán

Guilá Naquitz

CENTRAL AMERICA

West Indies

Central America: intensive seasonal hunting and gathering

PACIFIC OCEAN

Orinoco

Guiana Highlands

Amazon

San Isidoro

Real Alto

Amazon Basin

Amazon

Amazonia: forest hunting and gathering

São Francisco

Guitarrero Cave

SOUTH AMERICA

Pachamachay

Western South America: llama hunting

Andes

Parana

Patagonia

ATLANTIC OCEAN

Congo

West Asia

The world's earliest farmers settled in the fertile arc of land stretching from the Persian Gulf to the eastern Mediterranean. Large-seeded grains were domesticated in Jericho by 8000 BCE. Villages of mud-brick houses appeared in Anatolia, and in central Mesopotamia by the 7th millennium BCE and craftsmen were smelting copper and lead by 6000 BCE. By 5500 BCE the farmers of southern Mesopotamia were irrigating arid land to improve crop yields.

Terra-cotta figurines of goddesses with swollen abdomens were found at Çatal Hüyük, suggesting a fertility cult.

East Asia

In northern China, agriculture dates back to c.7000 BCE. At farming villages such as Banpo, millet was cultivated and kept in grain storage pits, and there is evidence that pigs and dogs were domesticated. In a separate development, rice cultivation was initiated in the lowlands of the Yangtze delta, probably by 6000 BCE. In Japan, the Jomon people lived by hunting, fishing, and gathering in the well-stocked mountains and coastal waters. Although the Japanese were making pottery by 10,500 BCE, their way of life would remain based on hunting and gathering for several thousand years.

The people of Banpo were producing and firing pottery such as this cord-scored amphora by the 5th millennium BCE.

SEE ALSO:

North America: pp.120–121

South America: pp.144–145

Africa: pp.158–159

Europe: pp.174–175

West Asia: pp.220–221

South and Southeast Asia: pp.240–241

North and East Asia: pp.258–259

Australasia and Oceania: pp.280–281

West Asia

9000: Wheat (einkorn) harvested in Mesopotamia

8000: First fully domesticated cereals harvested in Jericho

7000: Goat becomes main domesticated animal throughout region. Foundation of settlement of Çatal Hüyük, Anatolia

6000: At Hassuna in northern Mesopotamia; painted pottery and copper and lead smelting

6500: Earliest known Old World textiles (linen) from Çatal Hüyük

5500: Ubaid culture of southern Mesopotamia harnesses spring floods of Euphrates for irrigation

10,000 BCE — 9000 — 8000 — 7000 — 6000 — 5000 BCE

East Asia

9000: Limestone caves in central China give evidence of hunting, fishing, and gathering way of life

c.6000: Hunting and fishing villages in Yangtze river delta begin cultivating rice

5000: Jade imported into northern Manchuria from Central Asia or Siberia

6500: 'Jomon' pottery spreads throughout southern Japanese archipelago

10,000 BCE — 9000 — 8000 — 7000 — 6000 — 5000 BCE

South and Southeast Asia

The first South Asian farmers were cultivating wheat and barley in the fertile highlands of northern India by the 5th millennium BCE. At the same time there was a gradual transition from hunting to farming, primarily rice, to the south of the Ganges valley. In Southeast Asia, post-glacial rises in sea levels created many new islands and estuaries with a marked increase in maritime resources. By c.2000 BCE farming had gradually become established in this region.

South and Southeast Asia

7000: Evidence of drainage and cultivation in the highlands of New Guinea

6000: Pottery in grave goods from Mehrgarh indicates trade with Central Asia

6000: First pottery production in mainland Southeast Asia

10,000 BCE — 9000 — 8000 — 7000 — 6000 — 5000 BCE

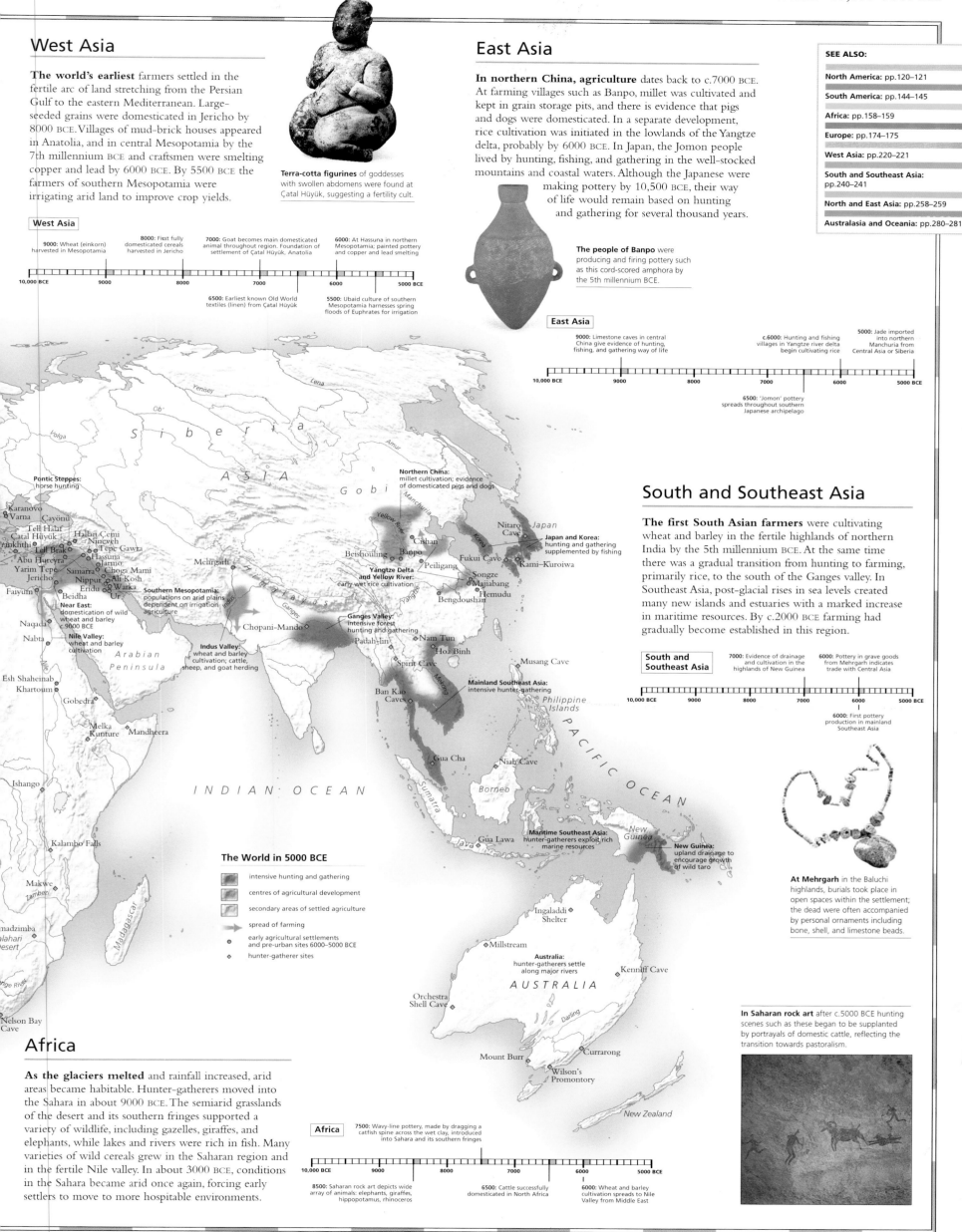

At Mehrgarh in the Baluchi highlands, burials took place in open spaces within the settlement; the dead were often accompanied by personal ornaments including bone, shell, and limestone beads.

The World in 5000 BCE

- intensive hunting and gathering
- centres of agricultural development
- secondary areas of settled agriculture
- → spread of farming
- early agricultural settlements and pre-urban sites 6000–5000 BCE
- hunter-gatherer sites

In Saharan rock art after c.5000 BCE hunting scenes such as these began to be supplanted by portrayals of domestic cattle, reflecting the transition towards pastoralism.

Africa

As the glaciers melted and rainfall increased, arid areas became habitable. Hunter-gatherers moved into the Sahara in about 9000 BCE. The semiarid grasslands of the desert and its southern fringes supported a variety of wildlife, including gazelles, giraffes, and elephants, while lakes and rivers were rich in fish. Many varieties of wild cereals grew in the Saharan region and in the fertile Nile valley. In about 3000 BCE, conditions in the Sahara became arid once again, forcing early settlers to move to more hospitable environments.

Africa

7500: Wavy-line pottery, made by dragging a catfish spine across the wet clay, introduced into Sahara and its southern fringes

8500: Saharan rock art depicts wide array of animals: elephants, giraffes, hippopotamus, rhinoceros

6500: Cattle successfully domesticated in North Africa

6000: Wheat and barley cultivation spreads to Nile Valley from Middle East

10,000 BCE — 9000 — 8000 — 7000 — 6000 — 5000 BCE

THE ADVENT OF AGRICULTURE

THE APPEARANCE OF FARMING transformed the face of the Earth. It was not merely a change in subsistence – perhaps in some regions a necessity caused by over-hunting, limited natural resources, and population growth – it also transformed the way in which our ancestors lived. Agriculture, and the vastly greater crop yields it produced, enabled large groups of people to live in permanent villages, surrounded by material goods and equipment. Specialized craftsmen produced these goods, supported by the community as a whole – the beginnings of social differentiation. These developments led ultimately to the emergence of the first cities, but in 5000 BCE only a limited number of regions were fully dependent on agriculture. In many parts of the globe, small-scale farming was being used to supplement hunting and gathering – the first steps in the gradual transition to the sedentary agricultural way of life.

Fragments of Egyptian wavy line pottery, decorated with a fish spine from c.7000 BCE

The agricultural revolution

The advent of farming brought large groups of people together into settled communities. Not only could food production be made more efficient, but animals could be tended communally, and food surpluses used to support villagers through the winter months. Some members of the community were therefore able to develop craft skills, engage in long-distance trade, and experiment with technology, such as pottery kilns, gold, and copper metallurgy and, by c.5500 BCE, irrigation. But sedentary coexistence also exposed people to infectious disease; the settlement of Çatal Hüyük, for example, was plagued by malaria.

Stone querns, dating to about 6000 years ago, were used by farmers for grinding grain into flour, which could then be kept in storage pits.

Ways of life

The exceptional productivity of the major cultivated species, in particular cereals, was vital to the viability of early farming villages. Cereals can be kept as a year-round resource, providing a staple supplement to more seasonal foods, thus creating a total dependence on farming. An inevitable, and necessary, by-product of this settled way of life was pottery – pottery containers could be used for both storing and cooking the harvested food. The technique of hand-modeling and firing clay pots evolved independently in many regions. Molds, wheels, and kilns were later innovations, and became the province of specialized craftsmen.

The earliest pottery had a round-based shape (*right*), and was sometimes decorated with incisions or impressions. A characteristic later vessel from western Europe was the flat-based beaker (*left*), again decorated with incisions. In other regions of Europe, notably the southeast, painted decoration was also used.

① The development of pottery

Earliest era of widespread pottery production

- 11th millennium BCE
- 9th millennium BCE
- 8th millennium BCE
- 7th millennium BCE
- 6th millennium BCE
- 3rd millennium BCE
- ◇ first known pottery-making sites

Settlement and innovation

c.10,5000: Earliest pottery in the world, from southern Japan

9000: Earliest Chinese pottery

7000: First pottery in the Near East
7000: Foundation of Çatal Hüyük, Anatolia, the largest neolithic site in the Near East

6500: Small-scale copper smelting at Catal Hüyük

5500: World's earliest irrigation system, at Choga Mami, Mesopotamia

5000: Gold and copper metallurgy in the Balkans

c.8500: Saharan rock art depicts wild animals, long since extinct in the region

c.7500: Characteristic "wavy line" pottery of the Sahara is produced

6500: Linen from Catal Hüyük is earliest known textile in the world

6000: Pottery produced at Mehrgarh, Central Asia; First pottery in mainland Southeast Asia

5200: Bandkeramik pottery produced by farmers of central Europe

10,000 BCE — 9000 — 8000 — 7000 — 6000 — 5000 BCE

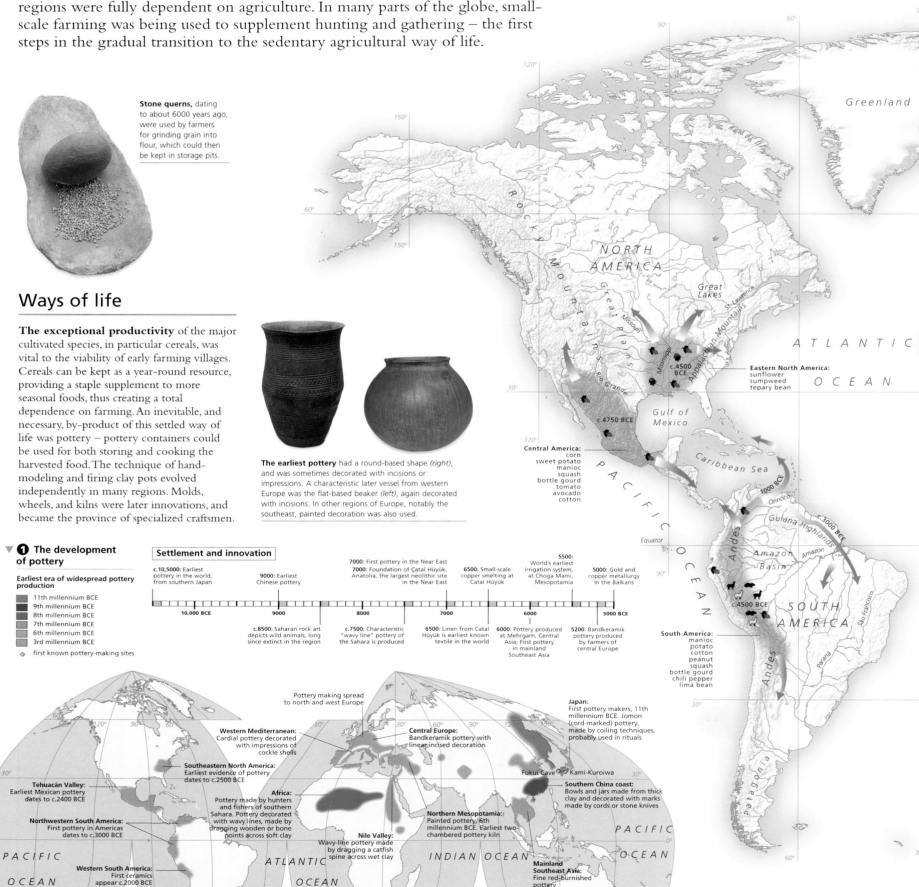

Map labels:

Greenland

NORTH AMERICA

Great Lakes

c.4500 BCE

Eastern North America: sunflower sumpweed tepary bean

ATLANTIC OCEAN

Gulf of Mexico

c.4750 BCE

Central America: corn sweet potato manioc squash bottle gourd tomato avocado cotton

Caribbean Sea

1000 BCE

Guiana Highlands

Equator

Amazon Basin

c.3000 BCE

c.4500 BCE

SOUTH AMERICA

South America: manioc potato cotton peanut squash bottle gourd chili pepper lima bean

Andes

PACIFIC OCEAN

Japan: First pottery makers, 11th millennium BCE. Jomon (cord-marked) pottery, made by coiling techniques, probably used in rituals

Pottery making spread to north and west Europe

Western Mediterranean: Cardial pottery decorated with impressions of cockle shells

Central Europe: Bandkeramik pottery with linear incised decoration

Southeastern North America: Earliest evidence of pottery dates to c.2500 BCE

Tehuacán Valley: Earliest Mexican pottery dates to c.2400 BCE

Africa: Pottery made by hunters and fishers of southern Sahara. Pottery decorated with wavy lines, made by dragging wooden or bone points across soft clay

Northwestern South America: First pottery in Americas dates to c.3000 BCE

Nile Valley: Wavy-line pottery made by dragging a catfish spine across wet clay

Fukui Cave Kami-Kuroiwa

Southern China coast: Bowls and jars made from thick clay and decorated with marks made by cords or stone knives

Northern Mesopotamia: Painted pottery, 6th millennium BCE. Earliest two-chambered pottery kiln

Mainland Southeast Asia: Fine red-burnished pottery

Western South America: First ceramics appear c.2000 BCE

PACIFIC OCEAN

ATLANTIC OCEAN

INDIAN OCEAN

PACIFIC OCEAN

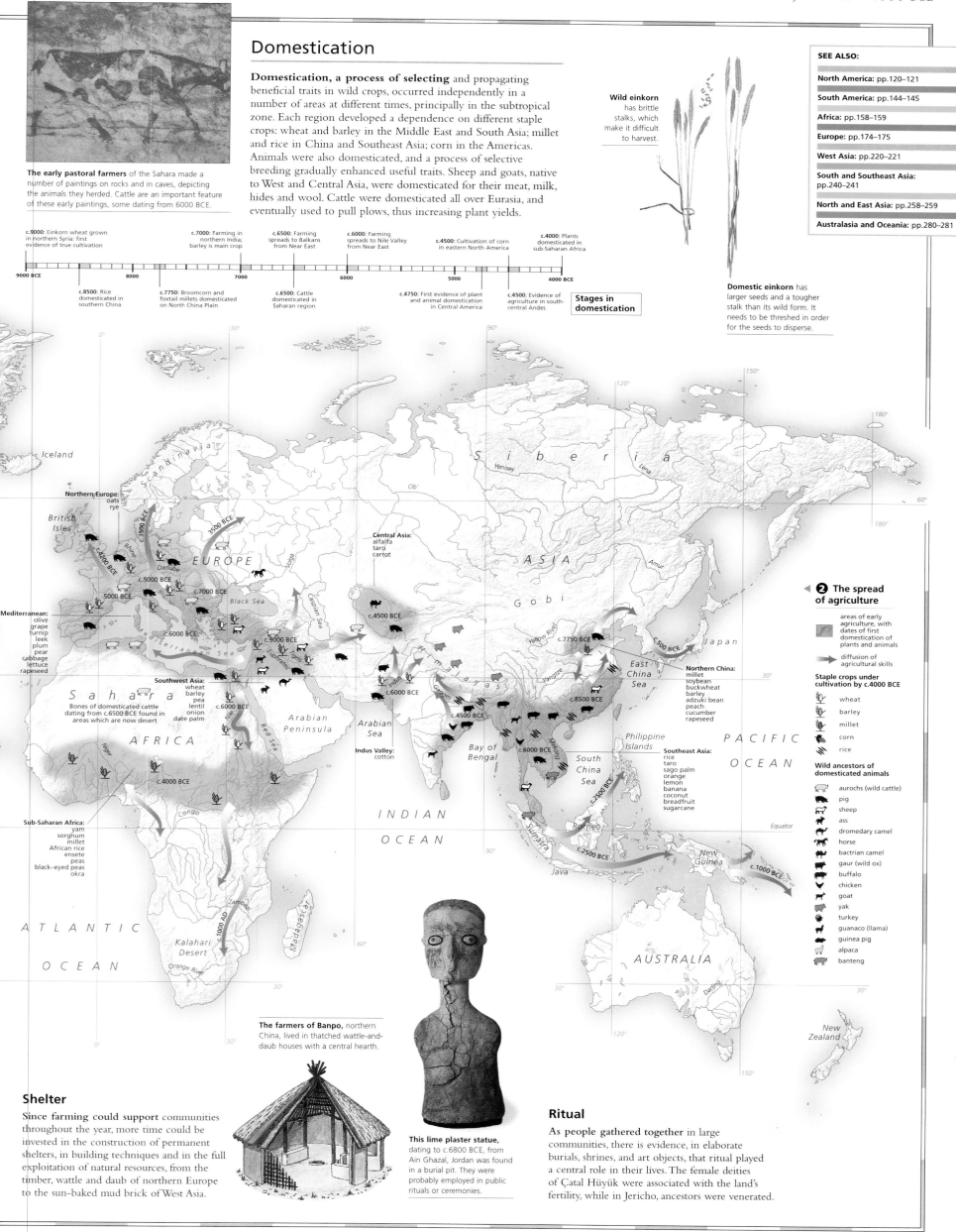

The early pastoral farmers of the Sahara made a number of paintings on rocks and in caves, depicting the animals they herded. Cattle are an important feature of these early paintings, some dating from 6000 BCE.

Domestication

Domestication, a process of selecting and propagating beneficial traits in wild crops, occurred independently in a number of areas at different times, principally in the subtropical zone. Each region developed a dependence on different staple crops: wheat and barley in the Middle East and South Asia; millet and rice in China and Southeast Asia; corn in the Americas. Animals were also domesticated, and a process of selective breeding gradually enhanced useful traits. Sheep and goats, native to West and Central Asia, were domesticated for their meat, milk, hides and wool. Cattle were domesticated all over Eurasia, and eventually used to pull plows, thus increasing plant yields.

Wild einkorn has brittle stalks, which make it difficult to harvest.

SEE ALSO:

North America: pp.120–121

South America: pp.144–145

Africa: pp.158–159

Europe: pp.174–175

West Asia: pp.220–221

South and Southeast Asia: pp.240–241

North and East Asia: pp.258–259

Australasia and Oceania: pp.280–281

Domestic einkorn has larger seeds and a tougher stalk than its wild form. It needs to be threshed in order for the seeds to disperse.

c.9000: Einkorn wheat grown in northern Syria: first evidence of true cultivation

c.7000: Farming in northern India; barley is main crop

c.6500: Farming spreads to Balkans from Near East

c.6000: Farming spreads to Nile Valley from Near East

c.4500: Cultivation of corn in eastern North America

c.4000: Plants domesticated in sub-Saharan Africa

9000 BCE — 8000 — 7000 — 6000 — 5000 — 4000 BCE

c.8500: Rice domesticated in southern China

c.7750: Broomcorn and foxtail millets domesticated on North China Plain

c.6500: Cattle domesticated in Saharan region

c.4750: First evidence of plant and animal domestication in Central America

c.4500: Evidence of agriculture in south-central Andes

Stages in domestication

Iceland

Northern Europe: oats rye

British Isles

Scandinavia

c.3500 BCE

3500 BCE

EUROPE

Rhine

c.4200 BCE

Danube

c.5000 BCE

5000 BCE

c.7000 BCE

Volga

Black Sea

Mediterranean: olive grape turnip leek plum pear cabbage lettuce rapeseed

c.6000 BCE

Mediterranean Sea

Caspian Sea

c.9000 BCE

Euphrates

Tigris

Central Asia: alfalfa taro carrot

c.4500 BCE

Ob

Yenisey

Lena

SIBERIA

ASIA

Gobi

Amur

Yellow River

c.7750 BCE

c.500 BCE

Japan

East China Sea

Northern China: millet soybean buckwheat barley adzuki bean peach cucumber rapeseed

Southwest Asia: wheat barley pea lentil onion date palm

Sahara

Bones of domesticated cattle dating from c.6500 BCE found in areas which are now desert

AFRICA

c.6000 BCE

Nile

Red Sea

Arabian Peninsula

Arabian Sea

Indus

c.6000 BCE

Ganges

c.4500 BCE

Himalayas

Yangtze

c.8500 BCE

c.4500 BCE

c.6000 BCE

Mekong

Bay of Bengal

South China Sea

Philippine Islands

PACIFIC OCEAN

30°

Indus Valley: cotton

Niger

c.4000 BCE

Congo

INDIAN OCEAN

Southeast Asia: rice taro sago palm orange lemon banana coconut breadfruit sugarcane

Sub-Saharan Africa: yam sorghum millet African rice ensete peas black-eyed peas okra

Zambezi

Madagascar

c.1000 AD

c.2500 BCE

Sumatra

Borneo

Java

c.2500 BCE

Equator

New Guinea

c.1000 BCE

ATLANTIC OCEAN

Kalahari Desert

Orange River

AUSTRALIA

New Zealand

Darling

◀ ② The spread of agriculture

areas of early agriculture, with dates of first domestication of plants and animals

diffusion of agricultural skills

Staple crops under cultivation by c.4000 BCE

🌾 wheat

🌾 barley

🌾 millet

🌽 corn

🌾 rice

Wild ancestors of domesticated animals

aurochs (wild cattle)

pig

sheep

ass

dromedary camel

horse

bactrian camel

gaur (wild ox)

buffalo

chicken

goat

yak

turkey

guanaco (llama)

guinea pig

alpaca

banteng

The farmers of Banpo, northern China, lived in thatched wattle-and-daub houses with a central hearth.

This lime plaster statue, dating to c.6800 BCE, from Ain Ghazal, Jordan was found in a burial pit. They were probably employed in public rituals or ceremonies.

Shelter

Since farming could support communities throughout the year, more time could be invested in the construction of permanent shelters, in building techniques and in the full exploitation of natural resources, from the timber, wattle and daub of northern Europe to the sun-baked mud brick of West Asia.

Ritual

As people gathered together in large communities, there is evidence, in elaborate burials, shrines, and art objects, that ritual played a central role in their lives. The female deities of Çatal Hüyük were associated with the land's fertility, while in Jericho, ancestors were venerated.

THE WORLD 5000–2500 BCE

THE FERTILE VALLEYS of the Nile, Tigris, Euphrates, Indus, and Yellow rivers were able to support very large populations, and it was here that the great urban civilizations of the ancient world emerged. Although cities developed independently in several regions, they shared certain characteristics. Urban societies were hierarchical, with complex labor divisions. They were administered, economically and spiritually, by an elite literate class, and in some cases, were subject to a divine monarch. Monuments came to symbolize and represent the powers of the ruling elite. Elsewhere, farming communities came together to create ritual centers or burial sites, while craftsmen experimented with new materials and techniques, such as copper and bronze casting, and glazed pottery. All these developments indicate that urban and non-urban societies were attaining a high degree of social organization.

EARLY PERCEPTIONS OF THE COSMOS

The stone circles and alignments of northwestern Europe are extraordinary prehistoric monuments which have mystified successive generations. Astronomical observations are central to the ritual purpose of these structures; many have chambers or stone settings arranged to be illuminated by the Sun only on certain days, such as the winter or summer solstice.

central axis

Stonehenge became the preeminent ritual center of southern Britain c.2500 BCE. The rising sun on midsummer's day shines along the central axis of the site, but little is known of the ritual enacted there.

WHEELED VEHICLES

The origin of the wheel is uncertain; humans probably first made use of rotary motion in log rollers, and then in the potter's wheel. Wheeled vehicles were known in southwest Asia by 3500 BCE – a Sumerian pictograph from this period depicts a sledge equipped with wheels – and their use had spread to Europe and India by 3000 BCE. Early vehicles were probably ox-drawn, two-wheeled carts, on wheels formed from planks of wood secured with crosspieces.

This ceramic model of a two-wheeled bullock cart is from a grave at Harappa in the Indus Valley.

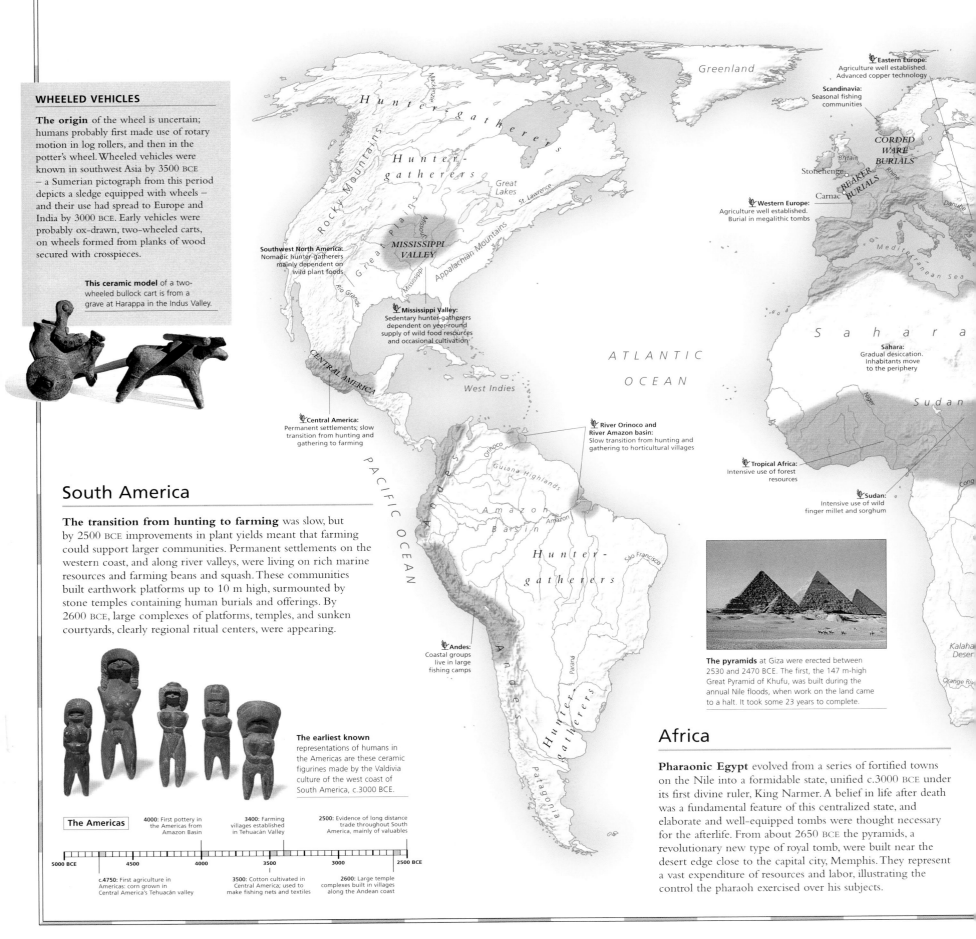

Southwest North America: Nomadic hunter-gatherers mainly dependent on wild plant foods

Mississippi Valley: Sedentary hunter-gatherers dependent on year-round supply of wild food resources and occasional cultivation

Central America: Permanent settlements; slow transition from hunting and gathering to farming

River Orinoco and River Amazon basin: Slow transition from hunting and gathering to horticultural villages

Eastern Europe: Agriculture well established. Advanced copper technology

Scandinavia: Seasonal fishing communities

Western Europe: Agriculture well established. Burial in megalithic tombs

Sahara: Gradual desiccation. Inhabitants move to the periphery

Tropical Africa: Intensive use of forest resources

Sudan: Intensive use of wild finger millet and sorghum

Andes: Coastal groups live in large fishing camps

South America

The transition from hunting to farming was slow, but by 2500 BCE improvements in plant yields meant that farming could support larger communities. Permanent settlements on the western coast, and along river valleys, were living on rich marine resources and farming beans and squash. These communities built earthwork platforms up to 10 m high, surmounted by stone temples containing human burials and offerings. By 2600 BCE, large complexes of platforms, temples, and sunken courtyards, clearly regional ritual centers, were appearing.

The earliest known representations of humans in the Americas are these ceramic figurines made by the Valdivia culture of the west coast of South America, c.3000 BCE.

The pyramids at Giza were erected between 2530 and 2470 BCE. The first, the 147 m-high Great Pyramid of Khufu, was built during the annual Nile floods, when work on the land came to a halt. It took some 23 years to complete.

Africa

Pharaonic Egypt evolved from a series of fortified towns on the Nile into a formidable state, unified c.3000 BCE under its first divine ruler, King Narmer. A belief in life after death was a fundamental feature of this centralized state, and elaborate and well-equipped tombs were thought necessary for the afterlife. From about 2650 BCE the pyramids, a revolutionary new type of royal tomb, were built near the desert edge close to the capital city, Memphis. They represent a vast expenditure of resources and labor, illustrating the control the pharaoh exercised over his subjects.

The Americas			
4000: First pottery in the Americas from Amazon Basin	3400: Farming villages established in Tehuacán Valley	2500: Evidence of long distance trade throughout South America, mainly of valuables	

5000 BCE   4500   4000   3500   3000   2500 BCE

c.4750: First agriculture in Americas: corn grown in Central America's Tehuacán valley

3500: Cotton cultivated in Central America; used to make fishing nets and textiles

2600: Large temple complexes built in villages along the Andean coast

Europe

Elaborate burials, from the megalithic tombs of northern Europe to the large cemeteries of central and eastern Europe, indicate an increasing level of social organization among the scattered farming communities of the European continent. By the 3rd millennium BCE small farming communities were gathering to build defensive enclosures and to create regional centers. Stone circles, such as Stonehenge, or stone avenues, such as Carnac, were major communal undertakings which acted as social, economic, and ritual centers.

Skara Brae is a magnificently preserved prehistoric village on the Orkneys. The village consists of one-room houses of undressed stone, with paved walkways between them and a drainage system.

Europe

4500: Large cemeteries, for example on the western coast of the Black Sea, contain rich burials with elaborate gold jewelry

3800: Ditched enclosures around settlements in Central Europe create defended villages

3200: Stone circles and rows of standing stones built throughout northern and western Europe

5000 BCE | 4500 | 4000 | 3500 | 3000 | 2500 BCE

c.5000: Metallurgy discovered in south-eastern Europe

c.4500: In western Europe, megalithic (large stone) chamber tombs, built as communal burial places

2900: Earliest burials containing Corded Ware pottery in northern and Central Europe

East Asia

As the early farming villages of China became more prosperous, new skills emerged. Farmers of the Longshan culture of eastern China invented the potter's wheel and were making eggshell-thin vessels by 3000 BCE; 250 years later they were raising silkworms and weaving silk. By 3000 BCE there was a marked difference between rich and poor burials, and walled settlements were appearing. The more complex social organization that these developments indicate was soon to lead to China's first urban civilization, the Shang.

This Kui (a pitcher with three hollow legs) is typical of Longshan pottery from the late 3rd millennium BCE.

East Asia

c.4000: Planned villages in northern China, with distinct residential, workshop, and burial areas

3000: First evidence of farming (millet cultivation) in Korea

2500: Banshan culture of western China produces boldly painted burial urns

5000 BCE | 4500 | 4000 | 3500 | 3000 | 2500 BCE

c.3000: Potter's wheel invented during formative phase of Longshan culture of eastern China

SEE ALSO:

North America: pp.120–121

South America: pp.144–145

Africa: pp.158–159

Europe: pp.174–175

West Asia: pp.220–221

South and Southeast Asia: pp.240–241

North and East Asia: pp.258–259

Australasia and Oceania: pp.280–281

South Asia

By 2500 BCE, an urban civilization had developed in the Indus Valley, dominated by Harappa and Mohenjo-Daro. At its height, the latter had a population of about 40,000. A network of residential streets, houses made with standardized bricks and sophisticated drains running into main sewers, overlooked by the "citadel," the religious and ceremonial focus of the city. Merchandise was traded as far afield as Mesopotamia.

The Harappans developed a pictographic form of writing which they used mainly on sealstones.

South Asia

5000: Evidence of use of pottery vessels at Mehrgarh and other Indus Valley settlements

2500: True cities emerge in Indus Valley. Cultural uniformity throughout Indus plain. Evidence of trade links with Central Asia and Mesopotamia

5000 BCE | 4500 | 4000 | 3500 | 3000 | 2500 BCE

4500: Introduction of irrigation techniques in Indus Valley increases size and prosperity of farming settlements

3500: Indus Valley lowlands settled by farmers; walled towns develop

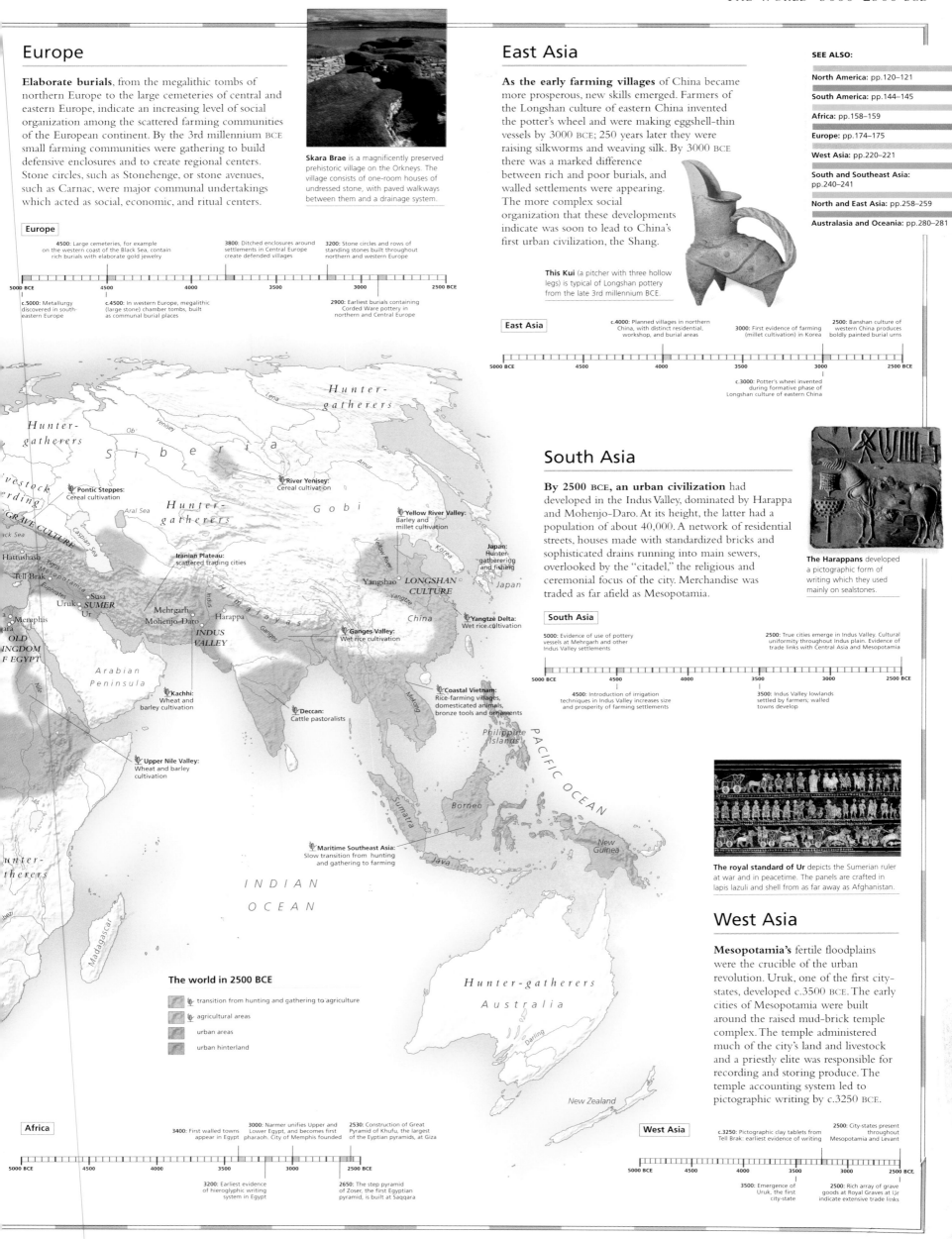

The royal standard of Ur depicts the Sumerian ruler at war and in peacetime. The panels are crafted in lapis lazuli and shell from as far away as Afghanistan.

West Asia

Mesopotamia's fertile floodplains were the crucible of the urban revolution. Uruk, one of the first city-states, developed c.3500 BCE. The early cities of Mesopotamia were built around the raised mud-brick temple complex. The temple administered much of the city's land and livestock and a priestly elite was responsible for recording and storing produce. The temple accounting system led to pictographic writing by c.3250 BCE.

Africa

3400: First walled towns appear in Egypt

3000: Narmer unifies Upper and Lower Egypt, and becomes first pharaoh. City of Memphis founded

2530: Construction of Great Pyramid of Khufu, the largest of the Egyptian pyramids, at Giza

5000 BCE | 4500 | 4000 | 3500 | 3000 | 2500 BCE

3200: Earliest evidence of hieroglyphic writing system in Egypt

2650: The step pyramid of Zoser, the first Egyptian pyramid, is built at Saqqara

The world in 2500 BCE

- transition from hunting and gathering to agriculture
- agricultural areas
- urban areas
- urban hinterland

West Asia

c.3250: Pictographic clay tablets from Tell Brak: earliest evidence of writing

2500: City-states present throughout Mesopotamia and Levant

5000 BCE | 4500 | 4000 | 3500 | 3000 | 2500 BCE

3500: Emergence of Uruk, the first city-state

2500: Rich array of grave goods at Royal Graves at Ur indicate extensive trade links

Map labels:

Hunter-gatherers

Siberia

Lena

Ob

Yenisey

Hunter-gatherers

Amur

Gobi

Pontic Steppes: Cereal cultivation

River Yenisey: Cereal cultivation

Aral Sea

Caspian Sea

Hunter-gatherers

Hattushash

Iranian Plateau: scattered trading cities

Yellow River Valley: Barley and millet cultivation

Korea

Japan: Hunter-gathering and fishing

Japan

Tell Brak

Susa

Uruk SUMER

Ur

Mesopotamia

Tigris

Euphrates

Memphis

OLD KINGDOM OF EGYPT

Nile

Arabian Peninsula

Mehrgarh

Mohenjo-Daro

Himalayas

Indus

Harappa

INDUS VALLEY

Ganges

Ganges Valley: Wet rice cultivation

Yangshao

LONGSHAN CULTURE

Yellow River

Yangtze

China

Yangtze Delta: Wet rice cultivation

Kachhi: Wheat and barley cultivation

Deccan: Cattle pastoralists

Mekong

Coastal Vietnam: Rice-farming villages, domesticated animals, bronze tools and ornaments

Philippine Islands

PACIFIC OCEAN

Upper Nile Valley: Wheat and barley cultivation

Sumatra

Borneo

New Guinea

Java

Madagascar

Hunter-gatherers

Maritime Southeast Asia: Slow transition from hunting and gathering to farming

INDIAN OCEAN

Hunter-gatherers Australia

Darling

New Zealand

TRADE AND THE FIRST CITIES

This Egyptian ivory label is inscribed with the name of King Djet (c.3000 BCE).

BY 2500 BCE, CITIES WERE ESTABLISHED in three major centers: the Nile Valley, Mesopotamia, and the Indus Valley, with a scattering of other cities across the intervening terrain. The culmination of a long process of settlement and expansion – some early cities had populations tens of thousands strong – the first urban civilizations all relied on rich agricultural lands to support their growth. In each case, lack of the most important natural resources – timber, metal, and stone – forced these urban civilizations to establish trading networks which ultimately extended from the Hindu Kush to the Mediterranean. They imported a diverse range of goods: metals and precious stones, such as lapis lazuli, gold, and turquoise, met the demands of the growing social elites for luxury goods; diorite, limestone, and timber were needed for the monumental construction programs which were an integral part of urban life. Where trading contacts led, cultural influence followed, and cities soon began to develop in the trading hinterlands of the Iranian Plateau and Anatolia.

Ur: a trading city

The ancient city of Ur, was the capital of a south Mesopotamian empire toward the end of the 3rd millennium. It was a major economic center, with extensive trade links extending as far as Dilmun (Bahrain) and the cities of the Indus. Ships laden with gold, copper, timber, ivory, and precious stones had access to the Persian Gulf via canals which linked the city to the Euphrates. Archives of clay tablets record, in minute detail, transactions and ships' cargoes. The wealth this trade generated is reflected in the grandiose buildings which adorned the city, most notably the ziggurat dedicated to the city's deity, Ur-Nammu, and in the lavishly furnished burials of Ur's so-called "Royal Graves."

Cities and trade

c.3500: Rise of city-state of Uruk

c.3100: Sumerian trading post at Habuba Kabira, Syria. Sumerian merchants have their own quarters in Persian city of Godin Tepe

c.2500: City of Ur in southern Mesopotamia is a major center of trade and manufacture

c.2500: Indus Valley trading colony of Shortughai, 1000 km from Harappa, supplies gold and lapis lazuli

c.3300: First walled towns in Egypt: Hieraconpolis and Naqada

c.3100: City of Byblos is founded on the Levantine coast

c.2500: The city of Ebla in western Mesopotamia begins to trade with Mediterranean peoples

3500 BCE — 3000 — 2500 BCE

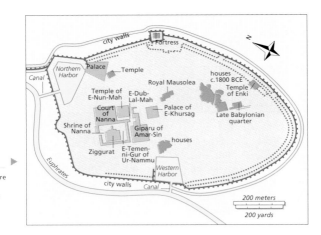

❶ Ur

sacred enclosure
royal palace
other building
..... inner walls
—— outer walls

200 meters
200 yards

Transportation

The long-distance trading networks of the ancient world required revolutionary developments in transportation. Much of the trade was maritime; the cities of Mesopotamia all had access, via rivers and canals, to the Persian Gulf and Indus Valley, and there is ample evidence for trade along the Gulf coast and Arabian Sea to the mouth of the Indus. The timber boats of the Nile, depicted carrying great columns of granite and alabaster, are known from tomb reliefs, models, and burials. Overland trade was dependent on newly-domesticated beasts of burden, such as donkeys and camels. Wheeled carts, pulled by oxen and bullocks, were also used.

A high-prowed reed boat can be seen on this impression from a cylinder seal from Uruk, dating to the 4th millennium BCE. The boat is being used to transport a priest or ruler, probably as part of a religious procession.

Egyptian culture was based on and around the Nile River, which offered the most effective means of transport. Some of the earliest vessels with sails were developed in Egypt.

This copper model from Tell Agrab, Mesopotamia, shows a two-wheeled chariot drawn by onagers, a type of wild donkey. Wheeled vehicles were used for both trade and warfare.

Levant: Coastal trade between Egypt and Mesopotamia

Egypt: The Nile enabled cargoes of precious metals and building materials to be shipped downriver from Nubia

Inventions and innovations

c.5000: Copper first used in Mesopotamia

c.4500: First use of sail, Mesopotamia

c.4000: Use of plow in Mesopotamia

c.3250: Pictographic tablets from Uruk, southern Mesopotamia; earliest evidence of writing

c.3200: Wheeled carts buried in tombs of rulers of Ur and Kish

5000 BCE — 4500 — 4000 — 3500 — 3000 BCE

c.3100: Development of cuneiform script in Mesopotamia. Experiments with bronze-working

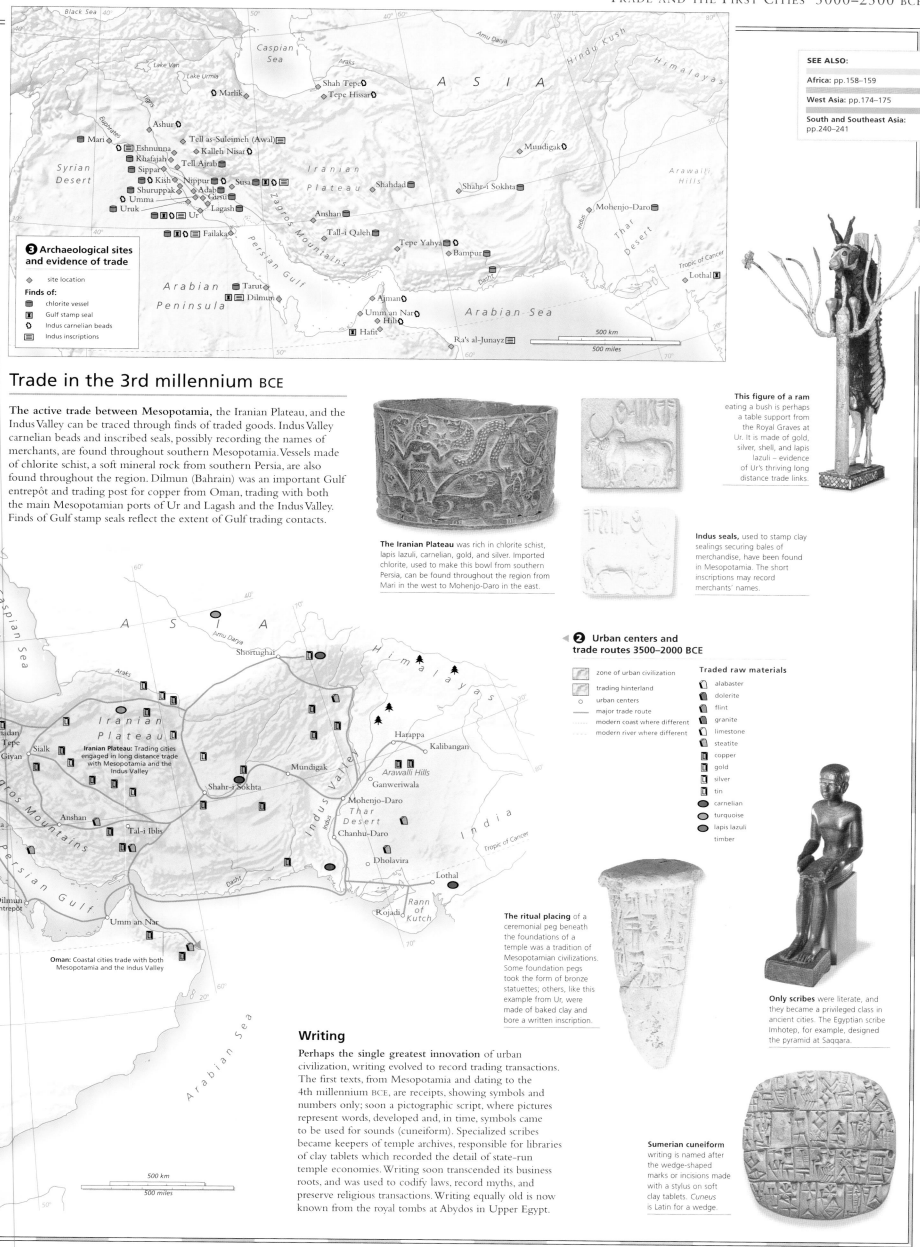

SEE ALSO:

Africa: pp.158–159

West Asia: pp.174–175

South and Southeast Asia: pp.240–241

❸ Archaeological sites and evidence of trade

◇ site location

Finds of:

▭ chlorite vessel

▣ Gulf stamp seal

◊ Indus carnelian beads

▤ Indus inscriptions

Trade in the 3rd millennium BCE

The active trade between Mesopotamia, the Iranian Plateau, and the Indus Valley can be traced through finds of traded goods. Indus Valley carnelian beads and inscribed seals, possibly recording the names of merchants, are found throughout southern Mesopotamia. Vessels made of chlorite schist, a soft mineral rock from southern Persia, are also found throughout the region. Dilmun (Bahrain) was an important Gulf entrepôt and trading post for copper from Oman, trading with both the main Mesopotamian ports of Ur and Lagash and the Indus Valley. Finds of Gulf stamp seals reflect the extent of Gulf trading contacts.

The Iranian Plateau was rich in chlorite schist, lapis lazuli, carnelian, gold, and silver. Imported chlorite, used to make this bowl from southern Persia, can be found throughout the region from Mari in the west to Mohenjo-Daro in the east.

This figure of a ram eating a bush is perhaps a table support from the Royal Graves at Ur. It is made of gold, silver, shell, and lapis lazuli – evidence of Ur's thriving long distance trade links.

Indus seals, used to stamp clay sealings securing bales of merchandise, have been found in Mesopotamia. The short inscriptions may record merchants' names.

❷ Urban centers and trade routes 3500–2000 BCE

▨ zone of urban civilization

▨ trading hinterland

○ urban centers

— major trade route

---- modern coast where different

----- modern river where different

Traded raw materials

▯ alabaster

▯ dolerite

▯ flint

▯ granite

▯ limestone

▯ steatite

▮ copper

▮ gold

▮ silver

▮ tin

● carnelian

● turquoise

● lapis lazuli

  timber

Iranian Plateau: Trading cities engaged in long distance trade with Mesopotamia and the Indus Valley

Oman: Coastal cities trade with both Mesopotamia and the Indus Valley

The ritual placing of a ceremonial peg beneath the foundations of a temple was a tradition of Mesopotamian civilizations. Some foundation pegs took the form of bronze statuettes; others, like this example from Ur, were made of baked clay and bore a written inscription.

Only scribes were literate, and they became a privileged class in ancient cities. The Egyptian scribe Imhotep, for example, designed the pyramid at Saqqara.

Writing

Perhaps the single greatest innovation of urban civilization, writing evolved to record trading transactions. The first texts, from Mesopotamia and dating to the 4th millennium BCE, are receipts, showing symbols and numbers only; soon a pictographic script, where pictures represent words, developed and, in time, symbols came to be used for sounds (cuneiform). Specialized scribes became keepers of temple archives, responsible for libraries of clay tablets which recorded the detail of state-run temple economies. Writing soon transcended its business roots, and was used to codify laws, record myths, and preserve religious transactions. Writing equally old is now known from the royal tombs at Abydos in Upper Egypt.

Sumerian cuneiform writing is named after the wedge-shaped marks or incisions made with a stylus on soft clay tablets. *Cuneus* is Latin for a wedge.

THE WORLD 2500–1250 BCE

AS THE FIRST CITIES expanded and proliferated, states developed, populations grew, and economic pressures increased. Rivalry for territory and power made the early states increasingly militaristic, and warfare, weapons, and diplomacy are conspicuous in the archaeology of this period. As these early societies became more stratified, distinct classes – warriors, priests, scribes, craftspeople, laborers – began to emerge. The great wealth of rulers and the social elite is reflected in the rich array of grave goods found in their burials. Urban civilizations still covered only a tiny fraction of the Earth's surface; in Europe, scattered agricultural communities were becoming more sophisticated, developing metallurgy and trade, and beginning to compete for land and resources. Hunter-gatherer groups still thrived in many areas, and many islands in the Pacific were yet to be settled at this time.

SUN SYMBOLISM

Symbolic representations of the Sun, suggestive of life, fertility, and creation, are found in almost all cultures. During this period in Egypt, the sun god Ra was the dominant figure among the high gods, his enhanced status culminating in the brief solar monotheism under Pharaoh Akhenaten c.1350 BCE. In Scandinavia, ritual finds such as the sun chariot found in a bog at Trundholm (below) attest to monotheistic sun worship and fertility rites in the region during the Bronze Age.

This bronze wheeled model of a horse drawing a disc, which dates to c.1650 BCE, may depict the sun's progress across the heavens.

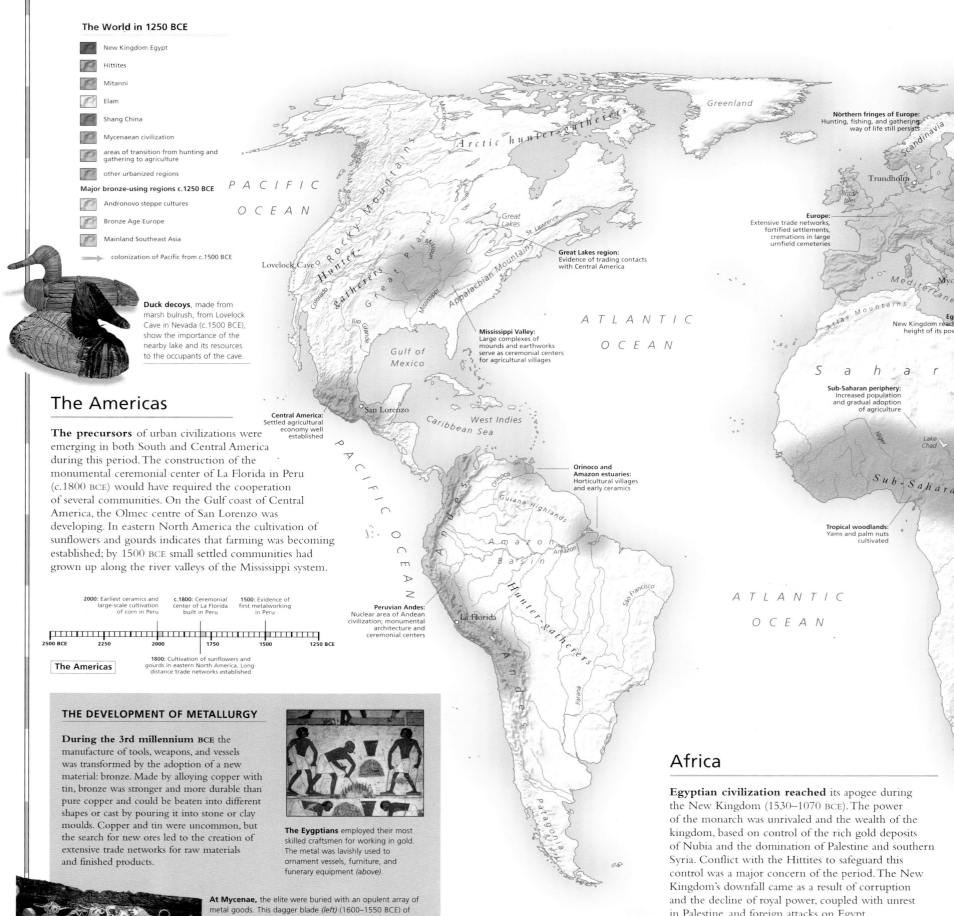

The World in 1250 BCE

- New Kingdom Egypt
- Hittites
- Mitanni
- Elam
- Shang China
- Mycenaean civilization
- areas of transition from hunting and gathering to agriculture
- other urbanized regions

Major bronze-using regions c.1250 BCE

- Andronovo steppe cultures
- Bronze Age Europe
- Mainland Southeast Asia
- → colonization of Pacific from c.1500 BCE

Duck decoys, made from marsh bulrush, from Lovelock Cave in Nevada (c.1500 BCE), show the importance of the nearby lake and its resources to the occupants of the cave.

Northern fringes of Europe: Hunting, fishing, and gathering way of life still persists

Europe: Extensive trade networks, fortified settlements, cremations in large urnfield cemeteries

Great Lakes region: Evidence of trading contacts with Central America

Mississippi Valley: Large complexes of mounds and earthworks serve as ceremonial centers for agricultural villages

Sub-Saharan periphery: Increased population and gradual adoption of agriculture

Tropical woodlands: Yams and palm nuts cultivated

Central America: Settled agricultural economy well established

Orinoco and Amazon estuaries: Horticultural villages and early ceramics

Egypt: New Kingdom reaching height of its power

Peruvian Andes: Nuclear area of Andean civilization; monumental architecture and ceremonial centers

The Americas

The precursors of urban civilizations were emerging in both South and Central America during this period. The construction of the monumental ceremonial center of La Florida in Peru (c.1800 BCE) would have required the cooperation of several communities. On the Gulf coast of Central America, the Olmec centre of San Lorenzo was developing. In eastern North America the cultivation of sunflowers and gourds indicates that farming was becoming established; by 1500 BCE small settled communities had grown up along the river valleys of the Mississippi system.

2000: Earliest ceramics and large-scale cultivation of corn in Peru

c.1800: Ceremonial center of La Florida built in Peru

1500: Evidence of first metalworking in Peru

| 2500 BCE | 2250 | 2000 | 1750 | 1500 | 1250 BCE |

1800: Cultivation of sunflowers and gourds in eastern North America. Long-distance trade networks established

The Americas

THE DEVELOPMENT OF METALLURGY

During the 3rd millennium BCE the manufacture of tools, weapons, and vessels was transformed by the adoption of a new material: bronze. Made by alloying copper with tin, bronze was stronger and more durable than pure copper and could be beaten into different shapes or cast by pouring it into stone or clay moulds. Copper and tin were uncommon, but the search for new ores led to the creation of extensive trade networks for raw materials and finished products.

The Eygptians employed their most skilled craftsmen for working in gold. The metal was lavishly used to ornament vessels, furniture, and funerary equipment (above).

At Mycenae, the elite were buried with an opulent array of metal goods. This dagger blade (left) (1600–1550 BCE) of bronze inlaid with silver portrays a lion hunt.

Africa

Egyptian civilization reached its apogee during the New Kingdom (1530–1070 BCE). The power of the monarch was unrivaled and the wealth of the kingdom, based on control of the rich gold deposits of Nubia and the domination of Palestine and southern Syria. Conflict with the Hittites to safeguard this control was a major concern of the period. The New Kingdom's downfall came as a result of corruption and the decline of royal power, coupled with unrest in Palestine, and foreign attacks on Egypt.

Europe

European settlements, ranging from hillforts to lake dwellings, indicate that increased pressures on land were causing conflict. New types of bronze weapons show the emergence of a warrior elite. The palace of Knossos on Crete marked the appearance of the first Mediterranean state, and on the mainland, the small, palace-based cities of Mycenaean Greece grew wealthy on east Mediterranean trade, but were all sacked or abandoned by the 12th century BCE.

Many aspects of Minoan life are depicted in the colorful frescoes at Knossos, a recurring theme being the acrobatic bull-leaping game on which a religious cult was possibly centered.

Europe

2300: Bronze technology reaches Europe	2000: Fortified settlements appear in Central and Eastern Europe	1550: Mycenaeans become dominant power on Greek mainland

2500 BCE — 2250 — 2000 — 1750 — 1500 — 1250 BCE

2000: Minoan civilization becomes established on island of Crete; palace of Knossos is built

1650: Linear A script comes into use on Crete

West Asia

Northern Mesopotamia was dominated by a number of city-states, such as Ashur and Mari, which centered on palaces and religious complexes. The palace administered each city's long-distance trade and tribute, and recorded these transactions on archives of clay tablets. In the 18th century BCE, the city-state of Babylon gained temporary control of the region. In central Anatolia, the Hittites ruled a powerful kingdom from their fortified citadel at Hattushash. Their attempts to gain contol over the wealthy trading cities of the Levant brought them into conflict with Egypt.

This gold figurine of a Hittite king dates to c.1400 BCE.

West Asia

2300: City-states of southern Mesopotamia temporarily united under Sargon of Agade	1775: Construction of palace of Zimri-Lim at Mari. Palace archive contained 17,500 clay tablets	1650: Emergence of Hittite kingdom, with capital at Hattushash	1500: Period of endemic warfare between Hittites, Egyptians, and Mitanni of northern Mesopotamia

2500 BCE — 2250 — 2000 — 1750 — 1500 — 1250 BCE

1760: City-state of Babylon gains political hegemony over northern Mesopotamia

1600: Phoenicians start to use Canaanite script – the first alphabetic script

1290: Battle of Kadesh: Egypt versus the Hittites

SEE ALSO:

North America: pp.120–121

South America: pp.144–145

Africa: pp.158–159

Europe: pp.174–175

West Asia: pp.220–221

South and Southeast Asia: pp.240–241

North and East Asia: pp.258–259

Australasia and Oceania: pp.280–281

East Asia

The urban civilization of Shang China developed in about 1800 BCE in the middle valley of the Yellow River. The Shang dynasty exercised an absolute power reflected in their incredibly rich burials. Yet this absolute power was based on the labor of farmers who cultivated beans and millet with tools of wood and stone. Elsewhere, in Southeast Asia, the transition to farming was slow, although agricultural villages in Thailand were producing bronze vessels using similar techniques to the Chinese.

Chinese mastery of bronze casting is evident in the exquisite vessels, created primarily for ceremonial use, that often accompanied the wealthy elite into the grave.

East Asia

		1800: Emergence of Shang dynasty in middle valley of Yellow River	1500: Evidence of bronze-working in mainland Southeast Asia	1400: Anyang succeeds Zhengzhou as the Shang capital

2500 BCE — 2250 — 2000 — 1750 — 1500 — 1250 BCE

2500: First domesticated animals and pottery in island Southeast Asia

1900 BCE: First Chinese city founded at Erlitou on the Yellow River

1800: First bronze vessels cast from ceramic molds

1400: First written inscriptions appear on oracle bones, which were used in a process of divination

When the Lapita people arrived in the western Pacific islands they were carrying a variety of food plants, the pig, and their distinctive style of pottery, the decoration of which was applied with short-toothed implements.

Oceania

One of the great population dispersals of the ancient world began c.1500 BCE, when the Lapita people, originally settlers from the East Indies, set off from New Guinea and the Solomons to explore and colonize the islands of the Pacific Ocean. The Lapita culture spread rapidly, reaching Tonga and Samoa, by 1000 BCE.

Map labels:

Arctic hunter-gatherers
Yenisey
Lena
Ob
Volga
Siberia
Lake Baikal
Steppes
Amur
Andronovo steppe cultures: Cattle herders and seasonal nomads
Aral Sea
Lake Balkhash
Gobi
China: Longshan groups form basis of Shang state c.1800 BCE
Japan
Caspian Sea
Black Sea
Troy
Anatolia
Hattushash
Knossos
Kadesh
Nineveh
Mesopotamia
Iranian Plateau: Scattered trading cities
Anyang
Yellow River
Erlitou   Zhengzhou
Japan: Jomon hunter-gatherers living in villages
Byblos
Tyre
Ashur
Euphrates
Babylon
Jericho
Jerusalem
El-Amarna
El-Lisht
Thebes
Nile
Nubia
Arabian Peninsula
Indus
Himalayas
Ganges
Yangtze
Deccan
Levant: City states repeatedly absorbed by neighboring empires; Hittite Empire, Elam and Kingdom of Mitanni vying with Egypt for control of region
Indus Valley: Disappearance of urban civilization; northwest India occupied by Aryan settlers
Ganges Valley: Rice-farming villages
Red River valley: Sophisticated bronze working; Dong Son drums
PACIFIC OCEAN
East Africa: Teff and ensete cultivation
Mainland Southeast Asia: Rice-farming villages, bronze tools and ornaments
Mekong
Philippine Islands
Maritime Southeast Asia: Slow transition from hunting and gathering to agriculture
Sumatra
Borneo
East Indies
Java
New Guinea
Bismarck Archipelago
Polynesian dispersal: Lapita population colonize the islands of Melanesia
pastoralists
Lake Victoria
Madagascar
Zambezi
Kalahari Desert
hunter-gatherers
INDIAN OCEAN
Hunter-gatherers Australia
Darling
New Zealand

Egyptian agriculture centered on the cultivation of cereals, primarily emmer wheat and barley. The fertile soils of the Nile floodplain produced high annual yields and large surpluses were a major source of the state's wealth.

Africa

	1633: Much of Egypt ruled by the Hyksos, an Asiatic people	c.1375: Egyptian prosperity, power and prestige reach high point under Amenophis III	

2500 BCE — 2250 — 2000 — 1750 — 1500 — 1250 BCE

2134: Egypt reunited under Middle Kingdom pharaohs after perod of dominance by nobles

1530: Rise of New Kingdom. New capital founded at Thebes

1350: Pharaoh Akhenaten introduces sun worship in Egypt

c.2500: Dingo introduced to Australia, probably from Southeast Asia	1500: Lapita colonists start to colonize Pacific Ocean, reaching Tonga and Samoa by c.1000 BCE

2500 BCE — 2250 — 2000 — 1750 — 1500 — 1250 BCE

Oceania

c.1600: Earliest examples of Lapita pottery in Bismarck Archipelago

WRITING, COUNTING, AND CALENDARS

The Greek inscription *(above)* is an offering of thanks to Asclepius, the god of healing.

THE INTERTWINED DEVELOPMENT of writing and counting was closely related to the advent of agriculture and the need to record and tally stored goods, livestock, and commercial transactions. The precursors of the first known writing and numerical systems were clay counting tokens, used in Sumer from c.3400 BCE to record quantities of stored goods. They were eventually sealed in clay envelopes, and marked on the outside with signs indicating their contents – the first written symbols. Within a thousand years, writing and numerical systems had spread throughout West Asia (they evolved separately in China and Central America), bringing a revolutionary change in human consciousness. The ability to count in abstract enabled humans to measure, assess, record, and evaluate their world – calendrical systems, weights and measures, coinage, astronomical calculations, and geometry all followed. Writing became a powerful tool of government, a means of communicating over increasing distances, codifying laws, and recording myths and history.

The evolution and spread of major scripts

The earliest symbolic records, of economic transactions, were used in Sumer from c.3400 BCE, and gradually evolved into a pictographic script, where pictures represented words. Cuneiform writing was used to record a variety of languages, and spread throughout West Asia. The system eventually became more complex, and written symbols also came to stand for concepts or sounds. Egyptian hieroglyphics probably developed under Sumerian influence, though the system was unique. Chinese pictographic writing developed independently, as did the Zapotec and Maya systems in Central America. The Proto-Canaanite alphabet, based on a selection of Egyptian hieroglyphs (developed by 1200 BCE), was the probable precursor of the Phoenician alphabet, adapted by the Greeks in the 8th century BCE.

This inscription in Egyptian hieratic is a record of a trading transaction. Hieratic was a form of cursive script, written with ink and a reed brush.

Writing in Ancient Egypt was the preserve of trained scribes, whose high status was reflected in their exemption from taxes.

This glyph from Central America, represents the word "grass."

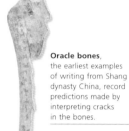

Oracle bones, the earliest examples of writing from Shang dynasty China, record predictions made by interpreting cracks in the bones.

The inscriptions on this black basalt pillar are the most complete example of the law code of Hammurabi, king of Babylonia (c.1790–1750 BCE), who is depicted on the top of the pillar.

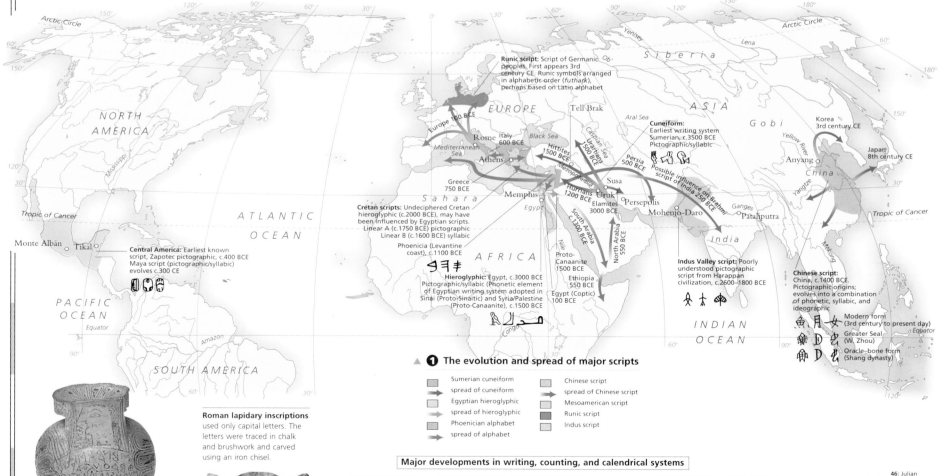

Roman lapidary inscriptions used only capital letters. The letters were traced in chalk and brushwork and carved using an iron chisel.

This perfume jar from Corinth in Greece is inscribed in the alphabetic script which was adapted from the Phoenician, and used in Greece from the 8th century BCE.

Runic script: Script of Germanic peoples. First appears 3rd century CE. Runic symbols arranged in alphabetic order (*futhark*), perhaps based on Latin alphabet

Cuneiform: Earliest writing system Sumerian, c.3500 BCE Pictographic/syllabic

Possible influence on Brahmi script of India 250 BCE

Korea 3rd century CE

Japan 8th century CE

Cretan scripts: Undeciphered Cretan hieroglyphic (c.2000 BCE), may have been influenced by Egyptian scripts. Linear A (c.1750 BCE) pictographic Linear B (c.1600 BCE) syllabic

Central America: Earliest known script, Zapotec pictographic, c.400 BCE Maya script (pictographic/syllabic) evolves c.300 CE

Hieroglyphic: Egypt, c.3000 BCE Pictographic/syllabic (Phonetic element of Egyptian writing system adopted in Sinai (Proto-Sinaitic) and Syria/Palestine (Proto-Canaanite), c.1500 BCE

Phoenicia (Levantine coast), c.1100 BCE

Proto-Canaanite 1500 BCE

Ethiopia 550 BCE

Egypt (Coptic) 100 BCE

Indus Valley script: Poorly understood pictographic script from Harappan civilization, c.2600–1800 BCE

Chinese script: China, c.1400 BCE. Pictographic origins; evolves into a combination of phonetic, syllabic, and ideographic

Modern form (3rd century to present day)
Greater Seal (W. Zhou)
Oracle-bone form (Shang dynasty)

▲ ❶ The evolution and spread of major scripts

Sumerian cuneiform	Chinese script
spread of cuneiform	spread of Chinese script
Egyptian hieroglyphic	Mesoamerican script
spread of hieroglyphic	Runic script
Phoenician alphabet	Indus script
spread of alphabet	

Major developments in writing, counting, and calendrical systems

c.3400: Sumerians use clay counting tokens and first written symbols

c.3000: Development of Egyptian hieroglyphic writing system

c.2500: Egyptian calendar pioneers division of day into 24 units

c.1400: First written inscriptions in China, on Shang oracle bones

c.1100: Introduction of Phoenician alphabet

46: Julian calendrical reforms; "Year of Confusion" is 445 days long

3500 BCE — 3000 BCE — 2500 BCE — 2000 BCE — 1500 BCE — 1000 BCE — 500 BCE — 1 CE

c.3250: Earliest writing in the world; clay pictographic tablets from Tell Brak, Syria

c.2000: Appearance of Cretan hieroglyphic writing

c.600: First Greek coins
c.600: First Central American script (Zapotec)
c.500: Hebrews evolve use of 7-day weeks
c.500: First coins used in China

The evolution of numerical systems

Wooden tally sticks were used over 30,000 years ago, probably to record numbers of animals killed. From c.3400 BCE the Sumerians used clay counting tokens to represent order of magnitude, and evolved the first written numbering system. As humans count using their fingers and toes, most systems used base 10, while the Maya, Aztecs, and Celts chose base 20. The Sumerian and Babylonian use of base 60 (still evident in our use of 60 minutes and seconds, and 360 degrees) remains mysterious. Alphabetic counting systems, used by Greeks, Hebrews, and Arabs, wrote numbers by using letters. The concept of zero and the positional numbering system were independent Indian and Maya inventions.

The Rhind mathematical papyrus dates to c.1575 BCE. It demonstrates that the Egyptians had some understanding of the properties of right-angled triangles.

This Babylonian mathematical text with cuneiform numbers dates to c.500 BCE. The use of the sexagesimal system was an important factor in the development of Babylonian astronomy.

SEE ALSO:

North America: pp.122–123

South America: pp.146–147

West Asia: pp.222–223

North and East Asia: pp.258–259

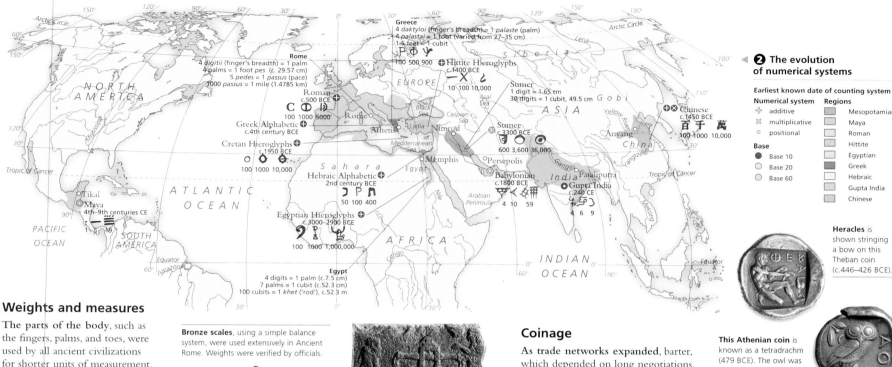

❷ The evolution of numerical systems

Earliest known date of counting system

Numerical system	Regions
✛ additive	Mesopotamian
⊠ multiplicative	Maya
○ positional	Roman
	Hittite
Base	Egyptian
● Base 10	Greek
◑ Base 20	Hebraic
○ Base 60	Gupta India
	Chinese

Heracles is shown stringing a bow on this Theban coin (c.446–426 BCE).

This Athenian coin is known as a tetradrachm (479 BCE). The owl was a symbol of Athena.

Weights and measures

The parts of the body, such as the fingers, palms, and toes, were used by all ancient civilizations for shorter units of measurement. Greater distances reflect the nature of the civilization; the Roman *passus* (1.6 m) reflects the Romans' road system and marching armies, the Greek stadion originates in the length of an athletic race track.

Bronze scales, using a simple balance system, were used extensively in Ancient Rome. Weights were verified by officials.

Mesopotamian weights were calculated according to the sexagesimal system. This 1st-millennium BCE relief from Nimrud, Iraq, shows tribute being weighed.

Coinage

As trade networks expanded, barter, which depended on long negotiations, became increasingly inconvenient. The need for an agreed system of equivalences of value led to the invention of coins, metal objects with a constant weight, marked with the official stamp of a public authority. The Greeks of Lydia developed the system in the 7th century BCE, and it was rapidly adopted elsewhere.

This early Egyptian counting stick was found with pieces of metal, used as money.

The evolution of calendrical systems

The development of calendars was linked to religion and the need to predict days of ritual significance, such as the summer solstice. Calendrical systems developed through astronomical observation and record-keeping, and were dependent on both writing and numeracy. All calendars had to resolve the incommensurate cycles of days, lunations and solar years, usually by intercalating extra days or months at regular intervals. Eras were assessed by different means, most commonly from the regnal years of monarchy, or from the year of birth of significant individuals, such as Buddha or Christ.

Light penetrates the neolithic tomb at Newgrange in Ireland at sunrise on 21 December, an example of the astronomical significance of many stone settings.

The Babylonians made systematic observations of the setting and rising of the planet Venus at the city of Kish, recorded on the Venus tablet (c.1700 BCE).

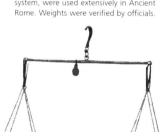
Fragments of a bronze Celtic lunisolar calendar have been found at Coligny, France. Pegs may have been inserted into holes to mark the passage of the days.

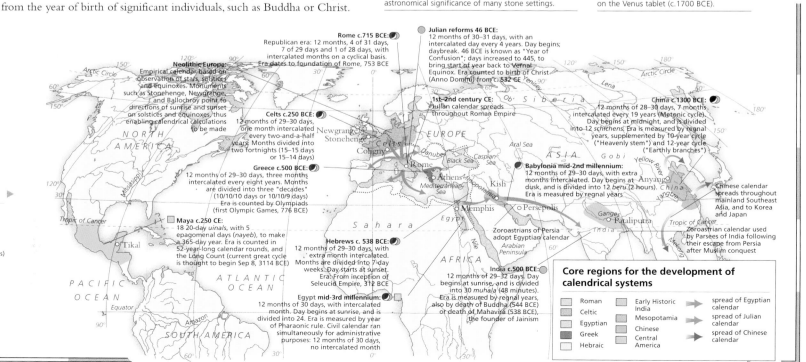

❸ The evolution and spread of calendrical systems

- ● lunar (months are kept in step with lunar cycle by intercalating days)
- ○ solar (lunar cycle is ignored; years are kept in step with the Sun by intercalating days)
- ◑ lunisolar (month are geared to lunar cycle; extra months are intercalated to key year synchronized with sun)
- □ wandering year (fixed number of days; lunar and solar cycles abandoned)
- ⋯⋯ extent of Roman Empire in 2nd century CE

Rome c.715 BCE: Republican era: 12 months, 4 of 31 days, 7 of 29 days and 1 of 28 days, with intercalated months on a cyclical basis. Era dates to foundation of Rome, 753 BCE

Neolithic Europe: Empirical calendar based on observation of stars, solstices and equinoxes. Monuments such as Stonehenge, Newgrange, and Ballochroy point to directions of sunrise and sunset on solstices and equinoxes, thus enabling calendrical calculations to be made

Julian reforms 46 BCE: 12 months of 30–31 days, with an intercalated day every 4 years; daybreak. 46 BCE is known as "Year of Confusion"; days increased to 445, to bring start of year back to Vernal Equinox. Era counted to birth of Christ (Anno Domini) from c.532 CE

1st–2nd century CE: Julian calendar spreads throughout Roman Empire

China c.1300 BCE: 12 months of 28–30 days, 7 months intercalated every 19 years (Metonic cycle). Day begins at midnight, and is divided into 12 *schichens*. Era is measured by regnal years, supplemented by 10-year cycle ("Heavenly stem") and 12-year cycle ("Earthly branches")

Celts c.250 BCE: 12 months of 29–30 days, one month intercalated every two-and-a-half years. Months divided into two fortnights (15–15 days or 15–14 days)

Greece c.500 BCE: 12 months of 29–30 days, three months intercalated every eight years. Months are divided into three "decades" (10/10/10 days or 10/10/9 days). Era is counted by Olympiads (first Olympic Games, 776 BCE)

Babylonia mid-2nd millennium: 12 months of 29–30 days, with extra months intercalated. Day begins at dusk, and is divided into 12 *beru* (2 hours). Era is measured by regnal years

Chinese calendar spreads throughout mainland Southeast Asia, and to Korea and Japan

Zoroastrian calendar used by Parsees of India following their escape from Persia after Muslim conquest

Maya c.250 CE: 18 20-day *uinals*, with 5 epagomenal days (*nayeb*) to make a 365-day year. Era is counted in 52-year-long calendar rounds, and the Long Count (current great cycle is thought to begin Sep 8, 3114 BCE)

Hebrews c. 538 BCE: 12 months of 29–30 days, with extra month intercalated. Months are divided into 7-day weeks. Day starts at sunset. Era: From inception of Seleucid Empire, 312 BCE

India c.500 BCE: 12 months of 29–32 days. Day begins at sunrise, and is divided into 30 *muhala* (48 minutes). Era is measured by regnal years, also by death of Buddha (544 BCE) or death of Mahavira (538 BCE), the founder of Jainism

Zoroastrians of Persia adopt Egyptian calendar

Egypt mid-3rd millennium: 12 months of 30 days, with intercalated month. Day begins at sunrise, and is divided into 24. Era is measured by years of Pharaonic rule. Civil calendar ran simultaneously for administrative purposes: 12 months of 30 days, no intercalated month

Core regions for the development of calendrical systems

Roman	Early Historic India
Celtic	Mesopotamia
Egyptian	Chinese
Greek	Central America
Hebraic	

→ spread of Egyptian calendar
→ spread of Julian calendar
→ spread of Chinese calendar

Map labels (numerical systems):
Greece: 4 *daktyloi* (finger's breadth) = 1 *palaste* (palm); 4 *palastai* = 1 foot (varied from 27–35 cm); 1.5 feet = 1 cubit
Rome: 4 *digitii* (finger's breadth) = 1 palm; 4 palms = 1 foot *pes* (c.29.57 cm); 5 *pedes* = 1 *passus* (pace); 1000 *passus* = 1 mile (1.4785 km)
Sumer: 1 digit = 1.65 cm; 30 digits = 1 cubit, 49.5 cm
Hittite Hieroglyphs c.1400 BCE
Roman c.500 BCE
Chinese c.1450 BCE
Greek Alphabetic c.4th century BCE
Cretan Hieroglyphs c.1950 BCE
Hebraic Alphabetic 2nd century BCE
Sumer c.3300 BCE
Babylonian c.1800 BCE
Gupta India c.240 CE
Egyptian Hieroglyphs c.3000–2900 BCE
Maya 4th–9th centuries CE
Egypt: 4 digits = 1 palm (c.7.5 cm); 7 palms = 1 cubit (c.52.3 cm); 100 cubits = 1 *khet* ('rod'), c.52.3 m

THE WORLD 750–500 BCE

THE CIVILIZATIONS OF EURASIA, although they only occupied a small portion of the Earth's surface, now lay in a more or less continuous belt from the Mediterranean to China. Both trade and cultural contact were well-established; understanding of iron metallurgy had spread from the Middle East as far as China, and by the 6th century BCE Chinese silk was beginning to appear in Europe, marking the beginning of 1,500 years of trans-Asian trade. All these civilizations, however, were increasingly subjected to incursions by tribes of nomadic pastoralists who were rapidly spreading across Central Asia, eastern Europe, and Siberia – a result of the invention of horse-riding. By 500 BCE, the Classical Age in Greece – a high point in the history of western civilization – was beginning. It was to have a profound impact on European political institutions, art, architecture, drama, and philosophy. In 505 BCE, the *polis* of Athens initiated radical political reforms and became the birthplace of democracy.

Europe

As the city-states of Greece became more prosperous, their civic pride was expressed through magnificent buildings. Greek colonies, which stretched from the Black Sea to the Iberian Peninsula, were major trading centers, importing raw materials and food supplies in exchange for manufactures, such as pottery. The expanding European population moved into more marginal areas, using iron tools for land clearance and agriculture. Northern Europe was occupied by Celtic and Germanic peoples, whose tribal societies centered on princely graves and hill-top fortresses.

Revelry is a common theme in the tomb frescoes of the Etruscans, whose urban civilization reached its height in 6th-century BCE Italy.

Europe

700: Scythians from Central Asia begin to settle in eastern Europe and Black Sea area	600: Foundation of Greek colony of Massalia. Trade between Greeks and Celts	505: Establishment of democracy in Athens

750 BCE — 700 — 650 — 600 — 550 — 500 BCE

750: First evidence of use of Greek alphabet
c.600: Defensive hill-top fortresses built throughout southern Germany and eastern France
510: Romans expel Etruscan overlords and establish a republic

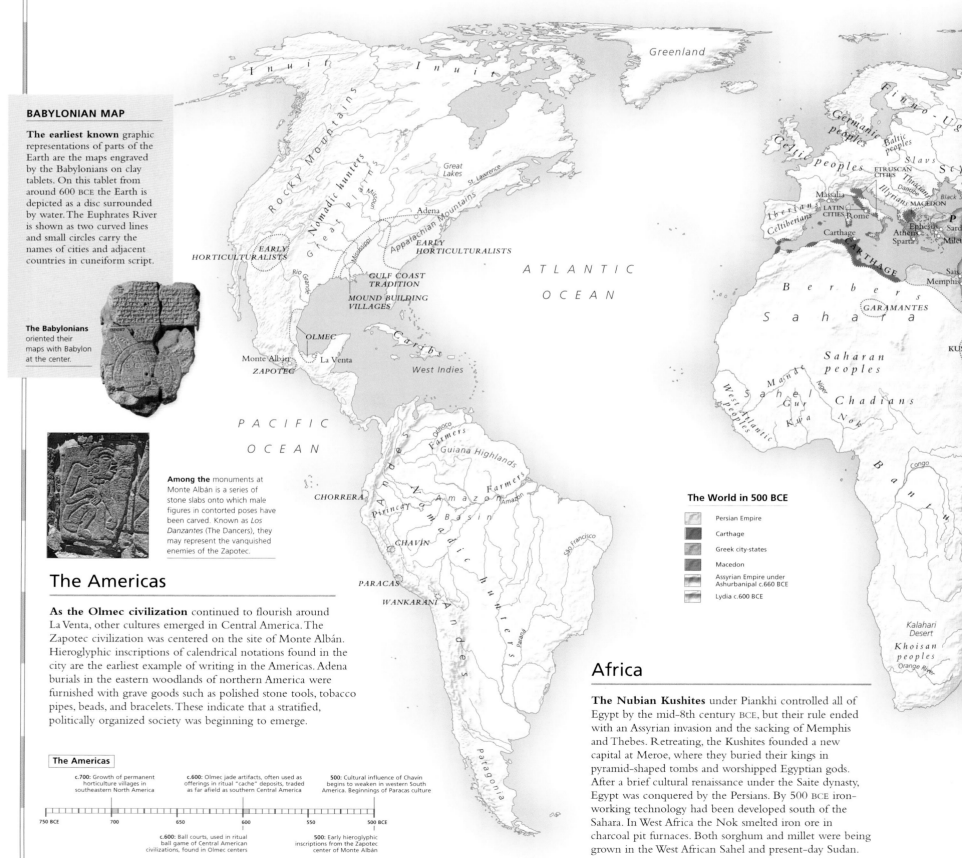

BABYLONIAN MAP

The earliest known graphic representations of parts of the Earth are the maps engraved by the Babylonians on clay tablets. On this tablet from around 600 BCE the Earth is depicted as a disc surrounded by water. The Euphrates River is shown as two curved lines and small circles carry the names of cities and adjacent countries in cuneiform script.

The Babylonians oriented their maps with Babylon at the center.

Among the monuments at Monte Albán is a series of stone slabs onto which male figures in contorted poses have been carved. Known as *Los Danzantes* (The Dancers), they may represent the vanquished enemies of the Zapotec.

The Americas

As the Olmec civilization continued to flourish around La Venta, other cultures emerged in Central America. The Zapotec civilization was centered on the site of Monte Albán. Hieroglyphic inscriptions of calendrical notations found in the city are the earliest example of writing in the Americas. Adena burials in the eastern woodlands of northern America were furnished with grave goods such as polished stone tools, tobacco pipes, beads, and bracelets. These indicate that a stratified, politically organized society was beginning to emerge.

The Americas

c.700: Growth of permanent horticulture villages in southeastern North America	c.600: Olmec jade artifacts, often used as offerings in ritual "cache" deposits, traded as far afield as southern Central America	500: Cultural influence of Chavín begins to weaken in western South America. Beginnings of Paracas culture

750 BCE — 700 — 650 — 600 — 550 — 500 BCE

c.600: Ball courts, used in ritual ball game of Central American civilizations, found in Olmec centers
500: Early hieroglyphic inscriptions from the Zapotec center of Monte Albán

The World in 500 BCE

- Persian Empire
- Carthage
- Greek city-states
- Macedon
- Assyrian Empire under Ashurbanipal c.660 BCE
- Lydia c.600 BCE

Africa

The Nubian Kushites under Piankhi controlled all of Egypt by the mid-8th century BCE, but their rule ended with an Assyrian invasion and the sacking of Memphis and Thebes. Retreating, the Kushites founded a new capital at Meroe, where they buried their kings in pyramid-shaped tombs and worshipped Egyptian gods. After a brief cultural renaissance under the Saite dynasty, Egypt was conquered by the Persians. By 500 BCE iron-working technology had been developed south of the Sahara. In West Africa the Nok smelted iron ore in charcoal pit furnaces. Both sorghum and millet were being grown in the West African Sahel and present-day Sudan.

THE FIRST COINS

The use of metals to make payments can be traced back more than 4000 years, but standardization and certification in the form of coinage did not arrive until the 7th century BCE. The first coins were issued by the Lydians of western Anatolia. They consisted of bean-sized pieces of electrum – a natural alloy of gold and silver – with punchmarks testifying to their weight and therefore their value in payments. By 570 BCE coinage had spread west to Greece and east to Persia. It was invented independently in China and India c.500 BCE.

The first Chinese coins, introduced c.500 BCE, were miniature bronze hoes or spades (*left*), copies of the tools that previously had been used for barter. Early Greek coins carried stamped designs, many derived from the animal world (*right*).

West Asia

Assyria's enemies united to overthrow the empire in 612 BCE, and for a brief period Babylon again enjoyed ascendancy in Mesopotamia. This changed with the arrival of the Medes and Persians, Indo-Europeans from Central Asia. In 550 BCE the Persian king, Cyrus the Great, defeated the Medes and united the two peoples, founding the Achaemenid Empire, which became the largest state the world had yet seen, stretching from the Nile to the Indus. A later Persian ruler, Darius I, consolidated imperial rule: subject peoples were divided into provinces, or satrapies; taxes were levied and the construction of the Royal Road from Sardis to Susa facilitated fast, efficient communications.

The king is the focus of the decoration of the palace at Persepolis, ceremonial capital of the Achaemenid Persians. Reliefs depict his court and processions of tribute-bearers from his empire.

West Asia

700: Nomadic Scythians begin to establish permanent settlements on western steppes

c.663: Assyrian Empire reaches greatest extent with sack of Thebes in Egypt

604: Nebuchadnezzar II rebuilds Babylon and captures Jerusalem

539: Cyrus takes Babylon, and Babylonian Empire, without bloodshed

612: Nineveh and Nimrud are sacked by Babylonians and Medes; end of Assyrian Empire

c.550: Cyrus the Great of Persia defeats Medes and founds Achaemenid Empire

521: Persian Empire reaches greatest extent, under Darius I

East Asia

With the beginning of the Eastern Zhou period in 770 BCE, China experienced several centuries of conflict as many former vassals of the Zhou competed for supremacy. This was a period of technological and cultural change. The widespread use of iron tools improved the productivity of the land and led to a marked population increase. At the same time new ideas stimulated feverish intellectual debate. The teaching of Confucius was a practical, ethical guide to good government and social behavior, while Taoism was a philosophy based on a mystical faith in natural forces.

During this period Chinese chariots were elaborately decorated to enhance their appearance in battle. This bronze bull's head chariot fitting is inlaid with gold.

East Asia

c.650: Introduction of iron technology to China. Silk painting, lacquerwork, and ceramics become highly skilled

605: Birth of Lao-tzu, founder of Taoism

551: Birth of Confucius

c.500: Bronze coinage introduced in China

c.500: Iron-casting used to manufacture huge quantities of tools and weapons in China

In India, early traditions, dating back before 2000 BCE, evolved into Hinduism. This stone statue portrays an early deity, Surya, the sun god.

South Asia

From about 1500 BCE the peoples of central north India began to adopt a sedentary life and expanded eastward to settle the Ganges plain. By the 7th century BCE, a patchwork of small states had emerged in northern India. Some were tribal republics, others absolute monarchies, but their common roots – apparent in the Hindu religion and the caste system – underpinned their religious and social organization. The Afghan region of Gandhara and the Indus Valley were absorbed into the Persian Empire in the late 6th century BCE.

From Meroe, the Cushites were able to maintain their rule over the middle Nile until the 4th century CE, while Egypt suffered a series of invasions. This stone ram lies among the ruins of a Meroitic temple at Naqa.

Africa

747: Rule of Egypt by Nubians

671: Assyrian king, Esarhaddon, captures Egyptian capital, Memphis

600: Nubian capital moves to Meroe

c.500: Darius I of Persia completes construction of a canal linking Nile and Red Sea

663: Egypt regains independence under 26th Dynasty, which rules from Sais in the Nile Delta until 525 BCE

550: Cyrus the Great founds Persian Empire

525: Egypt becomes part of Persian Empire

South Asia

c.600: 16 Aryan kingdoms are spread across northern India

c.540: Birth of Mahavira, founder of Jain religion

c.566: Birth of Buddha, who forsakes life of a nobleman to seek enlightenment through asceticism and good conduct

533: Kingdom of Gandhara becomes satrapy of Persia

THE ORIGINS OF ORGANIZED RELIGION

THE 6TH CENTURY BCE has been called the "axial age" in the development of religion. Judaism, Hinduism, and Taoism were well established. Reformers such as Deutero-Isaiah, Mahavira, Siddhartha Gautama, and Confucius were at work. Around the Mediterranean, a melting-pot of local cults was forming the roots of European Classical civilization, while in the Americas the first urban cultures brought with them organized religion. And frequently, it was the adoption by political rulers of a particular religion which would ensure its longevity and evolution – as in Buddhism, Confucianism, and, later, Christianity – into a world religion.

The development of a priestly class, as here at Sumer, was central in the organization of religious practice as a core social activity.

The development of organized religion

Zoroastrian worship focused on a supreme being, Ahura Mazda, who was widely worshiped at fire altars.

The development of organized religions was linked to the emergence of urban civilization. The earliest known state religion was that of Sumer in the 3rd millennium BCE, and the oldest coherent written mythology was that of Egypt, from the 2nd millennium BCE. By the 1st millennium a range of common characteristics and practices had emerged from local cults to acquire the trappings of organized religion: shamans became priests; myth became doctrine; sacrifice became ceremony; ancestor worship was celebrated in increasingly rich and elaborate burial practices and grandiose monumental architecture.

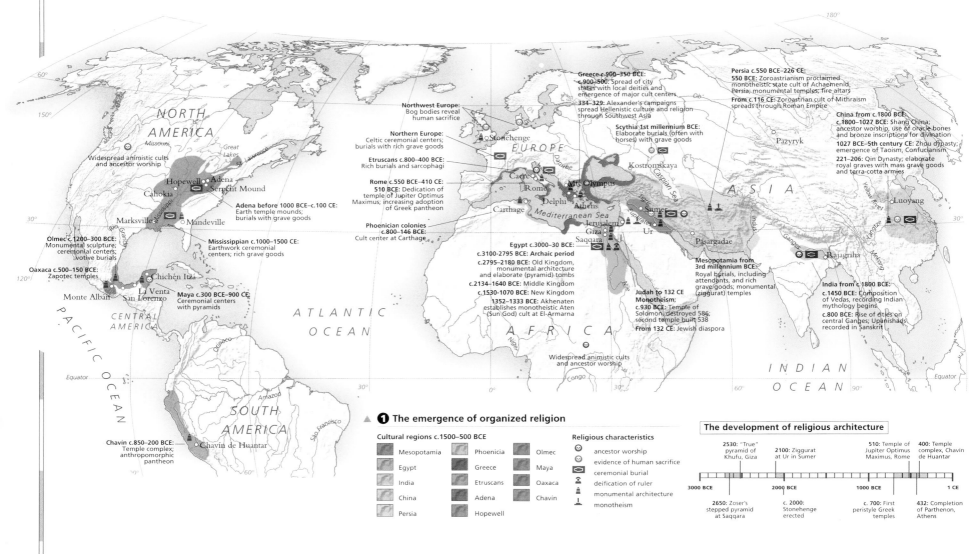

❶ The emergence of organized religion

Cultural regions c.1500–500 BCE

Mesopotamia · Phoenicia · Olmec
Egypt · Greece · Maya
India · Etruscans · Oaxaca
China · Adena · Chavin
Persia · Hopewell

Religious characteristics

- ancestor worship
- evidence of human sacrifice
- ceremonial burial
- deification of ruler
- monumental architecture
- monotheism

Map labels

North America: Widespread animistic cults and ancestor worship

Hopewell · Adena · Serpent Mound · Cahokia

Adena before 1000 BCE–c.100 CE: Earth temple mounds; burials with grave goods

Mississippian c.1000–1500 CE: Earthwork ceremonial centers; rich grave goods

Marksville · Mandeville

Olmec c.1200–300 BCE: Monumental sculpture; ceremonial centers; votive burials

Oaxaca c.500–150 BCE: Zapotec temples

Monte Albán · San Lorenzo · La Venta · Chichén Itzá

Maya c.300 BCE–900 CE: Ceremonial centers with pyramids

Chavin c.850–200 BCE: Temple complex; anthropomorphic pantheon · Chavin de Huantar

Northwest Europe: Bog bodies reveal human sacrifice

Northern Europe: Celtic ceremonial centers; burials with rich grave goods · Stonehenge

Etruscans c.800–400 BCE: Rich burials and sarcophagi

Rome c.550 BCE–410 CE: 510 BCE: Dedication of temple of Jupiter Optimus Maximus; increasing adoption of Greek pantheon

Phoenician colonies c.800–146 BCE: Cult center at Carthage

Greece c.900–350 BCE: c.900–500: Spread of city states with local deities and emergence of major cult centers; 334–329: Alexander's campaigns spread Hellenistic culture and religion through Southwest Asia

Carthage · Caere · Rome · Mt. Olympus · Delphi · Athens · Kostromskaya

Egypt c.3000–30 BCE:
c.3100–2795 BCE: Archaic period
c.2795–2180 BCE: Old Kingdom, monumental architecture and elaborate (pyramid) tombs
c.2134–1640 BCE: Middle Kingdom
c.1530–1070 BCE: New Kingdom
1352–1333 BCE: Akhenaten establishes monotheistic Aten (Sun God) cult at El-Armarna

Giza · Saqqara

Judah to 132 CE. Monotheism: 930 BCE: Temple of Solomon, destroyed 586; second temple built 538; From 132 CE: Jewish diaspora · Jerusalem

Scythia 1st millennium BCE: Elaborate burials (often with horses) with grave goods

Persia c.550 BCE–226 CE: 550 BCE: Zoroastrianism proclaimed monotheistic state cult of Achaemenid Persia; monumental temples; fire altars; From c.116 CE: Zoroastrian cult of Mithraism spreads through Roman Empire

Pasargadae · Pazyryk

Mesopotamia from 3rd millennium BCE: Royal burials, including attendants, and rich grave goods; monumental (ziggurat) temples · Sumer · Ur

China from c.1800 BCE: c.1800–1027 BCE: Shang China; ancestor worship, use of oracle bones and bronze inscriptions for divination; 1027 BCE–5th century CE: Zhou dynasty; emergence of Taoism, Confucianism; 221–206: Qin Dynasty; elaborate royal graves with mass grave goods and terra-cotta armies · Luoyang

India from c.1800 BCE: c.1450 BCE: Composition of Vedas, recording Indian mythology begins; c.800 BCE: Rise of cities on central Ganges; Upanishads recorded in Sanskrit · Rajagriha

Widespread animistic cults and ancestor worship (Africa)

The development of religious architecture

3000 BCE	2000 BCE	1000 BCE	1 CE
2650: Zoser's stepped pyramid at Saqqara; 2530: "True" pyramid of Khufu, Giza	2100: Ziggurat at Ur in Sumer; c. 2000: Stonehenge erected	c. 700: First peristyle Greek temples; 510: Temple of Jupiter Optimus Maximus, Rome	432: Completion of Parthenon, Athens; 400: Temple complex, Chavin de Huantar

---

A *trimurti* at the Temple of Shiva at Elephanta depicts the three principal Hindu divinities, Shiva, Vishnu, and Brahma.

Early religion in South Asia

The religion of the ancient Aryan tribes is known largely from the hymns of the *Rig Veda*, and the *Vedas*, *Brahmanas*, and *Upanishads*. It focused on sacrifices to a pantheon of deities and semigods. Vedic Hinduism spread over much of India before the rise of Buddhism and Jainism, which developed in reaction to the excesses of Aryan religious practices. These faiths emphasized *ahimsa* (nonviolence), meditation, and the suppression of desire for worldly possessions; these and other elements of Hinduism may derive from the religion of the Indus civilization (c.2600–1800 BCE).

❷ Religions of South Asia

UDICHYA broad cultural region recognised by ancient Aryans
MAGADHA other regions
Yamuna sacred river
core area of Buddhism and Jainism
Ashokan rock and pillar edicts

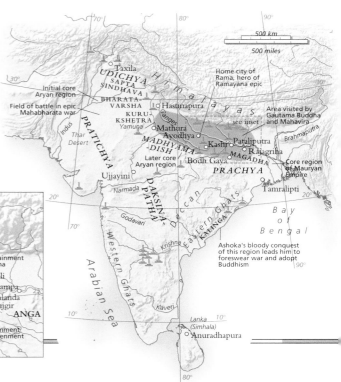

Map labels (South Asia):
Taxila · UDICHYA · SAPTA · SINDHAVA · BHARATA-VARSHA · PRATICHYA · Hastinapura · Home city of Rama, hero of Ramayana epic · Initial core Aryan region · Field of battle in epic Mahabharata war · Thar Desert · KURU · KSHETRA · Mathura · MADHYAMA-DISH · Ayodhya · Kashi · Pataliputra · Rajagriha · Area visited by Gautama Buddha and Mahavira · Bodh Gaya · Core region of Mauryan Empire · Later core Aryan region · Ujjayini · PRACHYA · DAKSINA-PATHA · Tamralipti · Narmada · Godavari · Deccan · Krishna · Eastern Ghats · KALINGA · Bay of Bengal · Western Ghats · Arabian Sea · Kaveri · Lanka (Simhala) · Anuradhapura

Ashoka's bloody conquest of this region leads him to foreswear war and adopt Buddhism

500 km · 500 miles

Early religion in South Asia

1400 BCE	1000	600	200 BCE
c.1550: Aryans settle northern India	c.800: Rise of urban culture in Ganges valley; c.600: Rise to dominance of Magadha	6th century: Life of Mahavira, founder of Jainism; 566: Birth of Siddhartha Gautama, founder of Buddhism	322: Chandragupta founds Mauryan dynasty; 272–232: Reign of Ashoka, who promulgates Buddhism as state religion

Inset map (Buddha)

Legendary descent of the Buddha from heaven · Kampilya · Samkashya · Kanauj · Ayodhya · Lumbini · Shravasti · Kapilavasthu · Kusinagara · KOSHALA · Yamuna · Vaishali · Prayaga · Sarnath · Pataliputra · Champa · Kaushambi · Benares · MAGADHA · Bodh Gaya · Gaya · Rajgir · ANGA · Nalanda

566: Birthplace
537: Great Renunciation
483: Attainment of Nirvana
528: Attainment of Enlightenment
528: Sermon in the Deer Park

200 km · 200 miles

Religions of the Mediterranean

The Mediterranean world in the 1st millennium BCE was the home of a range of discrete cultures, each supporting its own religious beliefs. However, many of these shared striking similarities in mythology, in the character and nature of their pantheons, and in religious practice and observance. Rivalry, warfare, and trade created an interaction of influences and cross-fertilizations, and with the rise of Classical Greece, Hellenistic culture, and then Rome, certain local beliefs and practices became widespread.

Greece

The Greek mythological pantheon, developed during the Mycenaean period, was described by writers such as Homer and became, during the Classic Greek period, a central force in Greek life. Each city-state practiced favored cults, but the emergence of oracles and other cult centers (such as Mount Olympus) codified a pan-Hellenic religious tradition which was spread widely by colonization and the campaigns of Alexander the Great (see pp.40–41).

Zeus (Jupiter for the Romans) was the supreme Greek deity.

SEE ALSO:

Africa: pp.160–161

Europe: pp.174–179

West Asia: pp.220–221

South and Southeast Asia: pp.242–243

North and East Asia: pp.258–259

❸ The Mediterranean cults ▶

Cult centers
- Egyptian
- Greek
- other
- Ares main divinity worshipped
- → spread of the cult of Cybele
- → spread of the Greek Pantheon
- → spread of Mithraism

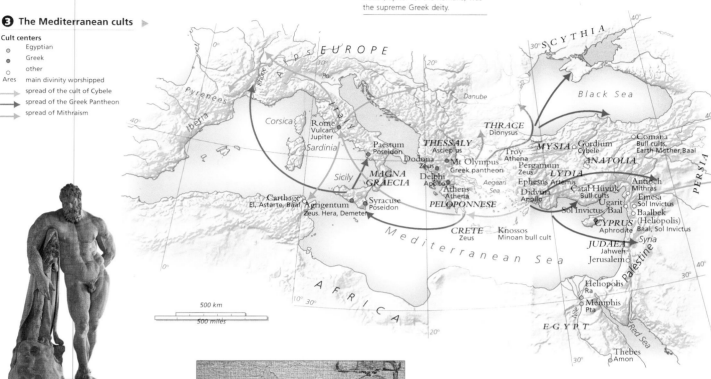

Judaism

The traditional religion of Israel and Judah was unusual in having a single deity, Jahweh. The Babylonian exile (587–538 BCE) strengthened Judaism and encouraged the crystallization of its core beliefs by Deutero-Isaiah and other prophets. The religion survived persecution to become the seedbed of Christianity.

The Jewish candelabra (menorah) symbolizes the eternal light (ner tamid) which burned in the first Temple of Solomon.

A dead man kneels before Anubis, god of mummification. Life after death was central to Egyptian theology, celebrated through a series of elaborate rituals.

Egypt

A detailed mythology and pantheon permeated Ancient Egyptian life and thought, and is recorded abundantly in votive statuary and hieroglyphic tomb paintings. The hierarchy and character of Egyptian cosmology probably influenced the development of the Mycenaean and Greek pantheon.

This Mycenaean ritual sprinkler takes the form of a bull's head.

Bull cults

Bull worshiping was widespread in the Mediterranean region, from Çatal Hüyük (c.7000 BCE) to the famous Minotaur cult in Crete (from c.2000 BCE); bulls also played a significant role in Egyptian, Mesopotamian, and Greek mythology.

The demigod Heracles (Hercules in Latin) formed part of the Greek mythological pantheon adopted by the Romans.

Rome

Rome's pantheon was largely adopted from that of Greece, although certain local cults gained popularity as the empire grew. One of the most widespread was that of Mithras, which spread from Persia to Syria, then throughout the empire; eventually the most influential was Christianity.

Taoism and Confucianism

Taoism developed during the Zhou dynasty as the most widespread of Chinese religions. Based on the worship of ancestors, nature spirits, and sacred places, it was codified by Lao-tzu (605–520 BCE). The philosopher Confucius (551–479 BCE) promulgated a system of filial observance, learning, obedience, and selflessness which became central to Chinese imperial policy and governance. Followers such as Mencius (c.370–300 BCE) ensured that his teachings survived the Warring States period (403–221 BCE).

❹ Taoism and Confucianism

- Chinese cultural area c.220 BCE
- YAN region associated with development of Taoism
- ▲ mountain sacred to Taoism

Centers of Confucianism
- Imperial capital
- Qin state capital by c.220 BCE

The teachings of Confucius ensured that even the most lowly could, by ability, correct behavior, and hard work, aspire to high office.

1027: Beginnings of Zhou dynastic rule

771: Decline of Zhou central administration

551–479: Confucius, author of the Analects, provides central philosophy for Chinese way of life

| 1050 BCE | 950 | 850 | 750 | 650 | 550 | 450 | 350 | 250 BCE |

Taoism and Confucianism in China

605–520: Lao-tzu, traditional founder of Taoism

403–221: Warring States period

c.370–300: Mencius continues Confucian teaching

THE WORLD 500–250 BCE

THE 5TH CENTURY BCE was an age of enlightened and innovative thought. It was the climax of the Classical Age in Greece, a period that was remarkable for its art, philosophy, drama, architecture, and political theory. At the same time the Buddhist religion, based on the precepts of renouncing all material desires as practiced by Siddhartha Gautama (c.566–486 BCE), was spreading throughout the Indian subcontinent. In China, the teachings of Confucius (551–479 BCE) were concerned with ethical conduct and propriety in human relations. Yet the ensuing centuries were a time of conflict and conquest. From 331–323 BCE Alexander the Great's military conquests created an empire which stretched from Macedon to the Indus. From c.272 BCE the emperor Ashoka absorbed most of the Indian subcontinent into his empire, while in China the Warring States period was a time of violent turmoil.

The shrine of Delphi was the site of the Pythian Games, one of four great athletic festivals that brought Greeks together at set intervals of years.

Europe

In the 5th century BCE, Greece reached the pinnacle of the Classical Age. Athens' conflict with Sparta in the Peloponnesian Wars weakened the Greek city-states, which in the 4th century fell to Philip of Macedon. Under his son, Alexander the Great, who conquered the Persian Empire, Macedon became a great imperial power. In Italy, by 264 BCE, Rome was poised to become a world power.

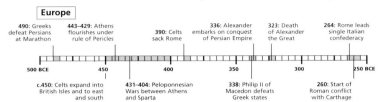

Europe

| 490: Greeks defeat Persians at Marathon | 443–429: Athens flourishes under rule of Pericles | 390: Celts sack Rome | 336: Alexander embarks on conquest of Persian Empire | 323: Death of Alexander the Great | 264: Rome leads single Italian confederacy |

500 BCE — 450 — 400 — 350 — 300 — 250 BCE

c.450: Celts expand into British Isles and to east and south • 431–404: Peloponnesian Wars between Athens and Sparta • 338: Philip II of Macedon defeats Greek states • 260: Start of Roman conflict with Carthage

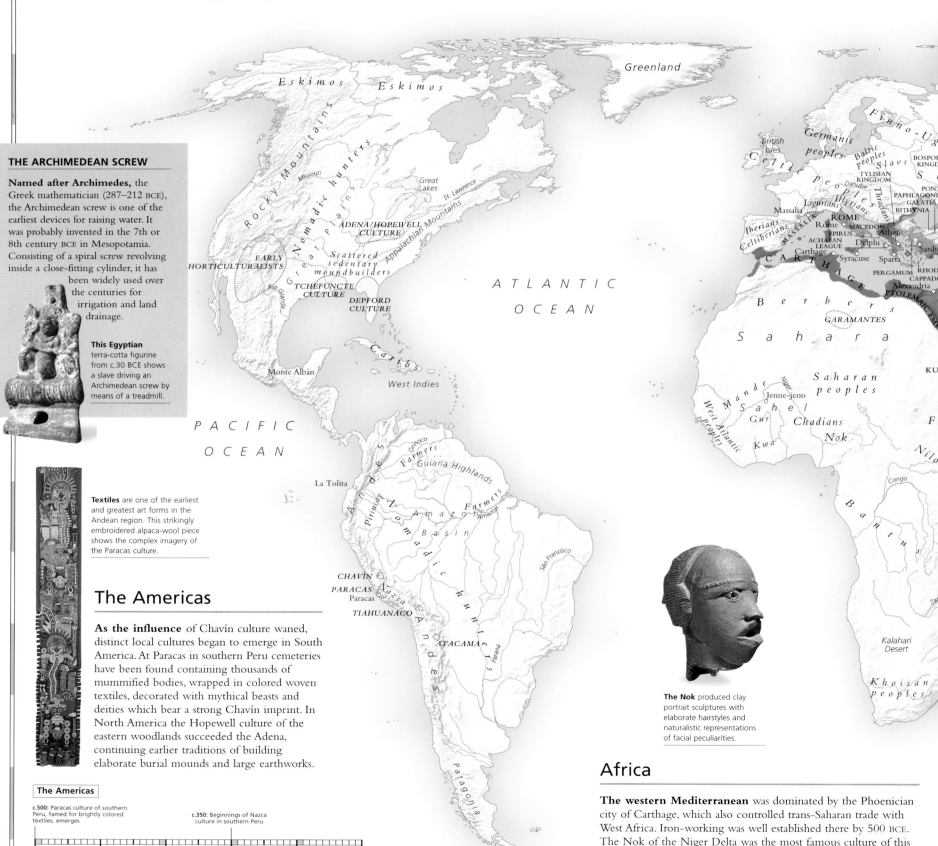

THE ARCHIMEDEAN SCREW

Named after Archimedes, the Greek mathematician (287–212 BCE), the Archimedean screw is one of the earliest devices for raising water. It was probably invented in the 7th or 8th century BCE in Mesopotamia. Consisting of a spiral screw revolving inside a close-fitting cylinder, it has been widely used over the centuries for irrigation and land drainage.

This Egyptian terra-cotta figurine from c.30 BCE shows a slave driving an Archimedean screw by means of a treadmill.

Textiles are one of the earliest and greatest art forms in the Andean region. This strikingly embroidered alpaca-wool piece shows the complex imagery of the Paracas culture.

The Americas

As the influence of Chavín culture waned, distinct local cultures began to emerge in South America. At Paracas in southern Peru cemeteries have been found containing thousands of mummified bodies, wrapped in colored woven textiles, decorated with mythical beasts and deities which bear a strong Chavín imprint. In North America the Hopewell culture of the eastern woodlands succeeded the Adena, continuing earlier traditions of building elaborate burial mounds and large earthworks.

The Americas

c.500: Paracas culture of southern Peru, famed for brightly colored textiles, emerges • c.350: Beginnings of Nazca culture in southern Peru

500 BCE — 450 — 400 — 350 — 300 — 250 BCE

c.400: Early Zapotec culture flourishing around city of Monte Albán • c.300: Hopewell culture in eastern North America develops traditions of earlier Adena culture

The Nok produced clay portrait sculptures with elaborate hairstyles and naturalistic representations of facial peculiarities.

Africa

The western Mediterranean was dominated by the Phoenician city of Carthage, which also controlled trans-Saharan trade with West Africa. Iron-working was well established there by 500 BCE. The Nok of the Niger Delta was the most famous culture of this early Iron Age. The Persian satrapy of Egypt was conquered by Alexander the Great in 332 BCE. On Alexander's death, Egypt fell to his successor, Ptolemy, who founded the Ptolemaic dynasty.

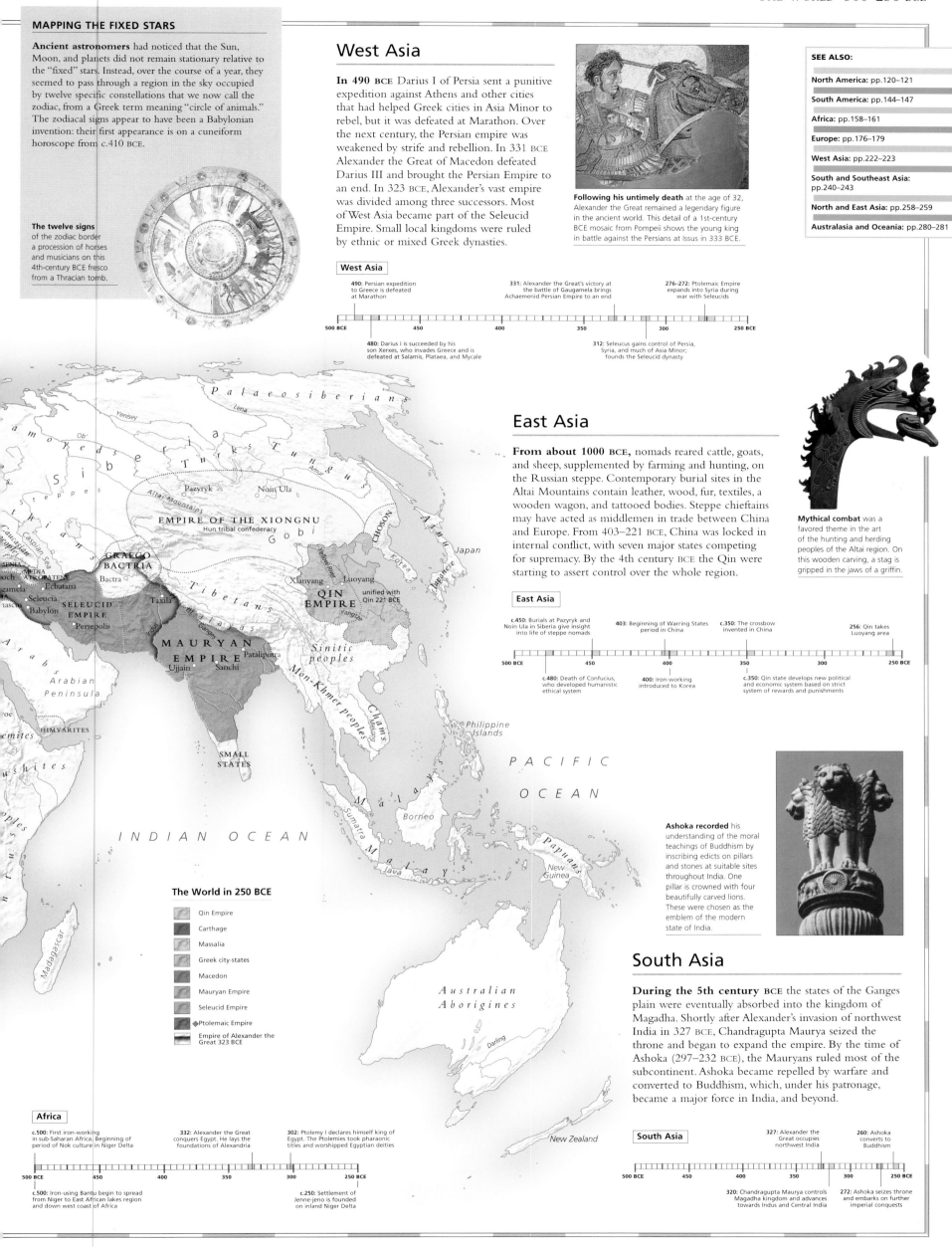

MAPPING THE FIXED STARS

Ancient astronomers had noticed that the Sun, Moon, and planets did not remain stationary relative to the "fixed" stars. Instead, over the course of a year, they seemed to pass through a region in the sky occupied by twelve specific constellations that we now call the zodiac, from a Greek term meaning "circle of animals." The zodiacal signs appear to have been a Babylonian invention: their first appearance is on a cuneiform horoscope from c.410 BCE.

The twelve signs of the zodiac border a procession of horses and musicians on this 4th-century BCE fresco from a Thracian tomb.

West Asia

In 490 BCE Darius I of Persia sent a punitive expedition against Athens and other cities that had helped Greek cities in Asia Minor to rebel, but it was defeated at Marathon. Over the next century, the Persian empire was weakened by strife and rebellion. In 331 BCE Alexander the Great of Macedon defeated Darius III and brought the Persian Empire to an end. In 323 BCE, Alexander's vast empire was divided among three successors. Most of West Asia became part of the Seleucid Empire. Small local kingdoms were ruled by ethnic or mixed Greek dynasties.

Following his untimely death at the age of 32, Alexander the Great remained a legendary figure in the ancient world. This detail of a 1st-century BCE mosaic from Pompeii shows the young king in battle against the Persians at Issus in 333 BCE.

SEE ALSO:

North America: pp.120–121

South America: pp.144–147

Africa: pp.158–161

Europe: pp.176–179

West Asia: pp.222–223

South and Southeast Asia: pp.240–243

North and East Asia: pp.258–259

Australasia and Oceania: pp.280–281

West Asia

490: Persian expedition to Greece is defeated at Marathon

331: Alexander the Great's victory at the battle of Gaugamela brings Achaemenid Persian Empire to an end

276–272: Ptolemaic Empire expands into Syria during war with Seleucids

| 500 BCE | 450 | 400 | 350 | 300 | 250 BCE |

480: Darius I is succeeded by his son Xerxes, who invades Greece and is defeated at Salamis, Plataea, and Mycale

312: Seleucus gains control of Persia, Syria, and much of Asia Minor; founds the Seleucid dynasty

East Asia

From about 1000 BCE, nomads reared cattle, goats, and sheep, supplemented by farming and hunting, on the Russian steppe. Contemporary burial sites in the Altai Mountains contain leather, wood, fur, textiles, a wooden wagon, and tattooed bodies. Steppe chieftains may have acted as middlemen in trade between China and Europe. From 403–221 BCE, China was locked in internal conflict, with seven major states competing for supremacy. By the 4th century BCE the Qin were starting to assert control over the whole region.

Mythical combat was a favored theme in the art of the hunting and herding peoples of the Altai region. On this wooden carving, a stag is gripped in the jaws of a griffin.

East Asia

c.450: Burials at Pazyryk and Noin Ula in Siberia give insight into life of steppe nomads

403: Beginning of Warring States period in China

c.350: The crossbow invented in China

256: Qin takes Luoyang area

| 500 BCE | 450 | 400 | 350 | 300 | 250 BCE |

c.480: Death of Confucius, who developed humanistic ethical system

400: Iron-working introduced to Korea

c.350: Qin state develops new political and economic system based on strict system of rewards and punishments

Ashoka recorded his understanding of the moral teachings of Buddhism by inscribing edicts on pillars and stones at suitable sites throughout India. One pillar is crowned with four beautifully carved lions. These were chosen as the emblem of the modern state of India.

South Asia

During the 5th century BCE the states of the Ganges plain were eventually absorbed into the kingdom of Magadha. Shortly after Alexander's invasion of northwest India in 327 BCE, Chandragupta Maurya seized the throne and began to expand the empire. By the time of Ashoka (297–232 BCE), the Mauryans ruled most of the subcontinent. Ashoka became repelled by warfare and converted to Buddhism, which, under his patronage, became a major force in India, and beyond.

South Asia

327: Alexander the Great occupies northwest India

260: Ashoka converts to Buddhism

| 500 BCE | 450 | 400 | 350 | 300 | 250 BCE |

320: Chandragupta Maurya controls Magadha kingdom and advances towards Indus and Central India

272: Ashoka seizes throne and embarks on further imperial conquests

The World in 250 BCE

- Qin Empire
- Carthage
- Massalia
- Greek city-states
- Macedon
- Mauryan Empire
- Seleucid Empire
- Ptolemaic Empire
- Empire of Alexander the Great 323 BCE

Africa

c.500: First iron-working in sub-Saharan Africa. Beginning of period of Nok culture in Niger Delta

332: Alexander the Great conquers Egypt. He lays the foundations of Alexandria

302: Ptolemy I declares himself king of Egypt. The Ptolemies took pharaonic titles and worshipped Egyptian deities

| 500 BCE | 450 | 400 | 350 | 300 | 250 BCE |

c.500: Iron-using Bantu begin to spread from Niger to East African lakes region and down west coast of Africa

c.250: Settlement of Jenne-jeno is founded on inland Niger Delta

Map labels

Palaeosiberians, Yenisey, Lena, Ob, Amoke, Reds, Siberia, Turks, Tungus, Amur, Altai Mountains, Pazyryk, Noin Ula, EMPIRE OF THE XIONGNU, Hun tribal confederacy, Gobi, CHOSON, Korea, Japan, Japanese, GRAECO-BACTRIA, Bactra, Tibetans, Xianyang, Luoyang, QIN EMPIRE, unified with Qin 221 BCE, Yellow River, Yangtze, Scythians, Caucasians, Caspian Sea, MEDIA, ATROPATENE, Ecbatana, Seleucia, SELEUCID EMPIRE, Babylon, Persepolis, Taxila, MAURYAN EMPIRE, Pataliputra, Ujjain, Sanchi, Sinitic peoples, Himalayas, Mon-Khmer peoples, Chams, Mekong, Arabs, Arabian Peninsula, HIMYARITES, SMALL STATES, Malays, Malaya, Sumatra, Borneo, Java, Philippine Islands, PACIFIC OCEAN, INDIAN OCEAN, Madagascar, Papuans, New Guinea, Australian Aborigines, Darling, New Zealand

THE EMPIRE OF ALEXANDER

Alexander the Great, (356–323 BCE), was king of Macedonia and conqueror of a great Afro-Eurasian empire.

THE CONQUESTS OF ALEXANDER took Greek armies to Egypt, Mesopotamia, the Hindu Kush, and India's western borders, and forced Achaemenid Persia, the most powerful empire in the world, into submission. This extraordinary and audacious military feat, accomplished in just ten years, was to create a truly cosmopolitan civilization. Hellenism permeated the cultures of West Asia: some Hellenistic kingdoms survived into the 1st century CE, while Greek remained the official language in many parts of West Asia until the 8th and 9th centuries CE; cities founded in the aftermath of Alexander's conquests, perpetuated the ideals of Greek civilization – some, such as Alexandria, Kandahar, and Tashkent, survive to this day. Ultimately, Alexander opened up new horizons; his followers encountered different peoples and cultures and established trade routes which linked the Mediterranean with East Africa, India, and Asia.

The battle between the Greeks and Persians is depicted with vigorous, high-relief realism on this sarcophagus, found at Sidon.

The conquests of Alexander

Alexander succeeded to the Macedonian throne after the assassination of his father, Philip, in 336 BCE. He crossed into Asia in 334 BCE, defeated the Persian provincial army at Granicus and liberated the old Greek cities of Asia Minor. After a brief sojourn in Egypt, he won a spectacular victory over the Persian emperor, Darius III, at Issus and pursued him into Persia, taking the cities of Babylon, Susa, and Persepolis. He pressed on to Bactria and Sogdiana, the eastern outposts of the Persian Empire, and crossed the Hindu Kush. At the Hyphasis River (Beas) his army refused to go farther. He died in Babylon in 323 BCE, aged 32.

❶ The Empire of Alexander

- Empire of Alexander
- dependent regions
- independent states
- → route of Alexander the Great
- → route of Nearchus
- → return route of Craterus
- ⚔ major battle
- Persian Royal Road

Scale varies with perspective

This 1st-century Roman mosaic (based possibly on a Macedonian original) shows Darius III, the Persian emperor, at the battle of Issus (333 BCE). His crushing defeat allowed Alexander to conquer the western half of the Persian Empire.

Hellenistic cities of West Asia

The most magnificent West Asian Hellenistic foundation was Pergamum, capital of the Attalid dynasty (282 to 133 BCE). Adorned by a new school of baroque architecture, characterized by its ornate and heavy style, the city had a spectacular theater and an impressive library, second only to Alexandria.

"The Dying Gaul" is a copy of one of the statues erected in Pergamum to commemorate the turning back of a Gaulish invasion in 241 BCE.

Spring 333 BCE: Over 30 cities in Lycia surrender to Alexander; he reaches Gordium, where he cuts Gordian Knot, said to be sign he will rule all Asia

1 Oct 331 BCE: Alexander's second battle with Darius III, whose army includes elephants and scythe-wheeled chariots. Victory for Alexander signals effective end of Persian Empire

May 334 BCE: Alexander visits Troy, where he appropriates so-called sword of Achilles

Feb 324 BCE: Returns to Su Mass marriage of Gre soldiers to Persian bric

Nov 333 BCE: Alexander's first meeting in battle with Darius III. Persian army taken by surprise, suffer heavy losses, and Darius flees

Nov 331 BCE: Following surrender of Babylon, Alexander enters city in triumph
10 Jun 323 BCE: Alexander dies in Babylon

Sep–Nov 332 BCE: Siege of key Persian fortress of Gaza. Alexander wounded by catapult bolt

Midwinter 331 BCE: Alexander visits oracle of Ammon at Siwa; kinship with Ammon-Zeus proclaimed

The growth of Macedonian power

359: Philip starts rise to power, and begins to extend Macedonian territory

342: Philip master of Thrace; one of conquered cities renamed Philippopolis

336: Philip is succeeded by his son Alexander

333: Persian king Darius III is defeated at Issus

326: Alexander reaches Taxila; prevented from advancing into India by revolt of his troops

356: Philip II takes title of king; birth of his son Alexander

346: War in Central Greece ends in uneasy peace between Philip and Athens

338: Battle of Chaeronea; Philip II defeats Greek states

332: Alexander founds the city of Alexandria in northern Egypt

331: Decisive defeat of the Persians at battle of Gaugamela

323: Death of Alexander

360 BCE   350   340   330   320 BCE

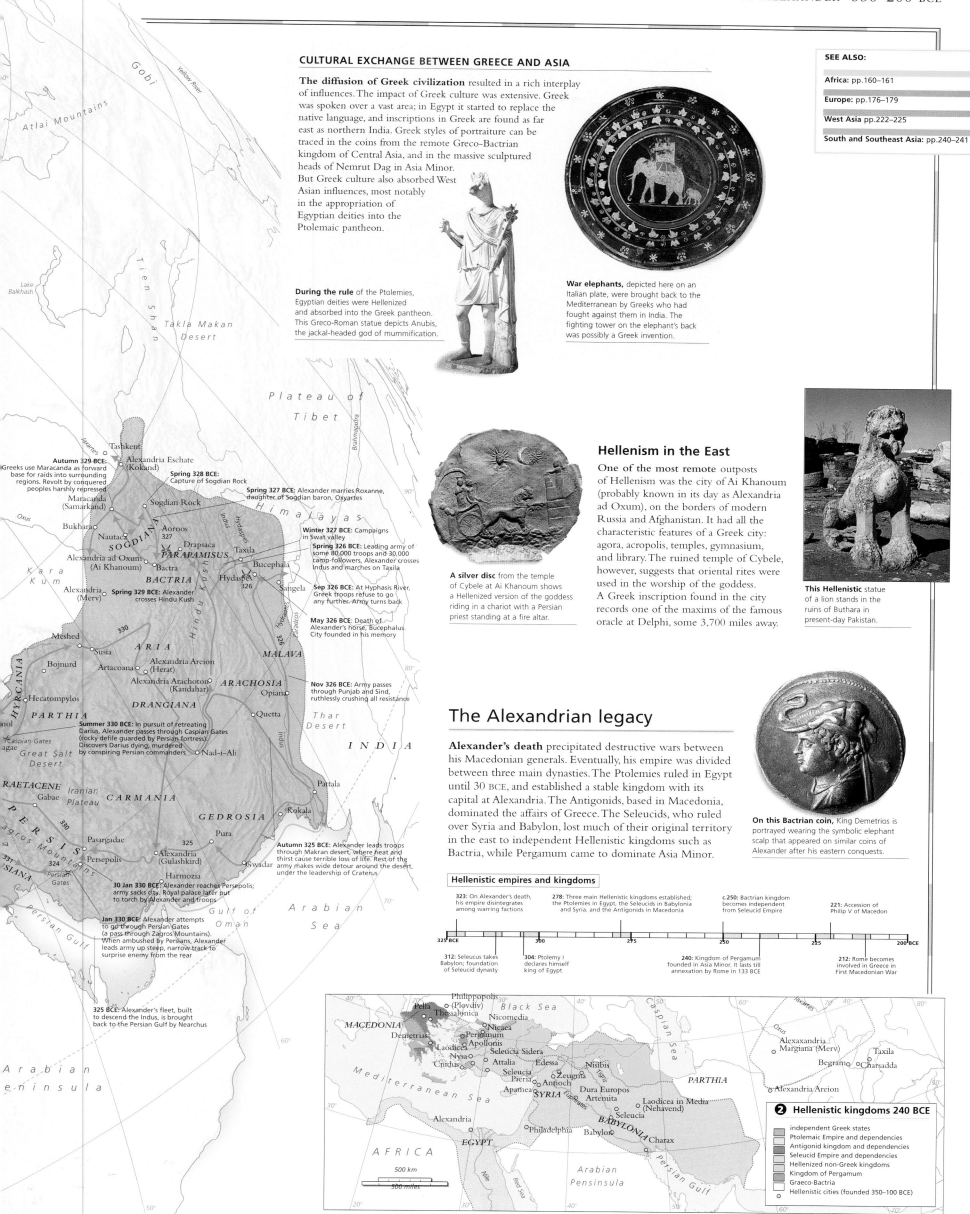

CULTURAL EXCHANGE BETWEEN GREECE AND ASIA

The diffusion of Greek civilization resulted in a rich interplay of influences. The impact of Greek culture was extensive. Greek was spoken over a vast area; in Egypt it started to replace the native language, and inscriptions in Greek are found as far east as northern India. Greek styles of portraiture can be traced in the coins from the remote Greco-Bactrian kingdom of Central Asia, and in the massive sculptured heads of Nemrut Dag in Asia Minor. But Greek culture also absorbed West Asian influences, most notably in the appropriation of Egyptian deities into the Ptolemaic pantheon.

During the rule of the Ptolemies, Egyptian deities were Hellenized and absorbed into the Greek pantheon. This Greco-Roman statue depicts Anubis, the jackal-headed god of mummification.

War elephants, depicted here on an Italian plate, were brought back to the Mediterranean by Greeks who had fought against them in India. The fighting tower on the elephant's back was possibly a Greek invention.

SEE ALSO:

Africa: pp.160–161

Europe: pp.176–179

West Asia pp.222–225

South and Southeast Asia: pp.240–241

Hellenism in the East

One of the most remote outposts of Hellenism was the city of Ai Khanoum (probably known in its day as Alexandria ad Oxum), on the borders of modern Russia and Afghanistan. It had all the characteristic features of a Greek city: agora, acropolis, temples, gymnasium, and library. The ruined temple of Cybele, however, suggests that oriental rites were used in the worship of the goddess. A Greek inscription found in the city records one of the maxims of the famous oracle at Delphi, some 3,700 miles away.

A silver disc from the temple of Cybele at Ai Khanoum shows a Hellenized version of the goddess riding in a chariot with a Persian priest standing at a fire altar.

This Hellenistic statue of a lion stands in the ruins of Buthara in present-day Pakistan.

The Alexandrian legacy

Alexander's death precipitated destructive wars between his Macedonian generals. Eventually, his empire was divided between three main dynasties. The Ptolemies ruled in Egypt until 30 BCE, and established a stable kingdom with its capital at Alexandria. The Antigonids, based in Macedonia, dominated the affairs of Greece. The Seleucids, who ruled over Syria and Babylon, lost much of their original territory in the east to independent Hellenistic kingdoms such as Bactria, while Pergamum came to dominate Asia Minor.

On this Bactrian coin, King Demetrios is portrayed wearing the symbolic elephant scalp that appeared on similar coins of Alexander after his eastern conquests.

Hellenistic empires and kingdoms

323: On Alexander's death, his empire disintegrates among warring factions

278: Three main Hellenistic kingdoms established; the Ptolemies in Egypt, the Seleucids in Babylonia and Syria, and the Antigonids in Macedonia

c.250: Bactrian kingdom becomes independent from Seleucid Empire

221: Accession of Philip V of Macedon

312: Seleucus takes Babylon; foundation of Seleucid dynasty

304: Ptolemy I declares himself king of Egypt

240: Kingdom of Pergamum founded in Asia Minor. It lasts till annexation by Rome in 133 BCE

212: Rome becomes involved in Greece in First Macedonian War

325 BCE · 300 · 275 · 250 · 225 · 200 BCE

Map labels (main map)

Gobi
Yellow River
Atlai Mountains
Tien Shan
Lake Balkhash
Takla Makan Desert
Plateau of Tibet
Brahmaputra
Himalayas
Kara Kum
Oxus
Tashkent
Autumn 329 BCE: Greeks use Maracanda as forward base for raids into surrounding regions. Revolt by conquered peoples harshly repressed
Alexandria Eschate (Kokand)
Spring 328 BCE: Capture of Sogdian Rock
Maracanda (Samarkand)
Bukhara
Nautaca
Sogdian Rock
Spring 327 BCE: Alexander marries Roxanne, daughter of Sogdian baron, Oxyartes
SOGDIANA
Aornos 327
Drapsaca
Taxila
Winter 327 BCE: Campaigns in Swat valley
Alexandria ad Oxum (Ai Khanoum)
PARAPAMISUS
Bactra
Bucephala
Hydaspes
Spring 326 BCE: Leading army of some 80,000 troops and 30,000 camp-followers, Alexander crosses Indus and marches on Taxila
Alexandria (Merv)
Spring 329 BCE: Alexander crosses Hindu Kush
BACTRIA
Hydaspes 326
Sangela
Sep 326 BCE: At Hyphasis River, Greek troops refuse to go any further. Army turns back
Hydaspes
Acesines
Hydraotes
May 326 BCE: Death of Alexander's horse, Bucephalus. City founded in his memory
Meshed
ARIA
MALAVA
Susia
Bojnurd
Artacoana
Alexandria Areion (Herat)
Alexandria Arachotorum (Kandahar)
ARACHOSIA
Opiana
Nov 326 BCE: Army passes through Punjab and Sind, ruthlessly crushing all resistance
Hecatompylos
DRANGIANA
Quetta
Thar Desert
PARTHIA
INDIA
Summer 330 BCE: In pursuit of retreating Darius, Alexander passes through Caspian Gates (rocky defile guarded by Persian fortress). Discovers Darius dying, murdered by conspiring Persian commanders
Caspian Gates
Great Salt Desert
Nad-i-Ali
Pattala
RAETACENE
Gabae
Iranian Plateau
CARMANIA
GEDROSIA
Kokala
Pasargadae
Pura
Persepolis
Alexandria (Gulashkird)
Swadar
Autumn 325 BCE: Alexander leads troops through Makran desert, where heat and thirst cause terrible loss of life. Rest of the army makes wide detour around the desert, under the leadership of Craterus
Harmozia
PERSIS
30 Jan 330 BCE: Alexander reaches Persepolis; army sacks city. Royal palace later put to torch by Alexander and troops
Persian Gates
Jan 330 BCE: Alexander attempts to go through Persian Gates (a pass through Zagros Mountains). When ambushed by Persians, Alexander leads army up steep, narrow track to surprise enemy from the rear
Gulf of Oman
Arabian Sea
325 BCE: Alexander's fleet, built to descend the Indus, is brought back to the Persian Gulf by Nearchus
Arabian Peninsula

Inset map (Hellenistic kingdoms 240 BCE)

Philippopolis (Plovdiv)
Pella
Thessalonica
Black Sea
MACEDONIA
Demetrias
Nicomedia
Nicaea
Pergamum
Apollonis
Laodicea
Nysa
Seleucia Sidera
Attalia
Edessa
Nisibis
Cnidus
Seleucia Pieria
Antioch
Zeugma
Dura Europos
Artemita
PARTHIA
Apamea
SYRIA
Laodicea in Media (Nehavend)
Alexandria
Philadelphia
BABYLONIA
Seleucia
Babylon
Charax
Alexandria
AFRICA
EGYPT
Arabian Pensinula
Mediterranean Sea
Caspian Sea
Oxus
Jaxartes
Tigris
Euphrates
Persian Gulf
Red Sea
Nile
Alexandria Margiana (Merv)
Taxila
Begramo
Charsadda
Alexandria Areion

② Hellenistic kingdoms 240 BCE

independent Greek states
Ptolemaic Empire and dependencies
Antigonid kingdom and dependencies
Seleucid Empire and dependencies
Hellenized non-Greek kingdoms
Kingdom of Pergamum
Graeco-Bactria
Hellenistic cities (founded 350–100 BCE)

500 km
500 miles

THE WORLD 250 BCE–1 CE

BY 1 CE HALF THE GLOBAL population, which had reached about 250 million, lived within three major empires – Rome, Parthia, and Han China. With the addition of the developing kingdoms of northern India and Southeast Asia, urban civilization now existed in a wide swathe across the Old World, from the Iberian Peninsula in the west to Korea in the east, surrounded by nomadic pastoralists, farmers, and increasingly marginalized hunter-gatherers. The opening up of the Silk Road in the 1st century BCE and the discovery of monsoon trade routes across the Indian Ocean led to an unprecedented degree of contact between empires, disseminating both religious and cultural influences. In the New World the increasingly sophisticated Nazca and Moche cultures were developing in Peru, while Teotihuacán in Mexico was poised to become one of the world's most populous cities.

Europe

The Ara Pacis (Altar of Peace) was set up in Rome in 9 BCE to commemorate the pacification of Gaul and Iberia by the Emperor Augustus.

Following the defeat of Carthage in the 2nd century BCE, Rome embarked on a program of expansion, which extended control to Greek territories in the east and Gaul to the north. In the 1st century BCE, a period of civil wars and rule by military dictators threatened the unity of the growing empire. In 27 BCE Octavian assumed imperial power (and the title Augustus), reuniting the Roman world and ushering in two centuries of stability and prosperity.

Europe

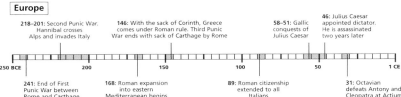

218–201: Second Punic War. Hannibal crosses Alps and invades Italy

146: With the sack of Corinth, Greece comes under Roman rule. Third Punic War ends with sack of Carthage by Rome

58–51: Gallic conquests of Julius Caesar

46: Julius Caesar appointed dictator. He is assassinated two years later

241: End of First Punic War between Rome and Carthage

168: Roman expansion into eastern Mediterranean begins

89: Roman citizenship extended to all Italians

31: Octavian defeats Antony and Cleopatra at Actium

This striking Nazca pottery figure shows a woman chewing coca leaves, an important cultural and ritual activity in the civilizations of the Andes.

The Americas

The Nazca people continued local traditions of fine textiles and pottery decorated with animals, birds, fish, plants, and human trophy heads. But the culture is best known for the Nazca Lines, long straight tracks and outlines of animals and mythical figures traced on the surface of the desert. Possibly created as offerings to the gods, their scale is so vast they can only be distinguished from the air. At the same time, the Moche culture of northern Peru, which has left a legacy of substantial urban and religious centers, fine pottery and goldwork, was beginning to emerge.

The Americas

c.200: Nazca Lines carved into the surface of the southern Peruvian desert

c.100: Adena culture of North America at its height

c.1 CE: The Moche, famous for their gold and pottery, dominate northern Peru

c.250: Many small coastal cultures, such as the Guangala, flourishing in present-day Ecuador

c.50: Teotihuacán in Valley of Mexico is largest city in the Americas, with population of 40,000

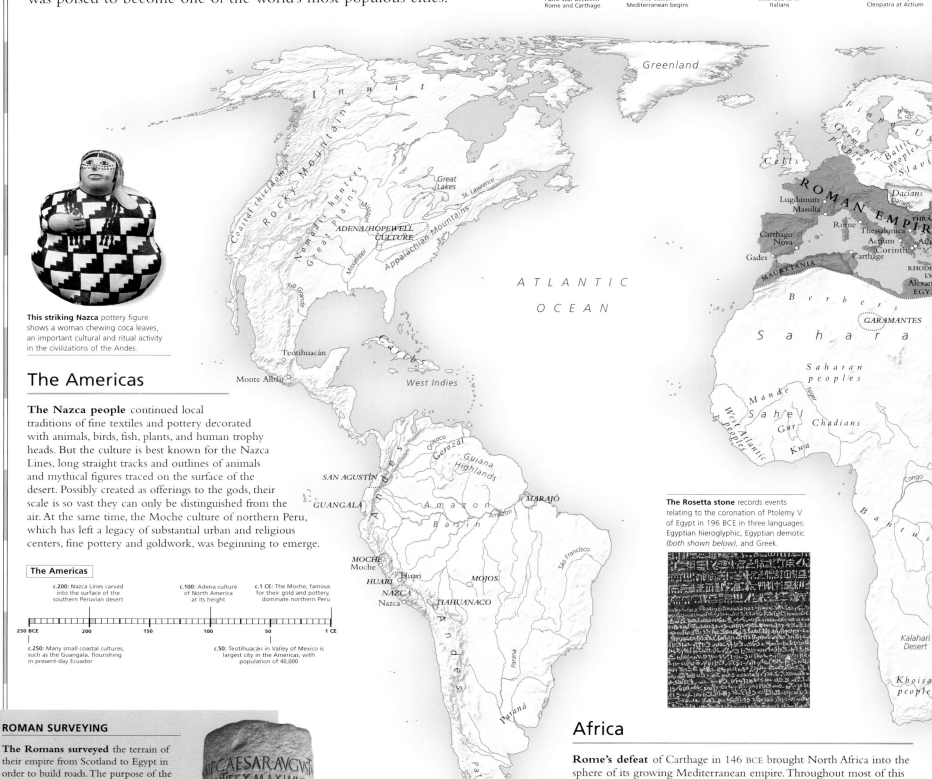

The Rosetta stone records events relating to the coronation of Ptolemy V of Egypt in 196 BCE in three languages: Egyptian hieroglyphic, Egyptian demotic (*both shown below*), and Greek.

Africa

Rome's defeat of Carthage in 146 BCE brought North Africa into the sphere of its growing Mediterranean empire. Throughout most of this period, Egypt was ruled by the Ptolemies, whose introduction of Greek language and writing hastened the decline of Egyptian civilization. In 31 BCE, when Octavian defeated Antony and Cleopatra at the battle of Actium, Egypt became a Roman province destined to serve as Rome's granary. To the south the kingdom of Meroe prospered, exporting frankincense to Rome along the Red Sea. The Bantu continued their progress into southern Africa, introducing agriculture and iron-working.

ROMAN SURVEYING

The Romans surveyed the terrain of their empire from Scotland to Egypt in order to build roads. The purpose of the roads was primarily military – to enable Roman legions to move quickly to trouble spots within the empire – but they also carried local commercial traffic. Distances were measured in thousands of paces (*milia passuum*) – hence the word mile – and milestones were placed at regular intervals. The Roman mile was about 1,680 yards (1,540 meters).

This Roman milestone stood on the Via Aemilia, which ran in a straight line across northern Italy. The inscription records road repairs undertaken in the reign of Augustus (27 BCE–14 CE).

West Asia

Following the secession of Bactria, Sogdiana, and Parthia from Seleucid rule in the mid-3rd century BCE, the nomadic Parthians took advantage of the upheaval to extend their territory. By the early 1st century BCE, their empire included Mesopotamia and stretched from Syria to Bactria. With their light, maneuverable mounted bowmen, the Parthians withstood the might of Rome at the battle of Carrhae (53 BCE), halting Rome's eastern expansion. The Parthian Empire lasted 500 years, growing wealthy from its control of the Silk Road linking China and Rome.

This ivory rhyton (horn-shaped drinking cup) was found at Nisa, the early capital of the Parthians after they expanded south from their homelands east of the Caspian Sea.

West Asia

247: Arsaces founds the Arsacid, or Parthian, dynasty

171: Mithridates II founds Parthian Empire

141: Parthians control Mesopotamia following capture of the old Seleucid capital, Seleucia-on-the-Tigris

53: Defeat of Roman infantry at the battle of Carrhae in northern Syria

250 BCE — 200 — 150 — 100 — 50 — 1 CE

124 : Accession of Mithridates II. Parthian Empire reaches greatest extent

90: Ctesiphon established as Parthian capital

40: Rome recognizes Herod the Great as ruler of Judaea

East Asia

The Qin unified China in 221 BCE, their leader taking the title "First Emperor" and introducing a harsh, centralized, bureaucratic regime. His death in 210 was followed by widespread revolts. By 206 the Han dynasty under Gao Zu had taken power. The Han, too, presided over a highly centralized bureaucracy, their state monopoly on iron and salt, combined with the opening up of the Silk Road to Central Asia, ensuring their prosperity.

Shi Huangdi, the Qin First Emperor, imposed his autocratic rule through military force. A symbolic army of thousands of life-sized, terra-cotta soldiers was assembled to guard his tomb.

East Asia

210: Death of Shi Huangdi leads to revolts throughout Qin Empire

206: Han dynasty, under Gao Zu, assumes control

119: State monopoly on iron-working established

108: Chinese take military control of Korea

55: Xiongnu confederacy breaks up; southern group becomes tributary of Han China

250 BCE — 200 — 150 — 100 — 50 — 1 CE

221: Great Wall built as protection against northern nomadic incursions

136: Confucianism becomes state religion of China

c.112: Opening up of Silk Road across Central Asia

ROMAN BUILDINGS

Architecturally, the Romans borrowed freely from the Greeks and other earlier civilizations. The most distinctive feature of their buildings, the arch, was inherited from the Etruscans. One of the Romans' major innovations was the use of *pozzolana,* concrete made of sand mixed with slaked lime and volcanic ash. This enabled them to build temples, bath houses, aqueducts, and amphitheatres on a prodigious scale.

The coffered dome of the Pantheon in Rome is made of *pozzolana.* It was still the largest in the world even when the dome of St Peter's was completed in the 16th century.

The great complex of rock-carved temples and monasteries at Ajanta in Central India became an important Buddhist center in the 1st century BCE. It is famous for its many fine ceiling paintings of the Buddha.

South and Southeast Asia

On the death of Ashoka in 232 BCE, the Mauryan Empire disintegrated and, in 185 BCE, was supplanted by the Shunga dynasty. The Greek colony of Bactria became independent and, in the Indus Valley region, Bactrians established kingdoms where Hellenic and Indian influences mingled. Much of Southeast Asia fell under Indian cultural influence as Hinduism and Buddhism spread eastward. Chinese contact was political and military; Annam fell under Han control in the 1st century BCE.

The World in 1 CE

- Han Empire
- Roman Empire and client states
- Empire of Pontus under Mithridates Eupator, c.100 BCE
- Numidia under Masinissa from 201 BCE
- Burebista's Dacian Kingdom, 45 BCE

Africa

146: Destruction of Carthage; Rome creates province of Africa from former Carthaginian possessions

105: Jugurtha, king of Numidia defeated by Roman general Gaius Marius

46: Foundation of Roman colony of Carthage

250 BCE — 200 — 150 — 100 — 50 — 1 CE

c.100: Camel introduced into Sahara by the Romans

31: Cleopatra's death marks end of Ptolemaic dynasty in Egypt

South and Southeast Asia

c.200: Bactrian Greeks establish small kingdoms

111: Annam falls to Han Empire

90: Bactrian kingdom of Gandhara falls to Scythians (Shakas)

250 BCE — 200 — 150 — 100 — 50 — 1 CE

232: Start of disintegration of Mauryan Empire

185: Pusyamitra founds Shunga dynasty

c.100: Indian influences spread to Southeast Asia via maritime trade routes

c.30: Shakas overrun Indo-Greek kingdoms of Indus Valley

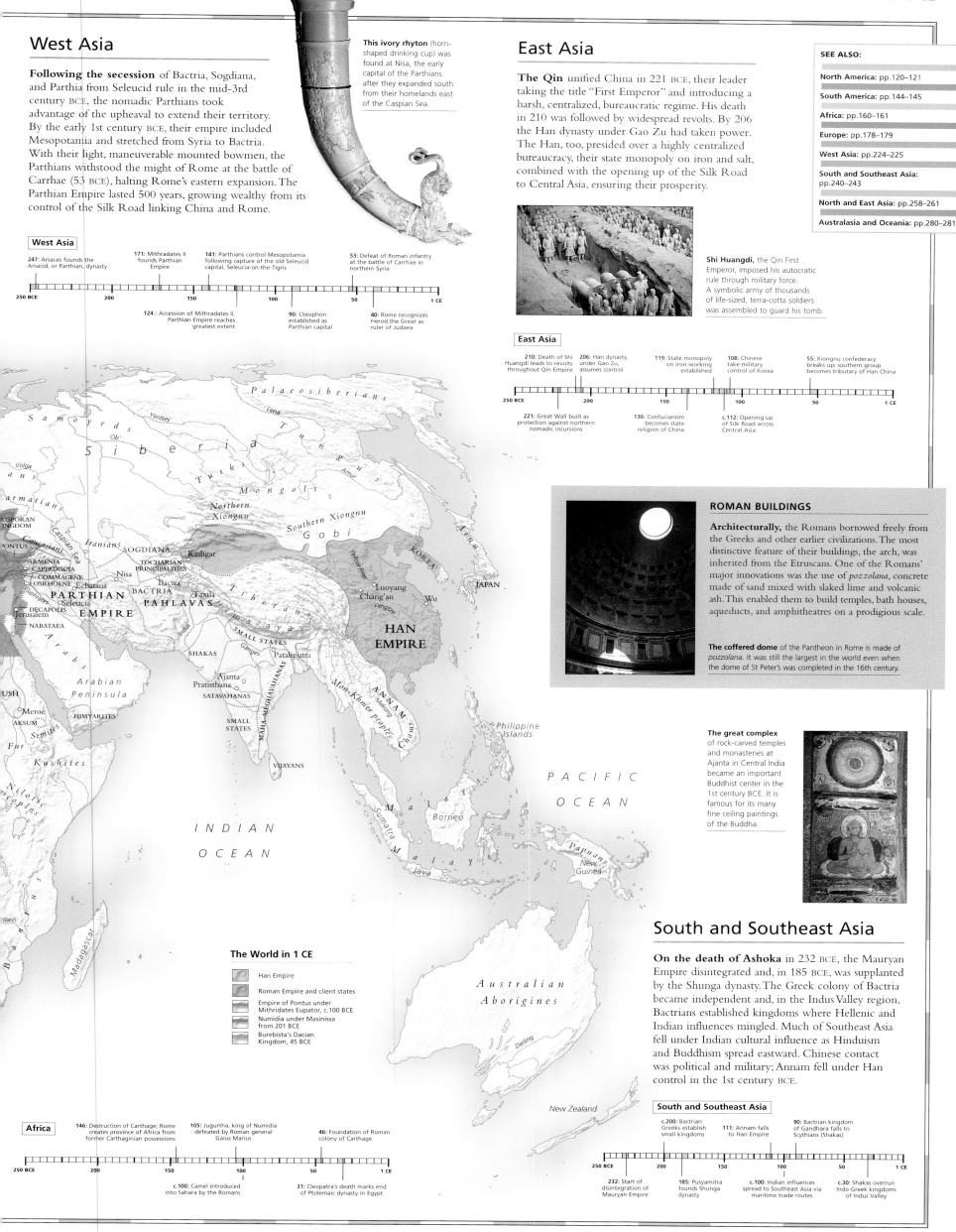

TRADE IN THE CLASSICAL WORLD

Fine Chinese silks from this period, lightweight and of high value, have been found throughout Eurasia, as far west as Egypt and Greece.

BY THE BEGINNING of the 1st millennium CE, a series of commercial and political networks had evolved which combined to form a nexus of trade which linked the eastern shores of the Atlantic Ocean, the Indian Ocean, and the western shores of the Pacific. At its extremes this network linked the Roman Empire, centered on the Mediterranean, and the land-based Han Empire of China. As the commercial and territorial influences of these two power bases spread beyond their political domains, so outlying regions were drawn into the web, from sub-Saharan Africa to the East Indies. However, the most important link to emerge was the Silk Road which spanned Asia, threading through the mountain ranges and deserts of the Central Asian landmass, and along which a chain of powerful trading cities and states came into being.

Han China and the wider world

The Han Dynasty, which emerged to take over the territorial extent of the Qin Empire from 206 BCE, was largely self-sufficient. Trade was not regarded as an imperial concern, although desirable goods were drawn into Han markets by successive middlemen on the empire's fringes – spices from South and Southeast Asia, trepang (dried sea cucumber) and mother-of-pearl from the East Indies and, with the extension of the empire into Central Asia, the swift cavalry horses of Ferghana became highly prized. Conversely, Chinese products such as silk and lacquerware commanded high prices across Asia.

Decorated Han votive mirrors were used as diplomatic gifts by the Chinese, and have been found as far away as Siberia, the Caucasus, and southern Russia.

The nimble "Horses of Heaven" from Ferghana provided the Chinese with the style of cavalry needed to keep the Xiongnu at bay.

Han trade
(in approximate order of value)

Exports	Imports
silk	horses
lacquerware	spices
	precious stones

The Classical world

141: Wudi expands Han power into Central Asia	**60:** Establishment of Kushan Empire

c.150: Ptolemy publishes first World Atlas

200: Han dynasty collapses

396: Roman Empire divided into eastern and western halves

200 BCE · 100 BCE · 1 CE · 100 · 200 · 300 · 400

31: Roman victory at Actium consolidates control of eastern Mediterranean

117: Roman Empire at greatest extent

224: Beginning of Sassanian control in Persia

238: First Germanic incursions into Roman Empire

370: Huns enter Europe

Roman trade

Rome, in contrast to Han China, was an empire largely dependent on trade. Rome's imports were prodigious. A single currency, common citizenship, low customs barriers, and the development of a broadly secure network of roads, inland waterways, harbors, and sea-routes provided a hub of commerce which drew in produce from far beyond the imperial boundaries.

The popular Roman taste for combat with exotic wild animals in the arena saw bears, bulls, and boars being imported from northern Europe, lions and tigers from Asia, crocodiles from Egypt, and rhinoceros, hippopotami, and a variety of large cats from sub-Saharan Africa.

Roman trade
(in approximate order of value)

Exports	Imports
gold	food
silver	slaves
wine	animals
olive oil	spices
glassware	silk
	incense
	ivory
	cotton

The Romans built many ports and harbors around the Mediterranean, elaborate complexes with lighthouses and docks, which serviced the Roman maritime trading network.

Knowledge of Classical Eurasia

There is some evidence of direct contact between Rome and the Han Empire and Europeans clearly had extensive knowledge of the general shape of Classical Eurasia. The Greek geographer Strabo gave a detailed description of the known world in his 17-volume *Geography* (c.20'CE) and by 150 CE the Alexandrian Ptolemy's *Geography* formally laid out the topography of Eurasia. His world view (*below*) names Sinae (China), Taprobane (Sri Lanka), and Sera Metropolis (Chang'an).

Reconstruction of Ptolemy's map of Classical Eurasia

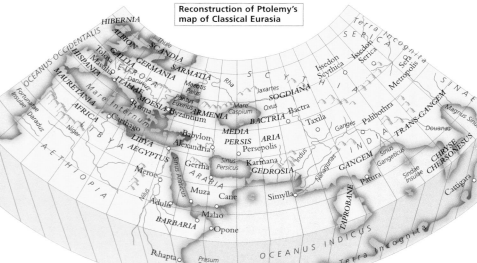

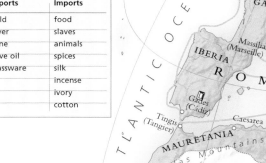

Central Asian trade

The development of the Silk Road saw the growth of a string of powerful cities and states which thrived, controlling the trade which passed through them. The greatest of these was the Parthian Empire of Persia (247 BCE–244 CE), while to the north Transoxiana, Bactria, and the Kushan Empire of modern Uzbekistan straddled the region in which the Silk Road converged and intersected with routes traveling north from India through the Hindu Kush, and on to the Caspian Sea and the river routes of Scythia.

The Silk Road

The campaigns by the Qin First Emperor, Shi Huangdi, and his Han successor Wudi against the nomadic Xiongnu opened a series of routes which traversed Central Asia, remaining the principal east–west trade route for centuries. The Silk Road linked Samarkand in the west with Anxi in the east; a summer route went north of the Tien Shan range, while the main route split to skirt the Takla Makan.

Fortified cities such as Jiaohei were established as *caravanserais* around the hostile wastes of the Takla Makan Desert.

This Greco-Roman bronze statuette of Serapis-Hercules, dating from 1st–4th century CE, was part of a hoard discovered at Bagram in the Hindu Kush, which also included Roman glassware, Chinese lacquerware, and Indian ivories.

SEE ALSO:
Africa: pp.160–161
Europe: pp.180–181
West Asia: pp.224–225
South and Southeast Asia: pp.240–24?
North and East Asia: pp.260–261

❶ Eurasian and African trade c.1 CE

Roman Empire and client states
Han Empire
Sinkiang (Han protectorate 73–94 CE)

Trade routes
Roman
Trans–Saharan (rudimentary route)
Indian Ocean
Silk Road
Scythian (rudimentary route)
China
East Africa
amber
incense
other (rudimentary route)

Goods traded
amber
animals
clothing
gold
silver
grain
horses
incense
ivory
olive oil
precious stones
silk
slaves
spices
timber
tin
tortoiseshell
wine

Trade in the Indian Ocean

Maritime trade routes in the Indian Ocean provided important links between the Roman Mediterranean, East Africa, the Persian Gulf, India, Taprobane (Sri Lanka) and beyond into the East Indies. Greek ships hugged the coasts, but lateen-rigged dhows, propelled by the regular seasonal pattern of the monsoon winds, were the first craft to move beyond coastal trade to establish direct routes across the ocean between major trading markets. The rich variety of goods they transported was described in a Greek manual from the 1st century CE, the *Periplus of the Erythraean Sea*; hoards of Roman coins have been found in southern India, Southeast Asia, and East Africa, while silks and spices from South and East Asia were transported westward.

Cana, on the southern coast of the Arabian Peninsula, one of the strategic fortified *entrepôts* which ringed the Indian Ocean, flourished on the local trade in incense.

Scale varies with perspective
720 km (450 miles)
17,810 km (11,070 miles)

Sea of Okhotsk
Kurile Islands
Sea of Japan (East Sea)
JAPAN
KOREA
Yellow Sea
East China Sea
Tropic of Cancer
PACIFIC OCEAN
Philippine Islands

Ural Mountains
Volga
Siberia
Altai Mountains
Xiongnu
Gobi
DZUNGARIA
Lake Balkhash
Kitai
Kuldja
Turfan
Jiaohei
Dunhuang
Anxi
Wuwei
Tien Shan
SINKIANG
Takla Makan Desert
Yellow River
Kaifeng
Luoyang
Chang'an
HAN EMPIRE
China
Hankou
Hangzhou
Ningbo
Fuzhou
Quanzhou
Guangzhou
Nathat
Kunming
Chengdu
Yangtze
Mekong

Aral Sea
Syr Darya
Tocharians
Aksu
Kashgar
Yarkand
Khotan
Plateau of Tibet
Tibetans
Himalayas
Taiwan
Hainan

FERGHANA
Iranians
TRANSOXIANA
Marakanda
SOGDIANA
Amu Darya
Pamirs
Mery
KUSHAN EMPIRE
Bactra
BACTRIA
Hindu Kush
Begram
Taxila
PAHLAVAS
Mathura
Patna
Brahmapura

ARMENIA
Caucasus
Caspian Sea
Hecatompylos
PARTHIA
Iranian Plateau
Persia
Alexandria Areion
Kandahar
Indus
Thar Desert
SHAKAS
Ganges
Patalipura
Nalanda
MAGADHA
Pataliputra
Tamluk
MAHA-MEGHAVAHANAS
Mon-Khmer peoples
Irrawaddy
Chams
South China Sea

Tigris
Ctesiphon
Ecbatana
Babylon
Euphrates
Zagros Mountains
Persepolis
Charax
Gerra
Persian Gulf
Ommana
Barbaricum
Barygaza (Broach)
Mandagora
SATAVAHANAS
MAHA-MEGHAVAHANAS
Masulipatam
Poduca
CHOLA
Bay of Bengal
Thaton
Oc Eo
Trang
Borneo
Celebes
Moluccas
Java Sea
Sumatra
Malays
Java

Arabian Peninsula
Arabs
Zenobia
Arabian Sea
Muziris
PANDYA
Colchi
Taprobane
Andaman Islands
Nicobar Islands

Sana
YEMEN
Cana
Aden
Gulf of Aden
Socotra
Emporion
Aromata
Aksum
KSUM
Avalites
Ethiopian Highlands
Maji
Kushites
Horn of Africa
Sarapion
Pemba
Zanzibar
Lake Victoria
INDIAN OCEAN

THE WORLD 1–250 CE

AS THE EMPIRES OF THE OLD WORLD expanded, the protection of their borders and far-flung imperial outposts became an urgent priority. Increasing threats from the mounted nomadic pastoralists of Asia, the Germanic tribes of Eastern Europe, and the Berbers of North Africa stretched resources to the limit, weakening Roman control, and leading to economic and social chaos. The empire of Han China collapsed in 220 CE, a victim of famine, floods, insurgency, and the growing power of regional warlords. By the early 3rd century CE, pressures on Rome's eastern borders precipitated a stormy century of civil wars, dynastic disputes, and army revolts. Against this troubled backdrop a new religion, Christianity, was beginning to spread throughout the Roman world. Originating with the teachings of Jesus of Nazareth in Palestine, the new religion proved remarkably resistant to Roman persecution.

Marcus Aurelius was one of the most conscientious Roman emperors: a Stoic philosopher and tireless campaigner on the German frontier.

Europe

In the 2nd century CE the Roman Empire stretched from West Asia to the Atlantic, united by one language, one coinage, a system of well-paved roads, and protected by fortified frontiers. The empire prospered under strong emperors, but stresses began to appear. Conflict over the imperial succession undermined central authority, leading to civil wars between rivals, economic breakdown, and revolts by the army. Pressure on imperial frontiers, especially from the Germanic tribes to the east of the Rhine, stretched the empire's resources, leading to inflation, famine, disease, and lawlessness.

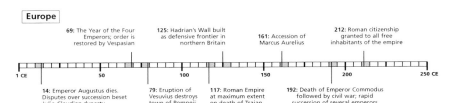

Europe

| 69: The Year of the Four Emperors; order is restored by Vespasian | 125: Hadrian's Wall built as defensive frontier in northern Britain | 161: Accession of Marcus Aurelius | 212: Roman citizenship granted to all free inhabitants of the empire |

1 CE — 50 — 100 — 150 — 200 — 250 CE

14: Emperor Augustus dies. Disputes over succession beset Julio-Claudian dynasty — 79: Eruption of Vesuvius destroys town of Pompeii — 117: Roman Empire at maximum extent on death of Trajan — 192: Death of Emperor Commodus followed by civil war; rapid succession of several emperors

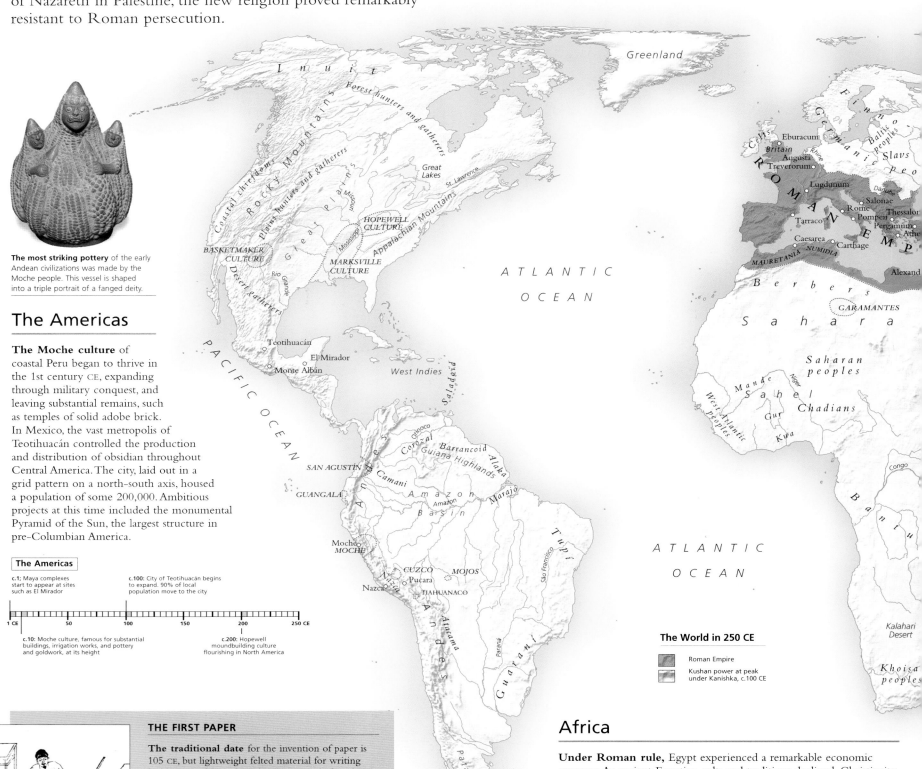

The most striking pottery of the early Andean civilizations was made by the Moche people. This vessel is shaped into a triple portrait of a fanged deity.

The Americas

The Moche culture of coastal Peru began to thrive in the 1st century CE, expanding through military conquest, and leaving substantial remains, such as temples of solid adobe brick. In Mexico, the vast metropolis of Teotihuacán controlled the production and distribution of obsidian throughout Central America. The city, laid out in a grid pattern on a north-south axis, housed a population of some 200,000. Ambitious projects at this time included the monumental Pyramid of the Sun, the largest structure in pre-Columbian America.

The Americas

c.1: Maya complexes start to appear at sites such as El Mirador — c.100: City of Teotihuacán begins to expand. 90% of local population move to the city

1 CE — 50 — 100 — 150 — 200 — 250 CE

c.10: Moche culture, famous for substantial buildings, irrigation works, and pottery and goldwork, at its height — c.200: Hopewell moundbuilding culture flourishing in North America

The World in 250 CE

Roman Empire

Kushan power at peak under Kanishka, c.100 CE

Africa

Under Roman rule, Egypt experienced a remarkable economic recovery. As ancient Egyptian cults and traditions declined, Christianity found converts among the Egyptians. To the west, the Romans extended their control to the Berber kingdoms of Numidia and Mauretania. The fertile coastal plains were fully exploited, but the southern borders of Roman territory were under constant threat of Berber invasion. By 100 CE the Red Sea kingdom of Axum, its wealth based on control of the incense trade, had become a major power.

THE FIRST PAPER

The traditional date for the invention of paper is 105 CE, but lightweight felted material for writing had been made in China for some time before then. The pulp was made of scraps of bark, bamboo, and hemp, finely chopped and boiled with wood ash. As techniques improved, paper replaced expensive silk and cumbersome wooden tablets.

A Chinese worker lifts a mesh screen covered with a thin layer of pulp that will drain and dry to form a sheet of paper.

West Asia

In the 1st century CE the Parthian Empire was torn by internal dissent and dynastic struggles. Between 114 and 198, the Romans invaded three times, sacking the cities of Seleucia and Ctesiphon. In 224 Ardashir Papakan defeated his Parthian overlords and founded the Sassanian dynasty. He introduced a centralized administration, and transformed vassal kingdoms into provinces, ruled by Sassanian princes. His son Shapur repelled the Romans and made Sassanian Persia the most stable power of late antiquity.

The ruined city of Petra contains remarkable rock-cut tombs. It was annexed by Rome in 106 as capital of the province of Arabia.

East Asia

In 25 CE, after a brief interregnum, Han emperors regained control of China, but their rule depended on the support of powerful landowners. The capital moved to Luoyang, and eastern and southern China exerted greater political influence. In the early 3rd century the empire, beset by rebellions and feuds, collapsed. Regional warlords carved out three new kingdoms and China remained fragmented for over 300 years. With the decline of the Han, small local states, notably Koguryo and Silla, took control of Korea.

This model horse and trap was found among the goods in the grave of a high-ranking officer of the Han period.

SEE ALSO:

North America: pp.120–121

South America: pp.144–145

Africa: pp.160–161

Europe: pp.180–181

West Asia: pp.224–225

South and Southeast Asia: pp.240–243

North and East Asia: pp.260–261

Australasia and Oceania: pp.280–281

West Asia timeline

70: Romans suppress Jewish revolt and destroy temple in Jerusalem
c.150: Petra, a major trading post for incense, at height of prosperity
165: Avidius Cassius sacks Seleucia and Ctesiphon
224: Sassanians take over Parthian Empire

1 CE — 50 — 100 — 150 — 200 — 250 CE

c.114: Trajan annexes Armenia, takes Seleucia and reaches Persian Gulf
c.132: Second Jewish revolt precipitates diaspora
197: Septimus Severus sails down Euphrates to invade Parthian Empire

East Asia timeline

9: Wang Mang seizes throne, founding short-lived Xin dynasty
159: Han imperial family feuds hand effective power to court eunuchs
c.220: Collapse of Han dynasty; replaced by three kingdoms: Shu, Wu, and Wei

1 CE — 50 — 100 — 150 — 200 — 250 CE

25: Han reassert control over China, but their power is limited
184: Rising of the Yellow Turbans, an insurgent group, in China
c.200: Emergence of native states in Korea

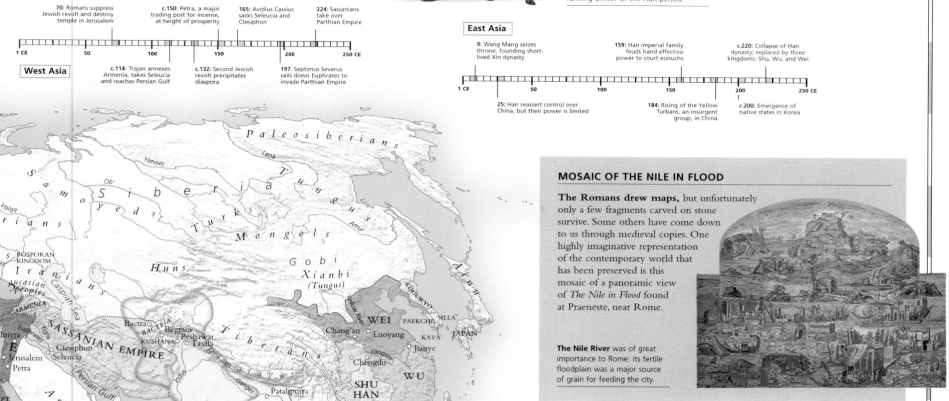

MOSAIC OF THE NILE IN FLOOD

The Romans drew maps, but unfortunately only a few fragments carved on stone survive. Some others have come down to us through medieval copies. One highly imaginative representation of the contemporary world that has been preserved is this mosaic of a panoramic view of *The Nile in Flood* found at Praeneste, near Rome.

The Nile River was of great importance to Rome: its fertile floodplain was a major source of grain for feeding the city.

South Asia

In the 1st century CE the nomadic Yuezhi were pushed westward from the borders of China. One of the tribes, the Kushans, united the others, moved into Bactria, and from there expanded into northern India, founding their capital at Peshawar. The Kingdom of Kushana crumbled at the end of the 2nd century, when native peoples – the Tamils of southern India and the Satavahanas of the Deccan – were beginning to assert their power.

The Kushans' wealth came from their control of east–west trade routes. This ivory plaque was part of a famous hoard found at Begram, which contained artifacts from Rome, Africa, India, and China.

Egyptian mummy cases took on a curious hybrid appearance under Roman rule. The portrait on this 2nd-century example shows the Egyptians' Hellenistic taste in art.

Africa timeline

c.50: Kingdom of Axum starts to emerge
c.100: Alexandria emerges as a center of Christian scholarship, seat of one of the earliest Christian bishoprics
c.150: Christianity starts to spread westward to Roman provinces of Numidia and Mauretania

1 CE — 50 — 100 — 150 — 200 — 250 CE

44: Mauretania annexed by Rome
69: Romans defeat powerful Saharan kingdom of Garamantes, but do not absorb it into empire

South Asia timeline

99: Indian embassy to court of Trajan in Rome, probably to announce Kushan conquests
c.102: Death of Kushans' greatest ruler, Kanishka
c.200: Cities appear for first time on Deccan plateau

1 CE — 50 — 100 — 150 — 200 — 250 CE

c.60: Kushans, under Kadphises I, unite Yuezhi tribes and advance into northern India
c.150: Kushans become Persian vassals

THE EMERGENCE OF GLOBAL RELIGIONS

This 7th-century silver plaque from Hexham, England is thought to depict a Christian saint.

BY 250 CE SOME OLD WORLD religions (*see pp.36–37*) had spread far beyond their areas of origin to become substantial bodies of faith. In the west, the Roman taste for monotheistic Mithraism, derived from Persian Zoroastrianism, spread throughout the empire, although it was always a minority cult. But in its wake the cult of Christianity was becoming firmly established. Further, the Roman suppression of the Jewish revolt in 132 CE had caused a diaspora through much of the empire. In South Asia, Hinduism became deeply rooted throughout the subcontinent as Dravidians and tribal peoples adopted the practices of their Aryan conquerors; meanwhile Buddhism was spread overland to Central Asia and China and beyond by missionaries of various sectarian schools.

Mithraism, Judaism, and Christianity

The worship of Mithras was arduous and limited to males; it was popular among the Roman legions, spreading to the corners of the empire. Its monotheism paved the way for Christianity which, in parallel to the Jewish diaspora, spread to centers throughout the empire. This was inaugurated by the missionary journeys of St. Paul, in the 1st century CE. By the time of Diocletian's persecutions (304 CE) centers had been established in Asia Minor, Mesopotamia, and around the Mediterranean. The fusion of Christian theology with the ethical concerns of Greek philosophy gave it intellectual respectability; and when Constantine (306–337) adopted the faith, Christianity became the official religion of the empire.

This 5th-century pottery amphora is decorated with two versions of the Christian cross, which became the most widely used symbol of the religion.

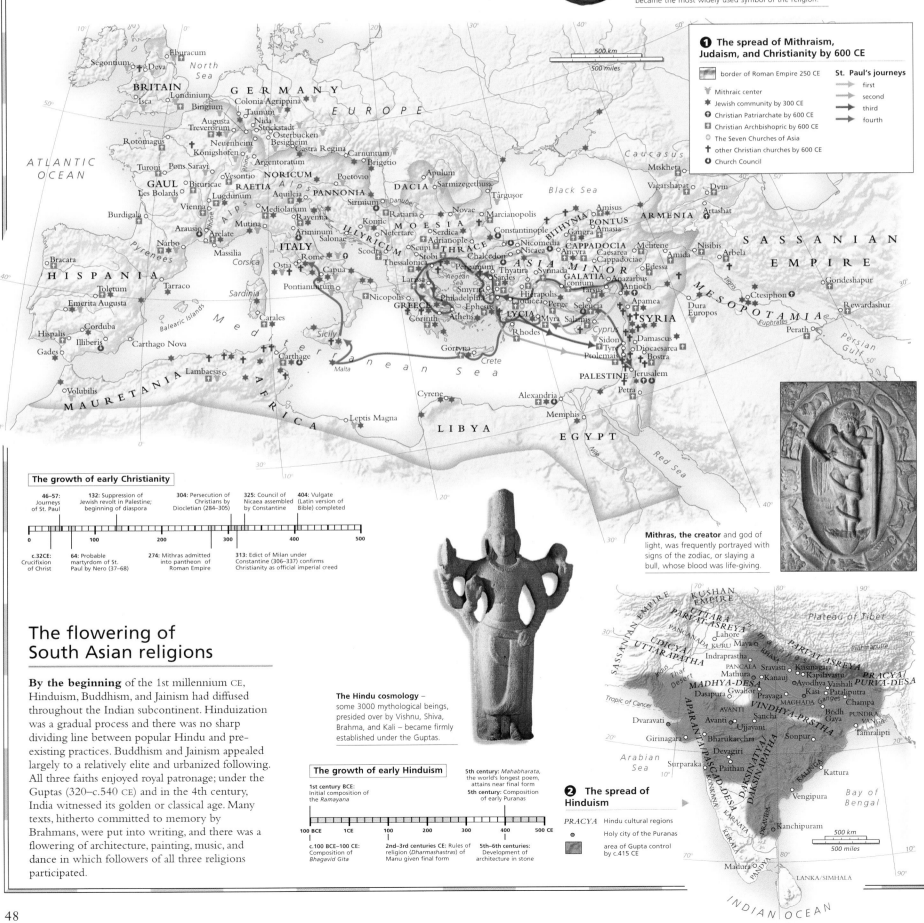

❶ The spread of Mithraism, Judaism, and Christianity by 600 CE

- border of Roman Empire 250 CE
- Mithraic center
- Jewish community by 300 CE
- Christian Patriarchate by 600 CE
- Christian Archbishopric by 600 CE
- The Seven Churches of Asia
- other Christian churches by 600 CE
- Church Council

St. Paul's journeys
- first
- second
- third
- fourth

The growth of early Christianity

46–57: Journeys of St. Paul

132: Suppression of Jewish revolt in Palestine; beginning of diaspora

304: Persecution of Christians by Diocletian (284–305)

325: Council of Nicaea assembled by Constantine

404: Vulgate (Latin version of Bible) completed

| 0 | 100 | 200 | 300 | 400 | 500 |

c.32CE: Crucifixion of Christ

64: Probable martyrdom of St. Paul by Nero (37–68)

274: Mithras admitted into pantheon of Roman Empire

313: Edict of Milan under Constantine (306–337) confirms Christianity as official imperial creed

Mithras, the creator and god of light, was frequently portrayed with signs of the zodiac, or slaying a bull, whose blood was life-giving.

The flowering of South Asian religions

By the beginning of the 1st millennium CE, Hinduism, Buddhism, and Jainism had diffused throughout the Indian subcontinent. Hinduization was a gradual process and there was no sharp dividing line between popular Hindu and pre-existing practices. Buddhism and Jainism appealed largely to a relatively elite and urbanized following. All three faiths enjoyed royal patronage; under the Guptas (320–c.540 CE) and in the 4th century, India witnessed its golden or classical age. Many texts, hitherto committed to memory by Brahmans, were put into writing, and there was a flowering of architecture, painting, music, and dance in which followers of all three religions participated.

The Hindu cosmology – some 3000 mythological beings, presided over by Vishnu, Shiva, Brahma, and Kali – became firmly established under the Guptas.

The growth of early Hinduism

1st century BCE: Initial composition of the *Ramayana*

5th century: *Mahabharata*, the world's longest poem, attains near final form

5th century: Composition of early Puranas

| 100 BCE | 1CE | 100 | 200 | 300 | 400 | 500 CE |

c.100 BCE–100 CE: Composition of *Bhagavad Gita*

2nd–3rd centuries CE: Rules of religion (*Dharmashastras*) of Manu given final form

5th–6th centuries: Development of architecture in stone

❷ The spread of Hinduism

PRACYA Hindu cultural regions
- Holy city of the Puranas
- area of Gupta control by c.415 CE

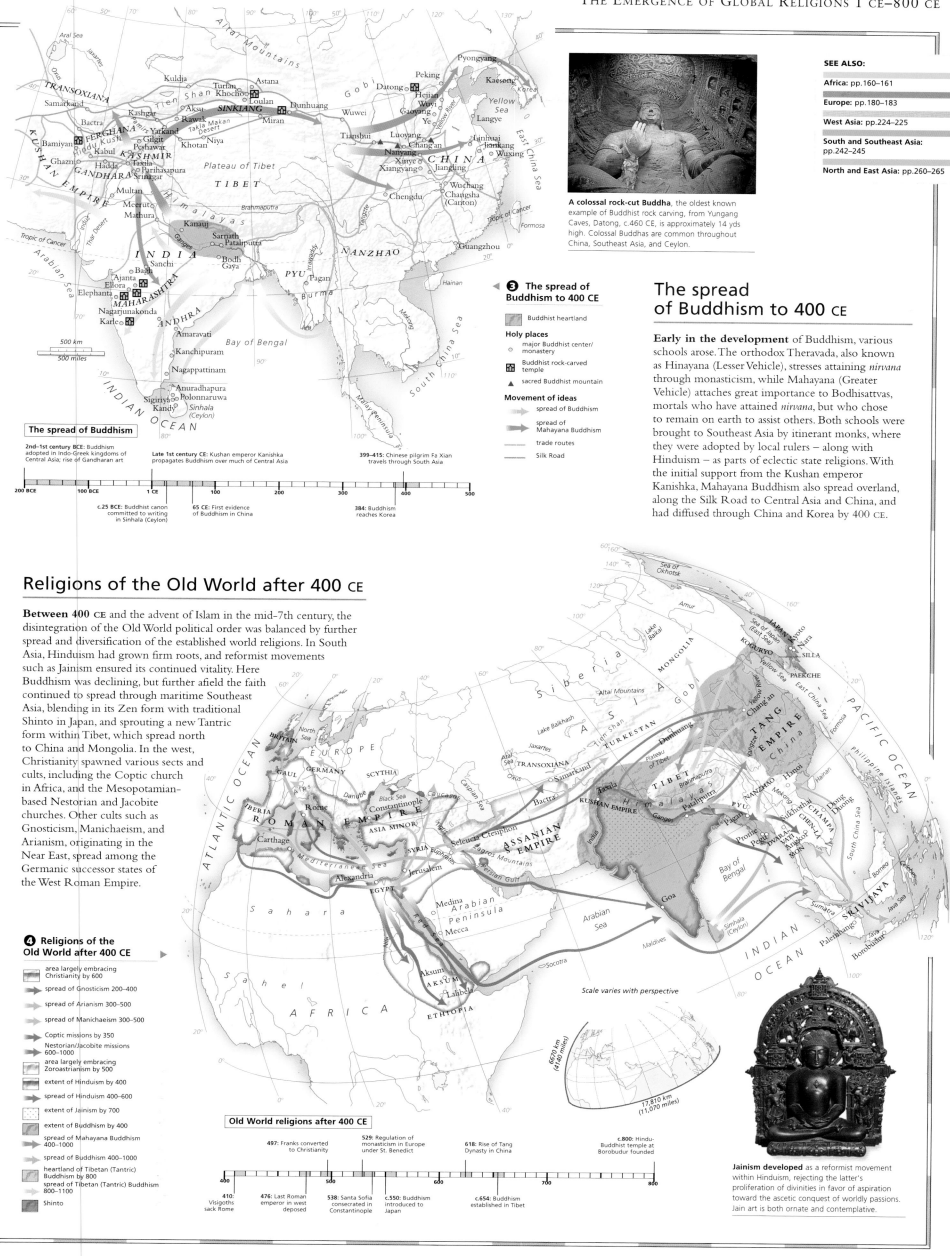

SEE ALSO:

Africa: pp.160–161

Europe: pp.180–183

West Asia: pp.224–225

South and Southeast Asia: pp.242–245

North and East Asia: pp.260–265

A colossal rock-cut Buddha, the oldest known example of Buddhist rock carving, from Yungang Caves, Datong, c.460 CE, is approximately 14 yds high. Colossal Buddhas are common throughout China, Southeast Asia, and Ceylon.

❸ The spread of Buddhism to 400 CE

Buddhist heartland

Holy places
- ○ major Buddhist center/ monastery
- 卐 Buddhist rock-carved temple
- ▲ sacred Buddhist mountain

Movement of ideas
- → spread of Buddhism
- → spread of Mahayana Buddhism
- ─ trade routes
- ─ Silk Road

The spread of Buddhism to 400 CE

Early in the development of Buddhism, various schools arose. The orthodox Theravada, also known as Hinayana (Lesser Vehicle), stresses attaining *nirvana* through monasticism, while Mahayana (Greater Vehicle) attaches great importance to Bodhisattvas, mortals who have attained *nirvana*, but who chose to remain on earth to assist others. Both schools were brought to Southeast Asia by itinerant monks, where they were adopted by local rulers – along with Hinduism – as parts of eclectic state religions. With the initial support from the Kushan emperor Kanishka, Mahayana Buddhism also spread overland, along the Silk Road to Central Asia and China, and had diffused through China and Korea by 400 CE.

The spread of Buddhism

2nd–1st century BCE: Buddhism adopted in Indo-Greek kingdoms of Central Asia; rise of Gandharan art

Late 1st century CE: Kushan emperor Kanishka propagates Buddhism over much of Central Asia

399–415: Chinese pilgrim Fa Xian travels through South Asia

| 200 BCE | 100 BCE | 1 CE | 100 | 200 | 300 | 400 | 500 |

c.25 BCE: Buddhist canon committed to writing in Sinhala (Ceylon)

65 CE: First evidence of Buddhism in China

384: Buddhism reaches Korea

Religions of the Old World after 400 CE

Between 400 CE and the advent of Islam in the mid-7th century, the disintegration of the Old World political order was balanced by further spread and diversification of the established world religions. In South Asia, Hinduism had grown firm roots, and reformist movements such as Jainism ensured its continued vitality. Here Buddhism was declining, but further afield the faith continued to spread through maritime Southeast Asia, blending in its Zen form with traditional Shinto in Japan, and sprouting a new Tantric form within Tibet, which spread north to China and Mongolia. In the west, Christianity spawned various sects and cults, including the Coptic church in Africa, and the Mesopotamian-based Nestorian and Jacobite churches. Other cults such as Gnosticism, Manichaeism, and Arianism, originating in the Near East, spread among the Germanic successor states of the West Roman Empire.

❹ Religions of the Old World after 400 CE

- area largely embracing Christianity by 600
- → spread of Gnosticism 200–400
- → spread of Arianism 300–500
- → spread of Manichaeism 300–500
- → Coptic missions by 350
- → Nestorian/Jacobite missions 600–1000
- area largely embracing Zoroastrianism by 500
- → extent of Hinduism by 400
- → spread of Hinduism 400–600
- extent of Jainism by 700
- extent of Buddhism by 400
- → spread of Mahayana Buddhism 400–1000
- → spread of Buddhism 400–1000
- heartland of Tibetan (Tantric) Buddhism by 800
- → spread of Tibetan (Tantric) Buddhism 800–1100
- Shinto

Scale varies with perspective

6670 km (4140 miles)

17,810 km (11,070 miles)

Old World religions after 400 CE

497: Franks converted to Christianity

529: Regulation of monasticism in Europe under St. Benedict

618: Rise of Tang Dynasty in China

c.800: Hindu-Buddhist temple at Borobudur founded

| 400 | 500 | 600 | 700 | 800 |

410: Visigoths sack Rome

476: Last Roman emperor in west deposed

538: Santa Sofia consecrated in Constantinople

c.550: Buddhism introduced to Japan

c.654: Buddhism established in Tibet

Jainism developed as a reformist movement within Hinduism, rejecting the latter's proliferation of divinities in favor of aspiration toward the ascetic conquest of worldly passions. Jain art is both ornate and contemplative.

THE WORLD 250–500

BY 500, MIGRATIONS IN ASIA AND EUROPE had so weakened the civilizations of the Old World that only the East Roman Empire and Sassanian Persia survived. Asian nomads broke the power of the Chinese and destroyed India's Gupta Empire. The Huns even invaded Europe, where the Romans repulsed them, but only with the aid of their Gothic allies. Rome relied increasingly on the aid of the Goths and other Germanic peoples, who settled within the empire and, as central authority waned, carved out new kingdoms for themselves. In contrast to the collapsing empires of the Old World, the great urban civilizations of Central America, Teotihuacán, the Maya, and the Zapotecs, were beginning to flourish.

Much of the best late Roman sculpture is found in the carving of Christian scenes on sarcophagi.

Europe

In 284, Diocletian divided the Roman Empire into eastern and western halves. With the advent of Christianity and the establishment of Constantinople as a new capital in 330, the empire's center of gravity shifted eastward. Meanwhile, Germanic and Slav peoples, living on Rome's northern borders, infiltrated imperial territory, at times peacefully, often by force. The Western Empire collapsed in 476 to be replaced by a series of Germanic kingdoms and the mantle of empire passed to Constantinople in the east.

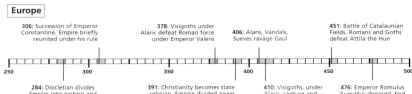

Europe			
306: Succession of Emperor Constantine. Empire briefly reunited under his rule	**378:** Visigoths under Alaric defeat Roman force under Emperor Valens	**406:** Alans, Vandals, Sueves ravage Gaul	**451:** Battle of Catalaunian Fields. Romans and Goths defeat Attila the Hun
284: Diocletian divides Empire into eastern and western halves	**391:** Christianity becomes state religion. Empire divided again	**410:** Visigoths, under Alaric, capture and sack Rome	**476:** Emperor Romulus Augustus deposed. End of Western Empire

(Timeline spans 250 to 500)

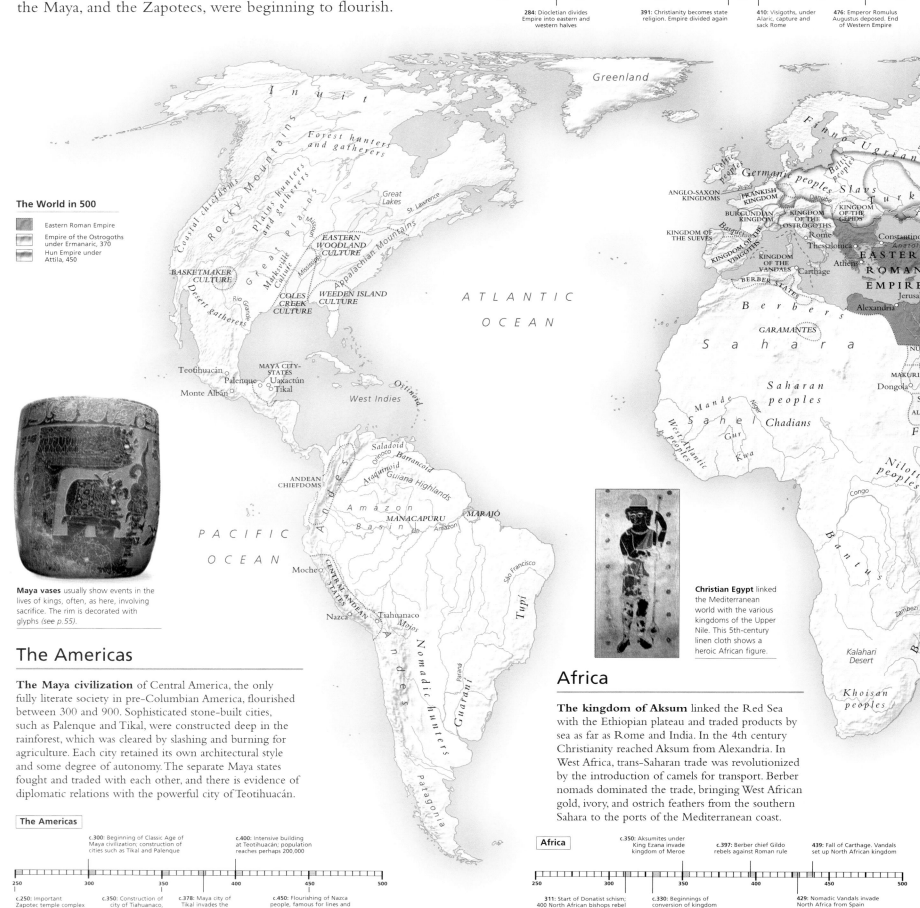

The World in 500

- Eastern Roman Empire
- Empire of the Ostrogoths under Ermanaric, 370
- Hun Empire under Attila, 450

Maya vases usually show events in the lives of kings, often, as here, involving sacrifice. The rim is decorated with glyphs *(see p.55)*.

The Americas

The Maya civilization of Central America, the only fully literate society in pre-Columbian America, flourished between 300 and 900. Sophisticated stone-built cities, such as Palenque and Tikal, were constructed deep in the rainforest, which was cleared by slashing and burning for agriculture. Each city retained its own architectural style and some degree of autonomy. The separate Maya states fought and traded with each other, and there is evidence of diplomatic relations with the powerful city of Teotihuacán.

The Americas			
c.300: Beginning of Classic Age of Maya civilization; construction of cities such as Tikal and Palenque	**c.400:** Intensive building at Teotihuacán; population reaches perhaps 200,000		
c.250: Important Zapotec temple complex built at Monte Albán	**c.350:** Construction of city of Tiahuanaco, near Lake Titicaca	**c.378:** Maya city of Tikal invades the city of Uaxactún	**c.450:** Flourishing of Nazca people, famous for lines and giant figures drawn in desert

(Timeline spans 250 to 500)

Christian Egypt linked the Mediterranean world with the various kingdoms of the Upper Nile. This 5th-century linen cloth shows a heroic African figure.

Africa

The kingdom of Aksum linked the Red Sea with the Ethiopian plateau and traded products by sea as far as Rome and India. In the 4th century Christianity reached Aksum from Alexandria. In West Africa, trans-Saharan trade was revolutionized by the introduction of camels for transport. Berber nomads dominated the trade, bringing West African gold, ivory, and ostrich feathers from the southern Sahara to the ports of the Mediterranean coast.

Africa			
c.350: Aksumites under King Ezana invade kingdom of Meroe	**c.397:** Berber chief Gildo rebels against Roman rule	**439:** Fall of Carthage. Vandals set up North African kingdom	
311: Start of Donatist schism; 400 North African bishops rebel against Roman Christian church	**c.330:** Beginnings of conversion of kingdom of Aksum to Christianity	**429:** Nomadic Vandals invade North Africa from Spain	

(Timeline spans 250 to 500)

THE STIRRUP

Most technological advances in equipment for horsemen were developed by the nomadic peoples of Central Asia, where the horse had first been domesticated. The Scythians may have used leather loops as a kind of stirrup as early as 400 BCE, although these were probably just an aid for mounting. Rigid metal stirrups, which provided a stable platform for warriors to fight effectively from horseback, were adopted some time before 400 CE in China, from where their use spread across Central Asia to Europe.

This Chinese ceramic figurine of a hunter attacked by a lion demonstrates one of the advantages of the stirrup as the rider turns to deal with his aggressor.

West Asia

By the end of the 4th century, Sassanian Persia stretched from the Euphrates to the Indus. Social stability was maintained by an elaborate and efficient bureaucracy, a healthy economy based primarily on agriculture, and widespread adherence to Zoroastrianism, the state religion. The Sassanians posed a major threat to Roman interests in Asia, and for 200 years there was conflict with the Roman Empire, especially over Armenia. In the 5th century Persia had to withstand incursions by eastern nomads, notably the Hephthalites or "White Huns", but survived intact.

A Sassanian Shahanshah (King of Kings), probably Bahram V, who ruled from 421 to 439, demonstrates his authority (and prowess as a lion-hunter) on this magnificent silver dish.

SEE ALSO:

North America: pp.120–123

South America: pp.144–147

Africa: pp.160–161

Europe: pp.180–183

West Asia: pp.224–225

South and Southeast Asia: pp.242–245

North and East Asia: pp.260–261

Australasia and Oceania: pp.280–281

West Asia

296: Sassanians occupy Armenia and defeat Roman emperor Galerius. Treaty ensures peace for next 40 years

337: Shapur II embarks on new warfare against Romans

c.450: Hephthalites attack northeastern borders of Sassanian Empire

260: At Edessa, Sassanians under Shapur I defeat and capture Roman emperor, Valerian

309: Accession of Shapur II. Persian borders are threatened by nomads

484: Hephthalites defeat and kill Sassanian ruler, but the empire survives

MOSAIC MAP OF JERUSALEM

The sites associated with the life of Christ all lay within the East Roman Empire. Jerusalem, as the scene of Christ's Passion, was a major center of pilgrimage and source of relics from the 4th century onwards. The city was depicted in great detail in a 6th-century mosaic found at Madaba in Jordan: a bird's-eye view of the city that indicates all the important churches and pilgrimage sites.

The Madaba map shows clearly the central colonnade which dates from Hadrian's rebuilding of Jerusalem in the 2nd century CE.

This fresco of two heavenly maidens decorated Kassapa's 5th-century fortified mountaintop palace at Sigiriya in Ceylon.

China's many Buddhist monasteries of this period have all been destroyed. Only the vast cave-temples, built with imperial patronage, such as this one at Longmen near Luoyang, have survived.

South Asia

The Gupta dynasty grew in power and influence throughout the 4th century, to dominate northern India. Sanskrit literature, poetry, sculpture, and architecture all flourished under the Hindu Guptas. It was also an age noted for its religious tolerance. In the mid-5th century, however, the Hephthalites advanced into Gupta territory, ending India's "golden age". In Ceylon, meanwhile, Buddhism became established as the dominant faith.

East Asia

After a period of fragmentation, China was briefly re-united in 280 under the Jin, but when nomads sacked Chang'an in 316, the Eastern Jin dynasty moved to Nanjing. They retained control over southern China, but the north suffered successive invasions by steppe nomads. In this climate of political uncertainty, Buddhism flourished and the monastic life grew in appeal. Japan's Yamato state emerged in the 4th century, gradually gaining hegemony over the south of the country.

South Asia

c.415: High point in career of Kalidasa, one of India's greatest poets and playwrights

c.500: Collapse of Gupta Empire under renewed Hephthalite attacks

320: Expansion of Gupta family, from Magadha, heralds start of Gupta dynasty

376: Gupta rule reaches its greatest extent under Chandra Gupta II

495: Death of Kassapa, self-appointed god-king of Sigiriya in Ceylon

East Asia

c.300: Emergence of Yamato state in Osaka region of Japan

420: Song rule in southern China: start of period of the Southern Dynasties

c.490: Northern Wei capital moved to Luoyang

280: Sima Yan, leader of the Jin dynasty, unites China

291: Steppe peoples from beyond Great Wall allowed to settle within empire

386: Toba Wei reunify northern China, intermarry with Chinese, and adopt Chinese culture

479: Rule of southern China passes to the Qi dynasty

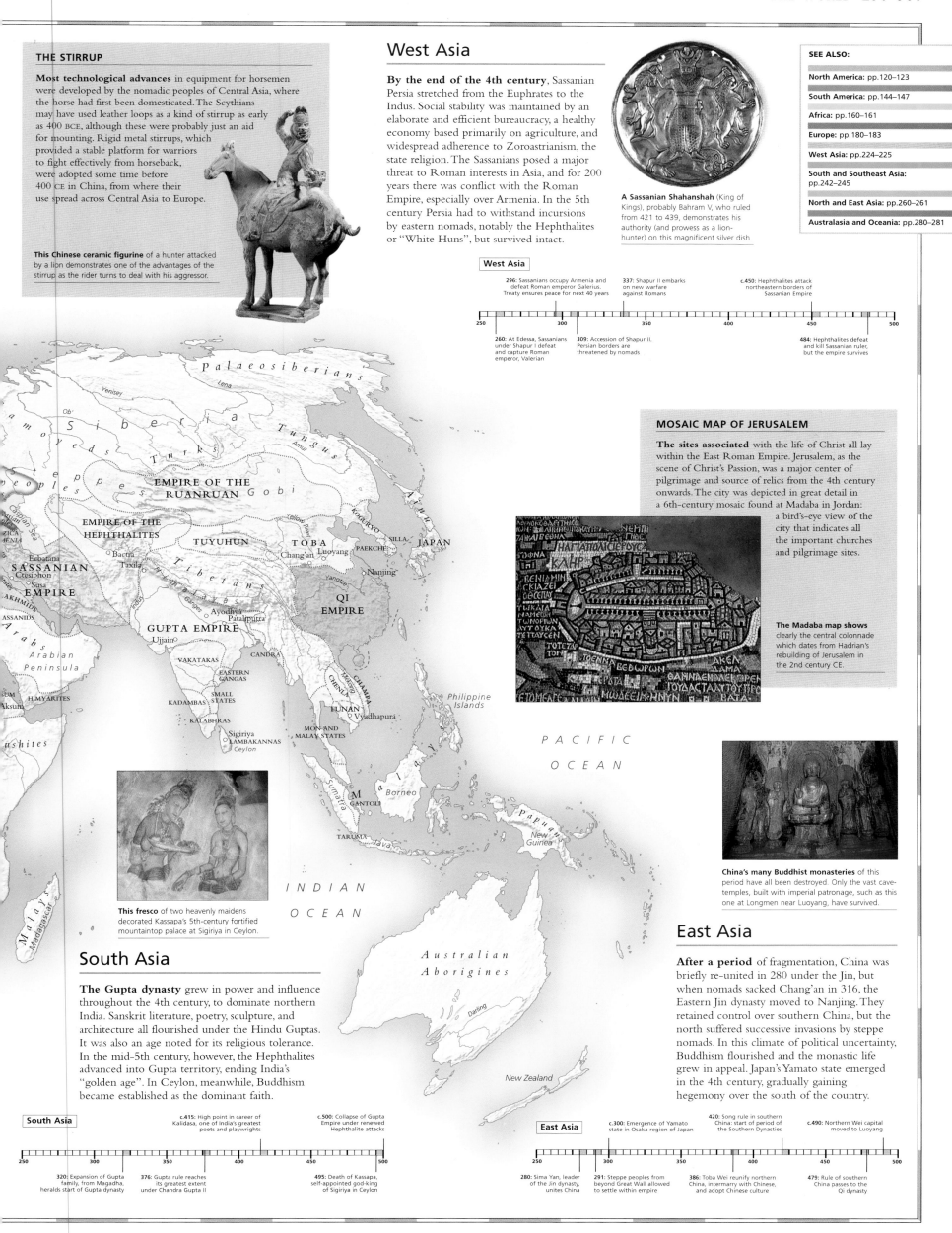

MIGRATIONS AND INVASIONS

The half-Vandal general Stilicho was regent during the reign of the child emperor Honorius.

THE GERMANIC PEOPLES who migrated into the Roman Empire during the 5th century were seeking to share in the fruits of empire, not to destroy it. They were spurred to move west in search of land by a combination of factors: famine, population pressure, and the prospects of a better standard of living. Rome initially accepted "barbarian" recruits into its depleted army as *foederati* (federates), and allowed them to retain their own leaders and laws. But when the Romans opposed the settlement of large groups or refused to reward them for their services, the results could be disastrous: campaigns of plunder, sacked cities, and the breakdown of imperial control.

The aims of the migrations

The peoples who invaded the Roman Empire in the 4th and 5th centuries were driven by a variety of motives. Some, like Alaric's Visigoths, sought official acceptance by the Roman authorities. Others, such as the peoples of the Great Migration of 406, were intent on finding land anywhere and by any means. The only invaders bent purely on destruction and plunder were the Huns. As steppe nomads, the Huns' strength lay in their mobility and their skill with bow, lance, and saber. They were able to smash the overstretched imperial defenses, but were repulsed when Goths and Romans joined forces against them. The Romans relied more and more on Gothic military support, and it was the Goths who emerged as the first inheritors of the Empire's western territories.

Turmoil in Italy

From the late 4th century, the Western Roman Empire was plagued by disputes over the imperial succession, which led to factionalism and civil wars. These were very destructive of Roman manpower and led to the recruitment of large numbers of barbarians under their own leaders. Emperors were often pawns in the power struggles of generals. Many of these, such as the half-Vandal Stilicho and the Suevian Ricimer, were of Germanic origin.

Honorius succeeded his father, Theodosius, as western emperor in 395 while still a child. He lived in comfortable seclusion while senior ministers governed.

Turmoil in Italy

324: Constantine becomes sole ruler	391: Theodosius makes Christianity religion of the Empire	402: Imperial court moved to Ravenna	476: Child emperor, Romulus Augustulus, deposed by Odoacer, "King of Italy"

300 — 350 — 400 — 450 — 500

| 395: Theodosius dies; West Roman Empire left to child emperor Honorius | 410: Sack of Rome by Visigoths | 455: Accession of Libius Severus, puppet emperor controlled by Ricimer |

The Great Migration

At Christmas 406, vast hordes of Vandals, Sueves, and Alans crossed the frozen Rhine River and poured into Gaul, where they greatly disrupted settled life. They then moved in a southwesterly direction and eventually reached the Iberian Peninsula. The Vandals pressed on to North Africa, crossing the Strait of Gibraltar in 429, while the Sueves and Alans set up kingdoms in Iberia.

Vandal nobles in North Africa led the same privileged life as their Roman predecessors, as this mosaic of a Vandal landowner shows.

The Great Migration

406: Vandals, Sueves, and Alans cross Rhine	c.411: Sueves establish kingdom in northwestern Iberia	439: Vandals reach city of Carthage	474: Rome recognizes Vandal kingdom

400 — 425 — 450 — 475 — 500

| 409: Vandals, Sueves, and Alans cross the Pyrenees | 429: Vandals cross Strait of Gibraltar | 455: Sack of Rome by Vandal king, Gaiseric |

Map labels

SCANDINAVIA

Baltic Sea

Vistula

North Sea

GERMANY

Alans

406-7

Elbe

Rhine

451

453: On death of Attila, Empire of the Huns collapses

Carpathian Mountains

EMPIRE OF THE HUNS c.420

Tisza

376

420

Dniester

Danube

452: Attila persuaded to leave Roman Empire

DACIA

Visigoths from 382

Adrianople

378

Danube

PANNONIA

Ostrogoths from 450

LOWER MOESIA

441

THRACE

395

Constantinople

c.410: Romans abandon Britain

Scotland

Picts

Scots

BRITAIN

Irish Celts

Ireland

Londinium

Thames

457

486

Augusta Treverorum

Seine Lutetia

Meuse

Moselle

Scheldt

Mogontiacum

Burgundians pre-413

Borbetomagus

ALPS

GAUL

Seine

443

418

ATLANTIC OCEAN

KINGDOM OF THE VISIGOTHS c.418

AQUITAINE

Tolosa

414

Narbo

456

409

Pyrenees

Tarraco

Massilia

KINGDOM OF THE BURGUNDIANS c.443

Rhône

Loire

Augusta Taurinorum

Genua

Mediolanum

Ticinum

Verona

Patavium

Aquileia

Ravenna

Po

489

410

Rome

Corsica

ITALY

Neapolis

410: Visigoths sack Rome
455: Vandals sack Rome

455

Sardinia

Panormus

Sicily

402: Capital of West Roman Empire moved to Ravenna

Adriatic Sea

410: Death of Alaric; Visigoths abandon plan to invade Africa

GREECE

Thermopylae

Aegean Sea

Athens

Corinth

Crete

EASTERN

ASIA

Ephesus

Philippopolis

Catalaunian Fields 451

414: Athaulf, leader of the Visigoths, marries Galla Placidia, daughter of late Emperor Theodosius. She had been captured during sack of Rome

WESTERN ROMAN EMPIRE from 395

Vandals, Alans, Sueves

Sueves

Alans

Doure

Tagus

Toletum

IBERIA

Corduba

Malaca

Carthago Nova

429

Balearic Islands

Hippo

439

Carthago

NUMIDIA

MAURETANIA

Atlas Mountains

AFRICA

Leptis Magna

c.456

Mediterranean Sea

430: City of Hippo taken by Vandals. St. Augustine, church father and bishop of the city, dies during siege

Vandals

429: Gaiseric leads Vandals into North Africa

Scale varies with perspective

6670 km
(4160 miles)

5310 km
(3310 miles)

① Migrations of peoples 300–500 CE

| | extent of Roman empire, c.390 CE | ⚔ | site of important battle, with date |

Movements of peoples, with dates:

→ Huns
→ Goths
→ Ostrogoths
→ Visigoths
→ Alans
→ Vandals, Alans, Sueves

→ Burgundians
→ Franks
→ Jutes, Angles, Saxons
→ Irish
→ Picts

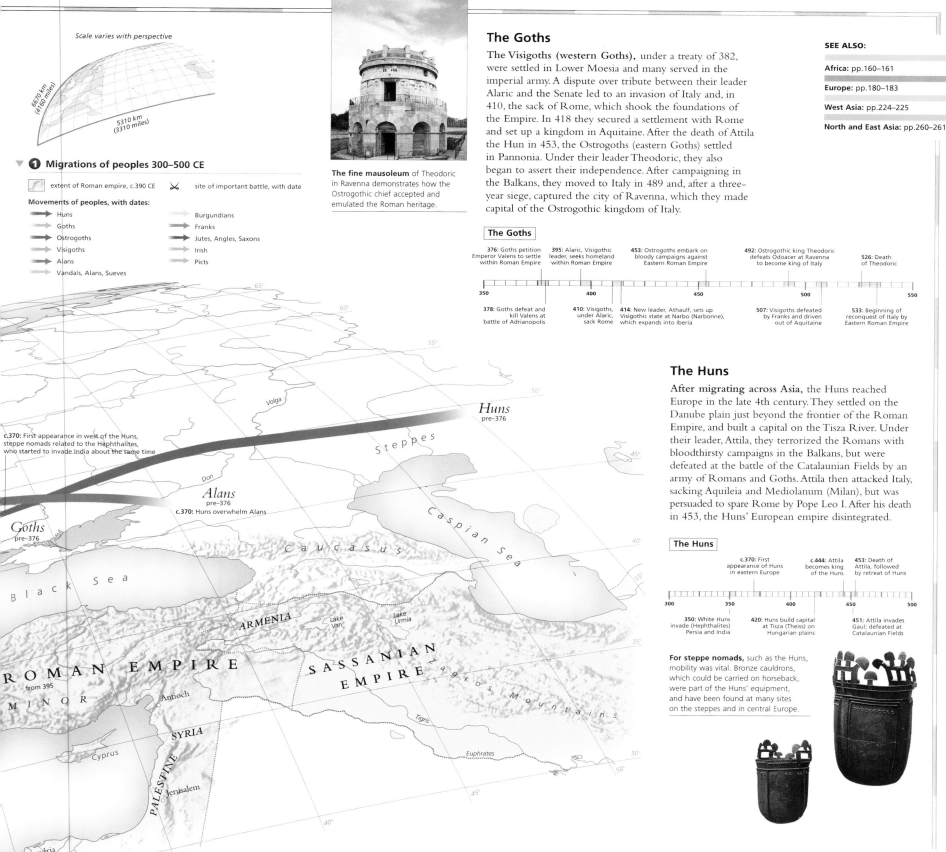

The fine mausoleum of Theodoric in Ravenna demonstrates how the Ostrogothic chief accepted and emulated the Roman heritage.

The Goths

The Visigoths (western Goths), under a treaty of 382, were settled in Lower Moesia and many served in the imperial army. A dispute over tribute between their leader Alaric and the Senate led to an invasion of Italy and, in 410, the sack of Rome, which shook the foundations of the Empire. In 418 they secured a settlement with Rome and set up a kingdom in Aquitaine. After the death of Attila the Hun in 453, the Ostrogoths (eastern Goths) settled in Pannonia. Under their leader Theodoric, they also began to assert their independence. After campaigning in the Balkans, they moved to Italy in 489 and, after a three-year siege, captured the city of Ravenna, which they made capital of the Ostrogothic kingdom of Italy.

SEE ALSO:

Africa: pp.160–161

Europe: pp.180–183

West Asia: pp.224–225

North and East Asia: pp.260–261

The Goths

376: Goths petition Emperor Valens to settle within Roman Empire

395: Alaric, Visigothic leader, seeks homeland within Roman Empire

453: Ostrogoths embark on bloody campaigns against Eastern Roman Empire

492: Ostrogothic king Theodoric defeats Odoacer at Ravenna to become king of Italy

526: Death of Theodoric

350 — 400 — 450 — 500 — 550

378: Goths defeat and kill Valens at battle of Adrianopolis

410: Visigoths, under Alaric, sack Rome

414: New leader, Athaulf, sets up Visigothic state at Narbo (Narbonne), which expands into Iberia

507: Visigoths defeated by Franks and driven out of Aquitaine

533: Beginning of reconquest of Italy by Eastern Roman Empire

The Huns

After migrating across Asia, the Huns reached Europe in the late 4th century. They settled on the Danube plain just beyond the frontier of the Roman Empire, and built a capital on the Tisza River. Under their leader, Attila, they terrorized the Romans with bloodthirsty campaigns in the Balkans, but were defeated at the battle of the Catalaunian Fields by an army of Romans and Goths. Attila then attacked Italy, sacking Aquileia and Mediolanum (Milan), but was persuaded to spare Rome by Pope Leo I. After his death in 453, the Huns' European empire disintegrated.

The Huns

c.370: First appearance of Huns in eastern Europe

c.444: Attila becomes king of the Huns

453: Death of Attila, followed by retreat of Huns

300 — 350 — 400 — 450 — 500

350: White Huns (Hephthalites) invade Persia and India

420: Huns build capital at Tisza (Theiss) on Hungarian plains

451: Attila invades Gaul; defeated at Catalaunian Fields

For steppe nomads, such as the Huns, mobility was vital. Bronze cauldrons, which could be carried on horseback, were part of the Huns' equipment, and have been found at many sites on the steppes and in central Europe.

Map labels: Volga, Huns pre-376, Steppes, Don, Alans pre-376, Caspian Sea, Goths pre-376, Caucasus, Black Sea, ARMENIA, Lake Van, Lake Urmia, ROMAN EMPIRE from 395, ASIA MINOR, Antioch, SASSANIAN EMPIRE, Zagros Mountains, SYRIA, Tigris, Euphrates, Cyprus, PALESTINE, Jerusalem, Alexandria, EGYPT

c.370: First appearance in west of the Huns, steppe nomads related to the Hephthalites, who started to invade India about the same time

c.370: Huns overwhelm Alans

The inheritors of Western Europe

By 526, the waves of migrations had redrawn the map of Western Europe. The Ostrogoths, under their charismatic leader Theodoric, controlled Italy, while the Visigoths had captured most of the Iberian Peninsula. The Vandals were established in North Africa, the Sueves in Galicia, and the Burgundians, who crossed the Rhine c.400, had settled in southeast France. The most enduring of the many Germanic kingdoms, however, would prove to be that of the Franks, founded in 456 by Clovis, which laid the foundations of modern France and Germany.

The magnificent votive crown of the 7th-century king Reccesuinth illustrates the importance of Christianity in Iberia under the Visigoths. Their rule lasted from the 5th century to the Arab conquest of 711.

② Europe in 526

Map labels: Picts, Jutes, Angles, Saxons, Celts, Anglos, Jutes, North Sea, Norsemen, Baltic Sea, Baltic peoples, Finno-Ugrians, Turkic peoples, Volga, Slavs, Dniester, ATLANTIC OCEAN, Bretons, Thuringians, Elbe, KINGDOM OF THE FRANKS, Alemanni, Meuse, Seine, Lombards, Gepids, Alans, Caucasus, BURGUNDIAN KINGDOM, Lyon, Rhône, Danube, KINGDOM OF THE OSTROGOTHS, Milan, Danube, Black Sea, KINGDOM OF THE SUEVES, Basques, Toulouse, Ravenna, Constantinople, Douro, Corsica, Rome, EASTERN ROMAN EMPIRE, SYRIA, SASSANIAN EMPIRE, KINGDOM OF THE VISIGOTHS, Toledo, Tagus, Balearic Islands, Sardinia, KINGDOM OF THE VANDALS, Sicily, Carthage, Crete, Mediterranean Sea, Cyprus, Berbers, Alexandria, AFRICA, EGYPT, Nile, Arabian Peninsula

500 km
500 miles

THE WORLD 500–750

THE RAPID RECOVERY of the ancient world from the onslaught of invading nomads is evident in the rise of two great empires in West Asia and China. The new religion of Islam was based on the teachings of Muhammad, an Arabian merchant from Mecca. Fired by a zeal for conquest and conversion, Islamic armies overran West Asia and North Africa, and by 750 had created an empire that stretched from the Indus to Spain. Under the Tang dynasty, Chinese civilization reached new heights; Tang control penetrated deep into Central Asia and Chinese cultural influence was widespread. In the Americas, the Maya remained the most advanced civilization, though their small city-states did not have the far-reaching influence of the great city of Teotihuacán.

Europe

The Franks became the most powerful of all Rome's Germanic successors. United under Clovis I, their overlordship was extended to the south of France and east of the Rhine. Constantinople was the Christian capital of the Byzantine Empire. The Emperor Justinian (527–65) reconquered North Africa and much of Italy, briefly creating an empire stretching from Spain to Persia. Over the next two centuries much of this territory was lost to Islam and, in the Balkans, to Slavic invaders.

The Byzantines were the champions of Christianity. This mosaic shows Emperor Justinian as God's representative on Earth.

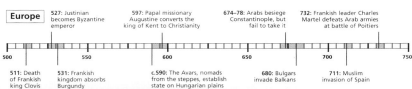

Europe				
527: Justinian becomes Byzantine emperor	**597:** Papal missionary Augustine converts the king of Kent to Christianity	**674–78:** Arabs besiege Constantinople, but fail to take it	**732:** Frankish leader Charles Martel defeats Arab armies at battle of Poitiers	

500 550 600 650 700 750

511: Death of Frankish king Clovis **531:** Frankish kingdom absorbs Burgundy **c.590:** The Avars, nomads from the steppes, establish state on Hungarian plains **680:** Bulgars invade Balkans **711:** Muslim invasion of Spain

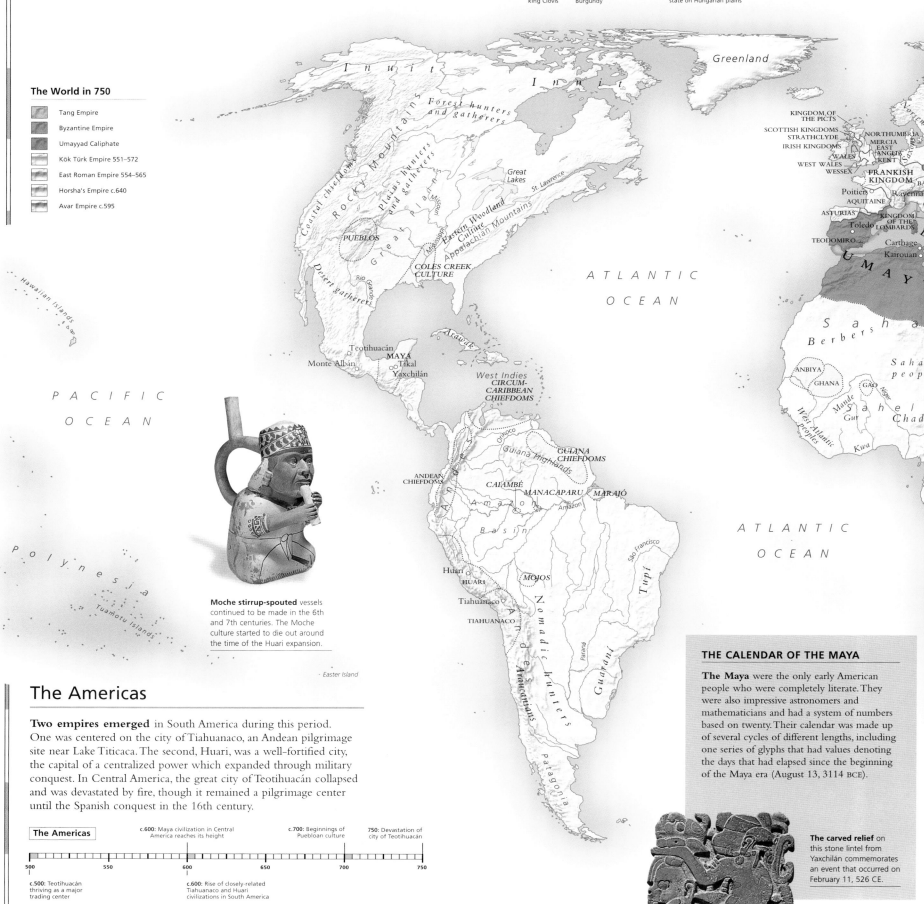

The World in 750

- Tang Empire
- Byzantine Empire
- Umayyad Caliphate
- Kök Türk Empire 551–572
- East Roman Empire 554–565
- Horsha's Empire c.640
- Avar Empire c.595

Moche stirrup-spouted vessels continued to be made in the 6th and 7th centuries. The Moche culture started to die out around the time of the Huari expansion.

The Americas

Two empires emerged in South America during this period. One was centered on the city of Tiahuanaco, an Andean pilgrimage site near Lake Titicaca. The second, Huari, was a well-fortified city, the capital of a centralized power which expanded through military conquest. In Central America, the great city of Teotihuacán collapsed and was devastated by fire, though it remained a pilgrimage center until the Spanish conquest in the 16th century.

The Americas			
c.600: Maya civilization in Central America reaches its height	**c.700:** Beginnings of Puebloan culture	**750:** Devastation of city of Teotihuacán	

500 550 600 650 700 750

c.500: Teotihuacán thriving as a major trading center **c.600:** Rise of closely-related Tiahuanaco and Huari civilizations in South America

THE CALENDAR OF THE MAYA

The Maya were the only early American people who were completely literate. They were also impressive astronomers and mathematicians and had a system of numbers based on twenty. Their calendar was made up of several cycles of different lengths, including one series of glyphs that had values denoting the days that had elapsed since the beginning of the Maya era (August 13, 3114 BCE).

The carved relief on this stone lintel from Yaxchilán commemorates an event that occurred on February 11, 526 CE.

The Dome of the Rock in Jerusalem was built in 692 over the ruins of the Jewish Temple. It is sacred to Islam as the site of Muhammad's journey to heaven.

West Asia

In the 7th century the whole of West Asia was overrun by Arabian armies, soldiers of Islam inspired to conquer and convert by the new religion founded by Muhammad. They were able to exploit the weaknesses of the two great powers in the region, the Sassanians and the Byzantines. Sassanian Persia had reached its peak under Khosrau I (531–79), who invaded Byzantine Syria and captured Antioch. But continuing conflict with the Byzantines led to a crushing defeat at Nineveh in 628.

CLASSICAL ARAB WORLD MAPS

When the Arabs took over much of the Greek-speaking eastern Mediterranean, they seized on the classical scholarship of Alexandria, including the famous *Geography* of Ptolemy *(see p. 44)*. Though no maps from this period survive, it seems that, while the map-making tradition died out in the west, it was kept alive by Arab scholars, albeit in the academic style of this later world map.

Al-Istakhri's world map, from the 10th century, uses a Ptolemaic projection, but with south at the top.

SEE ALSO:

North America: pp.122–123

South America: pp.142–145

Africa: pp.162–163

Europe: pp.182–185

West Asia: pp.226–227

South and Southeast Asia: pp.242–245

North and East Asia: pp.262–265

Australasia and Oceania: pp.280–281

West Asia

570: Prophet Muhammad born in Mecca
622: The Hegira: Muhammad and his followers move to Medina; start of Islamic era
656: Arabians overrun Persia
661: Start of Umayyad dynasty. Damascus is center of Islamic empire
698: Arabs capture Carthage

531: Beginning of reign of Sassanian ruler, Khosrau I Anohshirvanh
628: Defeat of Sassanians by Byzantine emperor Heraclius
637: Arabian armies capture Sassanian capital, Ctesiphon
674–78: Arabian siege of Constantinople
711: Islamic armies cross the Strait of Gibraltar and conquer Spain

Tang ceramics were of very high quality. This 7th-century figurine portrays one of the celebrated Ferghana horses, prized for their speed.

East Asia

538: Buddhism reaches Japan
589: Turko-Chinese Sui reunite China
640: Tang armies reach Turfan in Central Asia
c.660: Tang forces in India and Central Asia
710: Nara becomes Japanese capital

c.550: Kök Türk (Blue Turks) establish vast Central Asian empire
617: Sui dynasty collapses; succeeded in 618 by Tang
645: Buddhism reaches Tibet
668: Korean peninsula united under Silla dynasty

East Asia

After centuries of conflict, China was united under the Sui dynasty (581–617), which was succeeded by the Tang in 618. Chinese territory was again extended into Central Asia, protectorates were set up as far afield as eastern Persia, and they gained control of much of the Silk Road. Chinese culture exerted a strong influence over surrounding areas; Buddhism reached Japan from China in about 538. Under Chinese influence, Japan underwent a series of social and political reforms: the abolition of slavery, the creation of a civil service, and the adoption of a modified form of written Chinese.

Oceania

The island of Fiji was first settled around 1500 BCE, and it was there and in nearby islands that Polynesian culture developed. Descendants of these first settlers would eventually colonize the whole Pacific Ocean. The Polynesians sailed across the open ocean in twin-hulled outrigger canoes, using sails and paddles, with only their knowledge of the skies, winds, and ocean currents to guide them. By 400 CE they had reached Easter Island and the Hawaiian Islands, but did not colonize New Zealand until about 1200.

Oceania

c.600: Polynesian colonists settle the Tuamotu Islands
c.650: Easter Islanders start to build *ahus*, sacred stone platforms

Many deities with a clear common ancestry appear in slightly different forms throughout Polynesia. This wooden carving of the war-god Ku was made in Hawaii in the early 19th century.

THE IMPACT OF ISLAM

This richly-decorated copy of the Koran dates from 704.

THE RAPID SPREAD OF ISLAM was one of the most decisive developments of the medieval period. The Arabian Peninsula was conquered for Islam within ten years, and following the death of Muhammad in 632, the expansion of Islam continued unabated. By the early 8th century, Arab armies fired by the concept of *jihad* (holy war) had reached the borders of India in the east and were invading Spain in the west. With the establishment of the Abbasid Caliphate, by 750 the Muslim realm was second only to that of China in extent and cultural sophistication. The Caliphate controlled Eurasian trade on land and by sea – trade which would spread the faith further afield, deep into Africa, across the Indian Ocean, and north into Central Asia, over the subsequent centuries.

The early history of the Caliphate

Muhammad's first successors – who became known as caliphs – were early disciples (Companions of the Prophet): Abu Bakr (632–34), 'Umar (634–44), and 'Uthman, who was murdered in 656. The authority of 'Uthman's successor Ali – Muhammad's cousin and son-in-law – was challenged by 'Uthman's family, the Umayyads. Ali was murdered in 661, and the Umayyads gained power as caliphs; their supporters were known as Sunnites. A minority of Muslims, however, known as Shi'a, saw the descendants of Ali (the Imams) as the true successors of the Prophet. This fundamental division within the faith continues to this day.

Harun al-Rashid, the great Abbasid caliph, reigned from 786 to 809. This illustration shows him in an episode from the *1001 Nights* with a barber in a Turkish Bath.

The spread of Islam 623–751

The Great Mosque at Kairouan is one of the oldest surviving Islamic buildings. It was begun in 670, shortly after Arab armies had swept through the Byzantine possessions along the North African coast.

Muhammad's vision of the Archangel Gabriel in about 610 began a process of revelation, enshrined in the Koran, the holy book which lies at the heart of Islam. His opposition to polytheism and adherence to a strict code of observance and conduct led to hostility in Mecca, and his withdrawal to Medina (the Hegira) in 622. Here the first Muslim state was established. By 630, with an army of 10,000 followers, he reentered Mecca, and began the conquest of Arabia. Conversion swelled the Muslim ranks, and Muhammad's work was continued after his death in 632 by his disciples. Within a century the heartland of Eurasia was dominated by Islam. Although Muslim warriors believed it their duty to conquer in the name of Islam, conquered peoples, especially Christians and Jews, were treated with tolerance.

① The growth of the Islamic world

- Muslim lands by 634
- Muslim lands by 656
- Muslim lands by 756
- → Muslim raid, with date
- • new city founded by Muslims
- ▣ Muslim fortress
- ✕ Muslim victory, with date
- ✕ Muslim defeat, with date
- 649 date of Muslim conquest
- Byzantine Empire c.610
- Sassanian Empire c.610
- Frankish Empire c.610

674–78 and 717–18: Arab forces twice besiege Byzantine capital, but walls are impregnable

732: Frankish army under Charles Martel halts Arab advance

695–97: Byzantines driven from Carthage

711: Berber general Tariq leads troops across Strait of Gibraltar (Jabal al-Tariq, the Rock of Tariq)

The spread of Islam

622: Beginning of Islamic calendar, marked by the Hegira of Muhammad	**634:** Caliphate of 'Umar (to 644)	**641:** Conquest of Egypt	**644:** Caliphate of 'Uthman (to 646)	**661:** Umayyad Caliphate (to 750)	**670:** Foundation of Kairouan	**692:** Dome of the Rock mosque in Jerusalem	**732:** Arab armies halted at Poitiers	**751:** Arab armies defeat Chinese on Talas River	**762:** Baghdad becomes Abbasid capital

| 600 | 620 | 640 | 660 | 680 | 700 | 720 | 740 | 760 | 780 | 800 |

| **632:** Death of Muhammad; succession of Abu Bakr (to 634) | **637:** Conquest of Mesopotamia | **656:** Imamate of Ali (to 661) | **664:** Conquest of Kabul | **711:** Invasion of Iberian Peninsula by Tariq; rapid conquest of Visigothic kingdom | **718:** Christian victory at battle of Covadonga halts Muslim advance in Iberian Peninsula | **750:** Abbasid Caliphate established | **756:** Breakaway Umayyad Emirate established at Cordova (to 1031); claims status of caliphate in 928 |

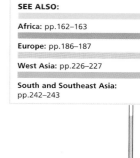

Preaching and teaching spread the Arabic language throughout the Islamic world. This 13th-century Persian illustration shows a preacher in the mosque at Samarkand.

Water-wheels for irrigation were introduced wherever the Arabs settled. This example stands at Hamah in Syria. The Arabs also introduced Asian fruits, such as peaches and apricots.

The Islamic imprint 1000–1200

By 1000, the Islamic world had become broadly divided into two caliphates: the Abbasids, based at Baghdad, and, in the west, the Umayyads (a branch of the Abbasids' predecessors), who ruled the Iberian Peninsula. So extensive were the Abbasid domains that many subsidiary rulers wielded local power in varying degrees and were able to found autonomous dynasties. Further, the movement of peoples into the Islamic world caused further decentralization of power. In the west, the Berbers gradually established a string of local dynasties along the Maghreb coast. The Shi'ite Fatimids emerged in North Africa, conquered Egypt, and claimed caliphate status; but the most significant blow to the Abbasid Caliphate was the invasion of the Seljuk Turks from Central Asia, who moved across southwest Asia, conquered Baghdad and drove back the frontiers of the Byzantine Empire, eventually occupying Anatolia.

SEE ALSO:

Africa: pp.162–163

Europe: pp.186–187

West Asia: pp.226–227

South and Southeast Asia: pp.242–243

The impact of the Islamic advance

935: Final text of Koran

969: Fatimids assume control of Egypt

1055: Seljuk Turks invade Baghdad

1056: Almoravids conquer North Africa and the Iberian Peninsula

1096: First Crusade; establishment of Latin kingdoms in Levant

1188: Saladin conquers Latin kingdoms in Levant

936: Buwayhids take effective control of Abbasid Caliphate

1071: Seljuks defeat Byzantine army at Manzikert

1135: Almohads control northwest Africa and the Iberian Peninsula

800 — 850 — 900 — 950 — 1000 — 1050 — 1100 — 1150 — 1200

② The Islamic imprint c.800–1200

Islamic world c.1000

Abbasid Caliphate at its greatest extent c.800

→ campaigns of Seljuk Turks

→ campaigns of Berbers

→ further expansion of Islam

ZIRIDS Muslim dynasty, with dates

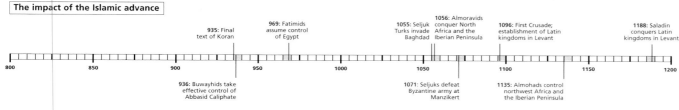

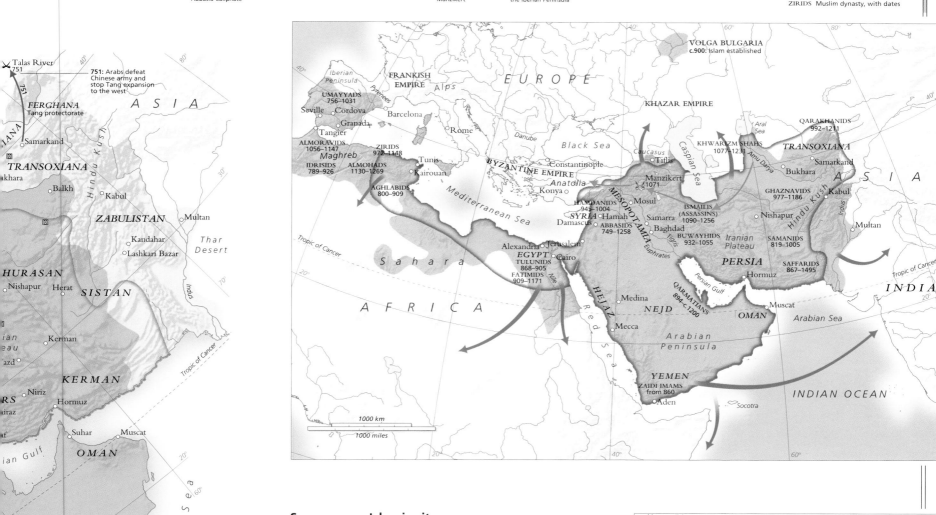

Samarra: an Islamic city

Founded by the Abbasid caliph al-Mu'tasim, Samarra was the Abbasid capital from 836–892, and grew to sprawl some 25 miles (40 km) along the east bank of the Tigris. The new city was based around earlier settlements; it was not walled, and was organized into residential cantonments arranged around central features such as palaces and mosques, and included luxurious facilities such as racetracks and a gigantic 11.6 square miles game reserve. Later caliphs added substantial areas, notably al-Mu'tasim's successor al-Mutawakkil, who built a new center to the north, Ja'fariyya. The Abbasid court returned to its original capital at Baghdad after the death of the eighth caliph, al-Mu'tamid.

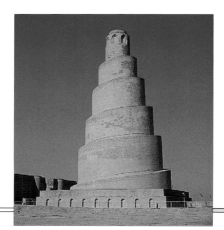

The spiral minaret of the Great Mosque of al-Mutawakkil at Samarra is one of the few standing remains of the city.

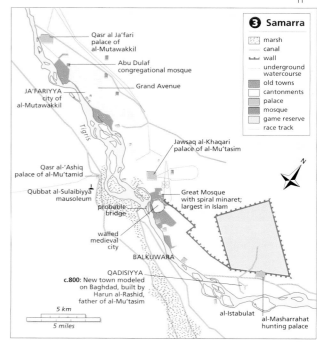

③ Samarra

- marsh
- canal
- wall
- underground watercourse
- old towns
- cantonments
- palace
- mosque
- game reserve race track

Qasr al Ja'fari palace of al-Mutawakkil

Abu Dulaf congregational mosque

JA'FARIYYA city of al-Mutawakkil

Grand Avenue

Qasr al-'Ashiq palace of al-Mu'tamid

Jawsaq al-Khaqari palace of al-Mu'tasim

Qubbat al-Sulaibiyya mausoleum

probable bridge

walled medieval city

Great Mosque with spiral minaret; largest in Islam

BALKUWARA

QADISIYYA
c.800: New town modeled on Baghdad, built by Harun al-Rashid, father of al-Mu'tasim

al-Istabulat

al-Masharrahat hunting palace

5 km / 5 miles

THE WORLD 750–1000

THE DISINTEGRATION OF GREAT EMPIRES and conflicts between warring dynasties were widespread throughout the 9th and 10th centuries. In Europe, Charlemagne was crowned western Emperor in 800, but his Frankish Empire was broken apart by disputes over inheritance. The Abbasid Caliphate, based in Baghdad, could not maintain central control over the vast Islamic world. New Islamic dynasties, such as the Fatimids of northern Africa, broke away from Baghdad's authority. In China, the mighty Tang Empire split into small warring states while in Central America, the Maya were in decline. In contrast to this political fragmentation, powerful new states developed in many parts of the world: the Khmers in Southeast Asia, Koryo in Korea, the Toltecs in Mexico, Ghana and Kanem-Bornu in Africa, and Kievan Rus in Eastern Europe.

Ireland suffered badly from Viking raids in the 9th and 10th centuries, so monasteries built distinctive round towers, such as these at Glendalough, as lookouts and refuges.

Europe

Charlemagne, king of the Franks, incorporated most of Western Europe into a single dominion. After disputes over his inheritance, the kingdom was divided into three parts. Henry I, the Saxon successor, extended his influence over the German duchies and conquered Italy. His son, Otto I, defeated the Magyars and was crowned Holy Roman Emperor. In the west, the Carolingian Empire and the British Isles fell prey to Viking raiders.

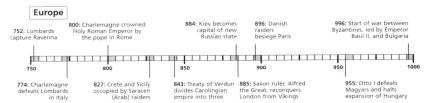

Europe

752: Lombards capture Ravenna	800: Charlemagne crowned Holy Roman Emperor by the pope in Rome	884: Kiev becomes capital of new Russian state	896: Danish raiders besiege Paris	996: Start of war between Byzantines, led by Emperor Basil II, and Bulgaria

750 — 800 — 850 — 900 — 950 — 1000

774: Charlemagne defeats Lombards in Italy · 827: Crete and Sicily occupied by Saracen (Arab) raiders · 843: Treaty of Verdun divides Carolingian empire into three · 885: Saxon ruler, Alfred the Great, reconquers London from Vikings · 955: Otto I defeats Magyars and halts expansion of Hungary

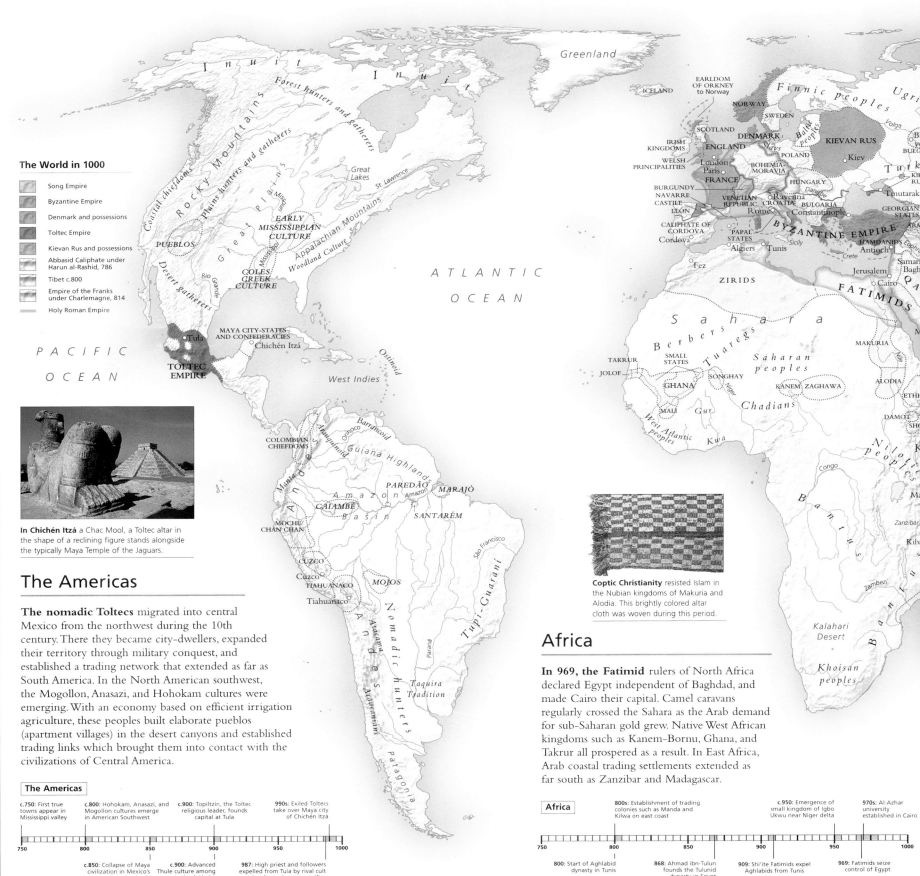

The World in 1000

- Song Empire
- Byzantine Empire
- Denmark and possessions
- Toltec Empire
- Kievan Rus and possessions
- Abbasid Caliphate under Harun al-Rashid, 786
- Tibet c.800
- Empire of the Franks under Charlemagne, 814
- Holy Roman Empire

In Chichén Itzá a Chac Mool, a Toltec altar in the shape of a reclining figure stands alongside the typically Maya Temple of the Jaguars.

Coptic Christianity resisted Islam in the Nubian kingdoms of Makuria and Alodia. This brightly colored altar cloth was woven during this period.

The Americas

The nomadic Toltecs migrated into central Mexico from the northwest during the 10th century. There they became city-dwellers, expanded their territory through military conquest, and established a trading network that extended as far as South America. In the North American southwest, the Mogollon, Anasazi, and Hohokam cultures were emerging. With an economy based on efficient irrigation agriculture, these peoples built elaborate pueblos (apartment villages) in the desert canyons and established trading links which brought them into contact with the civilizations of Central America.

The Americas

c.750: First true towns appear in Mississippi valley	c.800: Hohokam, Anasazi, and Mogollon cultures emerge in American Southwest	c.900: Topiltzin, the Toltec religious leader, founds capital at Tula	990s: Exiled Toltecs take over Maya city of Chichén Itzá

750 — 800 — 850 — 900 — 950 — 1000

c.850: Collapse of Maya civilization in Mexico's southern lowlands · c.900: Advanced Thule culture among Inuit of Alaska · 987: High priest and followers expelled from Tula by rival cult that favors human sacrifice

Africa

In 969, the Fatimid rulers of North Africa declared Egypt independent of Baghdad, and made Cairo their capital. Camel caravans regularly crossed the Sahara as the Arab demand for sub-Saharan gold grew. Native West African kingdoms such as Kanem-Bornu, Ghana, and Takrur all prospered as a result. In East Africa, Arab coastal trading settlements extended as far south as Zanzibar and Madagascar.

Africa

800s: Establishment of trading colonies such as Manda and Kilwa on east coast		c.950: Emergence of small kingdom of Igbo Ukwu near Niger delta	970s: Al-Azhar university established in Cairo

750 — 800 — 850 — 900 — 950 — 1000

800: Start of Aghlabid dynasty in Tunis · 868: Ahmad ibn-Tulun founds the Tulunid dynasty in Egypt · 909: Shi'ite Fatimids expel Aghlabids from Tunis · 969: Fatimids seize control of Egypt

PRINTING IN CHINA

The Chinese had been experimenting with ways of reproducing writing and illustrations for centuries, before they made their greatest breakthrough under the Tang in the 8th century. Carving characters and pictures in reverse onto wooden blocks was a time-consuming process, but it allowed many hundreds of copies to made before the wood's surface became too worn. All kinds of documents – from religious texts to tax receipts – were printed by this method.

The earliest printed document that can be dated with certainty is *The Diamond Sutra*, a work of Buddhist doctrine printed on a scroll, produced in 868.

After the fervor of the 7th-century *jihads*, many Arab tribes subsequently turned against one another as they competed to rule the various parts of the Islamic world.

West Asia

The Abbasid dynasty came to power in 750. Though the arts, culture, and trade flourished under their rule, disagreements over the succession meant that their authority was not universally recognized. Even in Baghdad the caliphs became figureheads, real power being in the hands of Turkish mercenary or slave troops and Persian administrators. Under a new dynasty of Macedonian rulers (867–1081) the Byzantine Empire reached its apogee, and came into conflict with the Arabs to the east. Byzantine troops regained control of most of Anatolia and, in 969, reconquered Antioch.

SEE ALSO:

North America: pp.122–123

South America: pp.144–145

Africa: pp.162–163

Europe: pp.184–185

West Asia: pp.226–227

South and Southeast Asia: pp.244–245

North and East Asia: pp.262–265

Australasia and Oceania: pp.280–281

West Asia

750: Umayyad Caliphate is overthrown and succeeded by the Abbasid dynasty
786: Under Caliph Harun al-Rashid Baghdad becomes center of arts and learning
863: Byzantines annihilate Arab forces to stem Muslim advance in Anatolia
945: Persian Buwayhids conquer Baghdad but allow caliph to reign as figurehead
976: Byzantine forces threaten to take Jerusalem
762: Abbasid capital founded at Baghdad
836: Baghdad terrorized by Turkish slave troops; Abbasid Caliph al-Mutasim builds new capital at Samarra
936: Caliphs of Baghdad lose effective power; caliphate under control of Turkish troops

ARAB STAR MAPS

Arab scientists and mathematicians were the finest in the world, and their astronomers added greatly to our knowledge of the heavens during this period. As well as using the night sky to set a course at sea and help them cross the desert, the Arabs continued to name stars and map constellations in the tradition of Ptolemy and other Greek astronomers. Many stars, such as Aldebaran, Rigel, and Rasalgethi, are still known by their Arab names.

The constellation of Andromeda is one of many attractive illustrations in *The Book of the Fixed Stars* compiled by Abd al-Rahman ibn Umar al-Sufi in the 10th century. The individual stars forming the constellation are shown in red.

Buddhism affected all aspects of life in Tang China, the Buddha assuming Chinese features, as in this wall painting from Dunhuang.

South and Southeast Asia

In the north, the Islamic kingdom of the Afghan ruler Mahmud of Ghazni stretched from the Oxus to the Indus, while states such as Gurjara-Pratiharas and the Buddhist Palas vied for the Ganges plain. To the south, the Tamil Cholas and the Chalukyas fought over the Godavari and Krishna rivers. Chola conquests expanded to include Ceylon and parts of the Malay Peninsula.

This bronze of the god Shiva was made under the Chola dynasty. In this period cults of individual Hindu deities grew in popularity.

South and Southeast Asia

802: Angkorian dynasty founded by King Jayavarman II
889: Khmer King Indravarman I begins construction of Angkor
997: Mahmud of Ghazni extends rule into northwest India
c.800: Construction of Buddhist temple at Borobudur, Java
886: Chola dynasty rules much of southern India
c.900: Gurjara-Pratiharas dominates northern India
962: Foundation of Afghan Ghaznavid dynasty

East Asia

Threats of internal rebellion in the middle of the 8th century weakened the Tang dynasty's control of China. As a result the empire became more inward looking and the political and economic center of gravity began to shift south to the Yangtze valley. The Tang dynasty eventually collapsed after massive peasant uprisings in the 9th century, and China split into ten separate states until 960–79, when it was reunified under the Song. Both Korea and Japan were governed by strong, centralized Buddhist dynasties.

East Asia

751: Defeat of Chinese by Muslim forces at battle of Talas River
794: Kyoto becomes capital of Japan
868: *The Diamond Sutra*, world's oldest surviving printed work
935: Foundation of kingdom of Koryo in Korea
979: Song establish power in China
756: Rebel general An Lushan captures Chang'an
763: Tang China is invaded by Tibetans
870s: Peasant uprisings throughout Tang China
907: End of the Tang dynasty
970: Paper money introduced by Chinese government

EXPLORERS OF THE OCEANS

The stylized image of a ship decorates this early Viking coin, which was minted at Hedeby in the 9th century.

IN THE 1ST MILLENNIUM CE, three peoples surpassed all others as navigators of the world's oceans: the Vikings, the Arabs, and the Polynesians. The traders and raiders of Scandinavia created the fast, efficient Viking longship, which took them along the rivers of Russia to the Black Sea, and across the Atlantic Ocean to Iceland and North America. The Arabs were already accomplished seafarers; the discovery, in the 8th century, of the sea route to China via the Strait of Malacca heralded a new era of long-distance trade, and Arab ships sailed to the East Indies, East Africa, and China. Perhaps the most extraordinary seafarers of all were the Polynesians, who by 1200 CE had completed the colonization of all the islands of the Pacific.

These 12th-century walrus ivory chesspieces are from Lewis in the Outer Hebrides. The islands were settled by Norwegians in the 9th and 10th centurie

The Viking world

Ocean-going ships allowed the Vikings to sail in search of new lands and trading opportunities. At first they dominated their Baltic neighbors, taking tribute in the form of amber, wax, fish, ivory, and furs. Norwegians and Danes exploited weaknesses in France, England, and Ireland, using their fast, maneuverable longships to conduct lightning raids, exacting tribute, conquering, and colonizing. Eventually, in a quest for land, they crossed the Atlantic, reaching Iceland in 860 and Newfoundland c.1000. Swedish traders penetrated the navigable rivers of Russia to dominate the lucrative trade with Constantinople and the Arab world. Varangians (as these eastern Vikings were called) founded Kievan Rus, the first Russian state, and their fighting qualities were recognized by the Byzantine emperors, who employed them as their elite mercenary guard.

Viking longships were oar-powered, ranging from 17–33 yds in length. Their light, flexible hulls "rode" the waves and made them ideal for raiding in shallow, coastal waters.

Viking voyages

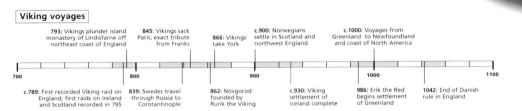

- 793: Vikings plunder island monastery of Lindisfarne off northeast coast of England
- 845: Vikings sack Paris; exact tribute from Franks
- 866: Vikings take York
- c.900: Norwegians settle in Scotland and northwest England
- c.1000: Voyages from Greenland to Newfoundland and coast of North America

- c.789: First recorded Viking raid on England; first raids on Ireland and Scotland recorded in 795
- 839: Swedes travel through Russia to Constantinople
- 862: Novgorod founded by Rurik the Viking
- c.930: Viking settlement of Iceland complete
- 986: Erik the Red begins settlement of Greenland
- 1042: End of Danish rule in England

The Polynesians

The first wave of colonization of the Pacific, between 2000 and 1500 BCE, took settlers from New Guinea and neighboring islands as far as the Fiji Islands. From there, they sailed on to the Tonga and Samoa groups. In about 200 BCE, the Polynesians embarked on a series of far longer voyages, crossing vast tracts of empty ocean to settle the Marquesas, the Society Islands, Hawaii, Rapa Nui (Easter Island), and New Zealand. By about 1200 CE they had discovered almost every island in the Pacific. They sailed in double-hulled canoes, laden with seed plants, chickens, and pigs. The canoes could tack into the wind, and they probably navigated by observating the sun and the stars, the direction of prevailing winds, and the flight patterns of homing birds.

Polynesian voyages 1500 BCE–1000 CE

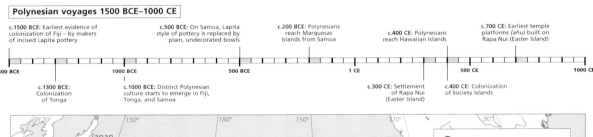

- c.1500 BCE: Earliest evidence of colonization of Fiji – by makers of incised Lapita pottery
- c.500 BCE: On Samoa, Lapita style of pottery is replaced by plain, undecorated bowls
- c.200 BCE: Polynesians reach Marquesas Islands from Samoa
- c.400 CE: Polynesians reach Hawaiian Islands
- c.700 CE: Earliest temple platforms (ahu) built on Rapa Nui (Easter Island)

- c.1300 BCE: Colonization of Tonga
- c.1000 BCE: Distinct Polynesian culture starts to emerge in Fiji, Tonga, and Samoa
- c.300 CE: Settlement of Rapa Nui (Easter Island)
- c.400 CE: Colonization of Society Islands

On their epic ocean voyages, the Polynesians used twin-hulled canoes, similar to the one in this 19th-century engraving, up to 33 yds long. Canoes with an outrigger, attached to the hull and kept to windward for balance, were probably for inshore sailing and shorter voyages. Both types of vessel could be powered by oars or sails.

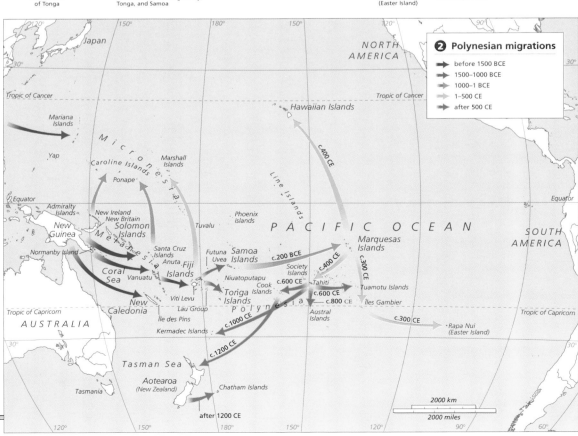

❷ Polynesian migrations
- before 1500 BCE
- 1500–1000 BCE
- 1000–1 BCE
- 1–500 CE
- after 500 CE

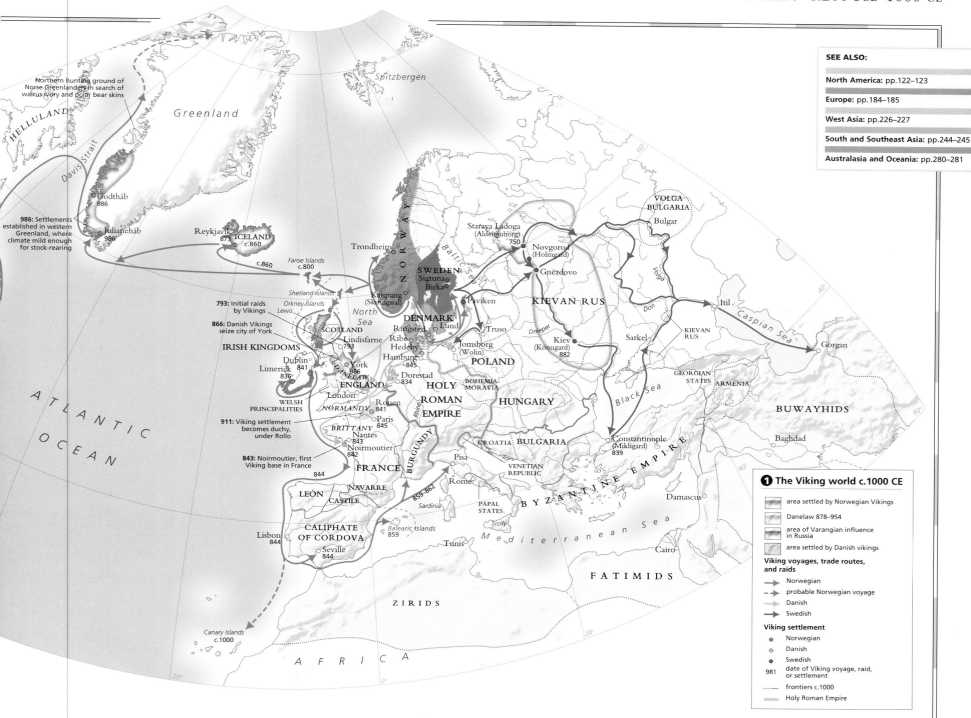

SEE ALSO:

North America: pp.122–123

Europe: pp.184–185

West Asia: pp.226–227

South and Southeast Asia: pp.244–245

Australasia and Oceania: pp.280–281

❶ The Viking world c.1000 CE

- area settled by Norwegian Vikings
- Danelaw 878–954
- area of Varangian influence in Russia
- area settled by Danish vikings

Viking voyages, trade routes, and raids
- → Norwegian
- ⇢ probable Norwegian voyage
- → Danish
- → Swedish

Viking settlement
- Norwegian
- Danish
- Swedish
- 981 date of Viking voyage, raid, or settlement
- ···· frontiers c.1000
- Holy Roman Empire

Arab traders in the Indian Ocean

The Arabs used the wind systems of the monsoon to propel their ships eastward from the Persian Gulf in November and to return them westward in the summer. In the 8th century, Arab traders discovered the sea route to Guangzhou (Canton) by way of the Malabar Coast, the Strait of Malacca, and Hanoi, a journey of 120 days, which nevertheless could take between 18 months and three years. The Arabs exported iron, wool, incense, and bullion in return for silk and spices. When the fall of the Tang Empire disrupted trade with China c.1000 CE, the Arabs turned to the East Indies, and Islam consequently became well established in the the islands of Southeast Asia. They also navigated the East African coast to Zanzibar and Madagascar, where they met the Malays who had colonized the island some 300 years earlier.

An Indian ship is depicted in an Arab manuscript of 1238. It has a square-rigged sail, suitable for running with the strong monsoonal winds, well known from the 1st century CE. The capacious hold could carry both passengers and cargo, essential for thriving Indian Ocean trade routes from the 8th century CE.

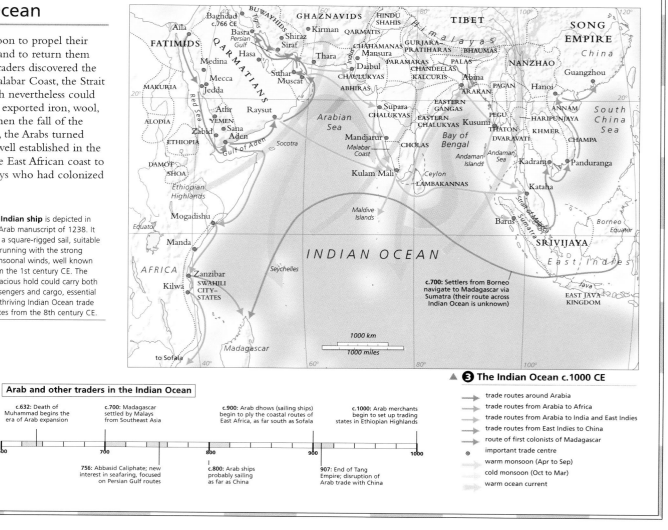

▲ ❸ The Indian Ocean c.1000 CE

The Indian Ocean c.1000 CE
- → trade routes around Arabia
- → trade routes from Arabia to Africa
- → trade routes from Arabia to India and East Indies
- → trade routes from East Indies to China
- ⇢ route of first colonists of Madagascar
- important trade centre
- warm monsoon (Apr to Sep)
- cold monsoon (Oct to Mar)
- warm ocean current

Arab and other traders in the Indian Ocean

c.632: Death of Muhammad begins the era of Arab expansion	c.700: Madagascar settled by Malays from Southeast Asia	c.900: Arab dhows (sailing ships) begin to ply the coastal routes of East Africa, as far south as Sofala	c.1000: Arab merchants begin to set up trading states in Ethiopian Highlands
600	700	800	900 1000
756: Abbasid Caliphate; new interest in seafaring, focused on Persian Gulf routes	c.800: Arab ships probably sailing as far as China	907: End of Tang Empire; disruption of Arab trade with China	

THE WORLD 1000–1200

IN MANY PARTS OF THE WORLD conflict over territory and religion was intense. This was a time when the Christian West was recovering from the tumult that followed the fall of Rome. As marginal land was cleared for agriculture, the population expanded. Trade routes crossed Europe and a mercantile economy developed and prospered. Yet the resurgence of Christian Europe brought it into direct confrontation with Islam when it launched the Crusades to conquer the Holy Land. This ultimately proved a failure, but in Spain and Portugal the Christian reconquest made intermittent progress. To the east, the states of northern India fell to Muslim invaders, and Buddhism was finally driven from the subcontinent. In China the Song Empire shrank under pressure from powerful nomadic peoples to the north, such as the Xixia and the Jin.

The power of the Church was expressed in new cathedrals built first in the Romanesque and then in the Gothic style, typified by the soaring facade of Chartres.

Europe

The assimilation in the 11th century of Poland, Hungary, and the Scandinavian kingdoms into the realm of Western Christianity brought it to a new peak of power and influence. As Western Europeans began to wrest control of the Mediterranean from the Arabs and Byzantines, a new era of prosperity based on trade began. Italian merchants became middlemen in Byzantine trade, and north Italian towns, such as Venice, Genoa, and Pisa, prospered. Elsewhere, forests and marginal land were cleared for agriculture, populations grew, and new towns were founded.

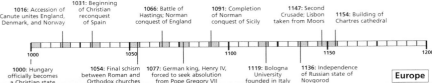

1016: Accession of Canute unites England, Denmark, and Norway
1031: Beginning of Christian reconquest of Spain
1066: Battle of Hastings; Norman conquest of England
1091: Completion of Norman conquest of Sicily
1147: Second Crusade; Lisbon taken from Moors
1154: Building of Chartres cathedral

1000: Hungary officially becomes a Christian state
1054: Final schism between Roman and Orthodox churches
1077: German king, Henry IV, forced to seek absolution from Pope Gregory VII
1119: Bologna University founded in Italy
1136: Independence of Russian state of Novgorod

Europe

AL-IDRISI'S WORLD MAP

Islamic geographers led the world in medieval times. Al-Idrisi (1100–65) was a Moroccan in the service of Roger II of Sicily. The island had been under Arab rule in the 10th century and became a meeting point of two cultures where much of the knowledge of the Islamic world was transmitted to the Christian West.

Al-Idrisi's map shows the lasting influence of Ptolemy (see p.44). However, he oriented his maps, as did most contemporary Islamic geographers, with the south at the top.

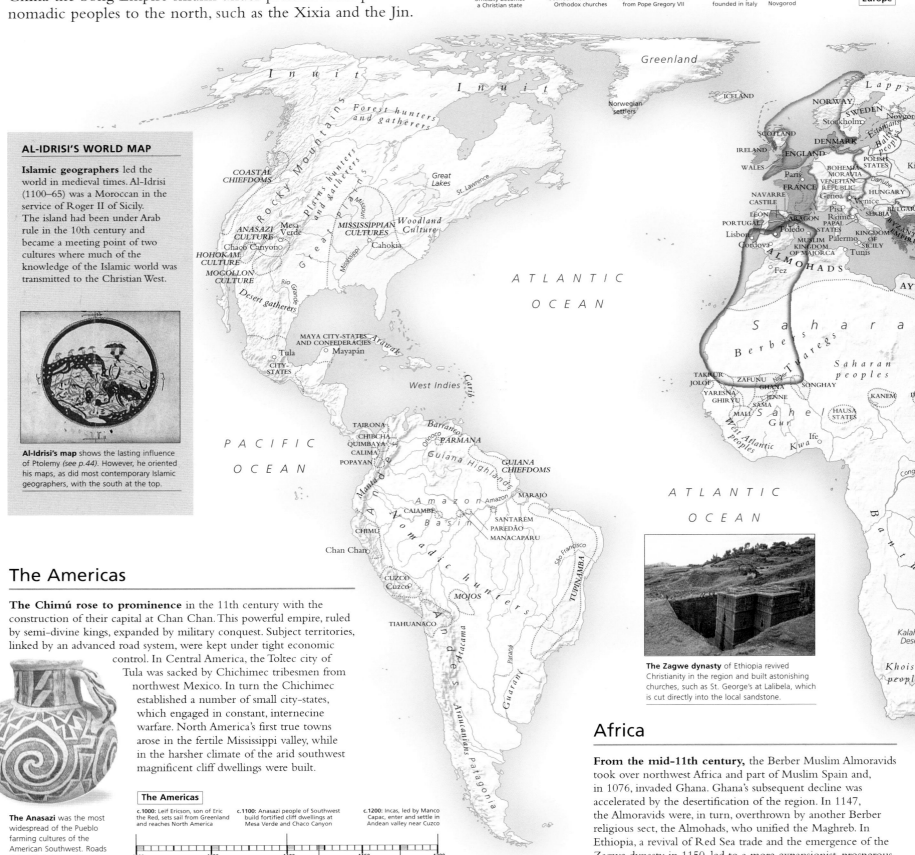

The Americas

The Chimú rose to prominence in the 11th century with the construction of their capital at Chan Chan. This powerful empire, ruled by semi-divine kings, expanded by military conquest. Subject territories, linked by an advanced road system, were kept under tight economic control. In Central America, the Toltec city of Tula was sacked by Chichimec tribesmen from northwest Mexico. In turn the Chichimec established a number of small city-states, which engaged in constant, internecine warfare. North America's first true towns arose in the fertile Mississippi valley, while in the harsher climate of the arid southwest magnificent cliff dwellings were built.

The Anasazi was the most widespread of the Pueblo farming cultures of the American Southwest. Roads linked their impressive canyon villages, where they produced fine black and white pottery.

The Americas

c.1000: Leif Ericson, son of Eric the Red, sets sail from Greenland and reaches North America
c.1100: Anasazi people of Southwest build fortified cliff dwellings at Mesa Verde and Chaco Canyon
c.1200: Incas, led by Manco Capac, enter and settle in Andean valley near Cuzco

c.1050: Settlements of mound-builders of Mississippi valley expand to become true towns
1121: Bishop Eirik visits North America from Greenland
c.1175: Toltec capital, Tula, is sacked by Chichimec

The Zagwe dynasty of Ethiopia revived Christianity in the region and built astonishing churches, such as St. George's at Lalibela, which is cut directly into the local sandstone.

Africa

From the mid-11th century, the Berber Muslim Almoravids took over northwest Africa and part of Muslim Spain and, in 1076, invaded Ghana. Ghana's subsequent decline was accelerated by the desertification of the region. In 1147, the Almoravids were, in turn, overthrown by another Berber religious sect, the Almohads, who unified the Maghreb. In Ethiopia, a revival of Red Sea trade and the emergence of the Zagwe dynasty in 1150, led to a more expansionist, prosperous era. In Egypt, the military leader Saladin became ruler in 1174, ending the Fatimid dynasty and founding that of the Ayyubids.

WINDMILLS

Wind power had been harnessed in various different ways, notably in Persia and China, for grinding corn and raising water. But it was not until the 12th century that the windmill started to take on its familiar European form. The mills of northern Europe differed from earlier versions in that the shaft turned horizontally rather than vertically and the sails were turned so that they kept facing the wind. The first northern European mills were simple post-mills. These evolved gradually into bulkier tower mills with rotating caps.

In Europe windmills were used only for grinding corn up until the 15th century, as illustrated in this English woodcut from c.1340. Their power was then adapted for tasks such as land drainage, particularly in Holland.

West Asia

Byzantium's resurgence under Basil II did not last, and in the 11th century most of the empire's Asian lands fell to the Seljuk Turks. The Islamic Turks, originally from Central Asia, established themselves in Baghdad in 1055. As "men of the sword," they formed a partnership with the Persians and Arabs, the "men of the law." Tens of thousands of Europeans answered Pope Urban II's call in 1095 to recapture Jerusalem for Christendom. In 1099 the holy city was taken and the Crusaders set up states in Antioch, Edessa, Tripoli, and Jerusalem. In the following century, Muslim leaders, notably Saladin, founder of the Ayyubid dynasty in Egypt, embarked on a campaign of reconquest.

The capture of Antioch in 1098 was one of the first Christian successes on the First Crusade. The strongly fortified city held out for seven months.

SEE ALSO:

North America: pp.122–123

South America: pp.146–147

Africa: pp.162–163

Europe: pp.186–187

West Asia: pp.228–229

South and Southeast Asia: pp.244–245

North and East Asia: pp.262–265

West Asia

- 1025: Death of great Byzantine emperor, Basil II
- 1055: Seljuk Turks capture Baghdad
- 1071: Seljuk Turks defeat Byzantines at Manzikert
- 1099: Jerusalem captured by Crusaders
- 1144: Fall of Edessa to Muslims
- 1174: Founding of Ayyubid Sultanate in Egypt
- 1187: Saladin recaptures Jerusalem
- 1188: Crusader states reduced to coastal enclaves by Saladin

East Asia

By 1110, Song China was the most advanced, prosperous, and populous state in the world. However the Song alliance with the Manchurian Jin to dislodge the hostile Liao from their northern border, fatally weakened the Song Empire. The Jin overran northern China and the Song were forced to regroup in the southeast, defensive and hostile to outside influences. In Japan, the emperors lost power to the Fujiwara family in the mid-12th century. A period of violent interclan warfare followed, ending with the victory of the Minamoto clan.

This Song scroll gives a vivid depiction of the bustling street life and prosperity of Kaifeng in the 12th century. In 1105 the city's population had risen to 260,000.

East Asia

- 1005: Song China becomes subject state of northern Liao kingdom, with capital at Beijing
- c.1045: Movable type printing invented in China
- 1125: Liao defeated by Jin from Manchuria
- 1130: Song capital moves to Hangzhou
- 1191: Zen Buddhist order founded in Japan
- 1192: Minamoto Yoritomo becomes Shogun and forms military government in Japan

The Khmer Empire was at its height in the 11th and 12th centuries. The artistic brilliance of the court, evident in these carvings decorating a temple at Angkor Wat, was in marked contrast to the conditions of the mass of the population.

South and Southeast Asia

Northern India was repeatedly invaded by the Ghazni Muslims of Afghanistan. In 1186 the last Ghazni ruler was deposed by the Turkish leader, Muhammad al Ghur, who continued to wage holy war in the region. Southeastern India was dominated by the Chola dynasty, who controlled the sea route between West Asia and China. The two most powerful states of Southeast Asia, the Khmer Empire and the kingdom of Pagan, both enjoyed an artistic golden age.

South and Southeast Asia

- 1014: Rajendra I becomes ruler of the Cholas of southeastern India
- 1018: Rajendra conquers Ceylon
- 1113: Accession of Suryavarman II, powerful warrior king of the Khmer
- 1152: Temple of Angkor Wat completed
- 1191: Muhammad al Ghur defeats Rajput clans
- c.1000: First Muslim raids into northern India, led by Sultan Muhammad of Ghazni
- 1044: Establishment of first Burmese state at Pagan
- 1077: Chola merchants send embassy to China
- 1186: Raids by Muhammad al Ghur herald end of Buddhism in northern India

The World in 1200

- Byzantine Empire
- England and possessions
- Venetian Republic
- Holy Roman Empire
- Almoravid Empire 1120
- Great Seljuk Empire 1071
- possessions of Canute 1028–1035

Africa

- 1048: Fatimids lose control of Ifriqiya (Libya)
- 1076: Ghana falls to Almoravids
- c.1110: Onset of serious desiccation of Sahel region
- 1128: Almohads start takeover of Almoravid dominions
- 1147: Almohads established in Morocco and southern Spain
- 1150: Zagwe dynasty established in Ethiopia
- 1171: Shi'ite Fatimid dynasty in Egypt suppressed by Saladin

Map labels: Paleosiberians, Samoyeds, Ugrians, RUSSIAN PRINCIPALITIES, Yenisey, Lena, Tungus, Siberia, Ob, Volga, VOLGA BULGARIA, Ugric peoples, Turkic peoples, RUSSIAN PRINCIPALITIES, Gobi, Mongols, Amur, KARA KHITAI EMPIRE, UIGHUR CITY-STATES, Manchuria, Liao, XIXIA, Yanjing, Beijing, KORYO, JAPAN, Constantinople, GEORGIA, RUM, Manzikert, Caspian Sea, Bukhara, KASHMIR, Kyoto, LITTLE ARMENIA, Edessa, EMPIRE OF THE KHWARIZM SHAH, Kabul, TIBET, JIN EMPIRE, Kaifeng, ANTIOCH, Baghdad, ABBASIDS, ALGHURIDS, GHURID EMPIRE, Delhi, Yellow River, Hangzhou, TRIPOLI, JERUSALEM, Jerusalem, Mecca, Red Sea, Beduins, PARAMARAS, Ganges, Yangtze, NANZHAO, SOUTHERN SONG EMPIRE, SULTANATE, MAKURIA, Nile, Arabian Peninsula, OMAN, CAULUKYAS, SMALL DYNASTIES, PAGAN, ANNAM, ALWA, YADAVAS, EASTERN GANGAS, Thais, Mekong, HARIPUNJAYA, ETHIOPIA, Lalibela, SILAHARAS, KAKATIYAS, ARAKAN, YEMEN, KADAMBAS, TELUGUCODAS, KHMER, Angkor, CHAMPA, Philippine Islands, GOJJAM, DAMOT, IFAT, HARAR, HOYSALAS, PANDYAS, CHOLAS, Nilotic peoples, SHOA, DAWARO, CERAS, Ceylon, SIMHALA, PACIFIC OCEAN, FETEGAR, Kushites, SWAHILI CITY-STATES, INDIAN OCEAN, SRIVIJAYA, Sumatra, Borneo, Papuans, New Guinea, Java, KEDIRI, Malays, Madagascar, Australian Aborigines, Darling, MAPUNGUBWE, Zambezi, New Zealand, Maoris

THE AGE OF THE CRUSADES

The idealism of a devout Crusader is captured in this 13th-century drawing.

THE IDEA OF A HOLY WAR was never part of the doctrine of the early Christian church. This changed in 1095, when Pope Urban II made an impassioned speech at Clermont, urging French barons and knights to go to the aid of the beleaguered Christians of the Byzantine Empire. In return, they were promised indulgences. When they got to the Holy Land and captured Jerusalem in 1099, the aims of the Crusaders became rather less spiritual. Those rewarded with land tried to recreate the society of feudal Europe, but there was always a shortage of manpower to maintain the Crusader states in their precarious two centuries of existence. Nevertheless, the crusading ideal became firmly established in European consciousness, and there were many subsequent expeditions to defend or recapture Jerusalem, but none was as successful as the first.

The most devout and determined of all the crusading kings of Europe was Louis IX of France (St. Louis). He sailed on two Crusades, once to invade Egypt, the second time to convert the King of Tunis. Both ended in disaster. In 1270, Louis and his men were struck down by disease as they camped before Tunis. Louis himself died. Here his coffin is being loaded on a ship to be carried back to France.

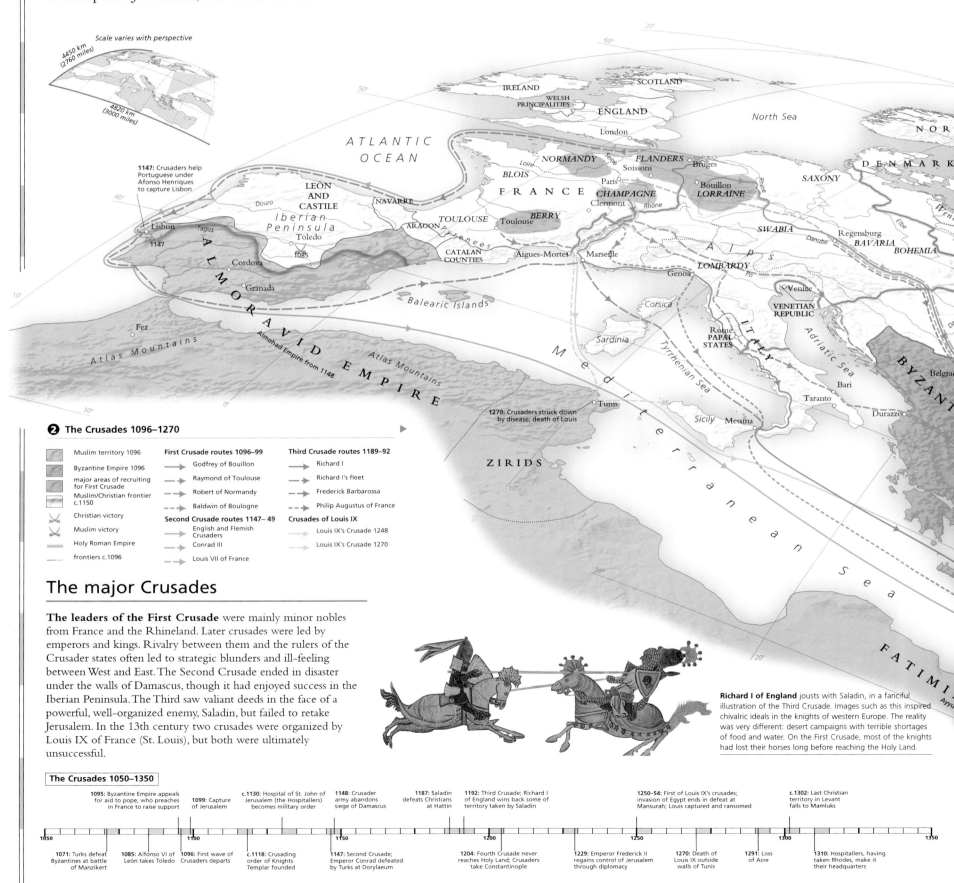

② The Crusades 1096–1270

▨	Muslim territory 1096
▨	Byzantine Empire 1096
▨	major areas of recruiting for First Crusade
▨	Muslim/Christian frontier c.1150
✕	Christian victory
✕	Muslim victory
▬	Holy Roman Empire
····	frontiers c.1096

First Crusade routes 1096–99
→ Godfrey of Bouillon
→ Raymond of Toulouse
⇢ Robert of Normandy
⇠ Baldwin of Boulogne

Second Crusade routes 1147–49
→ English and Flemish Crusaders
→ Conrad III
⇢ Louis VII of France

Third Crusade routes 1189–92
→ Richard I
→ Richard I's fleet
⇢ Frederick Barbarossa
⇠ Philip Augustus of France

Crusades of Louis IX
— Louis IX's Crusade 1248
— Louis IX's Crusade 1270

Map labels: Scale varies with perspective; 4450 km (2760 miles); 4820 km (3000 miles); IRELAND; SCOTLAND; WELSH PRINCIPALITIES; ENGLAND; London; North Sea; NOR...; DENMARK; ATLANTIC OCEAN; NORMANDY; FLANDERS; Bruges; SAXONY; Seine; Soissons; BLOIS; Paris; Bouillon; LORRAINE; Elbe; Wen...; LEÓN AND CASTILE; NAVARRE; FRANCE; CHAMPAGNE; Clermont; Rhône; SWABIA; Regensburg; BAVARIA; BOHEMIA; Iberian Peninsula; Douro; TOULOUSE; BERRY; ARAGON; Toulouse; Danube; Lisbon; Tagus; Toledo; Pyrenees; CATALAN COUNTIES; Aigues-Mortes; Marseille; LOMBARDY; Po; Venice; 1147; 1085; Cordova; Genoa; ALPS; Granada; Balearic Islands; Corsica; VENETIAN REPUBLIC; Fez; Rome PAPAL STATES; ITALY; Adriatic Sea; BYZANT...; Atlas Mountains; ALMORAVID EMPIRE; Almohad Empire from 1148; Atlas Mountains; Sardinia; Tyrrhenian Sea; Bari; Belgra...; Mediterranean Sea; Tunis; Sicily; Messina; Taranto; Durazzo; ZIRIDS; FATIMI...; Ayyu...

1147: Crusaders help Portuguese under Afonso Henriques to capture Lisbon

1270: Crusaders struck down by disease; death of Louis

The major Crusades

The leaders of the First Crusade were mainly minor nobles from France and the Rhineland. Later crusades were led by emperors and kings. Rivalry between them and the rulers of the Crusader states often led to strategic blunders and ill-feeling between West and East. The Second Crusade ended in disaster under the walls of Damascus, though it had enjoyed success in the Iberian Peninsula. The Third saw valiant deeds in the face of a powerful, well-organized enemy, Saladin, but failed to retake Jerusalem. In the 13th century two crusades were organized by Louis IX of France (St. Louis), but both were ultimately unsuccessful.

Richard I of England jousts with Saladin, in a fanciful illustration of the Third Crusade. Images such as this inspired chivalric ideals in the knights of western Europe. The reality was very different: desert campaigns with terrible shortages of food and water. On the First Crusade, most of the knights had lost their horses long before reaching the Holy Land.

The Crusades 1050–1350

1095: Byzantine Empire appeals for aid to pope, who preaches in France to raise support
1099: Capture of Jerusalem
c.1130: Hospital of St. John of Jerusalem (the Hospitallers) becomes military order
1148: Crusader army abandons siege of Damascus
1187: Saladin defeats Christians at Hattin
1192: Third Crusade; Richard I of England wins back some of territory taken by Saladin
1250–54: First of Louis IX's crusades; invasion of Egypt ends in defeat at Mansurah; Louis captured and ransomed
c.1302: Last Christian territory in Levant falls to Mamluks

1050 — 1100 — 1150 — 1200 — 1250 — 1300 — 1350

1071: Turks defeat Byzantines at battle of Manzikert
1085: Alfonso VI of León takes Toledo
1096: First wave of Crusaders departs
c.1118: Crusading order of Knights Templar founded
1147: Second Crusade; Emperor Conrad defeated by Turks at Dorylaeum
1204: Fourth Crusade never reaches Holy Land; Crusaders take Constantinople
1229: Emperor Frederick II regains control of Jerusalem through diplomacy
1270: Death of Louis IX outside walls of Tunis
1291: Loss of Acre
1310: Hospitallers, having taken Rhodes, make it their headquarters

The boundaries of Christianity and Islam

In the 9th and 10th centuries, the boundaries between the Islamic and Christian worlds shifted very little. A new threat to Christianity came in the mid-11th century with the advance of the Seljuk Turks, newly converted to Islam and effective rulers of the Abbasid Caliphate after reaching Baghdad in 1055. Following their victory over the Byzantines in 1071 at Manzikert, they won control of almost all Asia Minor, home to former Christian subjects of the Byzantine Empire. In the Iberian Peninsula, however, the Christian kingdoms won back land from the Muslims in the course of the 11th century.

❶ Islam and Christianity c.1090

- Muslim lands
- Greek Christians (Orthodox)
- Roman Church (under papal authority)
- Greek Christians in Muslim lands
- other Christians
- direction of Muslim expansion
- direction of Greek Christian expansion
- direction of Roman Church expansion
- city with important Jewish community

1000 km
1000 miles

SEE ALSO:

Africa: pp.162–163

Europe: pp.186–187

West Asia: pp.228–229

Godfrey of Bouillon leads the attack on Jerusalem in 1099. After all the hardship and the long journey there, the capture of the Holy City was hailed as a miracle. It was followed by the murder or brutal eviction of many of the city's Muslims and Jews.

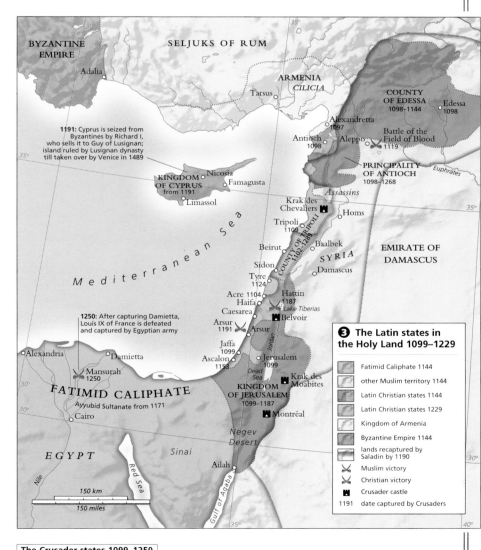

Krak des Chevaliers was one of many heavily fortified Crusader castles. Manned by the Hospitallers, it held out against Saladin's forces, but fell to the Mamluks in 1271 after a month's siege.

Crusader states in the Holy Land

How the Crusaders' conquests should be ruled was not considered until after Jerusalem had fallen. The solution – a feudal kingdom of Jerusalem buttressed by the counties of Edessa, Tripoli, and Antioch – alienated the Byzantines, who had hoped to regain their former territories. Jerusalem was always a weak state with a small population, heavily dependent on supplies and recruits from western Christendom. When a strong Islamic ruler such as Saladin emerged, the colonists had little hope against a determined Muslim onslaught. They held on to the coast through the 13th century, but in 1291, Acre, the last major city in Christian hands, fell to the Mamluks of Egypt.

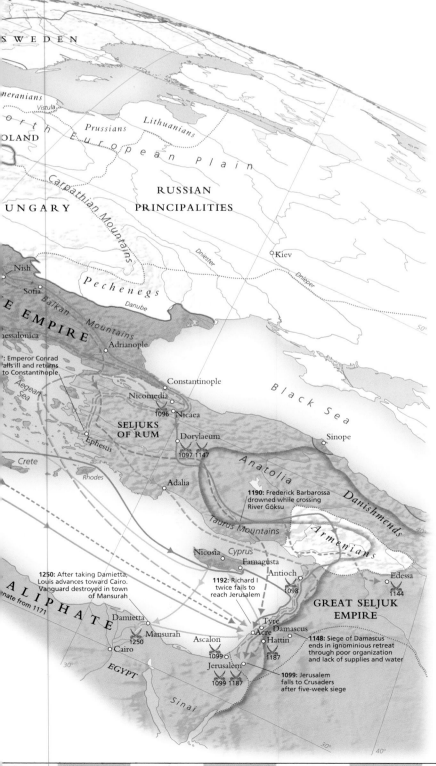

1191: Cyprus is seized from Byzantines by Richard I, who sells it to Guy of Lusignan; island ruled by Lusignan dynasty till taken over by Venice in 1489

1250: After capturing Damietta, Louis IX of France is defeated and captured by Egyptian army

1250: After taking Damietta, Louis advances toward Cairo. Vanguard destroyed in town of Mansurah

1190: Frederick Barbarossa drowned while crossing River Göksu

1192: Richard I twice fails to reach Jerusalem

1148: Siege of Damascus ends in ignominious retreat through poor organization and lack of supplies and water

1099: Jerusalem falls to Crusaders after five-week siege

❸ The Latin states in the Holy Land 1099–1229

- Fatimid Caliphate 1144
- other Muslim territory 1144
- Latin Christian states 1144
- Latin Christian states 1229
- Kingdom of Armenia
- Byzantine Empire 1144
- lands recaptured by Saladin by 1190
- Muslim victory
- Christian victory
- Crusader castle
- 1191 date captured by Crusaders

150 km
150 miles

The Crusader states 1099–1250

1099: Godfrey of Bouillon elected King of Jerusalem	1151: Last Christian stronghold in County of Edessa falls to Nur al-Din	1191–92: Richard I wins back Jaffa, but fails to reach Jerusalem	1229: Frederick negotiates agreement which wins back control over Jerusalem
1090 — 1120 — 1150 — 1180 — 1210 — 1240			
1098: Crusaders take Antioch	1124: Capture of important port of Tyre — 1144: Edessa lost to Zangi, governor of Mosul	1187–88: Crusaders states ravaged by Saladin's armies	1225: Emperor Frederick II inherits Kingdom of Jerusalem

THE WORLD 1200–1300

IN THE 13TH CENTURY Mongol horsemen burst out of their Central Asian homeland and conquered a vast swathe of the Eurasian landmass. By 1300, they had divided their conquests into four large empires that stretched from China to eastern Europe. Mongol campaigns brought devastation, particularly to China and the Islamic states of southwest Asia but, once all resistance had been crushed, merchants, ambassadors, and other travelers were able to move safely through the Mongol realms. Though the old political order of the Islamic world, centered on the Abbasid Caliphate and Baghdad, was swept away, the influence of Islam continued to spread as many Mongols adopted the religion. Powerful new Muslim states also emerged in Mamluk Egypt and the Sultanate of Delhi. Europe remained on the defensive in the face of the Mongols and Islam, but city-states such as Venice and Genoa prospered through increased trading links with the East.

The port of Venice was the richest city in western Europe. This illustration shows Marco Polo with his father and uncle setting off in 1271 on the first stage of their incredible journey to the court of the Great Khan.

Europe

The feudal monarchies of England and France consolidated large regional states, but conflict between popes and emperors prevented any similar process in Italy and Germany. In Spain, Christian forces took Córdoba and Seville, leaving only the small kingdom of Granada in Moorish control. In eastern Europe, the Mongols of the Golden Horde collected tribute from the Russian principalities. Western Europe, in contrast, prospered economically as Italian merchants linked northern lands to the commerce of the Mediterranean basin.

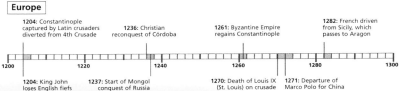

Europe

- 1204: Constantinople captured by Latin crusaders diverted from 4th Crusade
- 1204: King John loses English fiefs in northern France
- 1236: Christian reconquest of Córdoba
- 1237: Start of Mongol conquest of Russia
- 1261: Byzantine Empire regains Constantinople
- 1270: Death of Louis IX (St. Louis) on crusade
- 1271: Departure of Marco Polo for China
- 1282: French driven from Sicily, which passes to Aragon

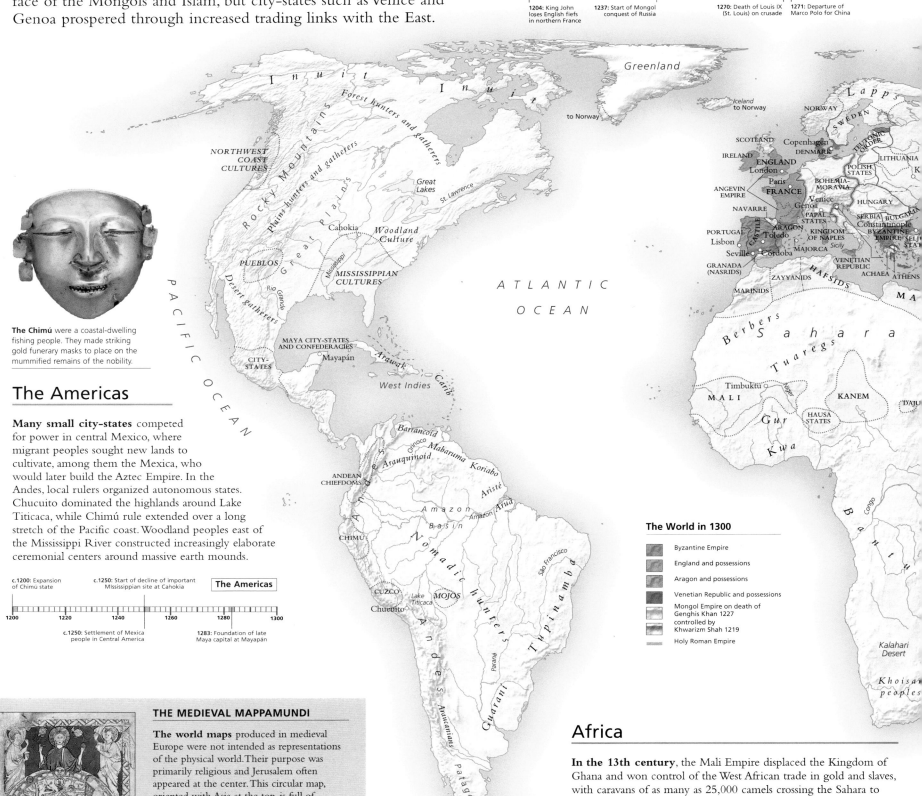

The Chimú were a coastal-dwelling fishing people. They made striking gold funerary masks to place on the mummified remains of the nobility.

The Americas

Many small city-states competed for power in central Mexico, where migrant peoples sought new lands to cultivate, among them the Mexica, who would later build the Aztec Empire. In the Andes, local rulers organized autonomous states. Chucuito dominated the highlands around Lake Titicaca, while Chimú rule extended over a long stretch of the Pacific coast. Woodland peoples east of the Mississippi River constructed increasingly elaborate ceremonial centers around massive earth mounds.

The Americas

- c.1200: Expansion of Chimú state
- c.1250: Settlement of Mexica people in Central America
- c.1250: Start of decline of important Mississippian site at Cahokia
- 1283: Foundation of late Maya capital at Mayapán

The World in 1300
- Byzantine Empire
- England and possessions
- Aragon and possessions
- Venetian Republic and possessions
- Mongol Empire on death of Genghis Khan 1227
- controlled by Khwarizm Shah 1219
- Holy Roman Empire

THE MEDIEVAL MAPPAMUNDI

The world maps produced in medieval Europe were not intended as representations of the physical world. Their purpose was primarily religious and Jerusalem often appeared at the center. This circular map, oriented with Asia at the top, is full of Christian symbolism, and is decorated with grotesque faces and mythical beasts.

A 13th-century English psalter contains this tiny world map or *mappamundi*, which measures just 4 inches across.

Africa

In the 13th century, the Mali Empire displaced the Kingdom of Ghana and won control of the West African trade in gold and slaves, with caravans of as many as 25,000 camels crossing the Sahara to North Africa. Meanwhile, the Swahili city-states on the East African coast exported goods through the trading networks of the Indian Ocean. Rulers of Mali and the Swahili city-states adopted Islam and built mosques and religious schools. Islam did not reach central and southern Africa, but the trade it generated led to the establishment of wealthy inland states such as the Kingdom of Great Zimbabwe.

West Asia

In 1258 the Mongols sacked Baghdad and overthrew the Abbasid Caliphate. Their leaders established themselves as Il-Khans, nominally subordinate to the Great Khan in China. Their empire extended almost to the Mediterranean, where their westward expansion was halted by the Mamluks of Egypt. By 1300 most Mongols of the Il-Khanate had embraced Islam, as had many of their fellow Mongols of the Golden Horde. Meanwhile, the Seljuks and other Turkic peoples consolidated their position in formerly Byzantine territory by establishing regional states.

This luster tile from 13th-century Persia is decorated with a verse from the Koran. The Mongols were too few to impose their beliefs on the peoples they conquered. Instead, many of them became Muslims.

THE MAGNETIC COMPASS

The Chinese had long known that a floating magnetized needle always points in the same direction. Their sailors started to make regular use of this fact in about 1100. By the 13th century, the magnetic compass was probably in widespread use among the Arab navigators of the Indian Ocean. In Europe, a written account of its principles appeared as early as 1190.

In the 13th century the Chinese simply floated a magnetized needle on water. This boxed compass is an early example.

SEE ALSO:

North America: pp.122–123

South America: pp.146–147

Africa: pp.162–163

Europe: pp.186–191

West Asia: pp.228–229

South and Southeast Asia: pp.244–245

North and East Asia: pp.262–265

West Asia

1219: Mongol invasion of Khwarizm Empire

1260: Battle of Ain Jalut; Mamluks defeat Mongol army north of Jerusalem

1299: Osman founds Ottoman state among the small Seljuk states in western Turkey

1200 — 1220 — 1240 — 1260 — 1280 — 1300

1231: Mongols reconquer resurgent Empire of the Khwarizm Shah

1258: Sack of Baghdad and fall of Abbasid Caliphate; Hülegü founds Il-Khanate

1265: Death of Hülegü

1295: Conversion of the Il-Khan Ghazan to Islam

North and East Asia

Genghis Khan invaded northern China in 1211, but the Southern Song Empire fell only after a long campaign (1260–79) directed by Kublai Khan. China was the richest of all the Mongol conquests. Kublai became emperor and founded the Yuan dynasty. He appointed many foreigners to govern the empire and fostered both maritime and overland trade with other lands throughout East Asia. From Korea (Koryo) the Mongols made two failed attempts to invade Japan.

Ghenghis Khan receives homage from the leaders of other Mongol tribes. White horsetails flying from his tent indicated that the Mongols were temporarily at peace. Black ones meant they were at war.

North and East Asia

1206: Temujin named Genghis Khan

1233: Mongols take Jin capital, Kaifeng

1264: Kublai elected Great Khan

1279: Foundation of Yuan dynasty

1294: Death of Kublai

1200 — 1220 — 1240 — 1260 — 1280 — 1300

1211: Mongols begin conquest of northern China

1274: First Mongol attempt to invade Japan

1292: Departure of Marco Polo from China

South and Southeast Asia

In 1206 Qutb al-din, leader of the Islamic raiders who had terrorized northern India for the past 30 years, fixed the capital of a new sultanate at Delhi. The Sultanate suffered occasional Mongol raids, while the Mongols made repeated forays from China into Annam and Pagan, without ever gaining secure control of the region. They also launched a massive seaborne attack on Java, but their tactics were ineffective in the island's tropical jungles.

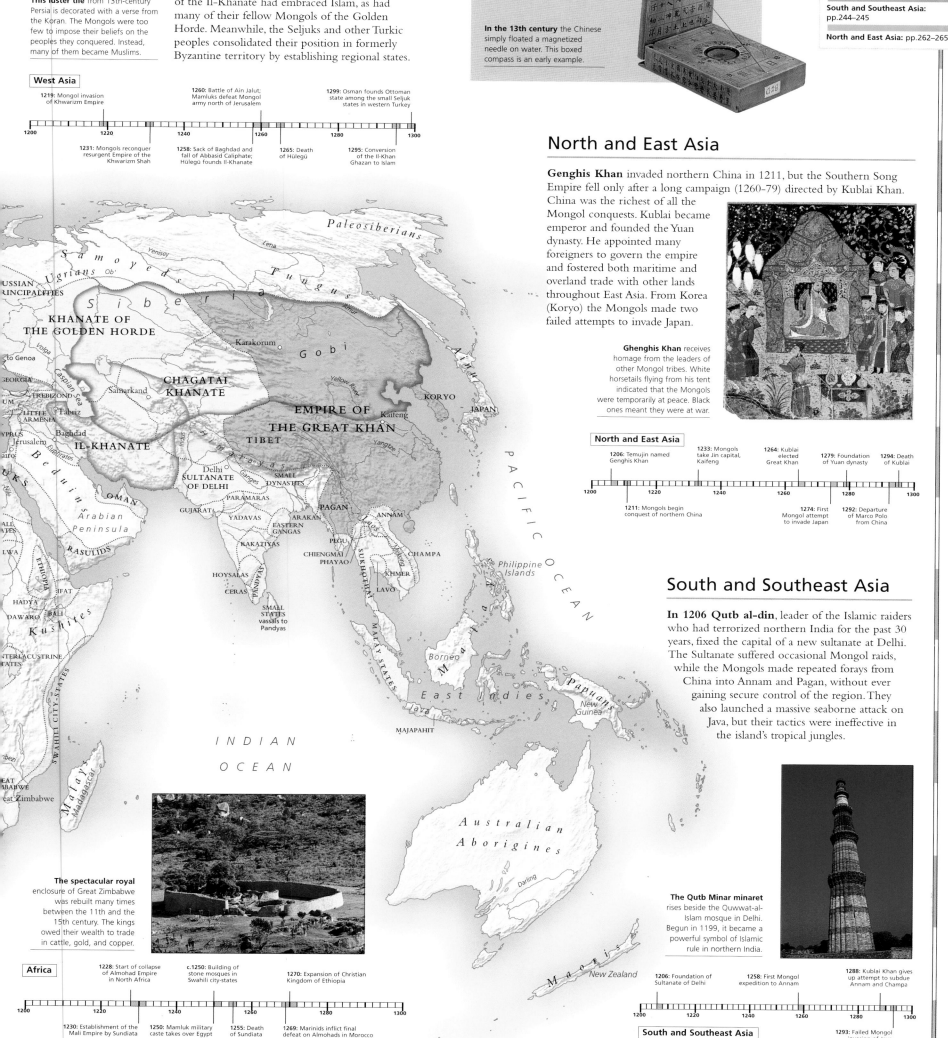

The spectacular royal enclosure of Great Zimbabwe was rebuilt many times between the 11th and the 15th century. The kings owed their wealth to trade in cattle, gold, and copper.

The Qutb Minar minaret rises beside the Quwwat-al-Islam mosque in Delhi. Begun in 1199, it became a powerful symbol of Islamic rule in northern India.

Africa

1228: Start of collapse of Almohad Empire in North Africa

c.1250: Building of stone mosques in Swahili city-states

1270: Expansion of Christian Kingdom of Ethiopia

1200 — 1220 — 1240 — 1260 — 1280 — 1300

1230: Establishment of the Mali Empire by Sundiata

1250: Mamluk military caste takes over Egypt

1255: Death of Sundiata

1269: Marinids inflict final defeat on Almohads in Morocco

1206: Foundation of Sultanate of Delhi

1258: First Mongol expedition to Annam

1288: Kublai Khan gives up attempt to subdue Annam and Champa

1200 — 1220 — 1240 — 1260 — 1280 — 1300

South and Southeast Asia

1293: Failed Mongol invasion of Java

THE AGE OF THE MONGOLS

Genghis Khan – the title means "universal ruler" – was born Temujin, son of a minor Mongol chief.

Genghis Khan, preceded by Jebe, one of his most trusted commanders, leads a cavalry charge. Jebe and another great general, Sübedei, made the astonishing raid into Russia in 1222 that first made Europe aware of the Mongols' existence.

THE NOMADIC HERDSMEN of the Mongolian steppe traded livestock, horses, and hides with the settled agricultural civilization of China to the south, but relations between the two were usually marked by hostility and suspicion. By the 13th century, the Chinese empire had become weak and fragmented. Into this power vacuum burst the Mongols, a fierce race of skilled horsemen, their normally warring tribes united under the inspired leadership of Genghis Khan. Genghis did not seek war at all costs; he first gave his enemies a chance to submit – on his terms. If they refused, he unleashed a campaign of terror, sacking cities and massacring entire populations. Although at first the Mongols numbered no more than a million, their ranks were swelled by Turks, Arabs, and other subject peoples. Genghis's successors extended his conquests across Asia and deep into Europe, but his empire then split into four khanates. By 1400, the Mongols were a divided and weakened force and most of their conquests had been lost.

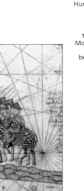

Caravan routes across Central Asia thrived in the climate of law and order imposed by Mongol rule. This illustration from the Catalan Atlas of 1375 shows a group of European merchants riding along the Silk Road.

The Mongol peace

The Mongols' chief aim was always to exact tribute from conquered peoples, but they also brought long periods of peace; travelers were able to cross Eurasia in safety along the old Silk Road. In the reign of Genghis Khan's grandson Möngke (1251–59) it was said that a virgin with a pot of gold on her head could walk unmolested across his empire. The two most famous travelers to benefit from the Mongol peace were the Venetian merchant Marco Polo, who claimed to have spent 17 years in the employment of Kublai Khan, and Ibn Battuta, a Muslim legal scholar from Tangier in Morocco, who also traveled as far as China.

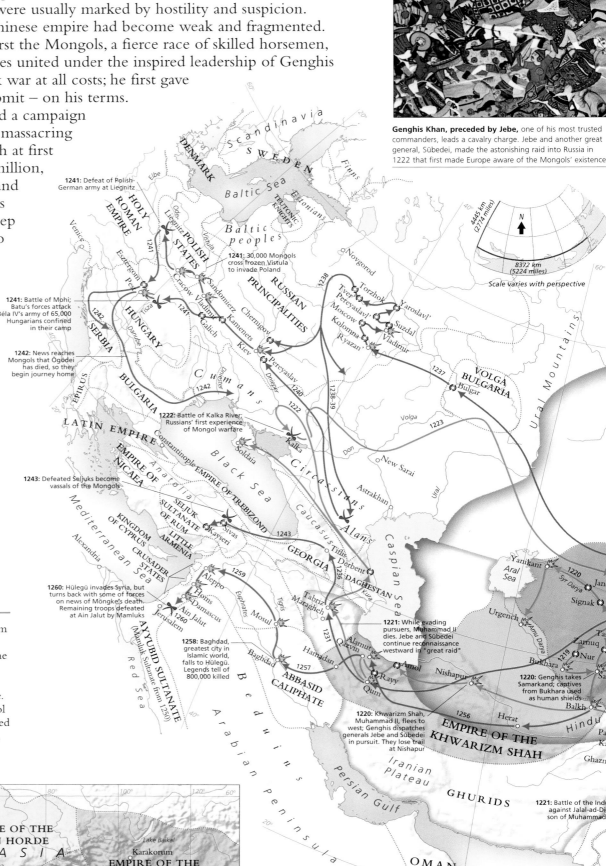

1241: Defeat of Polish-German army at Liegnitz

1241: 30,000 Mongols cross frozen Vistula to invade Poland

1241: Battle of Mohi; Batu's forces attack Béla IV's army of 65,000 Hungarians confined in their camp

1242: News reaches Mongols that Ögödei has died, so they begin journey home

1222: Battle of Kalka River; Russians' first experience of Mongol warfare

1243: Defeated Seljuks become vassals of the Mongols

1260: Hülegü invades Syria, but turns back with some of forces on news of Möngke's death. Remaining troops defeated at Ain Jalut by Mamluks

1258: Baghdad, greatest city in Islamic world, falls to Hülegü. Legends tell of 800,000 killed

1221: While evading pursuers, Muhammad II dies. Jebe and Sübedei continue reconnaissance westward in "great raid"

1220: Genghis takes Samarkand; captives from Bukhara used as human shields

1220: Khwarizm Shah, Muhammad II, flees to west; Genghis dispatches generals Jebe and Sübedei in pursuit. They lose trail at Nishapur

1221: Battle of the Indus against Jalal-ad-Din, son of Muhammad II

Scale varies with perspective

② Eurasia and Africa c.1300

route of Marco Polo 1271 — 1295   route of Ibn Battuta 1325 — 1345

⋮⋮⋮ disputed journeys of Ibn Battuta
— Silk Road

The Mongol peace

1235: Walled city built at Karakorum as fixed Mongol capital

1275: Marco Polo reaches Kublai's summer palace at Shangdu (Xanadu)

1325: Ibn Battuta's first pilgrimage to Mecca

1345–46: Ibn Battuta visits Southeast Asia and China

1264: Kublai defeats rival for title of Great Khan, ending civil war

1266: Kublai founds new capital at Khanbaliq (Beijing)

1292: Marco Polo given task of escorting Mongol princess to Hormuz

1334–41: Ibn Battuta serves as qadi (judge) in Delhi

1225   1250   1275   1300   1325   1350

The Mongol conquests

In less than 20 years, in a series of conquests without parallel in history, Genghis Khan shattered the Muslim states of Central Asia, overran northern China, and sent troops on a lightning raid into Russia. Genghis's immediate successor was his third son Ögödei, whose reign as Great Khan saw the destruction of the Jin and Khwarizm empires, continued fighting with Song China, and an invasion of Europe that reached Hungary and Poland. The conquest of the Song was completed by Kublai Khan, a grandson of Genghis, who became emperor of China, while Kublai's brother, Hülegü, founder of the Il-Khanate, destroyed the Abbasid Caliphate, sacking the great Islamic city of Baghdad. The first setback to Mongol expansion came at the hands of the Mamluks, who, in 1260, prevented their advance into Egypt at Ain Jalut.

Mongol conquests of the 13th century

1206: Mongols united by Genghis Khan
1211: First invasion of Jin Empire
1219: Genghis attacks Khwarizm
1227: Death of Genghis
1229: Ögödei elected Great Khan
1242: Batu founds Golden Horde
1260: Hülegü invades Syria; Mongols suffer first major defeat at Ain Jalut
1258: Sack of Baghdad
1279: Last Song resistance crushed
1281: Second failed invasion of Japan
1294: Death of Kublai

1200 1220 1240 1260 1280 1300

SEE ALSO:

Europe: pp.188–189

West Asia: pp.228–229

South and Southeast Asia: pp.244–245

North and East Asia: pp.262–265

At the siege of Hezhou in 1258–59, Mongol horsemen tried unsuccessfully to cross the Yangtze on a pontoon bridge of boats. The conquest of Song China was accomplished only after many protracted sieges.

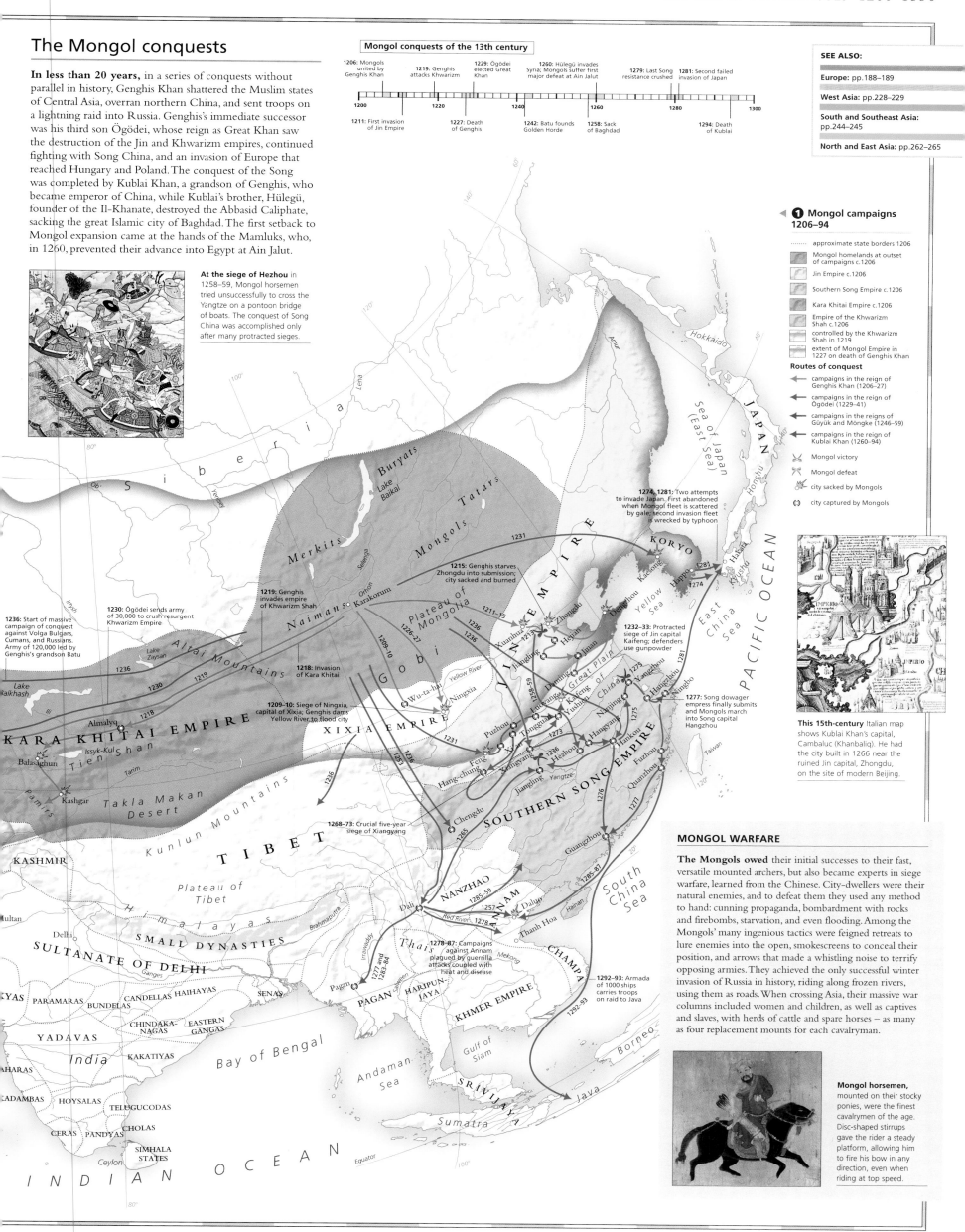

① Mongol campaigns 1206–94

- ········· approximate state borders 1206
- Mongol homelands at outset of campaigns c.1206
- Jin Empire c.1206
- Southern Song Empire c.1206
- Kara Khitai Empire c.1206
- Empire of the Khwarizm Shah c.1206
- controlled by the Khwarizm Shah in 1219
- extent of Mongol Empire in 1227 on death of Genghis Khan

Routes of conquest
- campaigns in the reign of Genghis Khan (1206–27)
- campaigns in the reign of Ögödei (1229–41)
- campaigns in the reigns of Güyük and Möngke (1246–59)
- campaigns in the reign of Kublai Khan (1260–94)
- ⚔ Mongol victory
- ⚔ Mongol defeat
- city sacked by Mongols
- city captured by Mongols

This 15th-century Italian map shows Kublai Khan's capital, Cambaluc (Khanbaliq). He had the city built in 1266 near the ruined Jin capital, Zhongdu, on the site of modern Beijing.

MONGOL WARFARE

The Mongols owed their initial successes to their fast, versatile mounted archers, but also became experts in siege warfare, learned from the Chinese. City-dwellers were their natural enemies, and to defeat them they used any method to hand: cunning propaganda, bombardment with rocks and firebombs, starvation, and even flooding. Among the Mongols' many ingenious tactics were feigned retreats to lure enemies into the open, smokescreens to conceal their position, and arrows that made a whistling noise to terrify opposing armies. They achieved the only successful winter invasion of Russia in history, riding along frozen rivers, using them as roads. When crossing Asia, their massive war columns included women and children, as well as captives and slaves, with herds of cattle and spare horses – as many as four replacement mounts for each cavalryman.

Mongol horsemen, mounted on their stocky ponies, were the finest cavalrymen of the age. Disc-shaped stirrups gave the rider a steady platform, allowing him to fire his bow in any direction, even when riding at top speed.

THE WORLD 1300–1400

DURING THE 14TH CENTURY epidemics of bubonic plague swept across the Old World from China and Korea to the west coast of Europe. Dramatic demographic decline led to economic and social disruption that weakened states throughout Eurasia and North Africa. In addition, the onset of the so-called "Little Ice Age," which would last till the 19th century, brought bad weather and poor harvests to many of the regions affected by plague. The Mongol empires, which had dominated Eurasia since the conquests of Genghis Khan in the 13th century, began to disintegrate, though the Khanate of the Golden Horde maintained its hegemony in southern Russia into the 15th century. In both China and Persia the Mongols were assimilated into the local population, but in China, a new dynasty, the Ming, introduced a Han Chinese aristocratic regime.

The Black Death reached Europe from Asia in 1347. In three years it probably killed one third of the population. The fear it generated is captured in this image of Death strangling a plague victim.

Europe

Europe struggled to recover from the social and economic disruption caused by the Black Death. Scarcity of labor led peasants and workers to seek improved conditions and higher wages, but landlords and employers resisted their demands, provoking many revolts in western Europe. France suffered too from the military campaigns of the Hundred Years' War, fueled by the dynastic ambitions of English kings. Religious differences also brought disorder. Rival popes residing in Rome and Avignon both claimed authority over the Catholic Church, while in England the Lollards challenged the authority and doctrine of the Church itself.

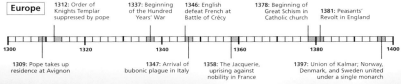

Europe

| 1312: Order of Knights Templar suppressed by pope | 1337: Beginning of the Hundred Years' War | 1346: English defeat French at Battle of Crécy | 1378: Beginning of Great Schism in Catholic church | 1381: Peasants' Revolt in England |

1300 · 1320 · 1340 · 1360 · 1380 · 1400

1309: Pope takes up residence at Avignon · 1347: Arrival of bubonic plague in Italy · 1358: The Jacquerie, uprising against nobility in France · 1397: Union of Kalmar; Norway, Denmark, and Sweden united under a single monarch

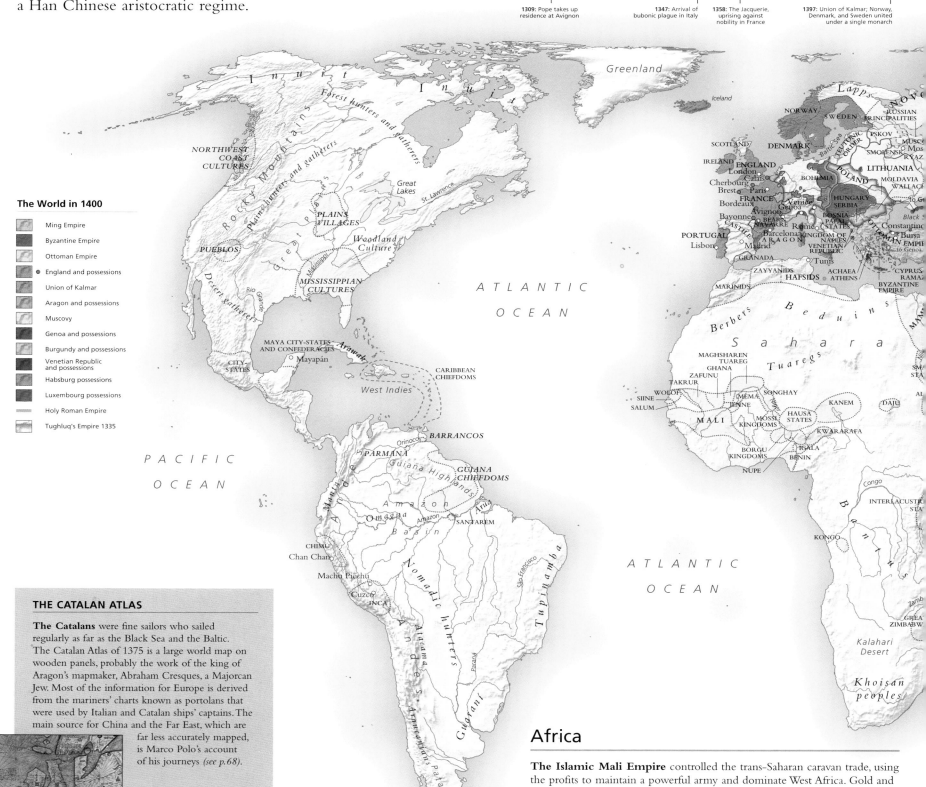

The World in 1400

- Ming Empire
- Byzantine Empire
- Ottoman Empire
- England and possessions
- Union of Kalmar
- Aragon and possessions
- Muscovy
- Genoa and possessions
- Burgundy and possessions
- Venetian Republic and possessions
- Habsburg possessions
- Luxembourg possessions
- Holy Roman Empire
- Tughluq's Empire 1335

THE CATALAN ATLAS

The Catalans were fine sailors who sailed regularly as far as the Black Sea and the Baltic. The Catalan Atlas of 1375 is a large world map on wooden panels, probably the work of the king of Aragon's mapmaker, Abraham Cresques, a Majorcan Jew. Most of the information for Europe is derived from the mariners' charts known as portolans that were used by Italian and Catalan ships' captains. The main source for China and the Far East, which are far less accurately mapped, is Marco Polo's account of his journeys (see p.68).

The Catalan map gives a comprehensive and accurate picture of the coastline and ports of Europe and North Africa.

Africa

The Islamic Mali Empire controlled the trans-Saharan caravan trade, using the profits to maintain a powerful army and dominate West Africa. Gold and slaves went north in exchange for salt, textiles, horses, and manufactured goods. Tales of the wealth of Mali spread to Europe and West Asia, especially after the ostentatious pilgrimage to Mecca made by one of the country's most powerful rulers, Mansa Musa. Many smaller states emerged in the region as rulers sought to ensure a regular supply of trade goods. The Swahili cities of East Africa were not hit by plague, but commercial traffic declined as their trading partners in Asia experienced social and economic disruption.

THE CANNON

The Chinese had a long tradition of using gunpowder weapons, including bamboo tubes that fired arrows and bullets. The English word "cannon" comes from the Italian *cannone*, meaning a large bamboo cane. Metal cannon were probably first used in China, but by the early 14th century were in action across Asia and in most of Europe. The earliest metal cannons in Europe were forged, but these were superseded by much larger ones cast using the technology initially developed for making church bells.

The cannon was primarily used as a siege weapon. Its effectiveness had a major influence on castle design.

West Asia

During the late 14th century the Turkish warrior chieftain Timur (Tamerlane), who claimed descent from Genghis Khan, carved out a vast Central Asian empire, and built himself a magnificent capital at Samarkand. Timur invaded India and sacked the city of Delhi, and he was planning an invasion of China when he died in 1405. One other empire expanded during this period – that of the Ottoman Turks, who seized Anatolia and encroached on Byzantine holdings in southeastern Europe. By 1400 the once-mighty Byzantine Empire consisted of Constantinople and a few coastal regions in Greece and western Anatolia that maintained maritime links with the capital.

Timur's ambition and cruelty revived memories of Genghis Khan. He instilled fear into conquered peoples and opponents of his rule by building towers studded with the severed heads of his victims.

SEE ALSO:

North America: pp.122–123

South America: pp.146–147

Africa: pp.162–163

Europe: pp.188–191

West Asia: pp.228–231

South and Southeast Asia: pp.242–243

North and East Asia: pp.262–267

West Asia

1326: Ottomans capture Byzantine city of Bursa and make it their capital
1347: Black Death reaches Baghdad and Constantinople
1370: Beginning of Timur's conquests
c.1380: Foundation of Janissary corps by Ottomans
1336: Birth of Timur
1354: First Ottoman conquests in southeastern Europe
1393: Sack of Baghdad by Timur
1300 1320 1340 1360 1380 1400

East Asia

Plague, floods, and famine all contributed to the buildup of Chinese resentment at Mongol rule. Local uprisings became increasingly frequent, culminating in 1356 in a rebellion in southeastern China, which carried Zhu Yuanzhang, founder of the Ming dynasty, to power. War with the Mongols continued for some years, but the Chinese drove them back to their original homelands in the north. Japan had successfully resisted Mongol attempts at invasion, but their own Kamakura shogunate collapsed in 1333. The new shoguns of the Ashikaga family never succeeded in exercising the same degree of control over the country.

The Ming emperors restored Chinese values after a century of Mongol rule. This statue portrays a guardian of the spirit world.

East Asia

1335: Rebellions against Mongol rule in China
1351: Massive flooding of Yellow River
1392: Foundation of Yi dynasty in Korea
1336: Foundation of Ashikaga shogunate in Japan
1368: Establishment of the Ming dynasty
1300 1320 1340 1360 1380 1400

South and Southeast Asia

In India, the Sultanate of Delhi reached its greatest extent in the reign of Tughluq, but by the end of the century had lost control of most of the peninsula. The small kingdoms of mainland Southeast Asia all maintained diplomatic and commercial links with Ming China. The new Thai kingdom of Siam proved especially skillful in its dealings with its powerful neighbor to the north. During the 14th century island Southeast Asia fell increasingly under the influence of the Majapahit empire based in Java. A Javanese navy, financed by taxes levied on the lucrative trade in spices, patrolled the waters of the archipelago and controlled maritime trade.

The marble dome of Tughluq's mausoleum rises above the ramparts of the fortified city he built at Delhi in 1321.

Mansa Musa, ruler of Mali, is depicted on the Catalan Atlas of 1375. Europeans were in awe of his reported wealth and the splendor of his court.

Africa

1331: Ibn Battuta's voyage to the Swahili cities of East Africa
1344: Ethiopia at its height at death of ruler Amde Sion
c.1390: Formation of the kingdom of Kongo
1324: Pilgrimage to Mecca by Mansa Musa of Mali
1347: Marinids take Tunis
1352: Ibn Battuta's travels to the Mali Empire
1300 1320 1340 1360 1380 1400

1320: Muhammad ibn Tughluq succeeds to Sultanate of Delhi
1343: Majapahit Empire completes conquest of Bali
1378: Sukhothai becomes vassal of Siam and is gradually absorbed
c.1350: Founding of Ayutthaya, capital of new kingdom of Siam
1398: Delhi sacked by Timur
South and Southeast Asia
1300 1320 1340 1360 1380 1400

Map labels

Paleosiberians
Samoyeds
Ugrians
Yenisey
Ob
Lena
Tungus
Amur
Siberia
KHANATE OF THE GOLDEN HORDE
KHANATE OF THE OIRATS
Gobi
BIZOND
Caspian Sea
Ardabil
LKADIR
Samarkand
CHAGATAI KHANATE
Yellow River
Beijing
KOREA
JAPAN
Baghdad
EMPIRE OF TIMUR
KASHMIR
TIBET
MING EMPIRE
Yangtze
Beduins
Himalayas
Delhi
SHARQIS
MALLA
SMALL STATES
SHAN STATES
IARES MEDINA
SIND
OMAN
Ganges
BENGAL
CHIENGMAI
ARIES OF MECCA
Mecca
Arabian Peninsula
KHANDESH
SMALL STATES
ARAKAN
EASTERN GANGAS
AVA
ANNAM
RASULIDS
BAHMANI KINGDOM
TELINGANA
TOUNGOO
LAOS
Mekong
THIOPIA
REDDIS
PEGU
IFAT
SUKHOTHAI
SIAM
CAMBODIA
CHAMPA
DAMA TATES
Ayutthaya
VIJAYANAGAR
SMALL STATES
Philippine Islands
ishites
PACIFIC OCEAN
Malay States
Borneo
Papuans
New Guinea
Malays Madagascar
PAJAJARAN
MAJAPAHIT
Java
Bali
INDIAN OCEAN
Australian Aborigines
Darling
New Zealand
Maoris

TRADE AND BIOLOGICAL DIFFUSION

The peripatetic black rat, at home in a wide range of human environments, was the host for plague-carrying fleas.

CAMPAIGNS OF IMPERIAL EXPANSION, mass migration, cross-cultural trade, and long-distance travel all facilitated the spread of agricultural crops, domesticated animals, and diseases throughout much of the Old World. From 500 to 1500 CE, an array of historical processes helped introduce biological species to new regions and peoples. Chinese rulers extended their authority south of the Yangtze River; Muslim armies pushed into India, Persia, and North Africa; Bantu-speaking peoples migrated throughout most of sub-Saharan Africa; Muslim merchants pursued commercial opportunities throughout the Indian Ocean basin and across the Sahara; and missionaries, pilgrims, diplomats, administrators, and other travelers ventured throughout Eurasia and North Africa. Biological exchanges resulting from these changes profoundly influenced the development of societies throughout the eastern hemisphere.

Skulls, crossbones, and other images of death were frequently represented in both religious and secular art during the period of the so-called "Black Death."

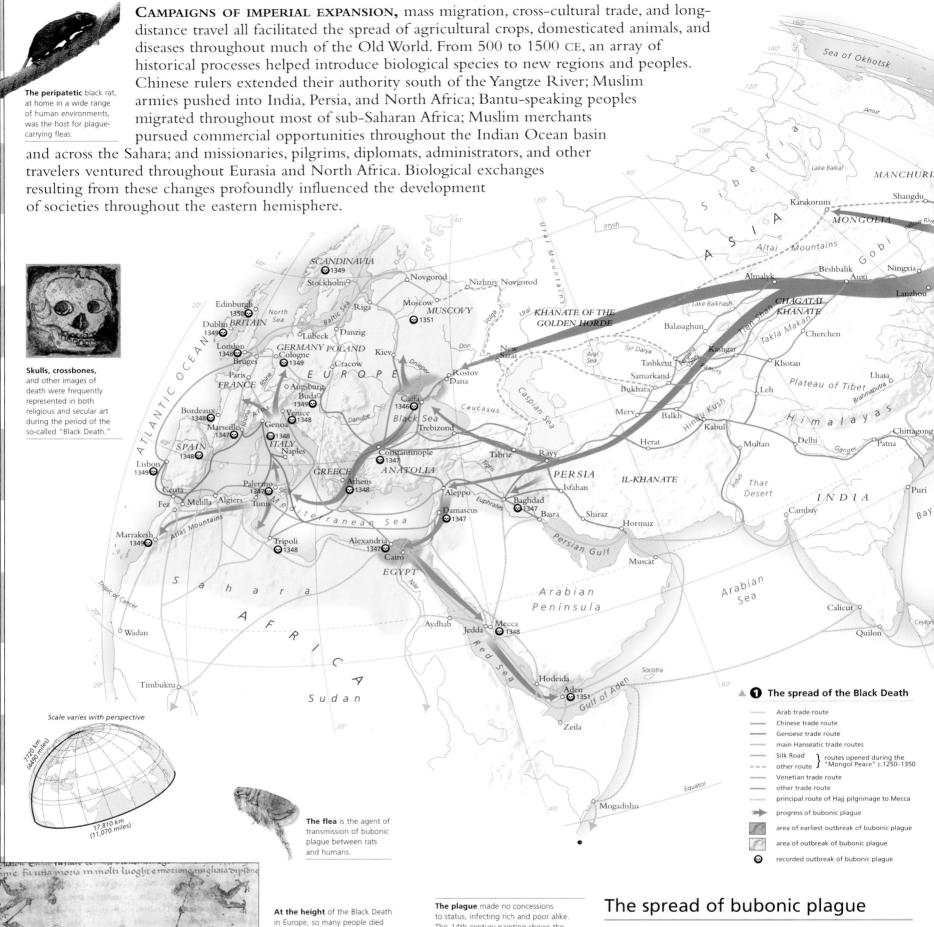

▲ ❶ The spread of the Black Death

- Arab trade route
- Chinese trade route
- Genoese trade route
- main Hanseatic trade routes
- Silk Road } routes opened during the
- other route } "Mongol Peace" c.1250–1350
- Venetian trade route
- other trade route
- principal route of Hajj pilgrimage to Mecca
- ➤ progress of bubonic plague
- ▨ area of earliest outbreak of bubonic plague
- ▨ area of outbreak of bubonic plague
- ☻ recorded outbreak of bubonic plague

Scale varies with perspective
7,720 km (4,800 miles)
17,810 km (11,070 miles)

The flea is the agent of transmission of bubonic plague between rats and humans.

At the height of the Black Death in Europe, so many people died daily that it was impossible to bury them all separately. The bodies were buried together in mass graves, usually outside the settlement walls. This manuscript illustration shows plague victims carried off by agents of Death.

The plague made no concessions to status, infecting rich and poor alike. This 14th-century painting shows the deathbed of Queen Anne of Bohemia, wife of King Richard II of England.

The spread of bubonic plague

Bubonic plague has long maintained an endemic presence in rodent communities in both Yunnan in southwest China and the Great Lakes region of East Africa. In the early 14th century, Mongol armies helped infected fleas spread from Yunnan to the rest of China. In 1331 an outbreak of plague reportedly carried away 90% of the population in parts of northeast China, and by the 1350s there were widely scattered epidemics throughout China. From China, bubonic plague spread rapidly west along the Silk Roads of Central Asia. By 1346 it had reached the Black Sea. Muslim merchants carried it south and west to southwest Asia, Egypt, and North Africa, while Italian merchants carried it west to Italy and then to northern and western Europe, where it became known as the Black Death. Up to one-third of Europe's population is thought to have died in this one episode.

The spread of plague during the 14th century

1320: Outbreak of plague in Yunnan province	**1330:** Plague reaches northeastern China	**1348:** Black Death hits Greece, Italy, France, Spain, Britain, and North Africa	**1351:** Black Death reaches much of northern Europe	

1310 — 1320 — 1330 — 1340 — 1350 — 1360

1320–30: Mongol armies help spread plague throughout China

1346: Plague reaches coast of Black Sea

1349: Black Death arrives in central Europe

The changing balance of world population

The spread of diseases and agricultural crops decisively influenced population levels throughout the Old World. In sub-Saharan Africa, for example, bananas grew well in forested regions that did not favor yams and millet, the earliest staples of Bantu cultivators. In 500 CE the population of sub-Saharan Africa was about 12 million, but following the spread of bananas it rose to 20 million by 1000 and 35.5 million by 1500. The spread of fast-ripening rice in China fueled an even more dramatic demographic surge: from 60 million in 1000, when fast-ripening rice went north from Vietnam to the Yangtze river valley, the Chinese population climbed to 100 million in 1100 and 115 million in 1200. However, beginning in the 14th century, bubonic plague raced through densely-populated lands from China to Morocco, thinning human numbers with drastic effect. By 1400, China's population had fallen to about 70 million.

SEE ALSO:

Africa: pp.162–163

Europe: pp.188–193

West Asia: pp.228–229

North and East Asia: pp.262–263

Many people were displaced by the depopulation of the Black Death and the societal changes that it wrought. Those reduced to begging often sought alms at the doors of churches or other religious foundations.

Some towns and villages suffered such depradations in population during the Black Death that they were abandoned by those who were left. The ruined church (left) is one of few remnants of the former village of Calceby, in the fenlands of eastern England.

❷ Distribution of world population c.1400 ▽

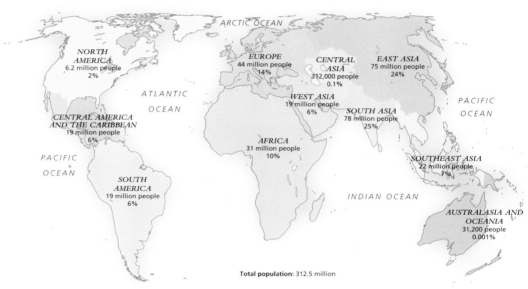

NORTH AMERICA
6.2 million people
2%

CENTRAL AMERICA AND THE CARIBBEAN
19 million people
6%

SOUTH AMERICA
19 million people
6%

EUROPE
44 million people
14%

CENTRAL ASIA
312,000 people
0.1%

WEST ASIA
19 million people
6%

EAST ASIA
75 million people
24%

SOUTH ASIA
78 million people
25%

AFRICA
31 million people
10%

SOUTHEAST ASIA
22 million people
7%

AUSTRALASIA AND OCEANIA
31,200 people
0.001%

ATLANTIC OCEAN

PACIFIC OCEAN

PACIFIC OCEAN

INDIAN OCEAN

ARCTIC OCEAN

Total population: 312.5 million

❸ The diffusion of staple crops to c.1500 ▶

Original source areas (pre-700)
- bananas
- sugarcane
- cotton
- sorghum

Spread of crops c.700–1500
- spread of bananas
- spread of sugarcane
- spread of cotton
- spread of sorghum

Areas to which crops had spread by 1500
- bananas
- sugarcane
- cotton
- sorghum

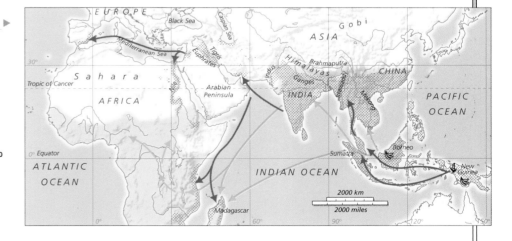

Sugar cane was taken westward to Europe from India from c.600 CE. This 16th-century engraving of a Sicilian sugar mill shows raw sugar being transformed into sugar loaves.

The diffusion of staple crops

A massive diffusion of agricultural crops took place between about 700 and 1400 CE. Most crops spread from tropical or subtropical lands in South and Southeast Asia to the more temperate regions of the eastern hemisphere. Many crops moved with the aid of Muslim merchants, administrators, diplomats, soldiers, missionaries, pilgrims, and other travelers who visited lands from Morocco and Spain to Java and southern China. Sugar cane, native to New Guinea, arrived in the Mediterranean basin as a result of this biological diffusion, along with hard wheat, eggplants, spinach, artichokes, lemons, and limes. Other crops that dispersed widely during this era included rice, sorghum, bananas, coconuts, watermelons, oranges, mangoes, cotton, indigo, and henna.

THE WORLD 1400–1500

BY 1500 MOST OF THE EASTERN HEMISPHERE had recovered from the depopulation caused by the Black Death in the 14th century. China began the 15th century by sponsoring naval expeditions in the Indian Ocean, but in the 1430s the Ming rulers ended these voyages and concentrated on their land empire. In Southwest Asia, two Turkish peoples established strong empires – the Ottomans in Anatolia and the Safavids in Persia. European states, meanwhile, were starting to build central governments with standing armies and gunpowder weapons. In the course of the 15th century Portuguese mariners settled the Atlantic islands, explored the west coast of Africa, and completed a sea voyage to India. It was, however, a Spanish expedition under the Genoese Columbus that crossed the Atlantic to make contact with the Americas, where the Aztec and Inca empires ruled over complex organized agricultural societies.

North America

The Aztec Empire reached its height in the late 1400s, exacting heavy tribute from the small city-states it had conquered. Through trade, Aztec influence reached far beyond the borders of the empire, extending across most of Central America as far as the Pueblo farmers north of the Rio Grande. In the woodlands around the Mississippi River, mound-building peoples maintained sizeable communities based on the cultivation of corn.

Human sacrifice to the sun god Huitzilopochtli was the core of the Aztec religion. Thousands of prisoners might be killed in a single ceremony.

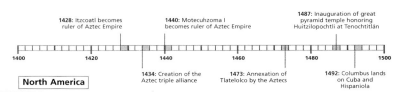

1428: Itzcoatl becomes ruler of Aztec Empire
1440: Motecuhzoma I becomes ruler of Aztec Empire
1487: Inauguration of great pyramid temple honoring Huitzilopochtli at Tenochtitlán

North America

1400 1420 1440 1460 1480 1500

1434: Creation of the Aztec triple alliance
1473: Annexation of Tlatelolco by the Aztecs
1492: Columbus lands on Cuba and Hispaniola

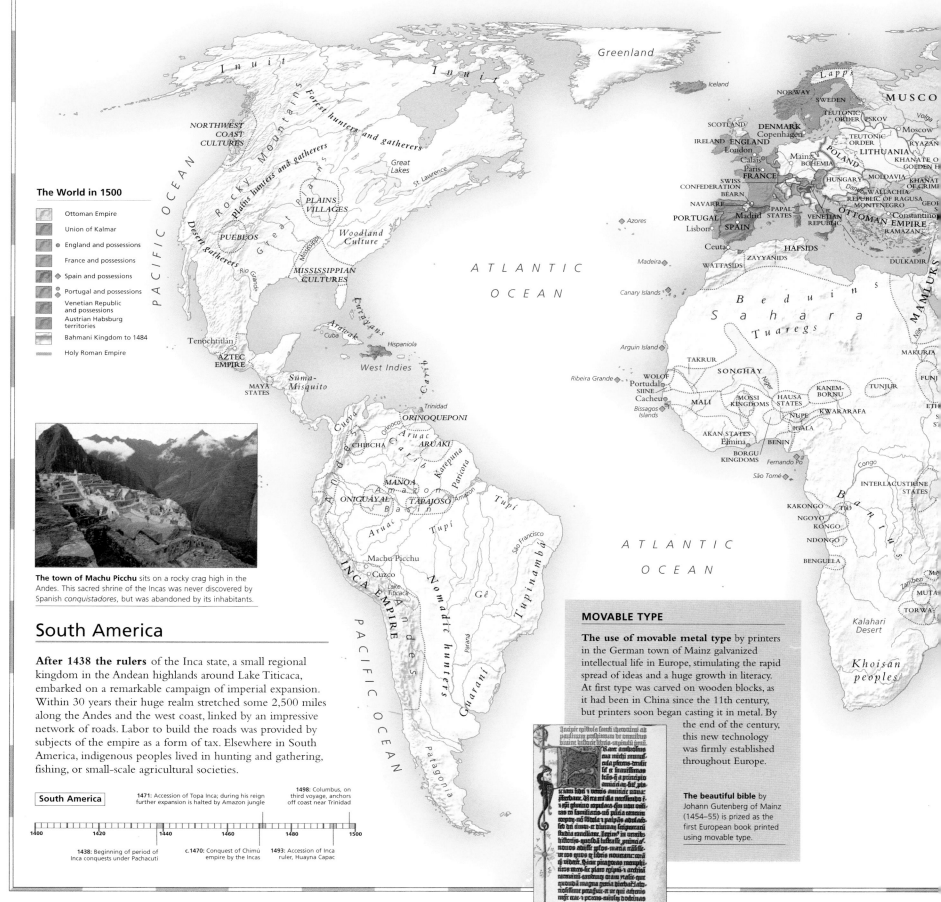

The World in 1500

- Ottoman Empire
- Union of Kalmar
- England and possessions
- France and possessions
- Spain and possessions
- Portugal and possessions
- Venetian Republic and possessions
- Austrian Habsburg territories
- Bahmani Kingdom to 1484
- Holy Roman Empire

The town of Machu Picchu sits on a rocky crag high in the Andes. This sacred shrine of the Incas was never discovered by Spanish *conquistadores*, but was abandoned by its inhabitants.

South America

After 1438 the rulers of the Inca state, a small regional kingdom in the Andean highlands around Lake Titicaca, embarked on a remarkable campaign of imperial expansion. Within 30 years their huge realm stretched some 2,500 miles along the Andes and the west coast, linked by an impressive network of roads. Labor to build the roads was provided by subjects of the empire as a form of tax. Elsewhere in South America, indigenous peoples lived in hunting and gathering, fishing, or small-scale agricultural societies.

South America

1400 1420 1440 1460 1480 1500

1471: Accession of Topa Inca; during his reign further expansion is halted by Amazon jungle
1498: Columbus, on third voyage, anchors off coast near Trinidad

1438: Beginning of period of Inca conquests under Pachacuti
c.1470: Conquest of Chimú empire by the Incas
1493: Accession of Inca ruler, Huayna Capac

MOVABLE TYPE

The use of movable metal type by printers in the German town of Mainz galvanized intellectual life in Europe, stimulating the rapid spread of ideas and a huge growth in literacy. At first type was carved on wooden blocks, as it had been in China since the 11th century, but printers soon began casting it in metal. By the end of the century, this new technology was firmly established throughout Europe.

The beautiful bible by Johann Gutenberg of Mainz (1454–55) is prized as the first European book printed using movable type.

Europe

Sixtus IV, elected in 1471, was typical of the popes of the Renaissance. A worldly, nepotistic prince, he commissioned great works of art and architecture, including the Sistine Chapel.

The 15th century saw the start of the Renaissance, a flowering of architecture, art, and humanist idealism inspired by Classical models. The city-states of Italy were the cultural leaders of Europe, but political power was shifting toward the "new monarchs," who created strong, centralized kingdoms in England, France, and Spain. Poland dominated eastern Europe, but here the future lay with Muscovy, where Ivan III launched Russian expansion to the east and south and in 1472 assumed the title of "tsar."

MARTIN BEHAIM'S GLOBE

Martin Behaim was a geographer of Nuremberg who visited Portugal and sailed down the west coast of Africa with Portuguese mariners in the 1480s. His globe, produced in 1490–92, is the oldest surviving globe in the world. Since he knew nothing of the existence of America, he depicted the island of "Cipangu" (Japan) and the east Asian mainland directly across the Atlantic from western Europe.

Martin Behaim's globe gives a very good picture of how Columbus must have imagined the world before he set sail across the Atlantic Ocean.

SEE ALSO:

North America: pp.122–123

South America: pp.146–147

Africa: pp.162–163

Europe: pp.192–193

West Asia: pp.228–231

South and Southeast Asia: pp.244–245

North and East Asia: pp.264–267

Europe

| 1415: English defeat French at Agincourt | 1429: English siege of Orléans relieved by Joan of Arc | 1454: Peace of Lodi ends wars in Italy | 1480: Muscovy throws off Mongol yoke | 1492: Muslim Granada falls to Spain |

1400 – **1420** – **1440** – **1460** – **1480** – **1500**

| 1417: End of Schism in Catholic church | 1453: Fall of Bordeaux to France ends Hundred Years' War | 1469: Marriage of Ferdinand of Aragon and Isabella of Castile | 1494: Invasion of Italy by Charles VIII of France |

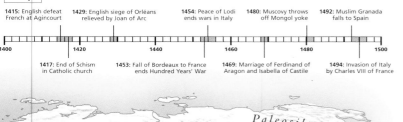

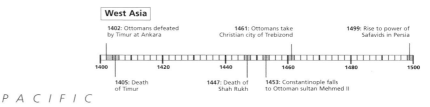

The fall of Constantinople removed the major Christian stronghold barring Islam's spread to the west. The small defending force of Byzantines and Italians was no match for the besieging army of 100,000.

West Asia

When Timur died in 1405, his empire was divided among his four sons. After a series of quarrels, Shah Rukh, who inherited the eastern part, presided over an era of peace, in which the arts and architecture flourished. The Shaybanids, who expanded south across the Syr Darya, were descendants of Genghis Khan. However, a new power was rising that would eclipse the Mongol dynasties that vied to control Persia – the Shi'ite Safavids. In the west, the Ottoman Turks, led by Sultan Mehmed II ("the Conqueror") and aided by powerful cannons, took Constantinople in 1453 and put an end to the Byzantine Empire.

West Asia

| 1402: Ottomans defeated by Timur at Ankara | 1461: Ottomans take Christian city of Trebizond | 1499: Rise to power of Safavids in Persia |

1400 – **1420** – **1440** – **1460** – **1480** – **1500**

| 1405: Death of Timur | 1447: Death of Shah Rukh | 1453: Constantinople falls to Ottoman sultan Mehmed II |

PACIFIC OCEAN

This painting on silk shows the courtyards of the Forbidden City, the compound of the imperial palace at the center of Beijing. The Ming capital was moved north from Nanjing to Beijing in 1421 during Yung Luo's campaign against the Mongols.

East and Southeast Asia

The Ming dynasty consolidated its hold on China, rebuilding the Great Wall to prevent raids by Mongol Oirats to the north. After Zheng He's epic but costly voyages in the Indian Ocean, the Ming rulers adopted a policy of self-sufficiency, discouraging travel and trade. In contrast to this defensive, inward-looking attitude, Southeast Asia thrived on trade. The most important entrepôt was Malacca. By 1500 its population was about 50,000, and it was reported that 84 languages could be heard in the city's streets.

East and Southeast Asia

| c.1400: Foundation of Malacca | 1424: End of long Ming campaign against Mongols | 1445: Conversion of Malacca to Islam | 1472: Birth of Neoconfucian philosopher Wang Yangming |

1400 – **1420** – **1440** – **1460** – **1480** – **1500**

| 1405: Beginning of Zheng He's voyages in Indian Ocean | 1449: Mongols defeat Chinese and capture emperor | 1471: Annamites expand to south by invading Champa |

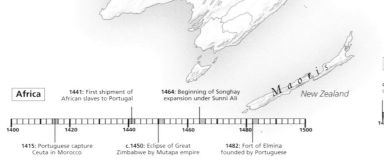

This bronze statue of a Portuguese soldier was made in Benin, one of Portugal's West African trading partners.

Africa

Between the 1460s and 1490s the Songhay ruler Sunni Ali conquered Mali and took over the Saharan caravan trade. Meanwhile, the Portuguese explored the west coast, where African rulers, seeing opportunities for trade, laid the foundations for the small kingdoms of Akan and Benin. Sailors from the Swahili city-states in East Africa helped Vasco da Gama understand the local monsoon winds and complete his voyage to India.

Africa

| 1441: First shipment of African slaves to Portugal | 1464: Beginning of Songhay expansion under Sunni Ali |

1400 – **1420** – **1440** – **1460** – **1480** – **1500**

| 1415: Portuguese capture Ceuta in Morocco | c.1450: Eclipse of Great Zimbabwe by Mutapa empire | 1482: Fort of Elmina founded by Portuguese |

GLOBAL KNOWLEDGE

Knowledge of the world and its peoples was colored by hearsay and travelers' tales.

THE GLOBAL WORLD VIEW is a relatively modern concept. The Americas were unknown to Old World Eurasia until 500 years ago, and each of the major cultural regions had discrete world views of varying extents. Each region had developed its own means of subsistence, and technologies which were direct responses to their immediate environment. In Eurasia, ideas, faiths, and technical achievements were spread by trade, migration, and cultural or political expansion; thus the imprint of Buddhism, Christianity, and Islam was widespread, and technical ideas as diverse as printing and gunpowder, originating in East Asia, had reached Europe. Mapping in one form or another was used by all cultures as a means of recording geographical information and knowledge, although pathfinding and navigation was usually a matter of handed-down knowledge, experience, and word of mouth.

❶ Global economies and technologies c.1500

Principal economies

- hunting and gathering
- herding/pastoralism
- hand cultivation
- plow cultivation
- hand cultivation and hunting and gathering
- slash and burn farming
- terraced farming
- uninhabited

The Americas

Both the Aztecs of Central America and the Incas of the Andes were still in the process of consolidating their young empires when the first Europeans arrived. Although there is evidence in both regions of extensive trading contacts, geographical obstacles (deserts, jungle) and relative immaturity meant their worlds were closely defined.

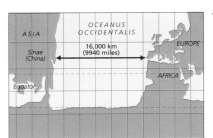

❷ The Americas ▲

- Aztec Empire
- known world 1500
- Inca Empire
- known world 1500

The size of the globe

The rediscovery of Classical texts was an important stimulus to the development of technology, science, and the arts, which flowered in the European Renaissance. European cartographers began to build a more detailed world map, using the works of Classical geographers such as Strabo and Ptolemy. The voyage of Bartolomeu Dias (1487–88) around the Cape of Good Hope established the limits of Africa; but in 1492, when Columbus made landfall in the Caribbean four weeks after leaving the Canary Islands, he assumed he had reached China (Cathay) rather than the West Indies. Although the circumnavigation by Magellan and del Cano some 30 years later (1519–22) dispelled many uncertainties, the accurate charting of the world's oceans and coasts would not be completed until the 20th century.

❽ The Ptolemaic map of the world ◀

❾ The Behaim map of the world 1492 ◀

→ Marco Polo 1271-75
Marco Polo assumed he had travelled 16,000 miles instead of 7000 miles

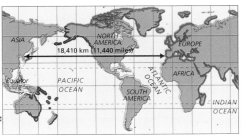

❿ The modern map of the world ◀

Coasts charted by

- 1500
- 1600
- 1700
- 1800
- 1900

❶ Global economies and technologies c.1500

Significant technologies

- **draft animals**
  - buffalo
  - oxen
  - horse/mule
  - camel
  - elephant
  - llama/alpaca
- **transport**
  - wheeled vehicles
  - dragged vehicles
- **hydraulics**
  - canals
  - aqueducts
  - irrigation
- **architecture**
  - temporary shelters
  - post and lintel
  - barrel vaulting
  - groin vaulting
- **navigation**
  - riverine
  - coastal
  - oceanic
  - lodestone/compass
- **warfare**
  - thrown missiles
  - archery
  - gunpowder
- **power**
  - windmills
  - watermills
  - X technology not developed
- **recording of knowledge**
  - knowledge recorded in writing
  - knowledge preserved orally
  - empirical cartographic tradition

The Muslim World

The most extensive and cosmopolitan of the Old World cultures, by 1500 Islam straddled large extents of three continents, stretching from the islands of the southwest Pacific to the shores of the Atlantic. Knowledge acquired from trade and travel underpinned much Muslim cultural hegemony and scholarship.

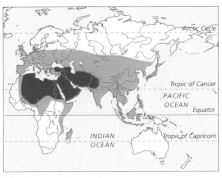

❸ The Muslim world ◀ ▲

- Muslim heartland
- known world 1500

❻ South Asia ▼

- South Asian states
- known world 1500

South Asia

In 1500, India was about to become subject to Muslim (Mughal) rule. Nevertheless its position on the crossroads of trade across the Indian Ocean, and overland routes from East and Southeast Asia, dated back many centuries, and its exports were known in Europe. Although essentially inward-looking, South Asian rulers and scholars had an extensive knowledge of the Old World.

Europe

By the end of the 15th century, Europe was poised on the brink of rapid territorial expansion. Technically sophisticated and resourceful, the Europeans had built up, through trade and travel, a fairly detailed knowledge of much of the Old World, from coastal Africa, through Arabia and southern Asia, to China and the many islands of the East Indies.

5 Europe

■ Western Christendom
□ known world 1492

East Asia

China, Korea, and Japan, although frequently isolationist – the Chinese "Middle Kingdom" regarded itself, with some justification, as the most powerful in the world – had nevertheless acquired considerable knowledge of the Old World, illustrated by the ambassadorial voyages of the Ming admiral Zheng He throughout the Indian Ocean (1405–33).

4 East Asia

■ charted by Chinese c.1500
□ known world c.1500

SEE ALSO:

North America: pp.118–119

South America: pp.142–143

Africa: pp.156–157

Europe: pp.172–173

West Asia: pp.218–219

South and Southeast Asia: pp.238–239

North and East Asia: 256–257

Australasia and Oceania: pp.278–279

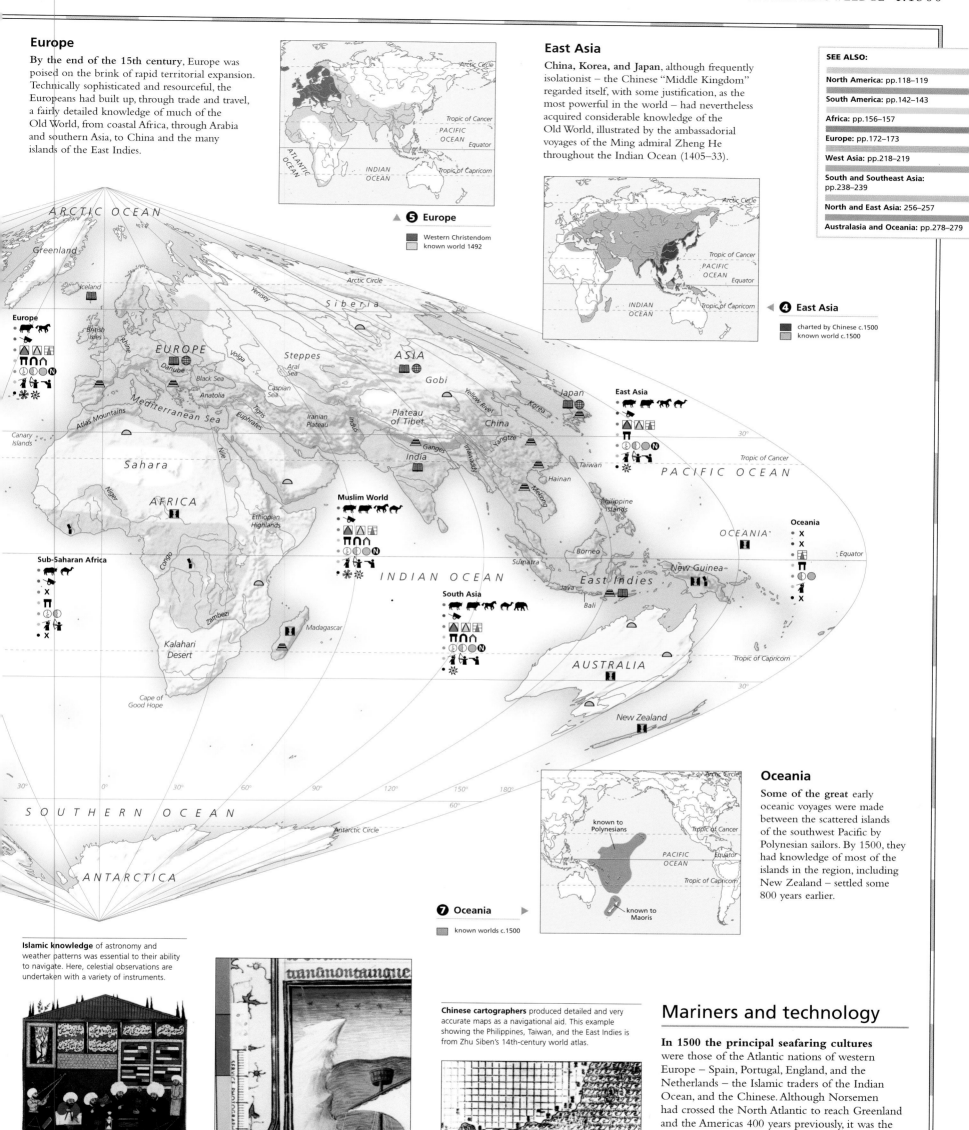

Oceania

Some of the great early oceanic voyages were made between the scattered islands of the southwest Pacific by Polynesian sailors. By 1500, they had knowledge of most of the islands in the region, including New Zealand – settled some 800 years earlier.

7 Oceania

■ known worlds c.1500

Islamic knowledge of astronomy and weather patterns was essential to their ability to navigate. Here, celestial observations are undertaken with a variety of instruments.

European navigators used an astrolabe, which gave an approximate postion in relation to the position of the stars. For lunar and solar measures, an almanac was also necessary.

Chinese cartographers produced detailed and very accurate maps as a navigational aid. This example showing the Philippines, Taiwan, and the East Indies is from Zhu Siben's 14th-century world atlas.

Mariners and technology

In 1500 the principal seafaring cultures were those of the Atlantic nations of western Europe – Spain, Portugal, England, and the Netherlands – the Islamic traders of the Indian Ocean, and the Chinese. Although Norsemen had crossed the North Atlantic to reach Greenland and the Americas 400 years previously, it was the navigators from Atlantic Europe who, in the 15th century, began the systematic exploration of Atlantic island groups and the African coastline. When they sailed east into the Indian Ocean, they benefited from the superior local knowledge of Arab, and later, Chinese navigators.

THE WORLD 1500–1600

IN THE 16TH CENTURY Spain seized a vast land empire that encompassed much of South and Central America, the West Indies, and the Philippine Islands. Meanwhile, the Portuguese acquired a largely maritime empire stretching from Brazil to Malacca and Macao. Ferdinand Magellan, a Portuguese in the service of Spain, demonstrated that all the world's oceans were linked and sea lanes were established through the Indian, Atlantic, and Pacific oceans, creating for the first time a genuinely global trading network. Although the Portuguese traded with the Ming Empire and Japan, cultural contact between Europeans and East Asia was limited. In Africa, too, European impact barely extended beyond the coast. Missionaries took the Catholic faith to distant parts of the Spanish and Portuguese empires, but in Europe the Church of Rome faced the threat of the Reformation, while Catholic kingdoms fought to stem Ottoman expansion in the Mediterranean and into the Habsburg lands of Central Europe.

Europe

The Protestant Reformation dominated 16th-century Europe. Rulers in Scandinavia, England, Scotland, and many German states abandoned the Roman church and took over monasteries and the running of church affairs. In France Protestants fought Catholics in a debilitating round of civil wars (1562–98) and religion was a major factor in the Dutch revolt against Spanish rule in 1565. The kings of Spain championed Catholicism and promoted missions worldwide. In the east, Russia's tsars extended their empire to the Caspian Sea and western Siberia.

Spanish troops raid a convoy in a scene typical of the atrocities of the Dutch Wars of Independence.

Europe					
	1519: Charles V elected Holy Roman Emperor	1545: Council of Trent called to counter threat of Protestantism	1580: Philip II of Spain seizes Portuguese crown		1598: Edict of Nantes ends over 30 years of religious wars in France
1500	1520	1540	1560	1580	1600
1517: Martin Luther's 95 Theses attack abuses of Catholic church	1534: Act of Supremacy; Henry VIII of England breaks with Rome	1565: Dutch Revolt starts long series of wars to gain independence from Spain	1588: English defeat Spanish Armada		

A Spanish *conquistador* rides a llama. The prime concern for most of the Spanish colonists granted large estates in the Americas was to exploit the labor of the native peoples.

The Americas

The arrival of the Spanish transformed the Americas. Their horses, iron weapons, and guns gave the *conquistadores* a military advantage over the indigenous peoples, but these alone might not have been sufficient without the devastating effect of the lethal diseases they introduced. The Spanish won control of all the major Caribbean islands by 1511, then in 1519–22 Hernán Cortés conquered the Aztecs, and in 1531–32 Francisco Pizarro overcame the Inca Empire. The more gradual colonization of Brazil by the Portuguese began in the 1530s, when nobles and entrepreneurs established plantations along its coast.

The Americas				
1502: Start of reign of last Aztec emperor, Montezuma II	1519: Cortés reaches Tenochtitlán (now Mexico), capital of the Aztec Empire	1545: Opening of vast silver mine at Potosí	1580: Philip II of Spain becomes king of Portugal and its Brazilian empire	
1500	1520	1540	1560	1580	1600
1510: First African slaves brought to Americas	1527: Death of Inca emperor Huayna Capac ignites civil war	1533: Pizarro captures Inca capital Cuzco	1549: Portuguese royal government established in Brazil	c.1575: Brazil becomes world's largest sugar producer

Columbus made his first crossing of the Atlantic in a square-rigged caravel similar to the model below.

SHIPS OF THE AGE OF EXPLORATION

The ships used by Columbus and other European explorers at the end of the 16th century were usually small caravels between 60 and 200 tons. Square-rigged on the main- and foremasts, they had a lateen sail for tacking against the wind. However, once the Spanish and Portuguese had learned to use the trade winds of the Atlantic and Indian oceans, they built huge square-rigged carracks with high castles in the stern. With a laden weight of up to 1,600 tons, they were designed to maximize the cargoes of spices and precious metals shipped back from the East Indies and the Americas.

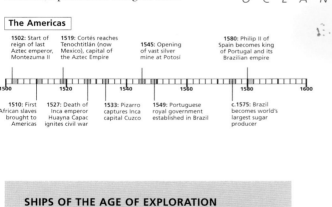

This cast bronze horse and rider is an impressive example of the stylized sculpture of Benin.

Africa

While most of North Africa fell to the Ottoman Empire, Morocco remained an independent champion of Islam, dealing a mortal blow to Portuguese expansion in the region and conquering Songhay to gain control of the valuable trans-Saharan caravan trade. Many of the small West African states had trade links both with Morocco and the Portuguese, who established a fortified trading post at Elmina.

West Asia

In the 16th century the Ottoman Empire expanded into Southwest Asia, North Africa, and southeastern Europe. The Ottoman navy was the preeminent power in the Mediterranean until its defeat by a Christian fleet at Lepanto in 1571, and Muslim vessels dominated the region's shipping. Ottoman rulers clashed constantly with the Safavids in Persia, and in the late 16th and early 17th centuries the two empires fought for control of Mesopotamia and the Caucasus. Many earlier Ottoman gains were reversed during the reign of Shah Abbas the Great, the Safavid ruler from 1588 to 1629.

Suleiman the Magnificent extended Ottoman rule far into southeastern Europe. In this miniature, he is seen receiving homage from his many Christian vassals.

West Asia

1507: Portuguese victory over Ottoman and Arab fleet at Diu	**1520:** Suleiman the Magnificent becomes Ottoman sultan	**1566:** Suleiman succeeded by Selim II	**1588:** Abbas I the Great becomes Safavid shah	

1500 — 1520 — 1540 — 1560 — 1580 — 1600

1514: Ottoman victory over Safavids at Çaldiran	**1526:** Battle of Mohács: Ottomans crush Hungarian army	**1571:** Battle of Lepanto; Ottoman navy defeated by united Christian fleet off Greek coast	**1587:** Isfahan becomes capital of Safavid Empire	

THE NEW WORLD BY ABRAHAM ORTELIUS

Abraham Ortelius was a mapseller from Antwerp whose *Theatrum Orbis Terrarum* of 1570 is considered the first modern atlas. He was not an original cartographer, but he traveled widely in search of reliable sources and his atlas sold well throughout Europe for over 40 years. His map of the New World was a fairly accurate summary of European explorers' knowledge of the Americas and the Pacific. The vast southern continent, *Terra Australis*, a relic of the Classical geography of Claudius Ptolemy, was a feature of most maps of the period. It includes Tierra del Fuego and part of the coast of New Guinea, but the rest is pure conjecture. Ortelius was a contemporary of Gerardus Mercator. Between them, the two great mapmakers did much to shift the center of European cartography from Italy to the Low Countries.

The map gives a fairly accurate picture of Central America and the Caribbean; however, many parts of America had still not been explored by Europeans at all.

SEE ALSO:

North America: pp.124–125

South America: pp.146–149

Africa: pp.162–163

Europe: pp.194–195

West Asia: pp.230–231

South and Southeast Asia: pp.244–247

North and East Asia: pp.264–267

South and Southeast Asia

South and Southeast Asia

1510: Portuguese conquest of Goa	**1526:** Babur conquers Sultanate of Delhi	**1563:** Burmese King Bayinnaung invades Siam	**1600:** English East India Company founded

1500 — 1520 — 1540 — 1560 — 1580 — 1600

1511: Portuguese take Malacca	**1556:** Akbar becomes Mughal emperor	**1565:** Spanish fleet claims Philippines in name of King Philip II	

In 1523 the Chagatai Turk Babur invaded northern India, founding the Mughal dynasty of Islamic rulers. The empire was consolidated by Babur's grandson, Akbar. Mughal rulers concentrated on their land empire and agriculture, allowing the Portuguese to maintain coastal trading posts and a flourishing colony at Goa. Portugal also conquered Malacca and the "Spice Islands" of the Moluccas. The dominant power in mainland Southeast Asia was Burma, which reached its largest extent under King Bayinnaung, who conquered Siam and Laos and installed puppet rulers.

The richest prize for European merchants in South and Southeast Asia was control of the valuable spice trade. This French illustration shows the pepper harvest in southern India.

Africa

c.1500: Establishment of forest states of Oyo and Benin	**1517:** Ottomans conquer Mamluks in Egypt	**1578:** Moroccans crush invading Portuguese	

1500 — 1520 — 1540 — 1560 — 1580 — 1600

1505: First Portuguese trading posts in East Africa	**1546:** Songhay destroys Mali Empire	**1570:** Establishment of Portuguese colony in Angola	**1591:** Songhay Empire falls to Morocco

The World in 1600

- Ming Empire
- Ottoman Empire
- Spain and possessions
- Portugal and possessions (ruled by Kings of Spain 1580–1640)
- England and possessions
- Austrian Habsburg territories
- France
- Denmark and possessions
- Venetian Republic and possessions
- United Provinces (fighting for independence from Spain)
- Dutch (United Provinces) possessions
- Mughal Empire at Akbar's accession, 1556
- under Burmese control, 1575
- Songhay to 1590
- Holy Roman Empire

THE AGE OF EUROPEAN EXPANSION

The Portuguese
Vasco da Gama was the first European navigator to reach India by sea.

THE 16TH CENTURY saw the expansion of several of the great European nations far beyond their continental limits. Explorers searching for new sources of luxury goods and precious metals began to open up new territories which monarchs such as Philip II of Spain quickly built up into great empires in the "New World." The Spanish and Portuguese, inspired by the voyages of Columbus and da Gama, led the way, closely followed by the Dutch and the English. The explorers were aided by technological advances in shipbuilding, navigational equipment, and cartography. At the start of the 16th century, the Americas were virtually unknown to Europeans; by 1700, outposts of a greater European empire had been established almost everywhere the explorers landed.

European voyages of expansion and discovery

Spain and Portugal were the leaders of world exploration in the 16th century. In search of maritime trade routes to Asia, the Portuguese found sea lanes through the Atlantic and Indian oceans to India. By 1512, fortified trading posts were in place at Goa and Malacca, and they had reached the "Spice Islands" of the Moluccas in eastern Indonesia. The Spanish, taking a westward route, found the Caribbean islands and the Americas instead. Magellan's three-year global circumnavigation revealed a western route through the Strait of Magellan and across the Pacific Ocean. English and French mariners sought northern passages to Asian markets and their voyages paved the way for the establishment of European settlements in North America.

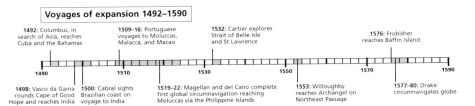

Voyages of expansion 1492–1590

1492: Columbus, in search of Asia, reaches Cuba and the Bahamas

1509–16: Portuguese voyages to Moluccas, Malacca, and Macao

1532: Cartier explores Strait of Belle Isle and St Lawrence

1576: Frobisher reaches Baffin Island

1498: Vasco da Gama rounds Cape of Good Hope and reaches India

1500: Cabral sights Brazilian coast on voyage to India

1519–22: Magellan and del Cano complete first global circumnavigation reaching Moluccas via the Philippine Islands

1553: Willoughby reaches Archangel on Northeast Passage

1577–80: Drake circumnavigates globe

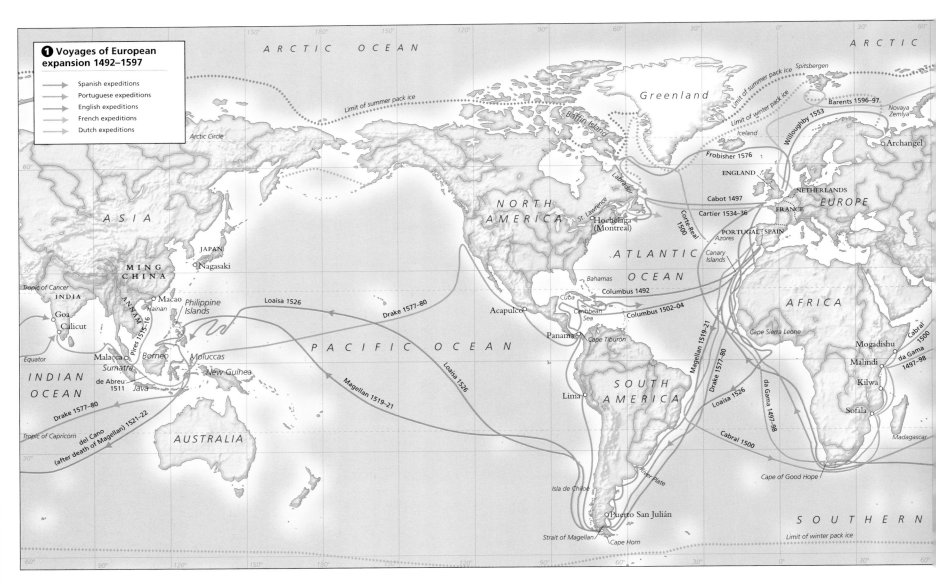

① Voyages of European expansion 1492–1597

→ Spanish expeditions
→ Portuguese expeditions
→ English expeditions
→ French expeditions
→ Dutch expeditions

EAST MEETS WEST

Europeans and the peoples they encountered in the East had much to learn from one another. Jesuit missionaries were particularly successful at establishing links between China and Japan and the West. During the 1580s, the Jesuit Matteo Ricci informed the Chinese emperor and his court about many European inventions. He presented them with elaborate clocks and taught them about astronomical equipment and weapons such as cannon. His primary purpose was to convert the Chinese to Christianity, using European scientific advances to demonstrate the superiority of European religion. Despite his efforts to accommodate Chinese culture – including the celebration of the mass in Chinese – large-scale conversion eluded him. But much future scientific endeavor was due to these cultural contacts: the revival of Chinese mathematics, the development of the suspension bridge, and early Western experiments in electrostatics and magnetism.

Magellan's global circumnavigation was so extraordinary that contemporary artists portrayed him abetted on his voyage by both the latest navigational technology and weaponry, and by mythical creatures such as monsters and mermaids. He was killed by hostile local people in the Philippine Islands in 1521.

The arrival of Portuguese merchants in Japan is shown below by a Japanese artist. From the mid-16th century, Portuguese traders provided a link between a hostile China and Japan and St. Francis Xavier began a mission to gain new Christian converts. They were soon perceived as a threat to Japanese security and ships which landed were ordered to be confiscated and their crews executed.

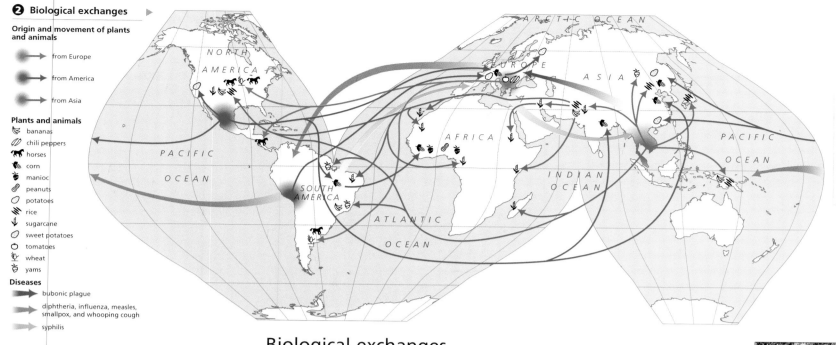

❷ Biological exchanges ▸

Origin and movement of plants and animals

- ➤ from Europe
- ➤ from America
- ➤ from Asia

Plants and animals

- 🌿 bananas
- 🌶 chili peppers
- 🐎 horses
- 🌽 corn
- 🌱 manioc
- 🥜 peanuts
- 🥔 potatoes
- 🌾 rice
- 🌿 sugarcane
- 🍠 sweet potatoes
- 🍅 tomatoes
- 🌾 wheat
- 🌿 yams

Diseases

- ➤ bubonic plague
- ➤ diphtheria, influenza, measles, smallpox, and whooping cough
- ➤ syphilis

SEE ALSO:

North America:
pp.118–119, 122–123

South America:
pp.142–143, 148–149

Africa: pp.156–157, 162–163

South and Southeast Asia:
pp.238–239, 246–247

North and East Asia:
pp.256–257

Australasia and Oceania:
pp.278–279

Biological exchanges

The plantain, a herb with medicinal properties, was known as "Englishman's foot" by native North Americans who believed it would grow only where the English had trodden.

European expansion had a profound biological impact. Travelers transported numerous species of fruits, vegetables, and animals from the Americas to Europe. At the same time, settlers introduced European species to the Americas and Oceania. Horses, pigs, and cattle were transported to the western hemisphere where, without natural predators, their numbers increased spectacularly. The settlers consciously introduced food crops, such as wheat, grapes, apples, peaches, and citrus fruits. Some plants, such as nettles, dandelions, and other weeds were inadvertently dispersed by the winds or on the coats of animals. European expansion also led to a spread of European diseases. Vast numbers of indigenous American peoples died from measles and smallpox, which broke out in massive epidemics among populations with no natural or acquired immunity. During the 16th century, syphilis – thought now to be the result of the fusion of two similar diseases from Europe and the New World – killed a million Europeans.

Many more indigenous Americans were killed by smallpox and measles than were slaughtered by the colonizers. Up to 90% of the total population may have perished from European diseases.

❸ The Spanish Empire in 1600 ▸

- ▪ Spanish Empire
- ▪ Portugal and possessions annexed by Philip II of Spain in 1580

Trade
- ➤ gold
- ➤ silver
- ➤ silk
- ➤ spices

New Spain: conquered by Cortés in 1521, Mexico, the former Aztec city of Tenochtitlán, became the center of the Spanish Empire in North America.

South America: based around the city of Lima, the Viceroyalty of Peru was the center of the Spanish Empire in South America.

The Manila galleon: brought silver once a year from Acapulco in New Spain to Manila. The silver was used to buy silk, porcelain, and lacquerware which were transported back to New Spain and then to Spain.

The Philippine Islands: first discovered in 1521 by Magellan and claimed for Spain. A governorship and Spanish settlement of the Philippines began in 1565.

Europe: by 1600, the Spanish Empire in Europe included Portugal, Flanders, Naples, and Sicily.

The Treaty of Tordesillas (1494)
Under this treaty between Spain and Portugal, the yet-to-be-discovered world was divided, with Spain taking the western portion and Portugal the east. In 1529 a further treaty divided the eastern hemisphere.

The Spanish Empire

By the end of the 16th century the Spanish Empire included Central America, the West Indies, western South America, and most of the Philippine Islands. The need to safeguard the new lands, their precious natural resources and the new trading networks which evolved, led to the development of a colonial administration of unparalleled scope. Royal authority was vested in the twin institutions of *audiencias*, with political, administrative, and judicial functions, and a series of viceroys, who acted primarily as powerful governors, though they possessed no judicial powers. All information relating to government in the Spanish territories was controlled by specially created councils, the Council of Castile and the Council of the Indies, which met regularly to ensure communication between Spain and the distant possessions of the Spanish Empire.

The New World empire Philip II inherited from his father, Charles V, was greatly expanded after 1580 following the annexation of Portugal, which added Brazil and the East Indies.

The Expansion of the Spanish Empire

- **1494:** Treaty of Tordesillas divides western hemisphere between Spain and Portugal
- **1509:** Spanish settlement of mainland Central America begins
- **1519–21:** Cortés conquers Aztec Empire
- **1540s:** Potosí becomes greatest single source of silver in the world
- **1564:** System of Atlantic convoys established
- **1580:** Union of Spanish and Portuguese crowns
- **1493:** Columbus establishes first Spanish settlement in western hemisphere
- **1532–40:** Pizarro conquers Inca Empire
- **1565–75:** Spanish conquest of Philippine Islands
- **1571:** Foundation of Manila
- **1590:** Silver shipped to Manila almost equal in value to Atlantic trade

(Timeline: 1480, 1500, 1520, 1540, 1560, 1580, 1600)

THE WORLD 1600–1700

DURING THE 17TH CENTURY Dutch, British, and French mariners followed Iberians into the world's seas. All three lands established colonies in North America, and all entered the trade networks of the Indian Ocean. British and French mariners searched for a northeast and a northwest passage from Europe to Asia and, although unsuccessful, their efforts expanded their understanding of the world's geography. Dutch incursions into the East Indies began to erode the dominance of the Portuguese empire in this region. Trade between Europe, Africa, North America, and South America pushed the Atlantic Ocean basin toward economic integration, while European trade in the Indian Ocean linked European and Asian markets.

Many European rulers believed that they governed by divine right. Louis XIV of France is here portrayed in a classical fashion which reflects both his supreme power and his belief in his godlike status.

Europe

The ramifications of the Protestant Reformation complicated political affairs in western and Central Europe. The Thirty Years' War (1618–48) ravaged much of Germany, but the Peace of Westphalia that ended the war established a system of states based on a balance of power. This system did not eliminate conflict but maintained relative stability until the French Revolution. The Russian Empire expanded to reach the Pacific Ocean by the mid-17th century as Cossacks and other adventurers established forts throughout Siberia while searching for furs.

Europe

1618: Start of Thirty Years' War
1643: Louis XIV becomes King of France
1648: Thirty Years' War ended by Peace of Westphalia
1682: Peter the Great becomes tsar of Russia

1611: Accession of Gustavus Adolphus signals Swedish expansion
1649: Execution of Charles I of England
1683: Siege of Vienna ends in Ottoman defeat

1600 1620 1640 1660 1680 1700

The World in 1700

- Ottoman Empire
- England and possessions
- France and possessions
- Denmark and possessions
- Spain and possessions
- Portugal and possessions
- Netherlands and possessions
- Hohenzollern possessions
- Sweden and possessions
- Venetian Republic and possessions
- Austrian Habsburg territories
- held temporarily by Netherlands during 17th century
- Holy Roman Empire

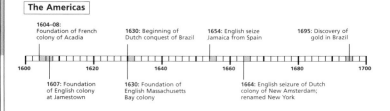

The French explorer Samuel de Champlain forged alliances with other Indian peoples as he fought the Iroquois in a series of violent struggles. He is seen here attacking an Iroquois fortress.

The Americas

The Spanish land empire expanded from bases in Central America and the Andes, and the Portuguese built a powerful and profitable plantation society along the coast of northeastern South America. English colonists established settlements along the Atlantic seaboard of North America, and sugar plantations on Jamaica and other Caribbean islands. French and Dutch colonists founded forts and trading posts in North America, with sugar plantations in the Caribbean and Guiana. French hunters traveled through the Great Lakes and the upper Mississippi valley in search of furs. However, indigenous peoples in the continental interior remained largely independent of European rule.

The Americas

1604–08: Foundation of French colony of Acadia
1630: Beginning of Dutch conquest of Brazil
1654: English seize Jamaica from Spain
1695: Discovery of gold in Brazil

1600 1620 1640 1660 1680 1700

1607: Foundation of English colony at Jamestown
1630: Foundation of English Massachusetts Bay colony
1664: English seizure of Dutch colony of New Amsterdam; renamed New York

Africa

By 1700 the Atlantic slave trade had started to affect African politics and society. In 1663 the Portuguese seized Ndongo territory to extend their colony in Angola, and made frequent attempts to conquer Kongo. The African population was boosted by the introduction of food crops from the Americas, including manioc, corn, and peanuts, but this increase was offset by the export of two million slaves from Africa – mainly to the Americas – during the 17th century. States such as Asante, Dahomey, and Oyo raided their neighbors in search of slaves to exchange for European guns.

OPTICAL INSTRUMENTS

The development of telescopes and microscopes geatly advanced human knowledge of both distant objects and those too small to see with the naked eye during the 17th century. The refracting telescope, using a combination of lenses, was first used for observation of the Moon and distant universe by Galileo in 1609. Newton's reflecting telescope, using lenses and mirrors, gave a still clearer picture of the stars and planets. In 1683, Anton van Leeuwenhoek made the first high-powered precision microscope.

A model of Newton's reflecting telescope, made in 1668.

The Qing dynasty began their rule with great energy, encouraging many projects for the improvement of their new lands. These workers are building a new dike constructed from timber and brushwood.

East Asia

In 1644 a Manchu army toppled the Ming dynasty, entered Beijing, and established the Qing dynasty (1644–1911). By the 1680s they had consolidated their hold on southern China, conquered the island of Formosa, and extended Chinese influence far into North and Central Asia. The Qing adapted to Chinese ways and largely preserved the Ming administrative structure. In Japan, the Tokugawa dynasty imposed a central government for the first time. Foreign trade was strictly controlled by both the Chinese and Japanese, confined mainly to Macao in China and Nagasaki in Japan.

SEE ALSO:

North America: pp.126–127

South America: pp.148–149

Africa: pp.164–165

Europe: pp.196–197

West Asia: pp.230–231

South and Southeast Asia: pp.244–245

North and East Asia: pp.268–269

Australasia and Oceania: pp.278–279

East Asia

1633: Closure of Japan by Tokugawa shoguns
1661: Kangxi becomes Qing emperor
1683: Conquest of Formosa by Kangxi
1603: Establishment of Tokugawa dynasty in Japan
1644: Manchu forces topple the Ming and establish the Qing dynasty
1689: Treaty of Nerchinsk between Russia and China; Russians withdraw from Amur basin

JOAN BLAEU'S EASTERN HEMISPHERE

During the 17th century, Dutch mariners and merchants pushed forward the boundaries of the world known to Europeans. Willem Blaeu and his son Joan were official cartographers to the Dutch East India Company (VOC), publishing maps and charts based on the most up-to-date and accurate information provided by explorers, as well as a series of world atlases.

The eastern hemisphere of Joan Blaeu's *Nova et accuratissima totius terrarum orbis tabula*, was first published in his *Atlas Major* in 1662. The map presents a familiar view of Africa, Europe, and most of Asia, although Australia is shown only sketchily.

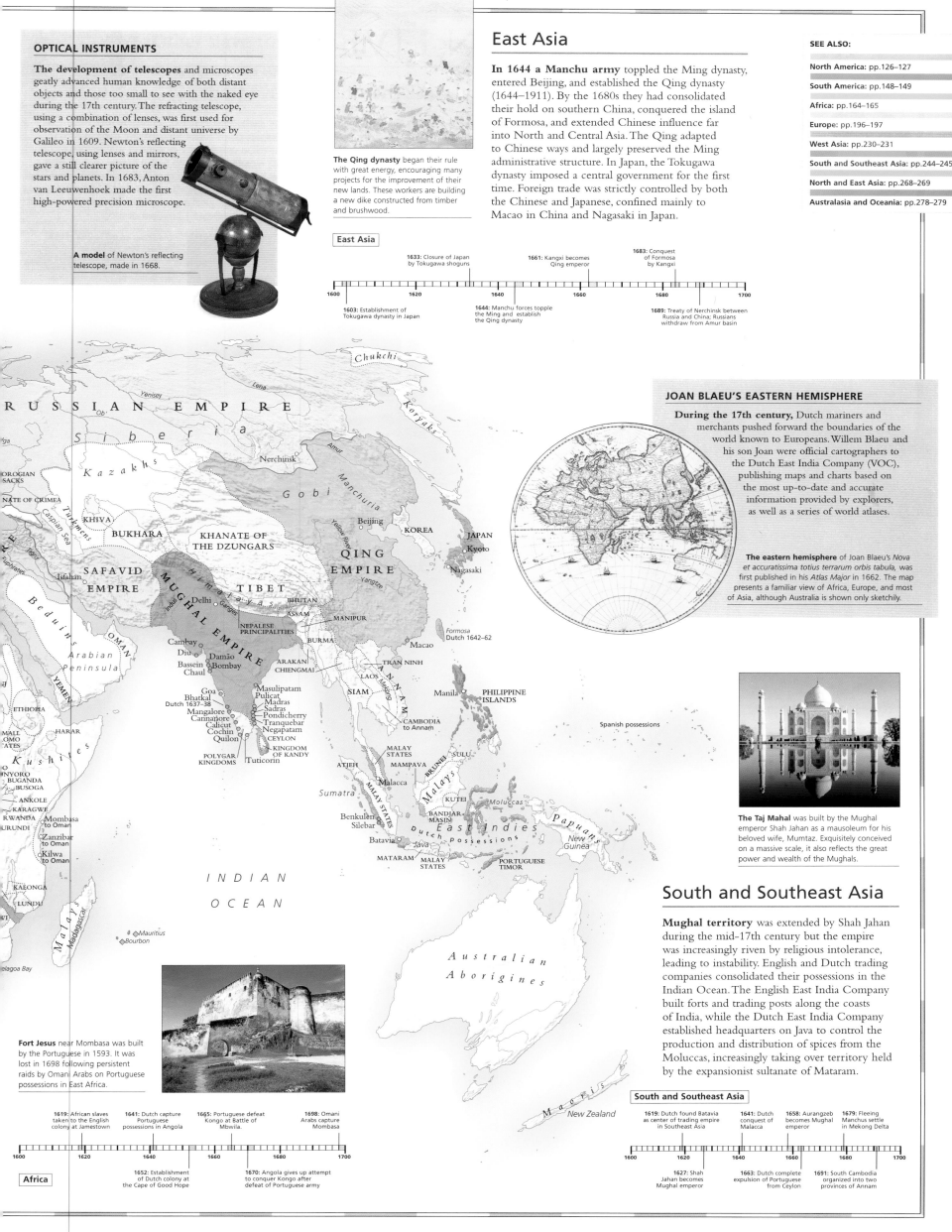

The Taj Mahal was built by the Mughal emperor Shah Jahan as a mausoleum for his beloved wife, Mumtaz. Exquisitely conceived on a massive scale, it also reflects the great power and wealth of the Mughals.

Fort Jesus near Mombasa was built by the Portuguese in 1593. It was lost in 1698 following persistent raids by Omani Arabs on Portuguese possessions in East Africa.

South and Southeast Asia

Mughal territory was extended by Shah Jahan during the mid-17th century but the empire was increasingly riven by religious intolerance, leading to instability. English and Dutch trading companies consolidated their possessions in the Indian Ocean. The English East India Company built forts and trading posts along the coasts of India, while the Dutch East India Company established headquarters on Java to control the production and distribution of spices from the Moluccas, increasingly taking over territory held by the expansionist sultanate of Mataram.

Africa

1619: African slaves taken to the English colony at Jamestown
1641: Dutch capture Portuguese possessions in Angola
1665: Portuguese defeat Kongo at Battle of Mbwila
1698: Omani Arabs capture Mombasa
1652: Establishment of Dutch colony at the Cape of Good Hope
1670: Angola gives up attempt to conquer Kongo after defeat of Portuguese army

South and Southeast Asia

1619: Dutch found Batavia as center of trading empire in Southeast Asia
1641: Dutch conquest of Malacca
1658: Aurangzeb becomes Mughal emperor
1679: Fleeing Manchus settle in Mekong Delta
1627: Shah Jahan becomes Mughal emperor
1663: Dutch complete expulsion of Portuguese from Ceylon
1691: South Cambodia organized into two provinces of Annam

THE WORLD 1700–1800

FROM THE BEGINNING of the 18th century, new ideas in science, philosophy, and political organization fueled change throughout the world. Popular reaction against the *ancien régime* in both France and North America led to the overthrow of the ruling governments. Improvements in agricultural techniques and land reform increased food production, and the population – especially in Europe – began to expand rapidly. Technological innovations in Europe led to the beginning of the Industrial Revolution and consequent urban growth. The expansion of European influence and territorial possessions throughout the world continued apace, with explorers charting the scattered islands of the Pacific and Britain establishing its power in India and Australia.

On January 21, 1793, the French king, Louis XVI, was guillotined in front of a huge Parisian crowd. His wife, Marie Antoinette, was executed later in the year.

Europe

Throughout Europe, government became more powerful, especially in the Russia of Peter the Great and the Prussia of Frederick the Great. In France, Bourbon monarchy had reached its peak during the reign of Louis XIV (1643–1715). Revolutionary ideas unleashed by the "enlightenment," combined with political relaxation, created an incendiary situation, leading in 1789 to the French Revolution whose effects reverberated throughout Europe.

Europe

	1740: Prussia launches War of Austrian Succession and becomes major European power	1756–63: Seven Years' War in Europe	1774: Ottoman decline follows Treaty of Kuchuk Kainarji	1799: Coup brings Napoleon to power in France
1700	1720	1740	1760	1780	1800

1703: Foundation of St. Petersburg by Peter the Great — 1715: Death of Louis XIV — 1768: War between Russia and the Ottomans — 1783: Russia conquers and annexes Crimea — 1789: French Revolution begins

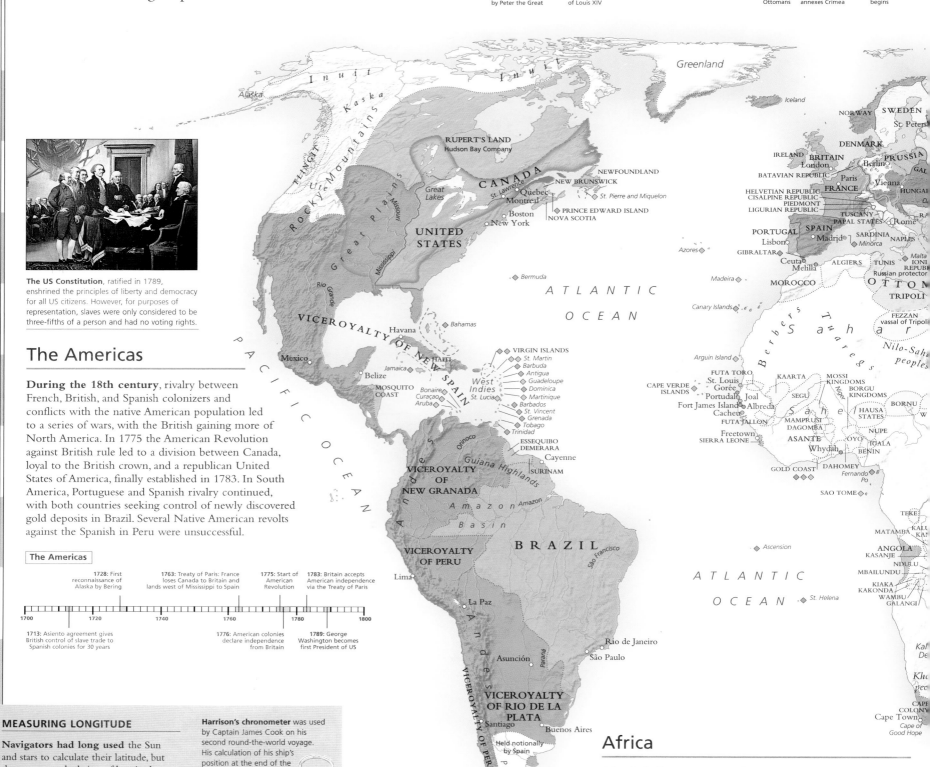

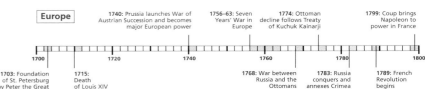

The US Constitution, ratified in 1789, enshrined the principles of liberty and democracy for all US citizens. However, for purposes of representation, slaves were only considered to be three-fifths of a person and had no voting rights.

The Americas

During the 18th century, rivalry between French, British, and Spanish colonizers and conflicts with the native American population led to a series of wars, with the British gaining more of North America. In 1775 the American Revolution against British rule led to a division between Canada, loyal to the British crown, and a republican United States of America, finally established in 1783. In South America, Portuguese and Spanish rivalry continued, with both countries seeking control of newly discovered gold deposits in Brazil. Several Native American revolts against the Spanish in Peru were unsuccessful.

The Americas

1728: First reconnaissance of Alaska by Bering	1763: Treaty of Paris: France loses Canada to Britain and lands west of Mississippi to Spain	1775: Start of American Revolution	1783: Britain accepts American independence via the Treaty of Paris
1700	1720	1740	1760	1780	1800

1713: Asiento agreement gives British control of slave trade to Spanish colonies for 30 years — 1776: American colonies declare independence from Britain — 1789: George Washington becomes first President of US

Africa

Islamic influence continued to expand in much of North Africa. The Asante and Yoruba were dominant in West Africa, but the slave trade which had flourished for centuries throughout much of Africa was internationalized and greatly magnified by European influence in this period. Over 13.5 million people left Africa as slaves during the 1700s. West Africans and Angolans were shipped to the New World – especially Brazil – and northern Africa traded with the Ottoman Empire. In southern Africa, Dutch and British colonists struggled for supremacy against organized Xhosa resistance.

MEASURING LONGITUDE

Navigators had long used the Sun and stars to calculate their latitude, but the accurate calculation of longitude depended on the precise measurement of local time in relation to the time at the Greenwich meridian. The invention by John Harrison of an accurate ship's chronometer in 1762 enabled navigators to calculate their position far more precisely, greatly reducing the risk of shipwrecks, and shortening journey times.

Harrison's chronometer was used by Captain James Cook on his second round-the-world voyage. His calculation of his ship's position at the end of the journey showed an error of only 8 miles.

CAPTAIN COOK'S MAP OF NEW ZEALAND

Until the 18th century Oceania and the South Seas remained a mystery to most navigators. The English sailor Captain James Cook made three exploratory voyages to the South Pacific between 1768 and 1779. This map of New Zealand was made on Cook's first voyage. His ship, the *Endeavour*, traced the coast to make this remarkably accurate map.

Cook's map was the first accurate representation of New Zealand and copies were issued to map publishers all over Europe.

By the late 18th century, many Indian rulers, such as the Nawab of Bengal, had assigned administrative powers to the British.

South and West Asia

The Persians under Nadir Shah began to challenge the Ottomans and pushed eastward into Mughal India, even sacking the city of Delhi in 1739. By the middle of the 18th century, the Marathas were emerging as successors to the Mughals, but they were comprehensively defeated by an Afghan army at Panipat in 1761. By the end of the century, the British East India Company had established firm control over much of India via a series of effective military campaigns.

SEE ALSO:

North America: pp.126–129

South America: pp.148–149

Africa: pp.164–165

Europe: pp.198–201

West Asia: pp.230–231

South and Southeast Asia: pp.246–249

North and East Asia: pp.268–269

Australasia and Oceania: pp.282–283

South and West Asia

1707: Death of Aurangzeb heralds decline of Mughal power in India
1736: Nadir Shah becomes Shah of Persia
1747: Foundation of Afghanistan by Ahmad Khan Abdali
1761: British destroy French power in India following seizure of Pondicherry
1799: Conquest of Mysore ends challenge to British power in southern India

1722–36: Subjugation of Afghans by Persia
1757: Robert Clive defeats Bengalis at battle of Plassey
1765: Bengal comes under British control
1775: First Anglo-Maratha war
1786: Start of Qadjar dynasty in Persia
1796: British conquest of coastal Ceylon

1700 1720 1740 1760 1780 1800

East Asia, Southeast Asia, and Oceania

The Qing dynasty extended its empire to include a protectorate over Tibet and the conquest of Xiankiang (Dzungaria) by 1760. By 1790, the Chinese population had virtually tripled to 300 million. Trade in tea, porcelain, and silk with Russia and the West boosted the economy, and Manchu China was able to resist European incursion. The kingdoms of Southeast Asia were frequently at war, and subject to invasion by the Chinese, as with Burma in 1765–69. Though the Portuguese and Dutch had set up trading ports, much of the East Indies had yet to be formally colonized.

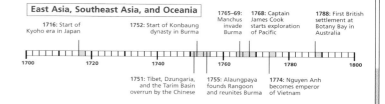

East Asia, Southeast Asia, and Oceania

1716: Start of Kyoho era in Japan
1752: Start of Konbaung dynasty in Burma
1765–69: Manchus invade Burma
1768: Captain James Cook starts exploration of Pacific
1788: First British settlement at Botany Bay in Australia

1751: Tibet, Dzungaria, and the Tarim Basin overrun by the Chinese
1755: Alaungpaya founds Rangoon and reunites Burma
1774: Nguyen Anh becomes emperor of Vietnam

1700 1720 1740 1760 1780 1800

Skilled Qing artists rendered images such as this vivid portrayal of an archery contest on silk. Silk and porcelain produced to a quality unknown in the West were prized by European traders.

Finely chased gold ornaments like this were worn as insignia by officials of the Asante court.

The World in 1800

Qing Empire
Persia and possessions
Ottoman Empire
Britain and possessions
France and possessions
Denmark and possessions
Spain and possessions
Portugal and possessions
Netherlands and possessions
Prussia and possessions
Russian Empire
Austrian Habsburg territories
Holy Roman Empire
Persia on death of Nadir Shah 1747
French possessions lost during 18th century

Africa

1705: Foundation of Husaynid dynasty in Tunis, which rules until 1957
1720: Dutch settlers reach Orange River from Cape
1730: Revival of ancient empire of Bornu in central Africa
1747: Oyo become main power in Niger Delta after defeat of Dahomey
1757: Muhammad III becomes Sultan of Morocco
1770s: Peak years of European slave trade with Africa
1779–80: Boers and Bantu at war in southern Africa
1787: Settlement of first freed slaves from Britain at Freetown
1795: British capture Cape of Good Hope from the Dutch
1798: Occupation of Egypt by Napoleon Bonaparte

1700 1720 1740 1760 1780 1800

THE WORLD 1800–1850

THE AFTERMATH OF THE FRENCH and American revolutions and the Napoleonic wars led to a new nationalism and demands for democracy and freedom. The colonial regimes of South America were overthrown, and in Europe, Belgium and Greece gained independence. The US and northern Europe were transformed by the Industrial Revolution, as mass production and transportation led to an economic boom. There were mass movements of peoples to the expanding cities or to new lives abroad. Hunger for raw materials to feed industry and the desire to dominate world markets was soon to lead to unprecedented colonial expansion. In the US, Australia, and New Zealand, indigenous peoples were fighting a futile battle for their homelands.

A series of major innovations put Britain at the forefront of industrial development. The Nielsen hot blast process, invented in 1824, made iron smelting more efficient.

Europe

The Napoleonic Empire convulsed the established European order, abolishing states and national institutions. While liberals preached democracy, the ruling class responded with repressive measures to restrict freedom of speech and political expression. By the late 1840s civil unrest in the growing cities, bad harvests, and economic crisis led to open rebellion. In 1848, Louis Philippe of France was forced to abdicate, and revolution broke out throughout Europe.

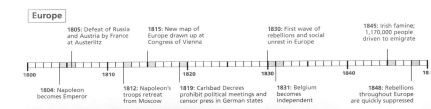

Europe				
1805: Defeat of Russia and Austria by France at Austerlitz	**1815:** New map of Europe drawn up at Congress of Vienna	**1830:** First wave of rebellions and social unrest in Europe		**1845:** Irish famine; 1,170,000 people driven to emigrate
1800 — 1810 — 1820 — 1830 — 1840 — 18				
1804: Napoleon becomes Emperor	**1812:** Napoleon's troops retreat from Moscow	**1819:** Carlsbad Decrees prohibit political meetings and censor press in German states	**1831:** Belgium becomes independent	**1848:** Rebellions throughout Europe are quickly suppressed

North America

The acquisition of new territories opened up the vast interior of North America to new settlement. Settlers pushing across the plains in search of fertile land and new wealth came into bloody conflict with Native Americans who, equipped with both horses and guns, proved to be formidable foes. The mechanization of agriculture increased exports of wheat, tobacco, and cotton and as the economy prospered, cities expanded and immigrants arrived in great numbers.

The intensive plantation economy of the southern US was dependent on slave labor to pick cotton and harvest tobacco.

North America			
	1819: Parts of Spanish Florida conquered by US	**1836:** Texans rebel against Mexican rule and declare Republic of Texas	**1849:** California Gold Rush
1800 — 1810 — 1820 — 1830 — 1840 — 1850			
1803: France sells territory between Mississippi and Rockies in Louisiana Purchase	**1821:** Mexico gains independence from Spanish colonists	**1846–48:** US victory in war with Mexico which cedes New Mexico and California to US	

South America

When Spain was cut off from her colonies by the Napoleonic wars, nationalist forces took advantage of the resulting disorder and weakness of the colonial regimes. Argentina's struggle for independence was led by José de San Martín, who marched an army across the Andes to liberate Chile and Peru from royalist control. Simón Bolívar led Venezuela and New Granada to independence, and helped found the new republic of Bolivia in 1825.

The Venezuelan Simón Bolívar (1783–1830) was known as the "liberator of South America."

South America		
1810: Argentina declares independence from Spain	**1821:** Bolívar secures Venezuelan independence	
1800 — 1810 — 1820 — 1830 — 1840 — 1850		
1817: San Martín wins a decisive victory over the Spanish and liberates Chile	**1822:** Empire of Brazil becomes independent from Portugal	

Africa

In sub-Saharan West Africa several Islamic leaders waged *jihad* against neighboring states. Under the Ottoman leader, Muhammad Ali, the viceroyalty of Egypt extended south to incorporate Sudan. The French invasion of Algeria in 1830 led to a war of resistance, led by Abd al-Qadir. In southeastern Africa, conflict broke out between different tribal groups (the *mfecane*) as natural resources became scarce. Shaka, the Zulu leader, established a united kingdom in southern Africa. In the late 1830s the "Great Trek" of the Boers from Cape Colony extended European influence into the African interior.

RAILROADS

The steam locomotive was first developed in Britain in the early 19th century to haul heavy industrial loads. By 1830, engines were being used to pull cars on iron rails and the first steam railroad – from Stockton to Darlington – had opened. By 1850, railroads had been built throughout Britain and were being introduced throughout its empire.

The steam engine *Locomotion*, built by Robert Stephenson and Co., hauled the first train at the opening of the Stockton-to-Darlington railroad in 1825.

East and Southeast Asia

Superior firepower such as that displayed by the merchant steamer *Nemesis* enabled the British to overwhelm the wooden junks used by the Chinese in the first Opium War.

In the early 19th century, British merchants began to exploit the Chinese desire for Indian opium. As the trade flourished and the problem of opium addiction grew, the Chinese authorities attempted to stamp out the trade. The British objected and the first Opium War ensued. Japan, ruled by the inward-looking, Tokugawa shogunate for the last two centuries, remained closed to all foreigners, except a small Dutch trading community.

GEOLOGICAL MAPS

In the 19th century newly-discovered fossil remains were used to classify rocks and determine the sequence of geological strata. Geographical names were often used in the naming of rock types; for example, the Jura Mountains gave their name to the dinosaur-bearing Jurassic rocks.

Geologists used cross sections to map the age of rocks. This one is taken from the Reverend William Buckland's *Bridgewater Treatise on Mineralogy and Geology.*

SEE ALSO:

North America: pp.128–131

South America: pp.150–151

Africa: pp.166–167

Europe: pp.200–205

West Asia: pp.232–233

South and Southeast Asia: pp.248–249

North and East Asia: pp.268–271

Australasia and Oceania: pp.282–285

East and Southeast Asia

1804: Russian envoy fails to agree commercial treaty with Japan

1819: Stamford Raffles, of the British East India company, founds Singapore

1837: Tokugawa Ieyoshi succeeds Ienari as Japanese shogun

1839–42: First Opium War in China

1802: Gia-Long proclaimed emperor of united Annam (Vietnam)

1834: Monopoly of China trade by East India Company abolished

1842: Treaty of Nanjing. Hong Kong ceded to British and five ports opened to foreign trade

Australasia and Oceania

New Zealand and Australia became British colonies in the first half of the 19th century. In Australia, settlement spread from the penal colony at Port Jackson, now part of Sydney. As settlers founded towns at Adelaide, Melbourne, and Perth, they expropriated Aboriginal lands, and infected the people with fatal diseases, destroying local Aboriginal communities.

The Treaty of Waitangi allowed the Maori to maintain control over their lands while ceding the sovereignty of New Zealand to Britain, an unequal exchange which soon led to resentment and further wars.

Australasia and Oceania

1810: Kamehameha I unites Hawaiian islands

1825: Dutch annex western New Guinea

1840: British takeover of New Zealand under Treaty of Waitangi

1829: Britain annexes the whole continent of Australia

1835–36: British found Melbourne and Adelaide

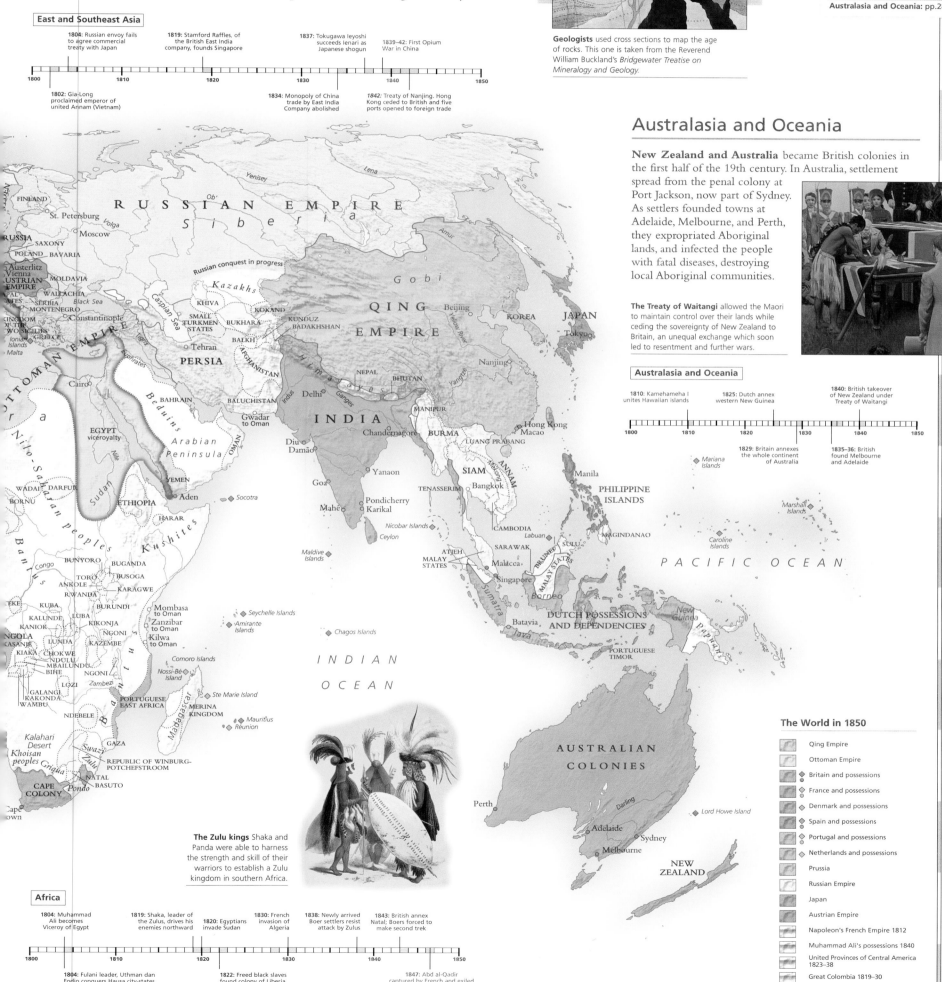

The Zulu kings Shaka and Panda were able to harness the strength and skill of their warriors to establish a Zulu kingdom in southern Africa.

The World in 1850

- Qing Empire
- Ottoman Empire
- Britain and possessions
- France and possessions
- Denmark and possessions
- Spain and possessions
- Portugal and possessions
- Netherlands and possessions
- Prussia
- Russian Empire
- Japan
- Austrian Empire
- Napoleon's French Empire 1812
- Muhammad Ali's possessions 1840
- United Provinces of Central America 1823–38
- Great Colombia 1819–30

Africa

1804: Muhammad Ali becomes Viceroy of Egypt

1819: Shaka, leader of the Zulus, drives his enemies northward

1820: Egyptians invade Sudan

1830: French invasion of Algeria

1838: Newly arrived Boer settlers resist attack by Zulus

1843: British annex Natal; Boers forced to make second trek

1804: Fulani leader, Uthman dan Fodio conquers Hausa city-states

1822: Freed black slaves found colony of Liberia

1847: Abd al-Qadir captured by French and exiled

THE WORLD'S ECONOMIC REVOLUTION

Innovative new constructions of the late-19th century included the Eiffel Tower, built in 1889.

IN THE FIRST HALF of the 19th century, world trade and industry was dominated by Britain; by the 1870s, the industrial balance was shifting in favor other nations, especially Germany, France, Russia, and the US, with rapid industrialization occurring throughout most of Europe by the end of the century. A stable currency, a standard (i.e., the price of gold) against which the currency's value could be measured, and an effective private banking system were seen as essential to the growth and success of every industrializing nation. The major industrial nations also began to invest heavily overseas. Their aims were the discovery and exploitation of cheaper raw materials, balanced by the development of overseas markets for their products.

The impact of the Industrial Revolution

The introduction of steam to oceangoing ships decreased journey times, and increased reliability because ships were no longer reliant on the wind.

World industrial output from 1870–1914 increased at an extraordinary rate: coal production by as much as 650%; steel by 2500%; steam engine capacity by over 350%. Technology revolutionized the world economy: the invention of refrigerated ships meant that meat, fruit, and other perishables could be shipped to Europe from as far away as New Zealand; sewing machines and power looms allowed the mass production of textiles and clothing; telephones, telegraphs, and railroads made communications faster.

The opening of the Suez Canal in 1869, linking the Red Sea to the Mediterranean, reduced the journey time from Europe to India by 50%.

By the 1880s almost all of the US was connected by long-distance rail networks including the Illinois Central Railroad *(below)*.

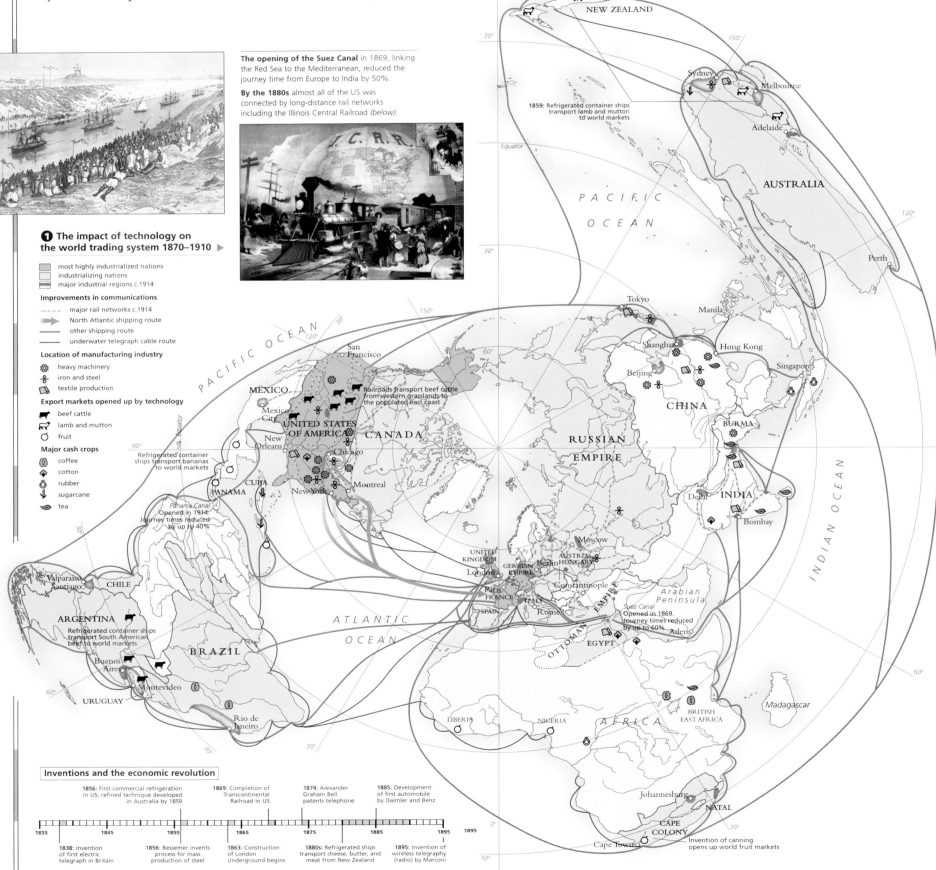

① The impact of technology on the world trading system 1870–1910 ▶

- most highly industrialized nations
- industrializing nations
- major industrial regions c.1914

Improvements in communications
- major rail networks c.1914
- North Atlantic shipping route
- other shipping route
- underwater telegraph cable route

Location of manufacturing industry
- heavy machinery
- iron and steel
- textile production

Export markets opened up by technology
- beef cattle
- lamb and mutton
- fruit

Major cash crops
- coffee
- cotton
- rubber
- sugarcane
- tea

Inventions and the economic revolution

1856: First commercial refrigeration in US; refined technique developed in Australia by 1859

1869: Completion of Transcontinental Railroad in US

1874: Alexander Graham Bell patents telephone

1885: Development of first automobile by Daimler and Benz

1838: Invention of first electric telegraph in Britain

1856: Bessemer invents process for mass production of steel

1863: Construction of London Underground begins

1880s: Refrigerated ships transport cheese, butter, and meat from New Zealand

1895: Invention of wireless telegraphy (radio) by Marconi

| 1835 | 1845 | 1855 | 1865 | 1875 | 1885 | 1895 |

The great mineral rush

The search for new sources of minerals, both precious and functional, reached new heights of intensity in the industrial 19th century. New finds of gold and diamonds in the US, Canada, Australia, and South Africa fueled the so-called gold and diamond rushes of the later 19th century. Though individuals could pan for gold in the Australian and North American rushes, the depth of gold and diamond deposits in South Africa meant that they could only be fully exploited with mechanical diggers owned by mining companies.

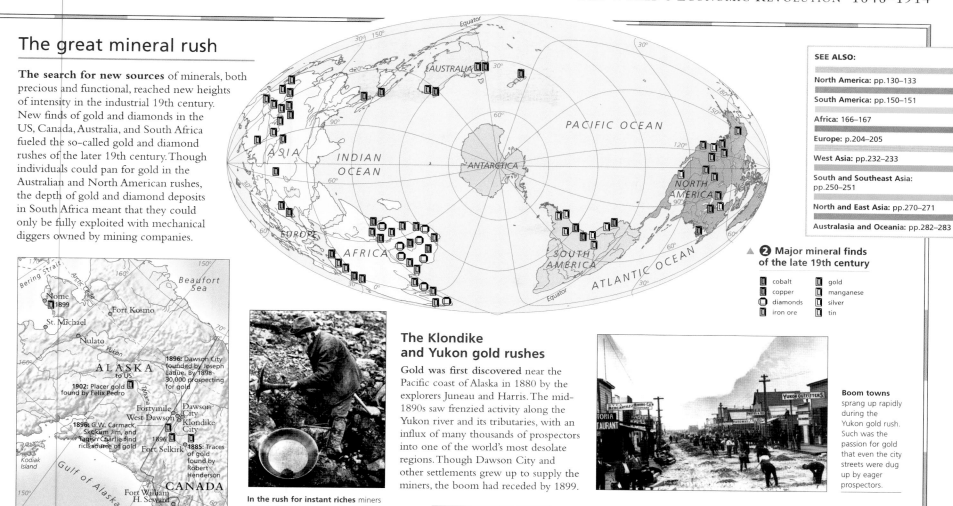

SEE ALSO:

North America: pp.130–133

South America: pp.150–151

Africa: 166–167

Europe: p.204–205

West Asia: pp.232–233

South and Southeast Asia: pp.250–251

North and East Asia: pp.270–271

Australasia and Oceania: pp.282–283

▲ **2** Major mineral finds of the late 19th century

▣ cobalt	▣ gold
▣ copper	▣ manganese
◯ diamonds	▣ silver
▣ iron ore	▣ tin

◀ **3** The Yukon and Klondike gold rushes

▣ major gold strike
◯ settlement or fort

In the rush for instant riches miners such as this man, panning for gold in British Columbia in 1900, were prepared to undergo extreme hardship.

The Klondike and Yukon gold rushes

Gold was first discovered near the Pacific coast of Alaska in 1880 by the explorers Juneau and Harris. The mid-1890s saw frenzied activity along the Yukon river and its tributaries, with an influx of many thousands of prospectors into one of the world's most desolate regions. Though Dawson City and other settlements grew up to supply the miners, the boom had receded by 1899.

Boom towns sprang up rapidly during the Yukon gold rush. Such was the passion for gold that even the city streets were dug up by eager prospectors.

Gold and diamond rushes

1849–50: Comstock Lode found near Virginia City, Nevada
1851: Rich gold deposits found in southern Australia
1869: Discovery of "Star of South Africa" diamond sets off diamond rush
1896–98: Yukon and Klondike gold rushes

1848: California Gold Rush starts near Sutter's Mill on the Sacramento River
1858: Gold discovered on Fraser River, northwest Canada
1867: Diamonds found at Kimberley, north of Cape Colony, South Africa
1876–78: Gold found near Black Hills of Dakota Territory
1886: Deep seams of gold discovered on the Witwatersrand, South Africa

(1840 — 1850 — 1860 — 1870 — 1880 — 1890 — 1900)

The politics of cotton

In the 1870s woven cotton in India was still produced on a local scale, by individuals, rather than factories, and traded at local markets (above).

5 The politics of cotton ▼

➤ raw cotton from US to Britain
➤ cotton textiles to India
➤ raw cotton from India to Britain
⬧ cotton producing region
▯ textile town
▦ major cotton-producing states

Cotton production was an early beneficiary of the Industrial Revolution. Eli Whitney's invention of the cotton gin led to a huge increase in the volume of cotton that could be processed; the invention of the power loom industrialized the weaving of cotton textiles. Britain's colonies in India and America supplied raw cotton for the cotton towns of Lancashire and Yorkshire; even with American independence, the southern states continued to provide much of Britain's cotton. The economic and political importance of cotton to the US was reflected in the Confederate states' decision to use it as a bargaining tool during their struggle for international recognition following secession in 1861. The ploy failed as a strategy; during the Civil War, Britain turned to India for its raw cotton supplies. British cloth woven with Indian cotton was then exported back to India, a policy which benefited British producers, while keeping the Indian textile industry at a local level until the end of the 19th century.

◀ **4** The cotton towns of Lancashire and Yorkshire

▯ cotton town
Peel textile firm
---- major railroad c.1850
— major canal

Cotton production in Lancashire

With plentiful water to power new machinery, Lancashire had developed as a major cotton-weaving center by the late 18th century. Textile towns such as Stockport, Blackburn, and Cromford, often containing several firms, grew up in the area around Manchester, which acted as a major market for finished cloth.

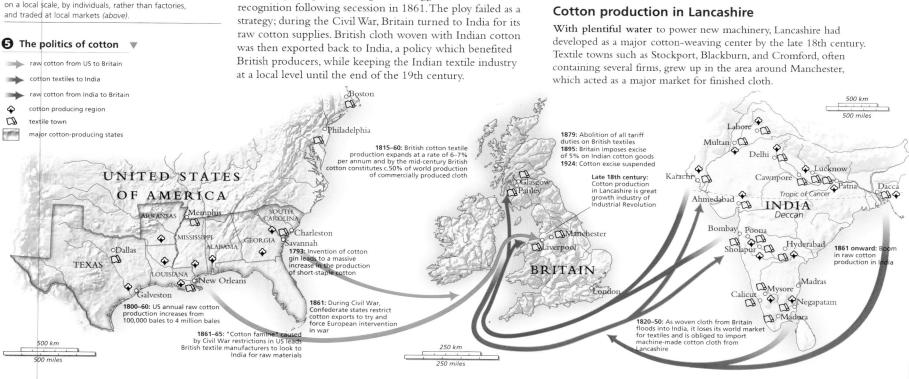

1815–60: British cotton textile production expands at a rate of 6–7% per annum and by the mid-century British cotton constitutes c.50% of world production of commercially produced cloth

1793: Invention of cotton gin leads to a massive increase in the production of short-staple cotton

1800–60: US annual raw cotton production increases from 100,000 bales to 4 million bales

1861–65: "Cotton famine" caused by Civil War restrictions in US leads British textile manufacturers to look to India for raw materials

1861: During Civil War, Confederate states restrict cotton exports to try and force European intervention in war

1879: Abolition of all tariff duties on British textiles
1895: Britain imposes excise of 5% on Indian cotton goods
1924: Cotton excise suspended

Late 18th century: Cotton production in Lancashire is great growth industry of Industrial Revolution

1820–50: As woven cloth from Britain floods into India, it loses its world market for textiles and is obliged to import machine-made cotton cloth from Lancashire

1861 onward: Boom in raw cotton production in India

THE WORLD 1850–1900

BY 1900 THE EUROPEAN POPULATION had more than doubled to 420 million, while the population of the US had reached 90 million. Industry and commerce were booming, and both Europe and the US were traversed by rail networks. The major European powers were extending their economic and political influence to the very ends of the globe, while fierce rivalries and competition were being enacted on the international as well as the domestic scene. Within two decades the European powers had colonized virtually the whole of the African continent, the British had claimed India for the Crown, and the western powers had exploited the fatal weaknesses of China's crumbling Qing dynasty to penetrate deep into the heart of Asia.

Kaiser Wilhelm II was determined to establish Germany as Europe's leading military power.

Europe

The emergence of new states, the rise of nationalism, and growing economic and political power led to rivalry and conflict. Expansionist Russia's activities in the Balkans led in 1854 to the Crimean War, between a Franco-British-Turkish alliance and Russia. In 1870 Bismarck, prime minister of Prussia, goaded the French into war; the French defeat led to the collapse of the Second Empire, providing the final impetus to the creation of the new German and Italian nations.

Europe

1854–56: Franco-British-Turkish alliance victorious against Russians in Crimea

1862: Otto von Bismarck prime minister of Prussia

1870: Franco-Prussian war; Prussian victory leads to collapse of Second Empire

1887: Bulgaria, independent of Ottoman empire, becomes leading Balkan state

1861: Abolition of serfdom in Russia

1867: Dual monarchy of Austria-Hungary established

1871: Rome becomes capital of united Italy; King Wilhelm I of Prussia declared German emperor

1896: Revival of Olympic Games at Athens, Greece

1850 1860 1870 1880 1890 1900

CAMPAIGN MAPS

During the American Civil War, new printing technology combined with up-to-date information from correspondents on the battlefields allowed US newspapers to produce simplified campaign maps to explain the stages of the war to a fascinated public.

This map shows the battle of Campbell's Station, Tennessee, as witnessed from the Union position by the *New York Tribune's* correspondent, Elias Smith.

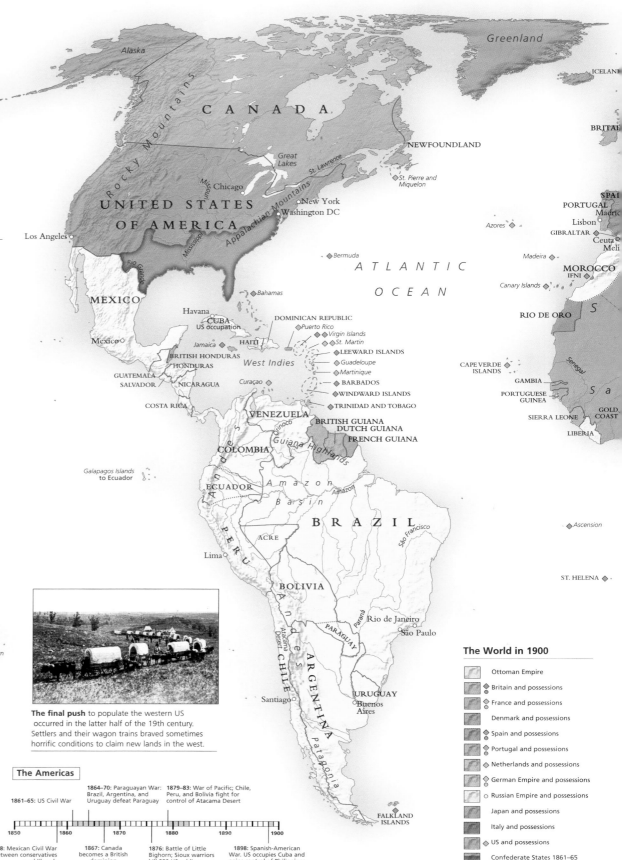

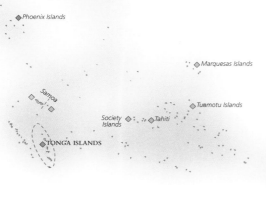

The final push to populate the western US occurred in the latter half of the 19th century. Settlers and their wagon trains braved sometimes horrific conditions to claim new lands in the west.

The Americas

In 1860-1 eleven southern states, fearful that the North was about to abolish slavery, left the Union and formed the Confederacy, beginning a conflict in which over 600,000 soldiers lost their lives. Following the Civil War, the US became the fastest growing economy in the world, its population swollen by waves of immigrants. In South America, economic prosperity, especially from the export of meat and rubber, was enjoyed by the ruling elite, while border disputes bedeviled the new republics.

The Americas

1861–65: US Civil War

1864–70: Paraguayan War: Brazil, Argentina, and Uruguay defeat Paraguay

1879–83: War of Pacific; Chile, Peru, and Bolivia fight for control of Atacama Desert

1850 1860 1870 1880 1890 1900

1858: Mexican Civil War between conservatives and liberals

1867: Canada becomes a British dominion

1876: Battle of Little Bighorn; Sioux warriors kill 250 US soldiers

1898: Spanish-American War. US occupies Cuba and gains control of Philippines

The World in 1900

- Ottoman Empire
- Britain and possessions
- France and possessions
- Denmark and possessions
- Spain and possessions
- Portugal and possessions
- Netherlands and possessions
- German Empire and possessions
- Russian Empire and possessions
- Japan and possessions
- Italy and possessions
- US and possessions
- Confederate States 1861–65

The great mineral rush

The search for new sources of minerals, both precious and functional, reached new heights of intensity in the industrial 19th century. New finds of gold and diamonds in the US, Canada, Australia, and South Africa fueled the so-called gold and diamond rushes of the later 19th century. Though individuals could pan for gold in the Australian and North American rushes, the depth of gold and diamond deposits in South Africa meant that they could only be fully exploited with mechanical diggers owned by mining companies.

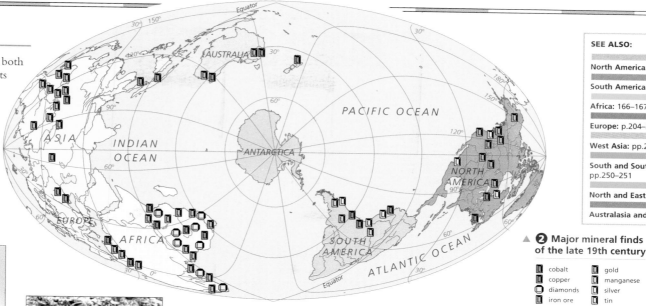

SEE ALSO:

North America: pp.130–133

South America: pp.150–151

Africa: 166–167

Europe: p.204–205

West Asia: pp.232–233

South and Southeast Asia: pp.250–251

North and East Asia: pp.270–271

Australasia and Oceania: pp.282–283

▲ **2** Major mineral finds of the late 19th century

- cobalt
- copper
- diamonds
- iron ore
- gold
- manganese
- silver
- tin

The Klondike and Yukon gold rushes

Gold was first discovered near the Pacific coast of Alaska in 1880 by the explorers Juneau and Harris. The mid-1890s saw frenzied activity along the Yukon river and its tributaries, with an influx of many thousands of prospectors into one of the world's most desolate regions. Though Dawson City and other settlements grew up to supply the miners, the boom had receded by 1899.

Boom towns sprang up rapidly during the Yukon gold rush. Such was the passion for gold that even the city streets were dug up by eager prospectors.

In the rush for instant riches miners such as this man, panning for gold in British Columbia in 1900, were prepared to undergo extreme hardship.

◄ **3** The Yukon and Klondike gold rushes

- major gold strike
- settlement or fort

Gold and diamond rushes

1849–50: Comstock Lode found near Virginia City, Nevada

1851: Rich gold deposits found in southern Australia

1869: Discovery of "Star of South Africa" diamond sets off diamond rush

1896–98: Yukon and Klondike gold rushes

1848: California Gold Rush starts neaer Sutter's Mill on the Sacramento River

1858: Gold discovered on Fraser River, northwest Canada

1867: Diamonds found at Kimberley, north of Cape Colony, South Africa

1876–78: Gold found near Black Hills of Dakota Territory

1886: Deep seams of gold discovered on the Witwatersrand, South Africa

1840 1850 1860 1870 1880 1890 1900

The politics of cotton

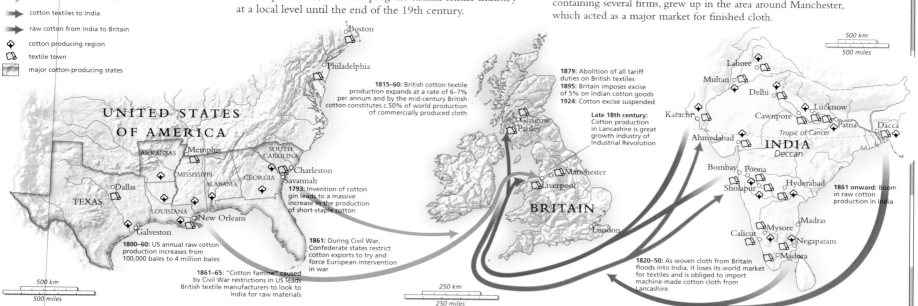

In the 1870s woven cotton in India was still produced on a local scale, by individuals, rather than factories, and traded at local markets (above).

Cotton production was an early beneficiary of the Industrial Revolution. Eli Whitney's invention of the cotton gin led to a huge increase in the volume of cotton that could be processed; the invention of the power loom industrialized the weaving of cotton textiles. Britain's colonies in India and America supplied raw cotton for the cotton towns of Lancashire and Yorkshire; even with American independence, the southern states continued to provide much of Britain's cotton. The economic and political importance of cotton to the US was reflected in the Confederate states' decision to use it as a bargaining tool during their struggle for international recognition following secession in 1861. The ploy failed as a strategy; during the Civil War, Britain turned to India for its raw cotton supplies. British cloth woven with Indian cotton was then exported back to India, a policy which benefited British producers, while keeping the Indian textile industry at a local level until the end of the 19th century.

5 The politics of cotton ▼

- raw cotton from US to Britain
- cotton textiles to India
- raw cotton from India to Britain
- cotton producing region
- textile town
- major cotton-producing states

◄ **4** The cotton towns of Lancashire and Yorkshire

- cotton town
- Peel textile firm
- major railroad c.1850
- major canal

Cotton production in Lancashire

With plentiful water to power new machinery, Lancashire had developed as a major cotton-weaving center by the late 18th century. Textile towns such as Stockport, Blackburn, and Cromford, often containing several firms, grew up in the area around Manchester, which acted as a major market for finished cloth.

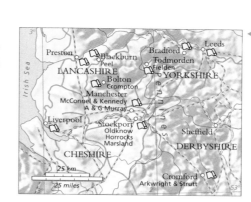

1815–60: British cotton textile production expands at a rate of 6–7% per annum and by the mid-century British cotton constitutes c.50% of world production of commercially produced cloth

1879: Abolition of all tariff duties on British textiles
1895: Britain imposes excise of 5% on Indian cotton goods
1924: Cotton excise suspended

Late 18th century: Cotton production in Lancashire is great growth industry of Industrial Revolution

1793: Invention of cotton gin leads to a massive increase in the production of short-staple cotton

1800–60: US annual raw cotton production increases from 100,000 bales to 4 million bales

1861: During Civil War, Confederate states restrict cotton exports to try and force European intervention in war

1861–65: "Cotton famine" caused by Civil War restrictions in US leads British textile manufacturers to look to India for raw materials

1861 onward: Boom in raw cotton production in India

1820–50: As woven cloth from Britain floods into India, it loses its world market for textiles and is obliged to import machine-made cotton cloth from Lancashire

THE WORLD 1850–1900

BY 1900 THE EUROPEAN POPULATION had more than doubled to 420 million, while the population of the US had reached 90 million. Industry and commerce were booming, and both Europe and the US were traversed by rail networks. The major European powers were extending their economic and political influence to the very ends of the globe, while fierce rivalries and competition were being enacted on the international as well as the domestic scene. Within two decades the European powers had colonized virtually the whole of the African continent, the British had claimed India for the Crown, and the western powers had exploited the fatal weaknesses of China's crumbling Qing dynasty to penetrate deep into the heart of Asia.

Kaiser Wilhelm II was determined to establish Germany as Europe's leading military power.

Europe

The emergence of new states, the rise of nationalism, and growing economic and political power led to rivalry and conflict. Expansionist Russia's activities in the Balkans led in 1854 to the Crimean War, between a Franco–British–Turkish alliance and Russia. In 1870 Bismarck, prime minister of Prussia, goaded the French into war; the French defeat led to the collapse of the Second Empire, providing the final impetus to the creation of the new German and Italian nations.

Europe

1854–56: Franco-British-Turkish alliance victorious against Russians in Crimea	**1862:** Otto von Bismarck prime minister of Prussia	**1870:** Franco-Prussian war; Prussian victory leads to collapse of Second Empire	**1887:** Bulgaria, independent of Ottoman empire, becomes leading Balkan state

| 1850 | 1860 | 1870 | 1880 | 1890 | 1900 |

1861: Abolition of serfdom in Russia	**1867:** Dual monarchy of Austria-Hungary established	**1871:** Rome becomes capital of united Italy; King Wilhelm I of Prussia declared German emperor	**1896:** Revival of Olympic Games at Athens, Greece

CAMPAIGN MAPS

During the American Civil War, new printing technology combined with up-to-date information from correspondents on the battlefields allowed US newspapers to produce simplified campaign maps to explain the stages of the war to a fascinated public.

This map shows the battle of Campbell's Station, Tennessee, as witnessed from the Union position by the *New York Tribune's* correspondent, Elias Smith.

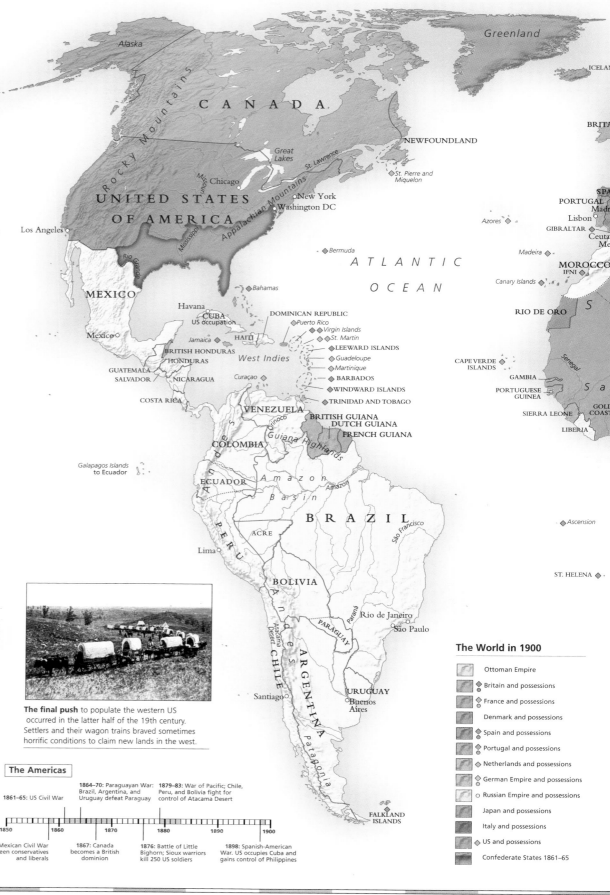

The final push to populate the western US occurred in the latter half of the 19th century. Settlers and their wagon trains braved sometimes horrific conditions to claim new lands in the west.

The Americas

In 1860-1 eleven southern states, fearful that the North was about to abolish slavery, left the Union and formed the Confederacy, beginning a conflict in which over 600,000 soldiers lost their lives. Following the Civil War, the US became the fastest growing economy in the world, its population swollen by waves of immigrants. In South America, economic prosperity, especially from the export of meat and rubber, was enjoyed by the ruling elite, while border disputes bedeviled the new republics.

The Americas

1861–65: US Civil War	**1864–70:** Paraguayan War; Brazil, Argentina, and Uruguay defeat Paraguay	**1879–83:** War of Pacific; Chile, Peru, and Bolivia fight for control of Atacama Desert

| 1850 | 1860 | 1870 | 1880 | 1890 | 1900 |

1858: Mexican Civil War between conservatives and liberals	**1867:** Canada becomes a British dominion	**1876:** Battle of Little Bighorn; Sioux warriors kill 250 US soldiers	**1898:** Spanish-American War; US occupies Cuba and gains control of Philippines

The World in 1900

- Ottoman Empire
- Britain and possessions
- France and possessions
- Denmark and possessions
- Spain and possessions
- Portugal and possessions
- Netherlands and possessions
- German Empire and possessions
- Russian Empire and possessions
- Japan and possessions
- Italy and possessions
- US and possessions
- Confederate States 1861–65

East Asia

Agrarian unrest in China in the 1850s led to rebellion and famine. Western powers were quick to exploit internal dissent, carving out spheres of influence and annexing territory. A wave of xenophobia led to the Boxer Rebellion of 1900. Western troops were sent to China and concessions were extracted from the weak government. In Japan, the overthrow of the Tokugawa shogunate in 1868 was followed by industrial and economic modernization.

From the late 19th century, the newly-modernized Japan reopened its doors to foreign trade.

East Asia

| 1850: Taiping Rebellion begins in Guangxi province | 1860: British and French occupy Beijing | 1871: Abolition of feudalism in Japan | | 1900: Boxer Rebellion: Christian missions and western legations attacked |

1850 — 1860 — 1870 — 1880 — 1890 — 1900

1853: Rebels capture Nanjing – recaptured a year later | 1868: Overthrow of Tokugawa shogunate | 1877–79: Famine in northern China leaves at least 10 million dead | 1894–95: Japanese overwhelm Chinese forces and annex Taiwan

South Asia

By 1850 the British East India Company emerged as the major power on the subcontinent. Hostility to the British, combined with suspicions about their attitude to India's traditional faiths, led to the Mutiny of 1857–59. Following the Mutiny, the British took administrative control of India, developed an extensive rail network, and began to industrialize the Indian economy.

The railroad station in Bombay was opened in 1887. The style and scale of the building reflected the great self-confidence of India's British rulers.

South Asia

| | 1878–79: Second Afghan War; British invade Afghanistan, which is coming under Russian influence | 1885: Foundation of Indian National Congress |

1850 — 1860 — 1870 — 1880 — 1890 — 1900

1857: Outbreak of Indian Mutiny | 1876: Queen Victoria declared Empress of India, and a Viceroy appointed as her representative | 1885–86: Third Burmese War leads to British annexation of Burma

SEE ALSO:

North America: pp.128–133

South America: pp.150–151

Africa: pp.166–167

Europe: pp.202–207

West Asia: pp.232–233

South and Southeast Asia: pp.248–251

North and East Asia: pp.268–270

Australasia and Oceania: pp.282–285

THE TELEPHONE

The telephone was invented in 1876 by the Scottish-born inventor and speech therapist Alexander Graham Bell. His device used a thin diaphragm to convert vibrations from the human voice into electrical signals. These were then reconverted into sound waves. Within a few years of its invention, the telephone had been installed in many city homes in Europe and the US.

This view of Broadway in 1880 shows its skyline crisscrossed by telegraph and telephone wires.

Africa

In 1850 Africa was a patchwork of kingdoms and states, mostly unknown to Europeans. But, by 1900, the major European powers had seized virtually the entire continent. Rivalries between European nations were played out in Africa as colonizing countries raced for territory, raw materials, and new markets. In 1898, open war between France and the British in the White Nile region was only just averted. In 1899, the Boer War, a bitter struggle between the British and Afrikaaners, began.

By 1872, rich seams of gold- and diamond-bearing rock in Cape Colony were being heavily mined by European prospectors.

Africa

| | 1869: Opening of Suez Canal | 1880: White Boers have appropriated most habitable land in Cape Colony | 1896: Abyssinia defeats Italians at Adowa | 1899: Boer War begins |

1850 — 1860 — 1870 — 1880 — 1890 — 1900

1863: Al-Hajj 'Umar clashes with French in Senegal Valley and creates a Muslim empire | 1879: Zulu War with British; Zulus defeated | 1882: British invade and occupy Egypt | 1893: French conquer Dahomey | 1898: British and French clash at Fashoda

THE ERA OF WESTERN IMPERIALISM

This *Punch* cartoon from 1890 depicts Germany as an eagle, with Africa as her prey. The caption reads, "On the Swoop."

THE LAST TWENTY YEARS of the 19th century saw unprecedented competition by the major European nations for control of territory overseas. The balance of imperial power was changing: having lost their American empires, Spain and Portugal were no longer preeminent. From the 1830s, France began to build a new empire, and Britain continued to acquire new lands throughout the century. Newly unified Italy and Germany sought to bolster their nation status from the 1880s with their own empires. Africa was the most fiercely contested prize in this race to absorb the nonindustrialized world, but much of Southeast Asia and Oceania was also appropriated in this period. Even the US, historically the champion of anticolonial movements, began to expand across the Pacific.

Other nations were frequently critical of the behavior of European imperialists in Africa. This German cartoon (*left*) has the caption: "Even the lions weep at the way the native Africans are treated by the French."

Many British officials in India maintained rituals of extreme formality (*below*), rather than adapting to native patterns of behavior.

The scramble for Africa

The race for European political control in Africa began in the early 1880s. The Berlin Conference of 1884–85, convened to discuss rival European claims to Africa, was the starting point for the "scramble." Some governments worked through commercial companies; elsewhere, land was independently annexed by these companies; sometimes Africans actually invited Europeans in. In most cases, however, European political control was directly imposed by conquest. By 1914, Africa was fully partitioned along lines that bore little relation to cultural or linguistic traditions.

Colonial administrators often required extreme obeisance from the people they controlled. A local Moroccan sultan is shown here kneeling before a French colonel.

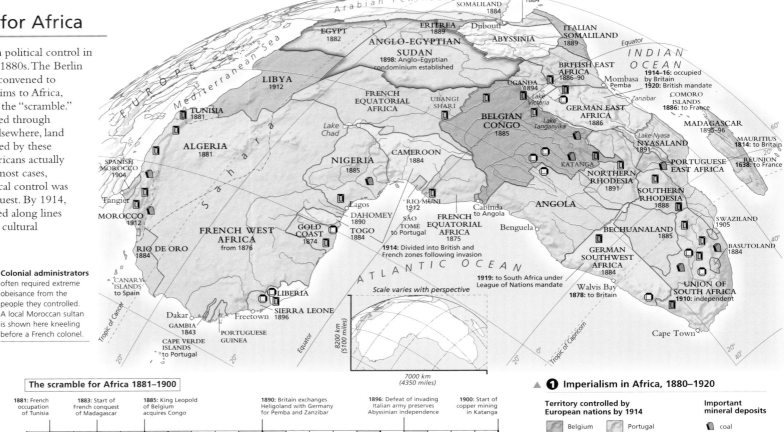

Scale varies with perspective

8200 km (5100 miles)

7000 km (4350 miles)

▲ ❶ **Imperialism in Africa, 1880–1920**

The scramble for Africa 1881–1900

1881: French occupation of Tunisia
1883: Start of French conquest of Madagascar
1885: King Leopold of Belgium acquires Congo
1890: Britain exchanges Heligoland with Germany for Pemba and Zanzibar
1896: Defeat of invading Italian army preserves Abyssinian independence
1900: Start of copper mining in Katanga

1880 · 1885 · 1890 · 1895 · 1900

1882: Revolt in Egypt prompts occupation by British
1884: Germany acquires South West Africa, Togo, and Cameroon
1886: Germany and Britain divide up East Africa
1889: Establishment of first Italian colony in Eritrea
1889: Cecil Rhodes' British South Africa Company begins colonization of Rhodesia
1894: Uganda occupied by Britain

Territory controlled by European nations by 1914

- Belgium
- Britain
- France
- Germany
- Italy
- Portugal
- Spain
- nominally Ottoman, under British control
- 1882 date of taking control
- — borders in 1914

Important mineral deposits

- coal
- copper
- diamonds
- gold

The struggle for South Africa

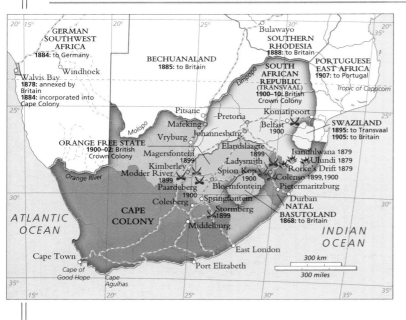

The British, with political control, the Afrikaners (Boers) – the first European settlers – and the Zulus all fought for control of South Africa in the 19th century. Seeking political autonomy, the Boers moved to found their own republics. The success of Transvaal, which grew rich from gold, led to annexation by Britain in 1877. British invasion of Zulu territory led to the First Zulu War, and British defeat, although this was swiftly reversed. In 1881, Boers in Transvaal rebelled against British rule, to set up the South African Republic. In 1899, the second Anglo-Boer war, broke out, lasting until 1902. The former Boer Republics became part of the British Empire as part of the Peace of Vereeniging.

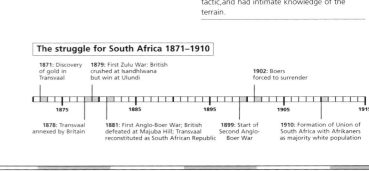

It took more than 300,000 British soldiers five years to subdue 75,000 heavily-armed Boers, who were skilled in guerrilla and siege tactic, and had intimate knowledge of the terrain.

❷ **The struggle for South Africa, 1854–1914**

- Cape Colony and Natal 1854
- territory under British control 1895
- South African Republic 1895
- Orange Free State 1895
- battle in Zulu wars

Boer War 1899–1902

- Afrikaner (Boer) victory
- British victory
- Afrikaner sieges
- Union of South Africa boundary 1910
- railroad

The struggle for South Africa 1871–1910

1871: Discovery of gold in Transvaal
1879: First Zulu War: British crushed at Isandhlwana but win at Ulundi
1902: Boers forced to surrender

1875 · 1885 · 1895 · 1905 · 1915

1878: Transvaal annexed by Britain
1881: First Anglo-Boer War; British defeated at Majuba Hill; Transvaal reconstituted as South African Republic
1899: Start of Second Anglo-Boer War
1910: Formation of Union of South Africa with Afrikaners as majority white population

Imperialism in Southeast Asia

Though the Dutch East Indian Empire had existed since the early 17th century, much of Southeast Asia was not colonized until the mid-19th century. Moving east from India, British ambitions concentrated on Burma, the Malay Peninsula, and north Borneo. Renewed French interest in empire-building began in earnest with the capture of Saigon in 1858 following a concerted naval effort. By 1893, France controlled Tongking, Laos, Annam, and Cambodia, collectively known as Indochina.

Imperialism in Southeast Asia 1858–1895

1855: Start of British trade with Siam
1863: French establish protectorate over Cambodia
1873: Dutch attack on Achin sultanate
1884: Annexation of northern New Guinea and Bismarck Archipelago by Germany
1886: Britain annexes Upper Burma after Third Burmese War

1859: Saigon captured by France
1859: Timor divided between Netherlands and Portugal
1867: French protectorate established in Cochin China
1885: French protectorate established in Annam and Tongking

SEE ALSO:

North America: pp.132–133

Africa: pp.166–167

Europe: pp.202–203, p.206

West Asia: pp.232–233

South and Southeast Asia: pp.250–251

North and East Asia: pp.268–271

Australasia and Oceania: pp.282–283

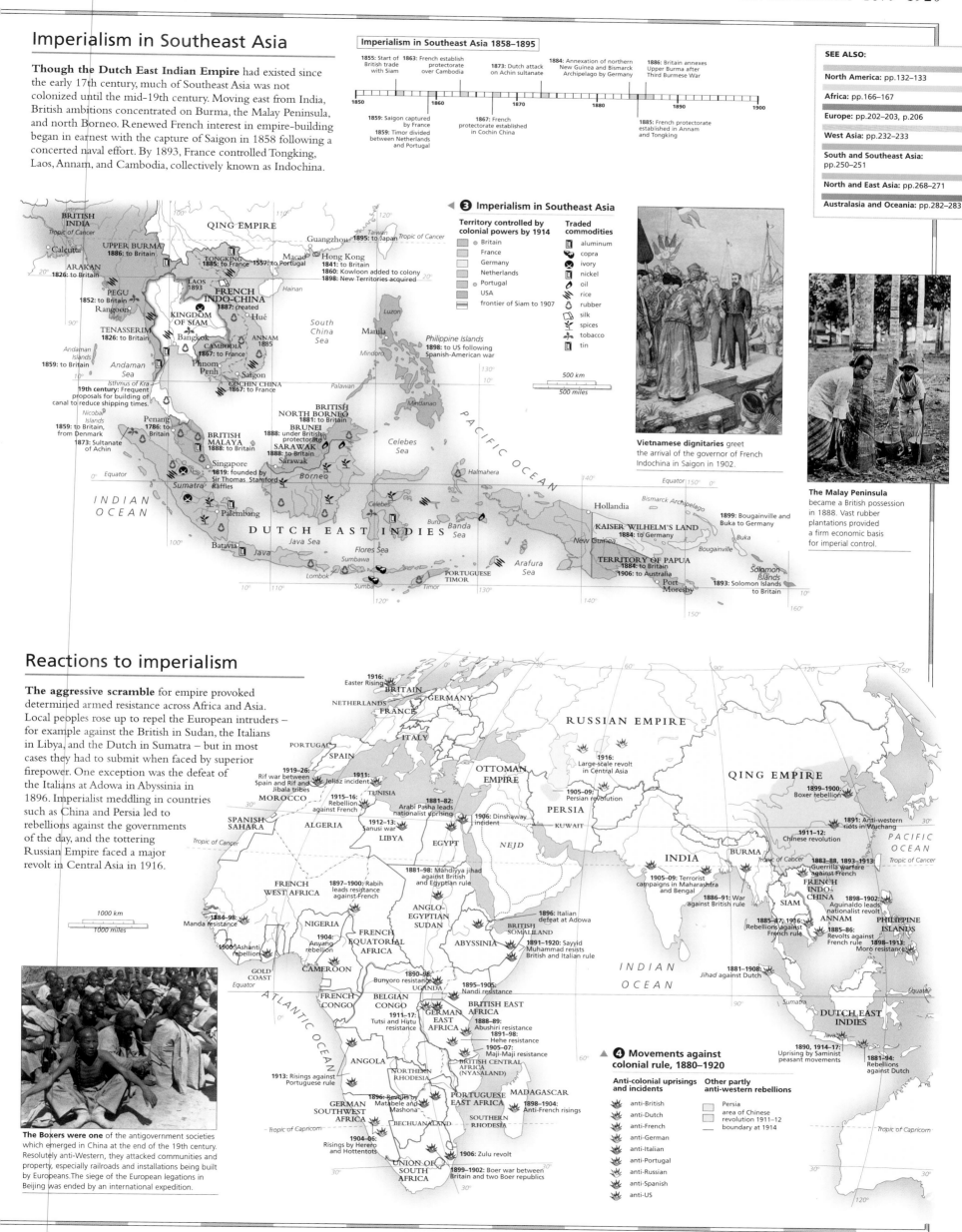

③ Imperialism in Southeast Asia

Territory controlled by colonial powers by 1914
- Britain
- France
- Germany
- Netherlands
- Portugal
- USA
- frontier of Siam to 1907

Traded commodities
- aluminum
- copra
- ivory
- nickel
- oil
- rice
- rubber
- silk
- spices
- tobacco
- tin

Vietnamese dignitaries greet the arrival of the governor of French Indochina in Saigon in 1902.

The Malay Peninsula became a British possession in 1888. Vast rubber plantations provided a firm economic basis for imperial control.

Reactions to imperialism

The aggressive scramble for empire provoked determined armed resistance across Africa and Asia. Local peoples rose up to repel the European intruders – for example against the British in Sudan, the Italians in Libya, and the Dutch in Sumatra – but in most cases they had to submit when faced by superior firepower. One exception was the defeat of the Italians at Adowa in Abyssinia in 1896. Imperialist meddling in countries such as China and Persia led to rebellions against the governments of the day, and the tottering Russian Empire faced a major revolt in Central Asia in 1916.

The Boxers were one of the antigovernment societies which emerged in China at the end of the 19th century. Resolutely anti-Western, they attacked communities and property, especially railroads and installations being built by Europeans. The siege of the European legations in Beijing was ended by an international expedition.

④ Movements against colonial rule, 1880–1920

Anti-colonial uprisings and incidents
- anti-British
- anti-Dutch
- anti-French
- anti-German
- anti-Italian
- anti-Portugal
- anti-Russian
- anti-Spanish
- anti-US

Other partly anti-western rebellions
- Persia
- area of Chinese revolution 1911–12
- boundary at 1914

THE WORLD 1900–1925

THE IMPERIAL AND MILITARY RIVALRY between Britain and France, and Germany and Austria-Hungary led, in 1914, to World War I, which left millions dead and redrew the map of Europe. The Habsburg and Ottoman empires broke up, leading to the emergence of a number of smaller nation states, while the end of the Ottoman Empire also created a territorial crisis in the Middle East. In 1917, the Russian Empire collapsed in revolution and civil war, to be transformed by the victorious Bolsheviks into the world's first Communist empire. The US's participation in the war confirmed its status as a world power, cemented by the central role played by President Wilson at the Versailles Conference, and by the nation's increasing economic dominance.

German soldiers wearing gas masks emerge from a dugout. Troops on both sides endured terrible conditions in the trench warfare which dominated the war in France.

Europe

Most countries in Europe and their colonies took part in World War I, which was fought on a scale unimagined in the 19th century. Years of rivalry between the major European powers, France, Britain and Germany had created an incendiary situation, finally touched off by a crisis in the Balkans. The Versailles Settlement of 1919 altered the balance of power in Europe irrevocably, setting up the conditions for a second European war 20 years later.

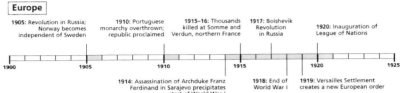

Europe

1905: Revolution in Russia; Norway becomes independent of Sweden

1910: Portuguese monarchy overthrown; republic proclaimed

1915–16: Thousands killed at Somme and Verdun, northern France

1917: Bolshevik Revolution in Russia

1920: Inauguration of League of Nations

1914: Assassination of Archduke Franz Ferdinand in Sarajevo precipitates start of World War I

1918: End of World War I

1919: Versailles Settlement creates a new European order

RADIO

Radio technology was first invented by Guglielmo Marconi in 1894. In 1901 he was able to send Morse Code messages across the Atlantic, and by 1920 the first commercial radio station was set up in Pittsburgh. By the mid-1920s, radio was established as an immensely effective means of mass communication.

This radio, advertised using the famous fox terrier listening to "His Master's Voice," dates from the 1920s.

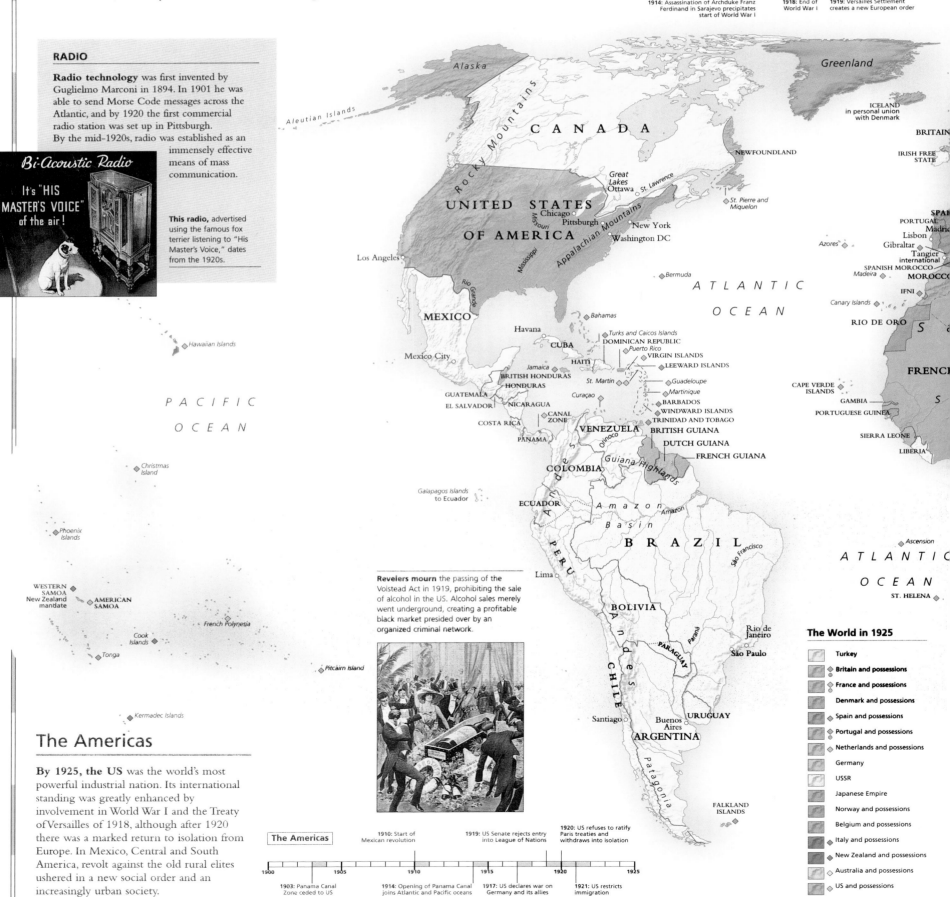

Revelers mourn the passing of the Volstead Act in 1919, prohibiting the sale of alcohol in the US. Alcohol sales merely went underground, creating a profitable black market presided over by an organized criminal network.

The Americas

By 1925, the US was the world's most powerful industrial nation. Its international standing was greatly enhanced by involvement in World War I and the Treaty of Versailles of 1918, although after 1920 there was a marked return to isolation from Europe. In Mexico, Central and South America, revolt against the old rural elites ushered in a new social order and an increasingly urban society.

The Americas

1910: Start of Mexican revolution

1919: US Senate rejects entry into League of Nations

1920: US refuses to ratify Paris treaties and withdraws into isolation

1903: Panama Canal Zone ceded to US

1914: Opening of Panama Canal joins Atlantic and Pacific oceans

1917: US declares war on Germany and its allies

1921: US restricts immigration

The World in 1925

- Turkey
- Britain and possessions
- France and possessions
- Denmark and possessions
- Spain and possessions
- Portugal and possessions
- Netherlands and possessions
- Germany
- USSR
- Japanese Empire
- Norway and possessions
- Belgium and possessions
- Italy and possessions
- New Zealand and possessions
- Australia and possessions
- US and possessions

West Asia

In 1918, the Ottoman Empire collapsed after more than 400 years. A new Turkish republic was inaugurated in 1923. In the post-war period much of the former Ottoman Empire, including Transjordan, Syria, and Iraq was controlled by Britain and France. A new Arab nationalism was becoming more strident, resulting in numerous political disturbances.

Kemal Atatürk was the first leader of the new Turkish republic. From 1923–38 he radically overhauled Ottoman institutions to bring Turkey into the modern age.

A Soviet propaganda poster encourages peasants to invest their savings in state projects. Much policy at this time was aimed at exerting control over the peasants.

Northeast Asia

Much of North and East Asia was destabilized by the collapse of the Chinese Empire into civil war in 1911, and the Russian Revolution of 1917. The victorious Bolsheviks hoped for the spread of revolution in other countries. Meanwhile, Japanese expansionism was rewarded by territorial gains in Siberia, China, and the Pacific islands.

SEE ALSO:

North America: pp.132–133

South America: pp.152–153

Africa: pp.166–167

Europe: pp.206–207

West Asia: pp.232–233

South and Southeast Asia: pp.250–251

North and East Asia: pp.270–271

Australasia and Oceania: pp.284–285

West Asia

- 1912–13: Ottomans lose most of their European lands in Balkan Wars
- 1915: Allied attack on Gallipoli
- 1917: Balfour Declaration commits Britain to creation of Jewish state in Palestine
- 1908: Ottoman sultan deposed in Young Turk Revolution
- 1914: Ottomans ally with Germany and Austria after Britan, France and Russia declare war
- 1918: Collapse of Ottoman Empire
- 1923: Foundation of modern Turkey by Kemal Atatürk

Northeast Asia

- 1910: Japanese annexation of Korea
- 1914: Japan takes over many German colonies in the Pacific
- 1918–20: Japan occupies part of Manchuria and Siberia
- 1904–05: Russo-Japanese War; series of Russian defeats
- 1911: Qing dynasty overthrown by Sun Yat Sen's nationalists and Republic of China declared
- 1922: Washington Naval Agreement limits Japanese naval power in the Pacific

ROAD MAPS

The growth in automobile use, a burgeoning road network and an increasingly mobile population, necessitated the creation of a new type of road map, more detailed than any made previously.

The cover of this 1920s road map emphasizes the link between car usage and leisure pursuits.

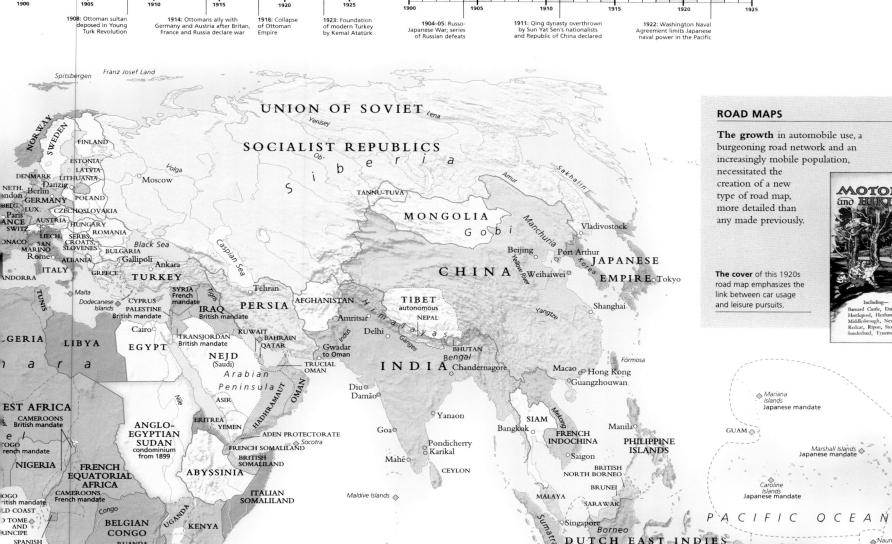

The European colonial powers maintained substantial armies within their empires, composed of both European and colonial troops.

The colonial world

By the end of the World War I, the vast overseas empires of Britain and France – which now included Germany's African lands – were becoming increasingly expensive and difficult to maintain. Colonialism was criticized by the US and the USSR, and independence movements developed in India and a number of African territories, alongside a growing nationalism in Southeast Asia.

The colonial world

- 1901: Commonwealth of Australia proclaimed
- 1904: Partition of Bengal: nationalist agitation in India
- 1910: Union of South Africa set up
- 1920: Mahatma Gandhi gains control of Indian National Congress
- 1902: End of Boer War in South Africa
- 1906: Foundation of All-India Muslim League
- 1911: Italian conquest of Libya
- 1919: Amritsar massacre leads to surge in Indian nationalism

GLOBAL MIGRATION

The Japanese shipping line *Osaka Shoshen Kaisha* carried thousands of immigrants to the US.

THE TECHNICAL INNOVATIONS of the Industrial Revolution made the 19th-century world seem a much smaller place. Railroads could quickly transport large human cargoes across continents, the Suez and Panama canals reduced travel times – sometimes by as much as 50%, and ships became larger, faster, and more seaworthy. The mechanization and centralization of industry required the concentration of labor on a scale never seen before. At the same time, the European imperial powers were exploiting their tropical possessions for economic benefit. Cash crops, grown on large plantations, needed a plentiful supply of labour as well. Political upheaval, wars, and economic hardship provided the most dramatic impetus to emigration – especially in the Russian Empire and Central Europe, and in southeastern China.

Migration in the 19th century

More than 80 million people emigrated from their country of origin during the 19th and early 20th centuries. Over half of them moved across the Atlantic to North and South America. The end of the American Civil War in 1865, and the opening up of Native American land to settlers saw the greatest period of immigration to the US and Canada. In the Russian Empire, movement was eastward from European Russia into Siberia and the Caspian region. Europeans moved south and east to take up employment in the colonies, while indentured laborers traveled to the Americas, Africa, and Southeast Asia.

Pogroms, or riots against Jews were frequent in late 19th-century Russia. Many fled following the riots; others were formally expelled from designated areas such as St. Petersburg (*above*).

❶ World migration c.1860–1920

Transatlantic migration
- → to North America
- → to South America and the Caribbean
- → to Europe from the Americas

Other European migration
- → to Australia and New Zealand
- → to North Africa

Asian migration
- → to the Americas and Australia
- → Russian migration into Siberia
- → Indian intercolonial migration
- ----- transcontinental railroad
- ▨ major exporters of people
- ▧ major importers of people

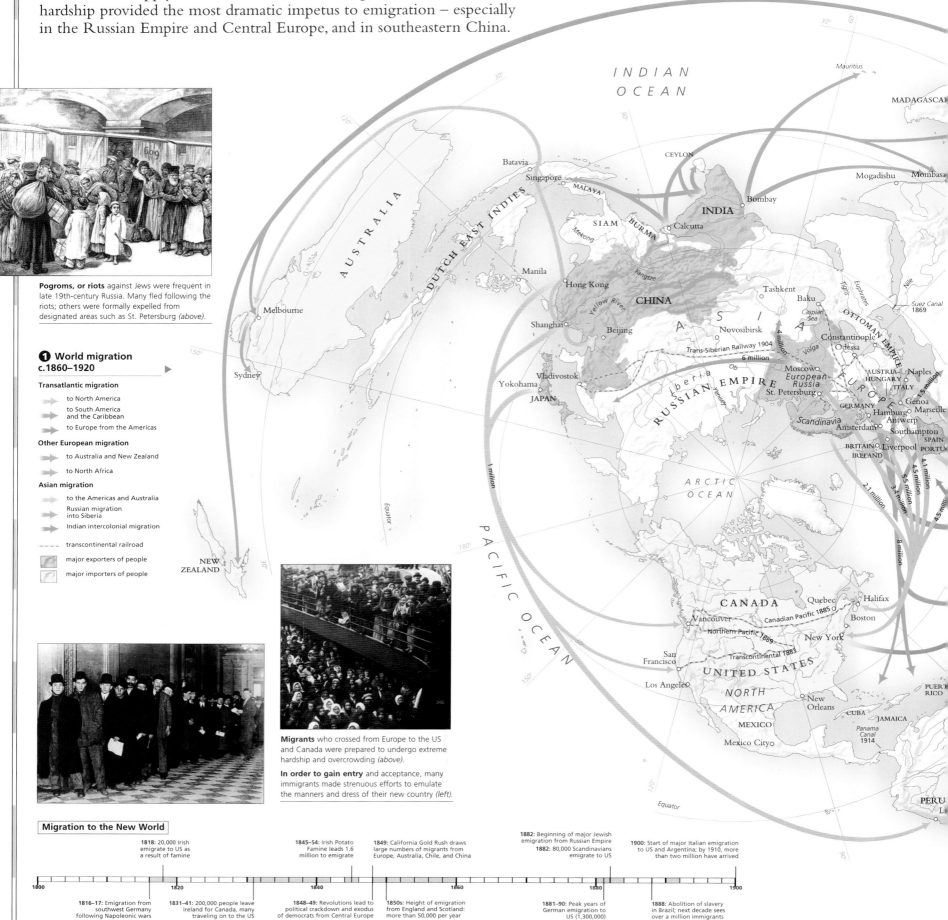

Migrants who crossed from Europe to the US and Canada were prepared to undergo extreme hardship and overcrowding (*above*).

In order to gain entry and acceptance, many immigrants made strenuous efforts to emulate the manners and dress of their new country (*left*).

Migration to the New World

1818: 20,000 Irish emigrate to US as a result of famine

1845–54: Irish Potato Famine leads 1.6 million to emigrate

1849: California Gold Rush draws large numbers of migrants from Europe, Australia, Chile, and China

1882: Beginning of major Jewish emigration from Russian Empire

1882: 80,000 Scandinavians emigrate to US

1900: Start of major Italian emigration to US and Argentina; by 1910, more than two million have arrived

1816–17: Emigration from southwest Germany following Napoleonic wars

1831–41: 200,000 people leave Ireland for Canada, many traveling on to the US

1848–49: Revolutions lead to political crackdown and exodus of democrats from Central Europe

1850s: Height of emigration from England and Scotland: more than 50,000 per year

1881–90: Peak years of German emigration to US (1,300,000)

1888: Abolition of slavery in Brazil; next decade sees over a million immigrants

❷ The great Jewish migration, 1880–1914

- major concentration of Jews in the Russian Empire (the "Pale")
- region with emigrating Jewish population
- region with substantial Jewish immigration
- region where pogroms occurring
- ● gateway city
- → Sephardic Jews
- → Ashkenazi Jews
- 70,000 number of Jewish immigrants 1880–1914

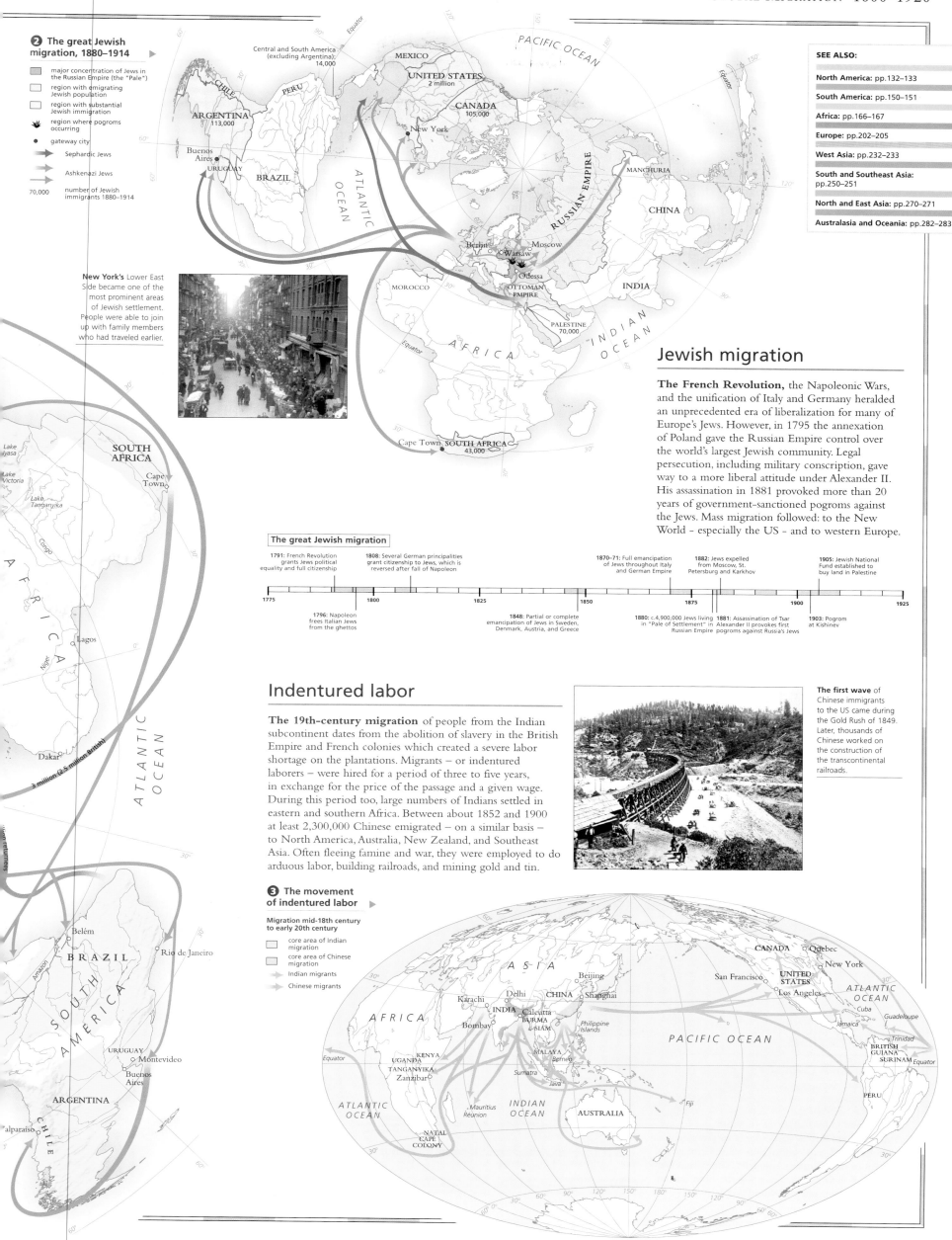

Central and South America (excluding Argentina); 14,000

MEXICO

UNITED STATES 2 million

CANADA 105,000

● New York

ARGENTINA 113,000

Buenos Aires ●

URUGUAY

BRAZIL

RUSSIAN EMPIRE

MANCHURIA

CHINA

Berlin ● Warsaw ● Moscow ●
Odessa ●

MOROCCO

OTTOMAN EMPIRE

INDIA

PALESTINE 70,000

Cape Town ● SOUTH AFRICA 43,000

New York's Lower East Side became one of the most prominent areas of Jewish settlement. People were able to join up with family members who had traveled earlier.

SOUTH AFRICA

Cape Town

Lake Nyasa
Lake Victoria
Lake Tanganyika
Congo

Lagos
Niger
Dakar

3 million (2.5 million British)

Belém

BRAZIL

Rio de Janeiro

Amazon

URUGUAY
Montevideo

Buenos Aires

ARGENTINA

Valparaíso

CHILE

SEE ALSO:

North America: pp.132–133

South America: pp.150–151

Africa: pp.166–167

Europe: pp.202–205

West Asia: pp.232–233

South and Southeast Asia: pp.250–251

North and East Asia: pp.270–271

Australasia and Oceania: pp.282–283

Jewish migration

The French Revolution, the Napoleonic Wars, and the unification of Italy and Germany heralded an unprecedented era of liberalization for many of Europe's Jews. However, in 1795 the annexation of Poland gave the Russian Empire control over the world's largest Jewish community. Legal persecution, including military conscription, gave way to a more liberal attitude under Alexander II. His assassination in 1881 provoked more than 20 years of government-sanctioned pogroms against the Jews. Mass migration followed: to the New World – especially the US – and to western Europe.

The great Jewish migration

1791: French Revolution grants Jews political equality and full citizenship

1796: Napoleon frees Italian Jews from the ghettos

1808: Several German principalities grant citizenship to Jews, which is reversed after fall of Napoleon

1848: Partial or complete emancipation of Jews in Sweden, Denmark, Austria, and Greece

1870–71: Full emancipation of Jews throughout Italy and German Empire

1880: c.4,900,000 Jews living in "Pale of Settlement" in Russian Empire

1881: Assassination of Tsar Alexander II provokes first pogroms against Russia's Jews

1882: Jews expelled from Moscow, St. Petersburg and Karkhov

1903: Pogrom at Kishinev

1905: Jewish National Fund established to buy land in Palestine

1775 — 1800 — 1825 — 1850 — 1875 — 1900 — 1925

Indentured labor

The 19th-century migration of people from the Indian subcontinent dates from the abolition of slavery in the British Empire and French colonies which created a severe labor shortage on the plantations. Migrants – or indentured laborers – were hired for a period of three to five years, in exchange for the price of the passage and a given wage. During this period too, large numbers of Indians settled in eastern and southern Africa. Between about 1852 and 1900 at least 2,300,000 Chinese emigrated – on a similar basis – to North America, Australia, New Zealand, and Southeast Asia. Often fleeing famine and war, they were employed to do arduous labor, building railroads, and mining gold and tin.

The first wave of Chinese immigrants to the US came during the Gold Rush of 1849. Later, thousands of Chinese worked on the construction of the transcontinental railroads.

❸ The movement of indentured labor

Migration mid-18th century to early 20th century

- core area of Indian migration
- core area of Chinese migration
- → Indian migrants
- → Chinese migrants

CANADA ○ Québec

New York

UNITED STATES

San Francisco
Los Angeles

ASIA

Beijing

Delhi
Karachi
INDIA
Bombay
Calcutta
BURMA
SIÁM

CHINA
Shanghai

Philippine Islands

AFRICA

KENYA
UGANDA
TANGANYIKA
Zanzibar

MALAYA
Borneo

Sumatra
Java

Mauritius
Réunion

INDIAN OCEAN

AUSTRALIA

Fiji

NATAL
CAPE COLONY

ATLANTIC OCEAN

PACIFIC OCEAN

Cuba
Jamaica
Guadeloupe
Trinidad
BRITISH GUIANA
SURINAM

PERU

Equator

THE WORLD 1950–1975

WORLD POLITICS IN THE ERA following the close of World War II were defined by the tense relationship between the US and the USSR. The "Cold War" between democratic capitalism and Communism saw each side constantly attempting to contain and subvert the other. The Korean War (1950–55), the Cuban Missile Crisis of 1962, and the Vietnam War (1954–75), as well as many smaller conflicts – particularly in Central America and Africa – were all manifestations of the Cold War. Though no nuclear weapons were ever used in anger, both sides built up huge nuclear arsenals whose potential for mass destruction acted as a deterrent to conflict on a global scale.

Europe

During the Soviet era the May Day parade in Moscow's Red Square became the focus for the USSR's display of its military might. Weapons such as these ballistic rockets were wheeled through the streets.

The 1950s and 1960s were a period of widespread prosperity and political stability in Western Europe, faltering only in the early 1970s. West Germany, banned from keeping a large army, rebuilt its shattered economy and infrastructure with stunning success. Eastern Europe was overshadowed by Soviet Communism, which restricted both economic development and the personal freedom of its citizens.

Europe

| 1955: Warsaw Pact created as Soviet-bloc opponent of NATO | 1957: Creation of European Economic Community (EEC) | 1961: Berlin Wall separates East and West Berlin | 1968: "Prague Spring" reforms in Czechoslovakia crushed by USSR | 1973: Oil crisis causes inflation and economic slowdown |

| 1950 | 1955 | 1960 | 1965 | 1970 | 1975 |

| 1956: Hungarian revolt crushed by Warsaw Pact | 1957: First artificial satellite, Sputnik II, launched by USSR | 1968: Student uprisings throughout Europe | 1969: De Gaulle resigns after defeat in referendum on regional reform |

SATELLITE IMAGERY

With space technology came the ability to keep artificial satellites in permanent orbit around the Earth. They are used to carry transmitters for telecommunications, as aids to navigation and as bases for space exploration. The data picked up by sensors can be digitally combined to create images of the Earth.

This satellite image of North and South America shows both vegetation cover and weather conditions at the time at which it was taken.

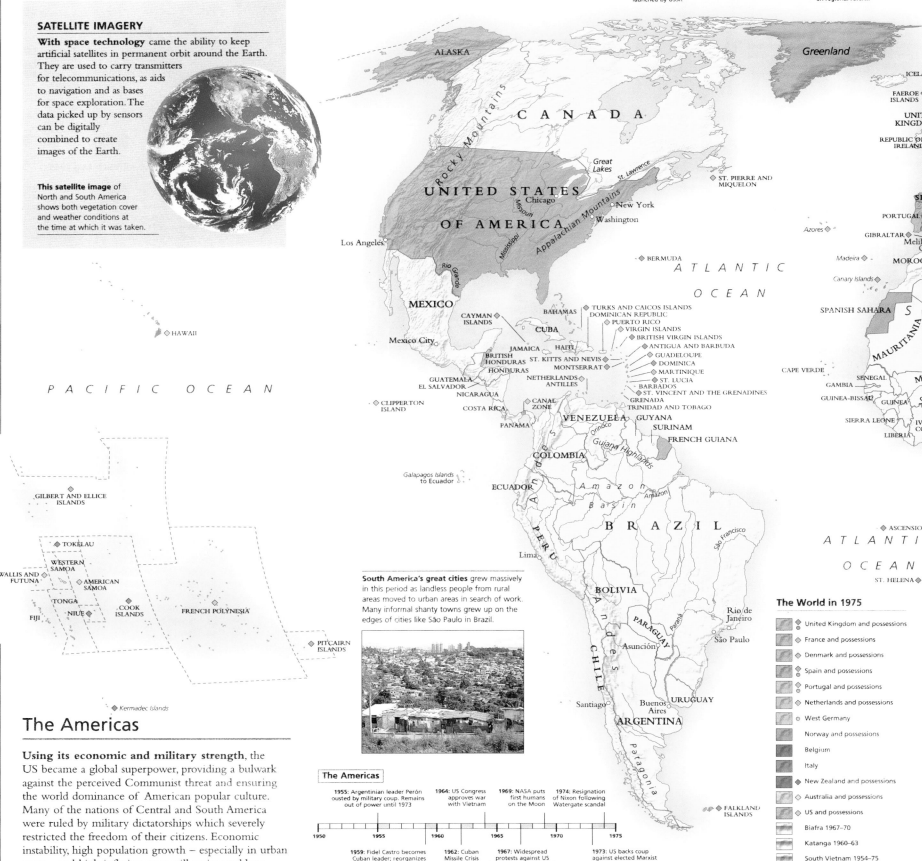

South America's great cities grew massively in this period as landless people from rural areas moved to urban areas in search of work. Many informal shanty towns grew up on the edges of cities like São Paulo in Brazil.

The Americas

Using its economic and military strength, the US became a global superpower, providing a bulwark against the perceived Communist threat and ensuring the world dominance of American popular culture. Many of the nations of Central and South America were ruled by military dictatorships which severely restricted the freedom of their citizens. Economic instability, high population growth – especially in urban areas – and high inflation were still major problems.

The Americas

| 1955: Argentinian leader Perón ousted by military coup. Remains out of power until 1973 | 1964: US Congress approves war with Vietnam | 1969: NASA puts first humans on the Moon | 1974: Resignation of Nixon following Watergate scandal |

| 1950 | 1955 | 1960 | 1965 | 1970 | 1975 |

| 1959: Fidel Castro becomes Cuban leader; reorganizes economy along Soviet lines | 1962: Cuban Missile Crisis | 1967: Widespread protests against US involvement in Vietnam | 1973: US backs coup against elected Marxist government in Chile |

The World in 1975

- ◇ United Kingdom and possessions
- ◇ France and possessions
- ◇ Denmark and possessions
- ◇ Spain and possessions
- ◇ Portugal and possessions
- ◇ Netherlands and possessions
- ○ West Germany
- Norway and possessions
- Belgium
- Italy
- ◇ New Zealand and possessions
- ◇ Australia and possessions
- ◇ US and possessions
- Biafra 1967–70
- Katanga 1960–63
- South Vietnam 1954–75

Intense rivalry between Israel and Egypt led in June 1967 to the Six Day War. Superior Israeli air power routed the Egyptian air force and the ground forces of Egypt, Jordan, Iraq, and Syria.

West and South Asia

Israel, supported by Western powers, fought a series of wars with its Arab neighbors to define its boundaries. The exploitation of extensive oil reserves brought immense wealth to the undeveloped Arabian Peninsula. Relations between India and Pakistan were strained by territorial disputes, and in 1971, the geographical separation of Pakistan proved unsustainable, with East Pakistan becoming Bangladesh.

West and South Asia

| 1952: First Indian general election won by Congress Party | 1961: Foundation of Organization of the Petroleum Exporting Countries (OPEC) | 1965: India–Pakistan War over sovreignty of Kashmir | 1971: Pakistan divides; East Pakistan becomes Bangladesh | 1973: OPEC restricts flow of oil to world markets |

1950 — 1955 — 1960 — 1965 — 1970 — 1975

1956: Pakistan constituted as Islamic Republic
1967: Israel defeats Egypt and other Arab nations in Six Day War
1973: Arab states fail to defeat Israel in Yom Kippur War

East and Southeast Asia

In China and mainland Southeast Asia, power passed to native Communist movements. Mao Zedong's Communist China became a superpower to rival the USSR, while the US intervened in Korea and Vietnam in response to the perceived threat of Communism. Japan began rebuilding its economy with American aid to become, by the mid-1970s, one of the world's richest nations. From 1950 onward, mainland Southeast Asia was destabilized by Cold War-inspired conflict: in Laos, Vietnam, and Cambodia.

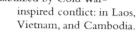

The political thoughts of Mao Zedong were published as the "Little Red Book" and distributed to all Communist Party members.

East and Southeast Asia

| 1950: Outbreak of Korean War | 1958: Start of Mao's "Great Leap Forward" in China | 1965: US troops sent to Vietnam – bombing of North begins | 1975: US-backed South Vietnam regime falls |

1950 — 1955 — 1960 — 1965 — 1970 — 1975

1954: Independence of Laos, Cambodia, and North and South Vietnam
1962: US military advisors sent to assist South Vietnamese regime
1966–70: Mao Zedong imposes Cultural Revolution in China

SEE ALSO:

North America: pp.136–137

South America: pp.152–153

Africa: pp.168–169

Europe: pp.212–213

West Asia: pp.234–235

South and Southeast Asia: pp.250–253

North and East Asia: pp.274–275

Australasia and Oceania: pp.284–285

THE MICROCHIP

The miniaturization of transistors and other electronic components, allowed complete electronic circuits to be created on a single slice of silicon about the size of a human fingernail. The first microprocessor chip, the Intel 4004, was produced in the USA in 1971.

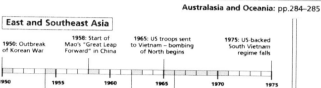

Most modern electronic devices use a number of integrated circuits like this.

Africa's post-colonial era provided rich pickings for a series of corrupt military dictators such as President Mobutu, who ruled Zaire from 1965–97.

Africa

A succession of former colonies became independent from 1957 onward; by 1975, 41 African countries had become independent. Few were fully prepared for the demands of independence, and many countries remained pawns in the Cold War, armed by the opposing powers, and fighting wars on behalf of their conflicting ideologies.

Africa

| 1956: UK fails to block Egypt's nationalization of Suez Canal | 1960: Fifteen African countries gain independence; South Africa leaves Commonwealth | 1962: Nelson Mandela, leader of ANC, given life sentence in South Africa | 1975: Angola and Mozambique gain independence from Portugal |

1950 — 1955 — 1960 — 1965 — 1970 — 1975

1954: Algerian uprising against French rule
1957: Ghana becomes first British colony to achieve independence
1960: Katanga province secedes from Republic of Congo (Zaire); UN intervention follows
1967–70: Civil war in Nigeria over secession of oil-rich east (Biafra). Over one million die

THE COLD WAR

Spies, such as the Rosenbergs, executed in 1953 for passing US nuclear secrets to the USSR, were endemic during the Cold War.

FROM THE MEETING OF US AND SOVIET FORCES on the Elbe River in April 1945 came a division of Europe and a confrontation between the former allies which would last for almost five decades. Defensive needs – for the US the security of Western Europe, for the USSR a buffer zone in Eastern Europe – which appeared to each other to be of offensive intents, overlaid by ideological, political, and economic rivalries. Thus the Cold War took shape, with the US committed to a policy of containment and attrition by all means just short of open conflict, and the USSR intent on supporting anti-Western revolutionary movements throughout the world. Strategic and armed stalemate gave rise to détente in the 1970s, but only the collapse of Soviet system in 1989–91 ended the Cold War.

The Cuban missile crisis 1961–62

The Cold War's most dangerous single episode arose from the Castro Revolution (1956–59) and subsequent US–Cuban estrangement. Castro's alignment with the Eastern bloc provided the USSR with an opportunity to offset its strategic inferiority by the creation of Cuban bases from which missiles could strike at the heart of the continental US. This was forestalled by a US blockade, and a stand-off following which the Soviets were forced to withdraw their missiles.

Cold warriors J. F. Kennedy and Nikita Khrushchev underestimated each other's strength and determination when they met in Vienna in 1961. By 1962 they had taken the world to the verge of nuclear conflict during the Cuban missile crisis.

Cold War crises 1956–64

1956–59: Cuban Revolution under Fidel Castro	**Apr 1961:** USSR launches first manned space flight		**1962:** Cuban missile crisis
1956	1958	1960	1962 1964
1957: USSR launches first space satellite	**1961:** Increasing US involvement in Vietnam		**1964:** Kubrick's film *Dr. Strangelove* alerts public to dangers of Mutually Assured Destruction (MAD)

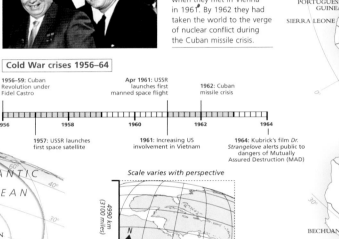

Scale varies with perspective

4990 km (3100 miles)

4440 km (2760 miles)

2 The Cuban missile crisis 1961-62

- potential range of Soviet missiles (1100 miles)
- US blockade zone
- Soviet missile and jet base
- US air base
- US naval base

★ Apr 1961: CIA-backed invasion force of Cuban exiles aborted at Bay of Pigs

On June 23, 1948, the Soviet army blockaded the Western-controlled sectors of Berlin, forcing the Allied powers to mount a massive airlift to supply the beleaguered enclave.

NATO and the Warsaw Pact

Deepening US-Soviet hostility, plus Western Europe's patent inability to defend itself, led to the creation of the North Atlantic Treaty Organization (NATO) in April 1949; in effect, the US provided guarantee of Western Europe's security. The latter's continuing war-weariness saw a buildup of US forces in Europe, and contributed to the decision to permit West Germany to have armed forces, admitting the nation to NATO in 1955. This in turn prompted the USSR and its satellite countries in Eastern Europe to form the Warsaw Pact. The building of the Berlin Wall in 1961 consolidated the "Iron Curtain" which divided Europe into two zones – East and West – until 1989.

The Cold War in Europe 1947–68

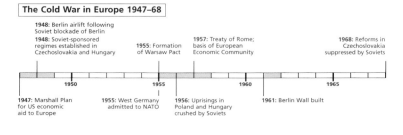

1948: Berlin airlift following Soviet blockade of Berlin		**1955:** Formation of Warsaw Pact	**1957:** Treaty of Rome; basis of European Economic Community	**1968:** Reforms in Czechoslovakia suppressed by Soviets
1948: Soviet-sponsored regimes established in Czechoslovakia and Hungary				
1950	1955		1960	1965
1947: Marshall Plan for US economic aid to Europe	**1955:** West Germany admitted to NATO	**1956:** Uprisings in Poland and Hungary crushed by Soviets	**1961:** Berlin Wall built	

3 The Cold War in Europe

- original NATO members in 1949
- later NATO members (with dates)
- Warsaw Pact members in 1955
- neutral states

From the early 1960s the Western allies depended increasingly on long-range nuclear-powered submarines to deliver missiles in the event of war. With the development of Trident submarines in the 1980s the range extended to 4,500 miles, a key factor in the Strategic Arms Reduction (START) negotiations of 1982–91.

SEE ALSO:

North America: pp.138–139

South America: pp.152–153

Africa: pp.168–169

Europe: pp.212–215

West Asia: pp.234–235

South and Southeast Asia: pp.252–253

North and East Asia: pp.274–275

Australasia and Oceania: pp.284–285

① The alliances of the Cold War

US, allies, and satellite states
- US and original NATO 1949
- later NATO
- NATO dependencies 1960
- other nations allied to the Western bloc by treaty
- ☾ CENTO Pact 1959
- major US and NATO overseas bases

USSR and allies
- USSR
- Warsaw Pact 1955
- Communist satellite states
- China
- major Soviet overseas base
- Cold War flashpoint
- major US fleet

Strategic manoeuvres in the Cold War

- 1947: Truman Doctrine seeks "containment" of USSR
- 1949: Formation of NATO
- 1972: SALT I strategic arms limitation talks
- 1979: SALT II arms limitation agreement signed
- 1990: NATO and Warsaw Pact agree on conventional arms limitation in Europe
- 1945: Yalta Conference; division between Allies; origins of Cold War
- 1955: Formation of Warsaw Pact
- 1989–90: Collapse of Communism in Europe
- 1991: US and USSR sign START arms reduction treaty

1945 · 1955 · 1965 · 1975 · 1985 · 1995

The strategic balance

In the Cold War's first decade the US sought to contain the threat of global Communism by a series of regional treaties and alliances backed by economic and military strength. But by 1960, with a rift in Sino-Soviet relations splitting the Communist bloc, and as the simultaneous process of decolonization (endorsed by the US) deprived its European NATO allies of their global outreach, so the theater of the Cold War shifted from Europe to the developing world. Here a series of conflicts from Cuba to Vietnam saw both the US and the Communist world frequently fighting a war by proxy.

THE ARMS RACE

As the Cold War arms race began, the US held technological, numerical, and positional advantages over the Soviet Union. In the 1960s, as US vulnerability increased, deterrence shifted from bombers to a triad built around submarine- and land-based intercontinental missiles (ICBMs). With the USSR acquiring ICBM capability by the late 1960s, both superpowers faced the future with secure second-strikes: MAD (Mutually Assured Destruction). This situation, and the development of multiple-warhead (MRV, MIRV) technology threatened a new round in the arms race. The 1970s saw ceilings on missile and warhead numbers, and antimissile defences (ABM) were limited (SALT I in 1972, and SALT II in 1979). The brief period of détente gave way to perhaps the most dangerous phase of the Cold War, one that witnessed ABM revival with the Strategic Defence Initiative (SDI, Star Wars) which only ended with the collapse of the USSR in 1991.

The Korean War 1950–53

Reluctantly sanctioned by the USSR, North Korea's invasion of the south in June 1950 was immediately seen as a test of US global credibility. The challenge was initially countered by a US-led UN force, which was met in turn by Chinese intervention. Thereafter the front stabilized around the prewar border. The US, confronted by the need to garrison Europe, and by a reluctance to carry the war beyond Korea's borders, accepted a policy of defensive self-restraint, which formed the basis of the Western Allies' Limited War doctrine.

The Korean War effectively ended in stalemate in July 1953, with the partition of Korea into a Communist North and a nominally democratic South along an armistice line straddling the 38th parallel. This border has remained a heavily armed military frontier ever since. These South Korean troops were photographed in 1996.

④ The Korean War 1950–53

- area controlled by North Korean forces Sep 15 1950
- front line Sep 15 1950
- US forces Sep 16–Oct 24 1950
- Chinese forces Oct 1950
- front line Nov 24 1950
- front line Jan 25 1951
- cease-fire line Jul 27 1953

The Angolan Civil War 1975–88

Ideological indoctrination by both East and West during the Cold War conflicts in the developing world was enforced irrespective of sex or age. The image of the child soldier is an enduring legacy of these conflicts in Africa.

By the 1970s Soviet naval and airlift capacity enabled it to give active support to anti-Western revolution globally. However, its major efforts in Africa, in Angola (1976–88) and Ethiopia (1977–89), were conducted by proxy via Cuba. In Angola, the three main organizations which had fought to end Portuguese rule were bitterly hostile to each other, and by 1975 there was a three-way civil war, the Marxist MPLA initially clearing the FNLA and UNITA from the north. The Soviets sustained the MPLA with Cuban troops, while the Western powers, through South Africa, secured southern borders in support of UNITA. The conflict lasted until 1988, the Cubans, MPLA and South Africa concluding an uneasy ceasefire. Throughout the struggle, UNITA dominated most of Angola through guerrilla warfare, but 50,000 Cuban troops ensured the survival of the MPLA.

⑤ The Angolan Civil War from 1975

- under FNLA control 1975
- under MPLA control 1975
- under UNITA control 1975
- area of MPLA control by mid-1976
- area under UNITA control by mid-1976
- Cuban troops and Soviet aid to MPLA from 1975
- area of effective South African occupation
- South African attacks in support of UNITA 1976–88
- limit of UNITA guerrilla activity 1976–92

PART TWO

REGIONAL HISTORY

INHABITANTS OF EACH PART of the globe view the history of the world through the lens of their regional heritage. The second section of this atlas presents the chronological story of eight principal geographic regions: North America, South America, Africa, Europe, West Asia, South and Southeast Asia, North and East Asia and, finally, Australasia and Oceania. Each regional narrative is prefaced by a map which examines its historical geography. This is followed by pages covering the exploration and mapping of the area, showing how it came to be known in its present form. Thereafter, the maps are organized to present the continuous historical development of each region through time.

By the 18th century, the modern world map was clearly emerging. This map, produced by the Dutch cartographer, Matthias Seutter in 1730, combines a series of detailed projections of the various hemispheres, with compass points depicted as a variety of different windheads.

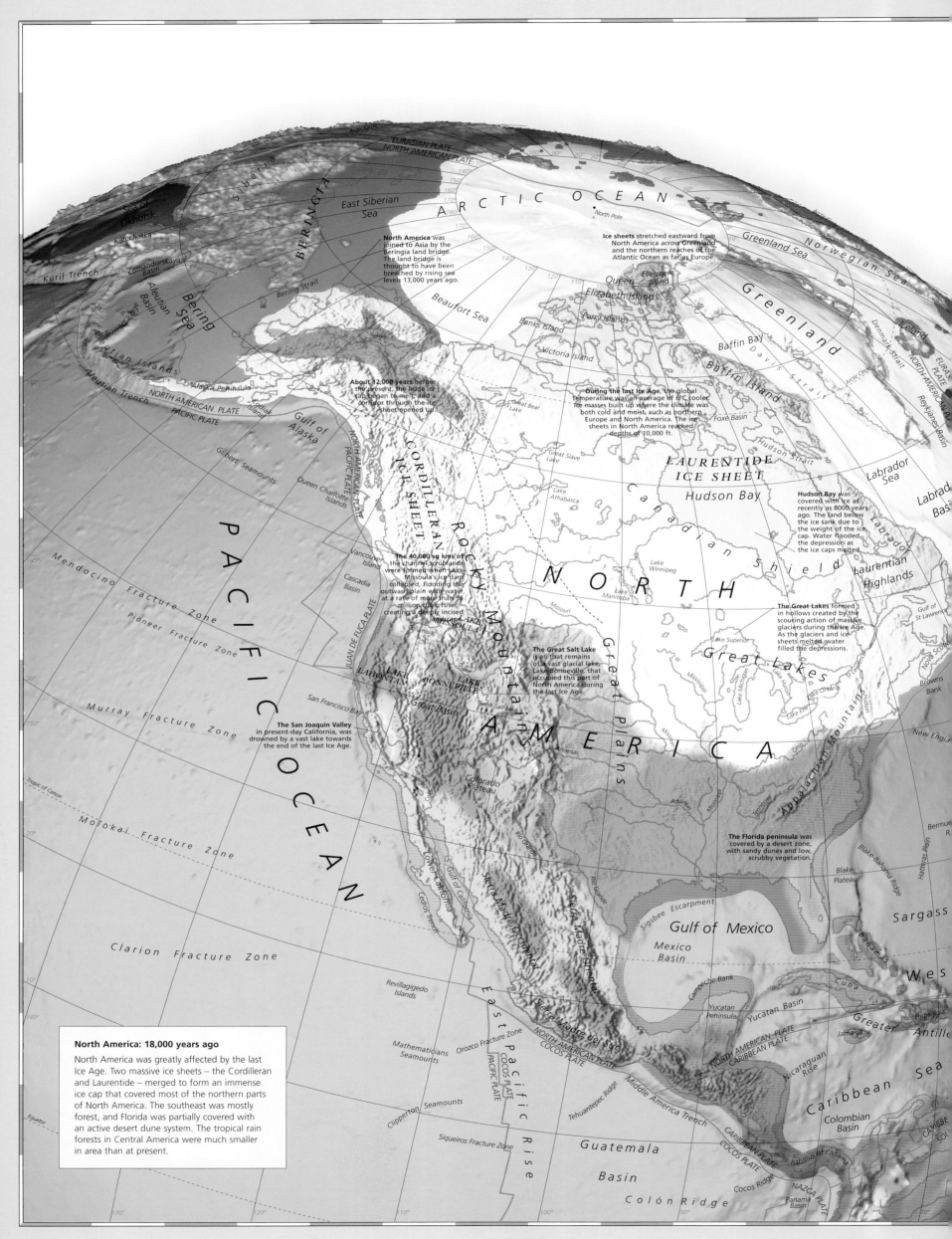

ARCTIC OCEAN

Ice sheets stretched eastward from North America across Greenland and the northern reaches of the Atlantic Ocean as far as Europe.

North Pole

North America was joined to Asia by the Beringia land bridge. The land bridge is thought to have been breached by rising sea levels 13,000 years ago.

EURASIAN PLATE
NORTH AMERICAN PLATE

Greenland Sea

Norwegian Sea

Queen Elizabeth Islands

Ellesmere Island

Greenland

Iceland

Denmark Strait

Reykjanes Ridge

EURASIAN PLATE

NORTH AMERICAN PLATE

BERINGIA

Siberia

Sea of Okhotsk

Kamchatka

East Siberian Sea

Beaufort Sea

Banks Island

Parry Islands

Baffin Bay

Davis Strait

Baffin Island

Arctic Circle

Komandorskaya Basin

Kuril Trench

Aleutian Basin

Bowers Ridge

Bering Sea

Bering Strait

Yukon

Victoria Island

Great Bear Lake

During the last Ice Age, the global temperature was an average of 6°C cooler. Ice masses built up where the climate was both cold and moist, such as northern Europe and North America. The ice sheets in North America reached depths of 10,000 ft.

Foxe Basin

Hudson Strait

Labrador Sea

Labrador Basin

Aleutian Islands

Alaska Peninsula

Kodiak Island

Gulf of Alaska

About 12,000 years before the present, the huge ice cap began to melt, and a corridor through the ice sheet opened up.

Mackenzie

Great Slave Lake

LAURENTIDE ICE SHEET

Hudson Bay

Hudson Bay was covered with ice as recently as 8000 years ago. The land below the ice sank due to the weight of the ice cap. Water flooded the depression as the ice caps melted.

Aleutian Trench

NORTH AMERICAN PLATE

PACIFIC PLATE

Gilbert Seamounts

Queen Charlotte Islands

CORDILLERAN ICE SHEET

Lake Athabasca

NORTH AMERICAN PLATE

PACIFIC PLATE

Vancouver Island

The 40,000 sq kms of the channel scrublands were formed when Lake Missoula's ice dam collapsed, flooding the outwash plain with water at a rate of more than 36 million cubic ft/sec creating a deeply incised landscape.

Lake Winnipeg

Lake Manitoba

Labrador Highlands

Laurentian Highlands

Mendocino Fracture Zone

Cascadia Basin

JUAN DE FUCA PLATE

Columbia

LAKE MISSOULA

Rocky Mountains

Canadian Shield

Missouri

NORTH

The Great Lakes formed in hollows created by the scouring action of massive glaciers during the Ice Age. As the glaciers and ice sheets melted, water filled the depressions.

Pioneer Fracture Zone

PACIFIC OCEAN

Cascade Range

Lake Superior

Great Lakes

Nova Scotia

Browns Bank

LAKE LAHONTAN

LAKE BONNEVILLE

Snake

Great Basin

The Great Salt Lake is all that remains of a vast glacial lake, Lake Bonneville, that occupied this part of North America during the last Ice Age.

Great Salt Lake

Great Plains

Lake Michigan

Lake Huron

Lake Erie

Lake Ontario

St Lawrence

Gulf of St Lawrence

Murray Fracture Zone

San Francisco Bay

Missouri

AMERICA

New England

Tropic of Cancer

The San Joaquin Valley in present-day California, was drowned by a vast lake towards the end of the last Ice Age.

Colorado Plateau

Arkansas

Arkansas

Missouri

Ohio

Appalachian Mountains

Molokai Fracture Zone

9

Colorado

Rio Grande

Tennessee

Bermuda Rise

The Florida peninsula was covered by a desert zone, with sandy dunes and low, scrubby vegetation.

Blake-Bahama Ridge

Lower California

Gulf of California

Sierra Madre Occidental

Sigsbee Escarpment

Blake Plateau

Hatteras Plain

Cedros Trench

Sargasso Sea

Clarion Fracture Zone

Gulf of Mexico

Mexico Basin

Revillagigedo Islands

Campeche Bank

Cuba

West

EAST PACIFIC RISE

Sierra Madre del Sur

Yucatan Peninsula

Yucatan Basin

Greater Antilles

Mathematicians Seamounts

Orozco Fracture Zone

COCOS PLATE

PACIFIC PLATE

NORTH AMERICAN PLATE

COCOS PLATE

Jamaica

Hispaniola

Clipperton Seamounts

Clipperton Fracture Zone

Tehuantepec Ridge

Middle America Trench

Nicaraguan Rise

Caribbean Sea

Siqueiros Fracture Zone

Guatemala Basin

Cocos Ridge

COCOS PLATE

CARIBBEAN PLATE

Isthmus of Panama

Colombian Basin

Equator

Colón Ridge

NAZCA PLATE

Panama Basin

Caribbean

North America: 18,000 years ago

North America was greatly affected by the last Ice Age. Two massive ice sheets – the Cordilleran and Laurentide – merged to form an immense ice cap that covered most of the northern parts of North America. The southeast was mostly forest, and Florida was partially covered with an active desert dune system. The tropical rain forests in Central America were much smaller in area than at present.

Vegetation type

ice cap and glacier

tundra

polar and alpine desert

semidesert or
sparsely vegetated

grassland

forest or open woodland

tropical rain forest

temperate desert

tropical desert

coastline (present-day)

coastline (18,000 years ago)

NORTH AMERICA
REGIONAL HISTORY

THE HISTORICAL LANDSCAPE

HUMANS FIRST ENTERED NORTH AMERICA FROM SIBERIA some 15,000 years ago. They migrated over the land bridge across the Bering Strait and, as the ice receded, moved south, into the rich gamelands of the Great Plains and onward to eventually populate Central and South America. As the ice melted and sea levels rose, these early settlers and their new homeland became isolated from Eurasia, and would remain so until the second millennium CE. The low population level and abundance of foods meant that sedentary agricultural life evolved only sporadically, some groups sustaining a hunting and gathering way of life to the present day. During this period of isolation, unique ecological, genetic, and social patterns emerged which proved disastrously fragile when challenged by the first European colonists in the 15th century CE. Within 500 years the indigenous cultures of North America had been destroyed or marginalized by waves of migrants from the Old World who, with astonishing energy and ferocity, transformed the continent into the World's foremost economic, industrial, and political power.

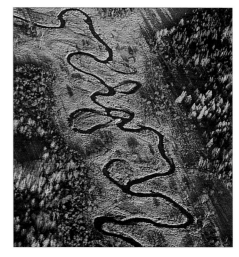

The gigantic basin drained by the Mississippi, spanning the entire tract between the Appalachians and the Rockies, provided a suitable environment for some of the first agricultural communities.

At the heart of the continent, it was the plains which provided homelands for Native North Americans, displaced and driven west by European immigrants.

The Central American mountain plateaus and uplands were where some of the earliest complex civilizations in the Americas developed. A combination of favorable climate and fertile land allowed plants to be cultivated and early agriculture to develop.

NORTH AMERICA
EXPLORATION AND MAPPING

Lewis *(above)* and Clark led an epic expedition to explore the west in 1805–06.

FOR MANY CENTURIES North America was untouched by contact with other continents. Viking seafarers en route from Iceland and Greenland made landfall at Newfoundland over 1,000 years ago, but their settlements were short-lived and their area of operation quite limited. Not until the early 16th century was the presence of a vast continent across the Atlantic fully accepted, and knowledge about it remained fragmentary. Once Europeans began to investigate North America, they were able to draw heavily on information from indigenous peoples, and use their preexisting trails to explore the continent.

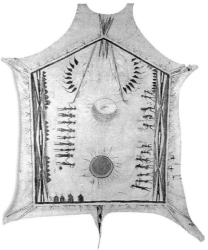

This map of three villages showing their positions relative to the Sun and Moon was painted on a cured buffalo skin by members of the Qapaw tribe.

Native American maps

The indigenous peoples of North and Central America had detailed knowledge of the continent long before the first European expeditions. Much knowledge was undoubtedly passed on orally. But the location of early petroglyph maps carved on rocks suggests that they may have been produced as guides for traveling hunters, and to define territorial boundaries. Later maps – sometimes produced at the request of Europeans – reveal an intimate knowledge of the landscape and principles of space and distance. Several tribes used maps to show the long history of their tenure of the land when they were fighting for territory during the Indian removals of the 19th century.

Early European explorers

Though the first Europeans to visit North America were 10th-century Vikings, European exploration began in earnest in the late 15th century when improvements in shipping made the longer exploratory voyages of Columbus and Cabot viable. By the mid-16th century Spanish-sponsored expeditions in search of gold and territory founded settlements in Florida, Central America, and the Caribbean, and explored the lands of the southeast and southwest. Meanwhile, English and French expeditions traced the Atlantic coast in detail, moving north in search of new routes to Asia.

❶ The first European explorers of North America

Norse expeditions
→ Bjarni Herjolfsson 985–86
→ Leif Eriksson 1003
⋯→ Thorvald Eriksson 1005–12

Spanish and Portuguese expeditions
→ Christopher Columbus 1492–93
→ Miguel Corte-Real 1501, 1502
⋯→ Christopher Columbus 1502–04
→ Hernán Cortés 1519–21
→ Juan Ponce de León 1513
→ Panfilo de Narváez and Álvar Núñez Cabeza de Vaca 1528–36
→ Francisco de Ulloa 1539–40
→ Hernando de Soto 1539–43
→ Francisco Vázquez de Coronado and Garcia Lopez de Cardeñas 1540–42
→ Sebastián Vizcaíno 1602–03

English expeditions
→ John Cabot 1497
→ Martin Frobisher 1576–77
⋯→ Francis Drake 1579
⋯→ John Davis 1585–87
⋯→ Henry Hudson 1610–11

French expeditions
→ Giovanni da Verrazano 1524
→ Jacques Cartier 1535–36
⋯→ Samuel de Champlain 1604–07

○ European settlement
1608 and date of foundation

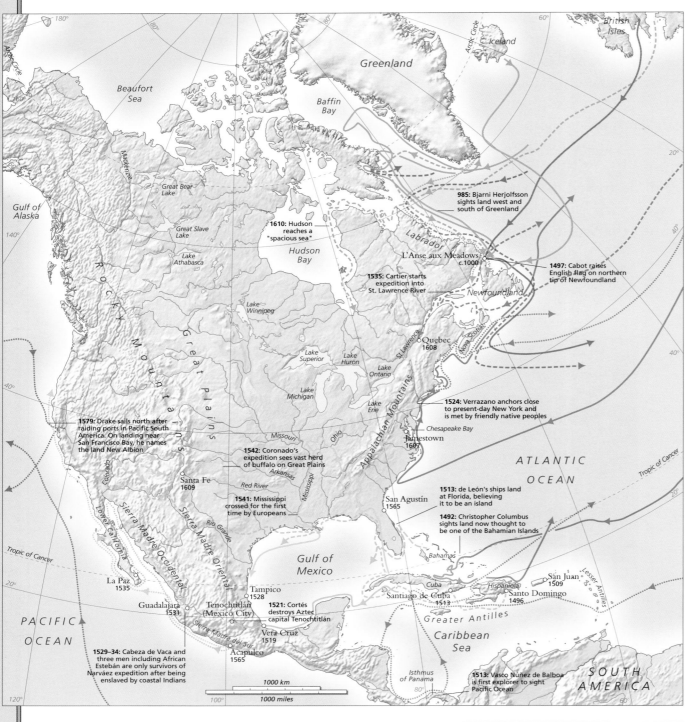

985: Bjarni Herjolfsson sights land west and south of Greenland
1610: Hudson reaches a "spacious sea"
L'Anse aux Meadows c.1000
1497: Cabot raises English flag on northern tip of Newfoundland
1535: Cartier starts expedition into St. Lawrence River
Quebec 1608
1524: Verrazano anchors close to present-day New York and is met by friendly native peoples
1579: Drake sails north after raiding ports in Pacific South America. On landing near San Francisco Bay, he names the land New Albion
1542: Coronado's expedition sees vast herd of buffalo on Great Plains
Jamestown 1607
Chesapeake Bay
Santa Fe 1609
1541: Mississippi crossed for the first time by Europeans
1513: de León's ships land at Florida, believing it to be an island
San Agustín 1565
1492: Christopher Columbus sights land now thought to be one of the Bahamian Islands
Bahamas
La Paz 1535
Tampico 1528
Guadalajara 1531
Tenochtitlán (Mexico City)
1521: Cortés destroys Aztec capital Tenochtitlán
Vera Cruz 1519
Acapulco 1565
1529–34: Cabeza de Vaca and three men including African Estebán are only survivors of Narváez expedition after being enslaved by coastal Indians
Cuba
Santiago de Cuba 1513
San Juan 1509
Hispaniola
Santo Domingo 1496
Greater Antilles
Lesser Antilles
Caribbean Sea
Isthmus of Panama
1513: Vasco Núñez de Balboa is first explorer to sight Pacific Ocean
SOUTH AMERICA
Greenland
Iceland
British Isles
Beaufort Sea
Baffin Bay
Gulf of Alaska
Great Bear Lake
Great Slave Lake
Lake Athabasca
Hudson Bay
Lake Winnipeg
Labrador
Newfoundland
Nova Scotia
Lake Superior
Lake Huron
Lake Michigan
Lake Ontario
Lake Erie
ROCKY MOUNTAINS
Great Plains
Appalachian Mountains
Sierra Nevada
Sierra Madre Occidental
Sierra Madre Oriental
Sierra Madre del Sur
Lower California
Rio Grande
Colorado
Missouri
Mississippi
Ohio
Arkansas
Red River
Mackenzie
St. Lawrence
PACIFIC OCEAN
ATLANTIC OCEAN
Gulf of Mexico
Tropic of Cancer
Arctic Circle
1000 km
1000 miles

This map of Florida and Chesapeake Bay *(above)* was painted in the late 16th century. The spatial relationships are very inaccurate, with the Caribbean islands depicted much too far to the north.

European explorers were astonished by the quantity of wildlife they encountered in North America *(left)*. Fur-bearing animals such as beavers were quickly exploited for their pelts.

15th- and 16th-century European expeditions

1497: Cabot lands on Newfoundland
1501: Miguel Corte-Real enslaves 50 Indians from Beothuk
1524: Verrazano sails up Atlantic coast as far as Nova Scotia
1539–43: De Soto explores southeastern North America

1490 | 1500 | 1510 | 1520 | 1530 | 1540

1492: Columbus lands in the Bahamas thinking he has reached Asia
1513: Ponce de León traces coast of Florida
1528: Cabeza de Vaca explores Gulf of Mexico and southwest
1534: Cartier begins exploration of St. Lawrence

Exploring the eastern interior

The rich Atlantic fisheries and the bounteous wildlife of the northeast were magnets for European hunters and fishermen, and many of the earliest settlements were fur-trading posts. Samuel de Champlain, aided by Iroquois and Montagnais, explored the St. Lawrence River and the Great Lakes, while Hudson and Davis ventured further west into Canada's great bays. Other expeditions were undertaken for missionary purposes, including Jolliet's Mississippian journey, where he was accompanied by Father Marquette. During the late 17th and early 18th centuries, several expeditions sought routes through the Appalachians, which would open up the Midwest to settlers.

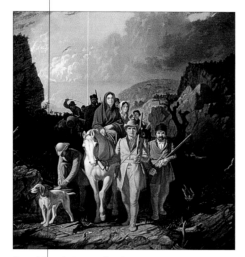

One of America's great frontiersmen, Daniel Boone, is shown here leading a group of settlers through the Cumberland Gap, a pass through the Appalachian system which provided a route to the West.

❷ Journeys into the North American interior 1600–1775 ▶

British expeditions
→ John Smith 1608
↛ Thomas Batts and Robert Fallam 1671
⇢ James Needham and Gabriel Arthur 1673
⋯ Dr. Henry Woodward 1674, 1685

French expeditions
→ Samuel de Champlain 1609–16
⇢ Medart Chouart des Groseillers and Pierre-Esprit Radisson 1659–1660
⋯ Father Claude Allouez 1665–67
→ Father Charles Albanel 1671–72
⋯ Louis Jolliet and Jacques Marquette 1672–73
→ René-Robert Cavelier Sieur de La Salle 1684–87
⋯ Louis Hennepin 1680
⋯ Chaussegros de Léry 1729

Dutch expeditions
→ Arnout Viele 1682–84
→ Johannes Rosebloom 1685–87

American expeditions
→ Christopher Gist 1750–51
→ Thomas Walker 1750
⋯ Daniel Boone 1769–71

By the late 17th century knowledge of the east coast of North America had improved significantly. This plate from Visscher's *Atlas Contractus* of 1671 shows the Atlantic coast from New England south as far as Chesapeake Bay. Detail of the lands further west and the Great Lakes remained limited.

1671: Guided by Indians, Batts and Fallam become first Europeans to cross Appalachians and reach Mississippi watershed

1607: Settlement founded by 120 colonists from England

1750: Walker reaches Cumberland Gap, the gateway to Kentucky

200 km
200 miles

17th- and 18th-century expeditions in eastern North America

1609–13: Champlain explores St. Lawrence and eastern Great Lakes	**1665–67:** Father Allouez explores Great Lakes	**1673:** Jolliet and Marquette explore Mississippi and Illinois Rivers		**1752:** John Finley realizes that Cumberland Gap is gateway to Kentucky lowlands
1600	1650		1700	1750
1607–08: John Smith leads colonizing expeditions in Virginia	**1673:** Needham and Arthur follow Occaneechee Path across Appalachians	**1682:** La Salle follows Mississippi to its mouth		**1729:** de Léry makes first proper survey of Allegheny and upper Ohio Rivers

Charting the West

The rapid expansion of the US created the need to survey and quantify the vast territories of the new nation. Lewis and Clark's famous cross-continental expedition was funded by Congress at the express request of President Jefferson. Fremont conducted his reconnaissance of the west under the auspices of the US Army's Corps of Topographical Engineers. The highly competitive railroad surveys of the 1850s were inspired by economic and political considerations, while Clarence King's survey of the western deserts was motivated primarily by scientific curiosity.

An illustration from Lieutenant Fremont's *Memoirs* shows members of his Great Basin survey team camped on the shores of the Pyramid Lake. The lake was later surveyed in detail by Clarence King.

❸ 19th-century exploration and surveys of the US and Canada ▶

Individual expeditions
→ Meriwether Lewis and William Clark 1804–06
→ Lt. Zebulon M. Pike 1806–07
→ Major Stephen Long 1819–20
→ Lt. John Franklin 1820–21
⇢ Lt. John Franklin 1825–27
→ Lt. John C. Fremont 1842–44
→ Lt. William Emory 1846
→ Lt. James Simpson and Capt. Lorenzo Sitgreaves 1849–51
→ Lt. John Palliser 1857–59

Other expeditions and surveys
→ Russian expeditions to Alaska 1816–65
→ Western Railroad surveys 1853–55
→ Western Union Telegraph survey 1865–67
→ Canadian Yukon Exploring expedition 1887–89

Survey areas
▨ Henry Hind 1857–58
▨ George Wheeler 1867–72
▨ Clarence King 1867–73

This watercolor of the Kanab Desert was painted by a member of the US Geological Survey team in 1880.

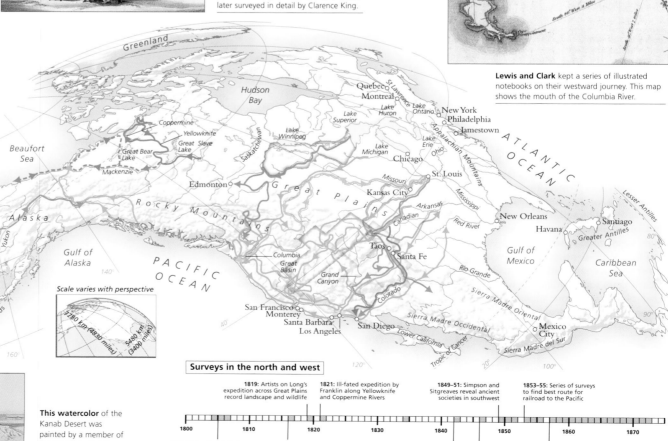

Scale varies with perspective

Lewis and Clark kept a series of illustrated notebooks on their westward journey. This map shows the mouth of the Columbia River.

Surveys in the north and west

1819: Artists on Long's expedition across Great Plains record landscape and wildlife	**1821:** Ill-fated expedition by Franklin along Yellowstone and Coppermine Rivers	**1849–51:** Simpson and Sitgreaves reveal ancient societies in southwest	**1853–55:** Series of surveys to find best route for railroad to the Pacific	
1800	1810	1820	1830	1840	1850	1860	1870
1804–06: Lewis and Clark explore new land acquired in the Louisiana Purchase and reach Pacific coast	**1816:** Start of Russian exploration of Alaska	**1842:** Fremont begins series of expeditions to map American west and encourage settlement	**1846:** Emory surveys Spanish territory during Mexican War	**1857–72:** Wheeler produces first contour maps of southwest

THE AMERICAN CIVIL WAR

Abraham Lincoln's 1863 Emancipation Proclamation freed the slaves of the south.

BETWEEN INDEPENDENCE in 1776 and 1860 there developed within the United States two very different regional societies. In the North there emerged an industrialized society, committed to liberal banking and credit systems, and protective tariffs. The south was a less populous agrarian society opposed to the sale of public land in the Midwest, high duties, and restrictions upon the institution of slavery. Moreover, the libertarian North increasingly resented Southern political and judicial overrepresentation. The Democratic Party held the two parts together until 1859; its split, and the election of a Republican president committed to opposing the spread of slavery, provoked the Union's collapse – even before Lincoln's inauguration, seven southern states had seceded, and war became inevitable.

The cotton gin invented by Eli Whitney in 1793 enabled the swift processing of short-staple cotton. Cotton production increased massively in the southern states, with a resultant rise in the number of slaves required to work the burgeoning plantations.

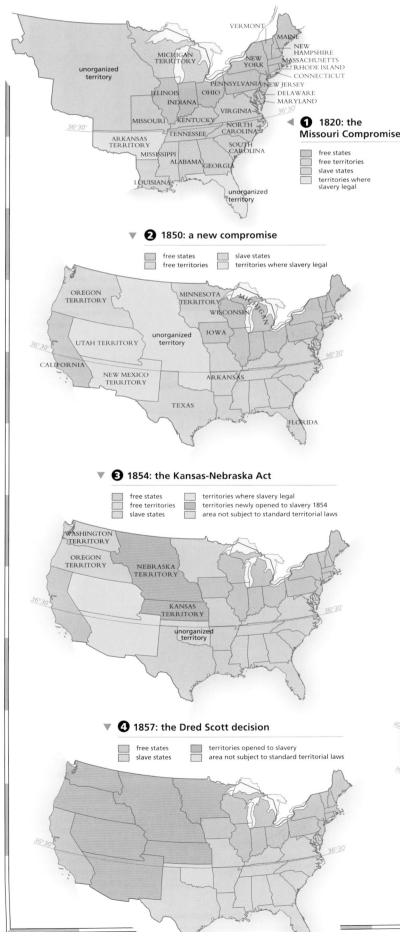

❶ 1820: the Missouri Compromise

- free states
- free territories
- slave states
- territories where slavery legal

▼ ❷ 1850: a new compromise

- free states
- free territories
- slave states
- territories where slavery legal

▼ ❸ 1854: the Kansas-Nebraska Act

- free states
- free territories
- slave states
- territories where slavery legal
- territories newly opened to slavery 1854
- area not subject to standard territorial laws

▼ ❹ 1857: the Dred Scott decision

- free states
- slave states
- territories opened to slavery
- area not subject to standard territorial laws

An unequal nation

By 1860 the US was composed of 18 "free" states – mainly in the North, and 15 "slave" states – mainly in the South. On the issue of slavery, as well as economics, the expanding nation was divided. Industry and finance dominated the North which also had 71% of the population, 81% of bank deposits, 72% of railroad mileage, and 85% of the country's factories. The South concentrated on farming, in particular on the production of cotton, tobacco, and sugar for export to Europe. In 1850, 347,000 Southern families out of a total population of 6,000,000 were slaveowners. The West was developing an agricultural economy, but produced a greater variety of crops, and sold most of its produce to the North.

Industrial production fueled the growth of Northern cities such as Chicago, seen here in the 1860s. The Southern states, largely dependent on agriculture, remained far less economically developed.

Compromises on the road to civil war

The addition of Missouri in 1820 was the first extension of Union territory west of the Mississippi. The question of whether slavery should be allowed in the new state was settled by the so-called Missouri Compromise, with an artificial limit of 36° 30' marking the boundary between slave and free territory. In 1854 the Kansas–Nebraska Act established two new territories and proposed to allow territorial legislatures to decide the issue of slavery. The Dred Scott decision of 1857 – in which a slave who had been taken west by his master claimed that he was free because slavery was not legal in the new territory – led to the ruling that slavery could not be excluded from new territories.

❻ The Civil War to the fall of Vicksburg Apr 1861–Jul 1863

- Union states 1861
- Confederate states 1861
- Union front line to Dec 1861
- Union front line to Dec 1862
- Union movement
- Confederate movement
- Union fort
- Confederate fort
- Union naval blockade
- Union victory
- Confederate victory
- Apr 12 1865 date of battle or attack

▼ ❺ North versus South: the state of the Union in 1861

- Union states
- Confederate states
- slavery legal
- major slave trade routes
- Jan 1861 date of secession from the Union

Resources and industry
- southern cotton belt
- northern corn belt
- coal
- iron ore
- precious metal
- textile production
- manufacturing city

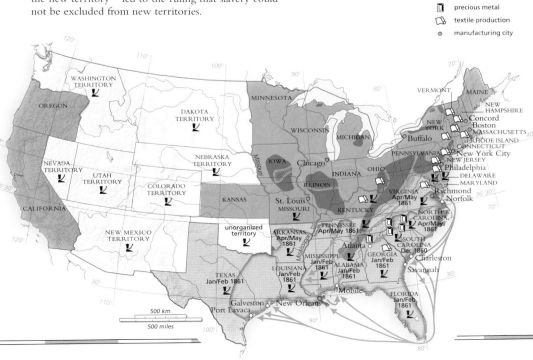

The Civil War 1861–65

In 1860, seven Southern states, fearing restrictions on slavery, seceded from the US. By 1861, they had been joined by four more and became known as the Confederacy. The remaining 23 so-called Union states remained loyal to the US. In April 1861, an attack on Fort Sumter in Charleston Harbor started a war for which neither side was prepared. The Civil War became a war of exhaustion. The superior demographic, industrial, and positional resources of the North, combined with sea power that ensured the Confederacy's isolation, slowly destroyed the capacity and will of the Confederacy to wage war. The Confederacy rarely tried to carry the war to the North, meeting crushing defeat at Gettysburg in July 1863. For the most part it waged a defensive war in order to sap the will of the Union. Certainly by 1864 war-weariness had set in in the North, but the successes of the 1864 campaign ensured Lincoln's reelection and sealed the South's defeat.

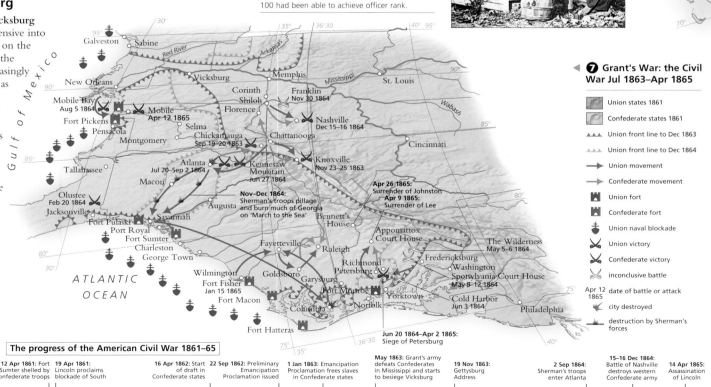

The Civil War was among the first wars to be recorded using photography. Field photographers such as Matthew Brady were able to record the true horrors of battles such as Gettysburg, the dead from which are seen above.

The Civil War to the fall of Vicksburg

During 1861–62 Union forces lost a series of battles to an enemy with superior military skills. However, the Northern naval blockade began to cut off both Southern exports and essential supplies. With no Confederate offensive on the upper Ohio which might have split the Union, the North was able to undertake offensives against the Confederate capital, Richmond, Virginia, and along the Tennessee and Mississippi. Repulsed before Richmond and obliged thereafter to move directly against the city, Union forces secured Memphis and New Orleans, capturing Vicksburg on July 4, 1863, to divide the Confederacy.

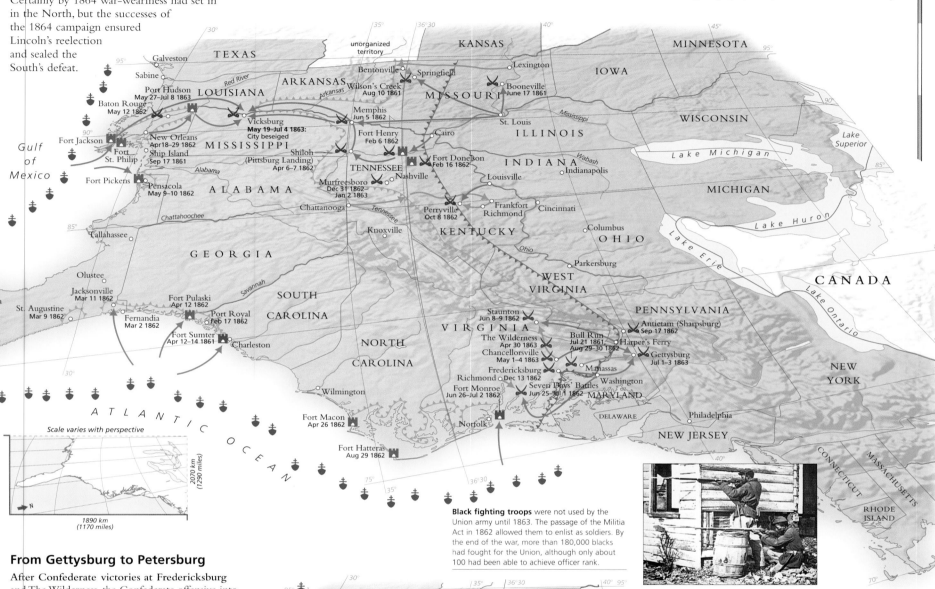

Black fighting troops were not used by the Union army until 1863. The passage of the Militia Act in 1862 allowed them to enlist as soldiers. By the end of the war, more than 180,000 blacks had fought for the Union, although only about 100 had been able to achieve officer rank.

From Gettysburg to Petersburg

After Confederate victories at Fredericksburg and The Wilderness, the Confederate offensive into Pennsylvania was defeated at Gettysburg, on the same day as Vicksburg fell. Thereafter on the defensive, Confederate armies were increasingly outnumbered: with Grant's appointment as commander, they were also increasingly outfought. Grant undertook an offensive against Richmond that broke the Confederate freedom of action in a series of battles and the siege of Petersburg: at the same time, Sherman's army broke into Georgia and South Carolina. With defeat in front of Petersburg, Confederate resistance collapsed in April 1865.

Ulysses S. Grant was appointed supreme commander of the Union forces in 1864.

7 Grant's War: the Civil War Jul 1863–Apr 1865

Union states 1861	
Confederate states 1861	
Union front line to Dec 1863	
Union front line to Dec 1864	
Union movement	
Confederate movement	
Union fort	
Confederate fort	
Union naval blockade	
Union victory	
Confederate victory	
inconclusive battle	
Apr 12 1865	date of battle or attack
	city destroyed
	destruction by Sherman's forces

The progress of the American Civil War 1861–65

12 Apr 1861: Fort Sumter shelled by Confederate troops

19 Apr 1861: Lincoln proclaims blockade of South

16 Apr 1862: Start of draft in Confederate states

22 Sep 1862: Preliminary Emancipation Proclamation issued

1 Jan 1863: Emancipation Proclamation frees slaves in Confederate states

May 1863: Grant's army defeats Confederates in Mississippi and starts to besiege Vicksburg

19 Nov 1863: Gettysburg Address

2 Sep 1864: Sherman's troops enter Atlanta

15–16 Dec 1864: Battle of Nashville destroys western Confederate army

14 Apr 1865: Assassination of Lincoln

1861   1862   1863   1864   1865

15 Apr 1861: President Lincoln issues call for troops

6–7 Apr 1862: Battle of Shiloh: heavy casualties on both sides

1 May 1862: Union fleet captures New Orleans

13 Dec 1862: Severe Union defeat at Fredericksburg

3 Mar 1863: Draft law passed in North

1–3 Jul 1863: Confederate defeat at battle of Gettysburg
4 Jul 1863: Vicksburg captured by Union troops

15 Nov 1864: Sherman begins 'March to the Sea'

9 Apr 1865: Lee surrenders to Grant at Appomattox

NORTH AMERICA 1865–1920

THE NATIONS OF NORTH AMERICA focused on the development of their own resources after 1865. The US worked to reconstruct itself after the Civil War and, like Canada, concentrated on the completion of transcontinental railroads to further exploit the continent's immense resources. Abroad, the US extended its influence in Central America and west across the Pacific, gaining new territory and economic advantage. In Mexico, Benito Juárez and his Republican forces felled the regime of Maximilian, ushering in a period of relative calm. Under Porfirio Díaz, Mexico attracted foreign investment and immigration, but its population remained brutally suppressed.

The Statue of Liberty came to symbolize the hope and freedom offered by the US.

Industrialization and urbanization

US manufacturing techniques and machinery were refined throughout the second half of the 19th century.

The growth of the railroads and industrialization transformed the North American landscape. The economic boom turned the continent into a magnet for immigration: thousands came to its shores seeking a better life. Inventions and innovations abounded; cities arose across the continent, supporting factories that had expanded rapidly because of the demands of the American Civil War. The new industrial cities became pressure cookers of societal and political discontent, with often bloody confrontations between organized labor, police, and even the military.

Theodore Roosevelt, president 1901–09, presided over the economic boom of the early 20th century.

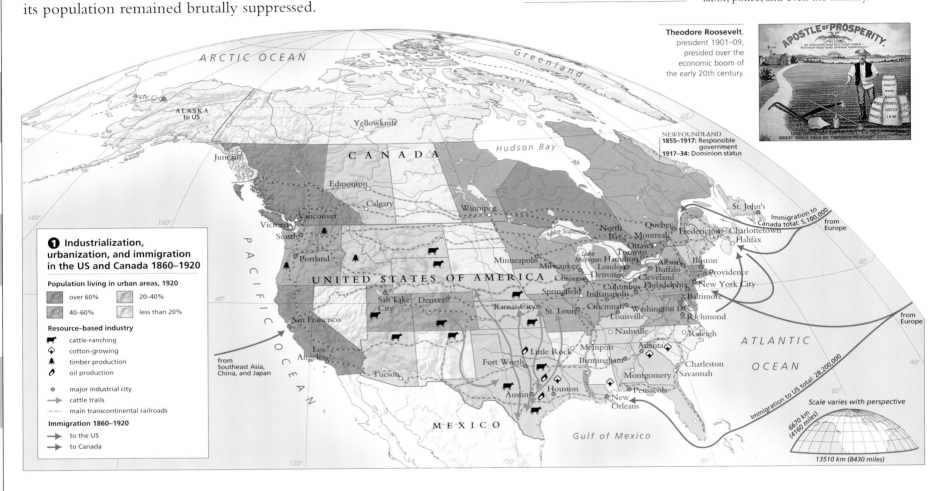

❶ Industrialization, urbanization, and immigration in the US and Canada 1860–1920

Population living in urban areas, 1920
- over 60%
- 20–40%
- 40–60%
- less than 20%

Resource–based industry
- cattle-ranching
- cotton-growing
- timber production
- oil production

- ○ major industrial city
- → cattle trails
- --- main transcontinental railroads

Immigration 1860–1920
- → to the US
- → to Canada

NEWFOUNDLAND
1855–1917: Responsible government
1917–34: Dominion status

Immigration to Canada total: 5,100,000 from Europe

Immigration to US total: 28,200,000 from Europe

Scale varies with perspective

6670 km (4160 miles)

13510 km (8430 miles)

WEST NEW YORK

◀ ❷ Ethnic neighborhoods in Manhattan c.1920
- African-American
- Chinese
- Czech, Hungarian
- French
- German
- Irish
- Italian
- Jewish
- Scandinavian, Finnish
- Syrian, Turkish, Armenian, Greek

QUEENS

2 km
2 miles

New York

New York City's Ellis Island was the point of entry for millions of immigrants between 1892 and 1920. Many people remained within the city, finding comfort and support in the ethnic neighborhoods which had grown up there. By the 1920s, the diversity of nationalities on Manhattan was a reflection of the diverse strains that made up the population of the US.

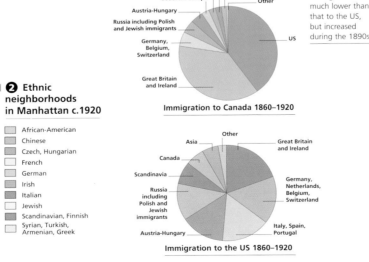

Canadian immigration was much lower than that to the US, but increased during the 1890s.

Immigration to Canada 1860–1920

Immigration to the US 1860–1920

The era of mass migration

During the 19th century nearly 50 million immigrants swelled the populations of Canada and the US. Immigration was initially from northern Europe: Germany, Scandinavia, Britain, and Ireland. From the 1880s, the bulk of migrants came from eastern and southern Europe. Most settlers were lured by the economic opportunities offered by the Americas, but others sought freedom from religious persecution and political uncertainty. After World War I, immigration was severely curtailed.

The majority of new arrivals to the Americas were able to gain entry. Only about 2% were refused entryy.

The US: 1865–1914

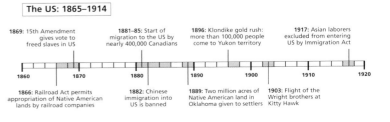

1869: 15th Amendment gives vote to freed slaves in US

1881–85: Start of migration to the US by nearly 400,000 Canadians

1896: Klondike gold rush: more than 100,000 people come to Yukon territory

1917: Asian laborers excluded from entering US by Immigration Act

1860   1870   1880   1890   1900   1910   1920

1866: Railroad Act permits appropriation of Native American lands by railroad companies

1882: Chinese immigration into US is banned

1889: Two million acres of Native American land in Oklahoma given to settlers

1903: Flight of the Wright brothers at Kitty Hawk

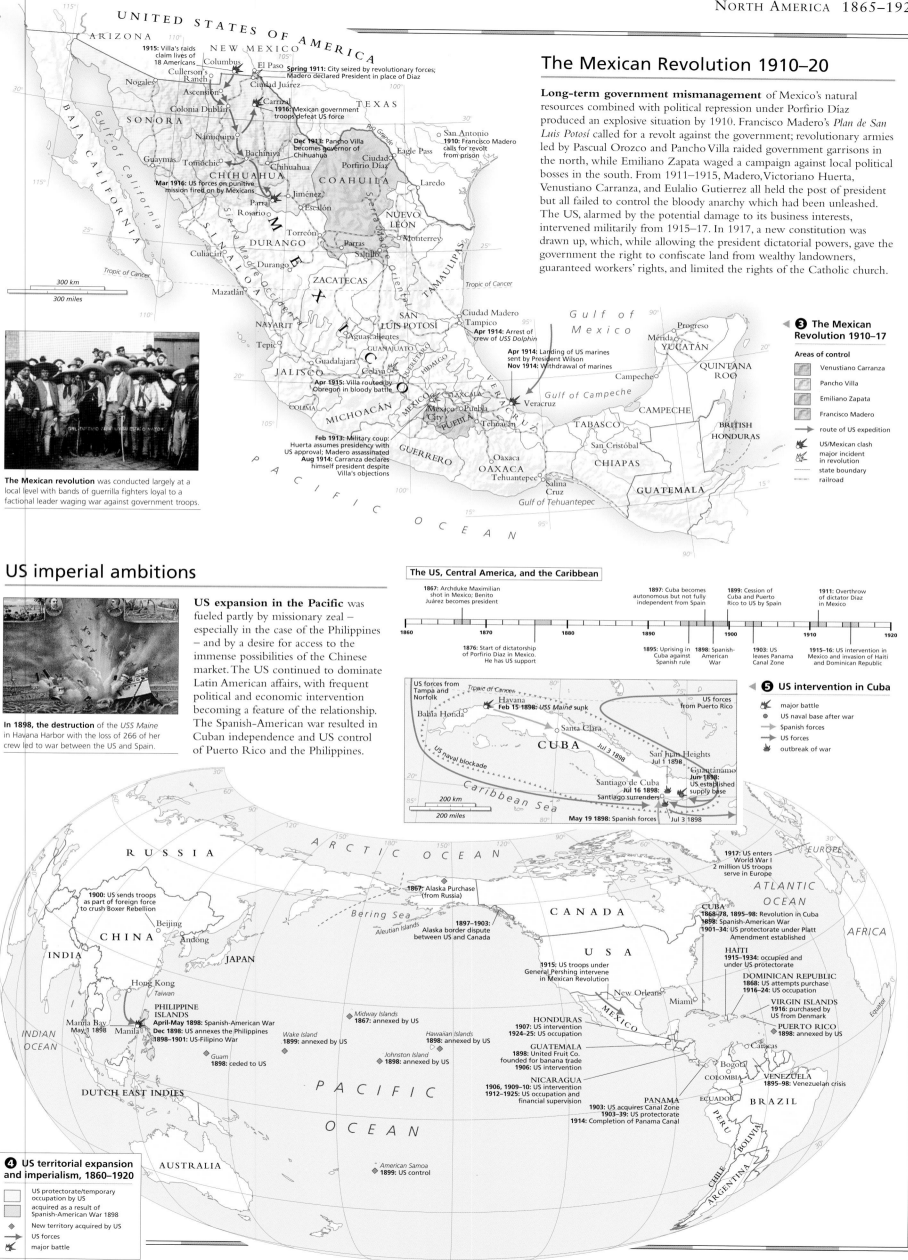

The Mexican Revolution 1910–20

Long-term government mismanagement of Mexico's natural resources combined with political repression under Porfirio Díaz produced an explosive situation by 1910. Francisco Madero's *Plan de San Luis Potosí* called for a revolt against the government; revolutionary armies led by Pascual Orozco and Pancho Villa raided government garrisons in the north, while Emiliano Zapata waged a campaign against local political bosses in the south. From 1911–1915, Madero, Victoriano Huerta, Venustiano Carranza, and Eulalio Gutierrez all held the post of president but all failed to control the bloody anarchy which had been unleashed. The US, alarmed by the potential damage to its business interests, intervened militarily from 1915–17. In 1917, a new constitution was drawn up, which, while allowing the president dictatorial powers, gave the government the right to confiscate land from wealthy landowners, guaranteed workers' rights, and limited the rights of the Catholic church.

3 The Mexican Revolution 1910–17
Areas of control
Venustiano Carranza
Pancho Villa
Emiliano Zapata
Francisco Madero
route of US expedition
US/Mexican clash
major incident in revolution
state boundary
railroad
UNITED STATES OF AMERICA
ARIZONA
NEW MEXICO
TEXAS
1915: Villa's raids claim lives of 18 Americans
Columbus
El Paso
Spring 1911: City seized by revolutionary forces; Madero declared President in place of Diaz
Ciudad Juárez
Cullerson's Ranch
Nogales
Ascensión
Colonia Dublán
Carrizal
1916: Mexican government troops defeat US force
SONORA
Namiquipa
Dec 1913: Pancho Villa becomes governor of Chihuahua
Bachiniva
Chihuahua
Guaymas
Tomóchic
CHIHUAHUA
Ciudad Porfirio Díaz
Eagle Pass
San Antonio
1910: Francisco Madero calls for revolt from prison
Laredo
COAHUILA
Mar 1916: US forces on punitive mission fired on by Mexicans
Parral
Jiménez
Escalón
Rosario
Torreón
NUEVO LEÓN
Monterrey
Parras
Saltillo
DURANGO
Durango
Culiacán
SINALOA
TAMAULIPAS
ZACATECAS
Mazatlán
Tropic of Cancer
300 km
300 miles
BAJA CALIFORNIA
Gulf of California
MEXICO
Sierra Madre Occidental
Sierra Madre Oriental
Rio Grande
SAN LUIS POTOSÍ
Ciudad Madero
Tampico
Apr 1914: Arrest of crew of USS Dolphin
Gulf of Mexico
NAYARIT
Tepic
Aguascalientes
GUANAJUATO
QUERÉTARO
HIDALGO
Guadalajara
JALISCO
Celaya
Apr 1915: Villa routed by Obregon in bloody battle
Apr 1914: Landing of US marines sent by President Wilson
Nov 1914: Withdrawal of marines
Veracruz
VERACRUZ
Gulf of Campeche
COLIMA
MICHOACÁN
MEXICO
TLAXCALA
Mexico City
Puebla
PUEBLA
Tehuacán
Feb 1913: Military coup: Huerta assumes presidency with US approval; Madero assassinated
Aug 1914: Carranza declares himself president despite Villa's objections
GUERRERO
Oaxaca
OAXACA
Tehuantepec
Salina Cruz
Gulf of Tehuantepec
PACIFIC OCEAN
Progreso
Mérida
YUCATÁN
Campeche
CAMPECHE
QUINTANA ROO
TABASCO
San Cristóbal
CHIAPAS
BRITISH HONDURAS
GUATEMALA

The Mexican revolution was conducted largely at a local level with bands of guerrilla fighters loyal to a factional leader waging war against government troops.

US imperial ambitions

In 1898, the destruction of the *USS Maine* in Havana Harbor with the loss of 266 of her crew led to war between the US and Spain.

US expansion in the Pacific was fueled partly by missionary zeal – especially in the case of the Philippines – and by a desire for access to the immense possibilities of the Chinese market. The US continued to dominate Latin American affairs, with frequent political and economic intervention becoming a feature of the relationship. The Spanish-American war resulted in Cuban independence and US control of Puerto Rico and the Philippines.

The US, Central America, and the Caribbean
1867: Archduke Maximilian shot in Mexico; Benito Juárez becomes president
1897: Cuba becomes autonomous but not fully independent from Spain
1899: Cession of Cuba and Puerto Rico to US by Spain
1911: Overthrow of dictator Diaz in Mexico
1860
1870
1880
1890
1900
1910
1920
1876: Start of dictatorship of Porfirio Díaz in Mexico. He has US support
1895: Uprising in Cuba against Spanish rule
1898: Spanish-American War
1903: US leases Panama Canal Zone
1915–16: US intervention in Mexico and invasion of Haiti and Dominican Republic

5 US intervention in Cuba
major battle
US naval base after war
Spanish forces
US forces
outbreak of war
US forces from Tampa and Norfolk
Tropic of Cancer
Havana
Feb 15 1898: USS Maine sunk
Bahía Honda
US forces from Puerto Rico
Santa Clara
CUBA
Jul 3 1898
US naval blockade
San Juan Heights
Jul 1 1898
Guantánamo
Jun 1898: US established supply base
Santiago de Cuba
Jul 16 1898: Santiago surrenders
Caribbean Sea
200 km
200 miles
May 19 1898: Spanish forces
Jul 3 1898

4 US territorial expansion and imperialism, 1860–1920
US protectorate/temporary occupation by US
acquired as a result of Spanish-American War 1898
New territory acquired by US
US forces
major battle
RUSSIA
ARCTIC OCEAN
1900: US sends troops as part of foreign force to crush Boxer Rebellion
Beijing
CHINA
Andong
INDIA
JAPAN
Hong Kong
Taiwan
PHILIPPINE ISLANDS
April-May 1898: Spanish-American War
Dec 1898: US annexes the Philippines
1898–1901: US-Filipino War
Manila Bay
May 1 1898
Manila
INDIAN OCEAN
Guam
1898: ceded to US
DUTCH EAST INDIES
AUSTRALIA
1867: Alaska Purchase (from Russia)
Bering Sea
Aleutian Islands
1897–1903: Alaska border dispute between US and Canada
Midway Islands
1867: annexed by US
Wake Island
1899: annexed by US
Hawaiian Islands
1898: annexed by US
Johnston Island
1898: annexed by US
PACIFIC OCEAN
American Samoa
1899: US control
CANADA
USA
1915: US troops under General Pershing intervene in Mexican Revolution
New Orleans
MEXICO
Miami
1917: US enters World War I
2 million US troops serve in Europe
EUROPE
ATLANTIC OCEAN
AFRICA
CUBA
1868–78, 1895–98: Revolution in Cuba
1898: Spanish-American War
1901–34: US protectorate under Platt Amendment established
HAITI
1915–1934: occupied and under US protectorate
DOMINICAN REPUBLIC
1868: US attempts purchase
1916–24: US occupation
VIRGIN ISLANDS
1916: purchased by US from Denmark
PUERTO RICO
1898: annexed by US
HONDURAS
1907: US intervention
1924–25: US occupation
GUATEMALA
1898: United Fruit Co. founded for banana trade
1906: US intervention
NICARAGUA
1906, 1909–10: US intervention
1912–1925: US occupation and financial supervision
PANAMA
1903: US acquires Canal Zone
1903–39: US protectorate
1914: Completion of Panama Canal
Caracas
Bogotá
COLOMBIA
VENEZUELA
1895–98: Venezuelan crisis
ECUADOR
BRAZIL
PERU
BOLIVIA
CHILE
ARGENTINA
Equator

AN ERA OF BOOM AND BUST

The NRA, set up in 1933, was the first New Deal recovery program.

INVOLVEMENT IN WORLD WAR I confirmed the US's position as a world power in the first quarter of the century. Immigration greatly magnified the population, but during the 1920s, laws were enacted to control the tide of European settlers. The economy grew quickly, but the boom proved vulnerable and in 1929 the stock market collapsed. Between 1930 and 1932, the number of unemployed rose from 4 million to between 12 and 15 million – 25% of the total workforce. The Republican government, which had promoted the boom and was blamed for the crash, was rejected by the electorate, leading to the political dominance of a Democrat, Franklin Delano Roosevelt, for 13 years.

The depression and the New Deal

The stock market crash of 1929 shattered millions of dreams and left many Americans destitute. Farmers were particularly hard hit, as banks withdrew funding. So were black people in both cities and rural areas. The Roosevelt administration devised a series of relief programs known as the "New Deal" to restart the economy and provide new jobs. Though millions of dollars of federal funding were spent on relief, 20% of Americans were still unemployed in 1939. Not until World War II did the economy recover.

The Works Progress Administration (WPA) provided work relief for 8.5 million unemployed. Projects included the building and repair of roads, bridges, schools, and hospitals.

▲ ❷ The impact of the Great Depression 1933–34

Unemployed	Families receiving relief
less than 10%	less than 10%
11–15%	10–15%
16–25%	over 15%
over 25%	

Migration in the US, 1914–41

Refugees from the Dust Bowl carry only the bare essentials as they walk towards Los Angeles in search of work (1939).

By the 1920s, more than 50% of Americans lived in urban areas. From 1917–20, more than 400,000 rural black southerners moved to northern cities, and 600,000 more went in the 1920s. In the mid-1930s, farmers from the drought-affected plains states abandoned their farms by the thousands and moved west – primarily to California's cities and valleys. Appalachia also saw a mass transference of people north to Indiana and Ohio and west to California.

The industrial boom

This Model-A Ford was the successor to the Model-T Ford, the first car to be built using production line techniques and initially produced only in black. By the 1930s, Henry Ford achieved his dream of "a car so low in price that no man making a good salary will be unable to afford one."

The early 1920s saw a massive growth in US production. Traditional industries such as iron and steel were in relative decline, but automobiles, petrochemicals, construction, and the service industries grew rapidly, as did speculation on the stock market. But the boom was built on shaky foundations. High rates of small business failure in the 1920s gave the first signs of fragility and it was clear that production was outstripping consumption. Paper fortunes that had accrued in stocks and shares were wiped out by the Wall Street Crash of 1929.

❶ Major US industries c.1925 ▼

- iron and steel
- meat processing
- oil and gas
- textile production
- timber
- vehicle manufacture
- coalfield
- major industrial city

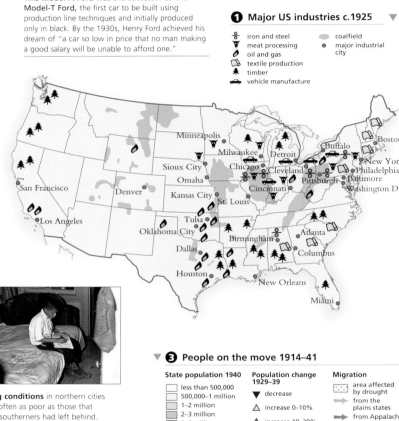

Living conditions in northern cities were often as poor as those that black southerners had left behind.

▼ ❸ People on the move 1914–41

State population 1940	Population change 1929–39	Migration
less than 500,000	▼ decrease	area affected by drought
500,000–1 million	△ increase 0–10%	from the plains states
1–2 million	△ increase 10–20%	from Appalachia
2–3 million	▲ increase over 20%	black migrants from South
3–6 million		other
over 6 million		

The US 1914–1941

1917–20: Start of migration of southern blacks to northern cities	**1918:** Armistice ends World War I	**1920:** American women granted the vote	**1923:** More than 13 million cars on US roads	**1929:** Wall Street Crash: collapse of US stock market leads to prolonged depression	**1930–31:** Over 3000 bank failures **1930:** Introduction of Smoot-Hawley tariff leads to worsening of depression worldwide	**1934–36:** Mass migration of farmers from the Great Plains to California	**1937:** Roosevelt attempts to "pack" Supreme Court to ensure passage of New Deal legislation

1915	1920	1925	1930	1935	1940	1945

| **1917:** US enters World War I | **1919:** Influenza kills 500,000 Americans | **1923:** Republican Calvin Coolidge becomes president after death of Warren Harding | **1928:** Republican Herbert Hoover elected president | **1932:** Democrat Franklin Roosevelt elected President | **1933:** NRA (National Recovery Administration) set up to regulate wage levels and child labor | **1941:** Bombing of Pearl Harbor; US enters World War II |

Popular culture in the US

Developments in technology during World War I improved communications throughout the US. By the 1920s virtually all of the nation was connected to the Bell Telephone network. Radio sets enabled news and information to reach even isolated areas. The movies became the first mass entertainment industry. From small beginnings in the early 1900s, by the 1930s, the film industry in Hollywood was exporting its glamorous products worldwide. During the Depression, cheap movie tickets kept audience numbers buoyant despite an initial downturn. Professional sports such as football, baseball, and boxing became of national interest for the first time, with huge attendances and highly paid celebrities.

❹ The major Hollywood studios in 1919

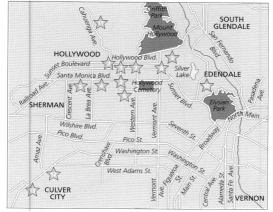

- Nestor
- Famous Players – Lasky Clater Paramount
- National Film Corporation of America
- Metro
- Chaplin
- Brunton
- Fox
- D.W. Griffith
- Vitagraph
- Mack Sennett
- Universal
- Ince
- Goldwyn

By 1919, most of the major movie studios had established themselves to the north of Los Angeles. Hollywood became the heart of the world motion picture industry and a magnet for all aspiring filmmakers.

Annual consumer expenditure on moviegoing ($ millions)

The growth in spending on movie tickets reflected wartime prosperity.

Number of radio sets in the US (millions)

By 1924, more than 2.5 million radios had been sold to American consumers.

Sales of records in the US ($ millions)

The growth in popularity of the radio led to a dramatic decline in record buying: within five years sales had virtually halved.

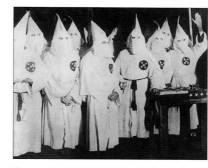

The growth of US popular culture spawned a new wave of national heroes including movie stars and athletes like the baseball star Babe Ruth, who scored 60 home runs in a season for the New York Yankees.

Though musicals and comedies took audiences away from the realities of the Depression, other films such as John Ford's *The Grapes of Wrath* dealt with themes inspired by the harshness of people's lives.

Walt Disney's Mickey Mouse first appeared as an animated cartoon in 1928. He became the symbol of the world's first international entertainment empire.

© Disney

Entertaining the masses 1914–41

- 1915: D.W. Griffith directs *The Birth of a Nation*
- 1917: First jazz recording made
- 1921: Charlie Chaplin produces *The Kid*, his first full-length film
- 1927: Al Jolson launches the talking picture with *The Jazz Singer*
- 1928: Mickey Mouse makes his first appearance on film
- 1929: First Academy Awards ceremony introduces the "Oscar"
- 1930: Weekly movie ticket sales reach more than 100 million
- 1934: More than 583 radio stations established nationwide
- 1935: Gate receipts exceed $1 million at World Heavyweight Boxing Championship
- 1939: *Gone With the Wind* becomes the highest-grossing film yet
- 1940: 86% of US population own radio sets

1915 | 1920 | 1925 | 1930 | 1935 | 1940 | 1945

THE FDR EFFECT

The political complexion of the US altered radically during the 1930s. Hoover's Republican party, so dominant at the height of the 20s boom, was routed by the Democrats in 1932. The patrician Franklin Delano Roosevelt attracted a "New Deal coalition" of Blacks, women, labor groups, and southern whites which dominated American politics for over 30 years.

Roosevelt spoke regularly to the American people via his "fireside chats" which were broadcast on national radio.

◀ ❺ Presidential elections

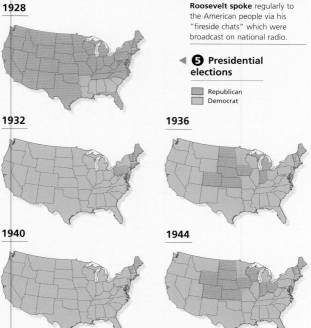

- Republican
- Democrat

1928

1932 | 1936

1940 | 1944

Intolerance

This period, particularly the 1920s, was marked by diverse displays of intolerance against perceived threats to the "American Way of Life." "New" immigrants, black migration, the increased freedom of women, and economic instability all fueled anxieties. The prohibition of alcohol, immigration "Quota Acts," and the formation of the FBI in response to the "Red Scare" of 1919–20 and the fear of Communism, were official responses to this new intolerance. Other – unofficial – reactions included race riots in the southern states and Midwest, and the revival of the white supremacist Ku Klux Klan, whose membership increased to more than two million in the 1920s.

The growth of the Ku Klux Klan in this period was largely an expression of insecurity among small-town White Anglo-Saxon Protestants toward a multitude of apparent threats to their power and influence.

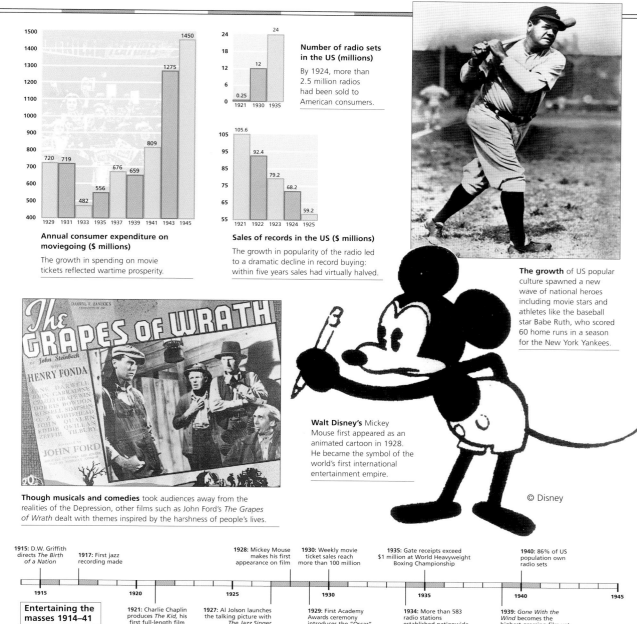

◀ ❻ Racial intolerance 1914–41

Membership of the Ku Klux Klan (% of total pop.)
- less than 1%
- 1–2%
- 2–3%
- 3–4%
- over 4%

Reported lynchings (by state) 1914–41
- 150–300
- over 300
- cities with over 10,000 Klan members
- race riot

Incidents of intolerance 1914–41

- 1919–20: Prohibition: Volstead Act and 18th Amendment make production, sale, and distribution of alcohol illegal
- 1919–20: "Red Scare" leads to deportations of radicals and subversives. Formation of the FBI
- 1920s: Height of revival of the Ku Klux Klan in South and Midwest
- 1917–21: Race riots in South and Midwest
- 1921–29: Immigration Restriction "Quota Acts" restrict annual immigration to 150,000 by 1929
- 1925: Scopes "Monkey Trial" condemns teaching of evolution
- 1933: Prohibition is repealed
- 1940s: Race riots in Harlem, Los Angeles, Detroit, and Chicago

1915 | 1920 | 1925 | 1930 | 1935 | 1940 | 1945

The cost of Prohibition 1920–28 ($ millions)

- the cost of enforcing Prohibition (monies voted by Congress)
- money collected from people prosecuted
- 20,000 people arrested

SOCIETIES IN TRANSITION

Martin Luther King, Jnr. harnessed the spontaneous protests of the 1950s to create a massive civil rights movement.

IN THE 1950s, THE UNITED STATES was labeled "the affluent society." This phrase reflected the experience of unprecedented economic prosperity and social progress in the years since World War II ended the Great Depression. Most Americans enjoyed rising incomes on the back of the postwar boom. The quality of life was further enhanced by the availability of new consumer goods, new leisure opportunities, and suburban housing. The people of Mexico, Central America, and the Caribbean continued to have a much lower standard of living than the US and Canada. And within the US, itself, not all regions and social groups experienced equal advances in affluence and status.

Postwar prosperity in the US

The idealized family unit, headed by a male breadwinner, became a favorite image for advertisers and politicians during the 1950s.

The economic stimulus provided by the war and, later, the arms race with the Soviet Union were key factors in creating the affluence of the immediate postwar decades. As manufacturing switched to a peacetime mode, consumer durables flowed into the domestic marketplace. Consumerism generated a flourishing service sector. America's position at the hub of the international trading system gave her access to foreign markets and raw materials crucial to economic success. The boom ended in the early 1970s, with the Vietnam War and the energy crisis producing prolonged inflation and recession. Europe and Japan were also challenging American economic dominance.

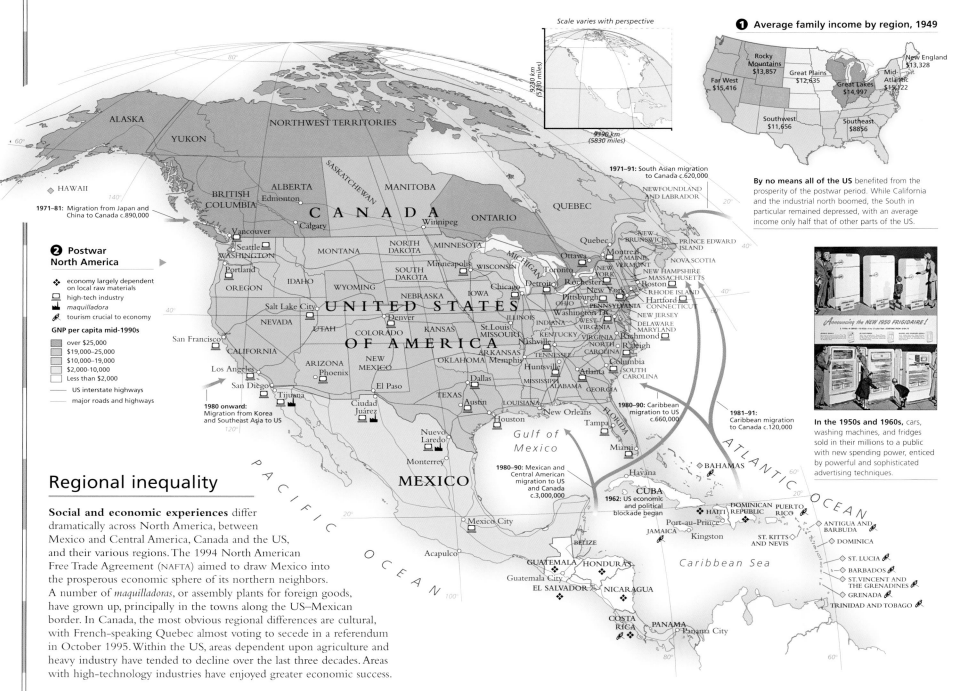

Scale varies with perspective

1 Average family income by region, 1949

Rocky Mountains $13,857 | Great Plains $12,635 | Great Lakes $14,997 | New England $13,328 | Mid-Atlantic $15,122
Far West $15,416 | Southwest $11,656 | Southeast $8856

By no means all of the US benefited from the prosperity of the postwar period. While California and the industrial north boomed, the South in particular remained depressed, with an average income only half that of other parts of the US.

1971–91: South Asian migration to Canada c.620,000

1971–81: Migration from Japan and China to Canada c.890,000

2 Postwar North America

- economy largely dependent on local raw materials
- high-tech industry
- *maquiladora*
- tourism crucial to economy

GNP per capita mid-1990s
- over $25,000
- $19,000–25,000
- $10,000–19,000
- $2,000–10,000
- Less than $2,000

— US interstate highways
— major roads and highways

1980 onward: Migration from Korea and Southeast Asia to US

1980–90: Caribbean migration to US c.660,000

1981–91: Caribbean migration to Canada c.120,000

1980–90: Mexican and Central American migration to US and Canada c.3,000,000

1962: US economic and political blockade began

In the 1950s and 1960s, cars, washing machines, and fridges sold in their millions to a public with new spending power, enticed by powerful and sophisticated advertising techniques.

Regional inequality

Social and economic experiences differ dramatically across North America, between Mexico and Central America, Canada and the US, and their various regions. The 1994 North American Free Trade Agreement (NAFTA) aimed to draw Mexico into the prosperous economic sphere of its northern neighbors. A number of *maquiladoras*, or assembly plants for foreign goods, have grown up, principally in the towns along the US–Mexican border. In Canada, the most obvious regional differences are cultural, with French-speaking Quebec almost voting to secede in a referendum in October 1995. Within the US, areas dependent upon agriculture and heavy industry have tended to decline over the last three decades. Areas with high-technology industries have enjoyed greater economic success.

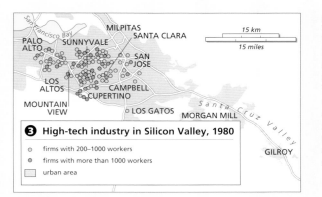

3 High-tech industry in Silicon Valley, 1980

- firms with 200–1000 workers
- firms with more than 1000 workers
- urban area

SILICON VALLEY

Without specific locational needs, many high-tech firms were able to site their businesses in nonurban areas in the South and West, helping to revitalize the economy of these regions. Silicon Valley near San Francisco, California, contains one of the world's highest concentrations of computing and electronic industries. Initially, many high-tech manufacturers relied upon contracts from the US military, but the age of the personal computer has allowed these manufacturers to play a key role in sustaining American exports and growth.

New high-tech industries including aerospace and electronics, as at Silicon Valley *(right)*, grew up in the late 1970s to fill the gaps left by the decline of traditional US heavy industries.

Changes in urban life

As black Americans migrated from the rural South to urban centers in the 1940s and 1950s, many whites abandoned city life for the suburbs. These areas became increasingly detached from the cities; instead of petitioning for access to the cities' municipal facilities, postwar suburban residents fought fiercely against annexation proposals. The tax dollars of prosperous whites were no longer available to maintain the city infrastructure. The financial crisis was made worse by the decline of traditional US industries, and many of America's cities sank into crisis during the 1960s and 1970s. Housing stock deteriorated, roads were not repaired, and poverty, crime, and racial tension were common features of many urban areas in the US. Poverty was not confined to the inner cities: people in rural areas in the deep South and the Appalachians were some of the most deprived in the US.

The centers of many of America's great cities declined physically as people move to the suburbs. Old housing stock was torn down but not replaced, and the infrastructure declined through lack of funding.

The growth of the suburbs

The 1950s saw the growth of suburban America. New construction techniques lowered the cost of new homes, and expressways improved access to and from urban centers. In the postwar era, cities like Chicago absorbed ever more of their surrounding areas.

The new suburbs provided a safe haven away from the cities. Mortgage assistance was readily available to those wishing to move to suburban areas. Until the 1960s, money was siphoned into the suburbs by federal housing officials, who simultaneously denied loans to people still living in urban areas.

❹ Chicago: 1850–1969

Urban growth
- 1850
- 1875
- 1900
- 1925
- 1950
- 1969

20 km / 20 miles

LAKE COUNTY · McHENRY COUNTY · ILLINOIS · KANE COUNTY · DU PAGE COUNTY · Chicago · Lake Michigan · COOK COUNTY · KENDALL COUNTY · WILL COUNTY · INDIANA · PORTER COUNTY · LAKE COUNTY

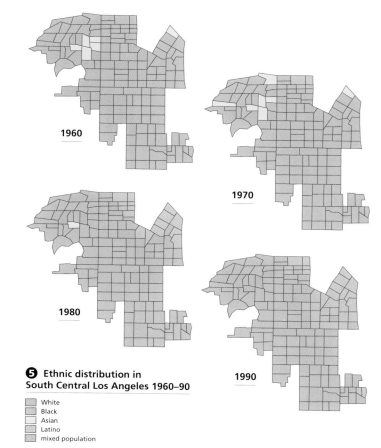

1960 · 1970 · 1980 · 1990

❺ Ethnic distribution in South Central Los Angeles 1960–90
- White
- Black
- Asian
- Latino
- mixed population

Poverty and ethnic balance in inner city Los Angeles

Los Angeles demonstrates how wealth and poverty live separate lives in postwar urban America. The central neighborhoods in an otherwise prosperous city have a massively disproportionate number of poor residents, with an ethnic mix in constant flux. In 1960, a substantial white population remained in South Central Los Angeles. By 1970, whites had largely left the area, which had a now predominantly black population. Twenty years later, Latinos formed a majority in many South Central neighborhoods.

Civil Rights and other protest movements

1955: Bus boycott against segregation in Montgomery, Alabama
1961: Student freedom riders go into South to protest against segregation
1963: March on Washington led by Martin Luther King, Jr.
1965: Voting Rights Act increases number of black voters; Watts Riots in Los Angeles
1968: Assassination of Martin Luther King, Jr. sparks riots in 124 US cities
1970: Four students killed at Kent State University, Ohio in protest over US involvement in Cambodia

1955 · 1960 · 1965 · 1970 · 1975

1957: Martin Luther King, Jr. heads coordinated resistance movement
1964: Civil Rights Act forbids segregation in public places
1966: Race riots in Atlanta
1968: Riots and protests follow Democrat rally in Chicago
1969: 250,000 people march on Washington in protest against war in Vietnam
1974: High Court gives go-ahead to busing for integration of US schools

In August 1969, 400,000 people gathered at a farm near Bethel in upstate New York to form the "Woodstock Nation," at a music festival which was also a celebration of peaceful, antiestablishment coexistence.

1970: Four students at Kent State University shot in protest over US entry into Cambodia
Aug 1967: Woodstock
Jul 1964: Riots in Harlem
Apr 1968: 5000 students in protest at Columbia University
1967: Riots leave 25 dead
1970: Two students killed at Jackson State University

WASHINGTON · OREGON · MONTANA · IDAHO · NORTH DAKOTA · SOUTH DAKOTA · MINNESOTA · WISCONSIN · MICHIGAN · MAINE · VERMONT · NEW HAMPSHIRE · NEW YORK · MASS. · R.I. · CONN. · CALIFORNIA · NEVADA · UTAH · WYOMING · COLORADO · NEBRASKA · IOWA · ILLINOIS · INDIANA · OHIO · PENN. · NEW JERSEY · DELAWARE · MARYLAND · WEST VIRGINIA · VIRGINIA · KENTUCKY · TENNESSEE · NORTH CAROLINA · SOUTH CAROLINA · GEORGIA · ALABAMA · MISSISSIPPI · LOUISIANA · ARKANSAS · OKLAHOMA · KANSAS · MISSOURI · ARIZONA · NEW MEXICO · TEXAS · FLORIDA

San Francisco 1966; **1967:** "Summer of Love"; **1969:** Anti-war protest
Fresno 1967
Santa Barbara **1970:** Bank burned by antiwar protestors
Los Angeles **Aug 1965:** Watts riots leave 34 dead
Oakland 1966
Phoenix 1967
Tucson 1967
Des Moines **1969:** Student protest
Omaha 1968
Kansas City 1968
Wichita 1967
Little Rock 1968
Houston 1967
New Orleans
Memphis; Nashville; Knoxville 1967; Chattanooga
Birmingham **1955, 1963**; Anniston; Montgomery 1962; Selma; Jackson 1962, 1967, 1968; Mobile; Tallahassee 1967
Chicago 1964, 1966, 1967; Milwaukee 1966; Detroit **1963, 1968**; **1967:** Riots leave 43 dead; Cincinnati 1967; Dayton 1966; Cleveland 1966, 1967; Pittsburgh 1968; Kent; Rochester 1964, 1967; Buffalo; Albany; Newark **1967:** Riots leave 25 dead; New York 1967, 1968; Philadelphia 1964, 1968; Baltimore 1968; Richmond 1968; Washington DC 1968; **Oct 1967, Nov 1969:** Antiwar protest; Greensboro 1968; Raleigh 1968; Charlotte 1968; Atlanta 1967; St Louis 1967

1968: Martin Luther King Jr. assassinated

VIRGINIA 38% / 52%
NORTH CAROLINA 44% / 43%
SOUTH CAROLINA 33% / 45%
GEORGIA 28% / 64%
ALABAMA 18% / 54%
MISSISSIPPI 6% / 60%
LOUISIANA 32% / 56%
ARKANSAS 42% / 81%
TENNESSEE 66% / 65%
FLORIDA 51% / 54%
Tampa 1967
Miami 1966

A woman prays for peace in Birmingham, Alabama, during a Civil Rights protest in May 1963, as fellow demonstrators dance and sing behind her.

❻ Protest movements and urban unrest of the 1960s

- ✹ antiwar protest
- ✸ center of civil rights activity
- ⚘ urban unrest/race riot

GEORGIA 28% / 64% Percentage of the black population of voting age registered to vote: before the Voting Rights Act of 1965, in 1971

Blacks as a % of state population
- more than 30
- 20–30
- 15–20
- 7–15
- less than 7

Moves for freedom

The opportunities presented by postwar America were denied to many black Americans, particularly in the still-segregated South, where they were prevented by whites from voting. Inspired by decolonization movements abroad, and aided by a 1954 Supreme Court judgement that segregation was unconstitutional, black Americans began to challenge discrimination. In 1955, a bus boycott in Montgomery, Alabama forced the bus company to end segregation. The success inspired similar protests throughout the South. In 1964 and 1965, the US Congress passed legislation banning racial discrimination and protecting the democratic rights of all Americans. The 1960s also saw a rise in political consciousness among other groups; protests against the Vietnam War grew in number throughout the late 1960s, as did the movement for women's rights.

THE USA: GROWTH OF A SUPERPOWER

John F. Kennedy, a charismatic and popular US president, was assassinated in 1963.

THE JAPANESE ATTACK on Pearl Harbor in December 1941 and the subsequent US entry into the Second World War caused a shift in the US view of the world. Thereafter, through alliances, military interventions, and trade, the United States dominated world affairs. Although challenged by the Cuban Revolution in 1959, the US maintained its position in the Americas, a secure base from which to fight the Cold War. The collapse of the Soviet Union in 1991 left the US as the world's only superpower. After the atrocities of 11 September 2001, the US embarked on a new phase of unilateralist interventionism, determined to stamp out terrorist and other threats to US security.

America and the world

During World War II, the US established military bases around the world, which remained important throughout the Cold War with the Soviet Union. The Cold War also encouraged the US to form alliances, such as the North Atlantic Treaty Organization (NATO) of 1949. After the Vietnam War, the US retreated from international politics, but the Soviet invasion of Afghanistan in 1979 revived the Cold War for another decade. With the collapse of the Soviet Union in 1991, the US was left as the sole superpower. After 11 September 2001, the United States took on a more assertive and unilateralist role in international affairs.

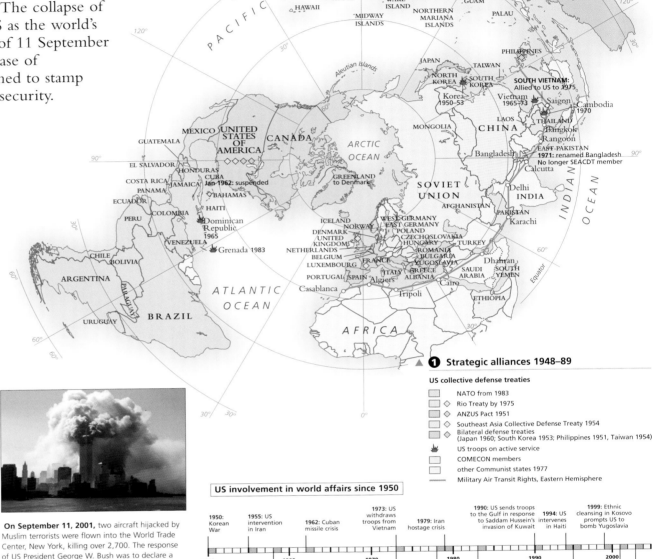

① Strategic alliances 1948–89

US collective defense treaties

	NATO from 1983
	Rio Treaty by 1975
	ANZUS Pact 1951
	Southeast Asia Collective Defense Treaty 1954
	Bilateral defense treaties (Japan 1960; South Korea 1953; Philippines 1951; Taiwan 1954)
	US troops on active service
	COMECON members
	other Communist states 1977
	Military Air Transit Rights, Eastern Hemisphere

US soldiers with a Viet Cong suspect during the Vietnam War (1950–73), the longest and most costly of US attempts to contain the perceived Communist threat during the Cold War.

On September 11, 2001, two aircraft hijacked by Muslim terrorists were flown into the World Trade Center, New York, killing over 2,700. The response of US President George W. Bush was to declare a 'War on Terror', stepping up security at home and invading Afghanistan (2001) and Iraq (2003).

US involvement in world affairs since 1950

1950: Korean War
1955: US intervention in Iran
1962: Cuban missile crisis
1973: US withdraws troops from Vietnam
1979: Iran hostage crisis
1990: US sends troops to the Gulf in response to Saddam Hussein's invasion of Kuwait
1994: US intervenes in Haiti
1999: Ethnic cleansing in Kosovo prompts US to bomb Yugoslavia

1950   1960   1970   1980   1990   2000

1950: Start of US involvement in Vietnam
1958: Eisenhower Doctrine commits US to prevent spread of Communism in Middle East
1973: US assists in right-wing coup in Chile
1978: US-brokered peace deal between Egypt and Israel
1983: US intervention in Grenada
1995: US troops withdraw from Somalia after failing to restore democracy
2001: Taliban ousted in Afghanistan by US-led forces
2003: US leads invasion of Iraq

US investment overseas

During the Cold War, investment overseas was seen as a way to bind other nations to the capitalist sphere. The Marshall Plan of 1948 aimed both to aid the postwar recovery of Western Europe and reduce the chances of Communist subversion. American firms also tried to secure access to valuable raw materials, most importantly oil in the Middle East. Since the end of the Cold War, US investment in Western Europe has grown significantly, as American companies have sought industrial partnerships and a share of the growing European economy.

② US investment overseas

US private direct investment abroad

	1960
	1984
	2003

Canada: 33% 21% 9%
Soviet Union (Russia) and Eastern Europe: 0% 0% 1%
Japan: 1% 3% 4%
Western Europe: 21% 47% 64%
Asia and Pacific (exc. Japan and Middle East): 3% 7% 8%
Middle East: 3% 1% 1%
Central and South America and the Caribbean: 28% 12% 9%
Africa (exc. South Africa): 2% 3% 1%
South Africa: 1% 1% 0.1%
Australia and New Zealand: 3% 4% 3%

The decline of the Democratic South

The migration of Southern blacks to northern cities in the 1940s and 1950s (in part due to the mechanization of cotton farming) killed off most of the remaining cotton plantations in the South, which had depended on their cheap labor, leading to a decline in the Southern economy. In the North, black Americans became an important political constituency. The Democratic Party tried to reconcile its desire for their votes with its desire for the continued support of white Southerners who traditionally voted Democrat. By the late 1960s, after the Civil Rights legislation of President Lyndon Johnson, many Southerners abandoned their traditional commitment to the Democratic Party.

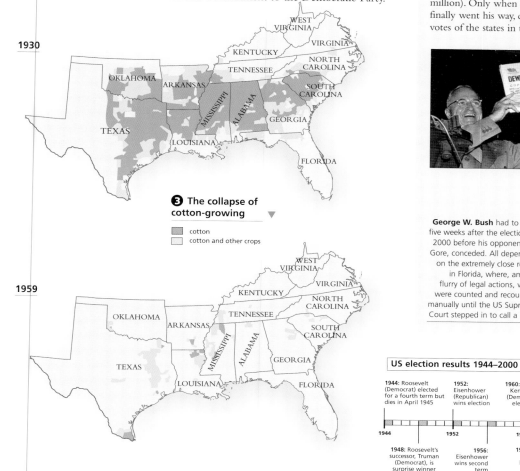

1930

1959

❸ The collapse of cotton-growing

- ▨ cotton
- ▫ cotton and other crops

US intervention in Central America

Historically the US has acted under the "Monroe Doctrine" to ensure stability and protect its business interests in Central America. During the Cold War, the US feared Communist subversion in its own backyard. In 1954, US agents organized the downfall of a left-wing government in Guatemala. In 1962, a crisis over Soviet nuclear arms in Cuba *(see p.108)* almost caused nuclear war. During the 1980s, President Reagan acted against leftists in Grenada and Nicaragua. After the Cold War, the US became more constructively engaged in combating the drugs trade in the region.

❺ US intervention in Central America and the Caribbean

- ⚔ Cuban-sponsored guerrilla activities 1959–68
- ▪ US intervention

KEY ELECTIONS 1948–2000

In 1948 Democrat President Harry Truman won a shock victory over the Republican Thomas Dewey. However, the success of the pro-segregationist States Rights Party indicated that the Democrats might have problems maintaining the support of both blacks and Southerners, and in 1968 the Democrats lost every Southern state except Texas. Though Republicans held the Presidency throughout the 1980s, the elections of 1992 and 1996 proved that the Democrats could still win despite a largely Republican South. The 2000 election was the most controversial for over a century. Republican George W. Bush secured a smaller share of the popular vote (49.8 million) than his Democrat rival, Al Gore (50.2 million). Only when the bitterly disputed result for Florida finally went his way, did Bush win the Presidency on the votes of the states in the electoral college (271 votes to 267).

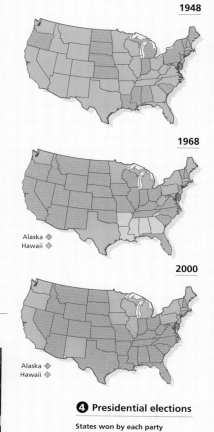

1948

1968

Alaska ◈
Hawaii ◈

2000

Alaska ◈
Hawaii ◈

The Chicago Daily Tribune was so confident of the outcome of the 1948 US Presidential elections that the paper was printed without confirmation of the results, leaving the victorious Democratic candidate Harry Truman to revel in the premature headline.

George W. Bush had to wait five weeks after the election in 2000 before his opponent, Al Gore, conceded. All depended on the extremely close result in Florida, where, amid a flurry of legal actions, votes were counted and recounted manually until the US Supreme Court stepped in to call a halt.

❹ Presidential elections

States won by each party
- ▨ Republicans
- ▫ Democrats
- ▪ States Rights
- ▪ American Independent

US election results 1944–2000

1944: Roosevelt (Democrat) elected for a fourth term but dies in April 1945

1948: Roosevelt's successor, Truman (Democrat), is surprise winner

1952: Eisenhower (Republican) wins election

1956: Eisenhower wins second term

1960: John F Kennedy (Democrat) elected

1963: Assassination of Kennedy. Johnson becomes President. Reelected in 1964

1968: Nixon (Republican) elected. Reelected 1972

1974: Nixon resigns over Watergate scandal. Replaced by Gerald Ford

1976: Jimmy Carter (Democrat) elected

1980: Ronald Reagan (Republican) wins. Wins second term in 1984

1988: George Bush (Republican) wins

1992: Bill Clinton (Democrat) elected

1996: Bill Clinton wins second term

2000: George W. Bush (Republican) wins closely-fought election after recount in Florida

2004: George W Bush reelected after another close campaign, endorsing his "War on Terror"

1944 · 1952 · 1960 · 1968 · 1976 · 1984 · 1992 · 2000

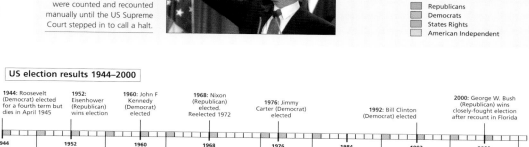

The Sandinista revolution of 1978 put an end to more than 40 years of military dictatorship in Nicaragua. The left-wing Sandinistas were distrusted by the US which sponsored Contra guerrillas based in Honduras *(left)* against the government.

US military advisors have been active, often working with the Drug Enforcement Administration (DEA), in training local troups in many Central and South American countries since its invasion of Panama in 1989.

UNITED STATES OF AMERICA

ATLANTIC OCEAN

Gulf of Mexico

US exploitation of cheap Mexican labor in free trade zone (see p.136)

Tropic of Cancer

MEXICO
- **1980s:** Serious economic difficulties
- **1993–94:** NAFTA creates free-trade community of US, Mexico, and Canada
- **1999:** Agreement with US to counter drugs-trafficking

BAHAMAS

CUBA

1961: Attempted invasion at Bay of Pigs by US-supported forces
1962: Cuban Missile Crisis
Apr–Sep 1980: Muriel boatlift: Migration of thousands of Cubans to US
1990: Severe economic distress following withdrawal of Soviet aid
2001: First US-Cuba trade agreement since 1962
2003: US government launches Commission for Assistance to a Free Cuba

Guantanamo Bay to US

1991: Ongoing unrest; military coup ousts elected government
2004: US troops assist in the removal of President Jean-Bertrand Aristide

BELIZE

1978–90: Staging area for anti-Sandinista rebel army (Contras) organized and financed by US

1954: Military, with US backing topples democratic government pledged to land and social reforms
1961: Appearance of revolutionaries
1968–70: US ambassador and military advisors killed by rebels
1980s–90s: Ongoing guerrilla activity

GUATEMALA

HONDURAS

EL SALVADOR

JAMAICA

HAITI

DOMINICAN REPUBLIC

1961: Assassination of President Trujillo
1965: US President Johnson intervenes with 22,000 troops

PUERTO RICO to US

1961: FSLN (Sandinista) rebels appear
1978: Sandinista revolution
1982–83: US finances guerrilla army fighting leftist Sandinista government
1990: Anti-Sandinista coalition wins election
2002: US agrees to resume military aid to Nicaraguan armed forces in their campaign against smuggling and terrorism

NICARAGUA

Caribbean Sea

1960s: The "model" of the Alliance for Progress
1970: First revolutionaries appear
1991: Right-wing government and opposition leaders sign unbrokered peace treaty
1990s: Continued reliance on US aid; heavy influence of US ambassador
2001: Adopts US $ as official currency

COSTA RICA

PANAMA

1959, 1964: Anti-US riots
1978: Panama Canal Treaties
Dec 1989: US invades Panama to capture General Noriega
1999: US returns control of Panama Canal to government of Panama

ST. KITTS AND NEVIS

ANTIGUA AND BARBUDA

DOMINICA

ST. VINCENT AND THE GRENADINES

ST. LUCIA

BARBADOS

GRENADA

Oct 1983: Radical left-wing government overthrown by US intervention

TRINIDAD AND TOBAGO

Caracas

PACIFIC OCEAN

Scale varies with perspective

5000 km (3110 miles)

5550 km (3450 miles)

Equator

COLOMBIA
- **1980s/1990s:** Flow of drugs to US causes serious crime
- **2000:** US launches 'Plan Colombia' to tackle drugs and violence

VENEZUELA

ECUADOR

GUYANA

SOUTH AMERICA
REGIONAL HISTORY

THE HISTORICAL LANDSCAPE

THE LAST CONTINENT – APART FROM ANTARCTICA – to be colonized
by humans (the first settlers arrived from North America no more than
13,000 years ago), South America remains a realm of harsh extremes of climate,
environment, and human society. The cordillera spine of the Andes was the
heartland of the first complex societies and civilizations. Early settlers spread
through the fertile tracts of the Amazon Basin, but few ventured to the sterile
salt pans of the Atacama Desert – one of the driest places on Earth – or
Patagonia – one of the least hospitable. European contact in the 16th century
brought, as elsewhere in the Americas, the decline of indigenous cultures.
Although here widespread intermarriage and the enforced importation of African
slaves to work on plantations created an extraordinarily varied genetic, linguistic,
and cultural pool. The continent struggled free of European colonialism in the
19th century only to be confronted by the challenge of economic, social, and
political modernization, which was met with varying success. This process brought
wealth for some, marginalization for many – especially in the continent's burgeoning
but scattered centers of population – and a threat to the global ecosystem, as the
resources of the Amazonian wilderness were increasingly placed under pressure.

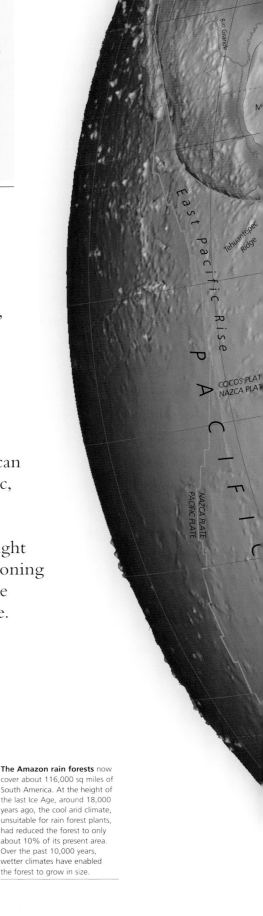

The Andes were one of the sites of the earliest agricultural
civilizations in South America, perhaps as many as 10,000 years
ago. The mountains and temperate climate provided a wide
range of habitats for wild plants. Tubers – such as potatoes and
sweet potatoes – grew naturally and were simple to cultivate.

The Amazon rain forests now
cover about 116,000 sq miles of
South America. At the height of
the last Ice Age, around 18,000
years ago, the cool arid climate,
unsuitable for rain forest plants,
had reduced the forest to only
about 10% of its present area.
Over the past 10,000 years,
wetter climates have enabled
the forest to grow in size.

The flat grassland plains of the
pampas of southeastern South
America were mainly desert
during the era covered by the
map *(opposite)*. Higher levels of
rainfall have allowed grasslands to
develop, but the area remains dry,
and has always been a region of
low human population.

Vegetation type

ice cap and glacier

tundra

polar and alpine desert

semi-desert or sparsely vegetated

grassland

forest or open woodland

tropical rain forest

temperate desert

tropical desert

coastline (present day)

coastline (18,000 years ago)

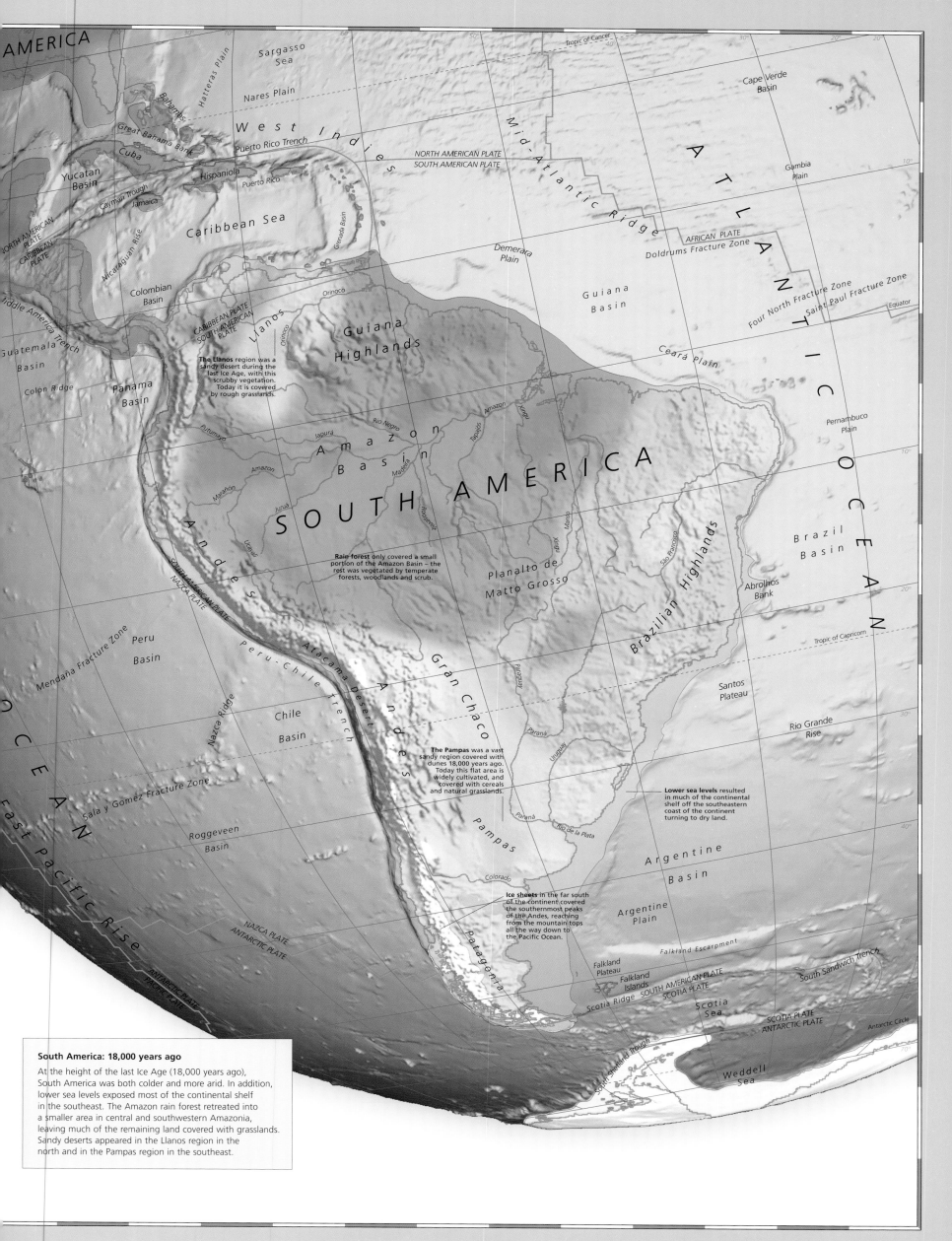

AMERICA

Sargasso
Sea

Hatteras plain

Nares Plain

Cape Verde
Basin

Tropic of Cancer

W e s t   I n d i e s

Bahamas

Great Bahama Bank

Cuba

Yucatan
Basin

Hispaniola

Puerto Rico Trench

Puerto Rico

Cayman Trough

Jamaica

NORTH AMERICAN PLATE
SOUTH AMERICAN PLATE

M i d - A t l a n t i c   R i d g e

AFRICAN PLATE

Gambia
Plain

A
T
L
A
N
T
I
C

Caribbean Sea

NORTH AMERICAN
PLATE
CARIBBEAN
PLATE

Nicaraguan Rise

Colombian
Basin

CARIBBEAN PLATE
SOUTH AMERICAN
PLATE

Doldrums Fracture Zone

Four North Fracture Zone

Saint Paul Fracture Zone

Equator

Middle America Trench

Guatemala
Basin

Colón Ridge

Panama
Basin

Llanos

Orinoco

Orinoco

Demerara
Plain

G u i a n a
Highlands

Guiana
Basin

Ceará Plain

The Llanos region was a
sandy desert during the
last Ice Age, with this
scrubby vegetation.
Today it is covered
by rough grasslands.

Pernambuco
Plain

Putumayo

Rio Negro

A m a z o n

Amazon

Japura

Tapajós

Xingu

Marañón

Juruá

B a s i n

Madeira

Roosevelt

SOUTH AMERICA

Brazil
Basin

Ucayali

Rain forest only covered a small
portion of the Amazon Basin – the
rest was vegetated by temperate
forests, woodlands and scrub.

Amazon

Tocantins

São Francisco

Planalto de
Matto Grosso

Brazilian Highlands

Abrolhos
Bank

O
C
E
A
N

A n d e s

SOUTH AMERICAN PLATE
NAZCA PLATE

Mendaña Fracture Zone

Peru
Basin

Peru - Chile Trench

Atacama Desert

Paraguay

Tropic of Capricorn

Santos
Plateau

Rio Grande
Rise

P A C I F I C

Nazca Ridge

Chile
Basin

A
n
d
e
s

Gran Chaco

Paraná

Uruguay

Sala y Gomez Fracture Zone

The Pampas was a vast
sandy region covered with
dunes 18,000 years ago.
Today this flat area is
widely cultivated, and
covered with cereals
and natural grasslands.

Lower sea levels resulted
in much of the continental
shelf off the southeastern
coast of the continent
turning to dry land.

Roggeveen
Basin

Paraná

Rio de la Plata

Pampas

O C E A N

Argentine
Basin

East Pacific Rise

Colorado

Ice sheets in the far south
of the continent covered
the southernmost peaks
of the Andes, reaching
from the mountain tops
all the way down to
the Pacific Ocean.

Argentine
Plain

NAZCA PLATE
ANTARCTIC PLATE

Falkland Escarpment

Patagonia

Falkland
Plateau

Falkland
Islands

SOUTH AMERICAN PLATE
SCOTIA PLATE

South Sandwich Trench

ANTARCTIC PLATE
PACIFIC PLATE

Scotia Ridge   SOUTH AMERICAN PLATE
SCOTIA PLATE

Scotia
Sea

SCOTIA PLATE
ANTARCTIC PLATE

Antarctic Circle

South Shetland Trough

Weddell
Sea

South America: 18,000 years ago

At the height of the last Ice Age (18,000 years ago),
South America was both colder and more arid. In addition,
lower sea levels exposed most of the continental shelf
in the southeast. The Amazon rain forest retreated into
a smaller area in central and southwestern Amazonia,
leaving much of the remaining land covered with grasslands.
Sandy deserts appeared in the Llanos region in the
north and in the Pampas region in the southeast.

SOUTH AMERICA
EXPLORATION AND MAPPING

THOUGH THE INCAS left no maps, their Andean empire's extensive road system was testimony to their topographical skills. It was a long time before any Europeans had a similar understanding of the continent. When Columbus first sighted the South American coast in 1498, he realized he had found a continental landmass, but thought it was part of Asia. This was disproved by the voyages of Vespucci and others along the Atlantic coast, culminating in Ferdinand Magellan's reaching the Pacific in 1520.

The name America was coined to honor Amerigo Vespucci, an Italian explorer in the service of Portugal.

In the wake of Pizarro's conquest of Peru and theft of the Incas' gold, many explorers were fired by dreams of instant riches. The net products of most expeditions, however, were the alienation of native tribes and the spread of European killer diseases. From the mid-17th century to the late 18th century, when serious scientific surveys began, exploration was largely the preserve of intrepid missionaries, notably the Jesuits, and slave-raiders from Brazil.

European conquerors and explorers

Throughout the first two decades of the 16th century Portuguese and Spanish explorers of the Atlantic coast sailed into every wide estuary in the hope that it would prove to be a passage to the Indies. Magellan eventually demonstrated that such a route existed, but it proved impracticable for the purpose of trade with the East. As a result, the Atlantic coastal regions of the continent were soon well understood and mapped, further information coming from Portuguese traders who sailed there in search of brazil wood, a tree that produced a valuable red dye and gave its name to the region. In the Andes, Pizarro, Benalcázar, and their fellow *conquistadores* were able to follow the well-maintained roads of the Inca Empire; but in most other parts of the continent, expeditions were forced back by hostile indigenous peoples, trackless swamps and forests, or impassable rapids.

This detail from a map of South America produced by John Rotz in 1542 shows Native Americans carrying logs of brazil wood for trade with Europeans.

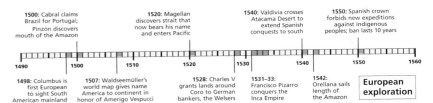

1500: Cabral claims Brazil for Portugal; Pinzón discovers mouth of the Amazon

1520: Magellan discovers strait that now bears his name and enters Pacific

1540: Valdivia crosses Atacama Desert to extend Spanish conquests to south

1550: Spanish crown forbids new expeditions against indigenous peoples; ban lasts 10 years

1498: Columbus is first European to sight South American mainland

1507: Waldseemüller's world map gives name America to continent in honor of Amerigo Vespucci

1528: Charles V grants lands around Coro to German bankers, the Welsers

1531–33: Francisco Pizarro conquers the Inca Empire

1542: Orellana sails length of the Amazon

European exploration

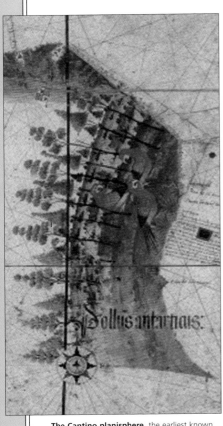

The Cantino planisphere, the earliest known map showing South America, was produced in Lisbon in 1502. It shows part of Brazil and the line agreed by the Treaty of Tordesillas in 1494, dividing the world between Portugal and Spain.

❶ First European explorers of South America ▶

Principal journeys

→ Spanish expedition
→ Portuguese expedition
→ German expedition
→ English expedition
→ Dutch expedition

Recife 1535 European settlement and date of foundation

Hispaniola

ATLANTIC OCEAN

Cape Verde Islands

Caribbean Sea

1498: Columbus anchors in Gulf of Paria

Jiménez de Quesada 1536–37

Santa Marta 1525

Coro 1527

Panama 1519

Diego de Ordás 1531–32

Christopher Columbus 3rd voyage 1498

Santa Fé de Bogotá 1539

Nikolaus Federmann 1537–39

Orinoco

Guiana Highlands

Vicente Yáñez Pinzón 1499–1500

Juan Díaz de Solís 1515–16

Amerigo Vespucci 3rd voyage 1501–02

Pedro Álvares Cabral 1500

Francis Drake 1577–80

Ferdinand Magellan 1519–21

Equator

Equator

Galapagos Islands

Quito 1534

Napo

Sebastián Benalcázar 1533–39

1542: Orellana, detached from expedition led by Gonzalo de Pizarro, decides to sail down Amazon

Amazon

Francisco de Orellana 1541–42

Cajamarca

Tomás de Berlanga 1535

1535: Berlanga, Bishop of Panama, sights Galapagos

Andes

Francisco Pizarro 1531–33

Madeira

Tapajós

Recife 1535

1533: Pizarro captures Inca Capital, Cuzco

Xingu

Tocantins

São Francisco

Lima 1535

Cuzco 1533

1543: Irala's party first to cross southern half of continent

Planalto de Mato Grosso

Bahia 1549

Brazilian Highlands

Willem Schouten and Jacob le Maire 1615–16

La Plata 1538

Diego de Almagro 1535–37

Potosí 1545

Domingo Martínez de Irala 1543–48

Gran Chaco

Paraguay

Paraná

Álvar Núñez Cabeza de Vaca 1541–42

1500: Cabral makes accidental landfall on journey to India

Pedro de Valdivia

Willem Schouten and Jacob le Maire 1615–16

Tropic of Capricorn

Tropic of Capricorn

PACIFIC OCEAN

Francis Drake 1577–53

Atacama Desert

Francisco de Aguirre 1553–65

Sebastian Cabot 1528

1502: Vespucci reaches point that he calls San Julian; exact location is uncertain

ATLANTIC OCEAN

Ferdinand Magellan 1519–21

1520: Magellan crosses Pacific in first circumnavigation of the world

Santiago 1541

Pampas

River Plate

Buenos Aires 1536

Amerigo Vespucci 3rd voyage 1501–02

Pedro Álvares Cabral 1500

1553: Valdivia killed in battle with Araucanians

1516: Díaz de Solís is first to reach mouth of River Plate, where he is killed by Native Americans

Andes

Patagonia

1000 km

1000 miles

1520: Magellan reaches Pacific after perilous 7-week journey through strait

Strait of Magellan

Falkland Islands

Tierra del Fuego

Cape Horn

1616: Schouten names cape after his home town of Horn

South Georgia

1578: Drake, blown south by gales, is first to sight Cape Horn

Jesuit missions in the interior

Spanish Jesuits created frontier settlements – often of three or four thousand people – known as *reducciones*. These had their own churches, workshops, foundries, even armories, and lands where the Native Americans grew crops and raised herds of cattle. Money was not used, but the Jesuits traded with local Spanish settlers, who envied their success, especially among the Guaraní tribes. For the authorities, however, the *reducciones* formed a defense against Portuguese encroachment on Spanish lands; Native Americans fought many battles with the slave-raiders from São Paulo known as Paulistas or *mamelucos*.

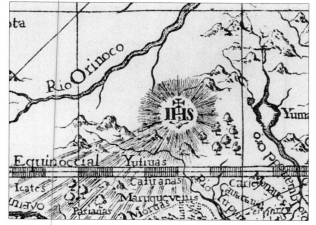

② South America 1750

Areas colonized
- Spanish by 1650
- Spanish by 1750
- Portuguese by 1650
- Portuguese by 1750
- Dutch
- French

Missionary activity
- principal areas of Jesuit *reducciones*
- other major Jesuit missions
- major Franciscan missions
- *CHACO 1732* *reduccion* with date of foundation
- 1630–32 active between these dates

Exploration of the interior
- Jesuits
- Franciscans
- Paulista raids

The area covered by the detail from Father Fritz's map *(shown left).*

From the 17th century, most serious exploration and mapping of the interior of South America was the work of missionaries. This detail is from a map of the Amazon compiled by Samuel Fritz, a Bohemian-born Jesuit, and published in 1707. Note the Jesuits' IHS monogram above the Equator.

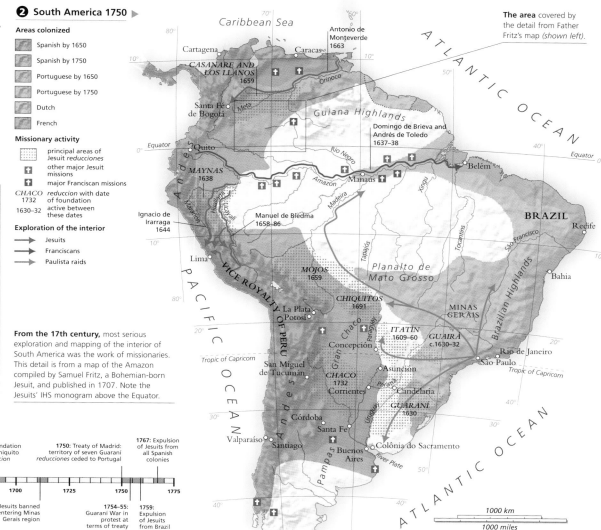

The Jesuits in South America

- **1550:** First Jesuits reach Brazil
- **1573:** Rules drawn up for planning Jesuit towns
- **1607:** Jesuits found province of Paraguay around Asunción
- **1631:** Father Ruiz de Montoya descends Paraná River with 12,000 Indians to escape slave-raiders
- **1641:** Indians and Jesuits defeat slave-raiders from São Paulo on Uruguay River
- **1640s:** Long-running quarrel between Jesuits and governor of Asunción
- **1649:** Viceroy grants *reducciones* virtual independence
- **1690:** Foundation of first Chiquito *reduccion*
- **1711:** Jesuits banned from entering Minas Gerais region
- **1750:** Treaty of Madrid: territory of seven Guaraní *reducciones* ceded to Portugal
- **1754–55:** Guaraní War in protest at terms of treaty
- **1759:** Expulsion of Jesuits from Brazil
- **1767:** Expulsion of Jesuits from all Spanish colonies

Later scientific exploration

Humboldt endured far greater hardship than this studio portrait suggests, as he traveled with French botanist, Aimé Bonpland, by canoe and on foot through the rainforests of the Orinoco.

For three centuries, the colonial authorities in South America did little to encourage scientific exploration. In the 19th century, however, scientists of all kinds began to explore the peaks of the Andes, the Amazon Basin, and even the wilds of Patagonia. The Prussian Alexander von Humboldt amassed unparalleled data on the geography, geology, meteorology, and natural history of South America. He mapped the course of the Casiquiare, a most unusual river in that it links the Amazon and Orinoco drainage basins. Of later travelers, the most famous was Charles Darwin, whose observations as a young naturalist aboard *HMS Beagle* in 1831–36 would inspire his theory of evolution expounded in *On the Origin of Species*. The French paleontologist Alcide d'Orbigny, who spent eight years studying the continent's microfossils, published the first detailed physical map of South America in 1842.

③ Scientific explorers

Humboldt's journey Aug 1799 — Mar 1803

Darwin's journey Feb 1832 — Sep 1835

Scientific exploration

- **1735:** Expedition to Quito led by French scientist La Condamine to test sphericity of the Earth
- **1783:** Spanish crown sponsors botanical expedition to South American colonies
- **1802:** Humboldt climbs to record height on the mountain of Chimborazo; correctly attributes altitude sickness to lack of oxygen
- **1826–34:** D'Orbigny studies continent's fossil-bearing strata
- **1832:** Darwin discovers fossils of giant mammals near Bahía Blanca, including *Megatherium*
- **1835:** Darwin encounters unique island fauna of the Galapagos Islands
- **1835–44:** Guiana region explored by Sir Robert Schomburgk, who fixes boundary of British colony
- **1859:** Naturalist Henry Bates returns to England with 8,000 insects new to science after 11 years in Amazon region
- **1872:** German Wilhelm Reiss scales Cotopaxi, which Humboldt had pronounced unclimbable

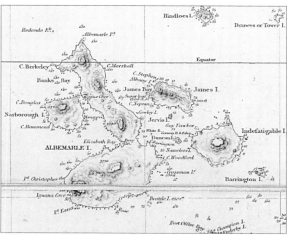

The Galapagos Islands are a volcanic group that lies on the equator. This chart was drawn by the officers of the *Beagle*, who were surveying the coast of South America for the British Navy. Darwin's interest was aroused by the peculiarities of the islands' fauna, such as the giant tortoises, which had evolved slightly different forms on each of the main islands, and the curious marine iguanas.

Large-billed seed-eating finch

Insectivorous warbler finch

The finches Darwin collected on the Galapagos Islands later provided powerful evidence for his theory of natural selection. Several closely related species had diverged from a common ancestor to occupy the various ecological niches on the islands.

EARLY CULTURES OF SOUTH AMERICA

The Bahia people of coastal Ecuador made clay sculptures such as this figure holding a swaddled child.

SOUTH AMERICA WAS COLONIZED by settlers from the north, possibly more than 13,000 years ago. By 10,000 BCE, hunter-gatherers had reached its southern tip and, by 5000 BCE, communities were beginning to exploit local resources, such as corn, manioc, and potatoes. Successful agriculture led to growing populations and increasingly stratified societies. The distinctive temple mounds of Peru appeared by c.2500 BCE, and characteristic elements of South American religious iconography were disseminated all over Peru from the site of Chavín de Huantar, from c.1200 BCE. By 300 CE, Peru was dominated by two major civilizations: the Nazca and the more expansionist Moche.

The earliest settlements

The first South American settlers were hunter-gatherers, exploiting the big game which flourished following the last Ice Age. Spearheads and arrowheads found at Fell's Cave indicate that this way of life had reached the far south of the continent by 10,000 BCE. In Chile, the site of Monte Verde (c.11,000 BCE) is a village of timber huts draped with animal hides. Finds of medicinal plants, potato peelings, digging sticks, wooden bowls, and mortars, reveal an intimate knowledge of plant resources which supplemented a diet of small game and mastodon.

Monte Verde, the earliest known settlement in the southern half of the continent, is thought to have existed by at least 11,000 BCE. Stone tools found there include devices for chopping, scraping, and pounding (left).

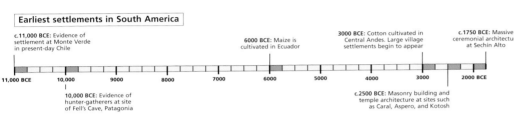

Earliest settlements in South America

c.11,000 BCE: Evidence of settlement at Monte Verde in present-day Chile

6000 BCE: Maize is cultivated in Ecuador

3000 BCE: Cotton cultivated in Central Andes. Large village settlements begin to appear

c.1750 BCE: Massive ceremonial architecture at Sechin Alto

11,000 BCE | 10,000 | 9000 | 8000 | 7000 | 6000 | 5000 | 4000 | 3000 | 2000 BCE

10,000 BCE: Evidence of hunter-gatherers at site of Fell's Cave, Patagonia

c.2500 BCE: Masonry building and temple architecture at sites such as Caral, Aspero, and Kotosh

① Settlement and agriculture in early South America

- .... Native American culture areas
- ◆ archaeological site before 10,000 BCE
- ◇ archaeological site 10,000– 2500 BCE
- early ceremonial center 2500 BCE–1000 BCE
- finds of early pottery, with date

The development of agriculture c.6000 BCE–c.1000 BCE

- earliest agricultural development
- early expansion of agriculture
- later expansion of agriculture
- initial diffusion of agriculture
- subsequent dispersal of agriculture
- distribution of shell middens

Domestication of plants and animals

- tobacco
- squash
- uxalis
- ullucu
- cacao
- sweet potato
- cotton
- potato
- guinea pig
- llama/alpaca
- beans
- avocado
- manioc
- maize
- pumpkin
- quinoa
- groundnut
- chili pepper
- amaranth
- dog
- sunflower

Symbols in red denote core areas of plant and animal domestication; symbols in green denote dispersal of domesticated plants and animals

This painted ceremonial vase shows a man hunting wild llamas. These versatile creatures were among the first animals to be fully domesticated by the early farmers of the Andes.

Scale varies with perspective

N

3560 km (1816 miles)

6224km (3864 miles)

Monumental centers

Spectacular improvements in plant yields sustained growing populations; villages grew into small towns, and the large temple mounds which appeared on the coast of central Peru from c.2500 BCE are evidence of organized, stratified societies. Major sites of this kind include Huaricoto, La Galgada, Caral, and Aspero, and the later El Paraíso.

This water vessel, dating from 900–200 BCE, was found near Cupisnique in the north of the Chavin region.

Agriculture

The first farmers of South America were located on the northern Pacific coast. Corn, the staple crop of the Americas, was cultivated in Ecuador c.6000 BCE; and the major high-altitude crop in the Andes, the potato, may have been grown by 4000 BCE. Llamas and alpaca, domesticated for their wool, were used as Andean pack animals. Manioc, which became a staple of tropical forest farmers, was cultivated in the Amazon Basin by 3000 BCE.

The peoples of the Amazon Basin and the Atlantic coast

Rock shelters and flaked stone tools dating to c.10,000 BCE provide the earliest evidence of settlement east of the Andes. The transition from hunting and gathering to agriculture – principally the cultivation of manioc – probably began c.3000 BCE. Large shell middens at the mouths of the Amazon and Orinoco rivers contain remains of pottery dating to c.5000 BCE – far earlier than the first pottery of Peru. When corn was introduced into the river flood plains in the 1st millennium BCE, populations expanded and hierarchical societies (chiefdoms) developed. Drainage earthworks on the Llanos de Mojos suggest that large populations were cooperating to farm the landscape.

◄ ② Early settlement of Amazonia and eastern South America

- ◇ early archaeological site 12,000–6000 BCE
- ⬙ early ceramic site 5000–1000 BCE
- early lithic site
- ▲ earthworks and hydrological systems
- shell midden

The cultures of Peru 1300 BCE–600 CE

The most influential culture of the middle Andes was that of the Chavín, which flourished at and around the major religious center of Chavín de Huantar between 850 BCE and 200 BCE. The Chavín were distinguished by the sophistication of their architecture and sculptural style and by technological developments including the building of canals. As Chavín influence waned, from c.200 BCE, many distinctive regional cultures developed in the Andean highlands. Coastal Peru, however, was dominated by two major civilizations, Nazca in the south, and Moche in the north. As these cultures developed a strong identity, military rivalries intensified, paving the way for the appearance of other major states from 500 CE including Tiahuanaco and Huari.

Large cemeteries in the Paracas region contained thousands of mummified bodies wrapped in colorful wool. The motif of a large-eyed deity, the Oculate Being, on these textiles shows a strong affinity with the Chavín deity, known as the Smiling God.

④ Coastal Peru c.600 BCE–600 CE

- Paracas cultural region c. 600–350 BCE
- ◆ major Paracas sites
- Ecuadorian cultural region c.500 BCE–500 CE
- Lima cultural region c.400 BCE–500 CE
- Nazca cultural region c.350 BCE–450 CE
- earliest Moche sites c.1 CE
- Moche cultural region c.1–600 CE
- Recuay cultural region c.500 CE
- ▽ irrigated river valley

Moche

Moche culture was centered on the capital of Moche, dominated by the famous Temple of the Sun, a massive structure of solid adobe 40 m high. The Moche state was powerful, well-organized, and expanded by military conquest. Mass labor was organized to participate in major public works and civil engineering projects and the construction of "royal" tombs.

The stirrup-spout on this drinking vessel is a typical feature of Moche pottery, as is the marvelously realistic and sensitive modeling of the facial features.

Nazca

Based on the south coast of Peru, Nazca culture is famous for its superb and graphic pottery, textiles, and above all, the enigmatic "Nazca lines," straight, geometric, or figurative designs etched onto the surface of the desert, possibly as offerings to the gods.

This aerial view shows Nazca lines etched into the shape of a hummingbird. Some of these images can be over 100 m across.

③ Chavín culture

- Chavín heartland
- ◇ early Chavín sites, 2000–850 BCE
- ◇ Chavín sites, 850–200 BCE
- → trade route

The Chavín

Chavín de Huantar (c.1200–200 BCE), with its large stone sculptures and grand temples, became a cult center. Chavín motifs, in architecture, textiles, pottery, and goldwork, are found throughout Peru.

Cultures of Peru 1300 BCE–1 CE

- 850 BCE: Florescence of Chavín de Huantar; Chavín style widely disseminated
- 500 BCE: Paracas culture in southern Peru produces textiles woven with Chavín-style images
- c.1 CE: Emergence of Moche culture of coastal Peru
- 1300 BCE: Cerro Sechin is earliest central Andean site with Chavín-style iconography
- 200 BCE: Regional cultures begin to appear in central Andes

1400 BCE | 1200 | 1000 | 800 | 600 | 400 | 200 | 1 CE

THE EMPIRES OF SOUTH AMERICA

THE EMPIRES WHICH DOMINATED the Andes between 500 and 1450, Tiahuanaco, Huari, and Chimú, were important precursors of the Inca, laying down the religious and social foundations, and the authoritarian government which were to serve the Inca so well. The Inca Empire (1438–1532) was the greatest state in South America exercising stringent control over its subjects through taxation, forced labor, compulsory migration, and military service. With its unyielding hierarchy and ill-defined line of succession, the empire was fatally weakened by a leadership crisis at the very point when Pizarro arrived in 1532, and was unable to prevent its own destruction at the hands of the Spanish *conquistadores*.

This gold knife in the form of a Chimú (or Sicán) sun god dates from c.1100 CE. The body is decorated with turquoises.

Empires of the Andean coast 250–1375

The empires of Tiahuanaco and Huari, which together dominated the Andes from 500 CE, shared a similar art style, and probably the same religion. The city of Tiahuanaco, on the windswept Altiplano of modern Bolivia, was a major pilgrimage center, and its cultural influence diffused throughout the south-central Andes from 500–1000. The contemporary Huari Empire, which controlled the coast around present-day Lima, was, by contrast, centralized and militaristic, expanding its influence through conquest. The Inca owed most to their direct predecessor, the Chimú Empire of the northern Andes, with its efficient administration, colonial expansionism, irrigation projects, and stress on an effective communication system.

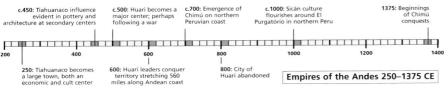

| c.450: Tiahuanaco influence evident in pottery and architecture at secondary centers | c.500: Huari becomes a major center; perhaps following a war | c.700: Emergence of Chimú on northern Peruvian coast | c.1000: Sicán culture flourishes around El Purgatório in northern Peru | 1375: Beginnings of Chimú conquests |

| 200 | 400 | 600 | 800 | 1000 | 1200 | 1400 |

| 250: Tiahuanaco becomes a large town, both an economic and cult center | 600: Huari leaders conquer territory stretching 560 miles along Andean coast | 800: City of Huari abandoned | **Empires of the Andes 250–1375 CE** |

Tiahuanaco

By 500 CE the city of Tiahuanaco on Lake Titicaca's southeastern shore had become a major population center, housing up to 40,000 people, and a focus of pilgrimage for the entire Andean region. It was dominated by palaces and a cult center, consisting of temples, monumental gateways, and large monolithic sculptures. The city's iconography, with its symbolism of water, sun, and weather, spread throughout the south-central Andes.

Carved from a single slab of andesite, the Gateway of the Sun at Tiahuanaco is a representation of the cosmos, with the creator god at the center of the frieze.

Huari

Thriving from 500–800 CE, the empire based on the city of Huari shared many of Tiahuanaco's cultural characteristics, but was a much more militaristic state which grew through conquest, reflected in finds of major trunk roads and regional centers with military barracks. Public works, such as road-building, were carried out as a labor tax by the empire's subjects.

The back of this Huari hand mirror contains a central face, with small heads at each side. The reflecting surface is of pyrite and the mosaic back of a variety of stones of contrasting texture and color.

Chimú

The Chimú Empire which ruled over the coast of northern Peru (c.700–1476) was centered on the capital of Chan Chan. A series of great royal compounds within the city served as both the palaces and tombs of ten successive monarchs. The empire stretched for 1,600 miles along the Peruvian coast, administered by a series of regional centers.

The Chimú people were skilled metalworkers, producing a wide variety of ceremonial objects such as this gold dove with turquoise eyes.

This small figure reflects the intricate casting and polishing typical of the goldsmiths of the Quimbaya chiefdoms. They also produced masks, spear tips, pendants, and helmets

Chiefdoms of the northern Andes

By the 15th century, many peoples of the northern Andes were organized into chiefdoms, based on large villages, supported by wetland farming, and capable of mobilizing sizable armies. Their gold-working skills gave rise to myths of "El Dorado" *(see p.149)*. Gold and copper resources were exploited by efficient mining operations — an indication of their impressive organizational ability.

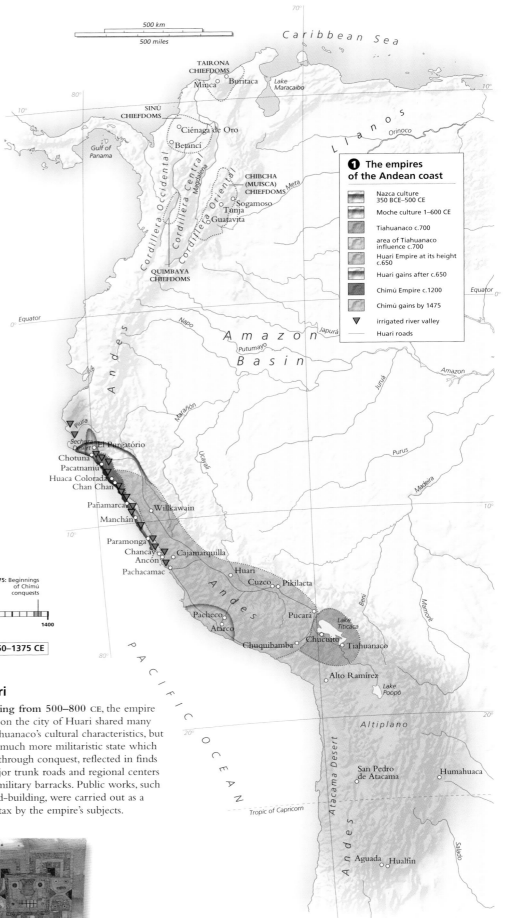

1 The empires of the Andean coast

- Nazca culture 350 BCE–500 CE
- Moche culture 1–600 CE
- Tiahuanaco c.700
- area of Tiahuanaco influence c.700
- Huari Empire at its height c.650
- Huari gains after c.650
- Chimú Empire c.1200
- Chimú gains by 1475
- ▽ irrigated river valley
- Huari roads

The Inca Empire

The Inca emerged, in less than a century, as the preeminent state in South America; from 1470 they ruled vast territories from their capital, Cuzco. Their hierarchical society, ruled by the Sapa Inca (believed to be descended from the sun), depended on the mass organization of labor. Adult men were liable for forced labor, and worked in the fields, on public works (terracing, building, mining), and served in the army. An extensive road network, interspersed with way stations and regional centers, bound the empire together. Yet this complex bureaucracy had no form of writing, although arithmetic records were used for administration, tribute, and taxation.

The Inca *quipumayoc*, or grand treasurer, is shown holding a *quipu*, a device made of knotted strings, used to record administrative matters and sacred histories. Information was encoded in the colors of the strings and the style of the knots.

▲ ❷ South America c.1500
- border of Inca Empire
- high civilization
- chiefdoms
- tropical forest farming villages
- other farming villages
- nomadic hunter-gatherers

Ona indigenous people

❸ The Inca Empire 1525

Expansion of the Inca Empire
- by 1400
- in reign of Pachacutec 1438–71
- in reign of Tupac Yupanqui 1471–93
- in reign of Huayna Capac 1493–1525
- border of Inca Empire 1525
- Inca road

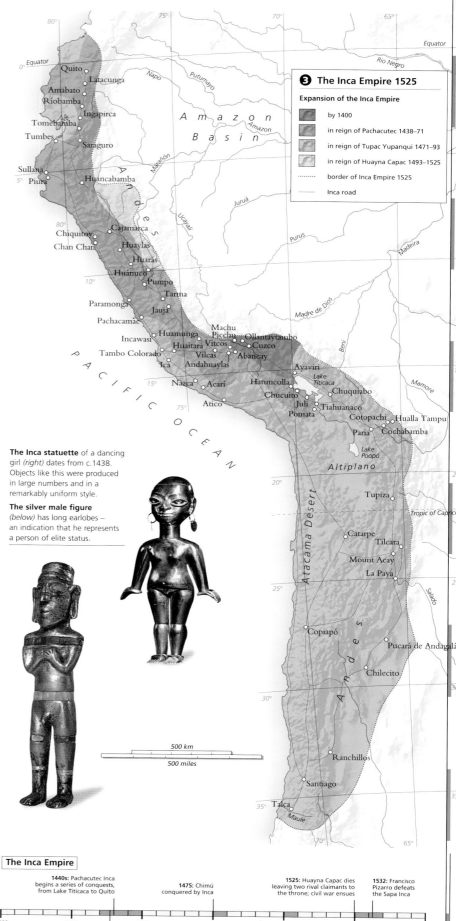

The Inca statuette of a dancing girl *(right)* dates from c.1438. Objects like this were produced in large numbers and in a remarkably uniform style.

The silver male figure *(below)* has long earlobes – an indication that he represents a person of elite status.

The peoples of South America c.1500

The golden raft, bearing a godlike figure surrounded by attendants, is a detailed example of a *tunjo* or offering piece, produced by the Muisca (Chibcha) people of the northeastern Andes.

A great diversity of indigenous cultures existed in South America by the start of the 16th century, ranging from the high civilization of the Incas to the hunter-gatherers of Patagonia. Large populations lived along the Amazon, the upper river dominated by the Omagua people, its lower reaches controlled by the warlike Tapajosó. Many chiefdoms held sway over huge areas, some extracting forced labor from subject peoples, who were often engaged on extensive building projects. Ancestor cults, based on the mummified bodies of chiefs, were widespread.

This stylized carving in the shape of a tree is etched on a hillside in the coastal desert above present-day Paracas.

THE VERTICAL ECONOMY OF THE ANDES

The rugged terrain of the Andes provided a series of contiguous, but contrasting environments, fully exploited by the Incas and their predecessors. High, treeless, grassy plains (the *puna*) were used for grazing llamas. Below this, at heights up to 4,400 yds above sea level, lay the *suni*, where potatoes and tubers could be cultivated. Corn, squash, fruits, and cocoa grew in lower, frost-free valleys (the *quechua*), while the lower slopes of the mountains (the *yunga*) were planted with peppers, coca plants, and other fruits. Sources of shellfish and fish from the ocean were periodically disrupted by El Niño, an irregular climatic disturbance which warmed the ocean, leading to torrential rains and disastrous flooding.

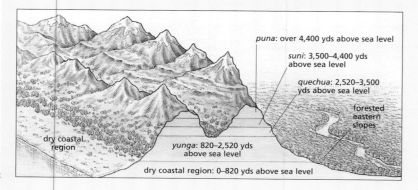

puna: over 4,400 yds above sea level

suni: 3,500–4,400 yds above sea level

quechua: 2,520–3,500 yds above sea level

forested eastern slopes

dry coastal region

yunga: 820–2,520 yds above sea level

dry coastal region: 0–820 yds above sea level

The Inca Empire

1440s: Pachacutec Inca begins a series of conquests, from Lake Titicaca to Quito

1475: Chimú conquered by Inca

1525: Huayna Capac dies leaving two rival claimants to the throne; civil war ensues

1532: Francisco Pizarro defeats the Sapa Inca

1400 — 1425 — 1450 — 1475 — 1500 — 1525 — 1550

1438: Incas rise to power; attack Lake Titicaca basin, and establish upland empire

1500: Protracted military campaigns at northern and southern extremes of empire lead to establishment of second capital at Tomebamba

COLONIAL SOUTH AMERICA

Christianity in South America blended with local traditions to produce colorful spectacles such as this 18th-century Corpus Christi procession in Cuzco.

IN THEIR CONQUEST of South America, the Spanish were so driven by the quest for gold and silver that it took the *conquistadores* less than ten years to take over the rich, organized states of the Andes. The Portuguese were slower to settle Brazil, first trading with the Indians, then turning to sugar production. Wherever Europeans settled, the native population declined rapidly, mainly through lack of resistance to alien diseases. There were also periodic wars against the colonists. Large cattle stations that destroyed native arable smallholdings were a further factor in their decline. Emigration to South America from both Spain and Portugal was light; settlers mixed with the natives, creating a mixed-race *mestizo* population. To make up for shortages in labor, they imported African slaves. Catholic missionaries, notably the Jesuits, were active throughout the colonial era, often defending the rights of the Indians against the settlers. Both colonial empires collapsed in the 19th century, but the religion and languages of the conquerors survived.

The silver mine at Potosí was the prime source of revenue to the Spanish crown between 1550 and 1650. At first the native population supplied all the labor and technology. The silver was extracted using mercury, mined at Huancavelica.

The conquest of Peru

In 1531 Francisco Pizarro sailed from Panama to conquer Peru. By the time the expedition had penetrated inland to Cajamarca, where the reigning Inca, Atahualpa, and 40,000 men were camped, Pizarro had only 180 men. Yet he succeeded in capturing Atahualpa, whom he held for ransom. When this was paid, Atahualpa was executed, and the *conquistadores* moved on to capture the Inca capital, Cuzco. The Incas were in awe of the Spanish horses and guns, but this astonishing feat of conquest would have been impossible had the Inca Empire not been weakened by a smallpox epidemic and civil war.

Atahualpa was given a summary trial by Pizarro and then garrotted, or – as this contemporary Inca illustration shows – beheaded.

❶ Pizarro's conquest of the Inca Empire

→ 1524 expedition
→ 1526 expedition
→ 1531–33 expedition
···· extent of Inca Empire
1526 date of foundation

400 km
400 miles

❷ Spanish South America

- Spanish territory before 1650
- Spanish territory after 1650
- region disputed by Spain and Portugal up to 1777
- Jesuit mission states, with dates
····· border with Brazil by Treaty of Madrid 1750
--- border with Brazil where modified by Treaty of San Ildefonso 1777
○ Portuguese settlement
▪ gold ⚘ drugs
▪ silver ✕ hides
▪ copper ▨ cocoa
▪ mercury

Inca ornaments, such as this gold llama, are very rare because most were melted down and shipped to Spain.

Spanish South America

Spain ruled her American colonies through two great viceroyalties, New Spain (centered on Mexico) and Peru. The viceroys' principal duty was to guarantee a steady flow of bullion for the Spanish Crown. When booty from the native empires was exhausted, the colonists turned to the region's mineral resources, using forced native labor *(mita)* to extract precious metals, in particular silver. Smaller administrative units called *audiencias* were presided over by a judge who enacted the complex laws devised in Spain for the running of the colonies. Attempts to expand the empire were thwarted in the south by the fierce Araucanian people, elsewhere by the inhospitable nature of the terrain.

The founder of Spain's South American empire, Pizarro was an aging soldier of fortune. Some of his own lieutenants rebelled against him and he was killed in a riot in Lima in 1541.

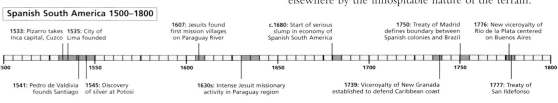

Spanish South America 1500–1800

1533: Pizarro takes Inca capital, Cuzco
1535: City of Lima founded
1607: Jesuits found first mission villages on Paraguay River
c.1680: Start of serious slump in economy of Spanish South America
1750: Treaty of Madrid defines boundary between Spanish colonies and Brazil
1776: New viceroyalty of Río de la Plata centered on Buenos Aires

1500 | 1550 | 1600 | 1650 | 1700 | 1750 | 1800

1541: Pedro de Valdivia founds Santiago
1545: Discovery of silver at Potosí
1630s: Intense Jesuit missionary activity in Paraguay region
1739: Viceroyalty of New Granada established to defend Caribbean coast
1777: Treaty of San Ildefonso

Portuguese South America

Brazil was formally claimed by Portugal in 1500. There were no conspicuous mineral resources, so colonization depended on agriculture. In the 1530s, in an attempt to encourage settlement, João III made grants of land to 12 hereditary "captains," each captaincy consisting of 50 leagues of coastline. Some failed completely and little of the coastal plain was settled before 1549 when a royal governor-general was sent to Bahia. The captaincy system continued, but the colonists' fortunes changed with the success of sugar. The native population living near the coast had been almost wiped out by disease and wars. The few that remained had no wish to labor on sugar plantations, so slaves were imported from Africa. In the 18th century, a gold boom opened up the Minas Gerais region, but apart from slave-raiders hunting for natives and prospectors searching for gold and diamonds, penetration of the interior was limited.

❸ Portuguese South America

	Portuguese territory by 1600
	Portuguese territory by 1750
	Portuguese frontier territory
	region disputed by Spain and Portugal up to 1777

PARÁ 1616 captaincy and date of foundation
□ capital city
🏠 gold
◯ diamonds
⊛ dyes
🗡 hides
↓ sugar

Between 1550 and 1800, some 2.5 million African slaves were taken to Brazil, more than 70% of them to work for the sugar plantations and mills which were the backbone of the economy.

Slaves were also employed at the gold and diamond mines of the interior. This early 19th-century print shows slaves washing diamond-bearing rock.

Brazil 1500–1800

1502: First expedition sent from Lisbon to exploit newfound coastline

1549: Direct royal rule imposed from new capital at Bahia

1580: Portugal and her empire come under rule of Spanish kings

1663: Brazil becomes viceroyalty

1674: Foundation of Manaus, 995 miles from mouth of Amazon

1750: Portugal renounces claim to Colônia do Sacramento

1500 – 1525 – 1550 – 1575 – 1600 – 1625 – 1650 – 1675 – 1700 – 1725 – 1750 – 1775 – 1800

1532: First captaincies granted for purposes of settlement

1562–63: War and disease kill much of Indian population

1621: Formation of separate Estado do Maranhão with its own governor-general

1680s: Portuguese found Colônia do Sacramento

1695: Gold discovered in Minas Gerais region

1763: Rio de Janeiro becomes Brazilian capital

THE SEARCH FOR EL DORADO

From the 1530s until well into the 17th century, fantastic tales of the kingdom of El Dorado (the gilded man) inspired many foolhardy expeditions through the Andes, the Orinoco basin, and the Guiana Highlands. The English sea captain Walter Raleigh twice sailed to the Orinoco, but both his voyages ended in failure, and on the second in 1617 his teenaged son was killed by the Spanish.

The legend of El Dorado took many forms. The most persistent was of a chieftain so rich that he was regularly painted in gold by his subjects.

Other colonial powers

For 150 years Portugal's hold on Brazil was far from secure. The French, who traded along the coast with the natives, made several attempts to found colonies. In the first half of the 17th century, the defense of Portuguese colonies was neglected by the ruling Spanish kings. This allowed the Dutch to capture a long stretch of the northeast coast. They were finally expelled in 1654 and had to be content, like the English and French, with a small colony in the Guianas.

Dutch Brazil thrived under the governorship of Prince Maurits of Nassau (1636–44), when many new towns were built. The artist Franz Post painted idealized views of the colony during this period. This detail shows the slave quarters on a plantation.

❹ Brazil and the Guianas c.1640

●	Portuguese possession and settlement
●	Dutch possession and settlement
●	French possession and settlement
—	temporary French colonies in Brazil

1558 and 1612: French attempts to colonize São Luís

1644: Dutch withdraw from São Luís following Portuguese rebellion

1630: Dutch take Recife; town rebuilt as Mauritsstad; regained by Portuguese in 1654

1555: French colonists found Henryville on the site of present-day Rio de Janeiro

Dutch, French, and English colonies 1550–1700

1555: 600 French settlers found short-lived colony of France Antarctique at Rio de Janeiro

1630: Dutch establish New Holland, covering much of northeastern Brazil

1654: Portuguese take Recife and regain control of Brazil

1550 – 1600 – 1650 – 1700

1568: French occupy northern Maranhão

c.1610: First Dutch settlements on the Essequibo

1625: Portuguese expelled from Maranhão

1667: Peace of Breda; some English territory in Guiana ceded to Dutch

AFRICA
REGIONAL HISTORY

THE HISTORICAL LANDSCAPE

THE GEOGRAPHY AND CLIMATE OF AFRICA has, to possibly a greater extent than in any other continent, determined its role in world history. The earliest human remains have been found here in the arid geological block faults of the Great Rift Valley and southern Africa. Although unaffected by the glaciation of the last Ice Age, attendant climatic changes witnessed a transformation of the Sahara from a desert during the Ice Age, into a belt of temperate grassland, inhabited by herds of game and groups of hunter-gatherers by 8000 years ago. By around 4000 BCE, the process of desiccation began which continues today, effectively isolating sub-Saharan Africa from the Mediterranean. Only the Nile Valley provided a link, and here one of the world's oldest civilizations emerged. South of the Sahara, a wide range of isolated cultures developed, their nature determined largely by their environment, linked by rich nonliterate oral traditions. The plateau nature of much of Africa, and the desert and jungle which dominate much of the landscape, meant that Africa was one of the last continents to be colonized by Europeans, and their brief and callous century of tenancy left a legacy of underdevelopment and political strife.

The Great Rift Valley was home to one of the earliest known human ancestors, *Australopithecus afarensis*, 3.8 million years ago. Modern humans (*Homo sapiens*) evolved here about 100,000 years ago before migrating to Asia and Australasia, Europe, and finally the Americas.

The Sahara covers much of northern Africa, although sand dunes account for only a quarter of the desert's area. The rest is made up of barren, rock-strewn surfaces. Desert has existed in this part of Africa for almost five million years, and the harsh climate and inhospitable landscape have prevented the establishment of permanent settlements.

The Nile River winds its way across the hostile Sahara to the Mediterranean Sea, flanked by fertile floodplains. Humans have inhabited the Nile region since the early Stone Age, making use of the fertile soils that have built up as a result of the annual flooding of the river.

Vegetation type

- semidesert or sparsely vegetated
- grassland
- forest or open woodland
- tropical rain forest
- tropical desert (18,000 years ago)
- desert (8000 years ago)
- coastline (present-day)
- coastline (18,000 years ago)

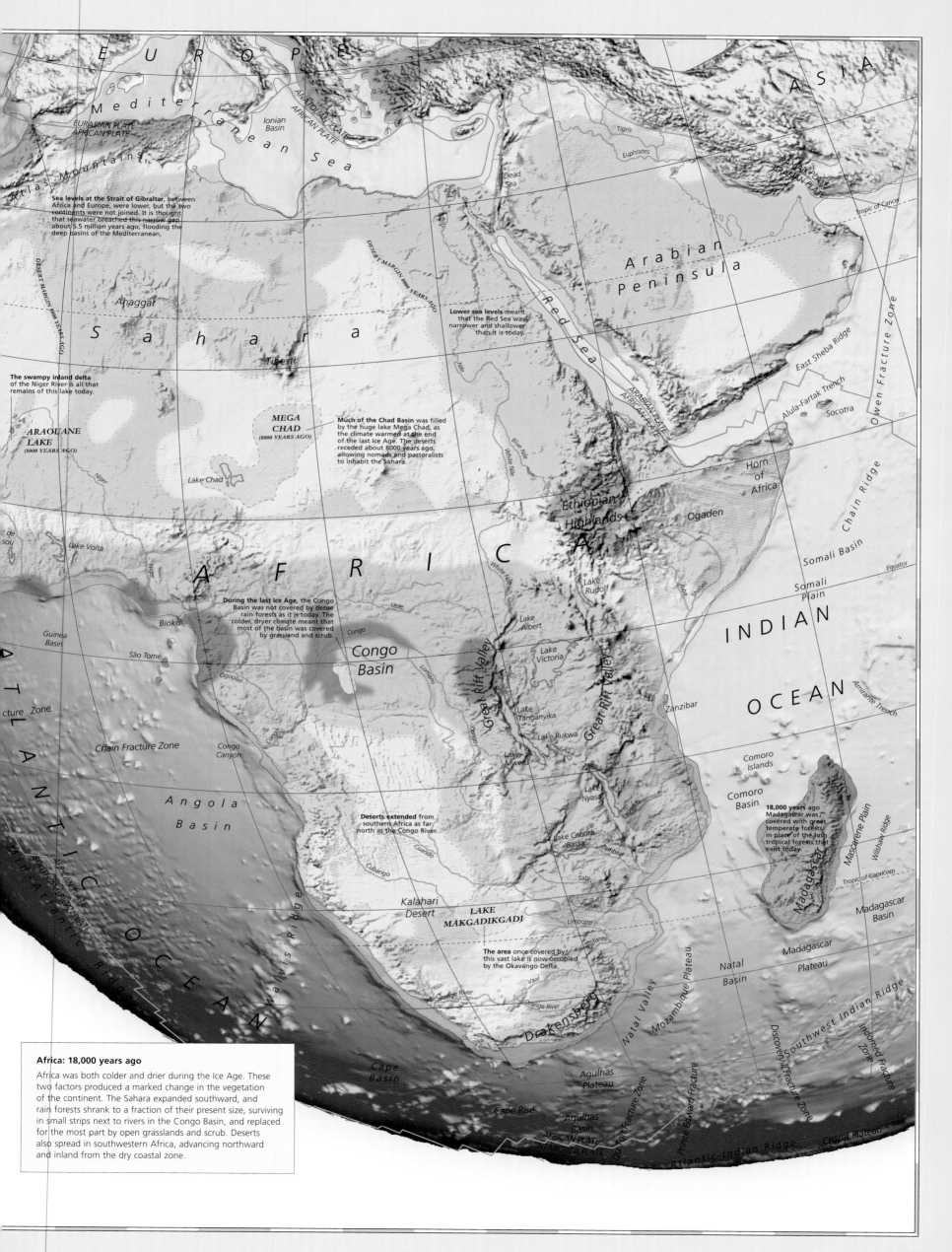

E U R O P E

Mediterranean Sea

EURASIAN PLATE
AFRICAN PLATE

Ionian
Basin

ANATOLIAN PLATE
AFRICAN PLATE

Anatolia

A S I A

Tigris

Euphrates

Dead
Sea

ARABIAN PLATE
AFRICAN PLATE

Tropic of Cancer

Atlas Mountains

Sea levels at the Strait of Gibraltar, between
Africa and Europe, were lower, but the two
continents were not joined. It is thought
that seawater breached this narrow gap
about 5.5 million years ago, flooding the
deep basins of the Mediterranean.

Arabian
Peninsula

DESERT MARGIN 8000 YEARS AGO

Ahaggar

S a h a r a

DESERT MARGIN 8000 YEARS AGO

Tibesti

Lower sea levels meant
that the Red Sea was
narrower and shallower
than it is today.

Red Sea

Owen Fracture Zone

East Sheba Ridge

Alula-Fartak Trench

Socotra

The swampy inland delta
of the Niger River is all that
remains of this lake today.

*MEGA
CHAD*
(8000 YEARS AGO)

Much of the Chad Basin was filled
by the huge lake Mega Chad, as
the climate warmed at the end
of the last Ice Age. The deserts
receded about 8000 years ago,
allowing nomads and pastoralists
to inhabit the Sahara.

Blue Nile

White Nile

Nile

*ARAOUANE
LAKE*
(8000 YEARS AGO)

Niger

Lake Chad

Horn
of
Africa

Chain Ridge

de
sou

Lake Volta

Niger

A F R I C A

White Nile

Ethiopian
Highlands

Ogaden

Somali Basin

Equator

Bioko

During the last Ice Age, the Congo
Basin was not covered by dense
rain forests as it is today. The
colder, drier climate meant that
most of the basin was covered
by grassland and scrub.

Uele

Lake
Rudolf

Somali
Plain

Guinea
Basin

São Tomé

Ogooué

Congo

Lomami

Congo
Basin

Lake
Albert

Lake
Victoria

I N D I A N

ture Zone

Chain Fracture Zone

Congo
Canyon

Congo

Great Rift Valley

Lake
Tanganyika

Great Rift Valley

Lake Rukwa

Zanzibar

O C E A N

Amirante Trench

Lake
Mweru

Angola
Basin

Congo

Comoro
Islands

Lake
Nyasa

Comoro
Basin

18,000 years ago
Madagascar was
covered with great
temperate forests
in place of the lush
tropical forests that
exist today.

MID-ATLANTIC RIDGE

AFRICAN PLATE
SOUTH AMERICAN PLATE

Deserts extended from
southern Africa as far
north as the Congo River.

Lugenda

Lake Cabora
Bassa

Zambezi

Madagascar

Mascarene Plain

Wilshaw Ridge

A T L A N T I C

Cuanza

Cubango

Cuando

Sabi

Kalahari
Desert

*LAKE
MAKGADIKGADI*

Runde

Madagascar
Basin

Tropic of Capricorn

O C E A N

Walvis Ridge

The area once covered by
this vast lake is now occupied
by the Okavango Delta.

Limpopo

Olifants

Natal
Basin

Madagascar
Plateau

Mozambique Plateau

Southwest Indian Ridge

Discovery II Fracture Zone

Indomed Fracture Zone

Orange River

Orange River

Vaal

Drakensberg

Natal Valley

Cape
Basin

Agulhas
Plateau

Du Toit Fracture Zone

Prince Edward Fracture

Crozet Plateau

Cape Rise

Agulhas
Plateau

AFRICAN PLATE
ANTARCTICA PLATE

Atlantic-Indian Ridge

Atlantic-Indian Ridge

Southwest Indian Ridge

Africa: 18,000 years ago

Africa was both colder and drier during the Ice Age. These
two factors produced a marked change in the vegetation
of the continent. The Sahara expanded southward, and
rain forests shrank to a fraction of their present size, surviving
in small strips next to rivers in the Congo Basin, and replaced
for the most part by open grasslands and scrub. Deserts
also spread in southwestern Africa, advancing northward
and inland from the dry coastal zone.

THE EARLY HISTORY OF AFRICA

Hatshepsut seized the throne in Egypt from her stepson and reigned from 1472 to 1458 BCE.

THREE EVENTS contributed to the growth and spread of farming in Africa: the spread of cattle pastoralism in the Sahara, the domestication of indigenous crops further south, and the introduction of cereals to Egypt. Asian wheat and barley spread along the Mediterranean coast, up the Nile Valley to the Sudan, and the Ethiopian Highlands. Drier conditions from 3000 BCE forced Saharan pastoralists to migrate to the Nile Valley, where from 5000 BCE crops had thrived in fertile soil deposited by annual floods. Egypt thereafter emerged as a powerful state, organized conventionally into 30 "Dynasties," broken down into three "Kingdoms" separated by two "Intermediate Periods" of disunity and instability.

The development of agriculture

From 4000 BCE bulrush millet was cultivated alongside sorghum in southern Sudan.

Both the herding of wild cattle in the Sahara and the cultivation of indigenous plants farther south began c.6000 BCE. From 5000 BCE, Asian wheat and barley were grown in Egypt. By 2000 BCE pastoralism was widespread north of the Equator. Farming and herding south of the Equator however, were impeded by dense forests and the presence of the parasitic tsetse fly. As a result, pastoralism progressed only slowly down the east coast, reaching southern Africa by 1000 CE.

Saharan rock art provide vivid pictures of what life was like in the region. This example from the Tassili n'Ajjer plateau dates from c.6000 BCE. It depicts the hunting of giraffes, now only found south of the Sahara.

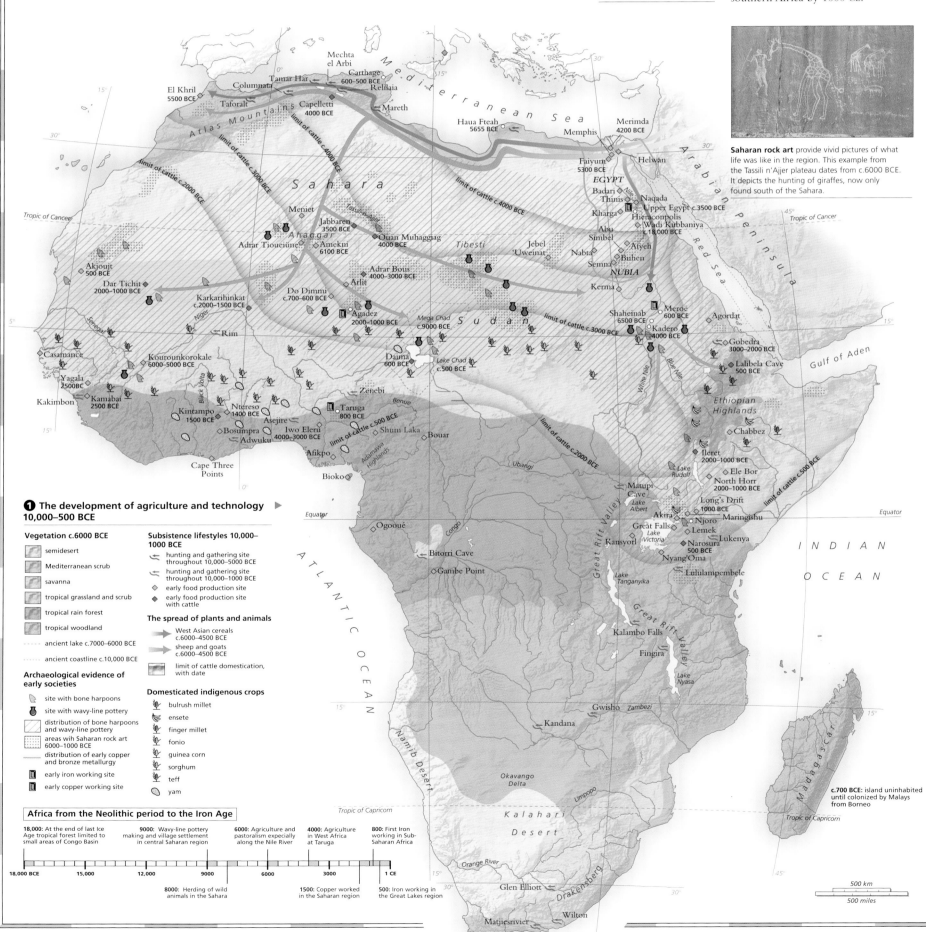

① The development of agriculture and technology 10,000–500 BCE

Vegetation c.6000 BCE
- semidesert
- Mediterranean scrub
- savanna
- tropical grassland and scrub
- tropical rain forest
- tropical woodland
- ancient lake c.7000–6000 BCE
- ancient coastline c.10,000 BCE

Archaeological evidence of early societies
- site with bone harpoons
- site with wavy-line pottery
- distribution of bone harpoons and wavy-line pottery
- areas with Saharan rock art 6000–1000 BCE
- distribution of early copper and bronze metallurgy
- early iron working site
- early copper working site

Subsistence lifestyles 10,000–1000 BCE
- hunting and gathering site throughout 10,000–5000 BCE
- hunting and gathering site throughout 10,000–1000 BCE
- early food production site
- early food production site with cattle

The spread of plants and animals
- West Asian cereals c.6000–4500 BCE
- sheep and goats c.6000–4500 BCE
- limit of cattle domestication, with date

Domesticated indigenous crops
- bulrush millet
- ensete
- finger millet
- fonio
- guinea corn
- sorghum
- teff
- yam

Africa from the Neolithic period to the Iron Age

18,000: At the end of last Ice Age tropical forest limited to small areas of Congo Basin

9000: Wavy-line pottery making and village settlement in central Saharan region

6000: Agriculture and pastoralism expecially along the Nile River

4000: Agriculture in West Africa at Taruga

800: First Iron working in Sub-Saharan Africa

| 18,000 BCE | 15,000 | 12,000 | 9000 | 6000 | 3000 | 1 CE |

8000: Herding of wild animals in the Sahara

1500: Copper worked in the Saharan region

500: Iron working in the Great Lakes region

c.700 BCE: island uninhabited until colonized by Malays from Borneo

500 km
500 miles

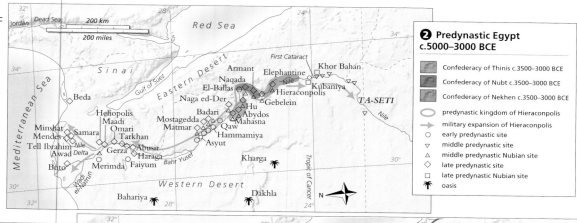

2 Predynastic Egypt c.5000–3000 BCE

- Confederacy of Thinis c.3500–3000 BCE
- Confederacy of Nubt c.3500–3000 BCE
- Confederacy of Nekhen c.3500–3000 BCE
- predynastic kingdom of Hieraconpolis
- military expansion of Hieraconpolis
- early predynastic site
- middle predynastic site
- middle predynastic Nubian site
- late predynastic site
- late predynastic Nubian site
- oasis

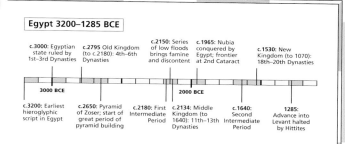

Egypt 3200–1285 BCE

c.3000: Egyptian state ruled by 1st–3rd Dynasties
c.2795 Old Kingdom (to c.2180): 4th–6th Dynasties
c.2150: Series of low floods brings famine and discontent
c.1965: Nubia conquered by Egypt; frontier at 2nd Cataract
c.1530: New Kingdom (to 1070): 18th–20th Dynasties

3000 BCE — 2000 BCE

c.3200: Earliest hieroglyphic script in Egypt
c.2650: Pyramid of Zoser; start of great period of pyramid building
c.2180: First Intermediate Period
c.2134: Middle Kingdom (to 1640): 11th–13th Dynasties
c.1640: Second Intermediate Period
1285: Advance into Levant halted by Hittites

The growth of Egypt 3500–2180 BCE

From 5000 BCE settled communities of farmers in the Nile valley gradually coalesced into urban centers under local rulers who developed efficient administrations. Narmer of the 1st Dynasty established the Egyptian state c.3000 BCE. From this time the use of hieroglyphic writing spread and Memphis was founded. With greater centralization of power the Old Kingdom emerged and the building of the great pyramids, which served as royal burial places, began. From 2400 BCE royal power began to decline and by 2180 BCE the Old Kingdom was divided between two rival dynasties in Upper and Lower Egypt. The years of political instability that followed became known as the First Intermediate Period.

3 Old Kingdom Egypt c.2795–2180 BCE

- regions of Egyptian control
- regions of contact
- Nubian chiefdoms
- kingdom capital
- pyramid
- oasis
- trade route

Traded materials:
- gold
- copper
- limestone
- turquoise
- red granite
- alabaster

The **step pyramid** of Zoser dating from c.2650 BCE was the earliest pyramid built in Egypt. Its construction required the large-scale mobilization of thousands of workers

4 Middle Kingdom Egypt c.2134–1640 BCE

- regions of Egyptian control
- regions of contact
- trading center
- Nubian fort
- Middle Kingdom temple
- oasis
- trade route

Traded materials:
- gold
- copper
- turquoise

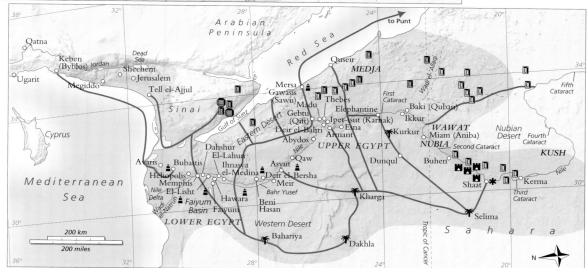

Hatshepsut's temple at Deir el-Bahri was built c.1473 BCE. A fine example of architecture from the 18th Dynasty, the building has a series of colonnades and courts on three levels.

Expansion and division in Egypt

The governors of Thebes emerged from the First Intermediate Period as rulers of Upper Egypt. They later successfully challenged Lower Egypt for control of the entire region, and the Middle Kingdom was established by c.2134 BCE. Its army and administration systematically enriched Egypt's economy by dominating, and eventually annexing, Wawat and northern Kush. The Second Intermediate saw Nubia lost from Egyptian control, and the division of the Nile Delta region into several kingdoms. From 1640 BCE much of Egypt was ruled by the Hyksos from the Mediterranean coast. They were later expelled by Ahmose, king of Thebes, who became the first ruler of the New Kingdom. During the New Kingdom Egypt embarked on a policy of expansion both north and south which made it the major commercial power in the ancient world. By 1000 BCE, however, the New Kingdom was in decline.

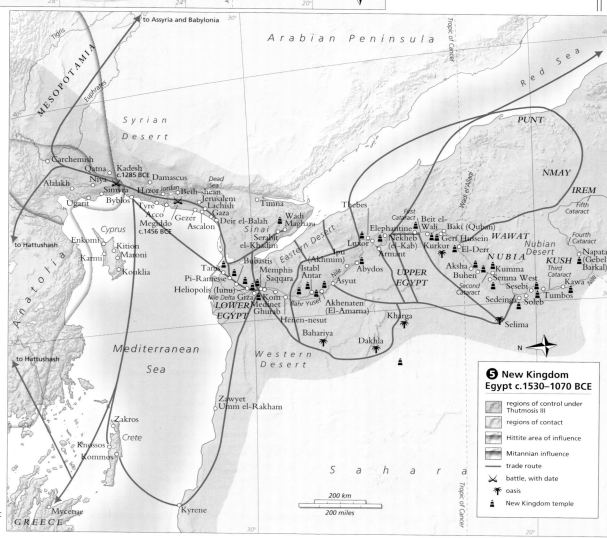

5 New Kingdom Egypt c.1530–1070 BCE

- regions of control under Thutmosis III
- regions of contact
- Hittite area of influence
- Mitannian influence
- trade route
- battle, with date
- oasis
- New Kingdom temple

ISLAM AND NEW STATES IN AFRICA

FROM THE 10TH CENTURY, A SERIES of empires arose in the sub-Saharan savannah. They attracted Muslim Arab traders who traveled south in search of salt, gold, and slaves. Through frequent contact, Islam gradually infiltrated the region by means of peaceful conversion. When the Muslim Berber Almoravids captured the capital of Ghana in 1076, causing the collapse of the empire, their conquest did little to advance the spread of Islam. Christian Ethiopia also withstood Muslim advances. However, Ghana's successors, Mali and Songhay, owed much of their wealth and civilization to the advent and adoption of Islam, as did the Kanem-Bornu Empire around Lake Chad, and, after the 15th century, the Hausa city-states. From the late 10th century, Arab merchant colonies were established in the coastal towns of East Africa, stimulating African trade with Arabia and India, and accelerating the southward spread of Islam.

African trade and the spread of Islam

Built in the 14th century, the great mosque at Jenne in Mali was constructed with sun-dried mud bricks.

Islamic expansion out of Arabia began in earnest following the death of the Prophet Muhammad in 632. By 640 Egypt had fallen into the hands of Muslim soldiers and settlers. From the 8th century, traders and clerics were the agents of Islam, spreading the religion along the commercial arteries of the Sahara which extended into West Africa, and up the Nile. By the 13th century the Saifawa kings of Kanem had adopted the faith. Islam had also traveled down the east coast of Africa, taken by seafaring Arabs who set up coastal trading centers. Trade between Arabs and Bantu necessitated a new language, so Swahili became the *lingua franca* of the east coast.

Carved by West African craftsmen, this 16th-century ivory horn (above) was produced for the European market. This is confirmed by its Portuguese-style inscriptions.

Dating from the 16th century, this blue and white Ming dynasty bowl (left) was found on the east coast of Africa, providing evidence of trade with China.

Islamic expansion in Africa from 600

632: Death of Muhammad	**635–40:** Conquest of Egypt by Arabs	**c.800:** Emergence of trading towns on East African coast.	**909:** Fatimid dynasty founded by Ubaydullah	**1050:** King of Takrur converts to Islam		**1270:** Beginning of Solomid dynasty in Ethiopia

600 — 700 — 800 — 900 — 1000 — 1100 — 1200 — 1300

625: First Islamic Arab invasion of Makuria
680: Arab armies reach Atlantic at Morocco
1076: King of Ghana converts to Islam

❶ African trade and the spread of Islam 500–1500 ▶

- ···· frontiers 1500
- → Muslim trade routes
- limit of Muslim influence by 900
- limit of Muslim influence by 1100
- limit of Muslim influence by 1300
- limit of Muslim influence by 1500
- limit of Muslim influence in Spain 1492
- Christians c.1100
- Christians c.1500
- ● Portuguese possession in 1500

- copper
- gold
- dates
- fish
- flour
- ivory
- kola nuts
- leather
- porcelain
- perfume
- saffron
- salt
- silk
- slaves
- spice
- wax
- wool

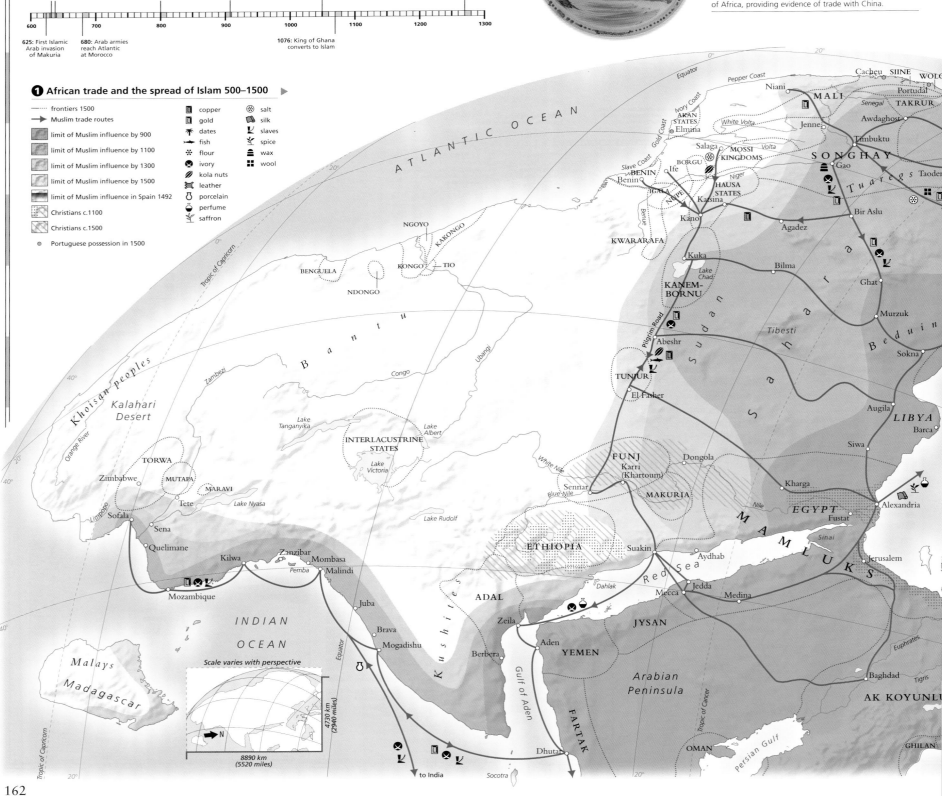

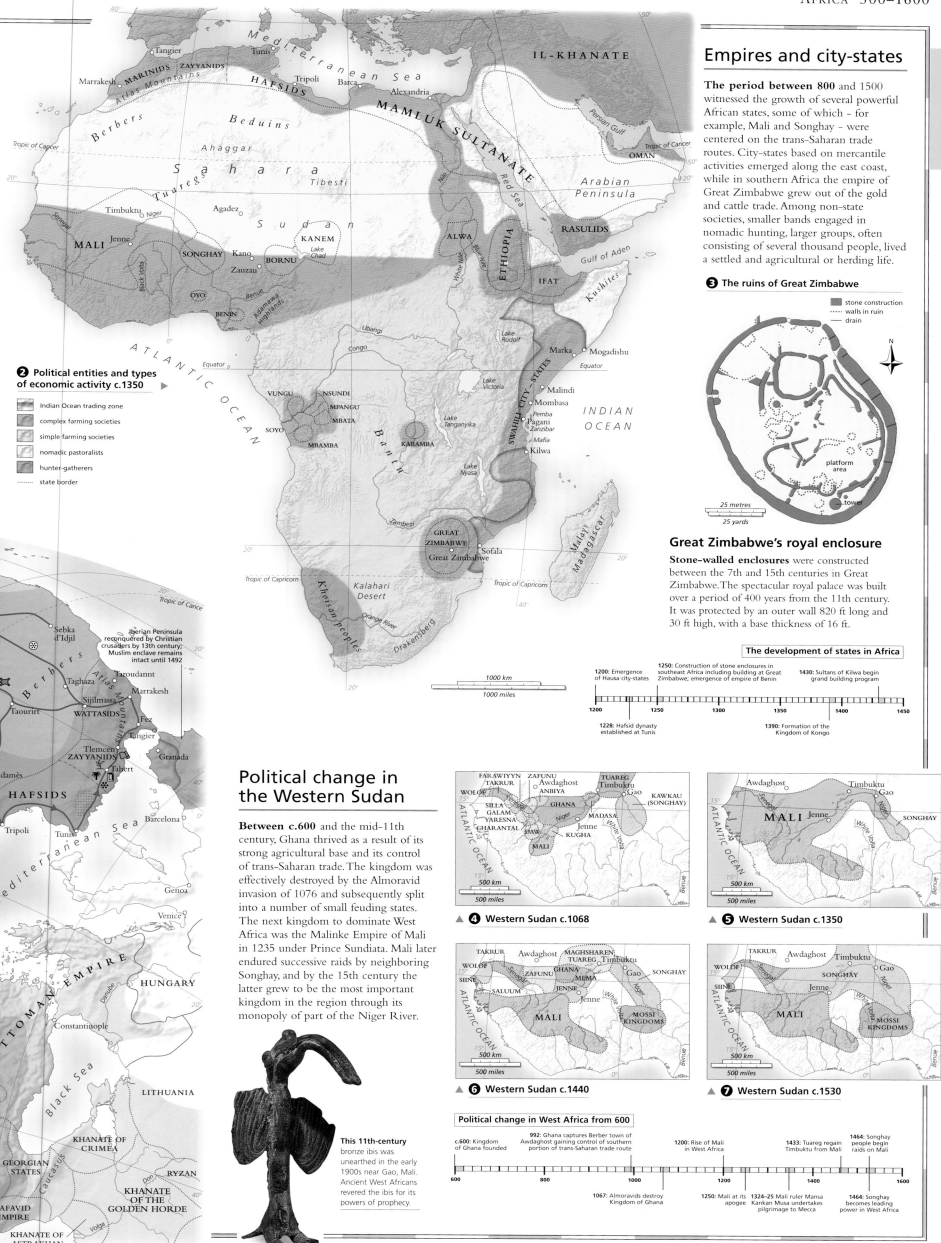

Empires and city-states

The period between 800 and 1500 witnessed the growth of several powerful African states, some of which – for example, Mali and Songhay – were centered on the trans-Saharan trade routes. City-states based on mercantile activities emerged along the east coast, while in southern Africa the empire of Great Zimbabwe grew out of the gold and cattle trade. Among non-state societies, smaller bands engaged in nomadic hunting, larger groups, often consisting of several thousand people, lived a settled and agricultural or herding life.

❸ The ruins of Great Zimbabwe

- ▬ stone construction
- ∙∙∙∙ walls in ruin
- ─ drain

platform area

tower

25 metres
25 yards

Great Zimbabwe's royal enclosure

Stone-walled enclosures were constructed between the 7th and 15th centuries in Great Zimbabwe. The spectacular royal palace was built over a period of 400 years from the 11th century. It was protected by an outer wall 820 ft long and 30 ft high, with a base thickness of 16 ft.

The development of states in Africa

1200: Emergence of Hausa city-states	1250: Construction of stone enclosures in southeast Africa including building at Great Zimbabwe; emergence of empire of Benin	1430: Sultans of Kilwa begin grand building program

1200 · 1250 · 1300 · 1350 · 1400 · 1450

1228: Hafsid dynasty established at Tunis

1390: Formation of the Kingdom of Kongo

❷ Political entities and types of economic activity c.1350 ▶

- Indian Ocean trading zone
- complex farming societies
- simple farming societies
- nomadic pastoralists
- hunter-gatherers
- ∙∙∙∙ state border

1000 km
1000 miles

Political change in the Western Sudan

Between c.600 and the mid-11th century, Ghana thrived as a result of its strong agricultural base and its control of trans-Saharan trade. The kingdom was effectively destroyed by the Almoravid invasion of 1076 and subsequently split into a number of small feuding states. The next kingdom to dominate West Africa was the Malinke Empire of Mali in 1235 under Prince Sundiata. Mali later endured successive raids by neighboring Songhay, and by the 15th century the latter grew to be the most important kingdom in the region through its monopoly of part of the Niger River.

This 11th-century bronze ibis was unearthed in the early 1900s near Gao, Mali. Ancient West Africans revered the ibis for its powers of prophecy.

Iberian Peninsula reconquered by Christian crusaders by 13th century; Muslim enclave remains intact until 1492

▲ **❹ Western Sudan c.1068**

▲ **❺ Western Sudan c.1350**

▲ **❻ Western Sudan c.1440**

▲ **❼ Western Sudan c.1530**

500 km
500 miles

Political change in West Africa from 600

c.600: Kingdom of Ghana founded	992: Ghana captures Berber town of Awdaghost gaining control of southern portion of trans-Saharan trade route	1200: Rise of Mali in West Africa	1433: Tuareg regain Timbuktu from Mali	1464: Songhay people begin raids on Mali

600 · 800 · 1000 · 1200 · 1400 · 1600

1067: Almoravids destroy Kingdom of Ghana

1250: Mali at its apogee

1324–25 Mali ruler Mansa Kankan Musa undertakes pilgrimage to Mecca

1464: Songhay becomes leading power in West Africa

EARLY MODERN AFRICA

AFTER THE PORTUGUESE had led European expansion into Africa in the 15th century, a few colonies were established – in Angola, along the Zambezi Valley, and in the region of the Cape of Good Hope – but for the most part, African rulers contained and controlled the activities of the newcomers. In parts of West Africa they allowed Europeans to establish coastal forts and trading

Asante's well-armed warriors made it the most powerful state on the Gold Coast.

posts. With this new presence came increased opportunities for external trade, principally in gold, ivory, and slaves. After 1700, however, the importance of all other goods was totally eclipsed by the value of the Atlantic slave trade.

The 16th century saw the Ottoman Empire advance across North Africa as far as the Atlas Mountains. To the south, the great empire of Songhay yielded to Moroccan invaders in 1591, though the cycle of empires continued in West Africa with Great Fulo. In the early 18th century powerful coastal kingdoms arose in Asante and Dahomey, while Rozwi replaced Mwenemutapa in southeast Africa.

Southern and East Africa

The Portuguese presence in the region was challenged in the 17th century by the Rozwi empire, which drove them from the highlands of Zimbabwe, while Omani fleets captured many of their coastal forts in East Africa. Portugal was left with the semi-independent *prazos* (estates) of the Zambezi valley and the coastal towns of Sofala, Mozambique, and Inhambane. In 1652 the Dutch East India Company founded its colony at Cape Town. Rapid expansion in the 18th century brought Dutch settlers into conflict with the many small states of the Nguni region.

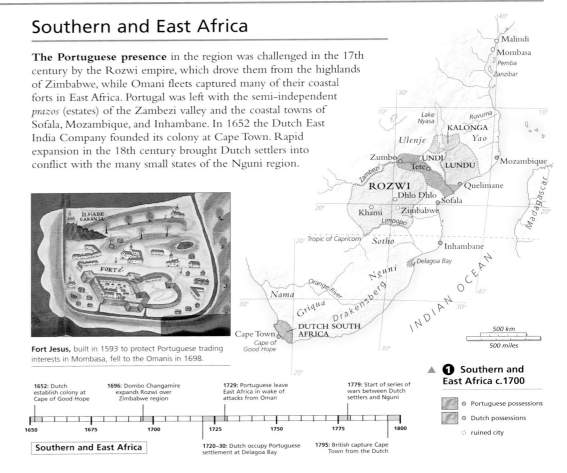

Fort Jesus, built in 1593 to protect Portuguese trading interests in Mombasa, fell to the Omanis in 1698.

1652: Dutch establish colony at Cape of Good Hope
1696: Dombo Changamire expands Rozwi over Zimbabwe region
1729: Portuguese leave East Africa in wake of attacks from Oman
1779: Start of series of wars between Dutch settlers and Nguni

| 1650 | 1675 | 1700 | 1725 | 1750 | 1775 | 1800 |

Southern and East Africa

1720–30: Dutch occupy Portuguese settlement at Delagoa Bay
1795: British capture Cape Town from the Dutch

▲ **1 Southern and East Africa c.1700**

- Portuguese possessions
- Dutch possessions
- ruined city

The Fulbe, who lived by raising cattle for their neighbors, were found throughout much of West Africa. This 1730 engraving shows a Fulbe town on the Gambia River with a plantation and a corral for livestock.

African political development

In the 17th century, much of sub-Saharan Africa consisted of many small, self-governing units, typically about 30 miles across. In West Africa some 70% of the population probably lived in these "ministates." Boundaries remained stable for long periods, the people choosing their leaders on the basis of heredity, election, or other local customs. There were extensive empires such as Songhay and Mali, but these lay in the sparsely populated region now known as the Sahel. These and the other larger states, which ruled the remainder of the population, usually grew by incorporating smaller units, although they continued to use the local polities to enforce the law and raise tribute. Taxation took the form of a head or house tax. There was no concept of land ownership; it could not be bought or sold. Land was regarded as belonging to whoever farmed it. Slave ownership, on the other hand, was an important measure of personal wealth.

The formidable Queen Njinga ruled the kingdom of Ndongo from 1624 to 1663. She fought the Portuguese to a standstill.

2 States of West and Central Africa 1625

- Portuguese possessions
- Dutch settlement

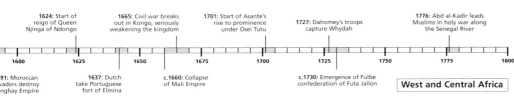

1624: Start of reign of Queen Njinga of Ndongo
1665: Civil war breaks out in Kongo, seriously weakening the kingdom
1701: Start of Asante's rise to prominence under Osei Tutu
1727: Dahomey's troops capture Whydah
1776: Abd al-Kadir leads Muslims in holy war along the Senegal River

| 1600 | 1625 | 1650 | 1675 | 1700 | 1725 | 1750 | 1775 | 1800 |

1591: Moroccan invaders destroy Songhay Empire
1637: Dutch take Portuguese fort of Elmina
c.1660: Collapse of Mali Empire
c.1730: Emergence of Fulbe confederation of Futa Jallon

West and Central Africa

The struggle for the Horn of Africa

Ethiopia's domination of the region came to an end in the 16th century. The Christian empire's expansion into Muslim lands to the south had often involved forced conversion and the destruction of Islamic literature and places of worship. In 1529 a dynamic imam from Adal, Ahmad Grañ, proclaimed a holy war against Ethiopia, winning many striking victories. In 1540 the Ethiopians sought aid from Portugal and Grañ was killed in battle in 1543. This ultimately inconclusive war laid waste the region, which allowed the Oromo to invade from the south. Organized in many independent mobile bands, they took over both Christian and Muslim lands and founded new kingdoms of their own. Many Oromo embraced Islam and some fought as mercenaries in civil wars in Ethiopia. The fortunes of the Ethiopian empire revived somewhat in the Gondar period in the 17th century, but its lands were much reduced.

1529: Ahmad Grañ leads *jihad* against Ethiopia

1540: Portuguese come to the aid of Ethiopia

1597: Start of period of civil war

1636: King Fasiladas founds permanent capital at Gondar

1682: Accession of Iyasu I, last great king of Gondar period

The decline of Ethiopia

1543: Death of Ahmad Grañ, shot by a Portuguese musketeer

1590: Oromo bands begin occupation of southern Ethiopia

1632: End of civil wars. Jesuit missionaries expelled from Ethiopia

❸ **Horn of Africa 1500–1700**

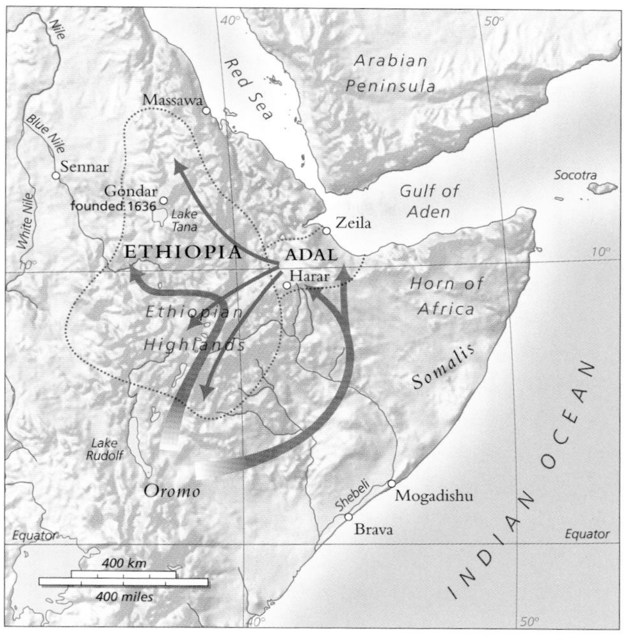

→ *Jihad* of Ahmad Grañ 1529–43
→ Oromo expansion 1550–1700
···· approximate state border 1500

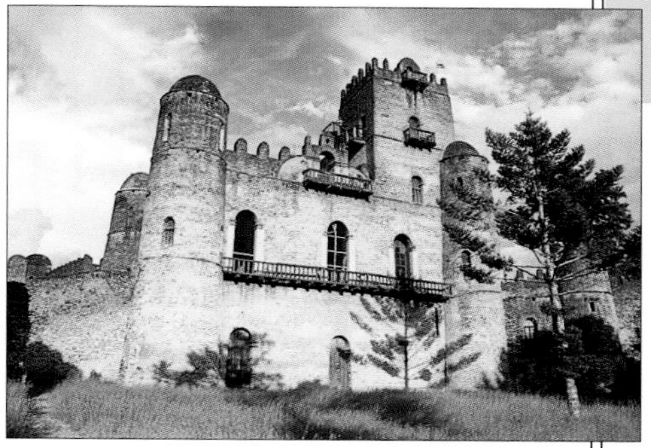

400 km
400 miles

Ethiopian King Fasiladas built the city of Gondar and this magnificent castle in 1636. Before his reign, the rulers of Ethiopia had never had a fixed residence, instead setting up a tented court for periods of six months to a year, then moving on to another part of the kingdom.

❹ **The African slave trade c.1750**

- Ottoman Empire
- Portuguese possessions
- Dutch possessions
- French settlement
- British settlement

Principal slave routes
→ Arab routes
→ British routes
→ Danish routes
→ Dutch routes
→ French routes
→ Moroccan routes
→ Portuguese routes

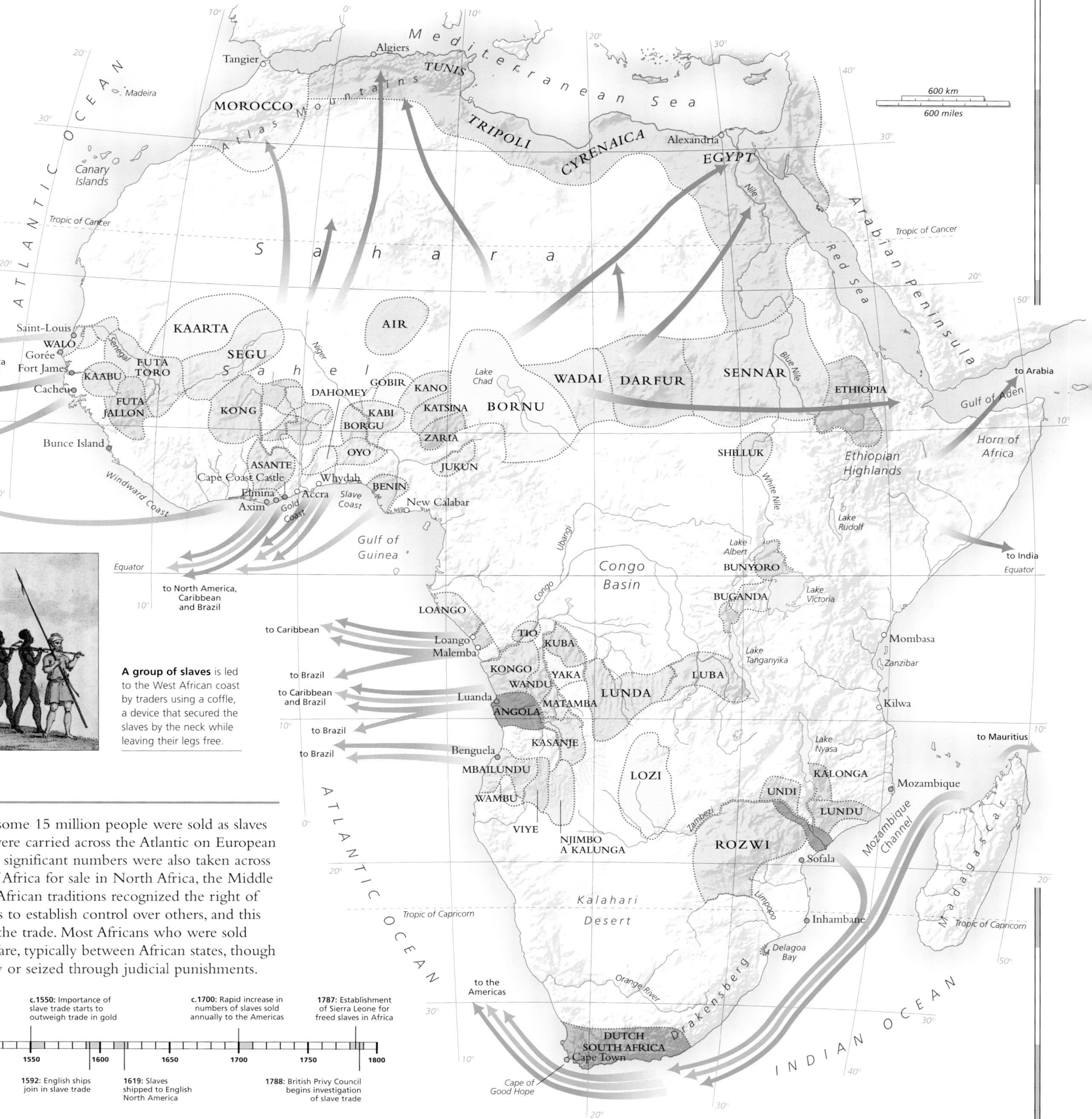

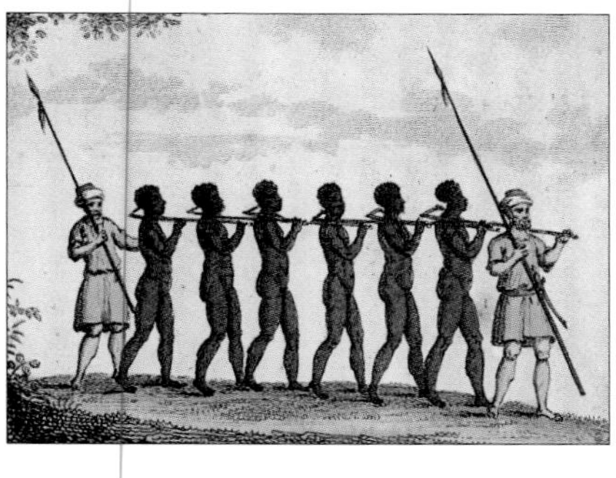

600 km
600 miles

A group of slaves is led to the West African coast by traders using a coffle, a device that secured the slaves by the neck while leaving their legs free.

The slave trade

Between 1500 and 1800 some 15 million people were sold as slaves from Africa. The majority were carried across the Atlantic on European and American ships, though significant numbers were also taken across the Sahara and the Horn of Africa for sale in North Africa, the Middle East, and southern Europe. African traditions recognized the right of states and private individuals to establish control over others, and this provided the legal basis for the trade. Most Africans who were sold were taken prisoner in warfare, typically between African states, though some were captured illegally or seized through judicial punishments.

1441: Portuguese export slaves from Atlantic coast to Europe

1502: First slaves taken to the New World

c.1550: Importance of slave trade starts to outweigh trade in gold

c.1700: Rapid increase in numbers of slaves sold annually to the Americas

1787: Establishment of Sierra Leone for freed slaves in Africa

The African slave trade

1592: English ships join in slave trade

1619: Slaves shipped to English North America

1788: British Privy Council begins investigation of slave trade

THE COLONIZATION OF AFRICA

Cecil Rhodes, the embodiment of colonialism, planned to extend British rule in Africa from Cairo to Cape Town.

THE 19TH CENTURY was a period of revolutionary change in Africa. The states of West Africa were convulsed by a series of reformist Islamic *jihads*, while in the south the rise of Zulu militarism had catastrophic consequences for neighboring peoples. By the mid-19th century Africa was also undergoing a commercial revolution. Europeans could now offer high-quality machined goods in large quantities. As a result, Africa was condemned to the role of producer of primary goods. By the end of the century, many African kingdoms and clan-based communities were being replaced by states organized along indigenous lines. However, this process was forestalled by the decision of the major European powers to carve up the continent between them.

Commerce in the 19th century

The Arab slave trader Tibbu Tib organized his own state and security system in 1875 with the help of armed followers.

The development of new export goods in Europe had social implications for Africa. Reduced shipping costs brought about by the introduction of the steamship meant that European textile and metal goods arrived in force. The resultant decline in local industries was accompanied by a growth in the internal slave trade. The substantial carrying trade, especially the porterage trade of East and Central Africa, was run by small-scale entrepreneurs. While such ventures did not bring large profit, those involved enjoyed new and elevated social positions. Often the carrying trade was organized from a particular region, giving it an ethnic character. Enterprising African traders took advantage of the expanding economy to gain political power – for example, the copper trader Msiri won himself a kingdom.

Commercial Africa from 1815

1816: Wool mills, flax mills, sugar refineries, indigo factories, and glassworks established in Egypt	**c.1850:** Atlantic slave trade, including clandestine operations, begins to die out	**1875:** Tibbu Tib establishes trading principality	

1815 1825 1835 1845 1855 1865 1875

1830: 20,000 slaves exported from central African ports to Brazil

1866: Copper trader Msiri establishes trading principality

① Commercial and political Africa c.1830

cloves
cocoa
coffee
copper
cotton
diamonds
gold
gum arabic
honey and wax
ivory
olives
palm products
peanuts
rubber
slaves/ migrant workers
wheat
wine
trade route

British possession
French possession
Ottoman territory
Portuguese possession
Spanish possession
commercial group

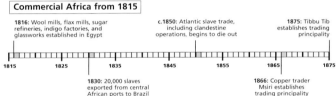

Zulu and Afrikaner expansion

Under the leadership of Shaka, the Zulu were organized into a highly militarized kingdom. They conquered neighboring Nguni tribes and set off a series of wars which depopulated large parts of the southern interior, leaving it vulnerable to Afrikaner expansion. Afrikaners left Cape Colony between 1835 and the 1840s in search of pastureland and to escape from unwelcome British rule. They successfully defeated powerful military kingdoms as they progressed northward.

British reforms, such as the abolition of slavery, caused the exodus of many Boers from Cape Colony. They undertook the "Great Trek" in ox-drawn wagons.

② The Afrikaner treks and the Mfecane wars

the nuclear Zulu chiefdom
Shaka's Zulu kingdom 1817
Sobhuza's Swazi kingdom 1820
Moshoeshoe's Lesotho kingdom 1824
Mzilikazi's Ndebele kingdom 1826
Nguni victory
British victory
Boer victory
main Boer trek route 1836–54
Nguni migrations
borders 1895

Shaka armed the Zulu with long-bladed stabbing *assegais*, which forced them to fight at close quarters. Shield markings and headdress distinguished different regiments.

Zulu and Afrikaner expansion

1820: Nguni clans disperse to avoid Mfecane wars brought about by rise of Zulu Empire	**1835:** Zwangendaba crosses the Limpopo taking the Mfecane northward	**1843:** Short-lived Boer republic of Natal annexed by Britain	**1852:** Independence granted by British to Voortrekkers in Transvaal

1820 1830 1840 1850 1860

1816: Shaka becomes leader of the Zulu, a clan of the Nguni

1836: Start of the Great Trek

1854: Boers found the Orange Free State

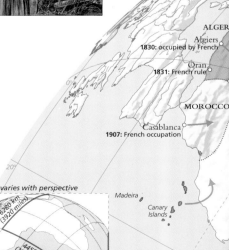

Scale varies with perspective

Islamic wars in western Africa

1807: Hausa kings replaced by Fulani emirs

1820: Usuman dan Fodio establishes Sokoto Fulani Kingdom

1852: 'Umar Tal conquers the Senegal valley

1861: 'Umar Tal's forces conquer Segu

| 1800 | 1810 | 1820 | 1830 | 1840 | 1850 | 1860 | 1870 |

1804: Jihad of Usuman dan Fodio

1816: Inspired by Usuman dan Fodio, Amadu Lobbo launches jihad in Masina

1863: Timbuktu falls to 'Umar Tal; he founds Tukulor Empire

1864: 'Umar Tal is killed attempting to suppress Fulani rebellion

The text of this richly decorated 19th-century Koran is written in West African Sudani script. The large rectangular design marks the end of a chapter.

Islamic reform in West Africa

The *jihads* of West Africa were a source of major turmoil in the 19th century. The idea that reformers could overthrow governments they thought were unjust was deeply rooted in the region, and dated back to the 11th century Almoravid movement. Holy men challenged rulers, often because of their tyranny and corruption, and demanded change. Social problems also promoted reform, for example, Fula herdsmen often backed reformers against those who taxed and mistreated them. In other cases, it was humble peasants or slaves who converted to Islam. Tukulor cleric Usuman dan Fodio's *jihad* in Hausaland in 1804 led to the establishment of the Islamic Sokoto Fulani Kingdom in 1820. Fulani cleric al-Hajj 'Umar Tal set about reforming the Segu region in 1851 and by 1863 had founded the Tukulor Empire.

❸ 19th-century West African *jihads* ▶

- Sokoto Fulani Kingdom c.1820
- Tukulor Empire c.1864
- ⊙ British possession
- ⊙ French possession
- ⊙ Portuguese possesssion
- → jihad route of al-Hajj 'Umar Tal
- ······ borders c.1850
- ✕ conflict

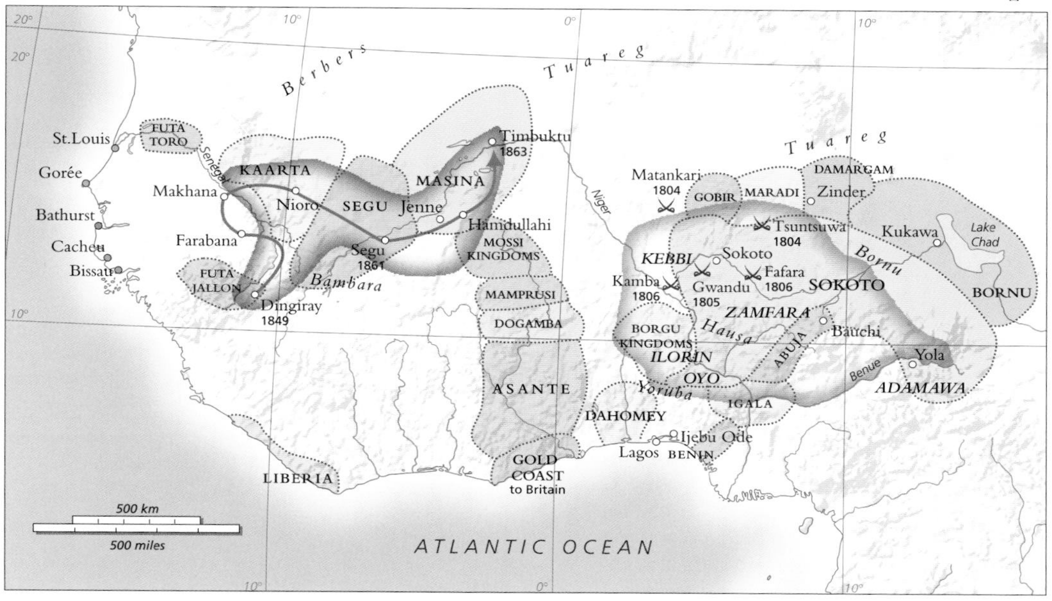

The conquest of the interior

The years after 1885 saw a race to complete the conquest of the African interior *(see p. 96)*. International rivalries between European powers, coupled with local merchant competition and the popularity of African conquest in the home arena, ensured European governmental interest in the continent. In many cases, initial conquests were funded by commercial interests, such as Cecil Rhodes' De Beers Consolidated Mines company. Most of the fighting personnel were Africans, hired mercenaries, or militarily trained slaves. The use of commercial contacts with African traders and the exploitation of local rivalries were as effective as brute force and the machine gun.

The conquest of Africa from 1880

1883: France begins its conquest of Madagascar

1884: Berlin Conference on Africa; Samore Touré proclaims his Islamic theocracy

1894: Britain occupies Buganda

1896: France takes Madagascar

1900–01: Britain annexes Asante

1908: Belgium takes over Congo Free State

| 1880 | 1890 | 1900 | 1910 |

1882: Britain occupies Egypt; Congo Free State formed by King Leopold of Belgium

1889: Italy establishes its first colony in Eritrea

1892: France destroys the Tukulor Empire

1904: French create federation of French West Africa

▼ ❹ European penetration of Africa

Colonial territory c.1880
- Ottoman suzerainty
- British
- Portuguese
- French
- Spanish
- Boer Republics
- frontier of Christian missionary activities c.1880

European routes of expansion
- → Belgian
- → British
- → French
- → German
- → Italian
- → Portuguese
- → Spanish
- → main lines of missionary advance
- **1888** foundation date of colonial settlement

Colonial settlements
- ⊙ Belgian
- ⊙ Boer
- ⊙ British
- ⊙ French
- ⊙ German
- ⊙ Italian
- ⊙ Portuguese
- ○ other settlement

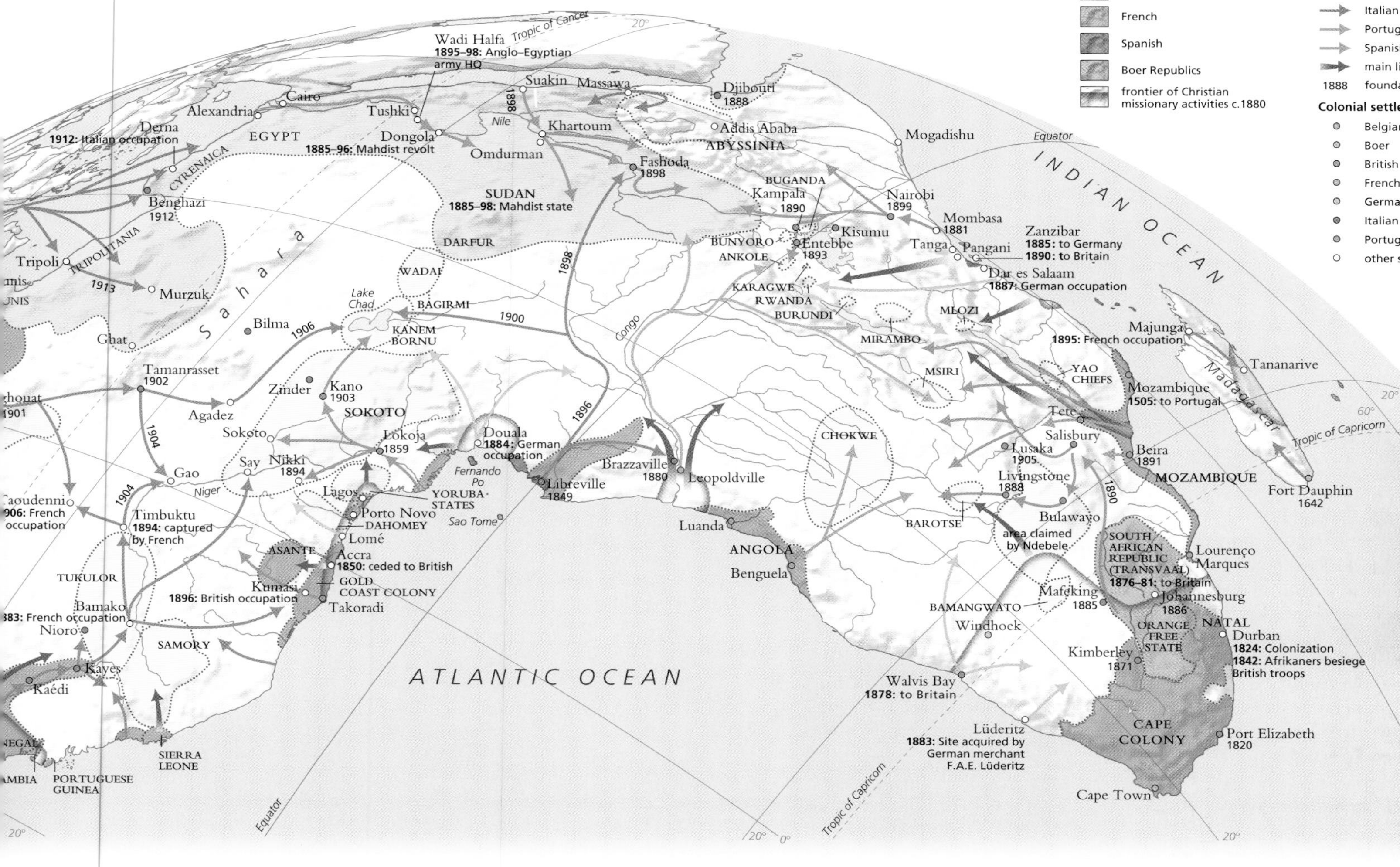

Armed and trained by France, these African soldiers, known as the Senegalese Rifles, helped France win territory in Africa.

Map labels (map 3)

Berbers · Tuareg · St.Louis · Gorée · FUTA TORO · KAARTA · Makhana · Nioro · MASINA · Timbuktu 1863 · Bathurst · Farabana · SEGU · Jenne · Matankari 1804 · DAMARGAM · GOBIR · MARADI · Zinder · Cachen · Bissau · Segu 1881 · Hamdullahi · MOSSI KINGDOMS · KEBBI · Tsuntsuwa 1804 · Kukawa · FUTA JALLON · Dingiray 1849 · Bambara · MAMPRUSI · Kamba 1806 · Sokoto · Fafara 1806 · Bornu · Lake Chad · DOGAMBA · Gwandu 1805 · SOKOTO · BORNU · ZAMFARA · BORGU KINGDOMS · ILORIN · ABUJA · Bauchi · ASANTE · OYO · IGALA · ADAMAWA · DAHOMEY · Yoruba · Benue · Yola · LIBERIA · GOLD COAST to Britain · Lagos · BENIN · Ijebu Ode · 500 km · 500 miles · ATLANTIC OCEAN · Niger

Map labels (map 4)

Wadi Halfa 1895–98: Anglo–Egyptian army HQ · Tropic of Cancer · 1912: Italian occupation · Alexandria · Cairo · Tushki · Suakin · Massawa · Djibouti 1888 · Derna · CYRENAICA · EGYPT · Dongola · Nile · Khartoum · Addis Ababa · ABYSSINIA · Mogadishu · Benghazi 1912 · 1885–96: Mahdist revolt · Omdurman · Fashoda 1898 · BUGANDA · Nairobi 1899 · Tripoli · TRIPOLITANIA · SUDAN 1885–98: Mahdist state · DARFUR · Kampala 1890 · Kisumu · Mombasa 1881 · 1913 · Murzuk · DARFUR · Entebbe 1893 · BUNYORO · ANKOLE · Tanga · Zanzibar 1885: to Germany 1890: to Britain · Ghat · Lake Chad · WADAI · BAGIRMI 1898 · 1900 · KARAGWE · RWANDA · BURUNDI · Dar es Salaam 1887: German occupation · Tamanrasset 1902 · Bilma 1906 · KANEM BORNU · MLOZI · Majunga 1895: French occupation · Tananarive · Agadez · Zinder · Kano 1903 · Douala 1884: German occupation · MIRAMBO · MSIRI · Sokoto · Sokoto · 1896 · Libreville 1849 · Brazzaville 1880 · Leopoldville · YAO CHIEFS · Mozambique 1505: to Portugal · Nikki 1894 · Lokoja 1859 · Fernando Po · Sao Tome · Luanda · BAROTSE · Tete · 1906: French occupation · Timbuktu 1894: captured by French · Gao · Niger · Say · Lagos · Porto Novo · DAHOMEY · YORUBA STATES · Salisbury 1905 · Beira 1891 · MOZAMBIQUE · Fort Dauphin 1642 · TUKULOR · Accra 1850: ceded to British · ANGOLA · Bulawayo 1888 · Livingstone 1888 · 1883: French occupation · ASANTE · 1896: British occupation · Kumasi · GOLD COAST COLONY · Takoradi · Benguela · area claimed by Ndebele · SOUTH AFRICAN REPUBLIC (TRANSVAAL) 1876–81: to Britain · Lourenço Marques · Bamako · Nioro · SAMORY · Kayes · BAMANGWATO · Mafeking 1885 · Johannesburg 1886 · NATAL · Kaedi · Windhoek · Kimberley 1871 · ORANGE FREE STATE · 1824: Colonization · 1842: Afrikaners besiege British troops · SIERRA LEONE · ATLANTIC OCEAN · Walvis Bay 1878: to Britain · Lüderitz 1883: Site acquired by German merchant F.A.E. Lüderitz · CAPE COLONY · Port Elizabeth 1820 · Durban · PORTUGUESE GUINEA · SENEGAL · Cape Town · Tropic of Capricorn · Equator · INDIAN OCEAN · Madagascar

Map labels (left map)

to Asia · Tropic of Cancer · Arabian Peninsula · HEJAZ · Red Sea · Socotra · ETHIOPIA · KAFFA · NYORO · Kamba · BUGANDA · to the Americas, Europe, India, Persian Gulf · Equator · INDIAN OCEAN · BUGANDA · Omani-Swahili · OMANI · to the Americas, Europe, India, Persian Gulf · Lake Nyasa · Yao · Madagascar · to East Indies, Europe, the Americas · ZAMBIQUE · to Seychelles · to East Indies, Europe, the Americas · Tropic of Capricorn · 1000 km · 1000 miles

POST-COLONIAL AFRICA

Julius Nyerere led the fight for independence in Tanganyika.

MOST AFRICAN COUNTRIES gained independence between 1956 and 1968. The new states, with few exceptions, were territorially identical to the European colonies they replaced. Following independence, leaders often became dictators, or the army seized power; many governments were corrupt and a number of countries were devastated by war. Moves were made towards multiparty democracy, most notably in South Africa where apartheid was dismantled in 1990. During the 1990s and 2000s, many western and central African states were gripped by bitter conflicts, stemming from ethnic rivalries and disputes over natural resources, such as timber and diamonds.

African independence

After World War II the colonial powers in Africa faced demands for self-determination, and most countries gained independence around 1960. In the face of widespread opposition, Portugal clung on to its territories through the 1960s. This resulted in long and bloody wars in Angola, Guinea-Bissau, and Mozambique. There were also protracted struggles for majority rule in the former British colonies of Zimbabwe and South Africa. The presidential election victory of Nelson Mandela in 1994 marked the end of white minority rule in South Africa.

The national flag is raised in Ghana during an independence ceremony. The country was declared a republic on July 1, 1960, with Dr. Kwame Nkrumah as the first president.

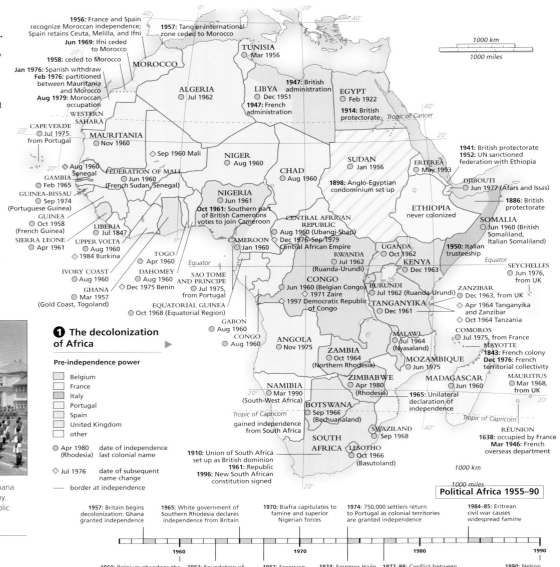

① The decolonization of Africa ▶

Pre-independence power

- Belgium
- France
- Italy
- Portugal
- Spain
- United Kingdom
- other

○ Apr 1980 (Rhodesia) — date of independence, last colonial name
◇ Jul 1976 — date of subsequent name change
— border at independence

1910: Union of South Africa set up as British dominion
1961: Republic
1996: New South African constitution signed

Political Africa 1955–90

1957: Britain begins decolonization: Ghana granted independence
1965: White government of Southern Rhodesia declares independence from Britain
1970: Biafra capitulates to famine and superior Nigerian forces
1974: 750,000 settlers return to Portugal as colonial territories are granted independence
1984–85: Eritrean civil war causes widespread famine

1960 — 1970 — 1980 — 1990

1960: Belgium abandons the Congo; required to return to restore order weeks later
1963: Foundation of Organization of African Unity (OAU)
1967: Secession of Biafra province in Nigeria
1974: Emperor Haile Selassie of Ethiopia deposed
1977–88: Conflict between Somalia and Ethiopia over claims to Ogaden region
1990: Nelson Mandela released; ban on ANC lifted

The African economy

Industrial growth is government policy in a number of countries in Africa, and is seen as the way to progress economically. Countries with large manufacturing sectors include South Africa and oil-rich states such as Nigeria, Algeria, and Libya. Many other states rely on a single resource or cash crop for export income, leaving them vulnerable to market fluctuations.

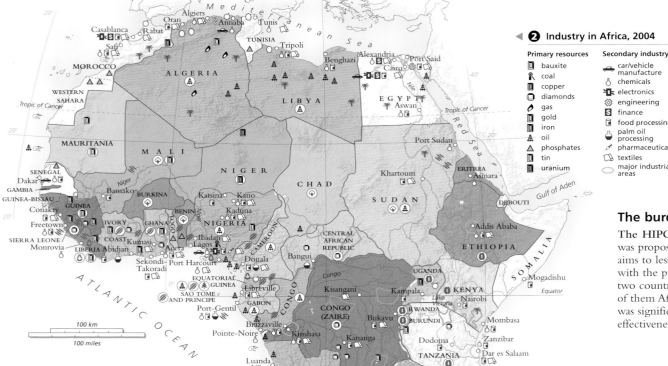

② Industry in Africa, 2004 ◀

Primary resources
- bauxite
- coal
- copper
- diamonds
- gas
- gold
- iron
- oil
- phosphates
- tin
- uranium

Secondary industry
- car/vehicle manufacture
- chemicals
- electronics
- engineering
- finance
- food processing
- palm oil processing
- pharmaceuticals
- textiles
- major industrial areas

Major cash crops
- cocoa
- coffee
- cotton
- dates
- fruit
- olives
- rice
- rubber
- shellfish
- spices
- timber
- tobacco
- vineyards

Ecological tourism
- national parks

Percentages of total export earnings
40–59   60–80   more than 80
agriculture and fishing
crude oil and petroleum products
metals and minerals

○ Main export product

The burden of debt

The HIPC (Highly Indebted Poor Countries) initiative was proposed by the World Bank and IMF in 1996. It aims to lessen the debt burden of the poorest countries, with the promise to erase $100 billion of debt. Forty-two countries were deemed eligible, 27 of which (23 of them African) have joined the scheme so far. There was significant early progress, but the fairness and effectiveness of the initiative are vigorously debated.

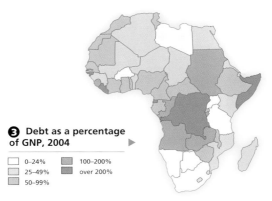

③ Debt as a percentage of GNP, 2004 ▶

- 0–24%
- 25–49%
- 50–99%
- 100–200%
- over 200%

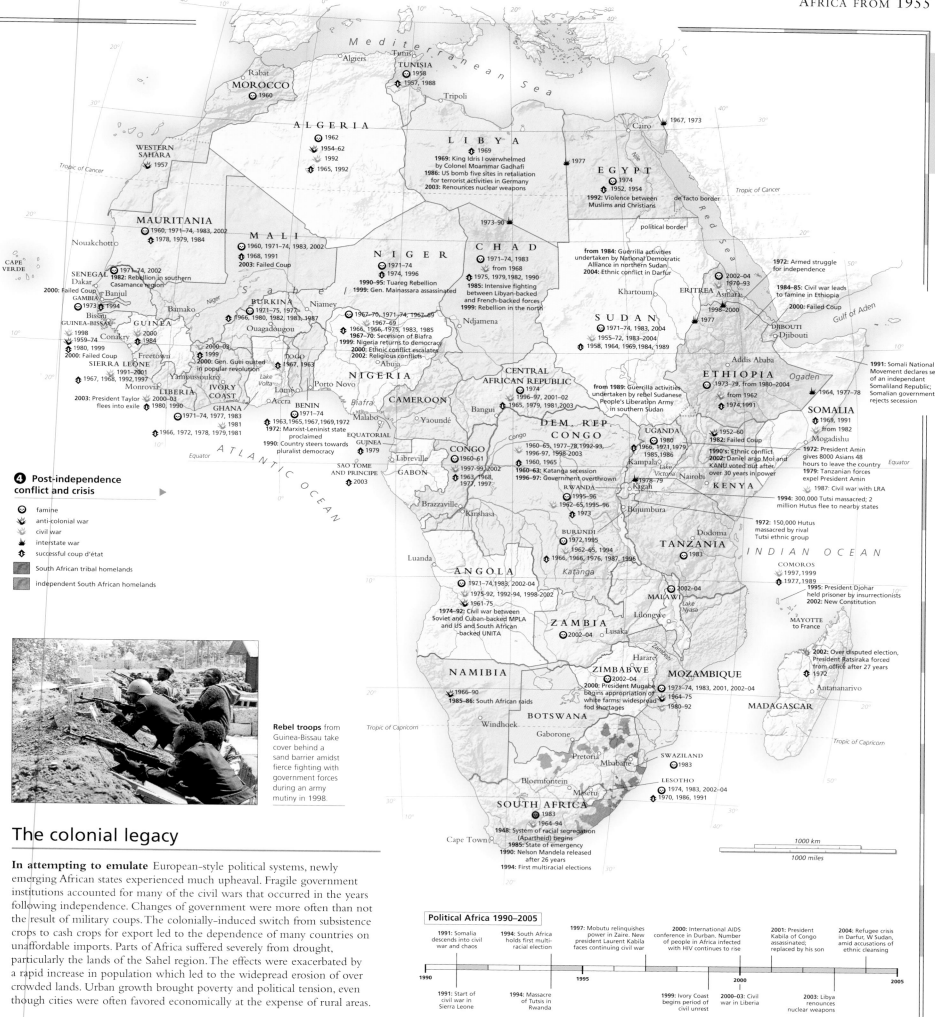

Map labels

Mediterranean Sea

Rabat
Algiers Tunis
MOROCCO ⊕ 1960
TUNISIA ⬩ 1958
⬩ 1957, 1988
Tripoli
Cairo ⬩ 1967, 1973

WESTERN SAHARA ☘ 1957

ALGERIA
⊕ 1962
☘ 1954–62
☘ 1992
⬩ 1965, 1992

LIBYA
⬩ 1969
1969: King Idris I overwhelmed by Colonel Moammar Gadhafi
1986: US bomb five sites in retaliation for terrorist activities in Germany
2003: Renounces nuclear weapons

⬩ 1977

EGYPT
⊕ 1974
⬩ 1952, 1954
1992: Violence between Muslims and Christians

de facto border
political border

MAURITANIA
⊕ 1960, 1971–74, 1983, 2002
⬩ 1978, 1979, 1984

MALI
⊕ 1960, 1971–74, 1983, 2002
⬩ 1968, 1991
2003: Failed Coup

NIGER
⊕ 1971–74
⬩ 1974, 1996
1990–95: Tuareg Rebellion
1999: Gen. Mainassara assassinated

CHAD
⊕ 1971–74, 1983
☘ from 1968
⬩ 1975, 1979, 1982, 1990
1985: Intensive fighting between Libyan-backed and French-backed forces
1999: Rebellion in the north

Khartoum

from 1984: Guerrilla activities undertaken by National Democratic Alliance in northern Sudan
2004: Ethnic conflict in Darfur

1972: Armed struggle for independence

ERITREA
Asmara
⬩ 2002–04
⊕ 1970–93
1984–85: Civil war leads to famine in Ethiopia
2000: Failed Coup
⬩ 1998–2000
☘ 1977

SUDAN
⊕ 1971–74, 1983, 2004
☘ 1955–72, 1983–2004
⬩ 1958, 1964, 1969, 1984, 1989

DJIBOUTI
Djibouti
Gulf of Aden

CAPE VERDE

SENEGAL
Dakar ⊕ 1971–74, 2002
1982: Rebellion in southern Casamance region
2000: Failed Coup
GAMBIA Banjul
⬩ 1973 ☘ 1994

Nouakchott

Bamako

Niger
Ouagadougou
BURKINA
⊕ 1971–75, 1977
⬩ 1966, 1980, 1982, 1983, 1987

Niamey

NIGERIA
⊕ 1967–70, 1971–74, 1967–69
☘ 1967–69
1967–70: Secession of Biafra
1999: Nigeria returns to democracy
2000: Ethnic conflict escalates
2002: Religious conflicts
⬩ 1966, 1966, 1975, 1983, 1985

Ndjamena

CENTRAL AFRICAN REPUBLIC
⊕ 1974
⬩ 1996–97, 2001–03
⬩ 1965, 1979, 1981, 2003

from 1989: Guerrilla activities undertaken by rebel Sudanese People's Liberation Army in southern Sudan

Addis Ababa

ETHIOPIA
⊕ 1973–79, from 1980–2004
☘ from 1962
⬩ 1974, 1991
Ogaden
☘ 1964, 1977–78

1991: Somali National Movement declares secession of an independant Somaliland Republic; Somalian government rejects secession

GUINEA-BISSAU
Bissau
GUINEA
Conakry
☘ 1998
☘ 1959–74
⬩ 1980, 1999
2000: Failed Coup
⬩ 2000
☘ 1984

SIERRA LEONE
☘ 1991–2001
⬩ 1967, 1968, 1992, 1997
Freetown

Monrovia
LIBERIA
2003: President Taylor flees into exile
☘ 2000–03
⬩ 1980, 1990

IVORY COAST
2000: Gen. Guei ousted in popular revolution
⬩ 1999
⊕ 2000–03
Yamoussoukro
Lake Volta
⬩ 1967, 1963

GHANA
⬩ 1966, 1972, 1978, 1979, 1981
Accra

Lomé
Porto Novo
TOGO
⊕ 1971–74, 1977, 1983
⬩ 1963, 1965, 1967, 1969, 1972

BENIN
⬩ 1971–74
1972: Marxist-Leninist state proclaimed
1990: Country steers towards pluralist democracy
Malabo

Abuja
Biafra

CAMEROON
Yaoundé

EQUATORIAL GUINEA
⬩ 1979

SAO TOME AND PRINCIPE
⬩ 2003

Libreville
GABON
CONGO
⊕ 1960–61
☘ 1997–99, 2002
⬩ 1963, 1968, 1977, 1997

Brazzaville
Kinshasa

DEM. REP. CONGO
⊕ 1960–65, 1977–78, 1992–93, 1996–97, 1998–2003
☘ 1960, 1965
1960–63: Katanga secession
1996–97: Government overthrown

UGANDA
⊕ 1980
⬩ 1966, 1971, 1979, 1985, 1986
1990's: Ethnic conflict
2002: Daniel arap Moi and KANU voted out after over 30 years in power

Kampala
Lake Victoria
Nairobi

RWANDA
⊕ 1995–96
☘ 1962–65, 1995–96
⬩ 1973
Kigali

KENYA

1972: President Amin gives 8000 Asians 48 hours to leave the country
1979: Tanzanian forces expel President Amin
1987: Civil war with LRA

SOMALIA
⊕ 1969, 1991
☘ from 1982
Mogadishu

1994: 300,000 Tutsi massacred; 2 million Hutus flee to nearby states

Luanda

BURUNDI
⊕ 1972, 1995
☘ 1962–65, 1994
⬩ 1966, 1966, 1976, 1987, 1996

1972: 150,000 Hutus massacred by rival Tutsi ethnic group

Dodoma
TANZANIA
⬩ 1983
Bujumbura

INDIAN OCEAN

COMOROS
⊕ 1997, 1999
⬩ 1977, 1989

1995: President Djohar held prisoner by insurrectionists
2002: New Constitution

MAYOTTE to France

ANGOLA
⊕ 1971–74, 1983, 2002–04
☘ 1975–92, 1992–94, 1998–2002
☘ 1961–75
1974–92: Civil war between Soviet and Cuban-backed MPLA and US and South African-backed UNITA

Katanga

MALAWI
⊕ 2002–04
Lake Nyasa
Lilongwe

ZAMBIA
⊕ 2002–04
Lusaka

2002: Over disputed election, President Ratsiraka forced from office after 27 years
⬩ 1972

Harare

NAMIBIA
☘ 1966–90
1985–86: South African raids

ZIMBABWE
⊕ 2002–04
2000: President Mugabe begins appropriation of white farms; widespread food shortages

MOZAMBIQUE
⊕ 1971–74, 1983, 2001, 2002–04
☘ 1964–75
⬩ 1980–92

Antananarivo

MADAGASCAR

Windhoek

BOTSWANA
Gaborone

Tropic of Capricorn

Pretoria
Mbabane
SWAZILAND
⊕ 1983

Bloemfontein
Maseru
LESOTHO
⊕ 1974, 1983, 2002–04
⬩ 1970, 1986, 1991

SOUTH AFRICA
⊕ 1983
☘ 1964–94
1948: System of racial segregation (Apartheid) begins
1985: State of emergency
1990: Nelson Mandela released after 26 years
1994: First multiracial elections

Cape Town

1000 km
1000 miles

Legend

4 Post-independence conflict and crisis

⊕ famine
☘ anti-colonial war
☘ civil war
☘ interstate war
⬩ successful coup d'état

South African tribal homelands
independent South African homelands

Rebel troops from Guinea-Bissau take cover behind a sand barrier amidst fierce fighting with government forces during an army mutiny in 1998.

The colonial legacy

In attempting to emulate European-style political systems, newly emerging African states experienced much upheaval. Fragile government institutions accounted for many of the civil wars that occurred in the years following independence. Changes of government were more often than not the result of military coups. The colonially-induced switch from subsistence crops to cash crops for export led to the dependence of many countries on unaffordable imports. Parts of Africa suffered severely from drought, particularly the lands of the Sahel region. The effects were exacerbated by a rapid increase in population which led to the widepread erosion of over crowded lands. Urban growth brought poverty and political tension, even though cities were often favored economically at the expense of rural areas.

Political Africa 1990–2005

1991: Somalia descends into civil war and chaos
1994: South Africa holds first multi-racial election
1997: Mobutu relinquishes power in Zaire. New president Laurent Kabila faces continuing civil war
2000: International AIDS conference in Durban. Number of people in Africa infected with HIV continues to rise
2001: President Kabila of Congo assassinated; replaced by his son
2004: Refugee crisis in Darfur, W Sudan, amid accusations of ethnic cleansing

| 1990 | 1995 | 2000 | 2005 |

1991: Start of civil war in Sierra Leone
1994: Massacre of Tutsis in Rwanda
1999: Ivory Coast begins period of civil unrest
2000–03: Civil war in Liberia
2003: Libya renounces nuclear weapons

The Rwandan crisis

Following a violent revolt in 1959 the Hutu ethnic group in Rwanda grasped political power from the Tutsi minority. In 1990, the Tutsi Rwandan Patriotic Front (RPF) mounted an invasion from Uganda. Genocidal violence broke out in 1994 and an estimated 500,000 Tutsi were massacred. Two million Hutus subsequently fled the country. An international criminal tribunal, set up to investigate the genocide, has indicted only a handful of those responsible.

Rwanda crisis map

UGANDA
Katale
CONGO (ZAIRE)
Goma
Byumbao
Lake Kivu
Apr 1994: RPF begin advance on Kigali
Aug 1994: RPF take control of Rwanda
RWANDA
Kigali
Gitarama
Bukavu
TANZANIA
Ngara
Ngozi
Muyinga
Uriva
BURUNDI
Lake Tanganyika
Bujumbura
Ruyigi

50 km
50 miles

5 Crisis in Central Africa

→ advancing RPF (Tutsi) forces
→ migrating Hutu refugees
⛺ refugee camp

In 1994 over two million Rwandans, the majority of whom were Hutu, fled to refugee camps in neighboring countries. Many were forced to live in unsanitary conditions and outbreaks of cholera in crowded camps killed thousands.

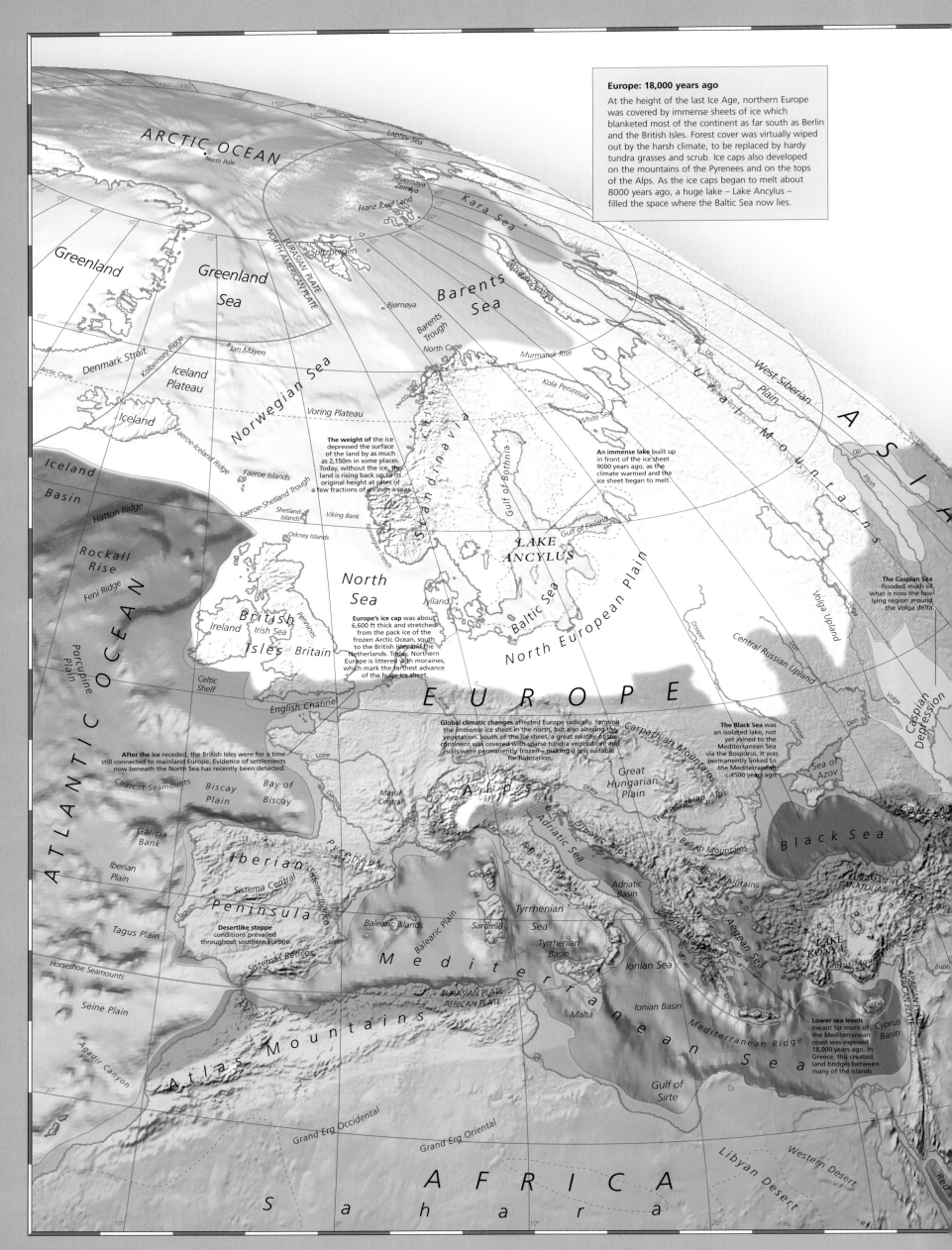

Europe: 18,000 years ago

At the height of the last Ice Age, northern Europe was covered by immense sheets of ice which blanketed most of the continent as far south as Berlin and the British Isles. Forest cover was virtually wiped out by the harsh climate, to be replaced by hardy tundra grasses and scrub. Ice caps also developed on the mountains of the Pyrenees and on the tops of the Alps. As the ice caps began to melt about 8000 years ago, a huge lake – Lake Ancylus – filled the space where the Baltic Sea now lies.

ARCTIC OCEAN
North Pole

Laptev Sea

Greenland

Greenland Sea

Severnaya Zemlya

Franz Josef Land

Spitzbergen

Kara Sea

Novaya Zemlya

ASIA

West Siberian Plain

EURASIAN PLATE
NORTH AMERICAN PLATE

Barents Sea

Bjørnøya

Barents Trough

North Cape

Murmansk Rise

Ural Mountains

Ob'

Ob'

Irtysh

Jan Mayen

Denmark Strait

Kolbeinsey Ridge

Iceland Plateau

Iceland

Faeroe-Iceland Ridge

Voring Plateau

White Sea

Kola Peninsula

Arctic Circle

Norwegian Sea

Scandinavia

Gulf of Bothnia

The weight of the ice depressed the surface of the land by as much as 2,150m in some places. Today, without the ice, the land is rising back up to its original height at rates of a few fractions of an inch a year.

An immense lake built up in front of the ice sheet 9000 years ago, as the climate warmed and the ice sheet began to melt.

Iceland Basin

Hatton Ridge

Rockall Rise

Feni Ridge

Faeroe-Shetland Trough

Shetland Islands

Viking Bank

Orkney Islands

Norwegian Trench

Gulf of Finland

LAKE ANCYLUS

The Caspian Sea flooded much of what is now the low-lying region around the Volga delta.

Volga Upland

Volga

ATLANTIC OCEAN

Porcupine Plain

North Sea

British Isles

Ireland

Irish Sea

Pennines

Britain

Jylland

Baltic Sea

Central Russian Upland

Dnieper

Europe's ice cap was about 6,600 ft thick and stretched from the pack ice of the frozen Arctic Ocean, south to the British Isles and the Netherlands. Today, Northern Europe is littered with moraines, which mark the farthest advance of the huge ice sheet.

Celtic Shelf

English Channel

E U R O P E

Rhine

Caspian Depression

After the ice receded, the British Isles were for a time still connected to mainland Europe. Evidence of settlements now beneath the North Sea has recently been detected.

Loire

Global climatic changes affected Europe radically, forming the immense ice sheet in the north, but also altering the vegetation. South of the ice sheet, a great swathe of the continent was covered with sparse tundra vegetation, and soils were permanently frozen – making it less suitable for habitation.

Carpathian Mountains

The Black Sea was an isolated lake, not yet joined to the Mediterranean Sea via the Bosporus. It was permanently linked to the Mediterranean c.4500 years ago.

Sea of Azov

Volga

Don

Dnieper

Charcot Seamounts

Biscay Plain

Bay of Biscay

Massif Central

Garonne

Alps

Great Hungarian Plain

Danube

Drava

Dinaric Alps

Transylvanian Alps

Balkan Mountains

Crimea

Black Sea

Galicia Bank

Iberian Plain

Pyrenees

Sistema Central

Sistema Ibérico

Tagus

Corsica

Adriatic Sea

Adriatic Basin

Rhodope Mountains

Aegean Sea

EURASIAN PLATE
ANATOLIAN PLATE

Tagus Plain

Iberian Peninsula

Balearic Islands

Balearic Plain

Sardinia

Apennines

Tyrrhenian Sea

Tyrrhenian Basin

Ionian Sea

Anatolia

Pindus Mountains

LAKE KONYA

Taurus Mountains

Euph

Horseshoe Seamounts

Sistemas Béticos

Desertlike steppe conditions prevailed throughout southern Europe.

Mediterranean Sea

Sicily

Malta

Ionian Basin

Mediterranean Ridge

ARABIAN PLATE
AFRICAN PLATE

Seine Plain

EURASIAN PLATE
AFRICAN PLATE

Crete

Cyprus

Cyprus Basin

Lower sea levels meant far more of the Mediterranean coast was exposed 18,000 years ago. In Greece, this created land bridges between many of the islands.

Agadir Canyon

Atlas Mountains

Gulf of Sirte

Sir

Grand Erg Occidental

Grand Erg Oriental

Libyan Desert

Western Desert

Re

A F R I C A

S a h a r a

Vegetation type

ice cap and glacier

polar or alpine desert

tundra

semidesert or sparsely vegetated

forest or open woodland

temperate desert

tropical desert

desert

coastline (present-day)

coastline (18,000 years ago)

EUROPE
REGIONAL HISTORY

THE HISTORICAL LANDSCAPE

EUROPE, THE SECOND SMALLEST OF THE WORLD'S CONTINENTS, has a great diversity of topography, climate, and ecology, a rich pattern which contributed greatly to its inordinate influence on global history. Extensive oceanic and inland shorelines, abundantly fertile soils, and broadly temperate conditions provided innumerable heartlands for a wide array of cultures. Internecine rivalries created shifting patterns, themselves frequently overlaid by successive waves of migration and incursion. The shores of the Mediterranean provided a cradle for many powerful cultural groups, which formed myriad states and several empires until the 15th century, when the power base shifted to the emergent nations of the Atlantic coast. It was these aggressive, mercantile and pioneering maritime powers who vaulted Europe to a globally dominant position, through trade and colonialism, during the closing centuries of the 2nd millennium. As they collapsed, a seemingly ineradicable linguistic, economic, technological, and cultural imprint remained, which in the 20th century was widely adopted and adapted, creating an almost universal global culture.

The fertile plains of rivers such as the Danube provided the setting for early agricultural settlements, which spread north from the shores of the Aegean Sea from around 7000 BCE.

During the Ice Ages, the Alps were covered with extensive glacier systems, vestiges of which remain today. As the ice receded, the mountains provided a barrier between the cultures of the Mediterranean and those of Northern Europe.

Europe's first cultures spread westward from Anatolia, reaching the fertile, often isolated coastal valleys around the Aegean between 7000 and 6000 BCE.

EUROPE

EXPLORATION AND MAPPING

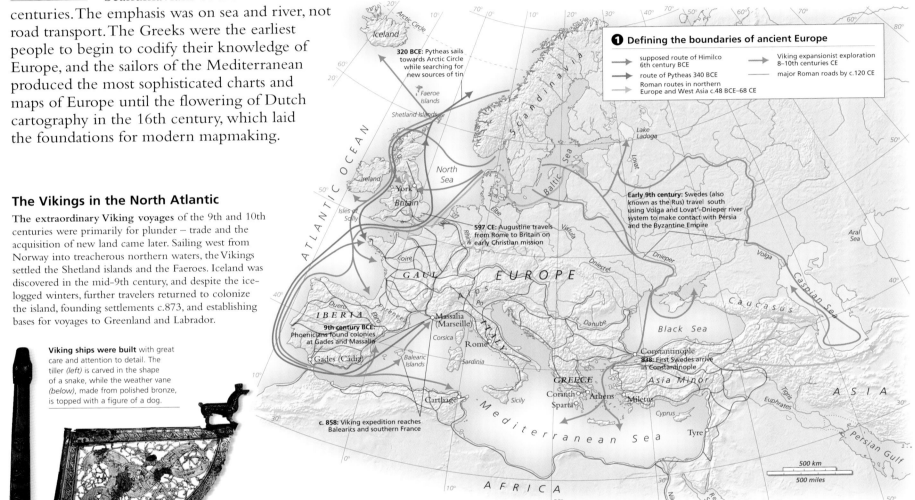

The theodolite was first used in the 17th century. This model, dating from 1765 could measure both altitude and azimuth.

EUROPEANS LEARNED TO KNOW their lands by practical experience and scientific study. Trade and the acquisition of new land provided an impetus for travel and exploration. Phoenician traders moving west in the 9th century BCE, and the Greeks from the 8th century BCE explored the Mediterranean. They were followed by the Romans, whose road system eventually covered much of southern and western Europe. Long-range travel was next developed by the wide-ranging Scandinavians of the 9th and 10th centuries. The emphasis was on sea and river, not road transport. The Greeks were the earliest people to begin to codify their knowledge of Europe, and the sailors of the Mediterranean produced the most sophisticated charts and maps of Europe until the flowering of Dutch cartography in the 16th century, which laid the foundations for modern mapmaking.

The Vikings in the North Atlantic

The extraordinary Viking voyages of the 9th and 10th centuries were primarily for plunder – trade and the acquisition of new land came later. Sailing west from Norway into treacherous northern waters, the Vikings settled the Shetland islands and the Faeroes. Iceland was discovered in the mid-9th century, and despite the ice-logged winters, further travelers returned to colonize the island, founding settlements c.873, and establishing bases for voyages to Greenland and Labrador.

Viking ships were built with great care and attention to detail. The tiller (left) is carved in the shape of a snake, while the weather vane (below), made from polished bronze, is topped with a figure of a dog.

Mapping in the Classical era

This map reconstructs the Europe known to Pytheas. His journey was the first scientific exploration of northern Europe by Greeks. The map is based on Eratosthenes' three-continent (Europe, Africa, and Asia) world view. The Mediterranean familiar to the Greeks is accurately plotted; the northern topography is far more speculative.

The peoples of the Mediterranean made the earliest attempts at a survey of Europe. In 340 BCE, the Greek Pytheas traveled from Massalia to Britain, visiting the Orkneys and Shetlands; he later visited Norway and north Germany. The first attempts at scientific mapping were made in the Mediterranean: Eratosthenes successfully measured the diameter of the earth; Hipparchus suggested lines of latitude and longitude as reference points, and Ptolemy tried to show the surface of the earth using two conical projections, and provided points of reference for more than 8000 places.

❶ Defining the boundaries of ancient Europe

- supposed route of Himilco 6th century BCE
- route of Pytheas 340 BCE
- Roman routes in northern Europe and West Asia c.48 BCE–68 CE
- Viking expansionist exploration 8–10th centuries CE
- major Roman roads by c.120 CE

320 BCE: Pytheas sails towards Arctic Circle while searching for new sources of tin

Early 9th century: Swedes (also known as the Rus) travel south using Volga and Lovat'–Dnieper river system to make contact with Persia and the Byzantine Empire

597 CE: Augustine travels from Rome to Britain on early Christian mission

9th century BCE: Phoenicians found colonies at Gades and Massalia

838: First Swedes arrive in Constantinople

c.858: Viking expedition reaches Balearics and southern France

❷ The Viking discovery of Iceland

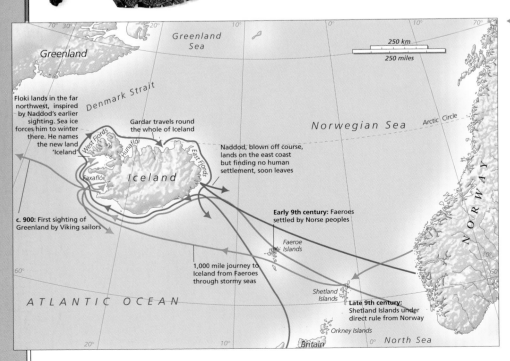

- Gardar Svavarsson c. 860
- Naddod c. 870
- Floki Vilgerdarsson
- other Viking explorers

Floki lands in the far northwest, inspired by Naddod's earlier sighting. Sea ice forces him to winter there. He names the new land 'Iceland'

Gardar travels round the whole of Iceland

Naddod, blown off course, lands on the east coast but finding no human settlement, soon leaves

c. 900: First sighting of Greenland by Viking sailors

Early 9th century: Faeroes settled by Norse peoples

1,000 mile journey to Iceland from Faeroes through stormy seas

Late 9th century: Shetland Islands under direct rule from Norway

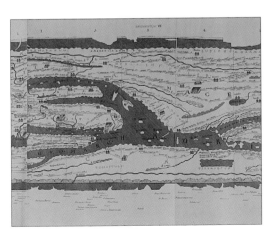

The Peutinger Table, a strip map 23 ft long and 1 ft wide, showed roads in the Roman Empire – such as the Via Appia – with little reference to the surrounding countryside. It was probably first drawn in the 3rd century CE and was a useful tool for actually planning journeys. Some 5000 places are recorded, mostly in Europe.

The Vikings in the North Atlantic

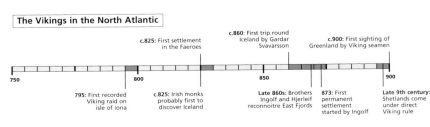

c.825: First settlement in the Faeroes

c.860: First trip round Iceland by Gardar Svavarsson

c.900: First sighting of Greenland by Viking seamen

750 — 800 — 850 — 900

795: First recorded Viking raid on isle of Iona

c.825: Irish monks probably first to discover Iceland

Late 860s: Brothers Ingolf and Hjerleif reconnoitre East Fjords

873: First permanent settlement started by Ingolf

Late 9th century: Shetlands come under direct Viking rule

Medieval mapping of Europe

Most of Europe was well known to travelers by the 11th century, but the accuracy with which it was mapped was extremely variable. The literate sailors of the Mediterranean were able to draw on the relatively sophisticated Portolan charts, which were made chiefly by Italian and Catalan navigators, but nothing comparable existed for the sailors of the north. Inland, largely imaginary wall maps represented Christian beliefs and the known world, with Jerusalem at the center of the earth, Europe at left, and Africa on the right. A second type of map was based on accumulated knowledge, and gave a recognizable, if distorted, picture of Europe. Examples include Gough's map, and the maps of Matthew Paris (1200–1259 CE). From the 15th century, Ptolemy's map of Europe *(see p.44)* was once again available and it was added to, and corrected in the light of new knowledge and re-published in the *Tabulae Modernae*. In 1425, Clavus, a Dane who had visited Iceland and Southern Greenland, added these, plus Norway, to the Ptolemaic base map.

The Hereford wall map *(left)* is perhaps the best known of the 600 or so "T-in-O maps" which are known to have survived. The T-shape of the Mediterranean Sea which divides the world into Europe, Africa and Asia is contained within a circle – the O.

Medieval mapping

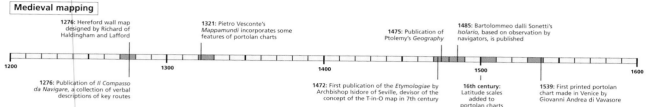

1276: Hereford wall map designed by Richard of Haldingham and Lafford

1321: Pietro Vesconte's *Mappamundi* incorporates some features of portolan charts

1475: Publication of Ptolemy's *Geography*

1485: Bartolommeo dalli Sonetti's *Isolario*, based on observation by navigators, is published

1200   1300   1400   1500   1600

1276: Publication of *Il Compasso da Navigare*, a collection of verbal descriptions of key routes

1472: First publication of the *Etymologiae* by Archbishop Isidore of Seville, devisor of the concept of the T-in-O map in 7th century

16th century: Latitude scales added to portolan charts

1539: First printed portolan chart made in Venice by Giovanni Andrea di Vavasore

Portolan charts *(above)* were available to Mediterranean sailors from early Medieval times. They recorded the ports of the Mediterranean and Black Sea, giving landmarks, bearings, and distances, based on the Roman mile of 1000 paces.

The beginnings of modern cartography

In early modern Europe, increasing trade and a growing gentry class interested in their surroundings encouraged a new phase of mapmaking. Overseas territories and the possessions of the rich were mapped using surveying instruments such as the theodolite. Dutch cartographers made some of the most important innovations. Gerardus Mercator was the first to break from the Ptolemaic model. Mercator's projection rejected Ptolemy's conical model to show bearings with a scale identical in all directions. This made it particularly useful for navigators, and it is still widely used today. Another Dutchman, Willebrord Snell (Snellius), was the first to use triangulation to survey a large area. After carefully measuring a base line, he then employed trigonometry to calculate the distances to far off landmarks.

This map of Europe was produced by Mercator in 1554. It gives a detailed picture of settlement patterns, river networks, forest cover, and country boundaries, but some of the surrounding details - for example the proportions of Scandinavia - are far from accurate.

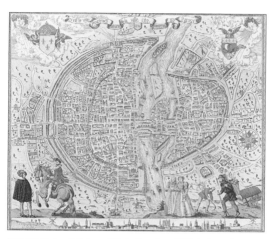

This detailed aerial view of Paris dates from 1576. It shows the original city wall, as well as building on the outskirts, agricultural areas – including windmills – and rough pasture on the edge of the city.

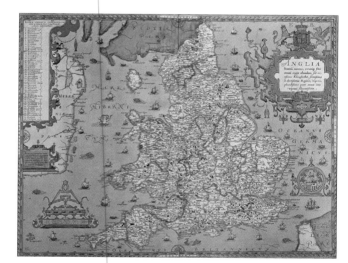

Saxton's county map of England and Wales, published in 1579, shows the detail and accuracy which was being achieved by the 16th century. Other similar examples include Norden's county maps of 1593, and Ogilvie's road map published in *Britannia*.

The Netherlands and the origins of modern cartography

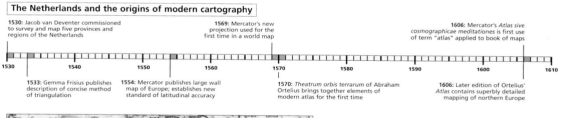

1530: Jacob van Deventer commissioned to survey and map five provinces and regions of the Netherlands

1569: Mercator's new projection used for the first time in a world map

1606: Mercator's *Atlas sive cosmographicae meditationes* is first use of term "atlas" applied to book of maps

1530   1540   1550   1560   1570   1580   1590   1600   1610

1533: Gemma Frisius publishes description of concise method of triangulation

1554: Mercator publishes large wall map of Europe; establishes new standard of latitudinal accuracy

1570: *Theatrum orbis terrarum* of Abraham Ortelius brings together elements of modern atlas for the first time

1606: Later edition of Ortelius' *Atlas* contains superbly detailed mapping of northern Europe

J.D. and C.F. Cassini continued Snellius' triangulation surveys in France. By 1744 all of France was covered by some 2000 triangles. The first sheets of a map of France on a scale of 1:86,400 were produced in 1756, but it was not until the Revolution that the last of the 182 sheets was published.

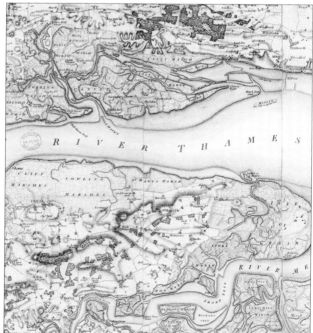

In England, fear of Napoleonic invasion and a need for detailed information about the land, led to a survey on a scale of two inches to the mile and publication on a scale of one inch to the mile. The first map of this series was sold as four sheets in 1801.

Surveyors from the Royal Engineers were responsible for making accurate maps of Britain and its Empire during the 19th century. Here they are shown undertaking a triangulation.

PREHISTORIC EUROPE

Mycenaean pottery, such as this goblet from Rhodes (c.1300 BCE), was traded throughout the eastern Mediterranean.

IN 7000 BCE, postglacial Europe, with its deciduous forests and increasingly temperate climate, was rich in natural resources and thinly populated by hunter-gatherers. By 1000 BCE, villages stretched from the Balkans to Scandinavia, and agriculture had reached even the marginal regions of the continent; there was a flourishing transcontinental traffic in salt, metals, and amber; and the first palace-based states had emerged on Crete and the Greek mainland. Although remains of settlements are rarely well preserved, a wide range of burials reveal, through grave goods as varied as woven textiles, ceramic vessels, and bronze axheads, an increasingly stratified society, in which individual possessions were a reflection of status.

The introduction of farming 7000–5000 BCE

As agriculture spread from Anatolia into the Balkans and beyond, farming practices were adapted to more northerly latitudes, with an increased reliance on cattle and pigs and new, hardy strains of cereal. The mud-brick hill villages (tells) of the Middle East were replaced, in the thickly forested river valleys of Central Europe, by clusters of timber longhouses. The location of early farming communities can be charted by different pottery styles; incised Bandkeramik pottery is found from Hungary to the North Sea, while Cardial pottery, decorated with shell impressions, is found along the Mediterranean.

The first potters of Central Europe used fired clay to make stylized human figures.

The spread of farming 7000–5000 BCE

c.7000: Farming spreads from Anatolia to southeastern Europe

c.6000: Farming starts to spread along the western coast of Mediterranean

c.5000: Agriculture well established in southern France and in the Netherlands

c.6500: Rising postglacial sea levels separate British Isles from the rest of the European continent

c.6000: First farming villages appear in southern Italy and Sicily

c.5600: Farming communities using Bandkeramik pottery in Central Europe

7000 BCE 6500 6000 5500 5000 BCE

Timber longhouses, such as this example from Bylany in the Czech Republic, were built by the earliest farmers of Central Europe. The basic framework, made from plentiful timber supplies, was covered with wattle and daub. The buildings could be up to 150 ft long, and housed one or more families, as well as livestock and stores of food.

❶ The introduction of farming 7000–5000 BCE ▶

→ spread of farming

▨ cultivated land by c.7000 BCE

▨ cultivated land by c.6000 BCE

▨ cultivated land by c.5000 BCE

▨ concentrations of Mesolithic settlements c.5000 BCE

⊙ early farming settlement

🏺 Balkan painted ware site

🏺 Bandkeramik pottery site

🏺 Cardial and incised pottery site

Europe in the Copper Age 4500–2500 BCE

This was an era of technological innovation and contact between communities. Both horses and wheeled vehicles spread westward from the steppes, reaching western Europe by c.2500 BCE, while the introduction of the scratch plow increased productivity. Copper technology, which was developed in eastern Europe c.5000 BCE, spread throughout Europe over the next millennium. Finds of high prestige metalwork in some individual burials indicate that society was becoming more hierarchical, while distinctive pottery styles, known as Beaker Ware and Corded Ware, became widespread in central and western European burials, indicating the existence of a network of contact and exchange.

Marble figurines, made in the Cycladic Islands of Greece from c.2600 BCE, were placed in burials.

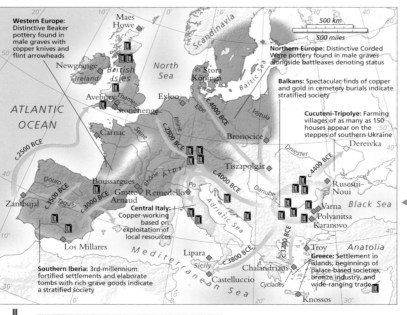

Western Europe: Distinctive Beaker pottery found in male graves with copper knives and flint arrowheads

Northern Europe: Distinctive Corded Ware pottery found in male graves alongside battleaxes denoting status

Balkans: Spectacular finds of copper and gold in cemetery burials indicate stratified society

Cucuteni-Tripolye: Farming villages of as many as 150 houses appear on the steppes of southern Ukraine

Central Italy: Copper-working based on exploitation of local resources

Southern Iberia: 3rd-millennium fortified settlements and elaborate tombs with rich grave goods indicate a stratified society

Greece: Settlement in islands; beginnings of palace-based societies, bronze industry, and wide-ranging trade

❷ Europe in the Copper Age 4500–2500 BCE

▨ early copper-working areas c.5000–4000 BCE

▣ copper resources

→ spread of copper-working, with date

▨ area of Corded Ware burials c.2900–2000 BCE

▨ area of Beaker burials c.2500–2000 BCE

◆ important archaeological site

Europe in the Copper Age 4500–2500 BCE

c.4000: Farming villages of the Cucuteni-Tripolye group appear in southern Ukraine

c.3500: Stone circles and alignments, henges, and menhirs appear throughout northwestern Europe.

c.3000: Copper-working begins in southern France

c.2500: Copper-working reaches British Isles. Bell beaker pottery found in individual burials in western Europe

c.4000: Copper mines being exploited in Bulgaria and Yugoslavia

c.3500: First wheeled vehicles in Central Europe

c.2900: Appearance of Corded Ware pottery and stone battleaxes in burials in northern Europe

4000 BCE 3500 3000 2500 BCE

The stone alignments at Kermario in northwestern France date to c.3000 BCE. They were probably associated with processions and seasonal rituals.

Europe in the Bronze Age 2300–1500 BCE

The Bronze Age in Europe was a period of remarkable cultural and technological uniformity. Limited tin resources in western Europe, vital for bronze manufacture, were transported along long distance trade routes in exchange for other valued commodities – Baltic amber and salt. Access to these resources was a major factor in creating a distinct social elite, interred under large burial mounds, replete with a rich array of grave goods. By 1500 BCE, marginal land was being brought into cultivation to feed growing populations. These social and economic pressures led to increasing conflict, evident in the appearance of fortified settlements and the emergence of a warrior elite.

Many of the bronze artifacts made in Europe during the 2nd millennium BCE, such as this ritual bronze ax from Teteven in the Balkan Mountains, were status objects for the emerging warrior elite.

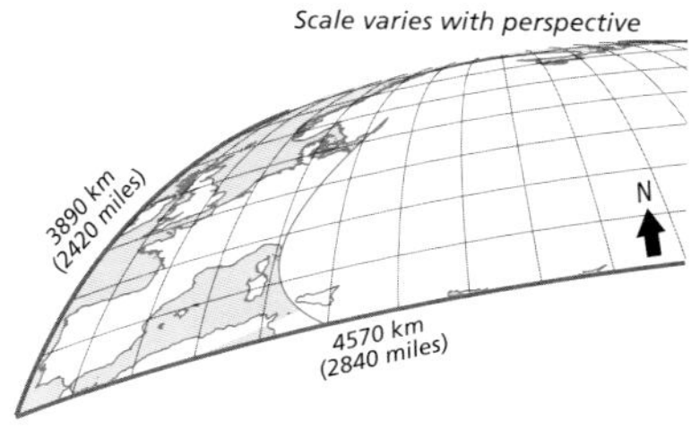
Scale varies with perspective
3890 km (2420 miles)
4570 km (2840 miles)
N

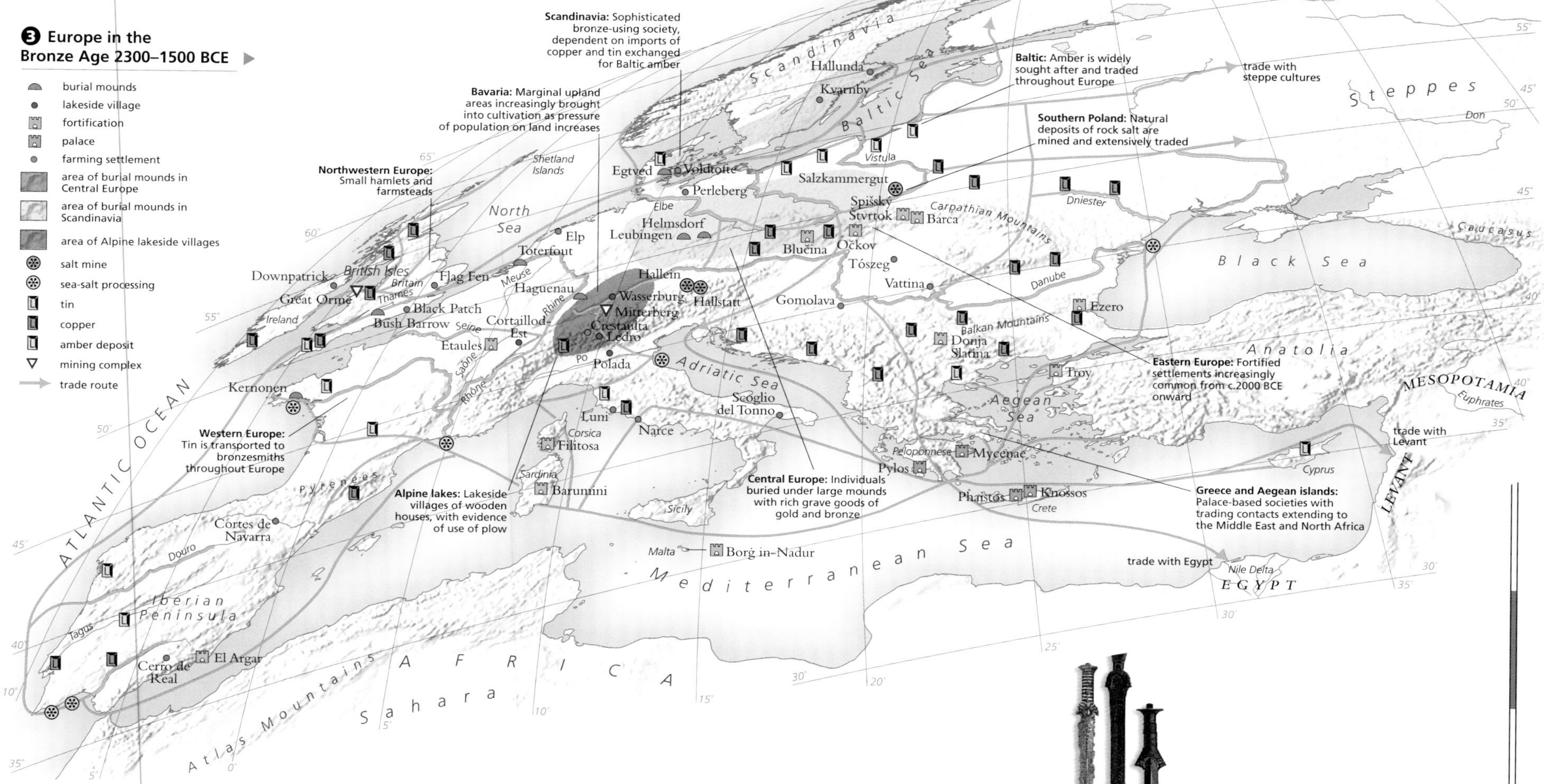
3 Europe in the Bronze Age 2300–1500 BCE
burial mounds
lakeside village
fortification
palace
farming settlement
area of burial mounds in Central Europe
area of burial mounds in Scandinavia
area of Alpine lakeside villages
salt mine
sea-salt processing
tin
copper
amber deposit
mining complex
trade route
Scandinavia: Sophisticated bronze-using society, dependent on imports of copper and tin exchanged for Baltic amber
Bavaria: Marginal upland areas increasingly brought into cultivation as pressure of population on land increases
Northwestern Europe: Small hamlets and farmsteads
Baltic: Amber is widely sought after and traded throughout Europe
Southern Poland: Natural deposits of rock salt are mined and extensively traded
trade with steppe cultures
Western Europe: Tin is transported to bronzesmiths throughout Europe
Alpine lakes: Lakeside villages of wooden houses, with evidence of use of plow
Central Europe: Individuals buried under large mounds with rich grave goods of gold and bronze
Eastern Europe: Fortified settlements increasingly common from c.2000 BCE onward
Greece and Aegean islands: Palace-based societies with trading contacts extending to the Middle East and North Africa
trade with Levant
trade with Egypt
Scandinavia
Hallunda
Kvarnby
Baltic Sea
Egtved
Voldtofte
Perleberg
Salzkammergut
Vistula
Spišský Štvrtok
Barca
Carpathian Mountains
Dniester
Steppes
Don
Caucasus
Black Sea
Shetland Islands
North Sea
Elbe
Helmsdorf
Leubingen
Elp
Toterfout
Blučina
Očkov
Tószeg
Vattina
Danube
Ezero
Downpatrick
British Isles
Britain
Thames
Great Orme
Flag Fen
Meuse
Haguenau
Hallein
Hallstatt
Wasserburg
Mitterberg
Crestaulta
Ledro
Black Patch
Bush Barrow
Seine
Rhine
Cortaillod-Est
Etaules
Ireland
Saône
Rhône
Po
Polada
Adriatic Sea
Gomolava
Balkan Mountains
Donja Slatina
Troy
Anatolia
Kernonen
Luni
Scoglio del Tonno
Narce
Aegean Sea
MESOPOTAMIA
Euphrates
Corsica
Filitosa
Peloponnese
Mycenae
Pylos
Cyprus
Sardinia
Barumini
Sicily
Phaistos
Knossos
Crete
LEVANT
ATLANTIC OCEAN
Pyrenees
Cortes de Navarra
Douro
Malta
Borg in-Nadur
Mediterranean Sea
Nile Delta
EGYPT
Iberian Peninsula
Tagus
Cerro de la Real
El Argar
AFRICA
Sahara
Atlas Mountains

Bronze Age Europe 2300–1500 BCE

- c.2300: Beginning of European Bronze Age – bronze objects begin to appear in tombs
- c.2200: Defensive enclosures built in southern Britain as communities compete for land and resources
- c.2000: Fortified settlements begin to appear in eastern and central Europe, a sign of increased social and economic pressure
- c.2000: First palace built at Knossos on Crete. Palace-based societies develop throughout island
- c.1900: Potter's wheel introduced to Crete
- c.1800: Finds of wooden plows in Scandinavian bogs. Bronze artifacts suggest sun worship

2300 BCE – 2200 – 2100 – 2000 – 1900 – 1800 BCE

These bronze slashing swords made in Europe toward the end of the 2nd millennium BCE, along with the widespread appearance of fortified settlements, were indications that society was becoming more militaristic.

Minoan Crete and Mycenaean Greece

The palaces of Minoan Crete were flourishing economic, royal and ritual centers. When catastrophe, possibly a volcanic eruption, struck c.1450 BCE, the Mycenaean kingdoms of mainland Greece gained supremacy. The Mycenaeans were able sailors and long-distance traders. Their well-fortified palaces, and the evidence of painted pottery, armor, and weapons, all attest to their military technology. But internal disorder and, possibly, foreign invasion precipitated their downfall, c.1100 BCE.

The snake goddess was revered as a household guardian in Minoan Crete. This figure is from Knossos, c.1500 BCE.

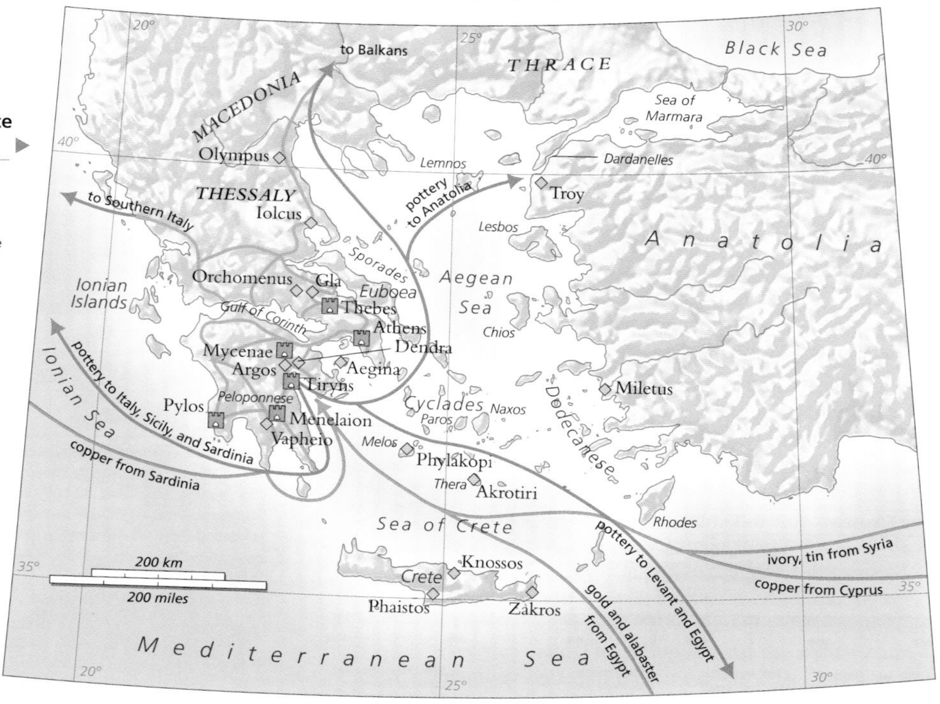
4 Mycenaean Greece c.1550–1150 BCE
Mycenaean major palace
Minoan and Mycenaean sites
major routes within the Mycenaean heartland
import routes
export routes
to Balkans
Black Sea
THRACE
MACEDONIA
Sea of Marmara
Olympus
Dardanelles
Lemnos
Troy
THESSALY
to Southern Italy
Iolcus
pottery to Anatolia
Lesbos
Anatolia
Sporades
Ionian Islands
Orchomenus
Gla
Euboea
Aegean Sea
Thebes
Gulf of Corinth
Athens
Chios
Dendra
Mycenae
Argos
Aegina
Tiryns
Ionian Sea
pottery to Italy, Sicily, and Sardinia
Miletus
Pylos
Peloponnese
Menelaion
Vapheio
Cyclades
Naxos
Paros
Dodecanese
copper from Sardinia
Melos
Phylakopi
Thera
Akrotiri
Rhodes
Sea of Crete
ivory, tin from Syria
200 km
200 miles
Knossos
Crete
copper from Cyprus
Phaistos
Zakros
pottery to Levant and Egypt
gold and alabaster from Egypt
Mediterranean Sea

Mycenaean Greece

- c.2000: Palace-based societies emerge on Crete
- c.1550: Kingdom of Mycenae rises to prominence
- c.1450–1250: Mycenae at height of power and prosperity linked by trading networks from the Levant to Sicily
- c.1450: Destruction of Minoan palaces of Crete. Mycenaeans take control of island
- c.1250: Defenses strengthened at several Mycenaean palaces, suggesting troubled conditions
- c.1100: Mycenaean palaces and towns sacked or abandoned

2000 BCE – 1800 – 1600 – 1400 – 1200 – 1000 BCE

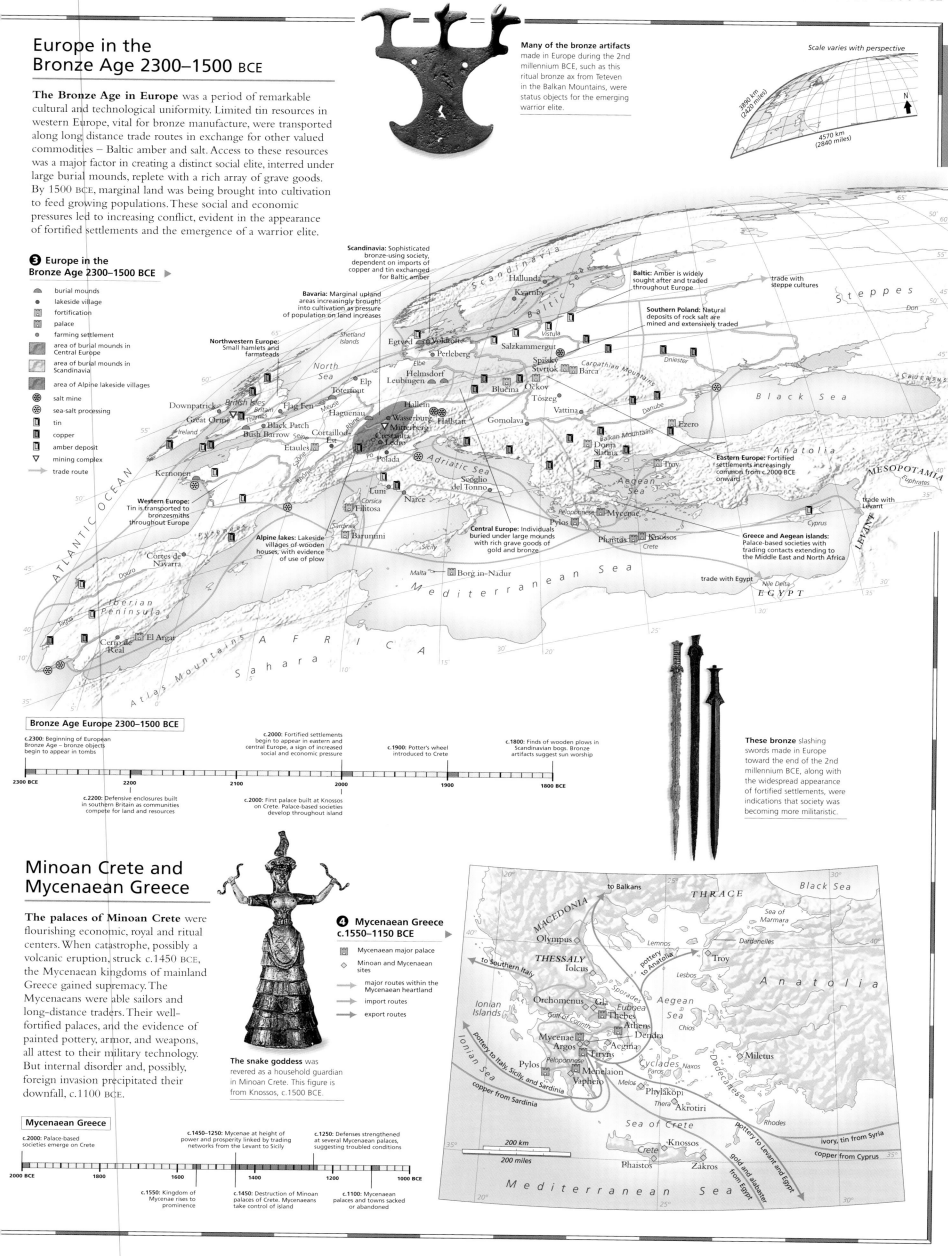

THE RISE OF ROME

The legionaries of Rome's citizen army were unmatched in discipline and skill.

ROME BEGAN THE 5TH CENTURY BCE as the most powerful city of the regional alliance known as the Latin League. By conquering the Etruscan city-state of Veii in 396 BCE, the Romans doubled their territory, and after the breakup of the Latin League in 338, they incorporated the whole Latin region. This gave them the manpower to defeat a coalition of Samnites, Etruscans, and Gauls in 295. When they faced the army of the Greek general Pyrrhus, they were able to sustain two crushing defeats before achieving victory in 275 BCE. With Italy now under its control, Rome turned its attention to foreign rivals. Following victory over Carthage in 202, it took less than a century to add North Africa, most of Iberia, southern Gaul, Macedon, Greece, and Asia Minor to its empire.

Rome and the Italian confederacy

Traditionally, this bronze bust of a stern Roman aristocrat has been identified as Lucius Junius Brutus, one of the founders of the Roman Republic in 509.

From the 5th to the 3rd century BCE, the city of Rome extended its area of domination to create a confederacy that united all Italy. Some cities were simply annexed and their inhabitants enjoyed the status of full Roman citizens, while others were granted a halfway form of citizenship that did not include the right to vote or hold office in Rome. Other peoples were considered "allies" and united to Rome by individual treaties. New towns known as "Latin colonies" extended the Roman presence throughout Italy, while "Roman colonies," where the inhabitants were full citizens, were established for defensive purposes, primarily along the Tyrrhenian coast. Beginning with the Via Appia in the 4th century BCE, the Romans built a road network that linked the whole peninsula.

Rome and its Latin allies c.495 BCE

Rome was the most powerful of the Latin city-states when the Republic was established in 509, though it controlled just 320 sq miles of territory.

The peoples of Italy in 500 BCE

Latin, the language Rome would spread throughout western Europe, was just one of many closely related Italic languages spoken by the tribes of central Italy. The most powerful peoples in the peninsula were the Greek colonists and the Etruscans, a sophisticated city-state people whose language suggests eastern Mediterranean origins. It had been the Etruscans' arrival in Rome in the 7th century BCE that transformed a cluster of small villages into a city.

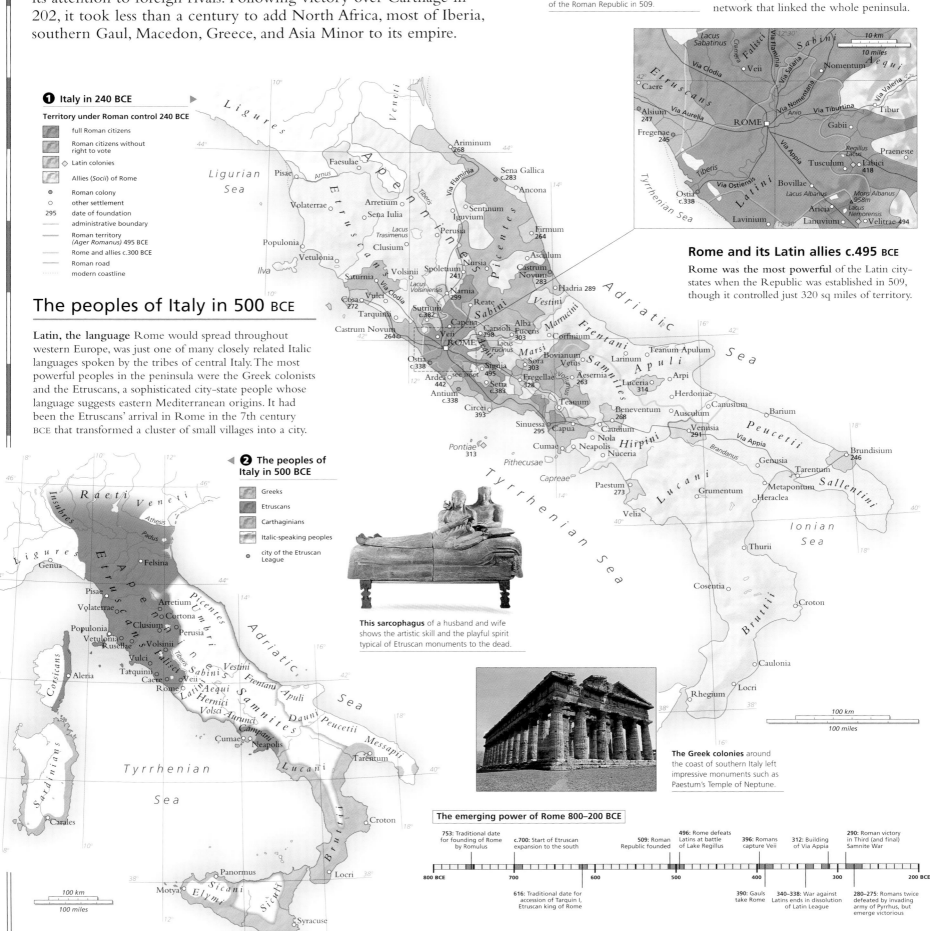

❶ Italy in 240 BCE

Territory under Roman control 240 BCE

- full Roman citizens
- Roman citizens without right to vote
- ◇ Latin colonies
- Allies (*Socii*) of Rome
- ● Roman colony
- ○ other settlement
- 295 date of foundation
- administrative boundary
- Roman territory (*Ager Romanus*) 495 BCE
- Rome and allies c.300 BCE
- Roman road
- modern coastline

❷ The peoples of Italy in 500 BCE

- Greeks
- Etruscans
- Carthaginians
- Italic-speaking peoples
- ● city of the Etruscan League

This sarcophagus of a husband and wife shows the artistic skill and the playful spirit typical of Etruscan monuments to the dead.

The Greek colonies around the coast of southern Italy left impressive monuments such as Paestum's Temple of Neptune.

The emerging power of Rome 800–200 BCE

753: Traditional date of founding of Rome by Romulus

c.700: Start of Etruscan expansion to the south

509: Roman Republic founded

496: Rome defeats Latins at battle of Lake Regillus

396: Romans capture Veii

312: Building of Via Appia

290: Roman victory in Third (and final) Samnite War

616: Traditional date for accession of Tarquin I, Etruscan king of Rome

390: Gauls take Rome

340–338: War against Latins ends in dissolution of Latin League

280–275: Romans twice defeated by invading army of Pyrrhus, but emerge victorious

800 BCE — 700 — 600 — 500 — 400 — 300 — 200 BCE

Rome and Carthage: the Punic Wars

Founded by Phoenicians *(Punici)* in 814 BCE, Carthage grew to be the preeminent naval power in the western Mediterranean. Rome came into conflict with the Carthaginians in 264, the start of a series of three wars. In the first, the Romans pushed their enemies out of Sicily. Then, in 218, Rome forced a second war by opposing Carthaginian actions in Iberia. Despite many defeats at the hands of Hannibal, the Romans won this war and stripped Carthage of its navy. The final war (149–146) ended in the destruction of Carthage and the enslavement of its people.

The Carthaginian general Hannibal *(left)* fought the Romans for 15 years in Italy. The smaller coin *(right)* shows an African elephant, used by the Carthaginians to strike terror into opposing armies.

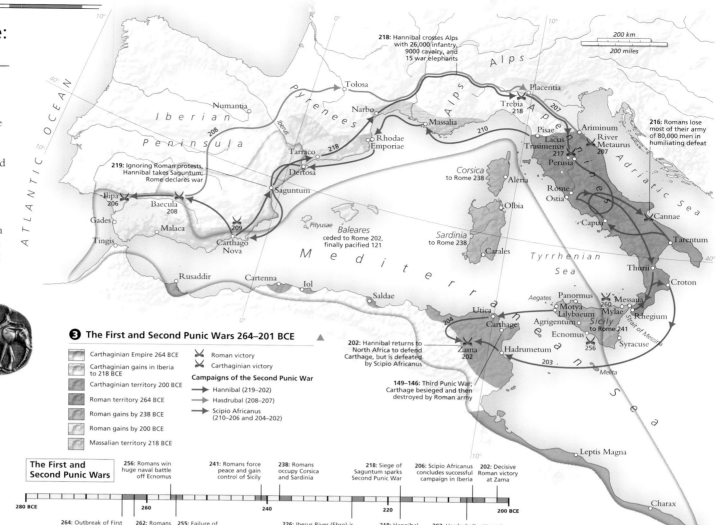

❸ The First and Second Punic Wars 264–201 BCE ▲

- Carthaginian Empire 264 BCE
- Carthaginian gains in Iberia to 218 BCE
- Carthaginian territory 200 BCE
- Roman territory 264 BCE
- Roman gains by 238 BCE
- Roman gains by 200 BCE
- Massalian territory 218 BCE
- ✕ Roman victory
- ✕ Carthaginian victory

Campaigns of the Second Punic War
- → Hannibal (219–202)
- → Hasdrubal (208–207)
- → Scipio Africanus (210–206 and 204–202)

218: Hannibal crosses Alps with 26,000 infantry, 9000 cavalry, and 15 war elephants

216: Romans lose most of their army of 80,000 men in humiliating defeat

219: Ignoring Roman protests, Hannibal takes Saguntum; Rome declares war

202: Hannibal returns to North Africa to defend Carthage, but is defeated by Scipio Africanus

149–146: Third Punic War; Carthage besieged and then destroyed by Roman army

The First and Second Punic Wars

256: Romans win huge naval battle off Ecnomus
241: Romans force peace and gain control of Sicily
238: Romans occupy Corsica and Sardinia
218: Siege of Saguntum sparks Second Punic War
206: Scipio Africanus concludes successful campaign in Iberia
202: Decisive Roman victory at Zama

280 BCE — 260 — 240 — 220 — 200 BCE

264: Outbreak of First Punic War over control of Strait of Messina
262: Romans capture Agrigentum
255: Failure of Roman invasion of North Africa
226: Iberus River (Ebro) is agreed as limit of Carthage's expansion in Iberian Peninsula
218: Hannibal crosses Alps
207: Hasdrubal's attempt to reinforce Hannibal in Italy ends in defeat

---

The subjugation of Greece by Rome

In 200 BCE the major powers of the Greek world were Macedon and the Seleucid Empire. Two Greek federations had also emerged: the Aetolian League and the Achaean League, which included Corinth, largest of the mainland Greek cities. Other city-states, such as Athens and Sparta, maneuvered to maintain their independence, as did the Asian kingdom of Pergamum. Political tensions and appeals to Rome for help gave the Romans excuses for five major military interventions in the 2nd century. Macedon became a Roman province in 148; Greece succumbed in 146 after the Achaean War.

❹ Greece in 200 BCE

- Macedon
- ally of Macedon
- Aetolian League
- ally of Aetolian League
- Achaean League
- Seleucid Empire
- Ptolemaic Empire
- independent Greek states and cities
- Roman Empire
- ally of Rome
- ✕ Roman victory

Corinth was first an ally of Rome, then an enemy. It was razed to the ground in 146 by the Roman general Mummius. The ruined temple *(left)* dates from the 6th century BCE.

This fine mosaic of a lion hunt decorated the royal palace in the Macedonian capital of Pella. Even before annexing Macedon and Greece, Rome eagerly embraced Hellenistic culture and customs.

Rome's overseas provinces in 120 BCE

Following the defeat of Carthage in 202 BCE, Rome's empire expanded rapidly. Greece and the Greek states of Asia Minor were won through a combination of diplomacy and war, but long, costly campaigns were needed to subdue the tribes of the Iberian Peninsula. Carthage itself was added to the empire in 146. As the Romans extended their rule beyond Italy, they largely abandoned the principles of incorporation that they had applied in Italy and instead set up provinces. These were ruled by governors, who served short one- or two-year terms, maintained order, and oversaw the collection of taxes. Corruption and plundering by governors were common enough for a special permanent court to be set up to try such cases in 149.

Roman expansion 200–120 BCE

200–196: Second Macedonian War
172–167: Third Macedonian War
148: Roman victory in Fourth Macedonian War
139: Defeat of Lusitani
133: Romans take Iberian city of Numantia

200 BCE — 180 — 160 — 140 — 120 BCE

192–189: War with Seleucid king Antiochus; Roman victories at Thermopylae and Magnesia
168: Romans crush Macedonians at Pydna
146: Roman armies destroy conquered cities of Corinth and Carthage
133: Rome bequeathed province of Asia by king of Pergamum

❺ Roman conquests to 120 BCE

- Roman Empire c.200 BCE
- Roman gains by c.120 BCE
- Massalia and possessions
- independent Greek states and cities
- Ptolemaic Empire and possessions
- Seleucid Empire
- ASIA 133 — Roman province and date of foundation
- *Volcae* 121 — people and date of conquest by Rome

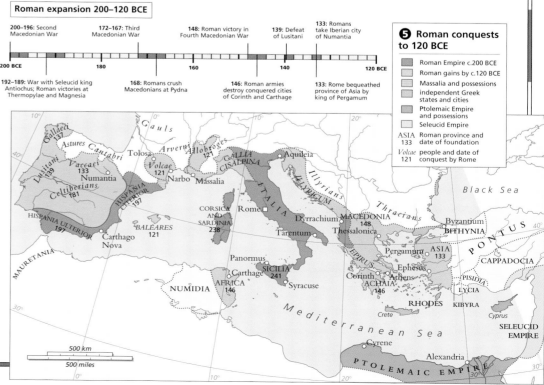

THE ROMAN EMPIRE

Constantine sealed the Empire's fate by moving the center of power to the east.

REPUBLICAN ROME asserted military control over most of the Mediterranean, but a century of internal political conflict and civil war prevented the development of an orderly imperial system. The first emperor, Augustus (27 BCE–14 CE), ended this period of disorder with his defeat of Mark Antony in 31 BCE and established the Principate – the military and political system that defended and governed the empire until the reforms of Diocletian and Constantine at the end of the 3rd century. At the height of its power in the 2nd century, Rome ruled over some 50 million people scattered in over 5000 administrative units. For the most part, subjects of the Empire accepted Roman rule, and, at least in the west, many adopted Roman culture and the Latin language. After 212 CE all free inhabitants of the Empire had the status of Roman citizens.

The Empire under Hadrian

The Empire reached its greatest extent early in the 2nd century under Trajan, who conquered Dacia, Arabia, Armenia, Assyria, and Mesopotamia. However, when Hadrian succeeded in 117 CE, he abandoned the last three provinces and adopted a defensive frontier strategy that would be followed by most of his successors. A professional army – under Hadrian it numbered just 300,000 – defended the frontiers and suppressed rebellions in trouble spots such as Britain and Judaea, while the navy kept the Mediterranean free of pirates. Fleets were also based on the Rhine and the Danube on the northeastern frontier.

The Pont du Gard, part of the aqueduct that supplied Nemausus (Nîmes) in the south of France, is a fine example of the Romans' skill in civil engineering.

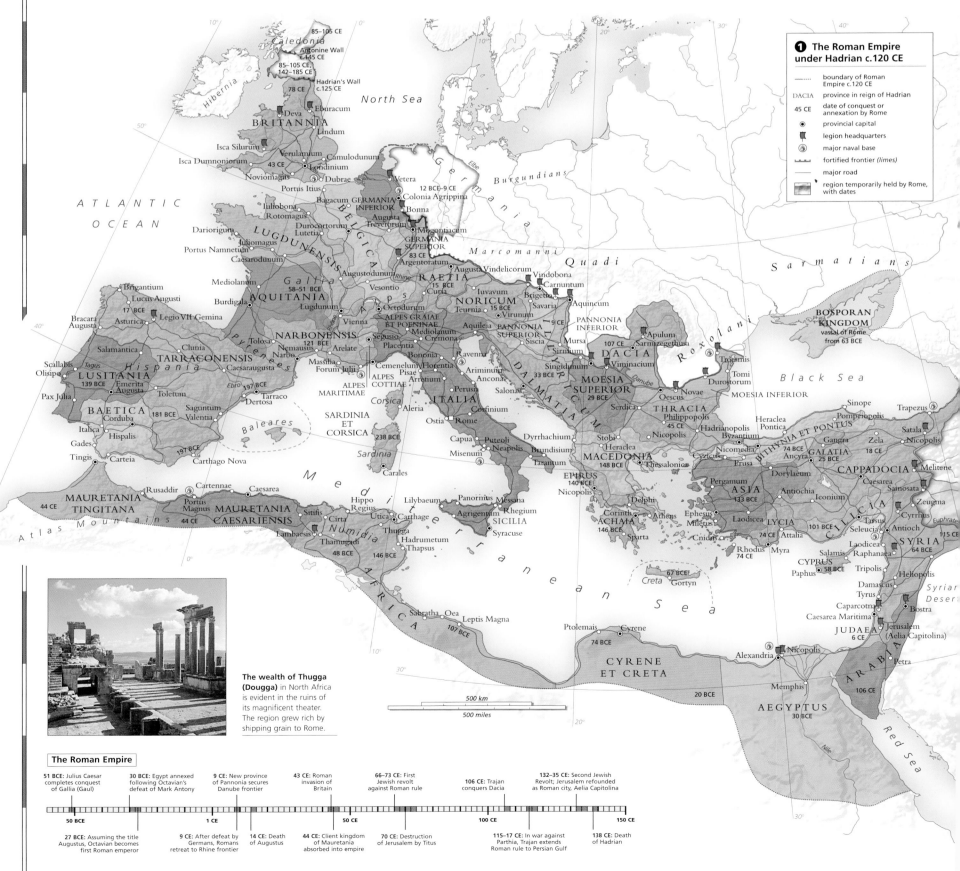

The wealth of Thugga (Dougga) in North Africa is evident in the ruins of its magnificent theater. The region grew rich by shipping grain to Rome.

① The Roman Empire under Hadrian c.120 CE

- .... boundary of Roman Empire c.120 CE
- DACIA — province in reign of Hadrian
- 45 CE — date of conquest or annexation by Rome
- ◉ provincial capital
- ▣ legion headquarters
- Ⓢ major naval base
- ▬▬▬ fortified frontier (limes)
- ——— major road
- region temporarily held by Rome, with dates

The Roman Empire

51 BCE: Julius Caesar completes conquest of Gallia (Gaul)	**30 BCE:** Egypt annexed following Octavian's defeat of Mark Antony	**9 CE:** New province of Pannonia secures Danube frontier	**43 CE:** Roman invasion of Britain	**66–73 CE:** First Jewish revolt against Roman rule	**106 CE:** Trajan conquers Dacia	**132–35 CE:** Second Jewish Revolt; Jerusalem refounded as Roman city, Aelia Capitolina

| 50 BCE | 1 CE | 50 CE | 100 CE | 150 CE |

| **27 BCE:** Assuming the title Augustus, Octavian becomes first Roman emperor | **9 CE:** After defeat by Germans, Romans retreat to Rhine frontier | **14 CE:** Death of Augustus | **44 CE:** Client kingdom of Mauretania absorbed into empire | **70 CE:** Destruction of Jerusalem by Titus | **115–17 CE:** In war against Parthia, Trajan extends Roman rule to Persian Gulf | **138 CE:** Death of Hadrian |

The city of Rome

As the empire grew, so did Rome, reaching a population of about one million in the 2nd century CE. The city was sustained by food shipped up the Tiber from Ostia and aqueducts that delivered 100 gallons of water per head per day. Many Romans did not work, but were eligible for the *annona*, a free handout of grain. Following the example of Augustus, every emperor aimed to leave his mark on the city by building magnificent forums, theaters, arenas, and temples.

The Colosseum, completed in 80 CE, vied with the Circus Maximus racetrack as Rome's most popular stadium. It regularly attracted a full house of 50,000 to its gladiatorial and wild animal combats.

Earthenware amphorae were used to transport and store wine, olive oil, and fish sauce.

Supplying the city of Rome

Feeding the citizens of Rome required regular shipments of grain from Egypt and North Africa. These were landed at Ostia and Portus, a new port built by Trajan at the mouth of the Tiber, from where they were shipped on smaller galleys up river to the capital. Goods were carried by ship wherever possible, as this was much cheaper and faster than road transport. Rome imported food and raw materials from all over its empire. Marble for the pillars and statues that graced the city's temples and palaces often came from as far afield as Greece and Africa. Unusual imports included *garum*, a fermented fish sauce which the Romans used, much like ketchup, to add flavor to a wide variety of dishes, and murex, a shellfish that produced the purple dye used for imperial togas. To give an idea of the volume of goods imported to the city, Mons Testaceus, a large hill, 165 ft in height, was created in imperial times from the shards of broken amphorae from the rows of warehouses that lined the banks of the Tiber in the southwest of the city.

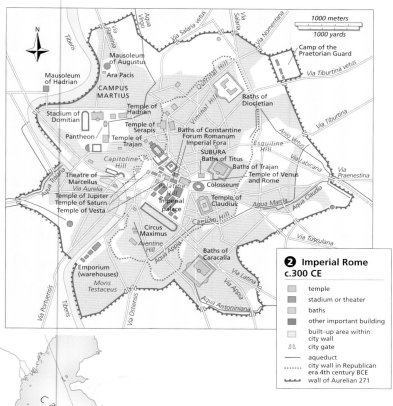

② Imperial Rome c.300 CE

- temple
- stadium or theater
- baths
- other important building
- built-up area within city wall
- city gate
- aqueduct
- city wall in Republican era 4th century BCE
- wall of Aurelian 271

③ Supply routes to Rome

- —— major shipping route
- major grain-producing region
- wine
- olive oil
- garum (fish sauce)
- honey
- slaves
- horses
- wool
- flax/linen
- murex (purple dye)
- marble
- timber
- gold
- tin
- copper

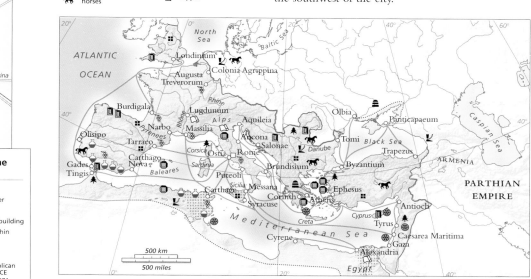

The Tetrarchy of Diocletian and the final division of the Empire

In the 3rd century CE the Empire was threatened by invasions by the Persians and Germanic peoples and by breakaway states such as the Kingdom of Palmyra. To counter this, Diocletian (284–305) and Constantine (307–337) reorganized the imperial administration. The existing provinces were divided into 100 smaller units, grouped in twelve larger regions called dioceses, each governed by a vicar. To share responsibility for defending the empire and to provide for an orderly succession, Diocletian established the Tetrarchy: two emperors with the title Augustus, one in the east, one in the west, each assisted by a junior emperor with the title of Caesar.

c.250: Period of civil wars and runaway inflation
270: Palmyra extends rule to Egypt
293: Diocletian establishes Tetrarchy and twelve dioceses
324: Constantine sole ruler
337: Constantine's death leads to fresh struggles over succession
395: Definitive division of empire into east and west on death of Theodosius

260: Gallic empire established by Postumus
273: Empire reunited by Aurelian
305: Abdication of Diocletian
312: Battle of Milvian Bridge, just north of Rome; Constantine defeats rival Maxentius
364: Rome loses war for control of Armenia to Sassanian Empire
378: Battle of Adrianople. Visigoths defeat Romans

The later Roman Empire 250–400 CE

④ The Roman Empire 240–395 CE

Parts of Empire ruled by:
- Diocletian
- Maximian
- Galerius
- Constantius
- □ principal residences of the tetrarchs
- Gallic Empire of Postumus 260–74 CE
- Kingdom of Palmyra 260–72 CE
- territory abandoned by Rome, with date
- —— division of Eastern and Western Empires 395 CE
- ····· boundary of Roman Empire 293 CE
- PONTUS diocese established by Diocletian 293 CE

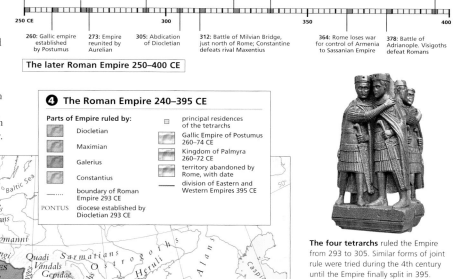

The four tetrarchs ruled the Empire from 293 to 305. Similar forms of joint rule were tried during the 4th century until the Empire finally split in 395.

This gold coin shows the heads of Diocletian and Maximian, first co-rulers of the Roman Empire.

This floor mosaic of Orpheus decorated a villa in Daphne, a wealthy suburb of Antioch, capital of the province of Syria.

EUROPE AFTER THE FALL OF ROME

THE END OF THE WESTERN ROMAN EMPIRE in 476 did not signal an immediate descent into barbarism. The rulers of the new kingdoms maintained relations with the eastern emperor in Constantinople, and most pretended to govern on his behalf. In much of western Europe, Roman laws and institutions were retained and, sooner or later, the so-called "barbarians" all converted to Christianity. The Eastern Roman (Byzantine) Empire continued to exert influence in the west. In the 6th century, Justinian, the most powerful emperor of the period, won back some of the Western Roman Empire. But, after failing to halt the Lombard invasion of Italy in 568, the Byzantines were unable to reassert their authority. The eventual successors to the Romans in the west were the Franks and the papacy.

This glass drinking horn would have been used at feasts of the Lombard rulers of Italy.

The kingdoms of the new order

On the death of the emperor Theodosius in 395, the Roman Empire was divided definitively in two. The 5th century saw the transfer of power in western Europe from the emperors to Germanic immigrants, for the most part groups recruited by the Romans to help them defend their lands (see pp.52–53). Chief beneficiaries were the Goths. By 480 the Visigoths had established a large kingdom in Aquitaine and Iberia, with its capital at Toulouse. In 492 the Ostrogoths took Italy and the Dalmatian coast.

Christianity maintained a sense of continuity between the Western Roman Empire and the kingdoms that replaced it. This late Roman sarcophagus is from Ravenna, capital of the Ostrogoths, successors to the Romans in Italy.

Classis was the port of Ravenna, capital of Ostrogothic and Byzantine Italy. This detail from a 6th-century mosaic shows the castle and ships riding at anchor in the harbor.

Europe in 500

One of the most powerful of the new kingdoms established in western Europe in 500 was that of Theodoric the Great, leader of the Ostrogoths. Though he ruled from Ravenna, the Senate still sat in Rome and relations between Romans and Goths were largely amicable. Royal marriages helped forge alliances with the Vandal and Visigothic kings in North Africa and Iberia. Theodoric hoped to create a power bloc to counter the might of the Eastern Roman Empire, but after his death in 526 he was succeeded by his infant grandson, who died young, and the dynasty collapsed.

① The inheritors of the Roman Empire at 500
- Frankish expansion
- Ostrogothic expansion
- Byzantine reconquests
- Sassanian expansion

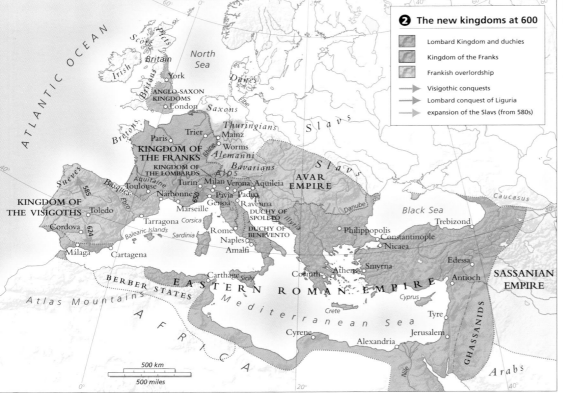

② The new kingdoms at 600
- Lombard Kingdom and duchies
- Kingdom of the Franks
- Frankish overlordship
- Visigothic conquests
- Lombard conquest of Liguria
- expansion of the Slavs (from 580s)

This Visigothic cross dates from the 6th century. Although Christian, the Visigoths were Arians (they denied the Trinity). This changed in 589, when King Reccared converted to the orthodox Catholicism of his Hispano-Roman subjects.

Europe in 600

The political map of Europe changed dramatically in the 6th century. In 600 the Visigoths still controlled the Iberian peninsula, but the Franks now ruled most of modern France. The Eastern Roman Empire had reconquered North Africa, Italy, Illyria, and even part of southern Iberia. The destruction of the Roman heritage was far greater during the long war waged by the Byzantines against the Goths than during the previous century. Italy then fell prey to the Lombards (Langobardi), Germanic invaders from the northeast.

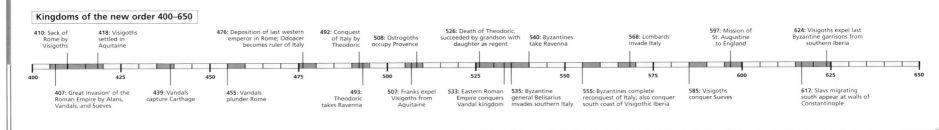

Kingdoms of the new order 400–650

410: Sack of Rome by Visigoths
418: Visigoths settled in Aquitaine
476: Deposition of last western emperor in Rome; Odoacer becomes ruler of Italy
492: Conquest of Italy by Theodoric
508: Ostrogoths occupy Provence
526: Death of Theodoric; succeeded by grandson with daughter as regent
540: Byzantines take Ravenna
568: Lombards invade Italy
597: Mission of St. Augustine to England
624: Visigoths expel last Byzantine garrisons from southern Iberia

407: 'Great Invasion' of the Roman Empire by Alans, Vandals, and Sueves
439: Vandals capture Carthage
455: Vandals plunder Rome
493: Theodoric takes Ravenna
507: Franks expel Visigoths from Aquitaine
533: Eastern Roman Empire conquers Vandal kingdom
535: Byzantine general Belisarius invades southern Italy
555: Byzantines complete reconquest of Italy; also conquer south coast of Visigothic Iberia
585: Visigoths conquer Sueves
617: Slavs migrating south appear at walls of Constantinople

❸ Britain c.750 ▶

- Anglo-Saxon kingdoms
- Mercia and dependencies
- Celtic kingdoms
- Pictish kingdoms
- ✗ battle
- † important monastery

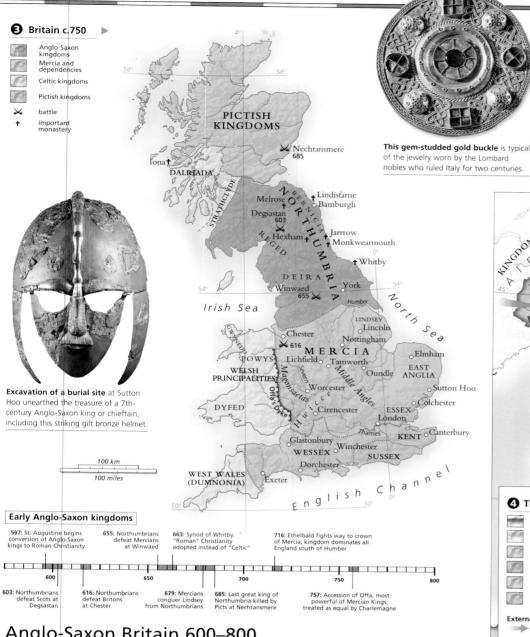

Excavation of a burial site at Sutton Hoo unearthed the treasure of a 7th-century Anglo-Saxon king or chieftain, including this striking gilt bronze helmet.

100 km
100 miles

This gem-studded gold buckle is typical of the jewelry worn by the Lombard nobles who ruled Italy for two centuries.

Byzantine and Lombard Italy

After the expulsion of the Goths, control of Italy was contested by the Byzantines and the Lombards, the latter gradually winning more and more territory after their invasion of 568. Only rarely did the Lombard kings, based at Pavia, exercise authority over the southern dukedoms of Benevento and Spoleto. Similarly, representatives of Byzantium, including the pope, often acted independently according to their own interests. The Byzantines were ousted from Ravenna in 751, but Lombard rule there lasted only until 756. At the pope's request, Pepin, king of the Franks, invaded northern Italy and crushed the Lombards.

Following Lombard invasion of Italy in 568, their former territories are occupied by Avars and Slavs

❹ The struggle for Italy 565–750

- East Roman Empire 565
- Lombard territories 565
- under Lombard rule 590
- Lombard gains by 650
- Lombard gains by 744
- East Roman territory 744

External threats to Italy in the 7th century
- → Franks
- → Avars and Slavs

100 km
100 miles

Early Anglo-Saxon kingdoms

597: St. Augustine begins conversion of Anglo-Saxon kings to Roman Christianity
655: Northumbrians defeat Mercians at Winwaed
663: Synod of Whitby. "Roman" Christianity adopted instead of "Celtic"
716: Ethelbald fights way to crown of Mercia; kingdom dominates all England south of Humber

600 | 650 | 700 | 750 | 800

603: Northumbrians defeat Scots at Degsastan
616: Northumbrians defeat Britons at Chester
679: Mercians conquer Lindsey from Northumbrians
685: Last great king of Northumbria killed by Picts at Nechtansmere
757: Accession of Offa, most powerful of Mercian Kings; treated as equal by Charlemagne

Anglo-Saxon Britain 600–800

For the two centuries that followed the Roman withdrawal in 410, there are no reliable accounts of events in Britain. The Celtic Britons fought each other, as well as Scottish invaders (from Ireland) and Angles, Saxons, and Jutes, who invaded across the North Sea from Denmark and north Germany. Around 600, following St Augustine's mission from Rome to convert the Anglo-Saxons, records appear of a number of kingdoms ruled by Anglo-Saxon kings (though some of these have British names). The west, notably Wales and West Wales (Dumnonia), remained in the hands of Celts. For most of the 7th century, the most powerful kingdom was Northumbria, whose kings briefly controlled much of Scotland. By 700, however, supremacy had passed to the midland kingdom of Mercia.

The struggle for Italy 550–750

568: Lombard invasion of Italy
590–604: Papacy of Gregory the Great, who negotiates with Lombards to save Rome
653: Conversion of Lombards to Christianity
712: Liutprand becomes Lombard king; tries to unite Italy
751: Lombards under Aistulf take Ravenna; end of Byzantine rule
753–56: Italy invaded by Pepin

550 | 600 | 650 | 700 | 750

554: Frankish invasion defeated; Italy under Byzantine control
643: Edict of Rothari: first book of Lombard law
663: Byzantine Emperor Constans II invades Italy and sacks Rome
773–74: Conquest of Lombards by Charlemagne; northern Italy comes under Frankish rule

The early Frankish kingdoms 481–650

The only Germanic kingdom of any permanence established in this period was the Kingdom of the Franks, foundation of modern France. The first Frankish dynasty, the Merovingians, expanded from lands around Tournai under Clovis, who pushed southwest to the Loire, then defeated the Visigoths in Aquitaine. Clovis's sons destroyed the Burgundians and exercised control over several Germanic tribes to the east. When a powerful king such as Clovis died, his territories were divided between his heirs, provoking dynastic civil wars. The three major kingdoms were Neustria and Austrasia (together referred to as Francia), and Burgundy.

Dagobert I's throne is a powerful emblem of the continuity of the French kingdom, which lasted till the Revolution in 1790.

200 km
200 miles

❺ The Kingdom of the Franks 486–537

- Frankish lands 486
- conquered by Clovis by 507
- conquered by 511
- Kingdom of Franks at the death of Clovis 511
- conquered by Clovis's sons 534
- conquered by Clovis's sons 537
- ✗ battle

The early Frankish kingdoms 481–650

c.481: Accession of Clovis I
c.497: Clovis converts to Christianity
558: Chlothar I sole king of the Franks
573: Beginning of major civil wars between the Franks
629: Chlothar II dies; succeeded by son, Dagobert I,
639: Death of Dagobert; kingdom divided between two sons

450 | 500 | 550 | 600 | 650

507: Clovis defeats Visigoths at Vouillé
511: Death of Clovis; his kingdom divided between four sons
561: Death of Chlothar I; kingdom divided between his four sons
613: Chlothar II king of all Gaul; civil wars end

❻ Division of the Frankish kingdoms 561 ▶

- Charibert
- Sigebert
- Guntram
- Chilperic
- territory of Frankish overlordship
- ○ royal residence

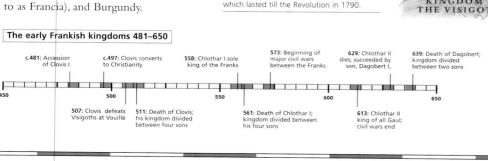

EUROPE IN THE AGE OF THE CRUSADES

Emperor Frederick
Barbarossa is shown in Crusader dress. He drowned in 1190 on his way to the Third Crusade.

FOLLOWING THE SUCCESS of the First Crusade *(see pp. 64–65)*, the spirit of the venture captured the imagination of Christian Europe. Expeditions to subdue the pagans of the Baltic and campaigns against the Muslims in Iberia were undertaken with papal blessing. Ideals of chivalry inspired the new religious orders of warrior clerics established to protect pilgrims to the Holy Land, such as the Templars and Hospitallers. These organizations became immensely wealthy with hundreds of priories and estates in Europe. At the same time, it was a period of great intellectual excitement. The rediscovery of Classical texts inspired an interest in philosophy; universities were founded and new religious orders gave renewed energy to the Catholic Church.

The crusading ideal in Europe

The Knights Templar were so well rewarded for their services in the Holy Land that they became a powerful political force throughout Europe.

The ideal of Holy War which inspired the Crusaders to fight in the Iberian Peninsula and the Holy Land was used to justify other wars, conflicts, and even racist atrocities. In 1096, German mobs attacked and massacred as "unbelievers" the Jews in their own communities. Missionary efforts to convert the pagan peoples of Livonia, Lithuania, and Prussia became a crusade, preached by Pope Innocent III. One crusade was mounted against "heretics" within Christian Europe – the Cathars (Albigensians) of southern France. In 1212 a French shepherd boy even set out to lead a children's crusade to Jerusalem. Most of his followers got no further than Genoa and Marseille.

The crusading ideal

1118: Founder of Knights Templar granted site close to Solomon's temple in Jerusalem
1126: Hospitallers of St. John adopt a military role
1208: Crusade against Cathars, or Albigensians, in southern France
1283: Conquest of Prussia completed by Teutonic Knights
1312: Templar Order accused of heresy and suppressed by Pope

1050 · 1100 · 1150 · 1200 · 1250 · 1300 · 1350

1096: Attacks on Jewish communities by Crusaders and their supporters
1197: Order of Teutonic Knights established in the Holy Land
1233: Inquisition established in Toulouse
1306–10: Hospitallers conquer Rhodes, which becomes their base

❶ The crusading ideal in Europe 1100–1300

- predominantly pagan lands c.1100
- Muslim lands c.1180
- main Cathar region
- Waldensian strongholds
- → direction of Reconquest in Spain

Crusades in the Baltic
- → Danish expeditions
- → Swedish expeditions
- → direction of advance of Sword Brothers
- → direction of advance of Teutonic Knights

Other crusades
- → Albigensian Crusade 1209–13
- → Children's Crusade 1212
- ✶ massacre of Jews 1096
- ⊕ major Templar house 1300
- ⊕ headquarters of crusading orders in Spain
- — frontiers 1180
- Holy Roman Empire
- first state of Teutonic Knights 1211–15

3650 km (2270 miles)
3890 km (2420 miles)

The Norman conquest of England

The Duchy of Normandy was established in northern France by 911. In 1066, William, Duke of Normandy led an expedition to win the English throne from Harold, the last Anglo-Saxon king. Harold had seen off the threat of another claimant, Harald Hardrada of Norway, but, after a long march south, he was defeated by William at Hastings. Once England had been conquered, it was parceled out in fiefs amongst William's Norman knights.

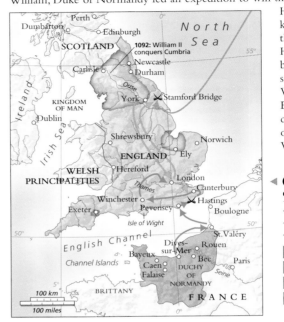

❷ The Norman conquest of England 1066–1095

- → Harald Hardrada's route 1066
- → Harold's route 1066
- → William's route 1066
- William's possessions 1066
- conquered by 1070
- additional conquest by 1095
- area of uprising against Norman rule c.1070
- ✕ battle

The Norman conquest of England 1066

5 Jan: Death of Edward the Confessor, king of England; Harold assumes throne
Apr: Harold's fleet drives off Tostig; guards English Channel until September
25 Sep: Harold defeats his brother Tostig and Harald Hardrada at Stamford Bridge
14 Oct: Battle of Hastings; Harold defeated and killed
25 Dec: William crowned in London

Jan 1066 · Apr 1066 · Jul 1066 · Oct 1066 · Jan 1067

Apr: Raids along south coast of England by Harold's exiled brother Tostig
Aug–Sep: William assembles fleet and army at Dives-sur-Mer
28 Sep: William lands at Pevensey

William's success depended on a large fleet to ship men and horses across the English Channel, but the Normans had long abandoned the seagoing life of their Viking forebears. Yet they managed to build a fleet, depicted here in a scene from the Bayeux Tapestry, large enough to transport an army of perhaps 7000 men to England.

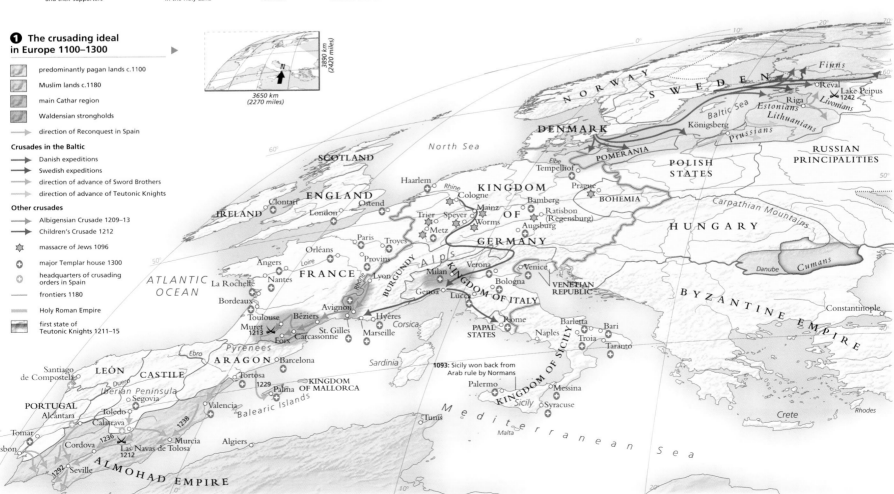

❸ The 12th-century renaissance in Europe ▶

- ▣ university with date of foundation
- ▣ other important theological school
- ▤ Muslim lands reconquered by Christians 1030–1200
- ▤ Muslim lands reconquered by Christians 1200–1300
- ○ center of contact with Arab scholarship
- † major Cistercian house with date of foundation
- ---- frontiers 1200
- ▬ Holy Roman Empire

c.1200: University of Paris has colleges for students from all over western Europe

1308: University of Lisbon transferred to Coimbra

The 12th-century renaissance

Christian idealism in this period was reflected in the growth of new monastic and teaching orders. The Cistercians, founded at Cîteaux in 1098, spread throughout Europe under the charismatic leadership of St. Bernard of Clairvaux. The early 13th century saw the even more rapid expansion of the orders founded by St. Francis of Assisi and St. Dominic. At the same time a renewed interest in scholarship led to the founding of new universities. The increased availability of the seminal texts of the ancient world, obtained through the medium of Arabic translations, was critically important for medieval scholars. By reconciling the science of Aristotle with Christian faith, St. Thomas Aquinas (d. 1274) gave Catholic theology an intellectual basis that lasted for centuries.

The Cistercians were founded in reaction to the idle life of monasteries financed by tithes. They worked their own land and were self-supporting, though they accepted gifts of marginal or recently conquered land. Their graceful architecture was plain and unadorned, as seen here in the refectory of Fountains Abbey in northern England.

The 12th-century renaissance

- **1098:** Foundation of new monastery at Cîteaux
- **1115:** Bernard founds Cistercian daughter house at Clairvaux
- **1126:** Birth of Muslim philosopher Averroes in Cordova
- **1158:** Frederick Barbarossa grants imperial protection to University of Bologna
- **1210:** St. Francis of Assisi gains papal recognition of his order of friars dedicated to poverty
- **1220:** First chapter of the Dominican order of friars
- **1249:** Foundation of Merton College, Oxford

`|1100|1150|1200|1250|1300|`

The Angevin Empire

The laws of inheritance of feudal Europe enabled Henry II, Count of Anjou and King of England, to acquire lands that included England, Ireland, and most of western France. His marriage to Eleanor of Aquitaine meant that he ruled more of France than the French king, even though he was nominally the latter's vassal. He spent much of his reign defending his empire against Louis VII of France and the ambitions of his children. After his death in 1189, the Angevin empire soon disintegrated. In 1214, Philip II of France defeated Henry's son, John, ending English rule in Normandy. England, however, did keep western Aquitaine, and, in the 14th century, would renew its claims to France in the Hundred Years' War.

English possessions 1154–89

- **1152:** Henry marries Eleanor of Aquitaine
- **1154:** Succession of Henry II to English crown
- **1151:** Henry succeeds Geoffrey as Count of Anjou
- **1173–74:** Henry quells French-backed rebellion by his sons
- **1189:** Succession of Richard the Lionheart
- **1199:** Accession of John
- **1214:** Defeat of English and German allies at Bouvines

`|1140|1160|1180|1200|1220|`

Henry II and Eleanor of Aquitaine had an intense, stormy relationship. She was imprisoned for intriguing against him on behalf of their eldest son Henry in 1173–74.

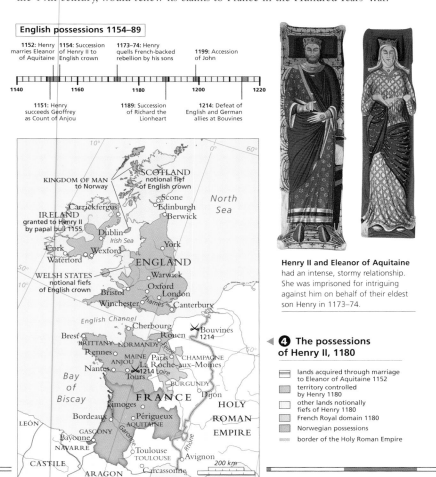

❹ The possessions of Henry II, 1180

- ▦ lands acquired through marriage to Eleanor of Aquitaine 1152
- ▦ territory controlled by Henry 1180
- ▢ other lands notionally fiefs of Henry 1180
- ▦ French Royal domain 1180
- ▦ Norwegian possessions
- ▬ border of the Holy Roman Empire

Venice and the Latin Empire

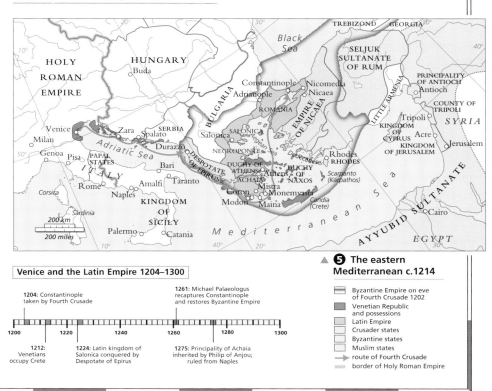

As well as being the principal emporium for east–west trade, Venice also made money shipping Crusaders to the Ho;y Land. When the Fourth Crusade gathered in Venice in 1203, the leaders did not have enough money to pay. The Venetians diverted the fleet first to capture the Adriatic port of Zara, long coveted by Venice, then to Constantinople, where in 1204, the Crusaders sacked the city and installed their own emperor. The Empire was divided into Venetian colonies and Latin fiefs. There were now two empires in the east; the "Latin" empire, ruled from Constantinople, and a rump Byzantine Empire, ruled from Nicaea.

The Crusaders' motive for attacking Constantinople in 1203 was financial reward for restoring Alexius IV (son of deposed emperor Isaac Angelus) to the imperial throne. When the population rebelled and killed Alexius in 1204, the Crusaders took over the city for themselves.

Venice and the Latin Empire 1204–1300

- **1204:** Constantinople taken by Fourth Crusade
- **1212:** Venetians occupy Crete
- **1224:** Latin kingdom of Salonica conquered by Despotate of Epirus
- **1261:** Michael Palaeologus recaptures Constantinople and restores Byzantine Empire
- **1275:** Principality of Achaia inherited by Philip of Anjou; ruled from Naples

`|1200|1220|1240|1260|1280|1300|`

▲ ❺ The eastern Mediterranean c.1214

- ▦ Byzantine Empire on eve of Fourth Crusade 1202
- ▦ Venetian Republic and possessions
- ▢ Latin Empire
- ▢ Crusader states
- ▢ Byzantine states
- ▢ Muslim states
- → route of Fourth Crusade
- ▬ border of Holy Roman Empire

EUROPE IN CRISIS

THE CONSOLIDATION of nation states on the eastern and western edges of Europe was matched, in the 13th century, by the decline of the Holy Roman Empire, its power depleted by long struggles with the papacy and the Italian city-states. In the east, raids by Mongols destroyed Kiev in 1240, and Russia, subject to Mongol overlords, developed in isolation until the 15th century. In the northeast, German colonization brought political and economic change, with a new trading axis around the Baltic Sea. During the 14th century, however, social unrest swept through Europe, compounded by famines, economic decline, dynastic wars, and the Black Death of 1347 *(see pp. 72–73)*, which wiped out a third of Europe's population in just two years.

The Empire and the papacy

Under the Hohenstaufen dynasty, the aspirations of the Holy Roman Emperors to universal authority were blocked by the papacy in central Italy, and the city-based communes of northern Italy. Emperor Frederick II (1211–50) clashed with Rome at a time when popes exercised great political power. After his death, the papacy gave the Kingdom of Sicily to Charles of Anjou, and Frederick's heirs were eliminated. Confronted with the growing power of France and England, the Empire lost any pretence to political supremacy in Europe; in Germany, a mosaic of clerical states, principalities, and free cities continued to undermine imperial authority.

Under Innocent III (1198–1216) the medieval papacy was at the height of its spiritual authority and temporal power.

England, Scotland, and Wales

The Scottish king, Robert Bruce, pictured here with his second wife, was a noble of Norman descent like his English enemies.

After a century of peace along the Anglo-Scottish border, Edward I (1272–1307) set out to assert his overlordship over all the British Isles. In 1284 he annexed Wales, bestowing the title of Prince of Wales on his son, but Scotland proved more intractable; Edward's attempts to subdue the Scots were met with resistance led by Robert Bruce, the victor at Bannockburn (1314). Hoping to extend his domains, Bruce sent an expedition to Ireland in 1315. His brother Edward continued fighting there until his death in 1318. In 1328, after a devastating period of guerrilla warfare and border raiding, England acknowledged Scottish independence.

England, Scotland, and Wales 1284–1337

1284: Edward I invades Wales	**1305:** Execution of William Wallace, Scottish nationalist leader
	1322: Scottish barons assert independence in Declaration of Arbroath
	1329: Death of Robert Bruce
	1337: Start of Hundred Years' War; Scots ally with French against England

1280	1290	1300	1310	1320	1330	1340	1350

1296: Edward I invades Scotland
1314: English defeated at Bannockburn
1318: Edward Bruce killed in Ireland
1328: Scottish independence confirmed by Treaty of Northampton

▼ ② The British Isles 1200–1400

100 km
100 miles

—	frontiers 1070
	to England 1092; to Scotland 1136
	southern limit of Scotland 1139–57
	to Scotland from Norway 1266
	northern limit of English control 1400
	Welsh Principalities, brought under English control gradually by 1247
→	campaigns of Edward I, with dates
→	Robert Bruce's campaign 1307–08
	region affected by Edward Bruce's invasions of Ireland 1315–18
MIDHE	Irish overkingdom c.1100
	Irish states brought under English control by Papal grant 1155; subdued gradually from 1169
	autonomous Irish chiefdoms 1300
	core area of Peasants' Revolt 1381

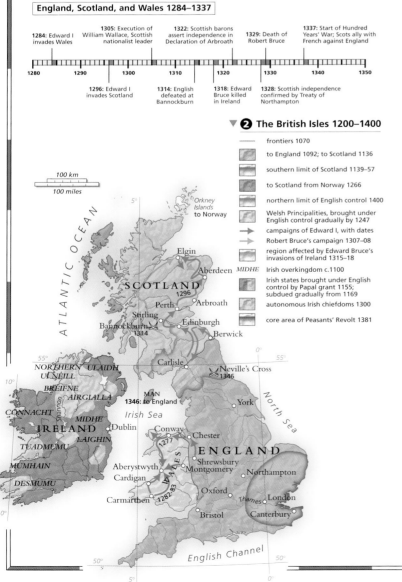

① The Empire of Frederick II ▲

	frontier of Holy Roman Empire 1250
	Kingdom of Germany
	Kingdom of Italy
	under effective Hohenstaufen control 1250
	German lands largely under imperial or Hohenstaufen ownership
	Papal States 1178
	added by 1219
	added by 1278
	Venetian Republic and possessions
●	member of Lombard League 1167
—	frontiers 1250

The Hohenstaufens and the papacy

1167: Lombard League formed to oppose Emperor Frederick I Barbarossa in northern Italy
1198: Accession of Pope Innocent III
1211: Frederick II becomes Emperor
1245: Innocent IV excommunicates Frederick
1268: Charles of Anjou defeats Conradin, Frederick's grandson, at Tagliacozzo
1282: Sicilian Vespers; Charles of Anjou defeated by Aragonese

1150	1170	1190	1210	1230	1250	1270	1290	1310

1194: Emperor Henry VI crowned King of Sicily
1237: Frederick II defeats Italian communes at Cortenuova
1250: Death of Frederick
1305: Pope Clement V takes up residency at Avignon, under French supervision

Eastward expansion in the Baltic

A German-led wave of migration, from 1100–1350, transformed eastern and Baltic Europe. As peasants moved east in search of land and resources, German language and law became predominant; New towns were bound together in the Hanseatic League, a trading association with links from Muscovy to London. Crusades in the east were spearheaded by the Knights of the Teutonic Order, who began to wage war on the pagans of Prussia and Lithuania in 1226. They also took over the Sword Brothers' lands in Livonia. The Livonians and Prussians were subdued, but Lithuania expanded to the southeast to become a powerful state. It was united with Poland in 1386.

Marienburg was the headquarters of the Teutonic Knights from 1309. Part abbey, part fortress, it was built of brick like many of the castles erected by the crusading order in Prussia and Livonia.

The Baltic 1200–1400

c.1200: Bishopric of Riga established
1242: Russians defeat Teutonic Knights at Lake Peipus
1309: Teutonic Order's subjugation of Prussia complete
1386: Poland and Lithuania joined through marriage alliance

1200 — 1250 — 1300 — 1350 — 1400

1226: Teutonic Knights invited to crusade in Prussia
1237: Start of Mongol invasion of Russia
1342: Death of Gedymin, founder of Lithuania

▲ ❸ **The Baltic states 1100–1400**

- frontier of Kievan Rus c.1100
- Holy Roman Empire, 1100
- added to Holy Roman Empire by 1380
- Sweden
- added to Sweden by 1323
- main thrusts of Danish expansion
- under Danish control c.1225
- eastern frontier of ethnic German settlement 1100
- frontier of ethnic German settlement 1400
- possessions of the Hungarian Angevins
- ○ member of Hanseatic League (not all shown)
- ---- frontiers 1380

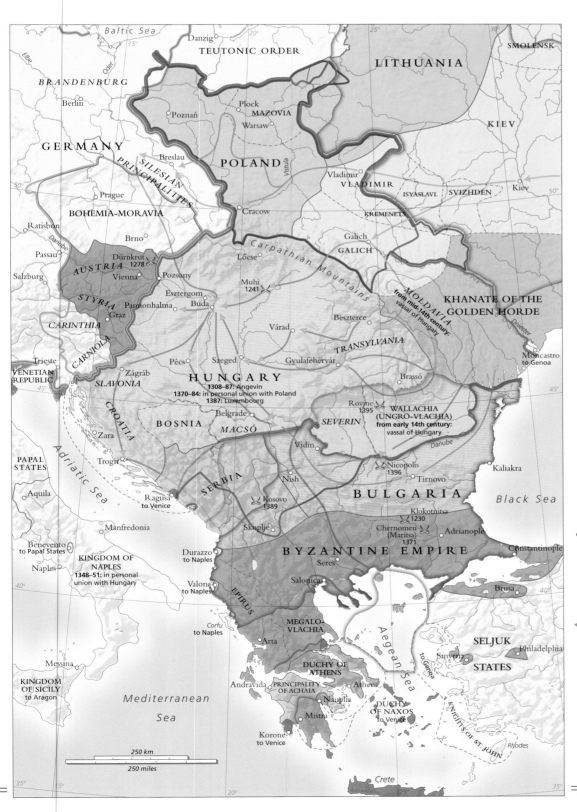

Central and southeastern Europe

After the setbacks of the early 13th century, when eastern Europe was devastated by Mongol invasions, the consolidation of powerful new states began. In Bohemia, the imperial ambitions of Ottakar II (1253–78) briefly expanded his domain from Silesia to the Adriatic, but he came into conflict with Bohemian and German princes, and the Habsburgs were able to seize power in Austria on his death. Powerful monarchies were established in Lithuania under Gedymin (c.1315–42), in Poland under Casimir the Great (1333–70), and in Hungary under Louis the Great (1342–82). Bohemia under the Luxembourg dynasty remained an influential state, especially when the king was elected as the Emperor Charles IV. In the Balkans, Stefan Dušan (1331–55) forged for himself a substantial Serbian Empire, but it fell to the Ottomans in 1389.

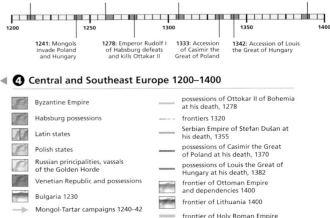

The Emperor Charles IV is shown with his Electors. His Golden Bull of 1356 set out clear rules for electing the emperor.

Central and southeastern Europe 1200–1400

1212: Golden Bull establishes Kingdom of Bohemia
1260: Ottakar II of Bohemia defeats Bela IV of Hungary
1306: Luxembourg dynasty acquires Bohemia
1389: Battle of Kosovo; Ottomans gain control of Balkans

1200 — 1250 — 1300 — 1350 — 1400

1241: Mongols invade Poland and Hungary
1278: Emperor Rudolf I of Habsburg defeats and kills Ottakar II
1333: Accession of Casimir the Great of Poland
1342: Accession of Louis the Great of Hungary

◀ ❹ **Central and Southeast Europe 1200–1400**

- Byzantine Empire
- Habsburg possessions
- Latin states
- Polish states
- Russian principalities, vassals of the Golden Horde
- Venetian Republic and possessions
- Bulgaria 1230
- → Mongol-Tartar campaigns 1240–42
- possessions of Ottakar II of Bohemia at his death, 1278
- ---- frontiers 1320
- Serbian Empire of Stefan Dušan at his death, 1355
- possessions of Casimir the Great of Poland at his death, 1370
- possessions of Louis the Great of Hungary at his death, 1382
- frontier of Ottoman Empire and dependencies 1400
- frontier of Lithuania 1400
- frontier of Holy Roman Empire

TRADE IN MEDIEVAL EUROPE

The seal of Lübeck shows a cog, the ship used for large cargoes in northern Europe.

THE EXPLOSION IN EUROPE'S POPULATION, which nearly doubled between the 10th and 14th centuries, was caused by greatly increased agricultural productivity, enhanced by technological innovations, in particular the use of the iron plow, and large land clearance projects, which brought marginal land, such as marshes and forests, under cultivation. This demographic surge inevitably led to increased trading activity; merchants traversed the continent, using the trans-Alpine passes which provided arterial routes between Italy and the North and, from c.1300, new maritime routes which opened up the North and Baltic seas. Trade and commerce went hand in hand with urban development. Commercial wealth had a cultural impact; cities were enhanced with magnificent buildings and churches and, from c.1200, universities. As cities prospered, a new class, the bourgeoisie, emerged.

Medieval trade

From the 11th century the Alpine passes had linked the textile towns of Lombardy and manufacturing centers of the Po valley with northern Europe, rich in natural resources, such as timber, grain, wool, and metals. Merchants converged from all over Europe to trade at vast seasonal fairs. International bankers, such as the Florentine Peruzzi, facilitated payments and promoted business. Around 1300, the Genoese opened a new sea route to the North Sea through the Strait of Gibraltar; Bruges, at the end of the route, became a major city. In the Mediterranean, Genoa competed with Venice for the carrying trade. Venice controlled the valuable eastern routes, profiting from trade in silks, sugar, spices, and gemstones from India and East Asia. In northern Germany, an association of trading cities centered on Lübeck, the Hanseatic League, promoted monopolies and sought exclusive trading rights with towns in England, Scandinavia, and Flanders.

Italian towns

Northern Italy was well-endowed with populous, wealthy cities, such as Milan and Florence. The Italian cities did not develop under the direct rule of kings, emperors, or the nobility, and took advantage of this to assert their municipal rights, evolving their own constitutions, codes of law, and military forces, the "communal movement."

The textile industry flourished in Flanders and northern Italy. The horizontal loom (above) was introduced to Europe in the 11th century.

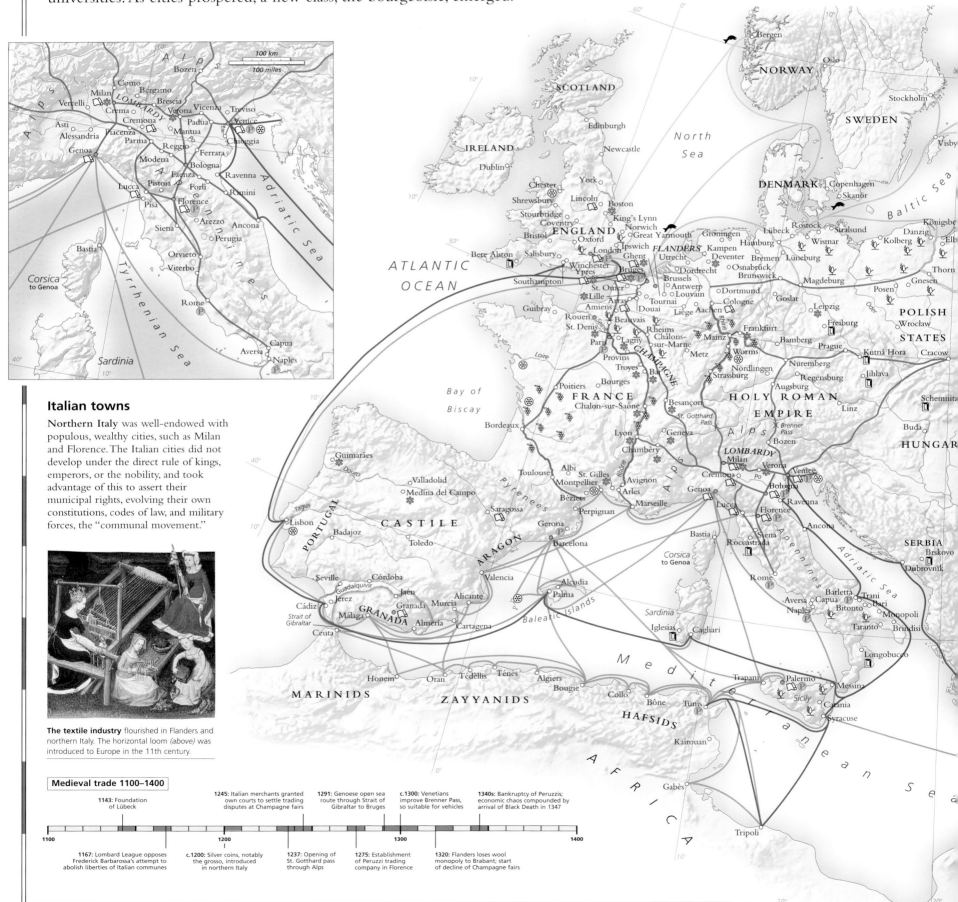

Medieval trade 1100–1400

1143: Foundation of Lübeck	**1245:** Italian merchants granted own courts to settle trading disputes at Champagne fairs	**1291:** Genoese open sea route through Strait of Gibraltar to Bruges	**c.1300:** Venetians improve Brenner Pass, so suitable for vehicles	**1340s:** Bankruptcy of Peruzzis; economic chaos compounded by arrival of Black Death in 1347

1100 — 1200 — 1300 — 1400

1167: Lombard League opposes Frederick Barbarossa's attempt to abolish liberties of Italian communes

c.1200: Silver coins, notably the grosso, introduced in northern Italy

1237: Opening of St. Gotthard pass through Alps

1275: Establishment of Peruzzi trading company in Florence

1320: Flanders loses wool monopoly to Brabant; start of decline of Champagne fairs

MONEY AND BANKING

Many gold and silver currencies circulated freely in Medieval Europe, irrespective of where they were minted, so money changing was inevitably an important profession. Traveling merchants left currency on deposit with money changers in exchange for a receipt, the first stage in the evolution of banking. By the 14th century the use of the bill of exchange, where one person instructs another to pay a sum of money to a third party, was widespread. The organization of bills of exchange was lucrative, and banking families, such as the Peruzzi and Bardi of Florence, became rich and powerful.

Venetian coinage included the silver grosso and the widely circulated gold ducat.

Medieval Italy gave the world the word "bank" from the *banco* (counter) where bankers transacted their business, as shown in this 14th-century illustration.

Medieval cities

Many of the cities of Medieval Europe owed their development to trade and commerce. The cities of northern Italy emerged from the 10th century onward, as entrepôts in the trade between Europe, Byzantium, and the Islamic world. In the 13th century, the demand for manufactured goods, such as glassware, textiles, and metalwork, led to the emergence of industrial centers, notably the Lombard textile towns and the wool centers of Flanders, such as Ghent, Bruges, and Ypres. By the mid-13th century, German expansion eastward had led to the growth of a thriving network of Baltic trading cities, including Lübeck, Hamburg, Danzig, and Riga.

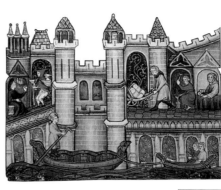

The Seine was vital to the economy of Paris. Boats of all sizes delivered goods along the river and the fortified bridges carried a constant flow of traders.

② Paris c.1400

- university and colleges
- other important building
- built-up area
- + church
- ⌒⌒ city gate
- ⚔ wall of Philip Augustus c.1200
- ⚔ wall of Charles V 1357

Medieval Paris

From the 11th century, Paris benefited from the return of order and stability under the Capetian kings. Streets were paved, city walls enlarged and three "divisions" of the city emerged; the merchants were based on the right bank of the Seine, the university (recognized in 1200) on the left bank, with civic and religious institutions on the Île de la Cité. In the 14th century, however, the city stagnated under the dual blows of the Black Death *(see pp. 72–73)* and the Hundred Years' War; repeatedly fought over by the contending forces, it was beset by riots and civil disorder.

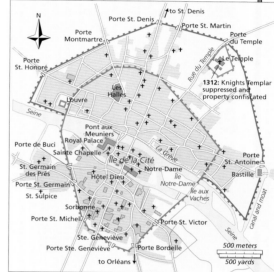

Medieval Paris

c.1200: Paris undergoes improvements; streets are paved

1257: Foundation of Sorbonne; it soon becomes most famous college of Paris University

1382: Tax riot is brutally suppressed; municipal government suspended

1100 — 1200 — 1300 — 1400

1171: King Louis VII grants river-merchants' guild a monopoly of river trade

1220: Citizens of Paris granted right to collect import duty

1356: Provost of merchants, Étienne Marcel, takes over running of Paris and orders building of new city wall

Medieval Venice

Venice was perceived as the symbolic center of a liberal government and divinely ordered religious, civic, and commercial life. Its political focus was the Doge's Palace, residence of the elected Doge and center of government. Since the city's wealth depended on maritime trade, the government maintained a vast shipyard – the Darsena – to build galleys for war and for merchant ventures.

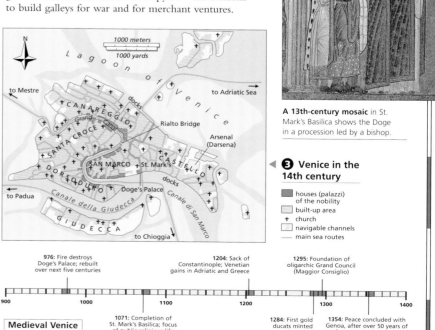

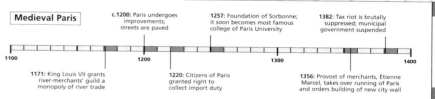

A 13th-century mosaic in St. Mark's Basilica shows the Doge in a procession led by a bishop.

❸ Venice in the 14th century

- houses (palazzi) of the nobility
- built-up area
- + church
- navigable channels
- main sea routes

976: Fire destroys Doge's Palace; rebuilt over next five centuries

1204: Sack of Constantinople; Venetian gains in Adriatic and Greece

1295: Foundation of oligarchic Grand Council (Maggior Consiglio)

900 — 1000 — 1200 — 1300 — 1400

Medieval Venice

1071: Completion of St. Mark's Basilica; focus of public religious life

1284: First gold ducats minted in Venice

1354: Peace concluded with Genoa, after over 50 years of warfare over trade supremacy

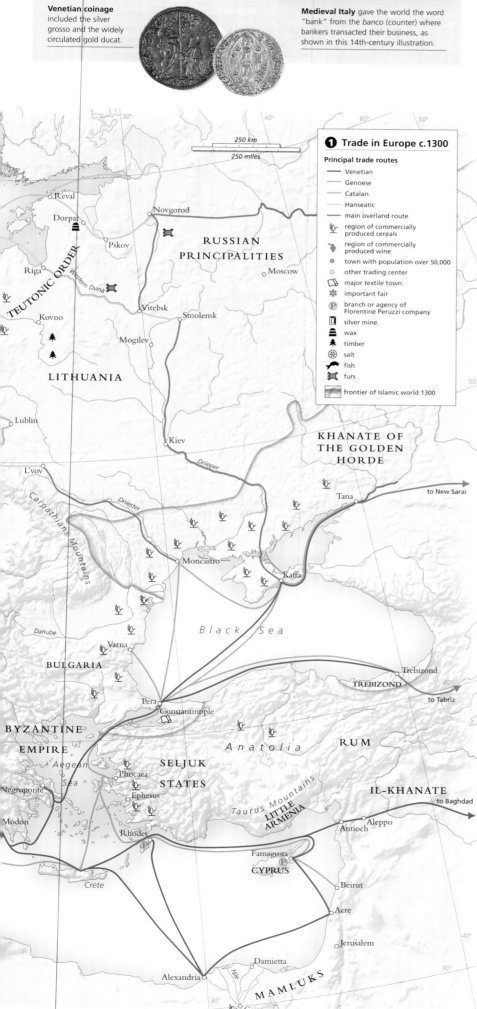

① Trade in Europe c.1300

Principal trade routes
— Venetian
— Genoese
— Catalan
— Hanseatic
— main overland route
- region of commercially produced cereals
- region of commercially produced wine
- ● town with population over 50,000
- ○ other trading center
- major textile town
- important fair
- branch or agency of Florentine Peruzzi company
- silver mine
- wax
- timber
- salt
- fish
- furs
- frontier of Islamic world 1300

Reval
Dorpat
Riga
Pskov
Novgorod
RUSSIAN PRINCIPALITIES
Moscow
TEUTONIC ORDER
Kovno
Vitebsk
Smolensk
Mogilev
LITHUANIA
Western Dvina
Lublin
Kiev
L'vov
Dnieper
KHANATE OF THE GOLDEN HORDE
Carpathians Mountains
Dniester
Tana
to New Sarai
Moncastro
Kaffa
Danube
Black Sea
Varna
BULGARIA
Trebizond
TREBIZOND
Pera
Constantinople
to Tabriz
BYZANTINE EMPIRE
Anatolia
RUM
Aegean Sea
SELJUK STATES
IL-KHANATE
to Baghdad
Negroponte
Phocaea
Ephesus
Taurus Mountains
LITTLE ARMENIA
Modon
Aleppo
Rhodes
Antioch
Crete
Famagusta
CYPRUS
Beirut
Acre
Jerusalem
Damietta
Alexandria
MAMLUKS
Nile
Cairo

250 km
250 miles

EARLY MODERN EUROPE

Cardinal Richelieu, was Louis XIII's chief minister and the architect of royal absolutism in France.

IN THE 17TH CENTURY, following years of destructive warfare, the modern European state system began to evolve. States were ruled centrally by autocratic (or absolutist) monarchs and bounded by clear, militarily secure frontiers. The Thirty Years' War laid waste large parts of central Europe, causing a decline in population from some 21 million in 1618 to 13 million in 1648. Under Louis XIV, France was involved in four costly wars, but emerged as the leading nation in Europe, eclipsing Spain, which entered a long period of decline. After a period of expansion under the Vasa kings, Sweden lost much of its Baltic empire by 1721. The Ottoman Turks struck once again at the heart of Europe, but were met by an increasingly powerful Austria, whose main rival in the region was Russia.

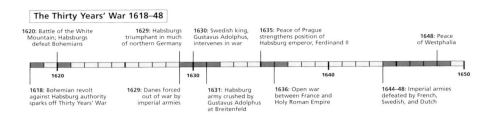

The Thirty Years' War 1618–48

1620: Battle of the White Mountain; Habsburgs defeat Bohemians

1629: Habsburgs triumphant in much of northern Germany

1630: Swedish king, Gustavus Adolphus, intervenes in war

1635: Peace of Prague strengthens position of Habsburg emperor, Ferdinand II

1648: Peace of Westphalia

1618: Bohemian revolt against Habsburg authority sparks off Thirty Years' War

1629: Danes forced out of war by imperial armies

1631: Habsburg army crushed by Gustavus Adolphus at Breitenfeld

1636: Open war between France and Holy Roman Empire

1644–48: Imperial armies defeated by French, Swedish, and Dutch

The Thirty Years' War

The Thirty Years' War provoked great advances in methods of mass destruction, and involved an unprecedented number of soldiers, over a million of whom died before it ceased. Much of Germany was devastated, towns were sacked, and their inhabitants raped and murdered.

The Thirty Years' War saw Protestant-Catholic rivalry and German constitutional issues subsumed in a wider European struggle. Habsburg attempts to control Bohemia and crush Protestantism coincided with the breakdown of constitutional mechanisms for resolving conflict in the Holy Roman Empire. Spain intervened to secure supply lines to the Netherlands; Danish and Swedish involvement followed as they competed for control of the Baltic. Fear of imperial absolutism, prompted by Austrian Habsburg victories in 1621 and 1634–35, led France to intervene in 1635 in support of Sweden. Prolonged negotiations from 1643 culminated in the Treaty of Westphalia, which fused attempts to secure peace in Europe with curbs on the emperor's authority in Germany.

① The Treaty of Westphalia, 1648

- Austrian Habsburg possessions
- Spanish Habsburg possessions
- Brandenburg possessions
- Danish possessions
- Swedish possessions
- Church lands
- ✠ electorate
- boundary of Holy Roman Empire, 1648
- frontiers 1648
- ⚔ major battle of Thirty Years' War

Political consolidation and resistance

European states were transformed in a process of internal political centralization and external consolidation. The legitimacy of these developments was often questioned, leading to civil wars and popular resistance. Foreign intervention turned local disputes into international conflicts, as in the Thirty Years' War. In western Europe, Spain's dominant position was broken by Portuguese and Dutch independence. The two rising powers in the region, France and England, developed in very different ways. In France, Louis XIV assumed absolute power, while in England, Charles I was arrested and executed for disregarding parliament, and although the English monarchy was restored, its powers were drastically curbed.

② Political consolidation and resistance in 17th-century Europe

- Austrian Habsburg possessions 1683
- Spanish Habsburg possessions 1683
- ⚔ civil war or widespread disturbance
- ⚔ local revolt or unrest
- civic autonomy suppressed by territorial rulers
- frontiers 1683
- Holy Roman empire 1683

Expansionist tendencies
- → Sweden
- → Russia
- → England
- → Ottoman Empire
- → Austrian Habsburgs
- → France
- → United Provinces

The union of Spain and Portugal was ended in 1640 when the native House of Braganza led a nationalist revolt. The relief of the siege of the frontier town of Elvas during the War of Independence is depicted in a Portuguese tile painting *(above)*.

As one of the leading generals of the Parliamentary army, Oliver Cromwell *(left)* played a decisive role in the English Civil War. After the execution of Charles I, he quelled the Royalists in Scotland and Ireland. Dissolving the "Rump" Parliament, he became Lord Protector of the Commonwealth.

Civil wars and revolts 1625–65

1628–29: Siege of Protestant stronghold of La Rochelle

1640: Portugal declares independence from Spain

1640: Catalan Revolt

1649: Execution of Charles I of England

1660: Restoration of English monarchy

1640: Civil War breaks out in England

1648–53: The Fronde: resistance to royal authority throughout France

❸ The Swedish Empire 1560–1721

- Sweden at the death of Gustavus Vasa 1560
- conquests by 1645
- conquests by 1658
- temporary Swedish acquisitions, with dates
- Russian gains from Sweden by treaty of Nystad, 1721
→ Swedish campaigns
→ Russians campaigns under Peter the Great
- trade routes
- frontiers, 1658

Habsburg–Ottoman conflict 1663–1718

In the mid-17th century, the Ottoman Empire resumed its expansion into southeastern Europe. Austrian attempts to challenge the Ottomans' control of Transylvania led to full-scale war in 1663. The Turkish advance on Vienna in 1664 was halted, but in 1683 the Turks besieged the city. The siege failed, and by 1687 the war had become a Habsburg war of conquest. The acquisition of Transylvania and Turkish Hungary transformed Austria into a great European power and loosened its traditional ties to the Holy Roman Empire.

In 1683 the Ottomans began their greatest onslaught on the Habsburg Empire by besieging Vienna with a huge army. Poland and the Papacy joined the German princes in an international relief effort which ended in Ottoman defeat.

Habsburg-Ottoman wars 1663–1718

- 1672: Greatest extent of Ottoman Empire
- 1699: Peace of Karlowitz confirms Austrian conquests
- 1716–18: Further Austrian victories, including capture of Belgrade
- 1664: Turkish advance on Vienna turned back at battle of St. Gotthard
- 1683: Siege of Vienna starts Great Turkish War

Sweden, Russia, and the Baltic

The 17th century witnessed the phenomenal growth of Sweden as an imperial power: by defeating regional rivals Denmark, Poland and Russia, it had by 1648 established a Baltic empire, the high point of which was reached during the reign of Charles X (1654–60). Lacking indigenous resources, however, Sweden's strength rested on its control of strategic harbors and customs points along the Baltic shore. Defense of these positions forced Sweden into a series of costly wars from 1655. After the Great Northern War, much of the empire was lost to the rising powers of Russia, Prussia, and Hanover.

Founded in 1703 by Peter the Great, St. Petersburg was modelled on European cities, its classical architecture and orderly street grid symbolizing the Tsar's westernizing policies.

The rise and fall of the Swedish Empire

- 1629: Sweden gains Livonia
- 1643: Sweden invades Denmark
- 1654: Start of reign of Charles X
- 1658: Peace of Roskilde; Denmark loses southern Sweden
- 1700: Great Northern War
- 1721: Peace of Nystad; Sweden cedes Ingria, Livonia, and Karelia to Russia
- 1632: Gustavus Adolphus dies at victorious battle of Lützen
- 1648: Substantial Swedish gains confirmed by Treaty of Westphalia
- 1675: Brandenburg defeats Sweden at Fehrbellin
- 1709: Charles XII's attempt to invade Russia halted at Poltava

❹ The Ottoman frontier 1683–1739

- Ottoman Empire 1683
- Habsburg possessions 1683
- Venetian Republic 1683
- Russia 1683
- Habsburg gains, with date
- temporary Habsburg gains, 1718–39
- aquired by Russia 1739
- Venetian gains 1699
- Habsburg-Ottoman frontier 1718
✗ Habsburg victory
- frontiers 1683
- Holy Roman Empire border

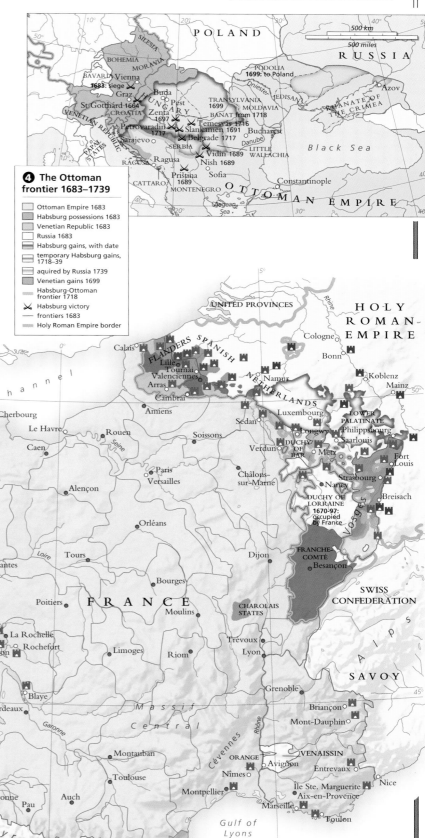

The French state under Louis XIV, 1660–1715

Under Louis XIV, France pursued an expansionist, anti-Spanish policy. The expense of maintaining a large army and building a ring of frontier fortresses was met by administrative reforms, and tax collection in the provinces was overseen by royal officials *(intendants)*. In 1667–68 Louis' armies secured parts of the Spanish Netherlands. Although this provoked international opposition to French aggression, further gains were made in the Dutch War (1672–79). The occupation of various territories in 1679–84 (known as the *Réunions*) rationalized France's eastern frontier, but after defeat in the Nine Years' War (1688–97), most of these had to be given up. The War of the Spanish Succession (1701–14) brought France no further gains.

A ring of defensive fortresses was built by Vauban, a great military engineer, to secure French territory.

During his long reign, Louis XIV *(left)* established France as cultural and political leader of Europe.

The growth of France under Louis XIV

- 1667–68: France acquires parts of Flanders from Spain
- 1679–84: *Réunions:* annexation of territory west of the Rhine
- 1701–14: War of the Spanish Succession
- 1661: Louis XIV assumes personal rule
- 1672–79: Dutch War brings significant territorial gains
- 1688–97: Nine Years' War: Peace of Ryswick (Rijswijk) partially reverses the *Réunions*
- 1715: Death of Louis XIV

❺ France 1648–1715

- France 1648
- frontier of Holy Roman Empire 1648
- French frontier 1713/14
- administrative regions under Louis XIV *(intendances or généralités)*
- French gains confirmed 1659
- French gains confirmed 1661
- French gains confirmed 1668
- French gains confirmed 1678–79
- areas temporarily annexed under the *Réunions*, 1684–97
- further French gains by 1697
⌂ Vauban fortress
⌂ fortified town
⌂ barrier fortress
● administrative center

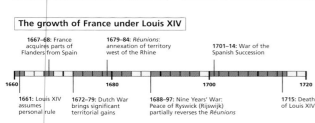

THE AGE OF ENLIGHTENMENT

Catherine the Great ruled the Russian Empire as an enlightened despot from 1762 to 1796.

THE 18TH CENTURY was a period of relative stability, when well-established monarchies ruled most of Europe and almost all the land was controlled by the nobility or the state. The Russian Empire and Prussia became leading powers. The rest of Germany remained a jigsaw of small states, as did Italy, while Poland was swallowed up by its powerful neighbors. Improved methods of cultivation fed Europe's escalating populations; towns and cities increased in size and number; trade and industry expanded to reach global markets; philosophy, science, and the arts flourished. Intellectual curiosity encouraged the radical political theories of the "Enlightenment," but alarmed reaction set in when the flag of liberty was raised in France in the last decade of the century. Though ultimately unsuccessful, the French Revolution would inspire many social and political reforms in the 19th century.

Cities and economic life 1700–1800

Despite the beginnings of industrialization in the 18th century, principally in textile production, in 1800 four out of five Europeans still depended on agriculture for their livelihood. The growing population – largely due to a fall in the death rate as a result of better health and hygiene – led to a rapid increase in the size of cities; in 1700 Europe had ten cities with over 100,000 inhabitants; by 1800 there were 17. At the same time, farmers adopted a more scientific approach to agriculture, introducing new, more productive crops and livestock. A general improvement in transportation by sea, road, river, and canal greatly stimulated trade throughout Europe and, as colonialism developed, with the rest of the world.

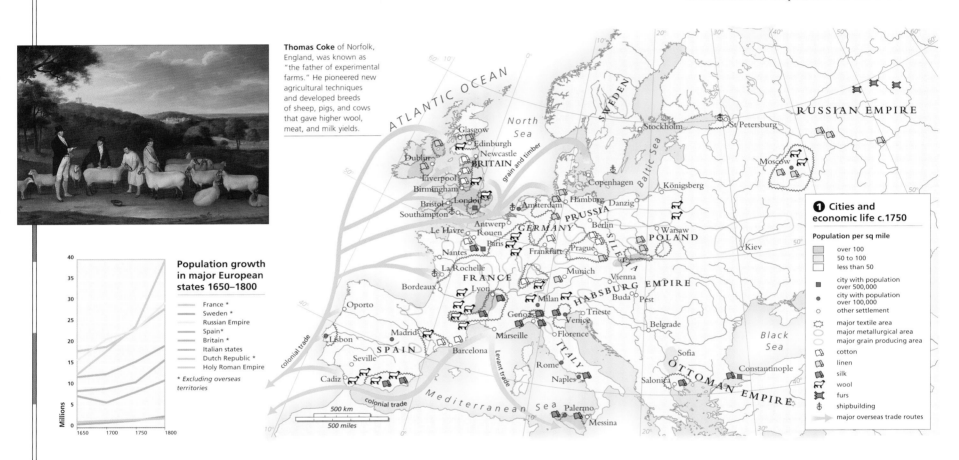

Thomas Coke of Norfolk, England, was known as "the father of experimental farms." He pioneered new agricultural techniques and developed breeds of sheep, pigs, and cows that gave higher wool, meat, and milk yields.

Population growth in major European states 1650–1800

- France *
- Sweden *
- Russian Empire
- Spain*
- Britain *
- Italian states
- Dutch Republic *
- Holy Roman Empire

* Excluding overseas territories

❶ Cities and economic life c.1750

Population per sq mile
- over 100
- 50 to 100
- less than 50

- ■ city with population over 500,000
- ● city with population over 100,000
- ○ other settlement
- major textile area
- major metallurgical area
- major grain producing area
- cotton
- linen
- silk
- wool
- furs
- shipbuilding
- major overseas trade routes

The partitions of Poland

17th-century Poland was one of Europe's largest states, but suffered frequent territorial losses to its neighbors, especially Russia. The elective monarchy allowed foreign powers to interfere in Polish affairs, and in the late 18th century the Russians, the Habsburgs, and Prussia settled their differences at Poland's expense in three partitions which removed the country from the map.

◀ ❷ The partitions of Poland 1772–95

- frontier of Poland in 1699

Partition of Poland in 1772
- to Prussia
- to Russian Empire
- to Habsburg Empire

Partition of Poland in 1793
- to Prussia
- to Russian Empire

Partition of Poland in 1795
- to Prussia
- to Russian Empire
- to Habsburg Empire
- frontiers in 1795

The decline of Poland 1550–1795

- 1569: Poland united with Lithuania
- 1660: East Prussia gains independence from Poland
- 1697: Start of rule by Electors of Saxony
- 1772: First partition of Poland
- 1795: Third partition

1550 — 1600 — 1650 — 1700 — 1750 — 1800

- 1629: Sweden acquires Livonia
- 1667: Russia acquires East Ukraine
- 1764: Russia secures Polish crown for Stanislas Poniatowski
- 1793: Second partition

THE ENLIGHTENMENT

The 18th-century "enlightened" writers, or *philosophes*, such as Voltaire and Diderot, appealed to human reason to challenge traditional assumptions about the Church, state, monarchy, education, and social institutions. "Man is born free, but everywhere he is in chains," wrote Jean-Jacques Rousseau in his *Social Contract* (1762), in which he sought to show how a democratic society could work.

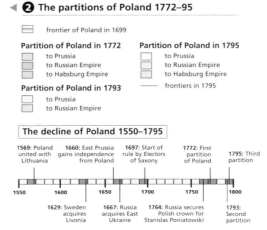

Voltaire (1694–1778) used poetry, drama, and satire to express his political views, including his opposition to the Catholic Church. His radicalism often led to periods of exile from his native France.

Published in 28 volumes from 1751–72, the *Encyclopédie* spread the philosophic and scientific ideas of the Enlightenment. It gave a comprehensive account of contemporary institutions and technologies, while fine engravings illustrated the work of all kinds of craftsmen, such as the instrument makers above.

The rise of Brandenburg Prussia

After the Peace of Westphalia in 1648, Germany consisted of some 300 small principalities, some Catholic, some Protestant. By the end of the 17th century Brandenburg was the dominant Protestant state. Frederick William (the "Great Elector") gained full sovereignty in Prussia and created a powerful state with a huge standing army. With the accession of Frederick II (the "Great") in 1740, expansion continued, including the acquisition of Silesia from the Habsburg Empire. With additional territory from the partitions of Poland, by the end of the century Prussia had become one of Europe's Great Powers.

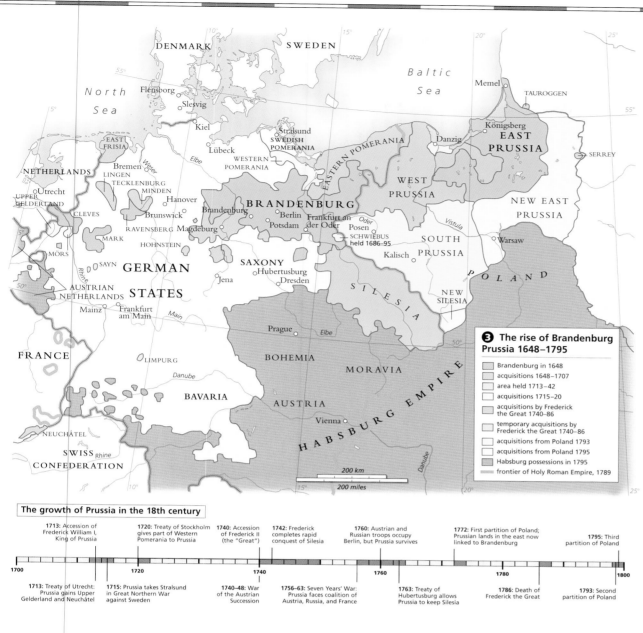

3 The rise of Brandenburg Prussia 1648–1795

- Brandenburg in 1648
- acquisitions 1648–1707
- area held 1713–42
- acquisitions 1715–20
- acquisitions by Frederick the Great 1740–86
- temporary acquisitions by Frederick the Great 1740–86
- acquisitions from Poland 1793
- acquisitions from Poland 1795
- Habsburg possessions in 1795
- frontier of Holy Roman Empire, 1789

These **splendidly uniformed cavalry** officers are representative of the highly disciplined and efficient army which, by 1763, enabled Prussia to emerge as the dominant military force in 18th-century Europe.

The growth of Prussia in the 18th century

1713: Accession of Frederick William I, King of Prussia
1720: Treaty of Stockholm gives part of Western Pomerania to Prussia
1740: Accession of Frederick II (the "Great")
1742: Frederick completes rapid conquest of Silesia
1760: Austrian and Russian troops occupy Berlin, but Prussia survives
1772: First partition of Poland; Prussian lands in the east now linked to Brandenburg
1795: Third partition of Poland

1713: Treaty of Utrecht: Prussia gains Upper Gelderland and Neuchâtel
1715: Prussia takes Stralsund in Great Northern War against Sweden
1740–48: War of the Austrian Succession
1756–63: Seven Years' War: Prussia faces coalition of Austria, Russia, and France
1763: Treaty of Hubertusburg allows Prussia to keep Silesia
1786: Death of Frederick the Great
1793: Second partition of Poland

1700 — 1720 — 1740 — 1760 — 1780 — 1800

The French Revolution 1789–95

In May 1789, a political crisis forced Louis XVI to summon the Estates-General, a parliament of nobles, clergy, and commoners. The third estate (the commoners) demanded reform and declared itself a National Assembly. Noble and clerical privileges were abolished; provincial uprisings were directed against landowners, many of whom fled into exile. In 1792 the Revolution gathered momentum: Louis was imprisoned, the monarchy abolished, and France declared a republic. Mass conscription was introduced to meet the threat of invasion by Austria and Prussia and the king was executed. Power shifted to the radical Jacobins, who ruled by means of "the Terror," executing all "enemies of the people." Many regions opposed these excesses, notably the Vendée in the west, but resistance was crushed. In 1794 the Jacobins shared the fate of their victims. France, however, had been saved from invasion, and there followed a period of moderate rule – the Directory.

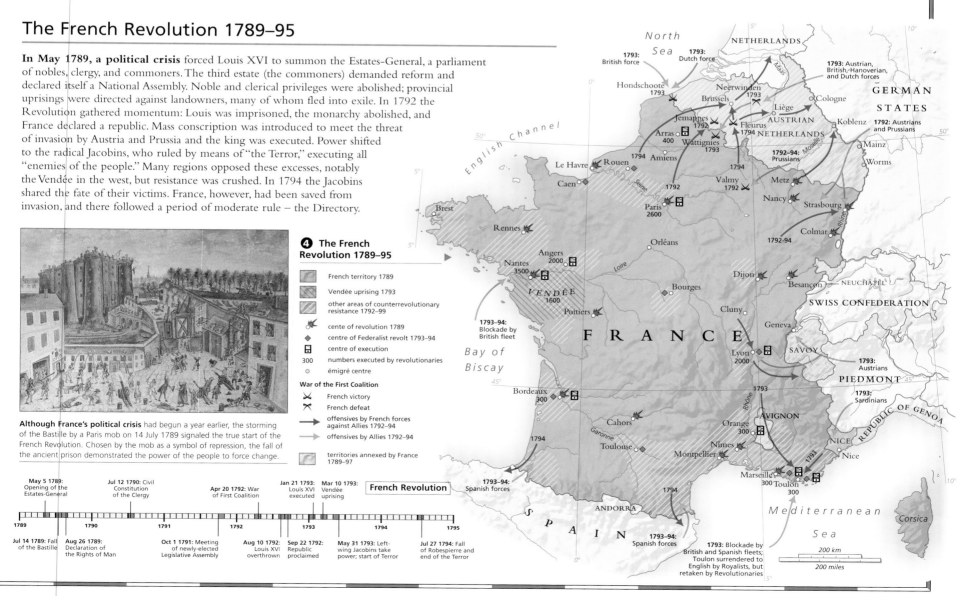

Although **France's political crisis** had begun a year earlier, the storming of the Bastille by a Paris mob on 14 July 1789 signaled the true start of the French Revolution. Chosen by the mob as a symbol of repression, the fall of the ancient prison demonstrated the power of the people to force change.

4 The French Revolution 1789–95

- French territory 1789
- Vendée uprising 1793
- other areas of counterrevolutionary resistance 1792–99
- centre of revolution 1789
- centre of Federalist revolt 1793–94
- centre of execution
- 300 numbers executed by revolutionaries
- émigré centre

War of the First Coalition
- French victory
- French defeat
- offensives by French forces against Allies 1792–94
- offensives by Allies 1792–94
- territories annexed by France 1789–97

French Revolution

May 5 1789: Opening of the Estates-General
Jul 12 1790: Civil Constitution of the Clergy
Apr 20 1792: War of First Coalition
Jan 21 1793: Louis XVI executed
Mar 10 1793: Vendée uprising

1789 — 1790 — 1791 — 1792 — 1793 — 1794 — 1795

Jul 14 1789: Fall of the Bastille
Aug 26 1789: Declaration of the Rights of Man
Oct 1 1791: Meeting of newly-elected Legislative Assembly
Aug 10 1792: Louis XVI overthrown
Sep 22 1792: Republic proclaimed
May 31 1793: Left-wing Jacobins take power; start of Terror
Jul 27 1794: Fall of Robespierre and end of the Terror

NAPOLEONIC EUROPE

THE BRILLIANT REVOLUTIONARY GENERAL Napoleon Bonaparte returned from his Egyptian campaign in 1799 to stage a *coup d'état* which made him ruler of France as First Consul. During the Consulate he began reforms of the administration, the legal system, the Church, and education. In 1804, just over ten years after revolutionaries had executed Louis XVI, Napoleon took the title of emperor and began to create a dynasty, members of his family being given the crowns of conquered states. His imperial ambitions were ultimately thwarted by Britain: its navy was used to blockade France and overrun French colonies, while a series of alliances completed an encirclement that contained and gradually reduced Napoleon's empire.

The Code Napoléon of 1804, the first modern law code, embraced many of the principles of the French Revolution.

The battle of Eylau in 1807 was fought in a blizzard, with the French heavily outnumbered and outgunned by the Russians. Though both sides claimed victory, the French lost more men. For the first time in his career, Napoleon had failed to win a major battle.

In this cartoon of 1812, Napoleon tries desperately to bridge the 2000 miles between Madrid and Moscow. The impossibility of personally masterminding both the Peninsular campaign in Spain and Portugal and the Russian campaign led to his downfall.

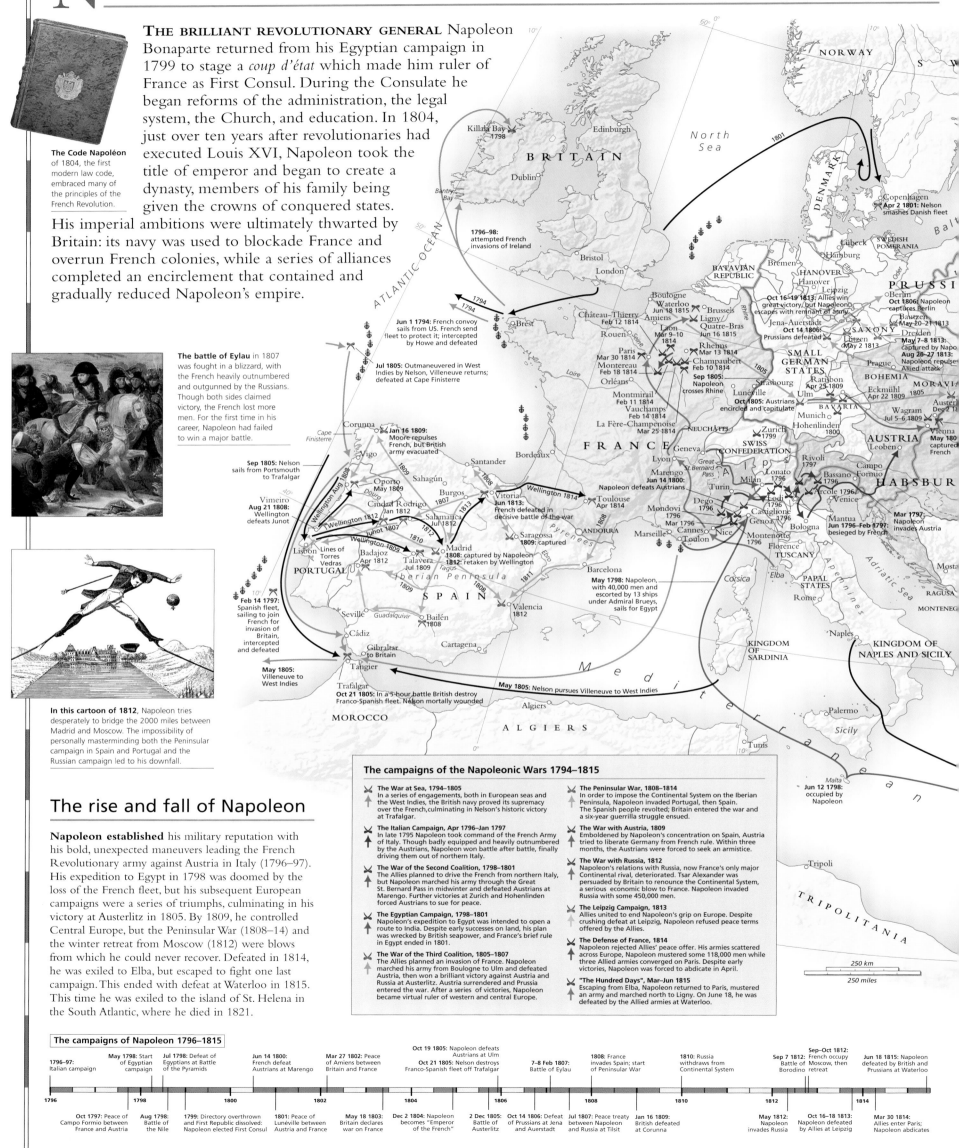

The rise and fall of Napoleon

Napoleon established his military reputation with his bold, unexpected maneuvers leading the French Revolutionary army against Austria in Italy (1796–97). His expedition to Egypt in 1798 was doomed by the loss of the French fleet, but his subsequent European campaigns were a series of triumphs, culminating in his victory at Austerlitz in 1805. By 1809, he controlled Central Europe, but the Peninsular War (1808–14) and the winter retreat from Moscow (1812) were blows from which he could never recover. Defeated in 1814, he was exiled to Elba, but escaped to fight one last campaign. This ended with defeat at Waterloo in 1815. This time he was exiled to the island of St. Helena in the South Atlantic, where he died in 1821.

The campaigns of the Napoleonic Wars 1794–1815

The War at Sea, 1794–1805
In a series of engagements, both in European seas and the West Indies, the British navy proved its supremacy over the French, culminating in Nelson's historic victory at Trafalgar.

The Italian Campaign, Apr 1796–Jan 1797
In late 1795 Napoleon took command of the French Army of Italy. Though badly equipped and heavily outnumbered by the Austrians, Napoleon won battle after battle, finally driving them out of northern Italy.

The War of the Second Coalition, 1798–1801
The Allies planned to drive the French from northern Italy, but Napoleon marched his army through the Great St. Bernard Pass in midwinter and defeated Austrians at Marengo. Further victories at Zurich and Hohenlinden forced Austria to sue for peace.

The Egyptian Campaign, 1798–1801
Napoleon's expedition to Egypt was intended to open a route to India. Despite early successes on land, his plan was wrecked by British seapower, and France's brief rule in Egypt ended in 1801.

The War of the Third Coalition, 1805–1807
The Allies planned an invasion of France. Napoleon marched his army from Boulogne to Ulm and defeated Austria, then won a brilliant victory against Austria and Russia at Austerlitz. Austria surrendered and Prussia entered the war. After a series of victories, Napoleon became virtual ruler of western and central Europe.

The Peninsular War, 1808–1814
In order to impose the Continental System on the Iberian Peninsula, Napoleon invaded Portugal, then Spain. The Spanish people revolted; Britain entered the war and a six-year guerrilla struggle ensued.

The War with Austria, 1809
Emboldened by Napoleon's concentration on Spain, Austria tried to liberate Germany from French rule. Within three months, the Austrians were forced to seek an armistice.

The War with Russia, 1812
Napoleon's relations with Russia, now France's only major Continental rival, deteriorated. Tsar Alexander was persuaded by Britain to renounce the Continental System, a serious economic blow to France. Napoleon invaded Russia with some 450,000 men.

The Leipzig Campaign, 1813
Allies united to end Napoleon's grip on Europe. Despite crushing defeat at Leipzig, Napoleon refused peace terms offered by the Allies.

The Defense of France, 1814
Napoleon rejected Allies' peace offer. His armies scattered across Europe, Napoleon mustered some 118,000 men while three Allied armies converged on Paris. Despite early victories, Napoleon was forced to abdicate in April.

"The Hundred Days", Mar–Jun 1815
Escaping from Elba, Napoleon returned to Paris, mustered an army and marched north to Ligny. On June 18, he was defeated by the Allied armies at Waterloo.

The campaigns of Napoleon 1796–1815

1796–97: Italian campaign
May 1798: Start of Egyptian campaign
Jul 1798: Defeat of Egyptians at Battle of the Pyramids
Jun 14 1800: French defeat Austrians at Marengo
Mar 27 1802: Peace of Amiens between Britain and France
Oct 19 1805: Napoleon defeats Austrians at Ulm
Oct 21 1805: Nelson destroys Franco-Spanish fleet off Trafalgar
7–8 Feb 1807: Battle of Eylau
1808: France invades Spain; start of Peninsular War
1810: Russia withdraws from Continental System
Sep 7 1812: Battle of Borodino
Sep–Oct 1812: French occupy Moscow, then retreat
Jun 18 1815: Napoleon defeated by British and Prussians at Waterloo

Oct 1797: Peace of Campo Formio between France and Austria
Aug 1798: Battle of the Nile
1799: Directory overthrown and First Republic dissolved; Napoleon elected First Consul
1801: Peace of Lunéville between Austria and France
May 18 1803: Britain declares war on France
Dec 2 1804: Napoleon becomes "Emperor of the French"
2 Dec 1805: Battle of Austerlitz
Oct 14 1806: Defeat of Prussians at Jena and Auerstädt
Jul 1807: Peace treaty between Napoleon and Russia at Tilsit
Jan 16 1809: British defeated at Corunna
May 1812: Napoleon invades Russia
Oct 16–18 1813: Napoleon defeated by Allies at Leipzig
Mar 30 1814: Allies enter Paris; Napoleon abdicates

The Napoleonic Empire

Napoleon's empire grew in two stages. In the first (1800–07), his brilliant military victories established France as the dominant power in Europe. Lands that came under his rule before 1807 – France, the Low Countries, northern Italy, and western Germany – formed an "inner empire." Here, French institutions and the Napoleonic legal code took root, surviving the empire's fall in 1814–15. Those areas taken after 1807 – Spain, southern Italy, northern Germany, and Poland – felt the effects of Napoleonic rule less, and often fiercely rejected French influence.

On December 2, 1804, Napoleon crowned himself "Emperor of the French" in the Cathedral of Notre Dame, Paris, as recorded in this famous painting by Jacques-Louis David.

The campaigns of Napoleon 1794–1815

Jul 1807: Treaty of Tilsit: ssia accepts humiliating terms. ssia joins France against Britain

Sep 7 1812: Despite Napoleon becoming ill and handing over command in mid-battle, Russians defeated and lose some 50,000 men

Sep 14 1812: Napoleon enters Moscow with some 95,000 men. City set on fire by inhabitants. On Oct 19 Napoleon forced to abandon Moscow

Borodino

left wing of army under Macdonald

Moscow

Aug 17 1812: Russians, led by Kutuzov, escape Napoleon's trap and retreat toward Moscow

Maloyaroslavets Oct 24 1812

Jun 24 1812: Napoleon crosses the Neman

Smolensk

Riga

Vilna

Tilsit

Krasnov Nov 16–17

Smorgon'

Nov 12 1812: French army, starved, frozen, and harried by regular and irregular Russian forces, continues retreat

Kovno Napoleon's main army

edland 1807

azig Eylau 1807

Studyanka

Dec 8 1812: Napoleon abandons army and returns to Paris to raise fresh troops

Nov 26–28 1812: Despite repulsing constant attacks by Russians, French cross frozen river on pontoon bridges. French lose over 30,000 men

Bereszina

Pripet Marshes

arsaw

Russian army abandons its pursuit; losses in the campaign, some 250,000

Kiev

① The campaigns of Napoleon 1794–1815

→ British forces
⚔ French victory (colored by campaign)
⚔ French defeat (colored by campaign)
⚓ British blockade
▲▲ defensive lines
⊙ French siege
—— frontiers 1797
▬▬ Holy Roman Empire 1797

RUSSIAN EMPIRE

St. Petersburg

ckholm

DEN

GALICIA

Cracow

ec 1805: Allies crushed; se 27,000 men, e French 9,000

spern-Essling ay 21–22 1809

Jassy

UNGARY OSSESSIONS

TRANSYLVANIA

MOLDAVIA

Odessa

Dniester

Dnieper

Don

Sebastopol

Black Sea

WALLACHIA

Belgrade

Bucharest

Danube

Sofia

Varna

OTTOMAN EMPIRE

Constantinople

Salonica

Ankara

Smyrna

Athens

Aleppo

Ionian Islands

1797: By Treaty of Campo Formio, islands taken from Venice by France in preparation for invasion of Egypt

Cyprus

1798: Sultan of Turkey declares holy war (jihad) on France; prepares to invade Egypt

Crete

Jun 1798

British fleet under Nelson

Mar 1799: besieged by French, but Turks resist and in May Napoleon begins retreat to Egypt

Beirut

Damascus

Acre

1799

Apr 17 1799: French defeat Turks

Aug 1 1798: Battle of the Nile (Aboukir Bay): Nelson, with 13 ships, destroys French fleet

Jaffa

Gaza

Jerusalem

Alexandria

S e a

EGYPT

Cairo

Jul 21 1798: Napoleon defeats the Mamluks; captures Cairo

Nile

to Aswan

Napoleon's invasion of Egypt in July 1798 was intended to secure an overland route to India, but the destruction of his fleet by the British under Nelson at the battle of the Nile left the French forces stranded.

③ Alliances in opposition to France 1792–1815 ▶

Alliances against France in the Napoleonic Wars:

⊗ wars of Second Coalition 1798–1800
⊗ wars of Third Coalition 1805–07
⊗ war with Austria 1809
⊗ war with Russia 1812
⊗ Wars of Liberation of France 1813–15

☐ France 1792
☐ annexed by France 1802
☐ satellites of France 1802
—— Napoleon's Continental System
▬▬ Holy Roman Empire
—— frontiers c.1802

② The Empire of Napoleon by 1812 ▲

☐ French territory ruled directly from Paris 1812
☐ dependent state 1812
☐ British or British occupied territory
⚜ state ruled by Napoleon or member of his family at some time between 1805–12

NORWAY

SWEDEN

North Sea

Edinburgh

Dublin

BRITAIN

Bristol

London

DENMARK

Copenhagen

Baltic Sea

Riga

Tilsit

RUSSIAN EMPIRE

Hamburg

Lübeck

REPUBLIC OF DANZIG

Bremen

HOLLAND

WESTPHALIA

PRUSSIA

Berlin

GRAND DUCHY OF WARSAW

Brussels

BERG

Hanover

Warsaw

Rouen

CONFEDERATION OF THE RHINE

Paris

Frankfurt

Prague

Cracow

Rhine

Loire

FRENCH EMPIRE

Corunna

Zürich

Munich

Vienna

AUSTRIAN EMPIRE

Geneva

HELVETIA

Buda

Pest

Bordeaux

Lyon

Milan

ILLYRIAN PROVINCES

KINGDOM OF ITALY

GUASTALLA

Venice

Toulouse

Marseille

LUCCA

Po

Bologna

PORTUGAL

Lisbon

Madrid

KINGDOM OF SPAIN

CATALONIA

Corsica

PIOMBINO

Florence

Belgrade

Danube

Barcelona

Rome

KINGDOM OF SARDINIA

KINGDOM OF NAPLES

OTTOMAN EMPIRE

Sofia

Cordova

Valencia

Balearic Islands

Tangier

Gibraltar to Britain

Algiers

Naples

Corfu to France

Ionian Islands to Britain 1809

Palermo

KINGDOM OF SICILY

Tunis

Athens

Malta to Britain 1800

Crete

Mediterranean Sea

ATLANTIC OCEAN

500 km

500 miles

Opposition to Napoleon

Between 1793 and 1815 France fought all the major European powers, either singly or in coalitions. After his defeat of the Third Coalition in 1807, Napoleon ruled virtually the entire continent. Only Britain opposed him. To cripple the British economically, Napoleon tried to prevent all trade between continental Europe and Britain, but this blockade, known as the Continental System, proved difficult to enforce. Russian withdrawal from the system provoked the fatal march on Moscow of 1812, which was to lead to his downfall.

In July 1807, Napoleon met King Frederick William III and Queen Louise of Prussia and Tsar Alexander I of Russia near Tilsit, Prussia, to discuss peace.

ATLANTIC OCEAN

North Sea

SWEDEN

Stockholm

BRITAIN

Copenhagen

Baltic Sea

Mar 1808: National revolt against French invasion supported by Britain, which sends armies under Moore and Wellington

London

Berlin

PRUSSIA

Warsaw

RUSSIAN EMPIRE

Brussels

SAXONY

Paris

Prague

FRANCE

Zürich

Vienna

AUSTRIAN EMPIRE

Geneva

PORTUGAL

Lisbon

Madrid

SPAIN

Milan

Venice

Florence

Belgrade

Bucharest

Black Sea

Marseille

Barcelona

Rome

NAPLES

Sofia

Constantinople

Gibraltar to Britain

Naples

Palermo

OTTOMAN EMPIRE

Athens

Ankara

Mediterranean Sea

500 km

500 miles

THE GROWTH OF NATIONALISM

Otto von Bismarck, prime minister of Prussia 1862–1890, was chief architect of the unification of Germany.

TO RESTORE PEACE and stability after the turmoil of the Napoleonic Wars, the Congress of Vienna was convened in 1814. Attended by all the major European powers, but dominated by Austria, Britain, Russia, and Prussia, the Congress redrew the political map of Europe and restored many former ruling houses. The result was three decades of reactionary rule, during which nationalist and republican movements, inspired by the American and French models, challenged the status quo. In eastern Europe, Greece and the Balkan states took advantage of the weakness of the Ottoman Empire to gain independence. In the west, Italy and Germany finally achieved their dreams of unification. But traditional rivalry between royal houses was now replaced by rivalry between industrialized nation states – a rivalry which led, ultimately, to World War I.

Europe under the Vienna system

The Congress of Vienna met to share out the spoils of victory over Napoleon, though painful compromise was required to achieve a workable balance of power in Europe. Political stability was reestablished by restoring the hereditary monarchs overthrown by Napoleon. France, though deprived of all its conquests, once more had a Bourbon on the throne. But the restored monarchs ruled with too heavy a hand: liberal, republican, and nationalist revolts began to break out, reaching a crescendo in 1848 when the governments of France, Italy, and Austria were all shaken by insurrection.

The Congress of Vienna was attended by five monarchs and the heads of 216 princely families. It was dominated by the Austrian chancellor, Prince Metternich, seen here standing on the left at the signing of the final settlement.

Threats to the Vienna system 1814–50

1806: Abolition of Holy Roman Empire	**1814:** Napoleon abdicates; opening of Congress of Vienna	**1820–23:** Revolts in Spain, Portugal, Naples, Sicily, Piedmont, and the Balkans	**1830–31:** Belgian War of Independence	**1848:** Second Republic in France with Louis-Napoleon as president	
1800	1810	1820	1830	1840	1850
1815: Napoleon escapes from exile, but is defeated at Waterloo; restoration of French monarchy	**1821:** Start of Greek War of Independence which lasts until 1833	**1830:** Revolution in Paris	**1833–39:** First Carlist War in Spain	**1848:** Revolutions throughout Europe	

❶ Europe after the Congress of Vienna 1815–52

MAIN MAP ▶

- small German states
- areas in revolt against Louis-Napoleon in 1851
- German Confederation
- ⚑ threat to Vienna System 1817–39
- ⚑ revolution in 1848–49
- ---- frontiers 1815

▼ INSET: Belgian independence 1831–39

- United Netherlands 1815–31
- boundary of German Confederation 1815
- boundary of German Confederation 1839
- .... boundary between French and Flemish speakers

400 km
400 miles

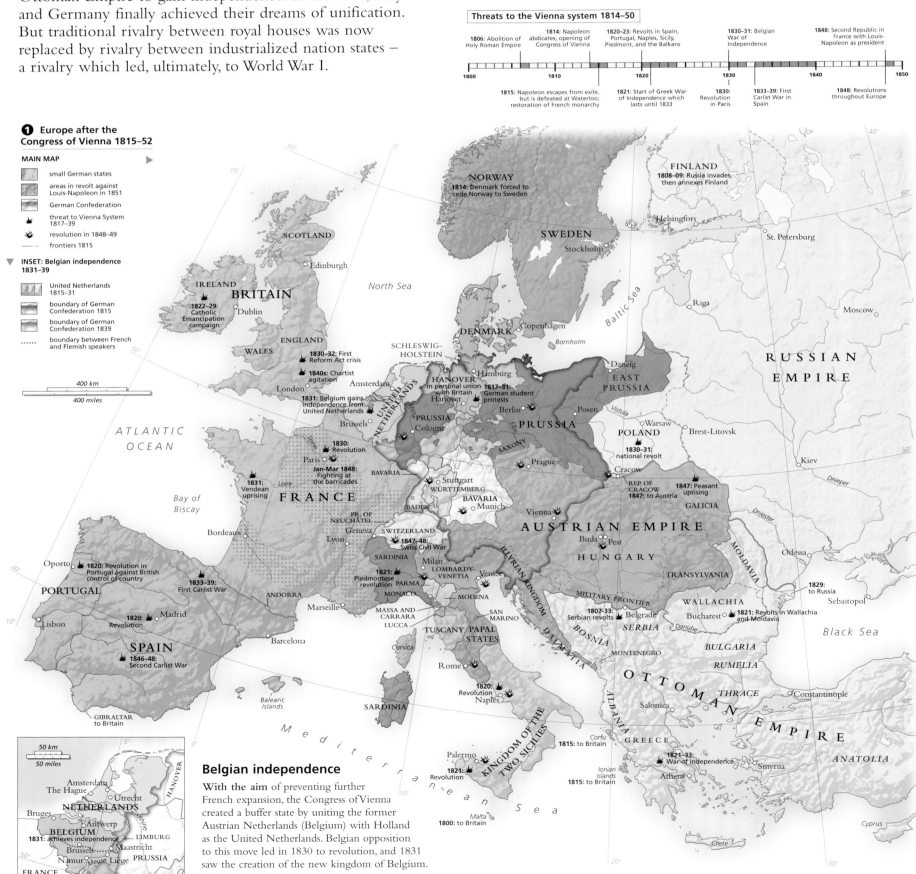

Belgian independence

With the aim of preventing further French expansion, the Congress of Vienna created a buffer state by uniting the former Austrian Netherlands (Belgium) with Holland as the United Netherlands. Belgian opposition to this move led in 1830 to revolution, and 1831 saw the creation of the new kingdom of Belgium.

The unification of Germany

In 1815 Germany's states were reduced to a Confederation of 39 under Austrian leadership. These states were further united in 1834 by the formation of a customs union (Zollverein). In 1866 Bismarck, prime minister of Prussia, proposed a German Confederation which would exclude Austria. When Austria refused, Bismarck – bent on German unification – declared war on Austria. Following Austria's defeat, Bismarck established the North German Confederation. The German Empire, including Bavaria and other south German states, was created after Prussia's victory in the Franco-Prussian War in 1870.

Spiked helmets such as this one worn by a dragoon officer became emblems of German militarism.

In 1870, alarmed at the intentions of Prussia, Napoleon III declared war, but the French were defeated. Here, Napoleon surrenders to the Prussian king Wilhelm I.

The unification of Germany

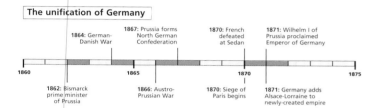

1864: German-Danish War
1862: Bismarck prime minister of Prussia
1867: Prussia forms North German Confederation
1866: Austro-Prussian War
1870: French defeated at Sedan
1870: Siege of Paris begins
1871: Wilhelm I of Prussia proclaimed Emperor of Germany
1871: Germany adds Alsace-Lorraine to newly-created empire

2 The unification of Germany
- boundary of German Confederation of 1815
- Prussia in 1815
- Prussian gains by 1866
- other states in North German Confederation 1867
- other German states 1866
- Austro-Hungarian Empire 1867
- frontiers in 1866
- → attack on Denmark by Austro-Prussian forces 1864
- ⇢ Prussian armies in war with Austria 1866
- ⇢ Prussian invasion of France in Franco-Prussian War 1870–71
- boundary of German Empire 1871

The unification of Italy

The restoration of the old order in 1815 provoked a movement to liberate and unite Italy. In 1859 Cavour, prime minister of Sardinia-Piedmont, enlisted the help of French emperor Napoleon III to drive the Austrians out of Lombardy. In 1860 Sicily and Naples were conquered by Garibaldi and his 1000 "Redshirts," then handed over to Victor Emmanuel II of Sardinia, who became king of a united Italy in 1861. Rome was finally added to the new kingdom in 1870.

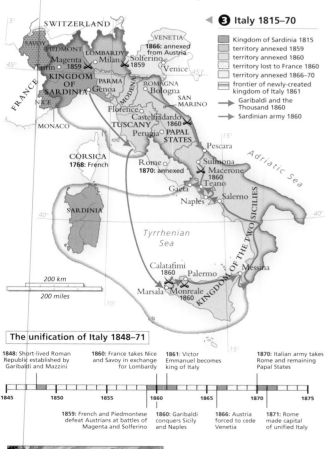

◀ 3 Italy 1815–70
- Kingdom of Sardinia 1815
- territory annexed 1859
- territory annexed 1860
- territory lost to France 1860
- territory annexed 1866–70
- frontier of newly-created kingdom of Italy 1861
- → Garibaldi and the Thousand 1860
- → Sardinian army 1860

The unification of Italy 1848–71

1848: Short-lived Roman Republic established by Garibaldi and Mazzini
1859: French and Piedmontese defeat Austrians at battles of Magenta and Solferino
1860: France takes Nice and Savoy in exchange for Lombardy
1860: Garibaldi conquers Sicily and Naples
1861: Victor Emmanuel becomes king of Italy
1866: Austria forced to cede Venetia
1870: Italian army takes Rome and remaining Papal States
1871: Rome made capital of unified Italy

At the meeting in 1860 between Victor Emmanuel II and Garibaldi at Teano, Garibaldi – a lifelong Republican – effectively presented the king with half of Italy.

Nationalism in the Balkans

In this cartoon of 1908, Ottoman sultan Abdul Hamid II sulks as more Balkan territory is whipped from under his feet by Austria and Bulgaria.

Nationalism proved most volatile in the Balkans, where many subject peoples aspired to independence from the Ottomans. Initially only the Greeks were successful. Meanwhile, Austria and Russia vied to replace the Turks as the dominant power in the region. Russian expansionism provoked the Crimean War in 1854, when Russia was defeated by Britain, France, Austria, and Turkey, and the Russo-Turkish War of 1877–78. At the Congress of Berlin in 1878, Turkey was forced to abandon all claims to Montenegro, Romania, and Serbia. In 1912, intent on seizing the Ottomans' last remaining European territories, Serbia, Bulgaria, and Greece were victorious in the First Balkan War. Resentment over the division of the spoils sparked a new war, from which Serbia emerged triumphant, but the precarious situation would be a major cause of World War I.

4 The Balkans and the Black Sea to 1913
- international boundaries 1913
- Ottoman Empire 1913
- Russian Empire 1913
- Austro-Hungarian Empire 1913
- Italy and possessions 1913
- Serbia 1833
- Serbian gain 1878
- Serbian gain 1913
- Greece 1830
- Greek gain 1864
- Greek gain 1881
- Greek gain 1913
- Romania 1861
- Romanian gain 1878
- Romanian gain 1913
- Bulgaria 1878
- Bulgarian gain 1885
- Bulgarian gain 1913
- Montenegro 1878
- Montenegrin gain 1913
- Albania 1913
- → Russian forces in Crimean War
- → Allied forces in Crimean War
- → Russian forces in 1877–78
- ✕ significant Ottoman defeat

The Balkans and the Black Sea 1850–1913

1854–56: Crimean War
1878: Treaty of San Stefano negotiated by Russia and Turkey
1877–78: Russia, Serbia, and Montenegro at war with Turkey
1878: Congress of Berlin alters terms of San Stefano treaty; Bulgaria becomes autonomous principality within Ottoman Empire
1885: Bulgaria granted Eastern Rumelia
1908: Bulgaria declares full independence
1912: Serbia, Bulgaria, Greece, and Montenegro form Balkan League; First Balkan War
1913: Treaty of London confirms independent Albania
1913: Second Balkan War

THE INDUSTRIAL REVOLUTION

Matthew Boulton's metal works in Birmingham developed the steam engine for industrial use.

IN THE LATTER HALF of the 18th century, rapid technological, social, and economic changes began to transform Britain from an agrarian into a largely urban, industrial society. This process, which became known as the Industrial Revolution, spread to Europe in the course of the 19th century. The population of the continent doubled in this period and was fed by a similar growth in agricultural production. Changes included the use of new power sources such as coal and steam; new building materials, chiefly iron and steel; and technical innovations and improved systems of transportation. These developments led to large-scale production and the growth of the factory system.

The move to the towns

Industrial chimneys dominate the Manchester skyline in this 19th-century engraving. Industry in Britain concentrated in cities where rich coal and iron deposits were in close proximity.

Urban development was inextricably linked to the process of industrialization. The most marked 19th-century urban growth occurred in areas where labor-intensive, mechanized, and often factory-based industries were emerging. Rapid urbanization first occurred in Britain, where the urban population grew from 20% of the total population in 1800, to 41% in 1850. By the 1850s, many other European countries experienced urban growth at a rate comparable with that of Britain in the first half of the century.

The Industrial Revolution in Britain

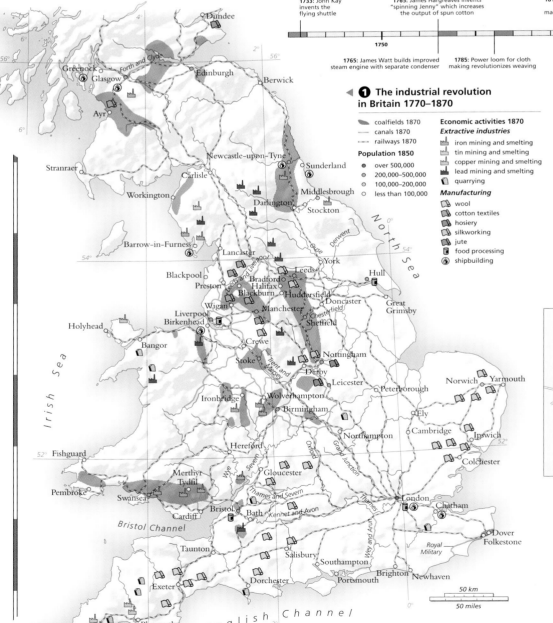

The replacement of water power with steam power greatly increased efficiency. Huge flywheels could drive machinery, such as that used here to make cable, at greater speeds.

A combination of geographical, political, and social factors ensured that Britain became the first industrial nation. The country possessed a number of natural ports facing the Atlantic, an established shipping trade, and a network of internal navigable waterways. It was richly endowed with coal and iron ore and could draw on a large market both at home and overseas. British colonies supplied raw materials and custom and an expanding population ensured buoyant demand at home. The textile industry in Britain was the first to benefit from new technical innovations which brought about greater production efficiency and output.

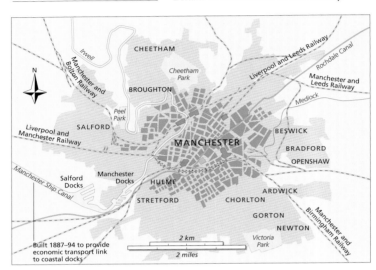

Built 1887–94 to provide economic transport link to coastal docks

2 km
2 miles

▲ ❷ The growth of Manchester 1840–1900

- – – railroad
- ▪ railroad station
- Manchester South junction viaduct
- park
- built-up area 1840
- growth of city 1840–1900

The advance of British technology from 1733

1733: John Kay invents the flying shuttle

1765: James Hargreaves invents the "spinning Jenny" which increases the output of spun cotton

1811–12: Luddite rioters wreck new textile machinery in Derbyshire

1837: First practical electric telegraph system produced by Cooke and Wheatstone

1838: Launch of I.K. Brunel's *Great Western* steamship

1842: Lord Shaftesbury's Mines Act; underground employment of women and children prohibited

1750 1800 1850

1765: James Watt builds improved steam engine with separate condenser

1785: Power loom for cloth making revolutionizes weaving

1825: First passenger steam railroad from Stockton to Darlington

1832: Outbreak of cholera kills 31,000 people in Britain

1840: Cheap postal system introduced; one penny per letter to anywhere in Britain

◀ ❶ The industrial revolution in Britain 1770–1870

- coalfields 1870
- canals 1870
- railways 1870

Population 1850
- ● over 500,000
- ● 200,000–500,000
- ○ 100,000–200,000
- ○ less than 100,000

Economic activities 1870
Extractive industries
- iron mining and smelting
- tin mining and smelting
- copper mining and smelting
- lead mining and smelting
- quarrying

Manufacturing
- wool
- cotton textiles
- hosiery
- silkworking
- jute
- food processing
- shipbuilding

URBANIZATION AND PUBLIC HEALTH

From the 1850s, industrial cities in Britain began to grow faster than the infrastructure needed to support the growing populations. Poorly built workers' tenement housing became severely overcrowded, and people drank water contaminated by sewage and industrial effluent. These poor standards of living resulted in the proliferation of diseases such as cholera, smallpox, dysentery, tuberculosis, and rickets. In 1854 and 1855, cholera broke out in Newcastle, where steep banks produced a concentration of settlement in the commercial areas along the river. Families lived five to a room, without sanitation or ready access to clean water, and of the 9453 houses in the city in 1854, 8032 were without toilets. During the cholera epidemic of 1854, 1500 of the 90,000 population died of the disease in a period of five weeks.

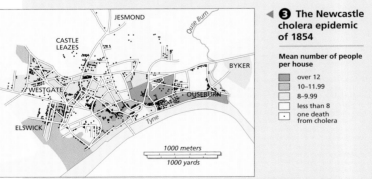

◀ ❸ The Newcastle cholera epidemic of 1854

Mean number of people per house
- over 12
- 10–11.99
- 8–9.99
- less than 8
- one death from cholera

1000 meters
1000 yards

The Public Health Act of 1848 was a turning point for public health in Britain. It allowed for the formation of local Boards of Health and the appointment of medical officers. This public health poster entitled *Cholera Tramples the Victor and the Vanquish'd Both*, warned people that no class was immune from the disease.

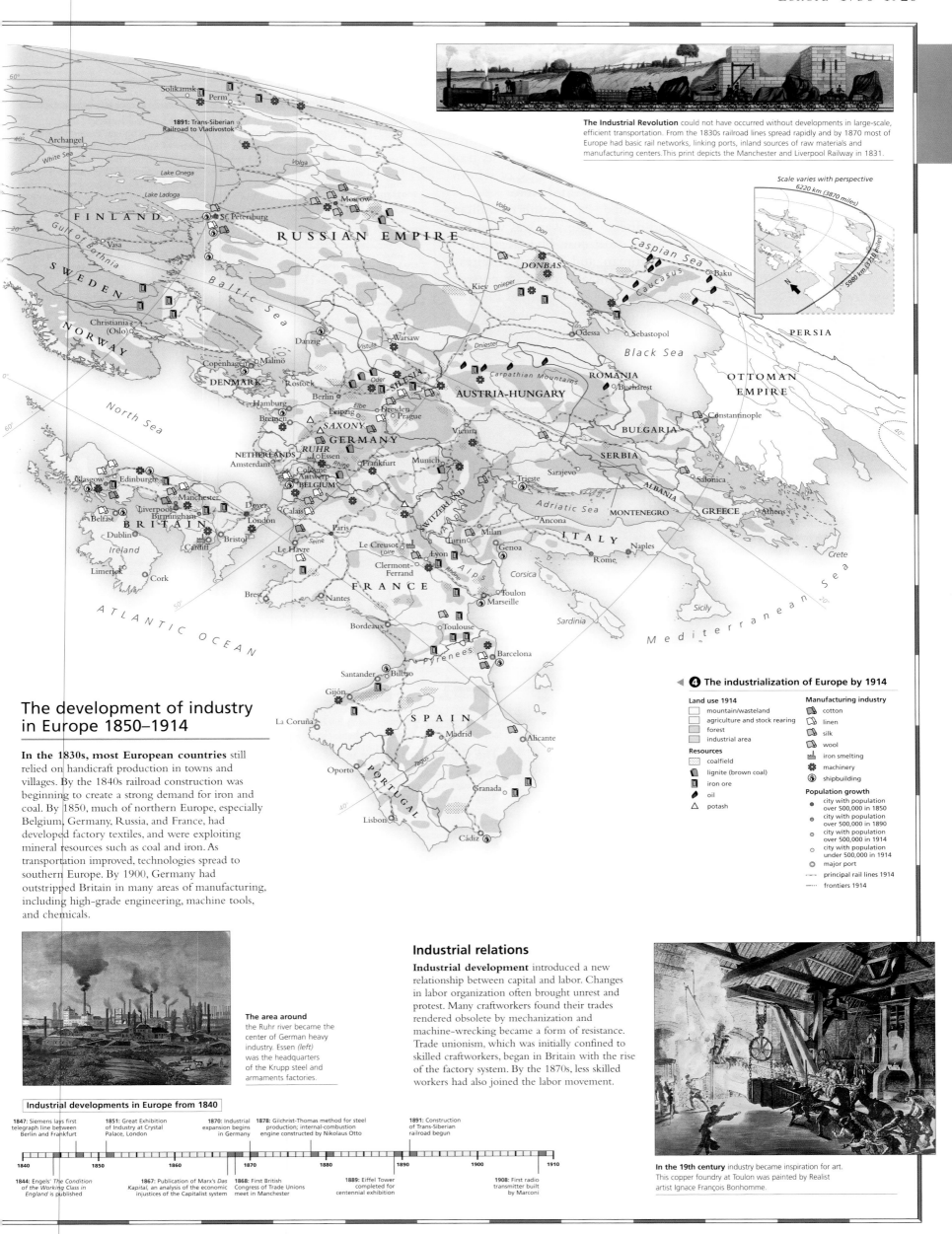

The Industrial Revolution could not have occurred without developments in large-scale, efficient transportation. From the 1830s railroad lines spread rapidly and by 1870 most of Europe had basic rail networks, linking ports, inland sources of raw materials and manufacturing centers. This print depicts the Manchester and Liverpool Railway in 1831.

Scale varies with perspective
6220 km (3870 miles)
5980 km (3710 miles)

1891: Trans-Siberian Railroad to Vladivostok

❹ The industrialization of Europe by 1914

Land use 1914
- ☐ mountain/wasteland
- ☐ agriculture and stock rearing
- ☐ forest
- ☐ industrial area

Resources
- ▦ coalfield
- ◧ lignite (brown coal)
- ▮ iron ore
- ● oil
- △ potash

Manufacturing industry
- cotton
- linen
- silk
- wool
- iron smelting
- ✿ machinery
- shipbuilding

Population growth
- ● city with population over 500,000 in 1850
- ● city with population over 500,000 in 1890
- ◐ city with population over 500,000 in 1914
- ○ city with population under 500,000 in 1914
- ○ major port
- --- principal rail lines 1914
- ---- frontiers 1914

The development of industry in Europe 1850–1914

In the 1830s, most European countries still relied on handicraft production in towns and villages. By the 1840s railroad construction was beginning to create a strong demand for iron and coal. By 1850, much of northern Europe, especially Belgium, Germany, Russia, and France, had developed factory textiles, and were exploiting mineral resources such as coal and iron. As transportation improved, technologies spread to southern Europe. By 1900, Germany had outstripped Britain in many areas of manufacturing, including high-grade engineering, machine tools, and chemicals.

The area around the Ruhr river became the center of German heavy industry. Essen *(left)* was the headquarters of the Krupp steel and armaments factories.

Industrial relations

Industrial development introduced a new relationship between capital and labor. Changes in labor organization often brought unrest and protest. Many craftworkers found their trades rendered obsolete by mechanization and machine-wrecking became a form of resistance. Trade unionism, which was initially confined to skilled craftworkers, began in Britain with the rise of the factory system. By the 1870s, less skilled workers had also joined the labor movement.

Industrial developments in Europe from 1840

1847: Siemens lays first telegraph line between Berlin and Frankfurt

1851: Great Exhibition of Industry at Crystal Palace, London

1870: Industrial expansion begins in Germany

1878: Gilchrist-Thomas method for steel production; internal-combustion engine constructed by Nikolaus Otto

1891: Construction of Trans-Siberian railroad begun

1844: Engels' *The Condition of the Working Class in England* is published

1867: Publication of Marx's *Das Kapital*, an analysis of the economic injustices of the Capitalist system

1868: First British Congress of Trade Unions meet in Manchester

1889: Eiffel Tower completed for centennial exhibition

1908: First radio transmitter built by Marconi

1840 | 1850 | 1860 | 1870 | 1880 | 1890 | 1900 | 1910

In the 19th century industry became inspiration for art. This copper foundry at Toulon was painted by Realist artist Ignace François Bonhomme.

WORLD WAR II IN EUROPE

Women were encouraged to join the war effort both as civilians and in the armed forces.

THE GREATEST WAR in Europe's history was initiated by a series of aggressive annexations and conquests by Hitler's Nazi Germany between 1939 and 1941. When the conflict ceased to be a series of campaigns and became a war, however, Germany was checked and then stripped of the initiative by an Allied force headed by two nations on the lateral extremes of Europe – Britain and the USSR – and from December 1941, a non-European nation, the US. Each of the latter proved more than Germany's equal in military and economic resources. The eventual Allied victory, following concerted assaults from the west, south, east, and the air, saved Europe from the scourge of Nazism but also completed Europe's devastation, bringing to an end 400 years of European global domination.

Blitzkrieg in Europe 1939–42

Between 1939 and 1941, lightning campaigns on land and in the air enabled Nazi Germany to conquer many of its weaker neighbors. In temporary alliance with the USSR, Germany annihilated Poland in the autumn of 1939. Denmark, Norway, Belgium, France, and the Netherlands were overrun in April–June 1940. Yugoslavia and Greece were occupied in April–May 1941, Britain was isolated, and Bulgaria, Romania, and Hungary brought under Nazi domination. Although a large contingent of German forces was committed to support Italy in North Africa, in June 1941 Hitler ordered a surprise attack on the USSR, hoping to destroy it in a single campaign. The attempt ended in failure because of the distances involved and unexpected Soviet resistance. In mid-winter 1941, the Nazi invasion forces were halted outside Moscow.

Following the Blitz (September 1940–May 1941) London became the first city in history to undergo ballistic missile attack from V1 flying bombs and V2 rockets (1944–45).

1 Blitzkrieg in Europe 1939–42

- Axis territory Sep 1939
- German offensive, 1939–41
- Italian offensive, 1939–41
- airborne attacks
- cities severely bombed
- Axis conquests 1939
- Axis conquests 1940
- Axis conquests 1941
- Soviet conquests 1939–40
- Axis satellites
- Allied territories Dec 1941
- British retreats
- Allied offensive 1941
- neutral states

The Second World War 1939–42

Aug 1939: Germany and USSR sign non-aggression pact

Apr 1940: German invasion of Denmark and Norway

Jul–Oct 1940: Battle of Britain in skies over southern England

Apr 1941: German invasion of Yugoslavia and Greece

Dec 1941: Germany declares war on US

Sep 1942: Start of German siege of Stalingrad

Nov 1942: Germans occupy Vichy France

Sep 1939: Germany and USSR invade Poland; France and Britain declare war on Germany

May–Jun 1940: Germany invades France, Netherlands, and Belgium

Oct 1940: Italy invades Albania and Greece

Jun 1941: Operation Barbarossa: German invasion of USSR

Nov 1941: USSR counterattacks against Germany

Oct–Nov 1942: UK defeats Germany at El Alamein

The Battle of the Atlantic

The battle over the supply of Europe was fought in the Atlantic. British destruction or containment of German surface warship raiders, following the sinking of the *Bismarck* in May 1941 and the blockade of supplies to "Fortress Europe," was followed by a German submarine (U-Boat) campaign against British shipping in western waters. Once the US entered the war in December 1941, U-boat attacks spread across the Atlantic. By summer 1943, US mass production of "Liberty" merchant ships, the use of the convoy system, increasing air cover, and the Allied interception of German radio traffic critically inhibited the effectiveness of the U-Boat "wolfpacks."

This Enigma encoding machine is being used by German naval personnel. By summer 1940, British counterintelligence experts had managed to crack the Enigma code, enabling them to interpret German radio traffic and disperse the intercepted messages (codenamed Ultra) throughout Allied High Command.

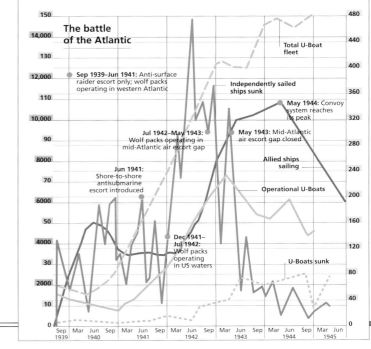

The battle of the Atlantic

Sep 1939–Jun 1941: Anti-surface raider escort only; wolf packs operating in western Atlantic

Jun 1941: Shore-to-shore antisubmarine escort introduced

Dec 1941–Jul 1942: Wolf packs operating in US waters

Jul 1942–May 1943: Wolf packs operating in mid-Atlantic air escort gap

May 1943: Mid-Atlantic air escort gap closed

May 1944: Convoy system reaches its peak

Total U-Boat fleet

Independently sailed ships sunk

Allied ships sailing

Operational U-Boats

U-Boats sunk

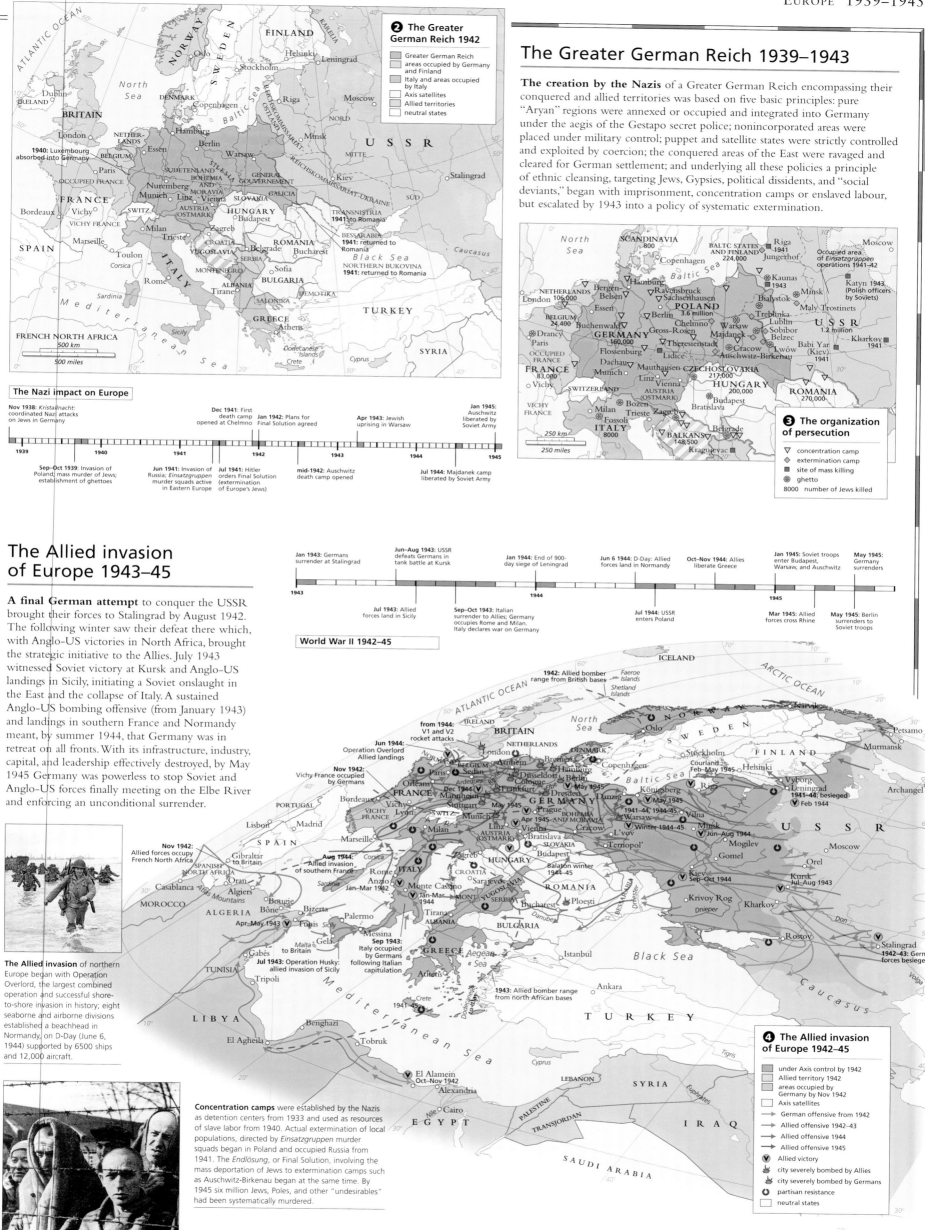

2 The Greater German Reich 1942

- Greater German Reich
- areas occupied by Germany and Finland
- Italy and areas occupied by Italy
- Axis satellites
- Allied territories
- neutral states

1940: Luxembourg absorbed into Germany

1941: to Romania (TRANSNISTRIA)

BESSARABIA 1941: returned to Romania

NORTHERN BUKOVINA 1941: returned to Romania

FRENCH NORTH AFRICA
500 km
500 miles

The Nazi impact on Europe

Nov 1938: *Kristallnacht:* coordinated Nazi attacks on Jews in Germany

Dec 1941: First death camp opened at Chelmno

Jan 1942: Plans for Final Solution agreed

Apr 1943: Jewish uprising in Warsaw

Jan 1945: Auschwitz liberated by Soviet Army

1939   1940   1941   1942   1943   1944   1945

Sep–Oct 1939: Invasion of Poland; mass murder of Jews; establishment of ghettoes

Jun 1941: Invasion of Russia; *Einsatzgruppen* murder squads active in Eastern Europe

Jul 1941: Hitler orders Final Solution (extermination of Europe's Jews)

mid-1942: Auschwitz death camp opened

Jul 1944: Majdanek camp liberated by Soviet Army

The Greater German Reich 1939–1943

The creation by the Nazis of a Greater German Reich encompassing their conquered and allied territories was based on five basic principles: pure "Aryan" regions were annexed or occupied and integrated into Germany under the aegis of the Gestapo secret police; nonincorporated areas were placed under military control; puppet and satellite states were strictly controlled and exploited by coercion; the conquered areas of the East were ravaged and cleared for German settlement; and underlying all these policies a principle of ethnic cleansing, targeting Jews, Gypsies, political dissidents, and "social deviants," began with imprisonment, concentration camps or enslaved labour, but escalated by 1943 into a policy of systematic extermination.

3 The organization of persecution

- ▽ concentration camp
- ◇ extermination camp
- ■ site of mass killing
- ⊕ ghetto
- 8000 number of Jews killed

SCANDINAVIA 800
BALTIC STATES AND FINLAND 224,000
Katyn 1943 (Polish officers by Soviets)
Occupied area of *Einsatzgruppen* operations 1941–42
NETHERLANDS 106,000
BELGIUM 24,400
POLAND 3.6 million
Maly Trostinets
GERMANY 160,000
USSR 1.2 million
OCCUPIED FRANCE
FRANCE 83,000
CZECHOSLOVAKIA 217,000
HUNGARY 200,000
ROMANIA 270,000
VICHY FRANCE
ITALY 8000
BALKANS 148,500
250 km
250 miles

The Allied invasion of Europe 1943–45

A final German attempt to conquer the USSR brought their forces to Stalingrad by August 1942. The following winter saw their defeat there which, with Anglo-US victories in North Africa, brought the strategic initiative to the Allies. July 1943 witnessed Soviet victory at Kursk and Anglo-US landings in Sicily, initiating a Soviet onslaught in the East and the collapse of Italy. A sustained Anglo-US bombing offensive (from January 1943) and landings in southern France and Normandy meant, by summer 1944, that Germany was in retreat on all fronts. With its infrastructure, industry, capital, and leadership effectively destroyed, by May 1945 Germany was powerless to stop Soviet and Anglo-US forces finally meeting on the Elbe River and enforcing an unconditional surrender.

World War II 1942–45

Jan 1943: Germans surrender at Stalingrad

Jun–Aug 1943: USSR defeats Germans in tank battle at Kursk

Jan 1944: End of 900-day siege of Leningrad

Jun 6 1944: D-Day: Allied forces land in Normandy

Oct–Nov 1944: Allies liberate Greece

Jan 1945: Soviet troops enter Budapest, Warsaw, and Auschwitz

May 1945: Germany surrenders

1943   1944   1945

Jul 1943: Allied forces land in Sicily

Sep–Oct 1943: Italian surrender to Allies; Germany occupies Rome and Milan; Italy declares war on Germany

Jul 1944: USSR enters Poland

Mar 1945: Allied forces cross Rhine

May 1945: Berlin surrenders to Soviet troops

The Allied invasion of northern Europe began with Operation Overlord, the largest combined operation and successful shore-to-shore invasion in history; eight seaborne and airborne divisions established a beachhead in Normandy, on D-Day (June 6, 1944) supported by 6500 ships and 12,000 aircraft.

Concentration camps were established by the Nazis as detention centers from 1933 and used as resources of slave labor from 1940. Actual extermination of local populations, directed by *Einsatzgruppen* murder squads began in Poland and occupied Russia from 1941. The *Endlösung*, or Final Solution, involving the mass deportation of Jews to extermination camps such as Auschwitz-Birkenau began at the same time. By 1945 six million Jews, Poles, and other "undesirables" had been systematically murdered.

4 The Allied invasion of Europe 1942–45

- under Axis control by 1942
- Allied territory 1942
- areas occupied by Germany by Nov 1942
- Axis satellites
- → German offensive from 1942
- → Allied offensive 1942–43
- → Allied offensive 1944
- → Allied offensive 1945
- Ⓥ Allied victory
- ✹ city severely bombed by Allies
- ✹ city severely bombed by Germans
- ✪ partisan resistance
- neutral states

1942: Allied bomber range from British bases

from 1944: V1 and V2 rocket attacks

Jun 1944: Operation Overlord Allied landings

Nov 1942: Vichy France occupied by Germans

Nov 1942: Allied forces occupy French North Africa

Aug 1944: Allied invasion of southern France

Sep 1943: Italy occupied by Germans following Italian capitulation

Jul 1943: Operation Husky: allied invasion of Sicily

Apr–May 1943

Jan–Mar 1944 (Monte Cassino)

Jan–Mar 1942 (Anzio)

1943: Allied bomber range from north African bases

El Alamein Oct–Nov 1942

Kursk Jul–Aug 1943

Stalingrad 1942–43: German forces besieged

1941–44, 1944–45 (Warsaw)

Jun–Aug 1944

Winter 1944–45

Balaton winter 1944–45

Kiev Sep–Oct 1944

1941–44: besieged (Leningrad)

Feb 1944

Courland Feb–May 1945

WEST ASIA
REGIONAL HISTORY

Vegetation type

ice cap and glacier
polar or alpine desert
tundra
semidesert or sparsely vegetated
grassland
forest or open woodland
temperate desert
tropical desert
desert
coastline (present-day)
coastline (18,000 years ago)

THE HISTORICAL LANDSCAPE

A SEEMINGLY INHOSPITABLE REALM, arid, largely desert or mountainous plateau, West Asia lays claim to a panoply of grand names – the Garden of Eden, the Fertile Crescent, the Promised Land, the Cradle of Civilization, the Crossroads of History. Lying at the meeting point of the three Old World continents - Africa, Europe, and Asia - the region was blessed with the fertile soils, beneficent climate, and diverse demography to earn these titles. As such it remained a pivotal point of Old World, or Afro-Eurasian, urbanization, culture, communications, trade, and – inevitably – warfare, until relatively recent times. In addition, possibly as a consequence of these factors, the region was also the birthplace of Judaism, Christianity, and Islam, which became three of the most widely observed world religions. Despite the attentions of European colonial powers, West Asia has upheld its inherent qualities and traditions; rivalries and divisions persist alongside ways of life and artistic traditions now centuries old, a cultural longevity sustained by religion on the one hand and, in the 20th century, by the region's control of the world's most valuable commodity – oil.

West Asia, apart from its fertile riverine lowlands, is a combination of dry sandy deserts and mountainous plateaus that remain sparsely populated, or totally uninhabited even today.

The mountainous Iranian Plateau is cut off from the moist ocean air, and temperatures fluctuate greatly between winter and summer and night and day. Humans lived in the mountain fringes, but did not settle in the plateau's interior because of the cold, dry climate.

The banks of the Euphrates and Tigris rivers were where the world's first towns and cities were established.

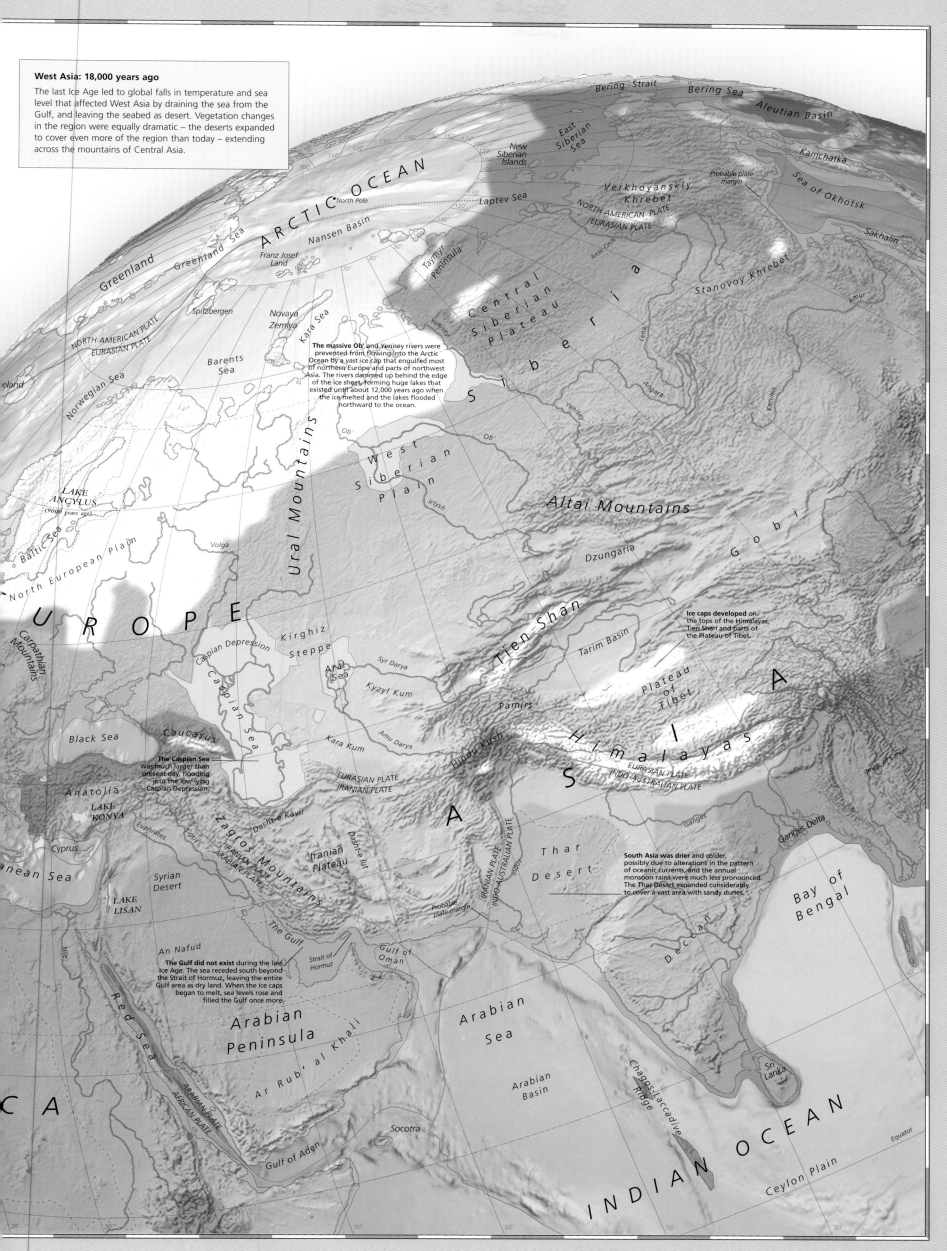

West Asia: 18,000 years ago

The last Ice Age led to global falls in temperature and sea level that affected West Asia by draining the sea from the Gulf, and leaving the seabed as desert. Vegetation changes in the region were equally dramatic – the deserts expanded to cover even more of the region than today – extending across the mountains of Central Asia.

ARCTIC OCEAN

Greenland

Greenland Sea

Nansen Basin

Franz Josef Land

Spitzbergen

Novaya Zemlya

Kara Sea

Barents Sea

Norwegian Sea

NORTH AMERICAN PLATE
EURASIAN PLATE

eland

LAKE ANCYLUS
(9000 years ago)

Baltic Sea

North European Plain

Volga

U R O P E

Carpathian Mountains

Ural Mountains

West Siberian Plain

Ob'

Ob'

Irtysh

The massive Ob' and Yenisey rivers were prevented from flowing into the Arctic Ocean by a vast ice cap that engulfed most of northern Europe and parts of northwest Asia. The rivers dammed up behind the edge of the ice sheet, forming huge lakes that existed until about 12,000 years ago when the ice melted and the lakes flooded northward to the ocean.

New Siberian Islands

East Siberian Sea

Laptev Sea

Taymyr Peninsula

Yenisey

Central Siberian Plateau

S i b e r i a

Arctic Circle

NORTH AMERICAN PLATE
EURASIAN PLATE

Verkhoyanskiy Khrebet

Stanovoy Khrebet

Lena

Angara

Yenisey

Kerulen

Amur

Bering Strait

Bering Sea

Aleutian Basin

Kamchatka

Sea of Okhotsk

Sakhalin

Probable plate margin

Altai Mountains

Dzungaria

Gobi

Kirghiz Steppe

Caspian Depression

Aral Sea

Syr Darya

Kyzyl Kum

Tien Shan

Tarim Basin

Pamirs

Plateau of Tibet

A

I

S

A

Ice caps developed on the tops of the Himalayas, Tien Shan and parts of the Plateau of Tibet.

Black Sea

Caucasus

Caspian Sea

Amu Darya

Kara Kum

Hindu Kush

Himalayas

EURASIAN PLATE
INDO-AUSTRALIAN PLATE

Ganges

Ganges Delta

The Caspian Sea was much larger than present day, flooding into the low-lying Caspian Depression.

Anatolia

LAKE KONYA

Cyprus

anean Sea

Syrian Desert

Euphrates

Tigris

Zagros Mountains

IRANIAN PLATE
ARABIAN PLATE

Dasht-e Kavir

Iranian Plateau

Dasht-e Lut

EURASIAN PLATE
IRANIAN PLATE

IRANIAN PLATE
INDO-AUSTRALIAN PLATE

Indus

Probable plate margin

Thar Desert

Deccan

Bay of Bengal

South Asia was drier and colder, possibly due to alterations in the pattern of oceanic currents, and the annual monsoon rains were much less pronounced. The Thar Desert expanded considerably, to cover a vast area with sandy dunes.

LAKE LISAN

An Nafud

The Gulf

Strait of Hormuz

Gulf of Oman

The Gulf did not exist during the last Ice Age. The sea receded south beyond the Strait of Hormuz, leaving the entire Gulf area as dry land. When the ice caps began to melt, sea levels rose and filled the Gulf once more.

Red Sea

ARABIAN PLATE
AFRICAN PLATE

Arabian Peninsula

Ar Rub' al Khali

Nile

Arabian Sea

Arabian Basin

Chagos-Laccadive Ridge

Sri Lanka

CA

Socotra

Gulf of Aden

INDIAN OCEAN

Ceylon Plain

Equator

WEST ASIA

EXPLORATION AND MAPPING

SINCE THE EMERGENCE of city–states and trade, West Asia has formed the crossroads between Europe, Africa, and Asia. The Sumerians and Babylonians accumulated local geographical knowledge, but it was the Greeks, following the conquests of Alexander the Great, who began a systematic recording of the region's geography. The Romans built on the knowledge of the Greeks, as did the Arabs when, in the 7th century, Islam spread throughout West Asia. In the 13th century, when the Mongols controlled Central Asia, traffic between China and the West flourished, leaving the way open for the great journeys of Marco Polo and William of Rubruck. The region least well-known to outsiders, though its geography was well understood by its desert tribes, was Arabia, finally mapped in the 19th and 20th centuries.

Invented by the Greeks, the astrolabe was developed by the Arabs into an indispensable tool of navigation.

The Greco-Roman view

Many merchants from Greek colonies in Asia Minor traded eastward to the Caspian Sea. Then, in the 4th century BCE, Alexander the Great led his army into West Asia, accompanied by a team of surveyors who recorded the route. Though none survive today, these records were a major source for subsequent geographers. Extending his quest for knowledge to the ocean, Alexander sent his admiral, Nearchus, to explore a route from the Indus to the Persian Gulf. The Greek merchant Hippalus was the first European sailor to recognize the regularity of the monsoon winds, harnessing them for his voyage to India. Arabia remained largely unknown, despite an exploratory expedition led by the Roman general Aelius Gallus.

This reconstructed map shows the world known to the Greeks in 5th century BCE. It is based on descriptions in the *History* of Herodotus, who traveled in Europe, Egypt, and West Asia, and gathered additional information from people he met en route.

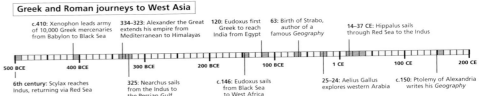

Greek and Roman journeys to West Asia

c.410: Xenophon leads army of 10,000 Greek mercenaries from Babylon to Black Sea

334–323: Alexander the Great extends his empire from Mediterranean to Himalayas

120: Eudoxus first Greek to reach India from Egypt

63: Birth of Strabo, author of a famous *Geography*

14–37 CE: Hippalus sails through Red Sea to the Indus

6th century: Scylax reaches Indus, returning via Red Sea

325: Nearchus sails from the Indus to the Persian Gulf

c.146: Eudoxus sails from Black Sea to West Africa

25–24: Aelius Gallus explores western Arabia

c.150: Ptolemy of Alexandria writes his *Geography*

Islamic travelers

Within a century of the death of Muhammad in 632, the Muslim world stretched from the Iberian Peninsula to the borders of Tang China. Building on knowledge acquired by earlier civilizations, in particular the Greeks, and incorporating information gathered by merchants, sailors, and other travelers, Arab geographers were able to create maps of the vast Islamic realms. By the 12th century they had an excellent understanding of West Asia, Europe, and North Africa. In 1325 Ibn Battuta *(see p.68)* began the first of the great journeys which were to take him to all corners of the Islamic world.

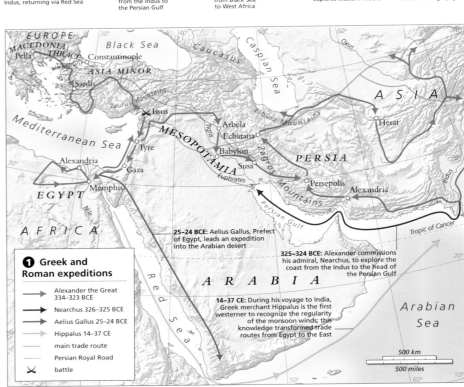

1 **Greek and Roman expeditions**

Alexander the Great 334–323 BCE

Nearchus 326–325 BCE

Aelius Gallus 25–24 BCE

Hippalus 14–37 CE

main trade route

Persian Royal Road

battle

25–24 BCE: Aelius Gallus, Prefect of Egypt, leads an expedition into the Arabian desert

325–324 BCE: Alexander commissions his admiral, Nearchus, to explore the coast from the Indus to the head of the Persian Gulf

14–37 CE: During his voyage to India, Greek merchant Hippalus is the first westerner to recognize the regularity of the monsoon winds; this knowledge transformed trade routes from Egypt to the East

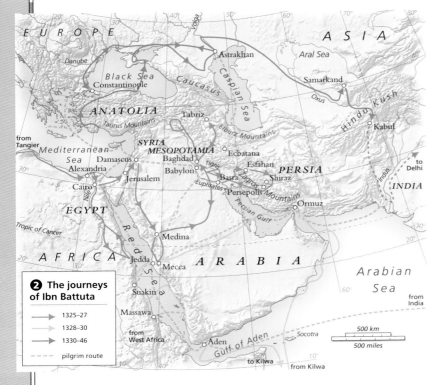

2 **The journeys of Ibn Battuta**

1325–27

1328–30

1330–46

pilgrim route

To a fanfare of trumpets, Muslims set out across the Arabian desert to make their pilgrimage to Mecca.

The Moroccan al-Idrisi was one of the most famous geographers of his day. The map shown here is a facsimile of the West Asian section of the beautiful world map he produced for Roger of Sicily c.1154. South is at the top, so the Mediterranean is on the right.

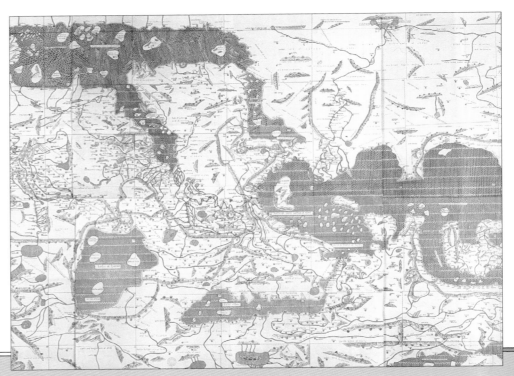

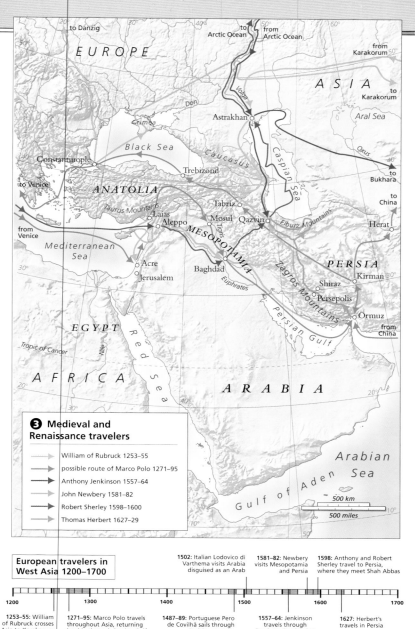

Medieval and Renaissance travelers from Europe

In the late 13th century, in the lull following the first Mongol invasions, Europeans began to venture east across Asia. Both William of Rubruck's mission to the Mongol Khan for Louis IX of France and Marco Polo's epic journeys yielded a wealth of geographical information. But with the rise to power of the Ottoman Turks, Central Asia's trade routes were once more closed to Europeans. Later explorers such as Sir Robert Sherley focused their attention on Persia, sworn enemy of the Turks.

European pilgrims visit the Holy Sepulchre in Jerusalem in this illustration from an illuminated manuscript of the travels of Marco Polo.

Juan de la Cosa's early 16th-century world map demonstrates how little Europeans of the period knew of West Asia to the east of the Holy Land. Inland from the Mediterranean coast, the cartographer compensated for lack of detail with an attractive illustration of the Three Kings on their journey to Bethlehem.

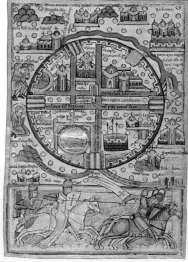

A 13th-century French map depicts the walled city of Jerusalem schematically, showing just the city's most important features, including the Holy Sepulchre and the Tower of David. Below, a crusader puts mounted Saracens to flight.

❸ Medieval and Renaissance travelers

→ William of Rubruck 1253–55
→ possible route of Marco Polo 1271–95
→ Anthony Jenkinson 1557–64
→ John Newbery 1581–82
→ Robert Sherley 1598–1600
→ Thomas Herbert 1627–29

MAPS FOR PILGRIMS

The Holy Land has possibly been the subject of more maps than any other part of the world. To medieval Christians, the holy city of Jerusalem was the center of their world, a concept depicted by many medieval maps which show a circular walled city, instead of a rectangular one, to symbolize the perfection of the Heavenly Jerusalem. Pilgrims and crusaders traveling to the Holy Land carried with them maps which were little more than illustrated itineraries of the towns they would pass through on their journey through Europe.

European travelers in West Asia 1200–1700

1200 — 1300 — 1400 — 1500 — 1600 — 1700

1502: Italian Lodovico di Varthema visits Arabia disguised as an Arab
1581–82: Newbery visits Mesopotamia and Persia
1598: Anthony and Robert Sherley travel to Persia, where they meet Shah Abbas

1253–55: William of Rubruck crosses Asia to Karakorum
1271–95: Marco Polo travels throughout Asia, returning by ship through Persian Gulf
1487–89: Portuguese Pero de Covilhã sails through Red Sea to India
1557–64: Jenkinson travels through Russia to Caspian Sea
1627: Herbert's travels in Persia

European travelers in Arabia

Although crisscrossed by Muslim pilgrim routes, maps of the interior of Arabia were rare until the 19th century. The region's hostile terrain and reputation for religious fanaticism remained considerable barriers to exploration by Europeans, despite the peninsula's wealth of valuable raw materials. Those that successfully penetrated Arabia did so armed with fluent Arabic and disguised as Muslims, particularly those who entered Islam's holy cities. The 19th century brought a rush of European explorers, especially the British, to Arabia. The last area to be explored was the Rub' al Khali (Empty Quarter), crossed first by Bertram Thomas in 1930–31 and explored more thoroughly by Wilfred Thesiger. The most detailed maps of the peninsula were made from the late 1920s following surveys by oil companies.

Europeans in the Arabian Peninsula 1800–1950

1800 — 1850 — 1900 — 1950

1812: Burckhardt discovers Petra, ancient capital of Nabataea
1853: Richard Burton visits Mecca and Medina in Arab disguise
1864: Guarmani travels through northern Nejd
1879: Wilfrid Scawen Blunt and his wife, Anne, travel to Nejd to buy horses
1930: Thomas first European to cross Empty Quarter
1946–48: Thesiger's double crossing of Empty Quarter

1814: Burckhardt visits Mecca
1818: Sadleir makes first east-west crossing
1862–63: Palgrave makes first west-east crossing through the Nafud
1876–78: Doughty's Arabian journeys
1888: Publication of Doughty's classic *Travels in Arabia Deserta*
1932: Philby crosses Empty Quarter

In 1762 a Danish surveyor, Carsten Niebuhr, took part in the first scientific expedition to the Arabian Peninsula. A team of Scandinavian and German experts recorded the flora and fauna of the Yemen and studied its peoples. Most of the party died, but Niebuhr survived and published an account of the expedition, *Descriptions of Arabia*, with several detailed maps of the region.

Non-Muslims entered Islam's holy cities at their peril. Richard Burton, seen here convincingly disguised as a Muslim pilgrim, visited both Mecca and Medina.

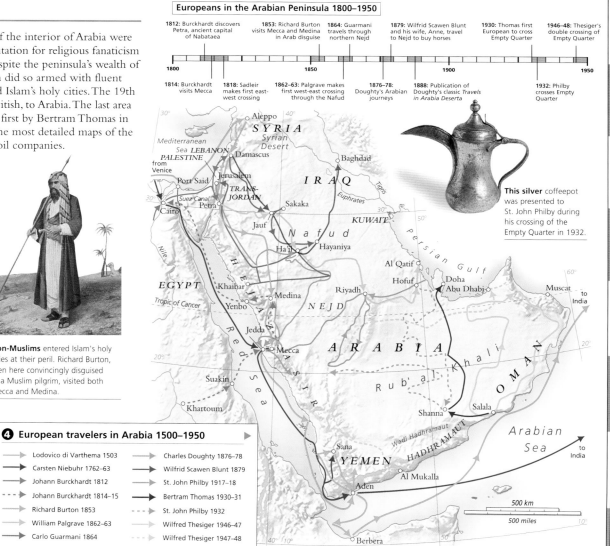

This silver coffeepot was presented to St. John Philby during his crossing of the Empty Quarter in 1932.

❹ European travelers in Arabia 1500–1950

→ Lodovico di Varthema 1503
→ Carsten Niebuhr 1762–63
→ Johann Burckhardt 1812
⇢ Johann Burckhardt 1814–15
→ Richard Burton 1853
→ William Palgrave 1862–63
→ Carlo Guarmani 1864

→ Charles Doughty 1876–78
→ Wilfrid Scawen Blunt 1879
→ St. John Philby 1917–18
→ Bertram Thomas 1930–31
⇢ St. John Philby 1932
→ Wilfred Thesiger 1946–47
→ Wilfred Thesiger 1947–48

SOUTH AND SOUTHEAST ASIA
REGIONAL HISTORY

Vegetation type

ice cap and glacier

polar or alpine desert

tundra

semidesert or sparsely vegetated

grassland

forest or open woodland

tropical rain forest

temperate desert

tropical desert

desert

coastline (present-day)

coastline (18,000 years ago)

THE HISTORICAL LANDSCAPE

LYING LARGELY BETWEEN THE TROPICS, this region enjoys a complex geography incorporating the world's greatest mountains, some of the world's largest river systems and tropical rain forests, and the globe's most extensive archipelago. During the last Ice Age, lower sea levels rendered the shallow seas surrounding Southeast Asia into dry land, allowing humans to migrate from the Asian mainland through the islands of Southeast Asia. From 3000 BCE, the Indian subcontinent was home to some of the world's earliest civilizations, founded on the banks of the Indus and Ganges rivers. Historically, the sheer size of the Indian subcontinent and variety of its peoples have attracted and resisted political unity in equal parts, and Hinduism, Buddhism, and Islam have provided the inspiration for remarkable eras of cultural, economic, and political efflorescence. The region is well-endowed with valuable natural resources and has attracted and fostered trade since the earliest times. Only in the recent centuries of colonial rivalry have concerns about self-determination been overtaken by the need to meet the demands of soaring population growth.

The Mekong is one of many great rivers which radiate south and east from the Plateau of Tibet. The alluvial soils that accumulate around the lower reaches of these rivers are exceptionally fertile, and have long been utilized by humans for agriculture – especially the cultivation of rice.

The Himalayas have always been a barrier to human migration between South and East Asia. The first settlers entered southern Asia by passes that still provide the only means of traversing the mountains.

The Indus River flows from the Himalayas, through mountain meadows and down across fertile plains to the sea. The Indus Valley civilizations were the most sophisticated early societies in southern Asia.

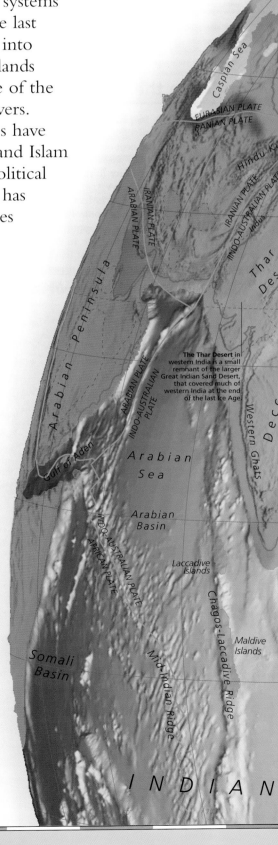

The Thar Desert in western India is a small remnant of the larger Great Indian Sand Desert, that covered much of western India at the end of the last Ice Age.

South and Southeast Asia: 18,000 years ago

Climatic changes and a global fall in sea level affected South and Southeastern Asia. The drop in sea levels turned much of the continental shelf surrounding the islands of Southeast Asia into dry land, forming a wide land bridge that encompassed Java, Sumatra, and Borneo. Rain forests covered a much smaller area, and many forested zones became grasslands and scrub. In India, sand dunes in the Thar Desert expanded to occupy a much larger area than today.

Ural Mountains

West Siberian Plain

Central Siberian Plateau

Siberia

Sea of Okhotsk

Kamchatka

Arctic Circle

NORTH AMERICAN PLATE

EURASIAN PLATE

Amur

Sakhalin

Great Khingan Range

Kurile Islands

Hokkaido

Kurile Trench

Altai Mountains

Aral Sea

Dzungaria

Gobi

Manchurian Plain

Sea of Japan (East Sea)

Japan Trench

Tien Shan

A S I A

Tarim Basin

Qilian Shan

Yellow River

Ordos Desert

Bo Hai

Korea

Honshu

PACIFIC PLATE

Kunlun Mountains

Yellow River

Yellow Sea

Plateau of Tibet

Qin Ling

Great Plain of China

East China Sea

Ryukyu Islands

PHILIPPINE PLATE

Himalayas

Red Basin

Yangtze

EURASIAN PLATE

Tropic of Cancer

Ganges

Brahmaputra

Patkai Range

Nan Ling

Taiwan

PACIFIC OCEAN

Eastern Ghats

Irrawaddy

Arakan Yoma

Salween

Xi Jiang

Ailao Shan

Gulf of Tongking

Hainan

Philippine Basin

Bay of Bengal

Colder, drier climates affected the vegetation of Southeast Asia. The rain forests that grew to blanket much of the area, covered much smaller portions of the continent.

South China Sea

Luzon

Philippine Trench

Yap Trench

Andaman Islands

Isthmus of Kra

Gulf of Thailand

South China Basin

Palawan

Sulu Sea

Mindanao

Sri Lanka

Nicobar Islands

Andaman Sea

Sri Lanka and India were linked by dry land at the end of the last Ice Age. Rising sea levels flooded the link between them, and made Sri Lanka an island, although even today the two are only separated by a narrow expanse of shallow sea.

18,000 years ago, many of the shallow seas surrounding maritime Southeast Asia were dry land. The Sunda Shelf was a low-lying, thickly forested plain, and many of the East Indian islands were joined together as a long peninsula which stretched eastward to Australia.

Celebes Sea

Ceylon Plain

EURASIAN PLATE

INDO-AUSTRALIAN PLATE

Malay Peninsula

Strait of Malacca

Sunda Shelf

Borneo

Makassar Strait

Celebes

Halmahera

Moluccas

Seram

PACIFIC PLATE

INDO-AUSTRALIAN PLATE

Equator

New Guinea

Ninetyeast Ridge

Cocos Basin

Sumatra

S U N D A

The Sunda Shelf was dissected by a complex river system; all of these ancient rivers were drowned when sea levels rose.

E a s t   I n d i e s

Banda Sea

O C E A N

Java Trench

Java

Bali

Flores

Timor

Arafura Sea

SOUTH AND SOUTHEAST ASIA

EXPLORATION AND MAPPING

THE RELIGIONS OF SOUTH ASIA all have a long tradition of cosmography, though surviving maps are of relatively recent date. While some early maps may have related to secular themes, most would have been associated with religion and the place of humankind in a greater universe, reflecting the sacred geography of the Hindu, Jain, and Buddhist traditions. Despite the sophistication of Indian science and the great distances traveled by Indian – especially Buddhist – missionaries and merchants, there is little evidence of conventional geographical mapping until well after the establishment of Islam in the region. Following the establishment of the Portuguese in western India after 1498, European colonists, with competing territorial claims, spurred on the Western mapping of South and Southeast Asia. Commercial, economic, and military motives, combined with a zeal for knowledge, led to the British Survey of India from 1767, an epic project to map and define their eastern empire.

This 18th-century Hindu globe shows the heavens *(in the top half)* and the earthly realm *(below)*.

The cosmographic tradition

A Jain diagram of the universe shows Mount Meru surrounded by concentric circles representing different continents and oceans.

The cosmographic conceptions of Hinduism, Buddhism, and Jainism, which attempted to locate the sacred places of this world in an imagined universe, were remarkably complex. Within each of them, Jambudvipa – the world inhabited by humans – formed only a very small part. In all cultures of Asia there is a strong belief that the fortunes of humans are affected by extraterrestrial forces whose influence can be foretold, in part, through astrology, with which astronomy was closely associated. Thus, mapping the heavens (on an astrolabe or other astronomical instruments) was a much more important concern than the geographic mapping of topography.

The lotus flower, redrawn here by Francis Wilford in 1805, was for Buddhists a symbol of the universe.

The astronomical observatory at Jaipur was one of five built by the Rajput king Sawai Jai Singh between 1722 and 1739. It contained remarkably accurate masonry instruments.

Indigenous mapping of South and Southeast Asia

Scarcely any surviving indigenous maps of the region are earlier than the 16th century. Maps were drawn for a variety of reasons: to provide information for the military; to illustrate itineraries or journeys; to legitimize territorial possessions. Maritime navigation charts from Gujarat date to the 17th century. Yet few surviving maps are strictly geographical, and virtually none are drawn to a fixed scale. Cosmographic views were sometimes combined with geographical knowledge of the known world.

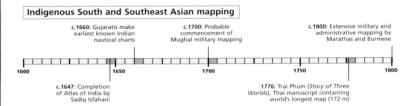

Indigenous South and Southeast Asian mapping

- c.1660: Gujaratis make earliest known Indian nautical charts
- c.1700: Probable commencement of Mughal military mapping
- c.1800: Extensive military and administrative mapping by Marathas and Burmese
- c.1647: Completion of Atlas of India by Sadiq Isfahani
- 1776: Trai Phum (*Story of Three Worlds*), Thai manuscript containing world's longest map (172 m)

1600 — 1650 — 1700 — 1750 — 1800

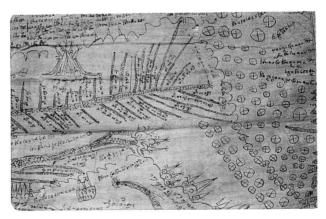

The sacred map of the Sundanese chiefdom of Timbanganten in western Java *(left)* was drawn in the late 16th century. It is still venerated by local villagers for its protective powers against the volcano clearly depicted on the left of the map.

The Mughal Emperor Jahangir is shown embracing Shah Abbas of Persia on a geographic globe, based on an Elizabethan model brought to the court by the first English ambassador in 1615 *(right)*.

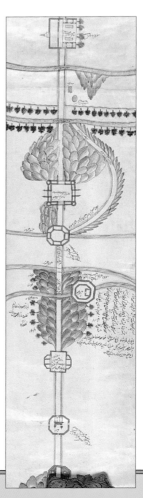

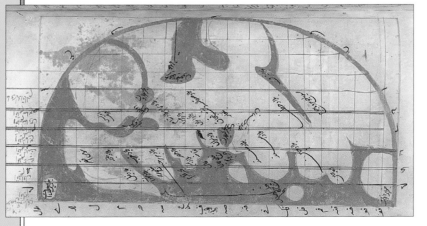

An encyclopedic work in Persian by Sadiq Isfahani of Jaunpur in northern India was finished in 1647. The section on travel contains a map *(left)* of the "inhabited quarter" (Africa and Eurasia), drawn in the traditional style of Islamic cosmography.

The detail *(right)* is from a Mughal map showing the route from Delhi to Kandahar by means of a system of straight lines and nodal points.

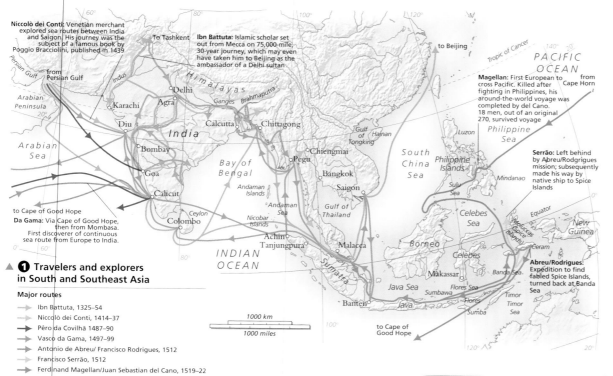

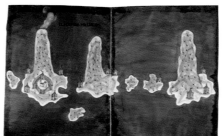

Travelers and explorers in South and Southeast Asia

Major routes

→ Ibn Battuta, 1325–54
→ Niccolò dei Conti, 1414–37
→ Pêro da Covilhã 1487–90
→ Vasco da Gama, 1497–99
→ Antonio de Abreu/ Francisco Rodrigues, 1512
→ Francisco Serrão, 1512
→ Ferdinand Magellan/Juan Sebastian del Cano, 1519–22
→ Ralph Fitch 1583–91
→ Jean Baptiste Tavernier 1639–67 (five visits)

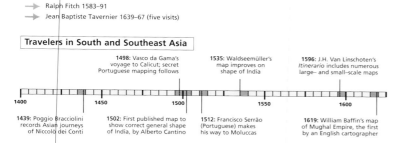

Travelers in South and Southeast Asia				
	1498: Vasco da Gama's voyage to Calicut; secret Portuguese mapping follows	**1535:** Waldseemüller's map improves on shape of India		**1596:** J.H. Van Linschoten's *Itinerario* includes numerous large– and small–scale maps
1400	1450	1500	1550	1600
1439: Poggio Bracciolini records Asian journeys of Niccolò dei Conti	**1502:** First published map to show correct general shape of India, by Alberto Cantino	**1512:** Francisco Serrão (Portuguese) makes his way to Moluccas	**1619:** William Baffin's map of Mughal Empire, the first by an English cartographer	

Travelers in South and Southeast Asia

The most celebrated medieval traveler in the region was Ibn Battuta of Tangier in the 14th century, even if his claim to have journeyed as far China may not be true. A century later Vasco da Gama was piloted across the Indian Ocean by a Gujarati Muslim. An even more southerly route opened up the richest prize of Southeast Asia – the fabled Spice Islands, subject of a Portuguese monopoly from 1512. In the 1590s the Dutch began to probe the southern Indian Ocean, using Mauritius as a staging-point.

This map of India and Ceylon dating from 1596 appears in Jan Huygen van Linschoten's *Itinerario*, a work instrumental in encouraging Dutch and English trade with India.

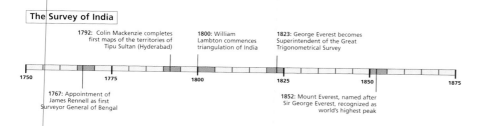

A **Portuguese map** of the Moluccas (1646) shows major settlements, volcanoes, and types of vegetation on the islands *(left)*.

This 17th-century French map shows the Kingdom of Siam, the Malay Peninsula, Sumatra, and Java, including political boundaries and areas of influence *(right)*.

The Survey of India

Although European mapping of India began in the wake of Vasco da Gama's 1498 landfall, it was not until after James Rennell's 1767 appointment as the first Surveyor General of the newly acquired province of Bengal that the British began to survey and map the country systematically. Initially, maps were based on observation, reports, and intelligence. From the late 18th century, British Army officers, such as Colin Mackenzie and William Lambton, began formal trigonometrical surveys. Sir George Everest, Lambton's successor, planned a vast network of triangulations, operated by a huge staff. He was careful to placate local princes, who feared that land surveys would infringe on their already eroded sovereignty.

James Rennell, surveyor of Bengal and Bihar, published this map in 1782, four years after his return to England. The cartouche depicts Britannia receiving the sacred scriptures of India from a Brahmin.

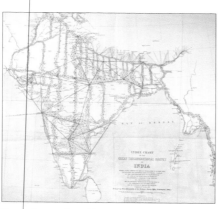

George Everest planned his trigonometrical triangulations on a grid overlying the entire subcontinent. His predecessor, William Lambton laid down the central north-south axis.

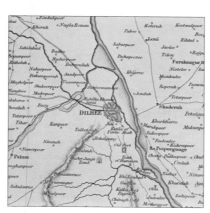

The Indian Atlas of J. & C. Walker was commissioned by the East India Company in 1823. It was produced at a scale of four miles to one inch.

The Survey of India					
	1792: Colin Mackenzie completes first maps of the territories of Tipu Sultan (Hyderabad)	**1800:** William Lambton commences triangulation of India	**1823:** George Everest becomes Superintendent of the Great Trigonometrical Survey		
1750	1775	1800	1825	1850	1875
	1767: Appointment of James Rennell as first Surveyor General of Bengal		**1852:** Mount Everest, named after Sir George Everest, recognized as world's highest peak		

The scientific exploration of Southeast Asia

In 1854, the British naturalist Alfred Wallace set out for Singapore, and spent the next eight years traveling around the islands of the East Indies and New Guinea. He observed and collected a vast number of animal species, many previously unknown to western science. Most importantly, he observed a dramatic change in fauna at the center of the region; the eastern species are distinctly Australian, the western, Asian. He argued that the eastern part of the archipelago was therefore once part of a Pacific continent. The boundary between the two faunal regions came to be called the Wallace Line.

Alfred Wallace's account of his Southeast Asian travels, published in 1869, contains many fine illustrations of the species encountered on his journey, such as this black cockatoo from the Aru Islands.

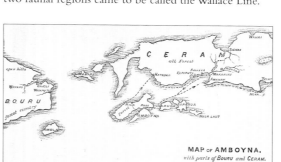

The series of maps published in Alfred Wallace's account of his journey to Southeast Asia show, in great detail, the terrain which he explored. This map, of Ceram in the Moluccas, shows the region where he encountered and carefully observed many different types of birds of paradise, and first began to devise his theories about species evolution.

The scientific journeys of Alfred Wallace in Southeast Asia

→ journeys of Alfred Wallace, 1854–62
— Wallace "line"
--- inferred ancient coastline
▢ eastern limit of transitional faunal zone

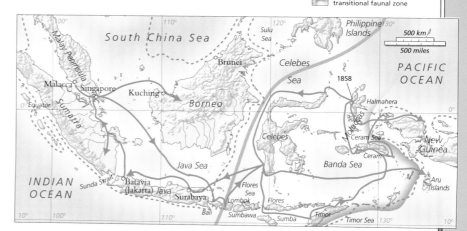

NORTH AND EAST ASIA
REGIONAL HISTORY

THE HISTORICAL LANDSCAPE

THE FRAGMENTED GEOGRAPHY of this, the world's largest uninterrupted land mass, has produced a wide variety of historical scenarios. The mountainous massifs at its heart – the Plateau of Tibet, the Altai, Tien Shan, and Pamir ranges – enclose the arid Takla Makan, Gobi, and Ordos deserts, which together comprise a hostile and sparsely inhabited realm. Stretching in a wide arc around this region are the massive steppes, long home to pastoral nomads whose turbulent history was punctuated by sorties against their sedentary neighbors and, occasionally, violent irruptions which impelled their skilled and fast-moving horsemen across Eurasia. Broad rivers flow north across Siberia to the Arctic, and west to inland deltas and landlocked seas such as the Aral and Caspian. To the east, the fertile floodplains of the Yellow River and the Yangtze were the focus of one the world's oldest civilizations, that of China, an enormous demographic and cultural fulcrum which dominates East Asia, and whose influence has been cast far across the peninsulas and archipelagos of the Pacific Rim.

Vegetation type

- ice cap and glacier
- polar or alpine desert
- tundra
- semidesert or sparsely vegetated
- grassland
- forest or open woodland
- tropical rain forest
- temperate desert
- tropical desert
- desert
- coastline (present-day)
- coastline (18,000 years ago)

Japan was settled by hunter-gatherers about 30,000 years ago. At the the time of the last Ice Age, most of the Japanese islands were densely forested, with settlement only in the coastal regions.

The Yellow River flows down to the plains of eastern China across a plateau of fertile *loess* – fine silty soils laid down along the edges of glaciers. The river cuts down through the soft sediments, washing them downstream and depositing them on the Great Plain of China, resulting in exceptionally fertile soils, suitable for a wide range of crops.

Siberia was a cold, frozen region at the time of the last Ice Age, sparsely inhabited by hunter-gatherers. Unlike northern Europe and North America, Siberia was not covered by an ice cap because of the lack of moisture across the region. The extreme cold preserved the remains of creatures such as mammoths, along with evidence of the shelters built by the people who hunted them.